W9-AGV-230

FIFTH EDITION

Contemporary Sociological Theory

Expanding the Classical Tradition

RUTH A. WALLACE

George Washington University

ALISON WOLF

University of London

Prentice Hall
Upper Saddle River, New Jersey 07458

Library of Congress Cataloging-in-Publication Data

Wallace, Ruth A.
    Contemporary sociological theory : expanding the classical
tradition / Ruth A. Wallace, Alison Wolf. — 5th ed.
        p.   cm.
    Includes bibliographical references and index.
    ISBN 0–13–787656–4
    1. Sociology.   2. Sociology—Philosophy.   I. Wolf, Alison.
II. Title.
HM51.W15   1998
301'.01—dc21   98-8360
                                                               CIP

Editorial Director: Charlyce Jones Owen
Editor in Chief: Nancy Roberts
Senior Acquisitions Editor: John Chillingworth
Managing Editor: Sharon Chambliss
Project Manager: Merrill Peterson
Prepress and Manufacturing Buyer: Mary Ann Gloriande
Marketing Manager: Christopher DeJohn
Cover Director: Jayne Conte

This book was set in 10/12 Palatino by DM Cradle
Associates and was printed and bound by
Courier Companies, Inc. The cover was printed by
Phoenix Color Corp.

 © 1999, 1995, 1991, 1986, 1980 by Prentice-Hall, Inc.
Simon & Schuster/A Viacom Company
Upper Saddle River, New Jersey 07458

All rights reserved. No part of this book may be
reproduced, in any form or by any means,
without permission in writing from the publisher.

Printed in the United States of America

10   9   8   7   6   5   4   3   2   1

ISBN 0-13-787656-4

PRENTICE-HALL INTERNATIONAL (UK) LIMITED, *London*
PRENTICE-HALL OF AUSTRALIA PTY. LIMITED, *Sydney*
PRENTICE-HALL CANADA INC., *Toronto*
PRENTICE-HALL HISPANOAMERICANA, S.A., *Mexico*
PRENTICE-HALL OF INDIA PRIVATE LIMITED, *New Delhi*
PRENTICE-HALL OF JAPAN, INC., *Tokyo*
SIMON & SCHUSTER ASIA PTE. LTD., *Singapore*
EDITORA PRENTICE-HALL DO BRASIL, LTDA., *Rio de Janeiro*

To Our Families and Students

Contents

CHAPTER THREE

Conflict Theory 67

CHAPTER FOUR

Evolution and Modernity: Macrosociological Perspectives   *154*

CHAPTER FIVE

Symbolic Interactionism   *189*

CHAPTER SIX

Phenomenology   *252*

CHAPTER SEVEN

Theories of Rational Choice   *293*

Preface

This book discusses and analyzes sociological theory as it is practiced today. It focuses on writers whose work has most influenced social theory and the way sociologists currently approach and analyze their subject matter.

Contemporary sociology, at almost every point, builds on and incorporates the classics, especially the work of Marx, Durkheim, Weber, Simmel, and Mead. We believe that the best way to study and understand theory is to follow the ways in which the work of classical writers has been expanded by later sociologists, and to see how theoretical insights are actually used by people to explain social developments. We therefore describe the contributions of classical theorists directly when discussing the historical roots of each perspective. Throughout the text we also point out the many ways in which contemporary theorists and researchers alike make active use of classical ideas.

In the last four editions of our book, the subtitle was "Continuing the Classical Tradition." Upon reflection, we still see a continuity with the early founders of the discipline in the work of contemporary theorists. But we have come to the conclusion that there is more than continuity in the theoretical work going on in sociology today. What has been happening recently in sociological theory is as exciting as the newly created technologies that are bringing the rest of the world closer to us, thus enriching us by a fuller appreciation of other cultures. Our contemporary theorists are, indeed, standing on the shoulders of the giants of sociology, but they are also expanding the horizons of our discipline at all three vantage points: the macrostructural, microinteractional, and interpretive levels of analysis. This is the reason for our new subtitle: "Expanding the Classical Tradition."

In the following pages we describe the central ideas and arguments of these thinkers and the ways in which they provide a number of quite distinct perspectives on society and social behavior. Although we also assess and criticize their theories, our purpose is to provide readers with a clear summary of sociological theory's arguments, not to engage in a detailed critique of each approach or to espouse a particular perspective. To give readers as clear an idea as possible of the authors' own style and presentation, we include a number of direct quotations in the text. We also try particularly to show how sociological theories inform social scientists' empirical research and to demonstrate the close links between sociological theory and the ways in which we all, sociologists and nonsociologists alike, deal with and try to understand our world. To this end we include throughout the book empirical examples of how a given perspective is used both by sociological researchers and by ordinary people as they interpret daily events.

While we have made every effort to avoid unnecessary jargon and to express ideas as simply and as clearly as possible, much of the subject matter is, inevitably, quite complex. We have tried, therefore, to follow Albert Einstein's dictum: "Everything should be made as simple as possible, but not one bit simpler." At the same time it is not a precondition for the reader to be a student of sociology already. We conceive of our audience as comprising anyone interested in the contributions social science can make to understanding our social world.

We have been very aware during our work of the old but still raging debate about whether any writers, but especially social scientists, can deal objectively with their subject matter. In one sense, namely our choice of what writers and what aspects of their work to present, our own values and preferences must obtrude. Within that framework, however, we have tried unashamedly to maintain the traditional scientific values of unbiased description, objectivity, and, indeed, reason; for while they may never be fully realizable, it seems to us of the utmost importance that scholars—and the world—not abandon them as standards. We have also paid particular attention to whether a given perspective is successful in dealing with and answering a range of concrete questions and problems.

PLAN OF THE TEXT

This revised text discusses five major perspectives of contemporary sociological theory: functionalism, conflict theory, symbolic interactionism, phenomenology, and theories of rational choice. It also provides an overview of recent theoretical developments. For this edition the text has been updated generally, and a number of significant additions have also been made. First, as in our previous edition, we refrain from creating a separate chapter for feminist theory because it draws on a wide range of theoretical orientations. Therefore we emphasize the ways in which feminist theorists have expanded the horizons of different sociological perspectives, and we discuss their work in the relevant chapters throughout this text. As in our previous editions, questions about the role of women in contemporary society form a research theme to which each chapter returns. This edition includes two new chapters. Chapter 4, a discussion of classical and modern social change theories, is entitled "Evolution and Modernity: Macrosociological Perspectives." It discusses in depth the evolutionary theories of Karl Marx, Talcott Parsons, Jürgen Habermas, and Anthony Giddens, and it introduces the work of Ulrich Beck. Chapter 8, "Rediscovering the Body," updates material from the previous edition and includes an expanded discussion of Foucault's work in this area as well as sociobiological material.

Other major changes include an expanded and updated treatment of the work of neofunctionalists: Jeffrey Alexander on the new theoretical movements and Neil Smelser's work on ambivalence (Chapter 2); an updated discussion of Erik Olin Wright's Marxian analysis of U.S. society and of research on class and the state (Chapter 3); expanded discussion of Erving Goffman's work on the sociology of gender, Arlie Hochschild's recent work on the sociology of the emotions, and Patricia Hill Collins's critique of the concept of complexity (Chapter 5); updated material from research using Dorothy Smith's standpoint theory (Chapter 6); a complete new section on James Coleman and an updating of work by other rational choice theorists (Chapter 7); and an expanded section on postmodernism (Chapter 9).

Chapter 1 discusses the structure of sociological theories and their practical importance as a way of analyzing and understanding how human societies work. It also introduces two important research themes. One of these—the role of women in contemporary society—has already been mentioned; the second is the working of the huge formal educational systems that characterize modern society. Each major theoretical perspective can provide important but partial answers to these questions about formal education and the role of women, themes woven throughout the book.

The following chapters on functionalism, conflict theory, symbolic interactionism, phenomenology, and theories of rational choice follow a common pattern. We set out the basic assumptions and key concepts of each theory and the questions it raises and attempts to answer. We identify the intellectual roots of the approach and discuss the insights derived from previous scholars by contemporary theorists. We then describe in detail the work of the perspective's major theorists, with particular emphasis on their most recent or current arguments. Throughout each section we stress the reciprocal relationship between theory on the one hand and sociological research and general social observation on the other. We show how contemporary theorists analyze concrete phenomena, including the educational system and the role of women, and how the research of their colleagues draws on and embodies different theoretical perspectives. We also illustrate how the outlook of contemporary theorists is reflected in the way nonsociologists look at and discuss the world. Chapter 8 discusses a theoretical development of interest to contemporary sociology: the sociology of the body. Finally, Chapter 9 discusses modernism and postmodernism, and synthesizes the major perspectives' contributions to answering the questions posed in Chapter 1 regarding education and the role of women.

This book has been a joint effort throughout, with no senior or junior authorship. Ruth Wallace took primary responsibility for the chapters on functionalism, symbolic interactionism, and phenomenology, and Alison

Wolf for the chapters on conflict theory, evolution and modernity, theories of rational choice, and rediscovering the body.

In writing this book we have learned a great deal and have both come to appreciate more fully the insights and achievements of the theorists we describe. We would like to acknowledge our intellectual debt to them and also to the many students whose questions and comments have contributed to our work.

Anthony Heath, Patricia Madoo Lengermann, J. Clyde Mitchell, Robert Moran, Whitney Pope, Neil Smelser, Martin Wolf, and the late Herbert Blumer all made major contributions to our thinking through their suggestions and questions on this and earlier editions. Our editors, Edward Stanford, Susan Taylor, Bill Webber, Nancy Roberts, and Sharon Chambliss, as well as a number of Prentice Hall reviewers, including Larry R. Ridener, Baylor University, and David G. Wagner, University of New York at Albany, gave us useful suggestions.

We would also like to acknowledge the help of Janet Saltzman Chafetz, Ralf Dahrendorf, Doug Goodman, Wade Hook, Heather Kane, Barbara Lal, Iain McLean, Frank Mars, Carlyle Maw, Bruce Mork, Kathryn Orlans, Sara Rab, Vernon Reynolds, David Sciulli, R. Stephen Warner, and Jacqueline Wiseman.

We thank Joy Alexander for encouraging us to write on theory and the late Edmund Wolf for his help in translating. Without the time so generously given by Winnie Potter, James Coriden, and the late Rebecca Wolf, this book would still be in manuscript. Jonathan, Benjamin, and Rachel Wolf maintained our sense of proportion and helped by being themselves.

R.A.W.
A.W.

CHAPTER ONE

The Understanding
of Society

Reading theory has not been something to which people have generally looked forward with delight. Often they see it as just so many groups of rarefied abstractions related only to each other, like a set of crossword puzzles, free-floating above the "real world" of schools, factories, and suburbs, elections, weddings, strikes, muggings, and tennis matches. This is a mistake. Far from being able to separate theory from real life, our whole way of looking at the world depends on our theoretical perspective. To read sociological theory is to understand a great deal more about what we and our world are like and how unordinary and ambiguous the most taken-for-granted and everyday aspects of our lives may be.

When sociologists "do sociology," they do not come to their subject matter cold, their minds blank. Whether their topic is the way people deal with death, or the whole evolution and probable future of modern society, they focus on particular aspects of what is going on.[1] They approach their subject with certain assumptions, they emphasize particular research methods, and they have particular types of questions they want answered. This means that their research is based on the ways of looking at things that sociological theories advance. The theories lay these out in an explicit and systematic way.

Very much the same is true of the world outside sociology. In some famous remarks John Maynard Keynes, whose own ideas dominated government economic management from the Second World War until the present, argued that ideas "both when they are right and when they are wrong, are more powerful than is commonly understood. Indeed, the world is ruled by little else. Practical men, who believe themselves to be quite exempt from any intellectual influences, are usually the slaves of some defunct economist. Madmen in authority, who hear voices in the air, are distilling their frenzy from some academic scribbler of a few years back."[2] The different ways of looking at our society that contemporary sociological theories advance are reflected in the arguments and observations of society's members as a whole.

The effect that sociological theory may have on people's behavior and on the course of history is demonstrated most dramatically by the work of Karl Marx. But a journalist trying to explain Watergate and the resignation of Richard Nixon, a marriage counselor grappling with rising divorce rates, and new students on campus trying to understand what is going on also draw on notions about how people behave and how social institutions work, notions that embody certain theoretical assumptions. Furthermore, our very ability to talk about "the president's unconstitutional behavior" or about

---

[1]For the use of theoretical perspectives to discuss these particular topics, see Chapter 3 (Collins), Chapter 5 (Part Two: Blumer), and Chapter 4 (Parsons and Habermas).

[2]John Maynard Keynes, *The General Theory of Employment, Interest and Money* (London: Macmillan, 1936), p. 383.

"granting someone a degree" depends on a whole range of facts about ourselves and our listeners. Sociological theories do not comprise a world of formal, empty boxes, irrelevant to the world of work and family, power, freedom, discrimination, and oppression. Far from it. They have everything to do with that world—how we see it, understand it, and explain it, as well as how we act in it and thus what it becomes.

THE STRUCTURE OF SOCIOLOGICAL THEORY

Sociological theorists are distinctive because they express their assumptions or hypotheses systematically and discuss in a comprehensive way how far their theories explain social life. Even more important, they provide new insights into behavior and the workings of societies. These, in turn, are disseminated, and in years to come they may affect the ideas of many who have never read the original work.

The systematic way in which sociological theory sets out its ideas is a quality it shares with the theory of any other discipline: psychology, physics, genetics, and the rest. Shared, too, is a second important quality: it relates innumerable events, with many apparent differences, to general principles that bring out their similarities. Student protests, strikes, and food riots may all be treated as examples of conflict within hierarchical organizations, and the important qualities they have in common may be thus defined.[3] Similarly, counselors' interviews with high school students and trials for murder may both be examined in the light of what they show about the shared ideas of a society's members and the creative and unpredictable dynamics of human interaction.[4]

However, although sociological theory shares the essential systematizing qualities of all theory, in other ways it often differs from what is usually meant by the term. The classical definition of a theory[5] is essentially a *deductive* one. It starts with definitions of some general concepts (and, often, a few clearly stated assumptions); lays out rules about how to classify the things we observe in terms of these different categories; and then puts forward a number of general propositions about the concepts. Once observers have classified their subject matter, a generalized theory allows them to deduce logically a number of quite specific statements about its nature and behavior. The laws of Mendelian genetics are a good example, for their general statements about the pairing of genes and distribution of characteristics among offspring can be used to deduce statements about an enor-

---

[3]See Chapter 3.

[4]See Chapters 5 and 6.

[5]One of the best such discussions can be found in Ernest Nagel, *The Structure of Science* (New York: Harcourt, Brace and World, 1961), especially pp. 90–105.

mous range of species. Because such theories are also powerful instruments in predicting and hence manipulating our environment, they are essential to almost every aspect of modern life, from stockbreeding to manufacturing rollerblades.[6]

Much sociological theory is of this clearly defined type, but much is not. Robert Merton, whose own functionalist theory we discuss later, has emphasized that "much of what is described in textbooks as sociological theory consists of general orientations toward substantive materials."[7] For example, if a theory puts forward a number of general propositions about human motivation, it may imply that some sorts of behavior are more likely than others and thereby provide the observer with a handle on a situation. However, it will supply little in the way of concrete propositions.

Such general propositions are not, in themselves, inconsistent with the idea of a deductive social science. Some theorists whose work is of this kind are interested in making predictive or testable statements about social organization and the development of society.[8] Others, however, are not concerned with such deductive scientific theory at all. Indeed, they may deny that such an approach is valid when one is dealing with the behavior of human beings.[9] Instead of being about regularities in the content of human behavior or the nature of social organization, their general statements describe how people's social interaction proceeds.[10]

Because of these differences, sociological theory may look like a group of perspectives with little in common except their general and formalizing approach and their concern with understanding human behavior. However, even those theories that are furthest removed from the deductive model involve a set of concepts, which are often described as the most elementary building blocks of any theory. Basically, a *concept* can be described as a word or symbol that represents a phenomenon (a label we use to name and clas-

---

[6]The actual process of scientific research and discovery is far more complex than this description of theoretical structure implies. Good (and very different) discussions of what is involved in scientific theory construction are to be found in Karl Popper, *The Logic of Scientific Discovery* (London: Hutchinson, 1959); Thomas Kuhn, *The Structure of Scientific Revolutions* (Chicago: University of Chicago Press, 1970); Stephen Toulmin, "From Form to Function: Philosophy and History of Science in the 1950s and Now," *Daedalus* 106, no. 3 (Summer 1977); Nagel, *The Structure of Science*.

[7]Robert K. Merton, *Social Theory and Social Structure*, enl. ed. (New York: The Free Press, 1968), p. 141.

[8]See, for example, the work of Dahrendorf on the importance of conflict, or much of Parsons' theory (Chapters 3 and 2).

[9]See, for example, the work of Garfinkel (Chapter 6) and Blumer (Chapter 5).

[10]For good discussions of the debate about whether social science is essentially different from natural science and whether it requires different and unique types of theory and argument, see Peter Wince, *The Idea of a Social Science and Its Relations to Philosophy* (London: Routledge and Kegan Paul, 1958); George Caspar Homans, *The Nature of Social Science* (New York: Harcourt, Brace and World, 1967); Randall Collins, *Conflict Sociology: Toward an Explanatory Science* (New York: Academic Press, 1975), chap. 1; Anthony Giddens, *The Constitution of Society* (Cambridge: Polity, 1984).

sify our perceptions and experiences) or an abstract idea generalized from particular instances. Durkheim's concept, anomie, and Marx's concept, alienation, are classic examples of sociological concepts.

The key concepts of a theory also enable us to see parts of social reality that may have escaped us otherwise. Concepts are an essential first step in understanding and analyzing social phenomena. Throughout this book we define the central concepts of each theory to enable the reader to see the various aspects of social reality revealed by each perspective and thus to better understand society.

Among the major dimensions along which sociological theories differ, we have already identified their acceptance or rejection of the deductive model drawn from natural science.[11] This is a crucial aspect of their *methodology*. Theories also differ in three other significant aspects. These are their *subject matter*, the *assumptions* underlying their approach, and the *types of questions* they believe social theory can and should answer. The following sections provide an overview of the current main alternatives as exemplified by the theories discussed in this text.

Subject Matter

In their subject matter, theoretical perspectives divide rather clearly between those perspectives that are concerned with the large-scale characteristics of social structure and roles, or *macrosociology*, and those concerned with person-to-person encounters and the details of human interaction and communication, or *microsociology*.

Functionalism and conflict theory are the two approaches concerned with the overall characteristics of social structure and the general nature of social institutions. They emphasize the relations between (and implications of) general categories of social position, such as Marx's classes or the affectively neutral relationships that Parsons saw as predominant in industrial societies. It is in the context of functionalism and conflict theory that discussions of social evolution, the most wide-ranging of all sociological subjects, are found.

This does not mean that macrosociological theories necessarily consider the perceptions and decisions of individual people to be irrelevant to their arguments. We would agree with Smelser that "hypotheses that link positions in the social structure with behavior always rest on at least implicit psychological assertions,"[12] and particularly on general ideas about human nature. But these theorists pay most attention not to individual psychology

---

[11]For a full discussion of the particular senses in which these terms are used, see the section on methodology later in this chapter.

[12]Neil J. Smelser, ed., *Sociology: An Introduction*, 2nd ed. (New York: John Wiley, 1973), p. 13.

but rather to organizations and institutions within society and to the socially prescribed roles that individuals play in them. They spend relatively little time analyzing the dynamics of individual action.

The perspectives of symbolic interactionism and phenomenology could hardly be more different, for they examine human interaction in the minutest detail. They discuss how, for example, the behavior of a super-market clerk, faced with an obstreperous customer and trying to make sense of the situation, depends on individual experiences and individual perceptions, as well as on social prescriptions; or how, sentence by sentence, a teacher and child understand (or fail to understand) each other. The concepts used by these microsociological approaches do not categorize aspects of social structure but instead consist of the vocabulary required to discuss the particular actions of people.

The rational choice theories discussed in Chapter 7 are less easily categorized. Although they concentrate on individuals' decisions and choices, these theories—Blau's in particular—attempt to link them to such structural qualities as a society's legitimacy. Nonetheless, compared to functionalists or conflict theorists, sociologists using a rational choice perspective are predominantly concerned with microsociological issues.

Assumptions

Sociological theorists' most important underlying assumptions concern human nature, and throughout the text we underline and contrast the different views of human beings. Theorists differ, in particular, in whether they view human behavior as essentially determined and so in principle *predictable*, or whether they emphasize human *creativity*. The clearest contrast is between, on the one hand, functionalism and theories of rational choice, and on the other, symbolic interactionism and phenomenology.[13]

The most explicit philosophical statement of the first view will be found in George Homans' work. Homans' arguments emphasize the role played by individuals' choices and decisions, but his whole approach is based on the belief that human behavior has causes and thus in principle is fully explicable. It may be *practically* impossible to find the underlying origins of different tastes and to predict any given decision, but they are nonetheless determined, Homans would argue, by a combination of particular prior circumstances and by universal principles or laws.

The same view is apparent in functionalism. Durkheim, Parsons, and Merton treat behavior as ultimately predictable, a function of certain underlying forces and needs and of the particular set of internalized norms and

---

[13]Rational choice theorists outside exchange theory use a rather less deterministic model in which individuals' given values and objectives nonetheless are treated as firm predictors of behavior.

values characteristic of a society. Again, it is not that functionalists' explanations ignore individual decisions; indeed, Parsons's action theory is built around individual motives. The point is, however, that functionalists see the behavior as ultimately determined and so in principle fully explicable—exactly the "scientific" attitude that Merton remembers exciting him and leading him into social science.[14]

Conflict theory is less wholeheartedly deterministic, but its underlying orientation is the same. The analytical theorists, Dahrendorf, Coser, and Collins, show this most clearly. Their search for general explanatory propositions implies that, by and large at least, behavior is determined and predictable. However, in general, the same is true for the more critical and utopian writers. Marx's whole theory of evolution is ultimately determinist.

What conflict theorists do emphasize is the point of view of *purposive individuals and groups* acting to secure their ends. The same is true of rational choice theorists. By contrast, functionalists are more interested in identifying and describing the general values and norms of a society or group, and in analyzing the roles these play in events, they treat behavior as considerably more *passive*.

However, it is the microsociological perspectives of symbolic interactionism and phenomenology that most emphasize human action, and their assumptions about human nature are fundamentally different. All the social sciences (and also, we would add, the biological sciences) differ from natural sciences, such as geology or physics, in that they deal with purposive behavior. In humans this involves a wide range of symbols and meanings—things that are intrinsically unobservable.[15]

Symbolic interactionists and phenomenologists believe that this view of the individual as active and creative also makes it impossible to predict behavior and develop sociological laws of a scientific type. Thus, although symbolic interactionists do not deny the existence of important regularities in behavior, they emphasize instead the *creative* way in which people interpret meaning during the course of an interaction. They distinguish between the "me" that incorporates learned attitudes and meanings and the innovative and unpredictable "I."[16] Phenomenology is also concerned with the continual nature of interpretation, but rather than contrasting the "I" with the "me," phenomenologists point to the pervasive nature of inferences and

---

[14]See Chapter 2.

[15]Behaviorist psychology is an attempt to dispense with any discussion of unobservables and to describe and predict behavior without going into what happens inside the "black box" of the human or animal mind. We feel that this is unlikely to be successful even with rats, and it is noticeable that Homans, one of the theorists who refers to this approach, nonetheless makes meanings and values a central part of his own explanations.

[16]It should be pointed out that predicting an individual's behavior and predicting average or group behavior are not the same; the impossibility of doing the first does not in itself imply that the second is also impossible. To predict group behavior, we need only know how most people will react most of the time.

assumptions. Our whole social world and experience of society and social interaction are, they argue, things that we build up as we go along, not things that are objectively real. Consequently, one should not develop concrete propositions that impose a misleading character of fixed meaning and structure on this process.

In addition to the crucial difference over whether human behavior is determined, perspectives also differ on whether they assume that human beings are motivated essentially by *interests* or by *values*. The difference is clearest in the case of functionalism and conflict theory, but it is also relevant to other perspectives.

Functionalists assume, more or less explicitly, that people's motives and behavior are largely a function of the social values they internalize. In other words, people's basic purposes are formed by their birth into a particular society; they do not exist independently. Functionalism also recognizes underlying "needs" or "functional imperatives" that are common to all human beings and that all societies must and do meet; but these tend to be sketched in cursorily. Socially instilled values are emphasized. Conflict theorists, by contrast, emphasize interests, which they often treat as self-evident but which include being free from subjugation, being in a position of power, and possessing more rather than less wealth and status. These theorists see interests as primary, common to all societies, and the main force behind human behavior in every case. Indeed, when conflict theorists discuss values specific to a given society, it is usually to describe their role in deceiving people about their true interests.

Other perspectives also imply that either values or interests are primary. Symbolic interactionism sees values as incorporated into the "me"; interests hardly appear in work done within this perspective. Phenomenology also emphasizes values rather than interests in its argument that people trust others to behave in certain situation-specific ways, and it sees such underlying trust as the basis of human behavior. Rational choice theorists, on the other hand, talk specifically about the importance of social values and tastes, which define people's preferences; but in practice they tend to base their arguments on objectives that are seen as universal—and therefore easily assumed—such as social acceptance or status. To that degree, they move closer to conflict theory's idea of universal interests.

Methodology

The third important respect in which the perspectives of modern theory differ is in their methods of argument and research, in particular whether they advocate deductive or inductive reasoning. With a *deductive* (or natural science) approach, one begins with explanatory hypotheses about a research problem and uses logical reasoning to deduce its empirical implications. In this approach the recipe for theory building requires that the basic concepts be spelled out before they are used in the formulation of hypotheses. For example, Durkheim's basic concepts (egoism, altruism, anomie, and fatalism) were used as key independent variables in his analysis of suicide rates.[17] The hypotheses are then tested on data in the real world.[18]

Scientists using the *inductive* approach begin instead by observing, by immersing themselves in the data. They feel that to start analysis with a clearly defined hypothesis is too rigid and may lead analysts to ignore important aspects of their subject. It is far better, they suggest, to get to know a subject and situation well and gradually build up, or induce, descriptions and explanations of what is really going on. In an inductive approach, the key concepts emerge in the final analysis of the research process. For example, Goffman's extensive observations in a mental hospital led him to create the concept "total institution."[19] Induction implies an inference from the particular to the general. In both deduction and induction, however, the theorist is concerned with clearly defined concepts that can be used to help understand what is going on.

Functionalism, conflict theory (with the exception of the Frankfurt School), and rational choice theory are essentially deductive. They logically derive, or "deduce," arguments and hypotheses from prior, more general propositions. For example, the functionalist Robert Merton argues that deviance results from a lack of congruence between values and opportunities;[20] the conflict theorist Ralf Dahrendorf explains industrial conflict by relating it to the more general principles of conflict of organization;[21] and Randall Collins devotes considerable effort to defending and advocating deductive scientific social analysis. Marxist theory can also be placed most easily on the deductive side of the divide. It relates social evolution to material changes, and the superstructure of politics and ideas to the substructure of economic life. However, its mode of argument is also consciously different in its emphasis on dialectical reasoning and identifying how social events emerge from contradictions within the existing order (rather than on tracing out a step-by-step progression).[22] Finally, rational choice, and especially exchange theory as presented by Homans, is also clearly and self-consciously deductive in form.[23] Homans sets out his basic propositions and then deduces

---

[17]See Chapter 2 for a discussion of Durkheim's approach.

[18]The argument is that, strictly speaking, you cannot prove that a hypothesis is *true* because there might always be some other explanation for your data that hasn't occurred to you. However, data that are clearly inconsistent with your hypothesis can show that it is *false*. See Karl Popper, *The Logic of Scientific Discovery* (London: Hutchinson, 1959).

[19]See Chapter 5 for a discussion of Goffman's approach.

[20]See Chapter 2.

[21]See Chapter 3.

[22]See Chapter 3. Marx's economics are especially close to mainstream deductive argument.

[23]Peter M. Blau's *Inequality and Heterogeneity: A Primitive Theory of Social Structure* (New York: The Free Press, 1977), although not a part of exchange theory, is quite as formally deductive in its approach.

others from them, showing how, for example, conformity to group norms may follow from individuals' valuation of social approval.[24]

Symbolic interactionism and phenomenology provide very clear contrasts, for their proponents observe and experience a situation first and then infer or "induce" from it what is going on. Symbolic interactionists feel that deductive reasoning implies falsely that action and interpretation are simplistically determined by prior events. Sociologists should instead concentrate on understanding—through the use, above all, of participant observation—how people in a particular situation see things and then build up from there. Phenomenologists are even more antagonistic toward deductive social science. This position is connected with the perspective's general assumptions. Phenomenologists believe that deductive theories, by proposing general positivist law, falsely imply the existence of a single objective reality about which one can advance testable generalizations. Instead, phenomenology argues, what any human being describes is his or her own view of reality, based on tacit assumptions. Ethnomethodologists, in particular, appear to be confident in their own ability to describe how people order their experiences. However, their view leads them to see sociology's task as not to derive general causal laws but to observe the ordering of experience directly and to use the documentary method of interpretation to identify regular patterns of meaning.

The deductive model is also rejected, for different reasons, by a third group, the "critical" theorists. They attack what they call "traditional," or "positivist," theory for suggesting that its deductive arguments can be assessed objectively and for aiming at pure knowledge. However, their work is not inductive in the fashion of symbolic interactionism or phenomenology. Its proponents have no faith in participant observation, and they have attacked phenomenology for relying on intuition.[25] Their critical theory assumes that fact and value are inseparable, and they propose their own antipositivist approach. In particular, they relate social phenomena to their notion of historical possibilities different from and superior to the current reality, and they believe in the possibility of reason as a standard against which to measure alternatives.[26]

Sociological theorists also differ in whether they advocate a heavy reliance on *quantitative data*. This aspect of their methodology tends to be related to whether they adopt a deductive model because the scientific idea of hypothesis testing is associated with using quantitative data. However, the link is by no means universal. A deductive exchange theorist like Homans is very quantitative in his approach; most conflict theorists, like Collins, are moderately so, within the limits set by historical information.

---

[24]See Chapter 7.

[25]Martin Jay, *The Dialectical Imagination* (Boston: Little, Brown, 1973), p. 82.

[26]Max Horkheimer, *Critical Theory* (New York: Herder and Herder, 1972).

However, a functionalist like Parsons makes fairly little use of quantitative data.

On principle, inductive theorists in sociology generally dislike quantitative techniques. Symbolic interactionists believe that quantitative techniques distance the observer from the area of life being studied and ignore important aspects of meaning not built into the measurement instrument. Phenomenologists distrust them because they imply that social phenomena can be measured objectively—although some, such as Cicourel, believe that they can be useful if analysts are aware of their limits. However, there is no necessary connection between induction and a distrust of quantitative methods. An analyst who believes in inducing propositions from experience may also believe in subsequently using quantitative methods for verification.

We present Table 1-1 as a means of summarizing some of the comparisons between the theories that we discuss in this section. Keep in mind that we have simplified the comparisons in this figure; therefore it doesn't do justice to the complexity of the differences between the perspectives and theorists involved.

TABLE 1-1 Comparison of Sociological Perspectives

Level of Analysis	Macro	Micro
	Functionalism Conflict	Symbolic Interactionism Phenomenology Rational Choice
View of Human Beings	**Predictable**	**Creative**
	Functionalism Conflict Rational Choice	Symbolic Interactionism Phenomenology
Motivation for Human Social Action	**Values**	**Interests**
	Functionalism Phenomenology Symbolic Interactionism	Conflict Rational Choice
Scientific Approach	**Deductive**	**Inductive**
	Functionalism Conflict Rational Choice	Symbolic Interactionism Phenomenology

We wish to thank an anonymous reviewer for suggesting this table.

Objectives

The final respect in which the major perspectives of sociological theory differ from each other is in their ultimate objectives—in particular, whether they aim largely at *describing* things or at *explaining*, or even *predicting*, them. Ultimately, all sciences and social sciences are concerned with increasing our comprehension of things, with providing accounts that make us feel that we now *understand* what is going on to a greater degree than we did before. But such accounts may range along a spectrum from more or less detailed redescriptions of what is happening (often employing unfamiliar terms and ways of looking at things but hardly concerned with identifying causal chains) to explanations that reinterpret things by relating them back to different and more general concepts. At their most precise and fully developed, such explanations may not only increase one's understanding but allow one to make specific predictions. This is what makes scientific deductive explanation such a powerful technological tool. Explanation and prediction are not identical, however. Important explanations that refer back to general principles may not permit much in the way of prediction; the theory of evolution is a case in point. Conversely, the ability to predict can rest simply on tight statistical correlations and not on much understanding at all.

One of our favorite examples of what this distinction means is the story of Dr. John Snow. During a nineteenth-century cholera epidemic, he suggested to the authorities that they could stop the spread of the disease if they simply removed the handles from all the water pumps! Snow was not a madman. He had noticed that the poorhouse inhabitants, who had their own well, were free from the disease, unlike people drinking water from the main pumps. But although Snow was quite correct about the correlation between catching cholera and drinking the water that carried it, he understood fairly little about the way cholera operates. This distinction between prediction and explanation has, in turn, encouraged many philosophers of science to emphasize explanation, not prediction, as the heart of deductive science.[27]

Among the major perspectives of sociological theory, we find, not surprisingly, that objectives are closely associated with methodology and with whether the perspective accepts a scientific model for social science. Thus, symbolic interactionism and phenomenology place relatively the greatest emphasis on descriptive analysis. Phenomenology's concern with describing events follows naturally from its rejection of the idea of general and objective laws about reality. Users and advocates of the symbolic interactionist perspective also tend to feel that general explanatory arguments are likely to ignore and miss so much of people's experiences that they are seriously flawed and inadequate. However, by taking into account numerous factors

---

[27]Toulmin, "From Form to Function," pp. 152–53.

and occurrences that can be missed in everyday, casual observation, such descriptions greatly increase our understanding.

Functionalism, conflict theory, and theories of rational choice aim at explaining phenomena in terms of more general principles. Of the three, functionalism is closest to the descriptive end of the spectrum. Talcott Parsons's work, for example, largely consists of redescribing society as a system and providing new classifications, but it does not explain how its parts develop, although other parts of functionalist theory are more fully explanatory.

Conflict theorists are more concerned with explanation than are functionalists. They also derive propositions that are generally predictive, though usually not to the extent of predicting particular historical events. Their work involves some redescription—as when they talk of "ideology" or "alienation"—but their main concern is to provide a detailed explanation of how events and institutions are created by the actions and interests of different groups with different resources and by changes in technology, economic organization, ritual, and ideas. In using such explanatory propositions as a basis for prediction Marx is by far the most ambitious, although other theorists, such as Habermas, have attempted to predict the future development of existing society.

Finally, of all the perspectives discussed in this text, rational choice, and especially exchange theory, is the least concerned with description and the most concerned with explanation and prediction. This is not to imply that its proponents are interested only in correlations of the pump-handle type, for they discuss in great detail what goes on inside people's minds in an attempt to understand the origins of actions and behavior. However, this objective further reinforces the tendency of exchange theorists and other rational choice theorists to concentrate on a limited range of subjects involving individual and small group behavior. On a wider scale, they would agree that the complexity of social affairs makes precise prediction impossible[28] and that by taking as its subject the whole sprawling complex of human society, sociology has chosen an area it cannot fully explain, let alone predict.

The fact that sociological theory does not form a cumulative body of work comparable to physics or even neoclassical economics does not mean that we have an impasse with one approach merely contradicting another. The test of a theory is ultimately whether it helps us to understand, and each of the theories discussed here sheds light on a different aspect of human society. In Popper's words, they are all "nets cast to catch what we call 'the world'—to rationalize, to explain and to master it";[29] and it is for this reason that each deserves recognition as part of contemporary sociological theory.

---

[28]Homans, in fact, would argue that at this level the distinction between history and sociology becomes meaningless.

[29]Popper, *The Logic of Scientific Discovery*, p. 59.

THEORY AND UNDERSTANDING: THE EXAMPLES
OF FORMAL EDUCATION AND THE ROLE OF WOMEN
IN CONTEMPORARY SOCIETY

Formal education and gender are two aspects of life in modern industrial society with which we all have direct experience and that affect our lives in countless ways. This makes them both excellent areas in which to see how well sociological theory illuminates our everyday world. In the chapters that follow we have consistently selected examples of sociological research and nonsociological writing that bear on education and gender. Each theoretical perspective can illuminate some but not all aspects of a social phenomenon; by returning frequently to the same themes we hope that the reader will understand more easily the strengths and weaknesses of each perspective.

In modern societies an increasing proportion of people's lives and a large part of national income are given to formal education. In 1994, for example, the proportion of the population in the United States completing secondary education was 85 percent, compared to 84 percent in Germany, 74 percent in Canada, 70 percent in Japan (1989 data), and 75 percent in the United Kingdom. Male and female rates were about the same in the United States, Canada, and Japan, but the male rate was 12 percent higher than females in Germany and 11 percent higher in the United Kingdom. Turning to the proportion completing higher education in these same countries, the percentages were as follows: United States, 24 percent; Canada, 17 percent; Japan, 13 percent in 1989; Germany, 13 percent; and the United Kingdom, 12 percent. The male rates were higher than females, with the difference ranging from 3 to 6 percent in all of these countries except Japan, where the gender gap was 17 percent.[30] Moreover, the length of people's education and their success in passing courses, getting good grades, and entering prestigious colleges have a considerable impact on their later opportunities and careers.

In the case of both education and gender, two questions in particular relate clearly to our experiences. Our questions for education are: First, why is the amount of time we spend in formal schooling so long, and the educational system of industrialized countries so big compared to the past? And second, within our own schools and classes, why do some students do well and continue through high school, college, and graduate school, while others drop out as soon as they possibly can after years of guerilla war with the authorities?

Our questions for gender both relate to the roles of women in contemporary society. First, why, among full-time workers, do females with *one to three years of college* in the United States make annual average salaries that are

---

[30]U.S. National Center for Education Statistics, *The Condition of Education* (Washington, D.C.: U.S. Government Printing Office, 1997), Table 23-1, p. 265.

lower than those earned by male high school graduates?[31] Second, why do boys and men, at home, school, and work, tend to be aggressive and to dominate the situation, while girls and women tend to be more caring and to exhibit more "supportive" behavior?

We suggest that our readers keep these general themes and research questions in mind as they progress through the text. Each theoretical perspective can effectively provide a piece of the puzzle. In Chapter 9 we assemble and synthesize what each offers. We hope that in bringing their contributions together it will be apparent how together these very different approaches can provide coherent explanations of apparently bewildering social phenomena.

[31]In 1995 the average annual earnings of full-time female workers in the United States with one to three years of college was $23,997; whereas the average earnings of male full-time workers who were high school graduates was $29,510. Among college graduates, male salaries averaged $45,266, compared to $32,051 for females. See U.S. National Center for Education Statistics, *Digest of Education Statistics* (Washington, D.C.: U.S. Government Printing Office, 1997), Table 378, p. 422.

CHAPTER TWO

Functionalism

INTRODUCTION

Because it held the dominant position among contemporary sociological theories for a number of years, and because other perspectives emerged as a challenge to it, we begin with functionalism. Typically a major portion of the required modern theory readings for sociology students in the United States has been devoted to works by Talcott Parsons and Robert Merton. Some sociologists have even taken the position that sociological analysis and functional analysis are one and the same. Such was the thrust of Kingsley Davis's presidential address to the American Sociological Association in 1959, titled "The Myth of Functional Analysis as a Special Method in Sociology and Anthropology."[1]

Davis argued that sociology involves (1) examining the role (or function) that an institution or type of behavior plays in society and the way it is related to other social features and (2) explaining it in essentially social terms.[2] This, Davis felt, is also the nature of functional analysis. The debate continues, however, for many sociologists disagree with Davis's arguments about the nature of sociology and oppose any effort to label the discipline as functionalist. Indeed, as we shall see in the ensuing chapters, other perspectives tend to define themselves in terms of and in contrast to functionalism.

This perspective is often labeled "structural-functionalism" because of its focus on the functional requisites, or "needs," of a social system that must be met if the system is to survive and on the corresponding structures that meet these needs. According to this view social systems tend to perform certain tasks that are necessary for their survival, and sociological analysis, therefore, involves a search for the social structures that perform these tasks or meet the needs of the social system. Over the years, the approach's two major theorists, Talcott Parsons and Robert K. Merton, have often been referred to as structural-functionalists. We call this perspective *functionalism* for two reasons. First, it clarifies the link to the functionalism of its forerunners, especially Émile Durkheim. Second, both of our major theorists prefer the term *functionalism*. Merton's use of the term *functional analysis* has been consistent over the years. Parsons abandoned the term "structural-functionalism" when he revised the concepts of function, structure, and process.[3]

---

[1]Kingsley Davis, "The Myth of Functional Analysis as a Special Method in Sociology and Anthropology," *American Sociological Review* 24 (1959): 757–72.

[2]It is interesting to compare Davis's arguments with the exchange theory of George Homans, who argues that satisfactory sociological explanation must ultimately be psychological. See George Homans on psychological reductionism, Chapter 7.

[3]See Talcott Parsons, "The Present Status of Structural-Functional Theory in Sociology," in Lewis A. Coser, ed., *The Idea of Social Structure: Papers in Honor of Robert K. Merton* (New York: Harcourt Brace Jovanovich, 1975), p. 67, where he states, "The hyphenated label 'structural-functionalism' has seemed to me to be decreasingly appropriate."

Functionalism Defined

In answer to the question "What is functionalism?" we turn first to *A Modern Dictionary of Sociology*, which defines functionalism as

> The analysis of social and cultural phenomena in terms of the functions they perform in a sociocultural system. In functionalism, society is conceived of as a system of interrelated parts in which no part can be understood in isolation from the whole. A change in any part is seen as leading to a certain degree of imbalance, which in turn results in changes in other parts of the system and to some extent to a reorganization of the system as a whole. The development of functionalism was based on the model of the organic system found in the biological sciences.[4]

Because it is concerned with the overall characteristics of social structure and the general nature of social institutions, functionalism has a macrosociological focus. What functionalists mean by the "interrelation of the parts of a social system" can be understood by looking at an airport. Its parts include the roles of airline ticketing and reservation personnel, maintenance crews, pilots and flight attendants, passengers, air traffic controllers, restaurant workers, and luggage carriers, to mention a few. All these parts are interrelated, and you need only think of a disturbance in any one of the parts to realize their interdependence. Many changes could lead to disequilibrium of the airport as a social system, including the closing of runways due to inclement weather, a malfunctioning of the radar control system, and the high volume of passengers during the holidays. Any of these disturbances can result in imbalance, often to the point of a temporary breakdown in the system.

In analyzing social systems along these lines, functionalists emphasize three elements:

1. The general interrelatedness, or interdependence, of the system's parts
2. The existence of a "normal" state of affairs, or state of equilibrium, comparable to the normal or healthy state of an organism
3. The way that all the parts of the system reorganize to bring things back to normal

One of functionalism's most important propositions is that there will always be some such reorganization and tendency to restore equilibrium. In the case of the airport, it is easy to define normal conditions and see how the system organizes to restore them: personnel will work harder, overtime will be set up, and additional staff will be hired. In other cases, as we shall see, restoring equilibrium may be more difficult.

---

[4]George A. Theodorson and Achilles S. Theodorson, ed., *A Modern Dictionary of Sociology* (New York: Thomas Y. Crowell, 1969), p. 167.

In analyzing how social systems maintain and restore equilibrium, functionalists tend to use *shared values* or generally accepted standards of desirability as a central concept.[5] Value consensus means that individuals will be morally committed to their society. The emphasis on values is the second most important feature of functionalism. As such, it contrasts directly with the other major macrosociological perspective, conflict theory. Whereas functionalism emphasizes the unity of society and what its members share, conflict theorists stress the divisions within a society and the struggles that arise out of people's pursuits of their different material interests.[6]

INTELLECTUAL ROOTS: ÉMILE DURKHEIM AND HIS FORERUNNERS

The most important intellectual ancestors of modern functionalism are the sociologists Auguste Comte, Herbert Spencer, Vilfredo Pareto, and Émile Durkheim. Comte, Spencer, and Pareto emphasized the interdependence of parts of the social system, while Durkheim emphasized integration or solidarity.

Auguste Comte (1789–1857), who is commonly identified as the founder of sociology, derived his interest in "statics" (order) and "dynamics" (progress) in society from his general investigation of the foundations of social stability. Comte stated functionalism's basic assumption of the social system's interdependence when he said, "The statical study of sociology consists in the investigation of the laws of action and reaction of the different parts of the social system."[7] The functional concept of equilibrium also emerged when Comte declared that a lack of harmony between the whole and parts of the social system was "pathological." The concept of equilibrium was borrowed from biology's treatment of homeostasis, which can be illustrated when you fall and scrape your knee, and eventually a scab forms as other parts of your body come to the rescue. Soon it heals and your body's system is in equilibrium again. Comte's work was replete with such comparisons between social and biological organisms.

Herbert Spencer (1820–1903) should also be mentioned as a forerunner of functionalism because of his concept of differentiation. By *differentiation* Spencer meant the mutual dependence of unlike parts of the system, which is brought about inevitably by an increase in society's size.[8] Modern functionalists similarly identify differentiation as an important aspect of a social system's interrelatedness and integration. Spencer's evolutionary theory

---

[5]See p. 25 for a functionalist definition of values.

[6]See Chapter 3.

[7]Auguste Comte, *The Positive Philosophy*, trans. Harriet Martineau (London: Bell, 1896), vol. II.

[8]Herbert Spencer, *The Principles of Sociology* (New York: Appleton, 1896).

generally resembled the theory that Durkheim later presented in *The Division of Labor in Society*—a theory that greatly influenced modern functionalists. However, there were two important differences. First, Durkheim did not insist on the inherent necessity of social differentiation, as did Spencer. Second, Durkheim's insistence that social facts were the proper subject matter for sociology directly contradicted Spencer's reductionist position that the cause of social progress was psychological; that is, that the determining factor was the individual's need for greater happiness. In these respects, functionalism follows Durkheim. Nonetheless, Parsons used Spencer's notion of social differentiation in his theory of social change.

Vilfredo Pareto (1848–1923) patterned his system of sociology on a physiochemical system characterized by interdependence of parts and adjustive changes, rather than on the biological organism. To Pareto, the "molecules" of the social system were individuals with interests, drives, and sentiments. He was the first sociologist to precisely describe a social system in terms of the interrelations and mutual dependencies among parts. In his discussion of how systems adapt and change while maintaining equilibrium, Parsons later borrowed Pareto's idea of a dynamic or "moving" equilibrium that produces harmony for the system.

Émile Durkheim

Émile Durkheim (1858–1917) is certainly the most important sociological forerunner of modern functionalism. Talcott Parsons has said that Durkheim was one of his most important intellectual role models.[9] Similarly, Robert Merton states that Durkheim was, besides those under whom he studied directly, one of the two from whom he learned most.[10]

However, Durkheim's theoretical influence extends beyond functionalism. Erving Goffman and Peter Berger have also incorporated some of Durkheim's ideas into their own symbolic interactionist and phenomenological perspectives. Randall Collins, a conflict theorist, incorporates Durkheim's ideas on ritual into his work.[11]

Émile Durkheim was born at Épinal in Lorraine, France. His father, grandfather, and great-grandfather had been rabbis, but though he studied for a time at a rabbinical school, Durkheim decided not to follow in their steps.[12] Family finances and his father's illness made Durkheim's early days as a college student difficult, but he finished his degree at the École Normale

---

[9]Talcott Parsons, "On Building Social System Theory: A Personal History," *Daedalus* (Fall 1970): 873.

[10]See Coser, *The Idea of Social Structure*, p. 96.

[11]See Chapters 3, 5, and 6.

[12]See Steven Lukes's *Émile Durkheim: His Life and Work* (New York: Harper and Row, 1972) for a comprehensive treatment.

Supérieure, and because of his many publications in philosophy and social science, he was invited to teach at the University of Bordeaux in 1887. In 1902 he moved to the University of Paris, where he taught until his death.

Durkheim viewed teaching as almost a sacred duty, for many of the students in his courses were the future secondary teachers of France. In addition to teaching and research, Durkheim found time to establish, with a small number of colleagues, the first French sociology journal, *Année sociologique*. He was also fiercely patriotic, and during World War I he helped to organize a committee for the publication of studies and documents on the war to explain the French position to other countries. Durkheim's only son, André, was killed while fighting for the French cause in 1916. That blow, combined with overwork, led to a stroke and Durkheim's subsequent death in 1917, at the age of 59.

Some of Durkheim's most important functionalist ideas are a result of his lifelong interest in the concept of *integration*, the incorporation of individuals into the social order. Integration (or social solidarity) is important for the maintenance of social equilibrium. *The Rules of Sociological Method* and his works on religion and education are often cited as his most important contributions to functionalism, but even in his first great work, *The Division of Labor in Society*, he was examining the function of the division of labor.

Durkheim viewed social evolution as a movement from the mechanical solidarity of tribal societies to the organic solidarity characteristic of industrial societies. He argued that primitive societies were characterized by a strong *collective conscience*, which he defined as "the totality of beliefs and sentiments common to average citizens of the same society." As the division of labor increased, so too did individualism. As a result, there was a corresponding decrease in collective conscience and a shift to organic solidarity, characterized by the interdependence of roles[13] and a lack of self-sufficiency that held people together. Nations on the brink of the third millenium have, however, experienced moments of increase in collective consciousness. Two examples come to mind: the students involved in the "velvet revolution" in Czechoslovakia who bravely faced down government tanks with flowers in their hands, and more recently, the outpouring of emotion in England on the death of Princess Diana that reverberated to other parts of the world.

Durkheim also set out to create a proper subject matter for sociology, the realm of social facts. He defined a *social fact* as that "which is general over the whole of a given society whilst having an existence of its own, independent of its individual manifestations." His examples of social facts are laws, morals, beliefs, customs, and fashions. Durkheim later elaborated on the meaning of social facts and used the term *institution*, meaning the

---

[13]Émile Durkheim, *The Division of Labor in Society* (Glencoe, Ill.: The Free Press, 1964), p. 49.

"beliefs and modes of behavior instituted by the collectivity." He defined sociology as "the science of institutions, their genesis and their functioning."[14] Durkheim thus made it clear that he viewed macrostructural (large-scale or societywide) phenomena as sociology's proper subject matter.

In *The Rules of Sociological Method*, where he discusses social facts, Durkheim sees functions as "general needs of the social organism."[15] He then proceeds to make his case for explanation of social facts by social rather than nonsocial causes. He applied his method in his well-known study *Suicide*, where he focused on suicide rates, a social fact, rather than on individual suicides.

Durkheim's discussion of punishment provides an excellent example of the strengths and weaknesses of both his and much later functionalist analysis. Punishment is, he argues, a social reaction to crime. It serves not simply the obvious functions of retribution for the criminal and general deterrence of crime; it also fulfills the generally unrecognized but critical function of maintaining the intensity of collective sentiments, or what modern functionalists call shared values (in this case, the objection to criminal activity). Punishment, Durkheim argues, "has the useful function of maintaining these sentiments at the same level of intensity, for they could not fail to weaken it if the offenses committed against them remained unpunished."[16]

However, Durkheim's explanation of what causes societies to adopt punishment is less satisfactory. He points out, quite correctly, that the function something performs does not explain its existence in the first place, and he states, "We will, therefore, discover more easily the function if the cause is already known." However, he then goes on to engage in exactly that circularity of reasoning he attempted to avoid in distinguishing cause from function; he argues that punishment exists *because* of the function it performs in maintaining collective sentiments, which then in turn "cause" punishment.

In other words, at first Durkheim says that punishment is a consequence, or dependent variable:

(Cause)	(Function)
X ————————————————→ Y	
intensity of	punishment
collective	
sentiments	

[14]Émile Durkheim, *The Rules of Sociological Method*, edited and with an introduction by Steven Lukes (New York: The Free Press, 1982), pp. 45 and 59.

[15]Durkheim, *The Rules of Sociological Method*, p. 123.

[16]Durkheim, *The Rules of Sociological Method*, p. 124.

But when he discusses the consequences of punishment for the society, he says

Thus, in Durkheim's argument, the cause is, after all, the function, as we can see in the illustration. One could ask the chicken or the egg question of Durkheim. We shall find that this problem of circularity and explaining things by the functions they perform recurs throughout functional analysis.

Durkheim's most famous concept, anomie, is central to his study *Suicide*.[17] Literally translated from the French, *anomie* means normlessness, a situation where rules or norms are absent. Besnard defined an anomic situation as one "characterized by indeterminate goals and unlimited aspirations, the disorientation or vertigo created by confrontation with an excessive widening of the horizons of the possible."[18] Durkheim described two types of anomie: acute anomie, which is the result of an abrupt change, like a business crisis or a divorce; and chronic anomie, a state of constant change, characteristic of modern industrial society. Durkheim focused on chronic anomie because he was concerned about what was going on in his own country and in other industrialized countries.

Durkheim did not take a neutral position regarding suicide; he saw it as a social problem and was concerned about the increasing rates of suicide in industrialized countries. He had also been touched personally by this phenomenon: it was the suicide of his closest friend, Victor Hommay, that prompted him to embark on an empirical study of suicide.[19]

A description of the central argument of Durkheim's *Suicide* may clarify the deductive (or natural science) approach. Durkheim's study does not simply describe the suicide rates in Europe in the nineteenth century. Instead he begins with the basic assumption that too much or too little integration or regulation (cohesion) is unhealthy for a society, and from this he derives specific hypotheses about suicide. To demonstrate Durkheim's approach and clarify what "middle-range" theory is about, Robert Merton restated Durkheim this way:

[17]Émile Durkheim, *Suicide: A Study in Sociology*, translated by John A. Spaulding and George Simpson, edited and with an introduction by George Simpson (Glencoe, Ill.: The Free Press, 1951).

[18]Phillippe Besnard, "The True Nature of Anomie," *Sociological Theory* 6 (1988): 91–95.

[19]See Ruth A. Wallace and Shirley F. Hartley, "Religious Elements of Friendship: Durkheimian Theory in an Empirical Context," in Jeffrey C. Alexander, ed., *Durkheimian Sociology: Cultural Studies* (New York: Cambridge University Press, 1988), pp. 93–106.

1. Social cohesion provides psychic support to group members subjected to acute stresses and anxieties.
2. Suicide rates are functions of unrelieved anxieties and stresses to which persons are subjected.
3. Catholics have greater social cohesion than Protestants.
4. Therefore, lower suicide rates should be anticipated among Catholics than among Protestants.[20]

In typical functionalist fashion, Durkheim bases his theory on social cohesion or solidarity and on two specific societal needs, integration and regulation. His hypothesis is that societies characterized by too much or too little integration or regulation will have high suicide rates. The corresponding types of suicide are altruism (too much integration), egoism (too little integration), fatalism (too much regulation), and anomie (too little regulation). Durkheim is deeply concerned about the effects of the latter type of suicide. Anomie, he says, is a pathological state for society, one aspect of which is a rise in suicide rates. As we shall see later, in his concern for the state of society Durkheim is similar to Marx. Whereas Durkheim saw modern society as afflicted with anomie, Marx described it as marked by alienation. The concept of anomie holds an important place in modern functionalism, as does alienation in conflict theory. However, whereas Durkheim emphasizes people's need for firmly established and common social norms, Marx sees alienation as the pernicious result of a social order that tightly controls its citizens, and he argues that mankind needs far greater freedom from regulation.[21]

Again unlike Marx, Durkheim attempted to make his theory of suicide empirically verifiable by further defining and operationalizing his concepts. For instance, he considered a situation clearly anomic when a crisis or a sudden social change causes discontinuity between people's actual experiences and their normative expectations. Events of this type, which Durkheim suggested will create anomie and on which empirical data can be collected, include the sudden death of a spouse and economic depressions. Anomie, Durkheim hypothesized, will in turn lead to high suicide rates. Using the deductive approach, Durkheim not only made his hypotheses testable; he actually tested some of his hypotheses with data that had been collected by government officials. He found, for example, that widows and widowers did indeed have higher suicide rates than married people and that suicide rates were higher during a depression than they were during periods of economic stability.[22]

[20]See Robert K. Merton, *Social Theory and Social Structure*, rev. and enl. ed. (New York: The Free Press, 1957), p. 151.

[21]See Chapter 3 for Marx's definition and discussion of alienation.

[22]See Durkheim, *Suicide*.

Durkheim's most important contribution to functionalism is *The Elementary Forms of the Religious Life*.[23] Here he shows how in the most primitive tribes religion was a strong integrative force through its instillation of common values and identification. We have already referred to the central role values play in functionalist explanation; functionalism again closely follows Durkheim's approach, referring to values as "widely shared conceptions of the good"[24] or "beliefs that legitimize the existence and importance of specific social structures and the kinds of behavior that transpire in social structure."[25] Smelser presents the example of belief in free enterprise as a societal value that "endorses the existence of business firms organized around the institution of private property and engaged in the pursuit of private profit."[26] Another of the hallmarks of functional analysis, the persistent search for integrative forces, is an aspect of the general stress on interdependence and equilibrium, which we have already mentioned.[27] Durkheim, who again shared modern functionalism's concerns, was interested in religion largely because he considered religion to be especially effective in developing common values—and so a good source of integration. Durkheim's search for an equally strong integrative force in modern society led him to see the public school system as the functional alternative to religion for the transmission of values in modern society.[28] Although modern functionalism has roots in the work of Comte, Spencer, and Pareto, it owes its greatest debt to Durkheim. We now turn to Durkheim's most important heirs, Talcott Parsons and Robert Merton.

[23]Émile Durkheim, *The Elementary Forms of Religious Life* (New York: Collier Books, 1961).

[24]Marie August Neal, *Values and Interests in Social Change* (Englewood Cliffs, N.J.: Prentice Hall, 1965), p. 9.

[25]See Neil J. Smelser, *The Sociology of Economic Life* (Englewood Cliffs, N.J.: Prentice Hall, 1963), p. 27.

[26]Smelser, *The Sociology of Economic Life*, p. 27. See also Robin M. Williams, Jr., "Change and Stability in Values and Value Systems," in Bernard Barber and Alex Inkeles, eds., *Stability and Social Change* (Boston: Little, Brown, 1971), pp. 123–59. Williams describes values as generalized criteria for desirability of conduct, and norms as specific obligatory demands, expectations, and rules that are legitimated by values.

[27]Amitai Etzioni, founder of the Communitarian Network in the United States, follows in Durkheim's footsteps. His recent efforts to move the public debate away from a preoccupation with rights to a balance between individual rights and social responsibilities are discussed in his recent books, such as *The Spirit of Community: Rights, Responsibilities, and the Communitarian Agenda* (New York: Crown, 1993) and *The New Golden Rule: Community and Morality in a Democratic Society* (New York: Basic Books, 1996).

[28]During the First World War, in which his own son was killed, Durkheim hailed the success of the public school system:

> All people . . . render homage to the virtues she (France) has shown, the heroism of her troops, to the grave and calm endurance with which the country has borne the frightful calamities of a war unparalleled in history. What does this mean if not that our educational methods have produced the best effects that could be expected of them; that our public school has made men of the children confided to it.

Émile Durkheim, "The School of Tomorrow," in Ferdinand Buisson and Frederic E. Farrington, eds., *French Educational Ideals of Today* (New York: World Books, 1919), pp. 185–92.

PART ONE

Talcott Parsons: Grand Theory

BACKGROUND

Talcott Parsons (1902–1979) was the son of a Congregational minister who later served as president of Marietta College in Ohio. Parsons did his undergraduate work at Amherst, where he majored in biology. As he describes it in his intellectual autobiography, he was "converted" to the social sciences in his junior year, but owing to faculty turnover he was unable then to pursue his interests in detail.[29] It is important to keep in mind this early interest in biology, however, because the direction he took in sociology was clearly rooted in biological studies and their concern with the interdependence of an organism's parts.

A year at the London School of Economics was followed by an exchange fellowship to Heidelberg, where he encountered Max Weber's work for the first time and where he wrote a doctoral dissertation on "The Concept of Capitalism in Recent German Literature," treating, among others, Marx and Weber. Parsons played an important part in introducing Weber to America when he translated *The Protestant Ethic and the Spirit of Capitalism* (1930) and later analyzed Weber's theoretical perspective in what is now Volume II of *The Structure of Social Action* (1937).

Following a year of teaching at Amherst, Parsons went to Harvard as an instructor in 1927[30] and taught there until he was retired as emeritus professor in 1973. In 1942 he was elected president of the American Sociological Association. After his retirement he continued to teach as a visiting professor at such universities as Pennsylvania, Rutgers, and California at Berkeley. Shortly before his death in May 1979 he was continuing work on such topics as sociobiology (the study of the biological bases of human behavior), interdisciplinary studies, and the cultural system level (the level of analysis that focuses on the question of meaning, or symbolic systems) in his general theory of action.[31] His critics, both positive and negative, are numerous; and although functionalism is no longer the dominant perspective, his work serves as a major reference point in modern sociological

---

[29]We have relied on Parsons's autobiographical statement and on Benton Johnson's monograph throughout this section. See Parsons, "On Building Social System Theory," pp. 826–81, and Benton Johnson, *Functionalism in Modern Sociology: Understanding Talcott Parsons* (Morristown, N.J.: General Learning Press, 1975).

[30]From 1927 to 1930 he was in the economics department. Harvard's sociology department was established in 1930.

[31]From a personal interview with Parsons on February 16, 1977.

theory.[32] Much of this chapter will be devoted to a discussion of Parsons's contributions to functionalism: his systems of action, his action schema, the pattern variables, and the system problems.

PARSONS'S SYSTEM LEVELS

The concept of a system is at the core of any discussion of Parsonian theory. Parsons stated, "The concept of system in the action field as in others, has been central to my thinking from a very early stage."[33] His general theory of action, in which he gives his overall pictures of how societies are structured and fit together, includes four systems: the cultural system, the social system, the personality system, and the behavioral organism as a system.

The basic unit of analysis at the cultural system level is "meaning" or "symbolic systems." Some examples of symbolic systems are religious beliefs, languages, and national values. In his view cultural traditions are made up of shared symbolic systems. As we would expect, at this level Parsons focuses on shared values. A key concept here is *socialization,* whereby societal values are internalized by a society's members; that is, they make society's values their own. In Parsons's view, socialization is a powerful integrative force in maintaining social control and holding a society together.

Heads of state often draw on the functionalist perspective in their speeches. The following excerpts from President John F. Kennedy's inaugural address on January 20, 1961, exemplify a leader's appeal to shared values on both national and international levels:

> Let every nation know . . . that we shall pay any price, bear any burden, meet any hardship, support any friend, oppose any foe to assure the survival and the success of liberty.
> . . . In your hands, my fellow citizens, more than mine, will rest the final success or failure of our course. Since this country was founded, each generation of Americans has been summoned to give testimony to its national loyalty.
> . . . And so, my fellow Americans: ask not what your country can do for you—ask what you can do for your country.
> My fellow citizens of the world: ask not what America will do for you, but what together we can do for the freedom of man.[34]

[32]Two festschrifts have been published. See Alex Inkeles and Bernard Barber, eds., *Stability and Social Change* (Boston: Little, Brown, 1971), and Jan J. Loubser, Rainer C. Baum, Andrew Effrat, and Victor Lidz, eds., *Explorations on General Theory in Social Science: Essays in Honor of Talcott Parsons* (New York: The Free Press, 1976). For a complete bibliography through 1977, see Talcott Parsons, *Action Theory and the Human Condition* (New York: Free Press, 1978).

[33]Parsons, "On Building Social System Theory," p. 849. See Walter Buckley's critique of the way functionalists like Parsons use "system" in his *Sociology and Modern Systems Theory* (Englewood Cliffs, N.J.: Prentice Hall, Inc., 1967).

[34]*Public Papers of the Presidents of the United States: John F. Kennedy* (Washington, D.C.: United States Government Printing Office, 1962), pp. 1–3. Thanks to Anne Kanour for drawing our attention to this source.

The social system is the next level in Parsons's scheme, and it is the one on which he has elaborated the most. Here the basic unit is "role interaction." Parsons defined the social system thus:

> A social system consists in a plurality of individual actors interacting with each other in a situation which has at least a physical or environmental aspect, actors who are motivated in terms of a tendency to the "optimization of gratification" and whose relation to their situations, including each other, is defined and mediated in terms of a system of culturally structured and shared symbols.[35]

In Parsons's definition of a social system, *plurality* can mean two or more, and *actors* can be people or collectivities. Thus a social system can be made up of anything from two people interacting in a restaurant to the relationships within the United Nations, where the actors are member nations. The relationship of the social system to the cultural system is apparent in Parsons's reference to "culturally structured and shared symbols," which define the way actors interact.

According to Parsons, the basic unit of the personality system is the individual actor, the human person. His focus at this level is on individual needs, motives, and attitudes, such as the "motivation toward gratification," which he emphasizes in his definition of the social system quoted above. As we shall see, motivation toward gratification corresponds to both conflict theory's and exchange theory's explicit assumptions that people are self-interested or profit maximizers.[36]

In the fourth system, the behavioral organism, the basic unit is the human being in its biological sense—that is, the physical aspect of the human person, including the organic and physical environment in which the human being lives. In referring to this system, Parsons explicitly mentions the organism's central nervous system and motor activity.[37] As we mentioned earlier, he returned to his interest in sociobiology toward the end of his life.[38]

Parsons's view of socialization will illustrate how all these systems are interrelated. At birth we are simply behavioral organisms; only as we develop as individuals do we gain any personal identity. How, then, do people become socialized? As we mentioned earlier, Parsons says that people internalize the values of a society; that is, they make the social values of the cultural system their own by learning from other actors in the social system what is expected of them. In other words, they learn role expectations and so become full participants in society. Thus the values come from the cultural

---

[35]Parsons, *The Social System* (New York: The Free Press, 1951), p. 5.

[36]See Chapters 3 and 7.

[37]Talcott Parsons, *The System of Modern Sociology* (Englewood Cliffs, N.J.: Prentice Hall, 1971), p. 5.

[38]See Chapter 8 for a discussion of the sociology of the body.

system; the corresponding normative or role expectations are learned in the social system; the individual identity comes from the personality system; and the biological equipment comes from the behavioral organism.

Let us take a concrete social system and see how socialization works within it. Consider an urban gang. If one of the values of the gang is the ability to steal cars or sell drugs, then juveniles who wish to become full members of that gang not only will have to make that value their own (cultural system), but they must also know how much of such behavior is expected of them. In social system terms, they must conform to normative expectations. Their own identity must also be involved in their membership: membership in the gang must answer certain needs or drives in their own personalities. The behavioral organism is also involved because potential gang members must possess a certain dexterity and the physical skills to steal cars or sell drugs without detection or bodily injury and live up to the expectations of the gang members.

This example should help illustrate the interpenetration of all four systems. Parsons does not consider his four system levels to be mutually exclusive; rather, they exhibit the interdependence that functionalism consistently stresses. In the following section, we discuss Parsons's theory of action, a framework for describing actual behavior within the context of the four systems.

PARSONS'S THEORY OF ACTION

Parsons's action theory starts with a role player, or "actor," who could be either a single person or a collectivity. In Figure 2-1 the actor (1) is Ann Doe. Parsons sees the *actor* as motivated to spend energy in reaching a desirable *goal* or end, as defined by the cultural system (2), which for Ann Doe is a B.A.

FIGURE 2-1   Parsons's Theory of Action

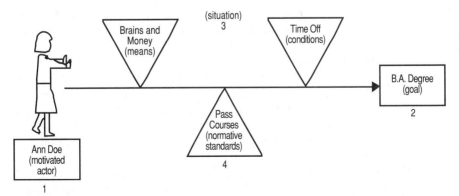

degree. The action takes place in a situation (3), which includes *means* (facilities, tools, or resources) and *conditions* (obstacles that arise in the pursuit of the goal). Ann Doe, for instance, has the intellectual ability and the money for tuition, but she is employed full-time. Taking courses that are scheduled after work hours, getting time off during work hours, or changing to a job that will allow her the needed time is essential in her situation. The means and conditions involved could, then, make a situation precarious. Finally, and this is extremely important in Parsons's action theory, all these elements are regulated by the *normative standards* of the social system (4); in Ann Doe's case, she must pass all courses required for her degree. Actors cannot ignore the rules of the game; the rules define their ends and how they behave, and normative expectations must be fulfilled by any actor who is motivated to pursue a goal. Because the norms have been internalized by the actor, she or he is motivated to act appropriately. Now we can see both why it could be said that norms are at the heart of Parsons' theory of action and why Parsons considers the "cultural system" that legitimates them to be primary.

In Chapter 1 we drew a distinction between theories in the scientific sense, from which one can logically deduce concrete propositions and hypotheses, and general orientations to analysis. We can see that Parsons's all-encompassing general theory of action belongs more to the latter than to the former category. It provides concepts that are appropriate for describing a wide range of behavior and for emphasizing the interdependence of society's components rather than direct statements about what people will do in different situations or the structure of actual societies. However, Parsons also provides some more specific arguments about how different societies work when he elaborates on the normative expectations and cultural goals that dominate his theory of action. The next section discusses this aspect of Parsons's thought.

THE PATTERN VARIABLES

As we saw in the preceding section, Parsons was initially preoccupied with the formulation of his theory of action. In it he portrayed purposive actors who were oriented to goals but had to fulfill certain conditions—themselves defined by normative expectations—before they could be gratified. Parsons felt that his next intellectual task was to develop clearer specifications of what different contingencies and expectations actors were likely to face. He wanted to show that their situation is not entirely unstructured and uncertain. Therefore he formulated the pattern variables, which categorize expectations and the structure of relationships. They make his abstract theory of action more explicit.

This portion of Parsons's work is based on Ferdinand Toennies's (1855–1936) *gemeinschaft-gesellschaft* typology. (A typology is an analysis based on types.) Toennies was interested in contrasting primitive communities (*gemeinschaft*) with modern industrial (*gesellschaft*) societies. Community (*gemeinschaft*) is characterized by a predominance of close personal bonds or kinship relations; society (*gesellschaft*) is characterized by a predominance of more impersonal or business-type relationships. Durkheim, following Toennies, analyzed the types of solidarity in primitive and modern societies. He labeled the former "mechanical solidarity" (where the collective conscience was strong) and the latter "organic solidarity" (where the collective conscience was weak owing to the rise of individualism).[39] Like Toennies and Durkheim, Parsons considers the difference between the two to be fundamental. He labels relationships in traditional societies, which are predominantly personal and informal, *expressive,* and relationships in modern society, which are predominantly impersonal or formal, *instrumental.*

Even in modern society both types of relationships exist and are needed. Parsons uses this need to analyze sex role differentiation in the family. He argues that the instrumental leadership role must be accorded to the husband-father, on whom the reputation and income of the family depend.[40] Likewise he states that because of the occupational responsibilities of the father, the mother must take on the expressive leadership role in the socialization of the children. Feminists have argued that Parsons's statement regarding the positive functions of this instrumental/expressive division of labor in the family was an attempt to justify the status quo. They have criticized Parsons's theory of gender socialization as oppressive for both genders, but particularly for women.[41]

As we mentioned in the preface, the work of feminist theorists will be presented throughout this book. At this point we present a definition of feminist theory:

> First, gender comprises a central focus or subject matter of the theory. Feminist theory seeks ultimately to understand the gendered nature of virtually all social relations, institutions, and processes. Second, gender relations are viewed as a problem. By this I mean that feminist theory seeks to understand how gender is related to social inequities, strains, and contradictions. Finally, gender relations are not viewed as either natural or immutable. Rather, the gender-related status quo is viewed as the product of sociocultural and historical forces which have been created, and are constantly re-created by humans, and therefore can potentially be changed by human agency.[42]

---

[39]See our earlier discussion of these two types of solidarity in the section about Durkheim.

[40]Talcott Parsons, *Essays in Sociological Theory* (New York: The Free Press, 1954), pp. 422–23.

[41]See the discussion of Patricia Hill Collins (Chapter 5) and Dorothy E. Smith (Chapter 6).

[42]Janet S. Chafetz, *Feminist Sociology: An Overview of Contemporary Theories* (Itasca, Ill.: Peacock, 1988), p. 5.

When Parsons worked out his pattern variable scheme, which was strongly criticized by feminists, he went beyond a simple twofold typology of expressive/instrumental. His pattern variables are a fivefold elaboration of the traditional-modern typology. Parsons's own definition of a pattern variable is "a dichotomy, one side of which must be chosen by an actor before the meaning of a situation is determinate for him, and thus before he can act with respect to the situation."[43] In other words, each pattern variable represents a problem or dilemma that must be solved by the actor before action can take place.

Table 2-1 summarizes the pattern variable scheme. In each case the choices that actors typically and appropriately make differ according to the type of society. The appropriate choices for traditional societies are on the left side (expressive), and the appropriate choices for modern societies are on the right side (instrumental).

The first choice actors must make is between *ascription and achievement*, or, as they are sometimes labeled, "quality" and "performance." The dilemma here is whether to orient oneself toward others on the basis of what they are (that is, on the basis of ascribed qualities, such as sex, age, race, ethnicity) or on the basis of what they can do or have done (that is, on the basis of performance). For example, in modern societies such as ours, employers are expected to orient themselves toward potential employees on the basis of the work that they have done in the past and that they could be expected to do in the future, not according to their color, age, gender, sexual orientation, or family connections. Thus employers should choose the performance, or achievement, side of the pattern variable dichotomy, rather than the ascriptive, or quality, side. When, for instance, a young member of a famous family is hired over others with better performance qualifications, an outcry from the public is to be expected. There remain situations, however, in which the recruitment or hiring choice is expected to be at least partly ascriptive. For example, one must be a certain age to qualify for acceptance into the armed services. If it could be proved that a person lied about age, negative sanc-

---

[43]Talcott Parsons, *Toward a General Theory of Action*, edited with Edward A. Shils (Cambridge: Harvard University Press, 1951), p. 77.

TABLE 2-1   Parsons's Pattern Variables

Expressive (Gemeinschaft)	Instrumental (Gesellschaft)
Ascription	Achievement
Diffuseness	Specificity
Affectivity	Neutrality
Particularism	Universalism
Collectivity	Self

tions from authorities in the armed services would be in order. It is important to keep in mind that what we are discussing here is the *appropriate* choice between ascriptive and achievement options. Parsons places normative expectations at the core of the decision; the either-or choice is not an arbitrary one. Thus, in Ann Doe's case, which we used in discussing Parsons's theory of action, normative standards dictate that she pass her courses; if she fails, she does not achieve the goal of a B.A. degree no matter what her ascriptive qualities.

The second pattern variable is *diffuseness or specificity*. Here the issue is the range of demands in the relationship. If the number and types of demands or responsibilities are wide-ranging, it is a diffuse relationship; if the scope is narrow or very limited, the relationship is functionally specific. For instance, you can expect a lot from your closest friend—from spending hours being a good listener to lending you a variety of things, including money. This is what Parsons means when he talks of a diffuse relationship. On the other hand, if the relationship in question is between dentist and patient, the dentist's interest in the patient is restricted to the care of the teeth, and the patient is expected to be on time for the appointment, to sit still, to open and close his or her mouth as directed, and to pay for the dentist's services. This is a functionally specific relationship. Moreover, the type of relationship predefines its limits. If the doctor makes demands that are not connected with the care of the teeth, such as asking personal questions about family, business, or sex life, a negative sanction can be expected; the patient will be angry and may even stop seeing the dentist altogether. In short, there aren't many things you can't ask your best friend to do for you; that relationship is based on nonexclusion. A specific relationship like the one between dentist and patient excludes all irrelevant behavior and specifically defines what is relevant. Parsons argues that in modern societies the appropriate choice generally involves specifically defined behavior, whereas in traditional societies, more relationships are diffuse.

The third pattern variable is *affectivity or affective neutrality*. Here the issue is simply whether the actor can expect emotional gratification in the relationship. An engaged couple can certainly expect to relate to each other with affectivity; on the other hand, a college teacher and student are expected to opt for neutrality. Parsons's view of the school system in the United States, incidentally, is that when children enter the system at approximately age six they are accustomed to the affective relationships of family life.[44] At school they learn that they can get away with some measures of affectivity, such as clutching the teacher's hand, but only in the first one or two years of schooling. Parsons describes how education becomes more of a "bloodless existence" as students progress through the grades; he argues

---

[44]The growing incidence of violence in the family makes this assumption more questionable today.

that this is important for children's survival in a society in which affective neutrality and instrumental, rather than expressive, expectations predominate in the labor force.[45] If children learn in school how to tread a predominantly instrumental path, then the school will provide the type of worker needed in modern society.

The fourth pattern variable is *particularism or universalism*. Here the choice is between reacting on the basis of a general norm or reacting on the basis of someone's particular relationship to you or one's membership in a particular group. Because a teacher in our society is expected to treat all students equally—that is, according to universalistic criteria—it would be difficult for parents or relatives to have their own students or relatives as students in their own classrooms. An example of particularism is the "old boy" network, which worked effectively as a glass ceiling for women and other "outsiders" in the United States when hiring was routinely done on a particularistic basis with no legal constraints. Although this used to be socially acceptable, and in many countries still is, it is not the orientation that U.S. employers are expected to take.[46] In general, questions of discrimination involve choices being made on the basis of particularistic criteria rather than the universalistic criteria that modern societies believe in and prescribe.

A fifth pattern variable, the *collectivity-self* orientation, involves the dilemma of whether private interests can be gratified, or some collective obligation or duty must be fulfilled. Self-interest is highly institutionalized in the business world, for example, where the profit motive is pursued legitimately. By contrast, civil servants are expected to carry out their duties in the best interests of the public, so appropriate role behavior is oriented to the interests of the collectivity rather than to self-interests. Although Parsons originally included collectivity-self, it tended to disappear from his own formulation of the pattern variables after 1953.[47]

Although Talcott Parsons admitted to being an "incurable theorist" (on the dedication page of *The Social System*), he was also concerned with the empirical application of the pattern variables. The results of one of his rare ventures into empirical research are reported in *The Social System* in a chapter

---

[45]Talcott Parsons, "The School Class as a Social System: Some of Its Functions in American Society," in A. H. Halsey, Jean Floud, and C. Arnold Anderson, ed., *Education, Economy, and Society* (New York: The Free Press, 1961), pp. 434–55. Expressive choices are appropriate in the private sphere of the family, however.

[46]Changes in normative expectations resulting from changes in laws or guidelines do not ensure conformity, as we have learned from the civil rights movement in the United States. Witness, for instance, the backlog of cases to be inspected by the Equal Employment Opportunity Commission.

[47]See Talcott Parsons, "Pattern Variables Revisited," *American Sociological Review* 25(1960): 467–88. Parsons said his view is that the collectivity-self orientation was "an unduly restricted formulation of an element in the organization of action components at the level next above that designated by the primary pattern variables." (480) In other words, he saw it on a more abstract level than the other four.

titled "Social Structure and Dynamic Process: The Case of Modern Medical Practice."[48] In this chapter Parsons utilized the pattern variable scheme as he described the doctor-patient relationship. In gathering data for his study of medical practice, Parsons engaged in both participant observation and interviews with physicians at Tufts Medical Center and Massachusetts General Hospital.[49] As might be expected, he depicted the doctor's role as predominantly instrumental. Because of the high levels of technical competence required, the doctor's position is seen as an achieved status: one is not born a doctor (though being the child of a doctor may help).[50] Parsons points out that the complexity and subtlety of the knowledge and skill required, and the consequent length and intensity of training, demand performance or achievement criteria as well as a universalistic orientation. For instance, a doctor must concentrate on making the patient well, and in this respect all patients must be treated the same.

Likewise, affective neutrality is necessary because the physician is expected to treat problems in objective, scientifically justifiable terms.[51] For this reason surgeons do not ordinarily operate on family members. Finally, because a doctor is a specialist in matters of health and disease, specificity of function is involved. Patients do not, for instance, ordinarily consult their doctors about their income taxes; even though physicians may be helpful in this matter, that is not their area of expertise.

Parsons points out that the particular patterning of the doctor's role is related to cultural tradition and that the specialization of technical competence is characteristic of that role in contemporary America. In tribal societies the role of medicine man could be an ascribed status, passed on from parents to children. A medicine man's behavior to others and theirs to him were defined by and varied according to particularistic variables. In addition, because the medicine man might often be consulted on many matters unrelated to health and sickness, diffuseness of function, rather than specificity, would be the norm. We might also expect to see more affectivity exhibited because of close tribal ties. Thus the patterning of the appropriate choices would be different in tribal societies. The contrast between the roles of medicine man and physician illustrates the general shift from an expressive orientation in *gemeinschaft* societies to an instrumental orientation in industrial, or *gesellschaft*, societies. As we explained earlier, this shift is at the heart of the pattern variable scheme.

[48]See Parsons, *The Social System*, pp. 428–79.

[49]See Parsons, "On Building Social System Theory," p. 835. This may come as a surprise to those who assumed that Parsons never engaged in empirical research.

[50]One could argue that there is an ascribed element inherent in the doctor's role, as the expense of medical school education makes it easier for those born of wealthy parents to aspire to the medical profession in the United States.

[51]Parsons, *The Social System*, p. 435.

If we assume, in the Parsonian framework, that individual actors are socialized and thus are motivated to meet the demands of societal expectations, then we can expect actors to make appropriate choices about the pattern variables, and we can predict their behavior on the basis of information about values and normative expectations. However, in some situations the choice is not simply a matter of one or the other. For instance, teacher-parents who have their own children as students in the classroom will find their parent role conflicting with the teacher role in many instances. The choice in this case is not always either a universalistic or a particularistic one; the blood relationship muddies the waters considerably because the decision involves both universalism and particularism. Parsons leaves little room for ambivalence on the part of the actor, who may both love and hate the person with whom he or she is planning to interact.[52]

Thus the pattern variable scheme is not as neat as it appears at first glance, either as a way of clarifying and describing role relationships or as a way of predicting people's appropriate choices. On their own the pattern variables do not tell the sociologist how people will behave when faced with role conflicts. In addition, it is questionable whether socialization is as effective, or people's behavior as simply and clearly a function of normative expectations, as Parsons's approach implies. In other words, people's appropriate choice may frequently not be their actual one. The occurrence of nonprescribed, or what Parsons would call "deviant," behavior will occupy us again in the context of our next topic: Parsons's work on "systems problems" and equilibrium.

THE FUNCTIONAL SYSTEM PROBLEMS—AGIL

Shortly after Parsons worked out the pattern variable scheme, he embarked on his next intellectual mission. He wanted to reduce the lack of certainty in his theory of action about what goals (like our Jane Doe's B.A. degree) actors would pursue, and he wanted to specify further the pattern variables. The ideas he developed—which have been referred to variously as the "system problems," the "functional imperatives," the "AGIL Model" (based on the first letters of the four functions he devised), or the "four-function paradigm"—were his attempt to incorporate into his theory propositions about the nature of goals.

This work evolved from Parsons's collaboration with Robert F. Bales in experiments on leadership in small groups. Bales observed changes in the quality of activity as the small groups attempted to solve their task problems. In a typical meeting the groups would begin by requesting and providing information that would solve the problem of a *common orientation* to the task. The groups would then attempt to solve the problem of *evaluation* and make decisions about the task at hand. Next they would attempt to

---

[52]See Neil Smelser's discussion of ambivalence in Part Three of this chapter.

ensure a degree of consensus through *social control*. The cycle, if successful, would conclude with activity expressing *solidarity* and *tension reduction*, like joking and laughing, to repair any damage done to social integration and to bring the groups back to a state of equilibrium.[53]

A careful reading of *Working Papers* will reveal that Bales's small groups were made up entirely of Harvard undergraduates, whom Bales recruited through the Harvard employment service. In the early 1950s those groups would have been made up almost entirely of white, upper-middle-class or upper-class, Protestant males. The group's homogeneity raises questions about the number, type, and range of Parsons's functional system problems and about their generalization.[54] Had the small groups included African Americans, Latinos, Asians, women, blue-collar workers, Catholics, and Jews, the types and sequences of group activities may have been different. Assuming that task orientation is seen differently by groups at or near the bottom of the social ladder, their view of social control would also differ. For example, more heterogeneous groups may have experienced more tensions, resulting in the emergence of conflict resolution as a major system problem. Thus the system problems could have had a different configuration.

Feminist theorists like Dorothy Smith[55] highlight the disjunction between how women experience the world and the mainstream concepts and theories about society and self-consciousness. Smith presents the following example:

> My early exploration of these issues included a graduate seminar in which we discussed the possibility of a women's sociology. Two students expressed their sense that theories of the emergence of leadership in small groups just did not apply to what had happened in an experimental group situation they had participated in. They could not find the correlates of the theory in their experiences.

Feminists are also critical of Bales's assumption that the same people cannot undertake task ("instrumental") behavior and social ("expressive") behavior, while both behaviors are necessary to a viable small group. Meeker and O'Neill show that subsequent research provides little support for the idea that task and social roles are incompatible. They conclude that the dimension of task versus social orientation is no longer justified as an explanation of sex differences in behavior in task groups.[56]

[53]See Talcott Parsons, *Working Papers in the Theory of Action*, with Robert F. Bales and Edward A. Shils (New York: The Free Press, 1953), pp. 140–43.

[54]For a feminist critique of the evolution of the functional system problems, see Ruth A. Wallace, "Introduction," pp. 1–19, in Ruth A. Wallace, ed., *Feminism and Sociological Theory* (Newbury Park, Calif.: Sage, 1989).

[55]See Dorothy E. Smith, *The Conceptual Practices of Power: A Feminist Sociology of Knowledge* (Boston: Northeastern University Press, 1990), p. 13. See Chapter 6 for a discussion of Dorothy Smith's standpoint theory.

[56]See Barbara F. Meeker and Patricia A. Weitzel-O'Neill, "Sex Roles and Interpersonal Behavior in Task-Oriented Groups," in Joseph Berger and Morris Zelditch, Jr., ed., *Status, Rewards, and Influence* (San Francisco: Jossey-Bass, 1985), pp. 379–405.

Parsons decided that Bales's categories for analyzing small group inter-action and the activities all small groups engage in could, if reconceptual-ized, be expanded beyond small groups to include *all* systems of action. This led Parsons to the four-function paradigm. In it Parsons identifies the major problems action systems must solve if they are to develop and survive—the problems existing systems cope with successfully.

Parsons's work in this area addresses in intricate detail the determi-nants of and requirements for his basic interest—equilibrium. *Equilibrium*, which basically means a state of balance of a system, was developed as a the-oretical concept in sociology by modern functionalists. The following defini-tion of "social equilibrium" illustrates the relationship between equilibrium and functionalism:

> [Social equilibrium is] the concept that social life has a tendency to be and to remain a functionally integrated phenomenon, so that any change in one part of the social system will bring about adjustive changes in other parts. The initial change creates an imbalance, but a functional adjustment of the parts occurs to recreate an integrated, adjusted, and relatively stable system.[57]

As we noted at the beginning of this chapter, functionalism's model of society as interdependent and self-equilibrating is similar to the biological model of an organism. Parsons traces his own early interest in equilibrium to W. B. Cannon's idea of homeostatic stabilization of physiological processes, as well as to his exposure to biology at Amherst.[58] In the case of society, he argues that certain institutions or structures maintain equilibrium by fulfilling needs and solving recurring problems—much as a biological organism does in its physical environment. These structures, in turn, func-tion because certain mechanisms ensure that they operate appropriately on a day-to-day basis. In his discussion of system problems, Parsons sets out his view on what any action systems needs to achieve equilibrium.

Parsons argues that all action systems face four major problems (or have four major needs): adaptation; goal attainment; integration; and pattern maintenance, or as he later renamed it, "latent pattern maintenance–tension management."[59] In the context of the social system, Parsons usually pictures society or the social system as a large square, that he divides into four equal parts. These parts are the four functional system problems, represented by the letters AGIL.[60] (See Figure 2-2.)

---

[57]George A. Theodorson and Achilles G. Theodorson, ed., *A Modern Dictionary of Sociology*, p. 133.

[58]Parsons, "On Building Social System Theory," p. 849.

[59]These four system problems are akin to Bales's categories we have mentioned: common orientation to the task, evaluation, social control, and tension reduction.

[60]For Parsons, a society and a social system are not synonymous. "A society," he says, "is a type of social system . . . which attains the highest level of self-sufficiency as a system in rela-tion to its environments" (*Societies; Evolutionary and Comparative Perspectives* [Englewood Cliffs, N.J.: Prentice Hall, 1966], p. 9). As mentioned earlier, a social system may range from an inter-national organization to a nuclear family.

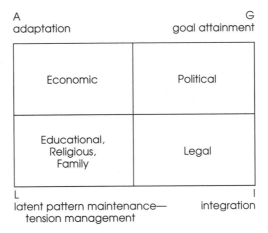

A
adaptation

G
goal attainment

Economic	Political
Educational, Religious, Family	Legal

L
latent pattern maintenance— tension management

I
integration

FIGURE 2–2 Parsons's Four-Function Paradigm Applied to the United States as a Social System.
(Adapted from Figure 3, p. 53 in Talcott Parsons and Neil J. Smelser, *Economy and Society* (Glencoe, Ill.: The Free Press, 1956), p. 53. Reprinted with permission of Routledge and Kegan Paul.)

What does Parsons mean by the letters AGIL in his famous square? By *A, adaptation*, he is pointing to the need to secure sufficient resources from the environment and distribute them throughout the system. *Social institutions* are interrelated systems of social norms and roles that satisfy social needs or functions and help to solve social system problems. Examples of social institutions are the economy, the political order, the law, religion, education, and the family. If it is to survive, a social system needs certain structures or institutions that will perform the function of adaptation to the environment. Taking the United States as a social system, a Parsonian analysis would point to the economy as the social institution that meets this need, or solves the problem of securing sufficient resources; it would identify production or the wealth that results as the central question.

The *G* stands for *goal attainment*, the system's need to mobilize its resources and energies to attain system goals and to establish priorities among them. In the United States this system problem of directing resources to collective ends is essentially the concern of political institutions. Basically the function of decision-making bodies, goal attainment's central question is the legitimate use of power to implement social decisions.

Integration, the *I* in the box, is at the heart of the four-function paradigm because solving this problem has been a priority for functionalists, especially since Durkheim. By integration Parsons means the need to coordinate, adjust, and regulate relationships among various actors or units within the system, thus preventing mutual interference, in order to keep the system functioning. In the social system of the United States, legal institutions and courts meet the need for social control; the central question is the implementation of norms, or influence.

The fourth system need, the *L* in Parsons's box (*latent pattern maintenance–tension management*) is twofold: first, the need to make certain that actors are sufficiently motivated to play their parts in the system or maintain the value "pattern"; and second, the need to provide mechanisms for internal tension management. This problem is one of keeping the value system intact and guaranteeing the conformity of the members of the system by transmitting societal values and by invoking value commitment. In the United States the relevant social institutions are family, religion, the media, and education, and the central question is moral commitment to shared values.

One of Parsons's later involvements in empirical research was related directly to the AGIL schema. With Gerald Platt, Parsons studied higher education by means of a sample survey of members of U.S. colleges and university faculties.[61] In *The American University*, the structure of higher education is described as "specializing in implementing the cultural patterns of cognitive rationality."[62] By cognitive rationality they mean the rational or "scientific" approach to generating knowledge and searching for truth and the whole range of teaching and learning within this framework. Parsons's and Platt's data on faculty teaching goals show that cognitive rationality is the paramount shared value within the American system of higher education.[63] Thus the American system of higher education transmits and maintains values central to modern American society; it has a pattern maintenance function and so is placed in the *L* box.

In Figure 2-2 we presented the four-function paradigm in terms of social structures and pictured the United States in Parsonian fashion. However, things are not necessarily so neat. In simpler societies there is more of a tendency to collapse functions. The Parsonian breakdown for the United States does not fit, for example, the pygmy tribes of the African forests who engage in little division of labor (typical of a *gemeinschaft* society). As members of the tribe, all participate in hunting, hut building, socialization of the young, and social control in general. Again, in a centrally planned totalitarian state, such as communist China, the party may be the institution responsible for both economic production and the direction of resources and setting of priorities, so that *G* and *A* are collapsed into one.

[61]Talcott Parsons and Gerald M. Platt, *The American University* (Cambridge: Harvard University Press, 1973). Although no major monograph with analysis of the data from this study has appeared, a number of articles have been published. See, for example, Gerald M. Platt, Talcott Parsons, and Rita Kirshstein, "Faculty Teaching Goals, 1968–1973," *Social Problems* 24(1976): 298–307; Gerald Platt, Talcott Parsons, and Rita Kirshstein, "Undergraduate Teaching Environments; Normative Orientations to Teaching Among Faculty in the Higher Educational System," *Sociological Inquiry* 51(1981): 155–65.

[62]Parsons and Platt, *The American University*, p. 394.

[63]See Platt, Parsons, and Kirshstein, "Undergraduate Teaching Environments."

Conversely, in a market economy the institutions concerned with G spill over into A: priorities are set by market forces affecting supply and demand and not by central political decision making.

This points to a general problem with Parsons's four functions. Because they are analytic categories, the four functions are not necessarily clearly separable. Institutions do not necessarily fit neatly into one box, and the scheme in itself cannot be used to predict what institutions a society will develop or what functions a given institution will fulfill. Rather, the paradigm serves as a way of classifying institutions after the event.

The complexity of applying the four-function paradigm becomes even more apparent when one realizes that Parsons believes the same problems face every system; this means not only the large social system but each of its subsystems as well. We can look at the family as a social structure that fulfills the larger social system's need for latent pattern maintenance–tension management, as in Figure 2-2; but we can also look at the family itself as a social system with the same four problems to be solved. Thus we can picture the L box in our diagram of the United States as itself a social system divided into four boxes of its own. Parsons's viewpoint regarding the family was consistently a traditional one, so it is not surprising to find him assuming that it is the father who solves the problem of adaptation by being the breadwinner. The father also makes the major decisions, thus fulfilling the goal attainment function, and he plays a dominant role in coordinating and adjusting family relationships to keep the system integrated. The mother's chief functions are to transmit family values to the children and to create and maintain an atmosphere where tensions can be released ($PM-L$). Once again, however, things may be far less neat and predictable than Parsons implies, especially in a period when the traditional family is less and less the statistical norm. Husband and wife may contribute equally to adaptation; or the wife may be the major breadwinner; or the state may play a crucial role through welfare, unemployment benefits, or social security payments. The other three functions may be shared as well. Parsons's scheme identifies universal functions but cannot in itself predict how they will be met.

AGIL and Equilibrium

The crucial point to remember about the four system needs is that Parsons considers them the prerequisites for social equilibrium. Their continuing daily operation is in turn ensured, according to Parsons's theory, by two mechanisms: socialization and social control. If socialization works, all members of a society will be committed to shared values, make the appropriate choices among the pattern variables, and generally do what is expected of them in terms of adaptation, integration, and so forth. For example, people will marry and socialize their children (L), and within the family, fathers will, as they "should," be the breadwinners (A). Moreover, such successful socialization produces what Parsons refers to as *complementarity of expectations*. This means that both parties involved in an interaction situation share and accept the same cultural values and normative expectations, so that each actor knows what the other expects, and their responses complement each other. Actors are motivated to meet the demands of societal expectations, and do interact appropriately: the happy result is equilibrium.

Parsons's work tends to imply that this situation of complementary expectations and behavior and of equilibrium is the one that obtains the bulk of the time. However, he also deals with situations of disequilibrium, in which the balance of society is disturbed and in which, he argues, forces come to play that restore equilibrium. Thus, from day to day, there will occur cases of deviance, and norms regarding role interaction will be transgressed, as in the case of a motorist who drives through a red light. In Parsonian terms, it is then that social control comes into play, and negative sanctions are used to make recalcitrant actors conform. A police officer will probably give a ticket to the deviant motorist. In Parsons's view every society has general social control mechanisms, like the police and courts, that operate to deal with deviance, bring behavior back into line with expectations, and restore equilibrium.

As mentioned earlier, role interaction is the basic component of a social system in Parsons's theory. However, Stacey and Thorne, in arguing against the term *sex and/or gender role*, or an emphasis on the process of sex and/or gender role socialization, state that the notion of role

> focuses attention more on individuals than on social structure, and implies that "the female role" and "the male role" are complementary (i.e., separate or different but equal). The terms are depoliticizing; they strip experience from its historical and political context and neglect questions of power and conflict. It is significant that sociologists do not speak of "class roles" or "race roles."[64]

In Parsons's view by ensuring appropriate role interaction, the two mechanisms of socialization and social control generally promote and maintain equilibrium in the social system. However, disequilibrium may arise because of changes or strains in the social system that affect the way the four system needs are met. Parsons is vague about the origins of strain. In introducing the concept, he says only, "Let us assume that, *from whatever source* (emphasis ours), a disturbance is introduced into the system";[65] thus the source of disequilibrium may be anything from an earthquake to a severe economic depression to a revolution. Whatever the source of the strain,

---

[64]Judith Stacey and Barrie Thorne, "The Missing Feminist Revolution in Sociology," *Social Problems* 32, no. 4 (April 1985): 307.

[65]Parsons, *The Social System*, p. 252.

Parsons believes society adjusts in response to disturbances in order to restore equilibrium.

At the beginning of this chapter we used the example of an airport to show what functionalists mean by systems adjusting to restore equilibrium. We can also show what this would mean in Parsonian terms by using the two social systems we have just been discussing: the family and the United States. Current debates about family breakdown often employ functionalist ideas. For example, British researcher Norman Dennis cites data showing that "the life chances of the child where both parents were married when the child was born, and where both parents successfully struggled to stay together to look after it . . . are much better than those of the child from the father-absent situation."[66] While he clearly recognizes that only some boys and girls today are in father-absent families, he argues thus:

> All boys and young men without exception . . . face their future with progressively reducing social pressure or social training to become responsible and competent husbands and fathers. . . . Fatherhood is learned like a language. . . . It is transmitted through the countless messages of reinforcement and restriction that come every day, from the moment of birth, through parents, other kinsfolk, neighbors, and passing strangers. These messages embody, like one's native tongue, the common sense of generations, derived from the experience of ordinary people as well as the contributions of geniuses, of what has proved benign and practicable in everyday life.[67]

Using functionalist concepts, Dennis argues that "socialization and social control are losing their power to produce . . . effective and successfully committed fathers."[68]

What happens when there is disequilibrium in a larger social system, such as the United States? Many Americans experienced such disequilibrium directly at the time of the assassination of President John F. Kennedy. In Parsonian terms, the G box, or the goal attainment function, was badly disturbed, because until Lyndon Johnson took the oath of office, the most important decision-making position in the government was vacant. Recall how rapidly the necessary actors were assembled for the oath-taking ceremony: Parsons would see this as an example of a system reacting quickly to an acute disequilibrium.

Parsons's model focuses our attention on the interdependence of different institutions, on the way human societies everywhere grapple with similar problems in spite of their surface differences, and on the continuities in social life and how they are secured. However, as many critics have pointed out, it leaves a great deal unexplained. In discussing the origins of

[66]Norman Dennis, *Rising Crime and the Dismembered Family: Choice in Welfare Series No. 18* (London: Institute of Economic Affairs, 1993), p. xii.

[67]Dennis, *Rising Crime and the Dismembered Family*, p. 8.

[68]Dennis, *Rising Crime and the Dismembered Family*, p. 4.

modern functionalism, we pointed out that Durkheim's explanation of something according to the function it performed was a recurring problem. This circularity is certainly apparent in Parsons's work. He fails to specify how systems develop ways to meet their needs or deal with functional exigencies, and he does not specify how systems respond to disequilibrium. Rather, Parsons's model assumes that the existence of various needs somehow ensures that they will be met. Again, the sources of deviance and disequilibrium are never dealt with in concrete detail, and Parsons's theory of deviance has been criticized because it "stands most in need of greater specification, of the conditions under which one type of deviance tends to excite one type of social control; and of the conditions under which social control tends to be effective or ineffective. Such specification would give his paradigm greater theoretical adequacy and bring it closer to direct testability."[69]

Parsons's concern with the interdependence of society's parts and his theory of social equilibrium have had enormous influence on sociology. From the start, however, he has also met with intense criticism; as we mentioned earlier, many sociologists have defined their work and their concerns in opposition to Parsons.[70] We have already touched on some of the problems with Parsons's theory: the fact that his classificatory schemes and list of essential functions, or needs, do not allow one to predict in advance the actual structure and institutions a society will develop; the way in which he fails to deal adequately with role conflict; and his failure to specify the mechanisms by which equilibrium will necessarily be restored. However, what has caused the most impassioned criticism is the fact that Parsons is not neutral about the survival and development of social systems. Instead, his formulation of functionalism implies that equilibrium is intrinsically desirable.

Above all else, Parsons's system is a system in equilibrium because each actor is morally committed to perform culturally and socially expected functions. As Parsons puts it, "Many complex processes are necessary to maintain the functioning of any societal system; if its members never did anything, a society would very soon cease to exist."[71] Indeed, if cultural values are fully inculcated and if all actors and all units do what is expected of them, the system can hardly fail to be in equilibrium. Suppose, however, that people do not do what is expected. Parsons treated deviance in a way that implies disapproval, saying very little about its origins or justification but instead discussing it as a source of disequilibrium to which negative sanctions are appropriately applied. But is it? Parsons's critics, especially those who apply a conflict perspective to social analysis, argue that his approach implies approval of the status quo at the expense of discounting

---

[69]Neil J. Smelser and R. Stephen Warner, *Sociological Theory: Historical and Formal* (Morristown, N.J.: General Learning Press, 1976), p. 204.

[70]See Chapters 3, 5, 6, and 7.

[71]Parsons, *Societies: Evolutionary and Comparative Perspectives*, p. 21.

the conflicts of interest, inequalities, or outright oppression that a social system may incorporate. As one such analyst argued,

> To maintain and transmit a value system, human beings are punished, bullied, sent to jail, thrown into concentration camps, cajoled, bribed, made into heroes, encouraged to read newspapers, stood up against a wall and shot, and sometimes even taught sociology. To speak of cultural inertia is to overlook the concrete interests and privileges that are served by indoctrination, education, and the entire complicated process of transmitting culture from one generation to the next.[72]

Does this suggest that Parsons would have approved of the atrocities committed under Hitler's regime? An answer to this question is found in a recent edited volume on Parsons's social scientific study of German fascism. According to Turner, "Parsons played an important intellectual and political role in explaining the problems and dangers of Nazi Germany to the American political establishment and in attempting to commit that establishment to participation in the war."[73]

In contrast to Barrington Moore's prior quote, another conflict theorist stated, "No one of his contemporaries developed a theory of society of comparable complexity. . . . Any theoretical work in sociology today that failed to take account of Talcott Parsons could not be taken seriously."[74]

PART TWO

Robert K. Merton: Middle-Range Theory

BACKGROUND

Robert King Merton was born in 1910 of Jewish immigrant parents in a South Philadelphia slum, where his father was a carpenter and truck driver. He grew up with a passion for learning and won a scholarship at Temple University. There he received his B.A. and became interested in sociology while taking an introductory sociology course taught by George E. Simpson. Recalling this experience, Merton has said, "It wasn't so much the substance of what Simpson said that did it. It was more the joy of discovering that it was possible to examine human behavior objectively and without using loaded moral preconceptions."[75]

---

[72]Barrington Moore, Jr., *Social Origins of Dictatorship and Democracy: Lord and Peasant in the Making of the Modern World* (Boston: Beacon Press, 1966), p. 486.

[73]See B. S. Turner's review of *Talcott Parsons and National Socialism*, edited by Uta Gerhardt (New York: Aldine de Gruyter, 1993) in *Contemporary Sociology* 23, no. 2 (March 1994): 325.

[74]Jürgen Habermas, "Talcott Parsons: Problems of Theory Construction," *Sociological Inquiry* 51(1981): 173–74. See also Chapter 4, pp. 171–76.

[75]Much of the background material here is based on the excellent biographical sketch by Morton M. Hunt, "How Does It Come To Be So?" Profile of Robert K. Merton, *The New Yorker*, 36(January 28, 1961): 39–63.

With the help of a fellowship, Merton received a doctorate from Harvard University, where he was one of Parsons's earliest and most important graduate students. Looking back over his career at Harvard, Parsons stated that of the significant relations he had with graduate students, "the most important single one was with Robert Merton." He adds, "For a considerable time, Merton and I came to be known as the leaders of a structural-functional school among American sociologists."[76]

While at Harvard, Merton was also influenced by Pitirim Sorokin, who was not sympathetic to Parsons's work.[77] Sorokin shared Parsons's propensity for large-scale theorizing, but he balanced this with an equally strong interest in empirical research and statistical studies. It was Paul K. Lazarsfeld who influenced Merton to become active in empirical research,[78] and Merton was closely associated with him at the Bureau of Applied Social Research at Columbia University until Lazarsfeld's death in 1976.[79] Parsons saw himself as an "incurable theorist," but Merton has been actively engaged in empirical research since 1941, when he joined the faculty at Columbia, where he is still at work. He currently holds the title of University Professor Emeritus, a rank for a handful of Columbia faculty who are professors-at-large.

Merton's two classic essays on the relationship between sociological theory and empirical research appear as chapters in his best-known book, *Social Theory and Social Structure*. Unlike Parsons, Merton does not stop with abstract theory and typology; he formulates empirical hypotheses and often tests them in the real world by gathering data himself and analyzing the results.[80]

In 1957 the American Sociological Society elected Robert K. Merton as its president. Not all of Merton's contributions to sociology are functionalist.[81] Some of his most important contributions to functionalism are his work on middle-range theory, his clarification and refocusing of functional analysis, and his theory of deviance.

[76]Parsons, "On Building Social System Theory," pp. 833 and 849.

[77]Parsons, "On Building Social System Theory," p. 832.

[78]See the dialogue between Lewis A. Coser and Robert Nisbet titled "Merton and the Contemporary Mind" in Lewis A. Coser, ed., *The Idea of Social Structure: Papers in Honor of Robert K. Merton* (New York: Harcourt Brace Jovanovich, 1975), pp. 3–10. This work also contains an excellent bibliography (see pp. 497–552).

[79]See Lazarsfeld's chapter, "Working with Merton," in Coser, *The Idea of Social Structure,* pp. 35–66.

[80]See, for example, his work on propaganda, which he describes in Chapter 16 of *Social Theory and Social Structure*, "Studies in Radio and Film Propaganda," pp. 563–82. See also his study (with George P. Reader, Patricia L. Kendall, and others) of the changing attitudes of medical students, *The Student-Physician: Introductory Studies in the Sociology of Medical Education* (Cambridge: Harvard University Press, 1957).

[81]The sociology of science, in particular, has been a central interest of Merton's. We recommend the festschrift edited by Lewis A. Coser, *The Idea of Social Structure: Papers in Honor of Robert K. Merton* (1975).

THEORIES OF THE MIDDLE RANGE

One of the most important ways in which Merton diverged from Parsonian functionalism was in his decision to abandon the quest for an all-encompassing theory. He chose, rather, to take the path of what he calls "middle-range theories." As Merton himself explains,

> At the summit of human thought, some sociologists are seeking a single unified theory—a generalized body of explanations as to what cements society together, how institutions fit into a social framework, how discrepant values arise and work their changes upon a society, and so on. My friend and occasional colleague, Talcott Parsons, is doing just that, and, I think, making useful progress. But for most of our energies to be channeled that way would be decidedly premature. Einstein could not have followed hard on the heels of Kepler, and perhaps we haven't even had our Kepler yet. Just as it would stifle sociology to spend all its time today on practical problems before developing theory sufficiently, so it would to spend all its time on abstract, all-encompassing theories. Our major task today is to develop *special* theories, applicable to limited ranges of data—theories, for example, of deviant behavior, or the flow of power from generation to generation, or the unseen ways in which personal influence is exercised.[82]

Theories of the middle range transcend sheer description of social phenomena. They are theories with limited sets of assumptions, from which specific hypotheses can be derived and tested empirically. In Merton's view, middle-range views would gradually consolidate into more general theory. What he sets out to do is to fill in the blanks between raw empiricism (what is referred to by some sociologists as the "fishing expeditions" of researchers who cross-tabulate data with abandon and with no guiding theoretical framework) and grand or all-inclusive theory of the type Parsons was working on in his general theory of action.[83]

In his plea for theories of the middle range, Merton is standing on the shoulders of such great sociologists as Durkheim and Weber. He presents two classical examples of middle-range theories: Durkheim's *Suicide*, which we discussed earlier, and Weber's *The Protestant Ethic and the Spirit of Capitalism*, an analysis of the importance of a religious belief system (Calvinist asceticism) in the rise of capitalism in the West.[84] What Merton advocates is not a new approach but a proliferation of works like these classics. His own work on such phenomena as medical students' attitudes and patterns of influence are good examples of middle-range theories. Durkheim's study of suicide rates provides an example of the kind of

---

[82]Merton in Hunt, "How Does It Come To Be So?", p. 44.

[83]See C. Wright Mills's critique of both Parsons's grand theory and of Lazarsfeld's abstracted empiricism in *The Sociological Imagination* (New York: Oxford University Press, 1959), pp. 25–75.

[84]See Chapters 3 and 5.

middle-range theory Merton advocates. It also furnished a concept, anomie, that Merton found fruitful in developing his own theory of deviance, though he defined anomie somewhat differently.

CLARIFYING FUNCTIONAL ANALYSIS

Merton has devoted considerable attention to what he calls the "codification of functional analysis in sociology."[85] This work displays some important differences from Parsons's functionalism. For one thing, Merton's functional paradigm is not open to criticisms of inherent conservatism and teleology (explaining things by their function). At the same time, however, Merton offers fewer specific propositions about the structure of societies than Parsons does. His notion of functionalism is closer to the general orientation that Kingsley Davis identified with sociology as a whole than it is to Parsons's own theories.

As we have seen, functionalists in general conceive of society as a system of interrelated parts. This is equally true of Merton, who argues that the central orientation of functionalism is expressed in the practice of interpreting data by establishing their consequences for larger structures in which they are implicated.[86] Merton is also deeply interested in social integration, or equilibrium. Like Durkheim and Parsons, he analyzes society with reference to whether the cultural and social structures are well or badly integrated;[87] is interested in the contributions of customs and institutions to the persistence of societies;[88] and defines functions as those contributions or consequences that "make for the adaptation or adjustment of a given system."[89] Finally, Merton thinks that shared values are central in explaining how societies and institutions work, thus sharing the other major distinguishing concern of all functionalist analysis.

However, through his paradigm Merton clarifies and refocuses some major aspects of functionalist theory. The most important are his emphasis on dysfunctions, his distinction between manifest and latent functions, his concept of functional alternatives, and his insistence on the importance of uncovering and understanding the mechanisms by which functions are fulfilled.

[85]Merton, *Social Theory and Social Structure*, p. 73.
[86]Merton, *Social Theory and Social Structure*, pp. 100–101.
[87]Merton, *Social Theory and Social Structure*, p. 217.
[88]Merton, *Social Theory and Social Structure*, p. 87.
[89]Merton, *Social Theory and Social Structure*, p. 105.

Dysfunctions

Talcott Parsons's work tends to imply that all existing institutions are inherently good or functional for society; this tendency has been one of the major points of attack on functionalism and the one that arouses the most emotion among its critics. Merton explicitly dissociates himself from such a position. Instead he emphasizes the existence of "dysfunctions" and encourages sociologists to actively identify them.

Merton's concept of dysfunctions involves two complementary but distinct ideas. The first is that something may have consequences that are generally dysfunctional; in his words, an item may have "consequences which lessen the adaptation or adjustment of the system."[90] The second is that these consequences may vary according to whom one is talking about; the sociologist must ask the crucial question, "Functional and dysfunctional for whom?"

An excellent example of what Merton means by generally dysfunctional consequences can be found in his own discussion of bureaucracy. On the whole, bureaucracy appears as a functional institution for industrial society in that bureaucratic specialization means better utilization of talent and more effective response to the exigencies of the environment. However, Merton's understanding of dysfunctions makes him aware of what may happen when adherence to bureaucratic rules becomes an end in itself—a situation he calls "ritualism" in his theory of deviance. He illustrates this aspect of bureaucracy with a pathetic incident involving Bernt Balchen, Admiral Byrd's pilot in the flight over the South Pole:

> According to a ruling of the Department of Labor Bernt Balchen . . . cannot receive his citizenship papers. Balchen, a native of Norway, declared his intention in 1927. It is held that he has failed to meet the conditions of five years' continuous residence in the United States. The Byrd Antarctic voyage took him out of the country, although he was on the ship carrying the American flag, was an invaluable member of the American expedition, and in a region to which there is an American claim because of exploration and occupation of it by Americans, this region being Little America. The Bureau of Naturalization explains that it cannot proceed on the assumption that Little America is American soil. This would be *trespass on international questions* where it has no sanction. So far as the bureau is concerned, Balchen was out of the country and *technically* has not complied with the law of naturalization.[91]

Although adherence to the rules is ordinarily a moral and social good and therefore functional for society, in this case it was dysfunctional—not only for Balchen but also for society because the rigidity resulted in the loss of a superb person as a citizen. Merton's knowledge of general dysfunction

[90]Merton, *Social Theory and Social Structure*, p. 105.
[91]Merton, *Social Theory and Social Structure*, p. 254.

thus makes him aware of the "dark underside" of bureaucracy in a way not generally associated with functionalism. He is close to Weber, who saw bureaucracy as an efficient, rational way of dealing with problems, necessary to a modern state and to the end of feudalism and yet prospectively tyrannical because of its inflexible ritualism, its insistence on rules for everything. Merton is even close to the neo-Marxist conflict theorist, Habermas, who sees rationalistic bureaucracy as an impressive technical development that threatens human freedom.[92]

Merton's second point—that an institution need not be generally functional or generally dysfunctional but may instead be functional for some people and groups and dysfunctional for others—is an even clearer shift away from a functionalism that implies approval of the status quo. In some ways it approaches conflict theory. Merton talks in terms of whether institutions and practices are functional or dysfunctional for people, whereas conflict theorists generally refer to people's interests and the degree to which these are served. However, they share a concern with the differing benefits that various groups obtain from the social order and with the way these benefits explain the origin, persistence, or decline of social institutions.

We can see what Merton means by dysfunctions and why it is important for sociologists to bear them in mind by looking at such supposedly indispensable institutions as marriage and family living. People commonly think of these institutions as crucial to the health of society. Yet marriage and family life may not be functional for some types of individuals at all. They may be happier with such functional alternatives as joining collectives, renting in singles' apartment complexes, living together as unmarried couples, or living in religious communities. Only by recognizing the dysfunctional aspects of marriage and family living can we explain the development and persistence of these alternatives. Again, as functionalists from Durkheim on have tended to emphasize, an institutionalized and established religion may help to integrate a society by creating common values and identification with the group. However, Merton points out, such a religion is hardly functional for dissidents who are victims of an inquisition, and religious conflicts and wars are dysfunctional for large segments of the societies involved.[93]

In *Social Theory and Social Structure* Merton asks, "What are the consequences, functional and dysfunctional, of positive orientation to the values of a group other than one's own?"[94] His interest in this phenomenon, labeled *anticipatory socialization*, is exemplified in a recent study by a former student of Merton's, Helen Ebaugh. Ebaugh explores the process of role exit—"disengagement from a role that is central to one's self-identity and the reestablishment of an identity in a new role that takes into account one's ex-role."

---

[92]See Chapter 3.
[93]Merton, *Social Theory and Social Structure*, pp. 96–99.
[94]Merton, *Social Theory and Social Structure*, p. 319.

Her study concerns a variety of social groups, including ex-convicts, ex-nuns, ex-alcoholics, divorced men and women, mothers without custody, ex-prostitutes, ex–air traffic controllers, and transsexuals.

Anticipatory socialization is functional for both the aspiring individual and for the group he or she eventually enters. This is true when the seeking and weighing of role alternatives is taking place and, especially, as individuals come closer to a final decision to exit a role. Prior identification with a group serves as a kind of bridge to membership in the group. Ebaugh found, for instance, that transsexuals identified with members of the opposite sex by cross-dressing and taking on the mannerisms of the opposite sex long before they underwent sex-change surgery. She states, "In addition to shifts in orientation, attitudes, and values, individuals at this point in the process also began rehearsing the roles they were anticipating."[95]

Gans's analysis of poverty demonstrates how a Mertonian functionalist approach can produce analyses that would generally be associated with radical left conflict theory rather than conservative functionalism. Gans points out that when one distinguishes between different groups in a society, one can see that the existence of poverty serves a number of positive functions for different groups. For example, he argues, poverty ensures the existence of a group willing to serve in a peacetime army, provides the upper classes with an outlet for charity and the gratification it brings, creates jobs for people in professions and occupations that serve the poor, and makes it possible for wealthier people to get dirty jobs and personal services performed at a slight cost. These functions, he suggests, help explain why poverty exists in technologically advanced societies: those who benefit from it wish to preserve it.[96]

Gans's analysis could also shed some light on a social problem of the 1990s—homelessness. We could point to the increase in homelessness in the United States as a dysfunction of the deinstitutionalization of mentally ill patients. By asking Merton's question "Who benefits?" we can uncover the travesty of leaving mentally ill people on the street in the name of civil liberties, and we can inquire where the funds that were recovered from a dismantling of the mental health systems will be allocated. Without attention to latent functions, we miss the significance of an analysis by President Reagan, who said in a television interview that many of the nation's homeless people "make it their own choice" not to seek shelter and who also claimed that a "large percentage" of the homeless are "retarded" people who have voluntarily left institutions in which they were placed.[97]

[95]Helen Rose Fuchs Ebaugh, *Becoming an Ex: The Process of Role Exit* (Chicago: University of Chicago Press, 1988), p. 111.

[96]See Herbert Gans, "The Positive Functions of Poverty," *American Journal of Sociology* 78 (1972): 275–89.

[97]Lou Cannon, "Reagan Cites 'Choice' by Homeless," *Washington Post* (December 23, 1988), p. A8.

Merton's concept of dysfunctions is also central to his argument that functionalism is *not* intrinsically conservative. It appears to be only when functionalists imply that everything is generally functional in its consequences[98]—something his concept of general dysfunctions denies—and when analysts treat society and its members as one and the same thing[99]— a view he sets out to demolish by asking, "Functional for whom?"

At the same time Merton does retain a distinctively functional perspective. Unlike most conflict theorists, Merton believes that institutions and values can be functional (or dysfunctional) for society as a whole, not just for particular groups. He suggests that researchers should start with the hypothesis that persisting cultural forms may have a "net balance of functional consequences"[100] for society as a unit as well as for subgroups. Merton's emphasis on dysfunctions balances Parsons's concern with social functions.

Manifest and Latent Functions

Merton's distinction between manifest and latent functions further clarifies functional analysis. *Manifest functions* are the consequences people observe or expect; *latent functions* are the consequences that are neither recognized nor intended. Parsons tends to emphasize the manifest functions of social behavior; Merton pays particular attention to the latent functions of things and the increased understanding of society functionalist analysis can bring by uncovering them.

The notion of latent functions is not a totally new one. Durkheim's discussion of social cohesion as a consequence of punishment, which we outlined at the beginning of this chapter, was an analysis of the latent function of punishment (the manifest function being retribution). Similarly, the functional analysis of religion as a social integrator, to which we have referred, is concerned with religion's latent function. Merton emphasizes both the distinction between manifest and latent and the way analysis of latent functions "precludes the substitutions of naive moral judgments for sociological analysis."[101] This distinction forces sociologists to go beyond the reasons individuals give for their actions or for the existence of customs and institutions; it makes them look for other social consequences that allow these practices' survival and illuminate the way a society works. As an example of the fruitfulness of such analysis, Merton cites Veblen's analysis of conspicuous

---

[98]This is what Merton labels the "Postulate of Universal Functionalism."

[99]This Merton calls the "Postulate of the Functional Unity of Society." Merton, *Social Theory and Social Structure*, pp. 79, 84.

[100]Merton, *Social Theory and Social Structure*, p. 86.

[101]Merton, *Social Theory and Social Structure*, pp. 124–25.

consumption, the latent function being the enhancement of one's status in the eyes of the world.[102]

Merton's own analysis of political machines shows how the distinction between manifest and latent functions can help explain the way institutions work and why they survive and thrive. The manifest function of political machines, especially in the context of ward politics, seems to be personal advancement through corruption, because it involves vote buying and similar law breaking. However, because they were so firmly rooted in the local neighborhood, ward politics and political machines were highly functional for such disadvantaged groups as new immigrants. They humanized welfare assistance by providing information about hospitals, marshaling legal aid, and furnishing jobs; thus they kept families together and broke down some of the isolation of immigrant groups. Merton started with the hypothesis that in spite of obvious surface dysfunctions, to survive and be influential the machine must have served important functions for some social groups. By asking "Who benefits?" and uncovering the machine's latent functions, he created a classic piece of sociological analysis.

Functional Alternatives

Functionalism's claim of providing specific propositions about how societies work, rather than simply general suggestions about how to set about analyzing and explaining things, rests in large part on its argument that in order to persist a society must have certain characteristics; and correspondingly, all societies will exhibit these characteristics. As we have seen, this argument is central to the work of Parsons, who lists such characteristics in his AGIL schema, and it is also apparent in the work of Durkheim. In much of Merton's work functionalism serves more as a way of orienting oneself to one's material than as a set of propositions about the structure of societies. But Merton does share this central view, and he puts forward the concept of functional prerequisites, or *"preconditions functionally necessary* for a society."[103] At the same time, however, he emphasizes that particular, given institutions are not the only ones able to fulfill these functions; therefore, a given social structure is in no way sacrosanct. On the contrary, a wide range of what he terms "functional alternatives," or substitutes may be able to perform the same task.

Merton's concept of functional alternatives also clarifies functionalist analysis because it explicitly rejects the idea that existing institutions are nec-

---

[102]It is worth noting that Veblen is generally considered essentially a conflict theorist (see Chapter 3), and conflict theorists are, on the whole, very interested in the unadmitted and unseen consequences of people's actions and their relationship to people's interests. Merton's use of Veblen to illustrate the notion of latent functions again underlines his point that there is nothing intrinsically conservative about analyzing society in terms of things' functions, dysfunctions, and general interrelatedness.

[103]Merton, *Social Theory and Social Structure*, p. 87.

essary and, by implication, good. Therefore, it encourages sociologists using a functionalist approach to question the indispensability of an existing social structure. For example, most functional theorists believe that religion maintains and inculcates certain norms and values central to the group[104] and thus combats the anomie that leads to both social disintegration and personal unhappiness. However, this function may be served by structures other than organized religion, and movements that might be interpreted as functional alternatives to religion seem to be cropping up almost yearly in certain parts of America, particularly in California, the birthplace of many occult and therapeutic groups.[105]

Other functional alternatives can be found among the different types of higher education and vocational training existing in modern industrial societies. All of these sort people into the adult world of work and classify them as qualified for different types of occupations. But the different ways they do so may be more or less functional for different people. As Burton Clark points out, American society places great emphasis on encouraging people to achieve and on ensuring equal opportunity to do so, and it practices something close to an open-door admission to college. However, in practice, not everyone can become a nuclear physicist, veterinarian, or corporate executive. Colleges impose fairly strict criteria on performance, and many students would, if they entered a four-year college, inevitably encounter standards of performance they could not meet. Using terminology derived directly from Merton's work on deviance, Clark says there is "dissociation between culturally instilled goals and institutionally provided means of realization; discrepancy between ends and means is seen as a basic social source of individual frustration."[106]

For students who would fail in a four-year college, the two-year or junior college provides a functional alternative. It performs the same function of sorting students for the labor market, and it makes it clear to less academically oriented students that certain careers are not possible for them. And it does so at much less personal cost to such students, for whom the straight academic failure of the conventional college might be personally dysfunctional. Clark describes the "cooling-out" function of these colleges, which permit transfer to four-year colleges but also redirect students through testing programs and extensive counseling that serve to reorient students who need to redefine their goals. Although a four-year college is both personally functional for those who succeed scholastically and an appropriate way to train people for some careers, Clark shows how the two-

[104]A view shared, as Merton points out, by Marxists. Merton, *Social Theory and Social Structure*, pp. 98–99.

[105]See Durkheim on the public school as a functional alternative, p. 25, fn. 28.

[106]Burton Clark, "The 'Cooling-Out' Function in Higher Education," *American Journal of Sociology* 65 (1960): 560. As Parsons might put it, the discrepancy creates strain or potential disequilibrium.

year college can be a functional alternative for others because it provides alternative achievements that alleviate the personal stress caused by failure. It may also function socially by helping to prevent discontentment and deviance and by directing people successfully into other occupations.

In the wake of the contemporary women's movement, many functional alternatives to traditional marriages have emerged, such as cohabitation and gay and lesbian families. The increasing use of day care facilities and, on a much smaller scale, househusbands are examples of functional alternatives to traditional families where the mother works as housewife at home, but not in the public sphere for a wage. Other examples of functional alternatives to traditional marriages are commuting relationships, equal parenting, and greater husband participation in household work.[107]

Merton's notion of functional alternatives is thus important because it alerts sociologists to the similar functions different institutions may perform, and it further reduces the tendency of functionalism to imply approval of the status quo. However, Merton makes little progress in specifying what the functional prerequisites are that can be served in a variety of ways. Merton apparently does not consider Parsons's schema to be the definitive statement on the subject, but neither does he provide any concrete alternative list of his own. He recognizes the idea of functional requirements as an essential part of any functional analysis,[108] and he refers frequently in his analysis to the degree to which society is well or poorly adjusted.[109] But he fails to define the functional requirements for such integration. Instead he refers to them as "one of the cloudiest and empirically most debatable concepts in functional theory."[110]

As might be expected from his remarks on middle-range theory, in general, Merton's achievement is to provide an excellent clarification of the requirements of functionalist theory and to show how a general functionalist orientation can be used fruitfully in empirical analysis, rather than to provide further general propositions about social structure and equilibrium.

[107]See William Beer, *Househusbands* (South Hadley, Mass.: Bergin and Garvey, 1982); Joseph H. Pleck, *Working Wives, Working Husbands* (Beverly Hills, Calif.: Sage, 1985); and Arlie Russell Hochschild, *The Second Shift: Working Parents and the Revolution at Home* (New York: Viking, 1989) and *The Time Bind: When Work Becomes Home and Home Becomes Work* (New York: Henry Holt, 1997).

[108]Merton, *Social Theory and Social Structure*, pp. 87 and 106.

[109]Merton, *Social Theory and Social Structure*; for example, p. 217. Merton's concept of integration seems to owe most to Durkheim and to include the necessity for cultural norms and actual institutions and opportunities to be in line with one another. See the discussion of his theory of deviance, which follows.

[110]Merton, *Social Theory and Social Structure*, p. 107.

MERTON'S THEORY OF DEVIANCE

Though Merton's contributions to sociology are legion, his theory of deviance, which has been reprinted several times in different languages, is one of his best known. In developing his theory of deviance, Merton utilizes explanatory factors that are typical of functional analysis—namely, cultural goals and institutionalized norms. He uses anomie as a major independent variable; as we have seen, anomie is a term also used by Durkheim to explain suicide, a form of deviance. Let us recall that Durkheim's general definition of anomie was a lack of regulation, or normlessness. Merton's definition differs somewhat; for him, anomie is a discontinuity between cultural goals and the legitimate means available for reaching them. He applies this analysis to the United States, where the goal of monetary success is heavily emphasized but there is no corresponding emphasis on the "legitimate avenues to march toward this goal."[111] The resulting anomie is, Merton argues, dysfunctional for American society in general and especially dysfunctional for those groups within the country who lack the means to the goal of monetary success. Thus it is a source of strain for the system, in the Parsonian sense, and it leads to a considerable amount of deviance.[112]

In depicting his model graphically Merton chose to use a plus sign (+) to indicate acceptance of the goal of monetary success or the means to the goal, and he used a minus sign (−) to indicate the rejection (or unavailability) of the goal or means to it. He thus arrives at five modes of adaptation, or types of deviance. Our schematic presentation (Figure 2-3) differs from Merton's original one in that we have presented the relationship between the goal and means (his independent variable, anomie) first, followed by the modes of adaptation, or deviance typology (his dependent variable).

[111]See Merton's chapter, "Social Structure and Anomie," in *Social Theory and Social Structure*, pp. 185–248.

[112]Parsons, in fact, borrowed from Merton's model in his own classification of deviant orientation. See Parsons, *The Social System*, p. 257.

FIGURE 2-3   Goals, Means, and Adaptations: Merton on Deviance

X ⟶		Y
(Anomie)		(Deviance)
Cultural Goals	Institutionalized Means	Modes of Adaptation
+	+	Conformity
+	−	Innovation
−	+	Ritualism
−	−	Retreatism
±	±	Rebellion

We can dispose of the mode of conformity easily, for a person who attains monetary success by working hard and getting an education is the prototype of the successful American. Next we can see that innovation (for example, racketeering) and ritualism (the type we mentioned earlier in discussing the Balchen case) are the only pure cases of anomie as Merton defined it, because in both of these there is discontinuity between the goals and means. Retreatism (for example, drug addiction) is a rejection (or unavailability) of both monetary success and the means to it, and rebellion is a combination of a rejection of societal goals and means and a substitution of other goals and means.

Merton's prediction for the United States, where monetary success is highly valued and the legitimate means to it are unavailable for many, is that our society should have a lot of deviance and that it should most likely occur among the lower classes, who experience the structural blockages most keenly. In general his model is not clear, however, about when the various types will emerge or in what degree.

Although Merton did not test his hypotheses on deviance himself, they were stated empirically enough to guide other researchers,[113] and it has been said that the publication of this essay on deviance in 1938 in the *American Sociological Review* established Merton "once and for all as a major figure in sociology."[114]

In concluding this section on Merton, we can see that in general he alerts functionalists to question and to evaluate critically the contributions of various social institutions. He also raises questions of inequality when he asks who benefits from certain structures, thus leading to a more critical view than Parsons.

PART THREE

Neofunctionalism

Neofunctionalism is a theoretical development that emerged in the mid-1980s in the United States and Germany. In 1984 the theory section of the American Sociological Association, then headed by Jeffrey C. Alexander, devoted two sessions to a conference on neofunctionalism at the annual meeting. Most of the papers presented reappraised and reconsidered the empirical applications of Parsonian theory. Alexander, recognized as the

---

[113]Light, for instance, stated that Merton's anomie theory is "still the orthodox sociological explanation of why ethnic and racial minorities have always been disproportionately involved in illegal enterprise in America." Ivan Light, "The Ethnic Vice Industry, 1880–1944," *American Sociological Review* (1977): 465.

[114]Hunt, "How Does It Come To Be So?" p. 52.

leading proponent of neofunctionalism in the United States, subsequently published a volume titled *Neofunctionalism*.[115]

In the introduction to *Neofunctionalism* Alexander suggests three similarities between neofunctionalism and neo-Marxism. Both include a critique of some of the basic tenets of the original theory, the incorporation of elements from antagonistic theoretical traditions, and a variety of competing developments rather than a single coherent form. Alexander then argues that neofunctionalism is a tendency rather than a developed theory, and he elaborates on the various tendencies of neofunctionalism: (1) to create a form of functionalism that is multidimensional and includes micro as well as macro levels of analysis; (2) to push functionalism to the left and reject Parsons's optimism about modernity; (3) to argue for an implicit democratic thrust in functional analysis; (4) to incorporate a conflict orientation; and (5) to emphasize contingency (uncertainty) and interactional creativity.

What remained at issue among neofunctionalists, however, were the following kinds of interrelated problems: How may researchers best characterize the relationship between conflict or contingency and social order? To what extent must Parsons's emphasis upon the relationship between social action and social order be reformulated in order to inform empirical research? In the 1980s and 1990s contributors to neofunctionalism in the United States, in addition to Alexander, include Paul Colomy, Dean Gerstein, Mark Gould, Frank Lechner, David Sciulli, and Neil Smelser, and in Germany Niklas Luhmann and Richard Munch. In the following section we briefly mention the work of Alexander, Smelser, and Luhmann.

Jeffrey C. Alexander

In his recent book entitled *Neofunctionalism and After*, Jeffrey Alexander confesses that he now considers the neofunctionalism project as finished. He argues that the transition from orthodox to reconstructed functionalism has been completed because the legitimacy of some of Parsons's central concerns has been established. In Alexander's view, neofunctionalism "has succeeded in helping to establish Parsons as a classical figure." This means that, like other classical theorists, Parsons's theoretical position, though historically eminent, will not dominate contemporary theoretical work. Alexander adds that Parsons's ideas are "no more important than some of the critical achievements of other classical theorists."[116]

On the other hand, Alexander continues to view functionalism as a "vital current in contemporary work . . . one strong strand in the fabric of

---

[115]See Jeffery C. Alexander (ed.), *Neofunctionalism* (Beverly Hills, Calif.: Sage, 1985), and David Sciulli and Dean Gerstein, "Social Theory and Talcott Parsons in the 1980s," *Annual Review of Sociology* (Palo Alto, Calif.: Annual Review, Inc., 1985).

[116]Jeffrey C. Alexander, *Neofunctionalism and After* (Malden, Mass.: Blackwell, 1998), 5–13.

the new theoretical movement." Further, he predicts that neofunctionalists will continue to produce creative and important sociological studies. But he adds, "The very success of neofunctionalism points beyond it as well."[117]

For Alexander the direction of the new theoretical movement is beyond reconstruction of already existing theories and toward creation of new ones. It is his position that what has stimulated these movements are "the emergence of new politically generated theories such as feminism, multiculturalism, civil society, and postcolonialism."[118] Alexander's departure from Parsons's focus on equilibrium at the macrosociological level is apparent when he states

> The divisive classes generated by economic life, the oligarchies generated by political and organizational power, the gender and age hierarchies of families, the demonology frequently legitimated by religious institutions, and the ethnic, regional, and racial dominations so often generated by the very construction of national civil states—such intrusions fragment and split civil society even while its very existence promises participation and restoration of the social whole.[119]

Daily newspapers throughout the world are filled with examples of these destructive intrusions in the lives of rich and poor, parents and children, husbands and wives, clergy and laity, and the majorities and minorities across racial, ethnic, and regional dimensions. With respect to empirical research, however, the American reconsideration of Parsons has not been successful in producing the quality and quantity of empirical research that we need in order to understand the conditions under which the fragmentations and restorations of civil society come about.

Alexander sees his work as a contribution to the new theoretical movement and confesses that he has shifted from following Parsons in his neglect of order in the lives of individual people, to theorizing much more directly in the microsociological tradition. An illustration of this is his new work on action. While Parsons consistently viewed actors as analytical concepts, Alexander defines *action* as the movement of concrete, living, breathing persons as they make their way through time and space. In addition, when he argues that every action contains a dimension of free will, or agency, in this respect he is expanding functionalism to include some of the concerns of symbolic interactionism.

---

[117]Alexander, *Neofunctionalism and After*, p. 13.
[118]Alexander, *Neofunctionalism and After*, p. 17.
[119]Alexander, *Neofunctionalism and After*, p. 227.

Neil J. Smelser

Neil Smelser, who coauthored *Economy and Society* with Parsons while a graduate student at Harvard, has been a key figure among neofunctionalists.[120] Though Smelser's work moved in directions different from Parsons's, their friendship endured until Parsons's death.[121] Smelser's presidential address at the 1997 meeting of the American Sociological Association, entitled "The Rational and the Ambivalent in the Social Sciences," exemplifies what was previously described as the movement toward creation of new theories. In this address Smelser sets out to establish the concept of ambivalence as an essential element for the understanding of individual behavior, social institutions, and the human condition in general. In contrast to Parsons and Merton, Smelser's approach, based on Freud's theory of ambivalence, takes intrapsychic processes, rather than roles, as the starting point. As he describes it, "the nature of ambivalence is to hold *opposing affective orientations* toward the same person, object, or symbol." The reason people look for ways to avoid experiencing ambivalence is that it is "such a *powerful, persistent, unresolvable, volatile, generalizable,* and *anxiety-producing* feature of the human condition."[122]

In applying the notion of ambivalence, Smelser refers to phenomena such as death and separation, retirement, and moving away from a community. He sees the postulate of ambivalence as most applicable, however, in a range of situations where persons are dependent on one another, such as lovers, partners, intimates, and friends. He argues that the form of dependence may vary:

> A subordinate person in a power relationship is politically dependent; a person who is committed to a religious or social movement is ideologically dependent; a person in love is emotionally dependent. The common element, however, is that freedom to leave—choice—is restricted because it is costly politically, ideologically, or emotionally. Thus, dependence entails entrapment.[123]

Smelser argues that certain types of organizations where people are "locked in" by personal or institutional commitment, like Goffman's "total institutions," are "seedbeds of ambivalence and its consequences—spite, petty wrangling, struggles for recognition, and vicious politics."[124] For example, Smelser points to academic departments, where "people are 'locked in' by

---

[120]See, for example, Neil J. Smelser, "Evaluating the Model of Structural Differentiation in Relation to Educational Change in the Nineteenth Century," pp. 113–29 in Jeffrey C. Alexander, ed., *Neofunctionalism*.

[121]For background on Smelser, see Ruth A. Wallace, "New ASA President Neil J. Smelser: A Bridge-Builder *Par Excellence,*" *Footnotes* 24.7 (September/October, 1996): 1, 10.

[122]Neil J. Smelser, "The Rational and the Ambivalent in the Social Sciences," *American Sociological Review* 63.1 (February 1998): 6.

[123]Smelser, "The Rational and the Ambivalent," p. 8.

[124]Smelser, "The Rational and the Ambivalent," p. 9. See Chapter 5 for Goffman's work on total institutions.

tenure or by the yearning and struggle for tenure, and can escape only at great cost unless a more attractive opportunity arises." And he adds, "People have to live with one another, but this does not mean they have to love one another; it implies, rather, that they both love and hate one another."[125]

Finally, Smelser makes a methodological point regarding ambivalence. He refers to the public opinion survey where a representative sample of citizens is asked to reply whether they approve or disapprove, and how strongly, in a series of questions regarding a political official. Smelser points out that most of our feelings about public figures in the United States—such as presidents Roosevelt, Eisenhower, Kennedy, Nixon, Bush, and Clinton—are ambivalent. We have mixed feelings not only about these public figures but also about social issues tapped by survey questions. Smelser argues, "We must regard attitude surveys not as revealed preferences but as a distorted structure of reality that minimizes and—in the process—delegitimizes both ambiguity and ambivalence."[126] As you will see in our chapter on symbolic interactionism, the late Herbert Blumer, a colleague and friend of Smelser's at Berkeley, would agree with this critique of public opinion surveys.[127]

Niklas Luhmann

German theorists, on the other hand, tend to read Parsons through the eyes of Niklas Luhmann, who spent a year in the early 1960s at Harvard studying under Parsons. Luhmann views Parsons's theory as a milestone because it "has been the only attempt to begin with a number of equally important functions and then to give a theoretical deduction to them. . . . No one else has dared to try this or even thought it was possible."[128] However, what Parsons's theory is missing, according to Luhmann, are the concepts of self-reference and complexity. His own work attempts to formulate a universal or grand theory of social systems that incorporates these concepts.

Luhmann argues that a social system exists "whenever the actions of several persons are meaningful, interrelated and are thus . . . marked off from an environment."[129] A social system thus emerges whenever any interaction takes place among individuals. According to Luhmann, there are three types of social systems: interaction systems (face-to-face interaction of human beings), organization systems (where membership is linked to specific conditions), and societal systems (the all-embracing social system, entire societies).[130]

[125]Smelser, "The Rational and the Ambivalent," p. 9

[126]Smelser, "The Rational and the Ambivalent," p. 11.

[127]See the section on Blumer in Chapter 5.

[128]See Niklas Luhmann, *The Differentiation of Society* (New York: Columbia University Press, 1982), p. 59.

[129]Luhmann, *The Differentiation of Society*, p. 70.

[130]Luhmann, *The Differentiation of Society*, pp. 71–75.

Self-reference, according to Luhmann, is a condition for the efficient functioning of systems. It means that the system is able to observe itself, can reflect on itself and what it is doing, and can make decisions as a result of this reflection. Self-referential systems have the ability to "delineate their self identities."[131] They can describe themselves by setting up boundaries regarding what they are and what they are not; in other words, the system has "structural autonomy."[132]

Self-referencing, in Luhmann's view, takes place in all subsystems, such as politics, science, economy, family, education, and law. He provides us with an example of the self-referencing of a system when he says that the scientific subsystem "reflects on itself in fundamental theorizing and in its decisions to continue or discontinue its historically given traditions."[133] "Self-referential systems are not only self-organizing or self-regulating systems. . . . They exist as a closed network of the production of elements which reproduces itself as a network by continuing to produce the elements which are needed to continue to produce the elements."[134]

To argue that a system is self-referencing is to confer on the system a capability for decision making. How much is gained by such a reification? It is one thing to suggest, as Parsons does, that a system has needs, but quite another to say that it can reflect on itself and make decisions. It seems to us that an example such as the one just given confuses the issue even further. After all, the scientific subsystem that reflects on itself consists, in the last analysis, of groups of scientists who do the reflecting and make the decisions.

Luhmann's position, however, is that the human subject or concrete social groups should not be the central point of social thought. Societal systems, according to Luhmann, are too complicated to be treated in this way. They must be treated not as being composed of human beings, but rather as being composed of communication units. Individuals, then, are merely part of the environment of the societal system. Subjective meaning is ruled out, as evidenced in his statement that "there is no plausible way to base systems theory on a Weberian concept of meaningful action."[135]

In Luhmann's theory the chief task performed by social systems is to reduce complexity.[136] Luhmann is convinced that Parsons's theory of action offers "only meager resources for handling complexity"[137] and that "a theory

[131]Niklas Luhmann, "Tautology and Paradox in the Self-Descriptions of Modern Society," *Sociological Theory* 6(1988): 26–37.

[132]Luhmann, *The Differentiation of Society*, p. 258.

[133]Luhmann, *The Differentiation of Society*, p. 265.

[134]Niklas Luhmann, "Society, Meaning, Religion—Based on Self-Reference," *Sociological Analysis* 46 (1985): 6. As this quote demonstrates, a combination of unclear definitions and highly abstract concepts makes Luhmann's theory difficult to grasp.

[135]Luhmann, *The Differentiation of Society*, p. 232.

[136]Luhmann, *The Differentiation of Society*, p. xxvi.

[137]Luhmann, *The Differentiation of Society*, p. 92.

of society will have to concern itself with ideas such as the reduction of the extreme complexity and contingency of the world."[138] In Luhmann's view, greater complexity brings more choices and more possibilities, and this means that choosing among alternatives is more difficult; it takes more noes to reach a yes. Think, for example, of the difficult decision arising from technological innovations that have produced an enormous variety of software programs for computers. How does one choose a word-processing program, a printer, a cellular phone, or a program for surfing the net for instance, when newer and more sophisticated versions are being introduced almost daily?

Luhmann argues that the fundamental problems of such a paradoxical world can be solved, or transformed into minor problems, by religion or by several functional equivalents of religion in modern society, including art, love, sovereign power, and making money.[139] What these alternatives have in common is that they provide at least some actors with shared standards of action accepted on faith. They allow complex sets of interactions to proceed in a world that would otherwise be chaotic and incomprehensible.

Luhmann is basically not as optimistic about the future as was Parsons. Luhmann argues that the modern world is too complex for shared norms or even value generalization, and he criticizes Parsons for overestimating not only the social consensus that is functionally necessary but also the consensus that exists in actuality. What unites us, according to Luhmann, is "common acceptance of schematized [or structural] contingency."[140]

In a later work Luhmann points to the negative aspects (dysfunctions) of modernity. He views society as confronted with the full consequences of its structural selections, such as the ecological problems resulting from its own "rationality."[141] Luhmann also points to the growing awareness of and anxiety about global risks nourished by modern ecological problems and the struggle to maintain the level of social welfare. In fact, Luhmann describes this as the "era of unmasked anxiety."[142]

In his book titled *Risk: A Sociological Theory*, Luhmann defines *risk* as a potential harm threatening an individual that is based on a decision made by the individual.[143] It is a calculation regarding potential loss and advantage in terms of time, like deciding whether or when or where to dispose of nuclear materials or to smoke a cigarette.

---

[138]Luhmann, *The Differentiation of Society*, p. 192. While Luhmann argues for the reduction of complexity, Patricia Hill Collins takes the opposite position. See Chapter 5.

[139]Luhmann, "Society, Meaning, Religion—Based on Self-Reference," p. 9.

[140]Luhmann, *The Differentiation of Society*, p. xix.

[141]Luhmann, "Tautology and Paradox in the Self-Descriptions of Modern Society," p. 36.

[142]Luhmann, "Tautology and Paradox in the Self-Descriptions of Modern Society," p. 33.

[143]Niklas Luhmann, *Risk: A Sociological Theory* (New York: Aldine De Gruyter, 1993), p. 11.

In this analysis Luhmann distingishes between risk and danger, the latter defined as a potential harm to which an individual is passively exposed, that is, without that particular individual having made a decision to do so—for example, a tornado, earthquake, or hurricane. In the case of danger, he explains, "the possible loss is caused externally, that is to say, it is attributed to the environment."[144]

Luhmann also argues that one individual's decision (risk) can be another individual's danger, like the smoker's effect on the nonsmoker. Thus the critical difference between the decision makers and the people affected by the decision is that what is a risk for one (the decision maker) is a danger for the other (the one affected).

Returning to his focus on communication units, Luhmann poses the question of how communication that seeks to raise the level of risk awareness must be constituted. He points to warnings against risks in product advertising, and he includes under that heading "the multifarious efforts to influence sexual behavior in the face of the AIDS risk."[145]

Whereas people in primitive societies were threatened primarily by dangers, Luhmann argues that the technological society makes decisions that affect the environment in a profound way, like decisions regarding nuclear power generation. In Luhmann's view we are primarily threatened by risks in modern society because we are dependent on the decision makers; thus he sees modern society as risk-prone. Luhmann states, "Modern risk-oriented society is a product not only of the perception of the consequences of technological achievement. Its seed is contained in the expansion of research possibilities and of knowledge itself."[146] The carcinogenic effects of X-rays, which became apparent only after use of the new technology, is one of the consequences of technological achievement mentioned by Luhmann. [147]

Luhmann's work and the work of Richard Munch have spearheaded the revival of functionalist theorizing in Germany.[148] Like neo-Marxism, the development of neofunctionalism involves a critique, a reinterpretation, and an expansion of the original work, rather than an attempt to repeat the debates of the 1950s and 1960s.

---

[144]Luhmann, *Risk: A Sociological Theory*, p. 22.

[145]Luhmann, *Risk: A Sociological Theory*, pp. 4 and 5.

[146]Luhmann, *Risk: A Sociological Theory*, p. 28. Our discussion of Luhmann's theory of risk was considerably enhanced by conversations with Frank Mars, a student of Luhmann.

[147]Luhmann, *Risk: A Sociological Theory*, p. 89. See Chapter 5, where we discuss Roentgen's discovery of X-rays.

[148]See Richard Munch, "Talcott Parsons and the Theory of Action I and II," *American Journal of Sociology* 86 (1981): 709–39 and 87 (1982): 771–826. For an American interpretation see Jeffrey C. Alexander, "The Parsons Revival in German Sociology," *Sociological Theory 1984* (San Francisco: Jossey-Bass, 1984), pp. 394–412.

CONCLUSION

In discussing the characteristics of functionalism and the contributions of the major theorists throughout this chapter, we have raised questions about certain features of the functionalist perspective. This was not done to discourage the reader from using the insights of functionalism. Rather, it was an attempt to uncover the weaknesses as well as the strengths of this perspective, and this, as we mentioned earlier, is one of our goals in writing this text.

As a matter of fact, those who prefer other perspectives could nonetheless profit by a more thorough knowledge and understanding of functionalism than is common among many contemporary sociologists. The perspective provides considerable insight into how societies work and why institutions and customs exist. If there is some wisdom in the saying, "You have to know the system to beat the system," then functionalism can help those who are dedicated to radical social change to a fuller understanding of how the system operates. Nor, to appreciate functionalism, need one take sides with Parsons when, for instance, he argues that his general theory of action encompasses conflict theory, and thus there are not two theories, but one. One may, instead, agree with Dahrendorf or Coser, who see consensus (or functionalist) theory and conflict theory as two different sides of the coin.[149]

Does the assumption that consensus lies at the basis of any social order make this theory ideologically conservative? In arguing that functionalism is independent of any ideological implications, Parsons argues that functional analysis has "nothing to do with political conservatism or a defense of the status quo."[150] In the past, however, functionalism has often been used as a conservative approach to the analysis of society because strain and conflict were seen as dysfunctional for the social system, and anomie as a pathological state to be avoided. Many of those who were attracted to functionalism tended, in practice, to be more or less satisfied with the present system, and they were not neutral about its survival. However, with the revitalization of functionalist theorizing in the 1980s and the critique and reinterpretation of Parsons by neofunctionalists through the 1990s, we expect to continue to see some new developments and extensions of this perspective.

To summarize, then, functionalism tends to stress values over interests, and although it shows the independent importance of ideas and the links between power and social consent, it neglects the coercive aspects of power and the significance of people's conflicting objectives. Similarly, it emphasizes social control over social change, thus analyzing adjustive but ignoring disruptive change, and overemphasizes the importance of security and the needs of society at the expense of interests and objectives that cannot be met without social change. In general, functionalism also stresses structure over

---

[149]See Chapter 3.
[150]In Coser, *The Idea of Social Structure*, p. 73.

process (although Parsons's work on evolutionary change takes into account processes as well as structures); and in general functionalism stresses macrostructural over microinteractional sociological analysis.

Its macrosociological emphasis means that one is taking an aerial view of society when one views society from the functionalist perspective. It is not a better picture than that taken from the ground where individuals are interacting; it is simply a picture taken from a different angle. If we consider, for instance, the locations of the numerous television cameras at a political convention, we realize that each camera captures a piece of reality but that no one camera by itself catches all of the action. So it is, we argue, with theoretical perspectives in sociology. In functionalism most of the pictures are taken from on high, focusing on social structures, and most of the pictures are developed as stills. Nonetheless, a part of the total reality is contained in those pictures. In the following chapters we shall see how other perspectives both challenge and differ from functionalism by emphasizing interests and change, the dynamic processes of individual behavior, and the close-up view of social interactions.

CHAPTER THREE

Conflict Theory

INTRODUCTION: THE TWO TRADITIONS

Conflict theory is the major alternative to functionalism as an approach to analyzing the general structure of societies; and it is increasingly popular and important in modern sociology. It is also a less unified perspective than the others discussed in this book, and the disagreements among its proponents are often more bitter than those they have with theorists who use other approaches. However, conflict theorists of all types share a number of important assumptions and preconceptions. Together these create a distinctive way of looking at the world.

Functionalists, as we have seen, look at societies and social institutions as systems in which all the parts depend on each other and work together to create equilibrium. They do not deny the existence of conflict; but they believe society develops ways to control it, and it is these that they analyze. Conflict theorists' perceptions of society could hardly be more different. Where functionalists see interdependence and unity in society, conflict theorists see an arena in which groups fight for power, and the control of conflict simply means that one group is able, temporarily, to suppress its rivals. Functionalists see civil law, for example, as a way of increasing social integration, whereas conflict theorists see civil law as a way of defining and upholding a particular order that benefits some groups at the expense of others.

We can see how different a view of things this perspective creates if we go back to the example we used in introducing functionalism—a modern airport. A functionalist perspective points out the way the different parts of an airport work together to keep the system functioning. Conflict theory is interested in the rivalries among different workers and management and in the position each group is in to do well for itself. A conflict theorist might point out that the air traffic controllers want more staff and additional expensive equipment; that the pilots are continually trying to restrict entry into the profession in order to keep salaries high; that the porters, maintenance staff, and cleaners all belong to militant unions; and that all these groups are at odds with the airlines and terminal management, who want to keep costs down and profits up. The focus is on the shifting balance of power among competing groups, not on the equilibrium of interdependence and cooperation.[1]

This general conflict orientation incorporates three central and connected assumptions. The first is that people have a number of basic interests,

---

[1]The contrast between equilibrium and conflict analyses of society is very old. One of the major modern theorists we discuss later, Ralf Dahrendorf, builds one of his expositions of conflict theory around the figure of Thrasymachus, a famous Greek sophist who appears in the work of Plato as a "conflict theorist" attacking the "equilibrium theory" that Plato puts in the mouth of Socrates. Ralf Dahrendorf, "In Praise of Thrasymachus," in *Essays on the Theory of Society* (Stanford, Calif.: Stanford University Press, 1968).

things they want and attempt to acquire that are not defined by societies but rather are common to them all. Conflict theorists are not always explicit about this view of humanity, but it is present in all their work.

Second, and central to the whole conflict perspective, is an emphasis on power as the core of social relationships. Conflict theorists always view power not only as scarce and unequally divided—and therefore a source of conflict—but also as essentially coercive. This analysis leads, in turn, to a concern with the distribution of the resources that give people more or less power. For example, any conflict theorist would consider what happened to the Native Americans to have been inevitable. The white settlers had greater numbers, greater wealth, and more advanced weapons; therefore, they were bound, such a theorist would argue, to seize lands and mineral wealth and give little in return. What is surprising, from a conflict perspective, is not that the settlers' religion and political beliefs did not stop them, but that the Native Americans were not simply exterminated.

The third distinctive aspect of conflict theory is that values and ideas are seen as weapons used by different groups to advance their own ends rather than as the means of defining a whole society's identity and goals. We shall find that conflict theorists have a great deal to say about ideas as an aspect of groups' interests, especially under the categories of "ideology" and "legitimacy." In the case of the U.S. treatment of the Native Americans, for example, conflict theorists would tend to interpret the notion of America's "manifest destiny" and the idea of "civilizing" the tribes as clear examples of how people develop ideas that suit their own interests.

The Two Traditions

The basic elements of conflict theory that we have described are common to all its proponents, but conflict theory can also be divided into two quite dissimilar traditions. These differ, above all, in their view of social science and in whether they believe that conflict can ever be eradicated. This chapter discusses each separately.

The first group of theorists believes social scientists have a moral obligation to critique society. It refuses to separate—or to admit that one can really separate—analysis from judgment or fact from value. Theorists in this group also often (but not always) believe that in principle a society could no longer have grounds for social conflict. The second group, by contrast, considers conflict to be an inevitable and permanent aspect of social life; it also rejects the idea that social science's conclusions are necessarily value-laden. Instead, its proponents are interested in establishing a social science with the same canon of objectivity as informs the natural sciences.

Theorists in the first group, where we discuss modern Marxism and neo-Marxism, the Frankfurt School, C. Wright Mills, and Pierre Bourdieu, are most influenced by the work of Karl Marx. In the second group, where we describe the work of Ralf Dahrendorf, Lewis Coser, and Randall Collins, Marx's influence is still apparent, but the most important continuities are with the writings of Max Weber. We therefore first discuss the roots of modern conflict theory in the work of these two classical thinkers, as well as the influence of such writers as Veblen, Simmel, the European elite theorists, and the American sociologists of the Chicago School.

INTELLECTUAL ROOTS

Power, Position, and Legitimacy: Marx and Weber

The basic elements of conflict theory were set out by two of the greatest early sociologists, Karl Marx and Max Weber. Much of Weber's work incorporates a debate with Marx and Marxist analysis, but in both these authors we find the same two concerns: first, with the way social positions bestow more or less power on their incumbents; and second, with the role of ideas in creating or undermining the legitimacy of a social position.

Karl Marx (1818–1883).   Conflict theory in sociology is the creation of Karl Marx. Indeed, Marxism and conflict theory are sometimes discussed as though the two were synonymous. There can also be no better example than Marxism of the close connection between a theorist's ideas and the events of the real world; for it is in the name of Marx's ideas that revolutionaries around the world attack existing forms of society and that organized Communist parties have ruled a large part of humanity.

Karl Marx was born in 1818 in Trier, Germany. His parents were Jews who had converted to Protestantism to avoid discrimination and loss of civil rights, and in particular to protect his father's law practice. Marx also began to study law. However, at the University of Berlin he became fascinated by the philosophy of Hegel, who interpreted the whole of history as the process by which "Spirit" (and consequently humanity) progressed toward complete self-knowledge and a rational and free society. Marx became a Young Hegelian, one of a group of young philosophers who questioned many parts of the master's teachings while remaining beholden to his approach. Indeed, in later years, Marx came to see his own writing as upending Hegel's, replacing Hegel's emphasis on mind as the crucial determinant of history with his own *materialist* philosophy, which demonstrated that material factors determined events. He also became an antireligious radical, and after completing his thesis he worked as a writer and publicist in Paris and Belgium. During this period he wrote *The Communist Manifesto*, which sets out a program for a revolutionary government and outlines his theory of social structures and social change. When the revolution of 1848 broke out in Germany, he returned to edit a radical newspaper. After the revolution failed, he went into exile again and settled in London, his home for the rest of his life.

During much of this period Marx and his family were extremely poor; help from his friend Friedrich Engels, a socialist textile manufacturer, was vital. Nonetheless, his theories became increasingly well known and influential, especially outside England. He was consulted more and more frequently by Russian and German radicals and revolutionaries, and since his death Communist parties have developed all over the world. Their dogma consists of the analyses of Marx and of Lenin, who led the first successful Communist revolution.

Because Marx's work is still used by so many writers in their analyses of contemporary society, we discuss it in additional detail later in the chapter. Of course, the ideas of many other long-dead writers are essential to contemporary analyses, but Marx's work is rather different. Marxist sociologists form a school whose analyses take place *within* the framework Marx created. In this sense, therefore, Marxism is an entirely contemporary theory.

The basic elements of conflict theory are all apparent in Marx's work. He believed, first of all, that people have an essential nature and clearly defined interests. Indeed, Marxists generally argue that if people do not behave in accordance with these interests it can only mean that they have been deceived about what their "true interests" are by a social system that works in others' favor. Second, Marx analyzed both historical and contemporary society in terms of conflicts between different social groups with different interests. Finally, he emphasized the link between the nature of ideas or *ideologies* and the interests of those who develop them, and he insisted that the ideas of an age reflect the interests of the "ruling class."

Marx emphasized the primacy of technology and of patterns of property ownership in determining the nature of people's lives and course of social conflict. Whereas Marxist and, to a lesser degree, other critical conflict theorists retain this emphasis, other analysts from Weber on have seen it as an important, but only partial, explanation. The divide between the two approaches thus derives from the central differences between Marx and Weber themselves.

Max Weber (1864–1920).   Max Weber was born into a prominent bourgeois German family. His father was an important member of the National Liberal Party, with a seat in the Reichstag (Parliament); his mother came from a wealthy but also intensely religious and cultured background. There was considerable tension in his parents' marriage. As a youth Weber tended to identify with his father. However, during his poststudent years, when he was still financially dependent and living at home, he came to resent the older man and his authoritarian behavior. These conflicts played an important part in the complete breakdown Weber suffered in his early thirties.

Before and after this period, Weber was enormously productive, both in his intellectual work and in political activities. He held chairs at the universities of Freiburg and Heidelberg and produced a range of works on topics that included economic policy, political development, the social psychology of industrial work, the sociology of religion, economic history, and the methodology of social science. At the same time he played an important role in Christian-Social political circles, producing papers on current issues. During this period his home was a center of German intellectual life.

The last years of Weber's life were also those of the First World War, of German defeat, of revolution and virtual civil war at home, and of the establishment of a German Republic. During this period Weber was intensely involved in politics. After initially supporting the war, he later urged peace overtures and called for widespread changes in the German political structure. He was a founding member of the Deutsche Demokratische Partei and was involved in writing the new constitution. But he also called the abortive 1918 revolution a "bloody carnival," something the left wing never forgave and that doomed proposals to have him join the government or become a candidate for president of the republic.

For all his lifelong concern with the relationship between politics and intellectual thought, Weber had none of the utopian prophet about him. Like Marx, Weber wanted to identify the origins of essential characteristics of modern society, but he did not see modernization as the road to perfection. On the contrary: modern rationality could be an "iron cage," creating a narrow, "disenchanted" world of bureaucratic officialdom.

Weber's analyses are complex and difficult to categorize, and they have had none of Marx's impact on the world. Nonetheless, a large proportion of non-Marxist intellectuals would nominate him as the greatest of sociologists, and his ideas are the single most important influence on analytic conflict theory.[2]

Like Marx, Weber saw people's activities as largely self-interested. However, he believed that a historian or sociologist must recognize, in addition to such universal interests as the acquisition of wealth, the importance of goals and values specific to a society. For example, he suggested that the Calvinists' desire to save their souls found expression in the unique goal of simply accumulating wealth. This was seen as evidence of God's favor, whereas actually enjoying its fruits would be sinful indulgence.[3]

Weber analyzed the way people maneuver in pursuit of advantage in terms of both particular values and circumstances and more general socio-

---

[2]Weber also, like Marx, continues to arouse considerable passion. Raymond Aron describes a Heidelberg conference to celebrate the centenary of Weber's birth. Emotions ran high, and Herbert Marcuse, one of the critical sociologists we discuss later, attacked with fury the long-dead Weber's hostility to and disbelief in socialist utopianism. Raymond Aron, *Main Currents in Sociological Thought* 2 (Harmondsworth, Middlesex: Penguin Books, 1970), pp. 252–56.

[3]Weber distinguishes among different types of social action, not all of which are rational and calculating in the sense implied here. See Chapter 5 for a discussion of Weber's ideas on the connection between action and meaning.

logical categories. He formulated *ideal types* by abstracting the typical or necessary properties of a concept from a variety of concrete instances. Real-life examples need not correspond exactly to the stylized ideal type: for example, it may be impossible to find any examples of bureaucracy that correspond in every particular to Weber's model. However, an ideal type is important in making historical and contemporary events intelligible. For example, Weber argues that an essential element of modern bureaucracies is that they are organized around written documents ("the files") and around fixed rules that define precisely what officials can and cannot do. American and Chinese bureaucracies may differ in certain ways because of general differences between the two countries. But insofar as both are examples of the ideal bureaucratic type, we can see that they will also be alike in crucial ways, including how they deal with the public.

Weber was very concerned with power and with the ways in which some people secure domination over others. He distinguished between unlegitimated domination and legitimated domination, which has *authority*, and involves claims that certain people have the *right* to be obeyed. He suggested that there are three main foundations for successful claims to authority—or three "ideal types."

Charismatic authority rests on a leader's personal qualities, so that "the governed submit because of their belief in the extraordinary quality of the specific *person*. . . . The legitimacy of charismatic rule thus rests upon the belief in magical powers, revelations, and hero worship."[4] Thus, Jesus' disciples followed him because of what he was, not because of some position that he held.

Traditional authority is also personal, but it is enjoyed because it has been handed down from the past. A king or a tribal chief may not personally be capable or effective, but he enjoys authority legitimated by custom. Weber argues that in general "patriarchalism is by far the most important type of domination the legitimacy of which rests upon tradition. Patriarchalism means the authority of the father, the husband, the senior of the house; . . . the rule of the master and patron of the lord over the domestic servants and household officials . . . of the patrimonial lord and sovereign prince."[5]

Finally, *rational-legal authority* is derived from formal rules. Thus modern bureaucrats are obeyed because and insofar as statutes empower them to do certain things and because our societies accept statutory laws as the ultimate source of authority. According to Weber, the anchoring of legitimacy in particular sorts of rules is central to modern society's ongoing "rationalization" of everything.

[4]*From Max Weber: Essay in Sociology,* edited and with an introduction by H. H. Gerth and C. Wright Mills (London: Routledge and Kegan Paul, 1970), pp. 295–96.
[5]*From Max Weber,* p. 296.

Weber did not disagree with Marx's view that economic interests often underlie people's behavior, even when not acknowledged. However, he believed Marx to be wrong in identifying economic characteristics as the *sole* crucial determinant of both social structure and people's chances in life. Someone's religion, education, or political faction may, he argued, be as important a source of power and success. Instead of relying on Marx's category of class, Weber distinguished among classes, status groups, and parties, all of which could be more or less important for people's lives and serve as foci of group organization and conflict.[6] By a *class* he meant people who shared the same position in economic life, whether this involved property, as in Marx's definition, or marketable skills. A *party* he defined as an association that exists to "secure power within a corporate group for its leaders in order to attain ideal or material advantages for its active members."[7] Examples include political parties seeking power in the modern state but also the factions that fought for control of Rome or the Italian city-states. Finally, *status groups*, as Weber's term *Stände* is generally translated, are groups whose distinctiveness lies not in their shared economic position but either in their shared mode of life—often founded on a common education—or in the prestige attached to their birth and family, as in the case of a hereditary aristocracy.[8]

Weber's argument has had great influence on modern analytic theorists who, like him, believe that economic factors are not always the major determinants of people's lives and power. His influence is also apparent in these theorists' discussion of the relationship between ideas and power. It is important to emphasize that, unlike Marx, Weber believed ideas and values to have an important, independent effect on history (as in the case of Calvinism and Confucianism) and did not consider them to be simply reflections of underlying interests. At the same time, he was aware of the role they could play in strengthening the position of a social group or a given social order. He emphasized, in particular, the importance of *legitimacy*, the belief that someone's position and the system incorporating it are right and proper. This concept recurs in much of modern conflict analysis and is also of central importance in the variety of evolutionary theories discussed in Chapter 4.

Power, Elites, and Classes

Although the major elements of conflict theory were set out by Marx and Weber, a number of other theorists developed comparable ideas that have also had a significant impact on modern analysts. The most important are

---

[6]Weber, *The Theory of Social and Economic Organization*, trans. A. M. Henderson and Talcott Parsons (New York: The Free Press, 1964), pp. 407–12, 424–29.

[7]Weber, *The Theory of Social and Economic Organization*, p. 407.

[8]Weber, *The Theory of Social and Economic Organization*, pp. 407–12 and 424–29. The medieval division of society into "estates" according to someone's degree of birth would correspond to Weber's idea of *Stände*.

the elite theorists (namely Pareto, Mosca, and Michels), and Thorstein Veblen.

Elite Theory. The most prominent elite theorists are Weber's contemporary, Vilfredo Pareto (1848–1923); Pareto's great rival, Gaetano Mosca (1858–1941); and Weber's friend, Robert Michels (1876–1936). Although in no sense did they form a school, they shared a number of important ideas.[9]

Their central argument was that only a small number of people in any organization can hold authority and that their occupation of these positions automatically places them at odds with those subjected to it. Moreover, these theorists contended, the elites who are in control generally share a common culture, and they are organized—not necessarily formally, but in the sense that they act together to defend their position, as well as using it to their own individual advantage. In other words, elite theory presents explicitly the argument that people's self-interest and the intrinsically unequal nature of power make conflict both inevitable and permanent.

Michels's main concern was with the so-called iron law of oligarchy, the proposition that small groups in authority come to run political parties essentially for their own ends. Mosca was primarily concerned with the conflict between holders of political power and those whom they dominate. Indeed, Mosca upended Marx, identifying political positions as the source of domination in all other spheres, including the economic. Pareto, on the other hand, recognized the existence of other nonpolitical elites; but he emphasized the governing elites who rule a society and the existence of ruling and subject classes who face each other like alien nations. The modern analytic theorists, especially Dahrendorf, have been most influenced by the elite theorists' insistence on authority and the state as dominant sources of power. Their general image of society as divided horizontally into an elite and a mass is also apparent in C. Wright Mills's social critique.

Thorstein Veblen (1857–1929). Veblen's major importance for modern conflict theory lies in the fact that he was one of the few early American sociologists to analyze the roots of power and conflict in a broad historical context. Early American sociologists were essentially empiricist and pragmatic in style, and only of America could it be said that here "sociology is practiced without socialism."[10] Instead they tended to be reformers, like the

---

[9]Vilfredo Pareto, *The Treatise on General Sociology* (New York: Dover, 1963); Robert Michels, *Political Parties: A Sociological Study of Oligarchical Tendencies of Modern Democracy*, trans. Eden and Cedar Paul (New York: The Free Press, 1949); Gaetano Mosca, *The Ruling Class* (New York: McGraw-Hill, 1960). In the case of Pareto, whose influence on Parsons we have noted, the theory of elites comprised only a small part of his work.

[10]A. Solomon, *The Tyranny of Progress* (New York: Noonday Press, 1955), p. 22. As so often, the United Kingdom stood midway between America and the rest of Europe: more openly ideological than America, less so than the European mainland.

highly influential Lester Ward, who approached social problems with a faith in government policies and gradualist reforms.[11] Veblen, by contrast, analyzed society in terms of the conflicting interests of different social groups, and he also denounced passionately much of the existing order. Among modern theorists, C. Wright Mills both continued this tradition and drew directly on Veblen in his discussion of status struggles.

Veblen, like Marx, believed that modern society is characterized by the conflict between opposing economic groups. In his case they are the *industrial class*, who actually make goods, and the *pecuniary class*, who are involved in finance and sales and whom he characterized as parasites living off the innovation and productiveness of the rest of the population.[12] Veblen was also interested in the constants of human nature that underlie social behavior. He argued that people desire passionately the esteem of others and that esteem is essentially a competitive affair because for everyone to enjoy high status is a contradiction in terms. A large part of people's behavior, Veblen argued, especially styles of consumption and leisure, can be explained by the struggle for high standing in the eyes of one's neighbors.

The Web of Conflict: Simmel and the Chicago School

In addition to the central tradition of conflict analysis, which we have just described, there exists a rather different approach to the study of conflict. It emphasizes the abstract qualities of a social order rather than the origins and progress of actual conflicts, and it is exemplified by the writings of Georg Simmel and the Chicago School.

Georg Simmel (1858–1918).   Among the great early sociologists Simmel was the most interested in identifying universal patterns in human behavior. Whereas Marx and Weber wanted to understand what made a particular society operate, Simmel concentrated on developing what is almost a mathematics of society: a collection of statements about human relationships and social behavior that apply irrespective of the historical setting. He has influenced a whole range of modern theorists who are similarly interested in interpersonal relationships, including some conflict theorists, symbolic interactionists, exchange theorists, and network analysts.[13]

Simmel's sensitivity to how human relationships form and change was related to his own background and his feelings of insecurity and rootlessness. He was born in Berlin, the youngest child of a Jewish businessman who had converted to Christianity. His father died when Simmel was still a child,

---

[11]"Radicals" of the period, such as E. A. Ross, often found it difficult to make a career on American campuses.

[12]Thorstein Veblen, *The Theory of the Leisure Class* (New York: Modern Library, 1934).

[13]See pp. 129, 192, and 297.

and the boy was never close to his mother. He studied history and philosophy at the University of Berlin and stayed on there as a Privatdozent, an unpaid lecturer dependent on student fees. His lectures were enormously popular, and he published widely. Among his friends were many of the foremost academics and writers of the time, including Weber. Yet although he applied constantly for senior positions in German universities, he was constantly turned down, partly because of anti-Semitism and partly because he refused, in his work, to stay within a single academic discipline. It was only in 1914, at the age of fifty-six, that he was appointed finally to a chair at the University of Strasbourg.

The most important part of Simmel's analysis for later conflict theory is his insistence that association and conflict between individuals and social groups not only can exist side by side but indeed are intimately related. One cannot divide people neatly into self-contained groups with common interests that are different from those of people in other, self-contained, antagonistic groups. Marx's image is of a society divided horizontally into antagonistic blocks; Simmel's is of a society integrated by numerous crosscutting conflicts, in which those who stand together in one respect are opposed in another.

Simmel's insistence that "social action always involves harmony *and* conflict, love *and* hatred"[14] did more than reinforce the tendency of analytic conflict theorists to consider conflict a permanent condition. It also alerted them to the way varying degrees of social contact and interdependence affect the nature of conflict. For example, Lewis Coser's discussion of how conflict can actually stabilize a society is based directly on Simmel's writing.

Robert Park and the Chicago School. An emphasis on conflict as a general and abstract principle of social life has been more typical of American than of European sociology. Robert Park (1864–1944), whose only formal training was in Simmel's courses in Berlin, built up the "Chicago School" of sociology, which is renowned for research into the social life and culture of the city.[15] He also developed a system of general concepts that described what were, for him, the central characteristics of social life: competition, conflict, accommodation, and assimilation into a common culture.[16] Park argued that competition, which is universal and continuous among individuals, determines individual careers. Conflict arises rather over status and over the way superordination—power—is allocated socially. Conflict

---

[14]Lewis A. Coser, *Masters of Sociological Thought: Ideas in Historical and Social Context* (New York: Harcourt Brace Jovanovich, 1971), pp. 184–85.

[15]This demonstrates an emphasis on understanding people's definitions of their own situation similar to the approach developed by symbolic interactionism, which is discussed in Chapter 5.

[16]Robert E. Park and Ernest W. Burgess, *Introduction to the Science of Sociology* (Chicago: The University of Chicago Press, 1921).

may thus involve groups as well as individuals. Park and his colleagues were more interested in analyzing racial antagonisms and conflict among different ethnic groups than the class struggles stressed by Marx and other Europeans, whose own societies were much more racially and culturally homogeneous. Once again, the influence of this rather different tradition is especially apparent in the work of Lewis Coser, one of the most important of American conflict theorists.

Summary

The most important historical influences on modern conflict theory are the writings of Karl Marx and Max Weber, and modern theorists can be divided into two groups according to who is the dominant influence upon them. A number of other sociologists who share the same general conflict perspective have also influenced modern theory; and American sociology, in particular, has been influenced by a different tradition of conflict analysis deriving from Simmel.

PART ONE

Conflict Theory and the Critique of Society

This section covers the conflict theory of Marx and modern Marxist sociologists, of the Frankfurt School analysts, of C. Wright Mills, and of Pierre Bourdieu. All the writers in this group are distinguished by their view of social science and their image of society as divided hierarchically into exclusive groups. Most also share a belief in the possibility of an ideal social order. In general, we refer to them as "critical" theorists because they all use social science to criticize society—in particular, the "ruling class," the "power elite," or what is often called the "establishment." However, "critical theory" also more narrowly refers to the work of the Frankfurt School.

Critical conflict theorists believe that social analysts should not separate their work from their moral commitments, and they see their theories as a force for change and progress. They also believe that objectivity is more or less impossible. For them social science is inextricably bound up with the particular views of a writer, which are in turn a function of his or her society. In other words, they reject the usual scientific view that whatever writers' own values or motives in writing may be, their theories stand or fall by whether independent factual evidence supports them. At the same time, critical conflict theorists feel sure that their own values and standards are the right ones and therefore constitute a justified basis for social critique.

The particular focus of their critique is the way wealth, status, and power are distributed in society. Theorists of this type generally see society as divided rather clearly between a small group of powerful and privileged people and an exploited or manipulated mass. They are also inclined to use a unicausal theory of social structure and to see people's circumstances as primarily determined by one set of institutions, most often property. At the same time, they do not believe that society need be highly segmented and unequal. They contrast the societies they analyze with a better order of things and often compare the "irrational" present, in which human development is stunted, with an ideal and "rational" state of affairs, in which human potential will be fulfilled. This vision of a society based on values that they presume to be absolutely valid, as well as their concept of "real" human nature, are the starting points for their criticisms of actual societies.

In all of this Marx is the dominant influence. The argument that ideas are a product of social circumstances *and for that reason not objectively correct* is his. Moreover, although he believed that his own theory was not open to the charge of being an *ideology*, Marx also regarded his work as a form of political and moral action—an expression of the ideas that would guide the proletariat to inevitable victory. Marxists use the term *praxis* to describe actions informed in this way by theoretical considerations and, more precisely, revolutionary consciousness. In addition, Marx presented a two-class model of society, divided between oppressors and oppressed on the basis of property, and looked forward to the communist utopia in which humanity would realize its essential nature.

For the most part conflict theory of this type has developed in Europe, particularly western Europe. In countries under one-party Communist rule, Marxism or Marxism-Leninism has been treated as essentially a state religion and not open to critical analysis and development. Philosophers, sociologists, and political theorists, such as Leszek Kolakowski, who engaged in such analysis, frequently have been forced into exile.[17] On the other hand, in western Europe intellectuals have continued to be greatly influenced by Marx. Although the organized Communist parties have themselves produced some important Marxist theorists, such as Antonio Gramsci in Italy, they too insist on doctrinal orthodoxy; and the major source of modern critical conflict theory is Marxist intellectuals outside the party hierarchies.

In America there was a strong Marxist and Communist element in intellectual life during the 1930s and 1940s. Nevertheless, although a number of sociologists and economists (such as Norman Birnbaum and Paul Sweezy) continued to use Marxist categories, Marxist analysis had little

---

[17]Kolakowski, one of the most eminent of modern European political philosophers, was expelled from the Communist Party in 1966 and dismissed from his chair of philosophy at Warsaw University in 1968. He was accused of corrupting youth by his reexamination of Marxist tenets. He is now a fellow of All Souls' College, Oxford.

direct impact on American sociology in the twenty years immediately after the Second World War. During this period, the only widely known and influential critical sociologist was C. Wright Mills, who was heavily influenced by Marx but not in any clear sense a Marxist. During the Vietnam period, however, many younger American sociologists were involved with the New Left and were heavily influenced by various radical writers, but quite specifically by Marx. Consequently, the critical sociology of the Frankfurt tradition and other Marxist and neo-Marxist writings became increasingly known and influential in American sociology. Marxian journals have been founded specifically devoted to this approach.[18]

MARXIST AND NEO-MARXIST SOCIOLOGY

This section discusses in some detail Marx's own analyses, as well as those of later Marxist scholars. As we have noted, Marxism remains an entirely contemporary theory because so many sociologists work *within* it, and we therefore present it as an integrated perspective. We describe Marx's theory of the economic basis of social organization, the classes and class conflict that arise around economic interests, and the importance of ideology in both maintaining and undermining a social order; and we look at how some modern theorists[19] incorporate political and cultural factors into Marxist class analysis.[20] In Chapter 4, which considers theories of modernity and evolution, Marx's ideas and prophecies are again considered in depth.

The Economic Basis of Society

The distinguishing mark of Marxist analysis is that it identifies economic factors as the fundamental determinant of social structure and change. Other spheres of social life and the ideas and values that people hold are seen as shaped by and dependent on the nature of economic production. In

---

[18]The cohort of sociologists most influenced by Marxist perspectives was in college in the middle to late 1960s. See Michael Burawoy and Theda Skocpol, ed., *Marxist Inquiries: Studies of Labor, Class and States*, Supplement to Vol. 88 of the *American Journal of Sociology*.

[19]A common distinction is between more or less orthodox "Marxists" and those "Marxian" scholars who depend largely on Marx's categories and perspectives but whose theories diverge substantially from his.

[20]The books that have most influenced our interpretation of Marx are Joseph Schumpeter, *Ten Great Economists: From Marx to Keynes* (London: George Allen and Unwin, 1952); John Plamenatz, *Man and Society* (London: Longmans, 1963); George Lichtheim, *Marxism* (London: Routledge and Kegan Paul, 1961); Robert C. Tucker, *Philosophy and Myth in Karl Marx* (Cambridge: Cambridge University Press, 1964); Shlomo Avineri, *The Social and Political Thought of Karl Marx* (Cambridge: Cambridge University Press, 1970); Leszek Kolakowski, *Main Currents of Marxism* (Oxford: Oxford University Press, 1981); and Anthony Giddens, *A Contemporary Critique of Historical Materialism*, Vol. I (London: Macmillan, 1981) and Vol. II (Cambridge: Polity, 1985).

Schumpeter's analogy they play the role of "transmission belts," through which the social forces and group interests created by economic arrangements emerge into social life.[21]

Marx distinguished between three aspects of social organization. They are, first, the "material forces of production," or the actual methods by which people produce their livings; second, the "relations of production" that arise out of them and that include property relations and rights; and third, the "legal and political" superstructures and the ideas, or "forms of social consciousness," that correspond to the first two. He argued that in production "men enter into definite . . . relations of production [which] correspond to a definite stage of development of their material productive forces. The sum total of these relations of production constitutes the economic structure of society, the real foundation . . . . The mode of production of material life conditions the social, political, and intellectual life-process in general."[22]

In other words, in Marx's view, the actual mode of production is the basic causal factor that ultimately determines how societies are organized. In this sense his is a "materialist" theory of history, whereby "in changing their mode of production . . . [men] change all their social relations. The hand-mill gives you society with the feudal lord; the steam-mill society with the industrial capitalist."[23] At the same time, however, both the mode and the relations of production—the technology *and* the form of economic organization—are the *substructure* that defines both the nature of a particular society and its *superstructure* of law, government, and ideas.

In practice both Marx and later Marxist writers tend to pay more attention to the effects of economic organization than those of the mode of production alone. Indeed, this is a far more plausible approach. There was little difference in technology between, for example, the Roman Empire and medieval Europe, yet their social structures were very different. These differences were, moreover, often clearly related to differences in economic organization, such as Rome's use of numerous slaves and feudalism's system of serfdom.[24]

However, if one admits that economic organization rather than technology is the primary determinant of social structure, one also undermines, to a considerable degree, Marx's claim that a single principle unlocks the workings of society. If different forms of economic organization can coexist with a given technology, then these forms must result, at least partly, from other, noneconomic factors—the ideas and legal principles that Marxism rel-

[21]Schumpeter, *Ten Great Economists*, p. 12.

[22]Karl Marx, Preface to *A Contribution to the Critique of Political Economy*, in *Karl Marx and Frederick Engels, Selected Works*, Vol. I (London: Lawrence and Wishart, 1962), p. 362.

[23]Marx, *The Poverty of Philosophy* (Moscow: Foreign Language Publishing House, n.d.), p. 122.

[24]See Marc Bloch, *Feudal Society*, trans. L. A. Manyon (Chicago: University of Chicago Press, 1962), for a discussion of the major differences between serfdom and slavery.

egates to the superstructure, for example, or the principles of military organization, which Marxists generally ignore. Thus many historians would argue that the different forms of economic organization in Rome and feudal Europe (and the wide-ranging differences in their social structure) can themselves only be understood in terms of their different legal codes and systems and their different military organization. A society with a centralized standing army is obviously different from one in which fighting is the task of feudal lords who owe service to the king but who are paid with grants of land—of which they are virtually independent rulers. And in that case, Marx's economic theory of history becomes, as its critics would argue, an insight of genius into the role of economic factors but not an all-embracing explanation.

Class and the Economic Base of Conflict

Marx argued that all forms of economic organization that had existed at the time he wrote inevitably generated conflict between social classes, which were defined by their common economic position. *The Communist Manifesto* opens with a now-famous declaration: "The history of all hitherto existing society is the history of class struggles."[25] This statement embodies three important but separate propositions. The first is that people whose economic position, or class, is the same also tend to act together as a group. The second is that economic classes are the most important groups to be found in society; their history is the history of human society. The third is that these classes are mutually antagonistic, and the outcome of their conflicts defines how society develops. Marx's theory of class is thus not simply a theory of social structure; it is also a theory of change.

Property and Class.   Although we have been describing the Marxist concept of class as economic, Marx actually used a more specific and restrictive definition. A class is made up of people who are alike in their relationship to property: they have none, or they have the same type.[26] Ultimately, the sort of work people do is not what matters. Thus manual workers, clerks, technicians, and engineers belong to the same class because they own and are paid for their labor. They belong to a different class from capitalists and landlords, who own the instruments of production; from serfs, who only partly own their own labor because they are bound to a given lord and cannot go to work for someone else; and from slaves, who own no property at all.

[25]Karl Marx and Friedrich Engels, *The Communist Manifesto* (Harmondsworth, Middlesex: Penguin Books, 1967), p. 79.

[26]Marx distinguishes between a class "in itself" and a self-conscious (or "class-conscious") class "for itself." See p. 85. For discussions of what creates class consciousness or group mobilization see also Dahrendorf's work (pp. 123–25) and the work of rational choice theorists (pp. 336–37 and 341–44).

If you look around a university campus, you will find the only factor of production most people own is their labor. In Marxist terms they therefore belong to the same class: the proletariat. This will certainly be true of most of the students and also of a good number of the faculty, who work for a salary and who, although they probably own their homes, do not own any "means of production." On the other hand, some faculty and some students probably own a fair number of shares of stock; some mature students may also be running businesses; and, especially if the campus is M.I.T., some of the faculty are likely to be founders and owners of high-technology industries, which are offshoots of their work. Because they own property of this type, all the people in the second group belong to another, different class: capitalists. Marx, we should note, does not differentiate between shareholders, who simply provide capital, and entrepreneurs.[27]

Marxist theory argues that different classes inevitably have incompatible interests because under systems of property ownership if one class makes economic gains, it must be at the expense of another. According to Marx, each of the major economic systems that existed in the past strengthened one particular class, which could then exploit others. He wrote that "Freeman and slave, patrician and plebeian, lord and serf, guild-master and journeyman, in a word, oppressor and oppressed, stood in constant opposition to one another, carried on an uninterrupted, now hidden, now open fight,"[28] and that "An oppressed class is the vital condition for every society founded on the antagonism of classes."[29] In bourgeois society capitalists are the oppressors and the proletariat the oppressed.

In explaining what Marx meant by this we must reiterate that Marx's general theory is the work of an analytical economist. His theory of exploitation is based on an economic theory of value,[30] and it is important to note that in its essentials, his was the value theory of the "classical" economist Ricardo. Nowadays this labor theory of value is seen as a distinguishing aspect of Marxism because only Marxist economists continue to hold it. However, in Marx's own time it was standard theory.

Marx states that the *value* of a commodity is equal to the quantity of labor that went directly into making it. In a market economy, workers selling their labor will get for it the price of the labor that went into making them—that is, the cost of rearing, feeding, educating, clothing, and housing them.

---

[27]Marx tends to assume that people will belong clearly to one class or another. If this is not the case, then it is also a great deal less likely that a well-defined class conflict will develop.

[28]Marx and Engels, *The Communist Manifesto*, p. 79.

[29]Marx, *The Poverty of Philosophy*, p. 196.

[30]For good critical discussions of Marxist economics, see Joseph Schumpeter, *History of Economic Analysis* (London: George Allen and Unwin, 1954), and Paul Samuelson, *Collected Scientific Papers*, ed. J. Stiglitz (Cambridge, Mass.: M.I.T. Press, 1966 and 1972). A good modern Marxist economic analysis is Paul M. Sweezy, *The Theory of Capitalist Development* (New York: Modern Reader Paperbacks, 1968).

However, what each of them produces at work will likely amount to considerably more than this, and this "surplus value" will go not to them but to the capitalist. In Marx's theory any surplus value appropriated by someone other than the worker is by definition *exploitation* because only labor produces value. All systems of property therefore involve a basic conflict of interest because one group expropriates the product of another's labor.[31]

Modern Marxist and Marxian sociologists retain Marx's emphasis on property relationships. Norman Birnbaum, for example, uses Marxist categories to analyze the United States. He attacks the argument that property ownership is no longer a crucial determinant of power and opportunity and that a meritocratic education system decides people's success. Birnbaum argues that educational success and "access to some of the more privileged educational institutions" are a function of family background. The technocratic elite is thus far from being a new group with interests and objectives quite separate from those of capitalists.[32] Rather, Birnbaum contends, it operates modern organizations in the interests of property and is backed by government, with which it has a symbiotic relationship.

Marxist feminists retain this emphasis while extending the definition of property. They argue that "Marxism is an analysis of exploitation in capitalism, where exploitation is defined as the appropriation of surplus value from its producers, including people (mainly women) who engage in unwaged domestic labor. This exploitation is possible where individual producers (and reproducers) do not control the means of production. Thus workers are exploited to the extent that they produce value (in the form of commodities) for which they are not paid. . . . (W)omen's unpaid household labor, in reproducing labor power, produces surplus value, just as surplus value is produced by so-called productive labor. . . . (C)apital exploits women's labor, both waged and unwaged, just as it does men's."[33]

---

[31]Marx's analysis is rejected by modern neoclassical economics, which explicitly separates judgments of how prices ought to be determined from descriptions of how they actually are, and so avoids discussions of what the real or just price of, say, a diamond may be. Modern economics argues that price is related to the "marginal cost" of producing goods, not to the sum of the cost of labor and surplus value. It also argues that providing capital for production involves genuine costs for which people must be recompensed. For example, if you put money in the stock market or a bank savings account, thus enabling companies to borrow, invest, and expand, you thereby deny yourself the enjoyment of the things you could have bought. Your recompense for this cost is the interest or dividends you receive. Modern neoclassical economists argue that people are paid for saving because providing capital (and so forgoing consumption) involves genuine costs.

[32]Norman Birnbaum, *The Crisis of Industrial Society* (New York: Oxford University Press, 1969), p. 13. See also the work of Harry Braverman, such as *Labor and Monopoly Capital: The Degradation of Work in the Twentieth Century* (New York: Monthly Review Press, 1974), and Michael Burawoy, *Manufacturing Consent: Changes in the Labor Process Under Monopoly Capitalism* (Chicago: University of Chicago Press, 1979).

[33]Beth Anne Shelton and Ben Agger, "Shotgun Wedding, Unhappy Marriage, No-Fault Divorce? Rethinking the Feminism-Marxism Relationship" in Paula England, ed., *Theory on Gender: Feminism on Theory* (New York: Aldine de Gruyter, 1993), pp. 25–26.

Class Conflict. Marx argued that at any one time class struggle defines the essential character of a society. It is the product of, first, the irreconcilable differences in interest between classes and, second, the fact that a class's common interests will encourage its members to group together for common action. However, at any given time, the degree to which members of a class recognize their interests will depend on their level of *class consciousness.* The dominant ideas of any era may stand in the way of their recognizing their class identity, but so too may the circumstances of their lives. The French peasants of the nineteenth century, for example, did not "form a class" in the active sense, according to Marx, because "there is merely a local interconnection among these small-holding peasants, and the identity of their interests begets no community, no national bond, and no political organization among them."[34] It is the task of the Marxist to encourage people—specifically the members of the exploited proletariat—to recognize and act upon their interests and to encourage and accelerate change and revolution, as well as understand its roots. Thus a prominent American Marxist sociologist has argued that "class interests in capitalist society are . . . potential objectives." They are "hypotheses about the objectives of struggles which would occur *if the actors in the struggle had a scientifically correct understanding of their situations.*"[35]

What Marx provides here is a powerful theory of how groups form in society. However, critics have queried the degree to which members of a property class always have common interests or tend to act in unison. For example, innovations are favored by those who introduce them but feared by all those involved with established firms, whether as owners, employees, or union officials. Government policy often benefits one part of an industry at another's expense, for example, by limiting imports of cheap foreign coal or oil and so increasing energy costs. In America, Northern businessmen wishing to relocate to small Southern towns are often opposed by local employers, who fear the impact of higher wages and benefits, and welcomed by prospective workers for the same reasons.

Class and Patriarchy. Marxist theory has always seen women as oppressed by capitalist society and the "bourgeois family." Marx and Engels argue that "the bourgeois sees in his wife a mere instrument of production."[36] In *The Origin of the Family* Engels argues that with the move from a

---

[34]Karl Marx, "The Eighteenth Brumaire of Louis Bonaparte," in *Karl Marx and Frederick Engels, Selected Works*, Vol. I (London: Lawrence and Wishart, 1962), p. 334.

[35]Erik Olin Wright, *Class, Crisis, and the State* (London: New Left Books, 1978), p. 89. Italics ours. Marxists differ in how far they emphasize individual action and purpose. The "structuralist" Louis Althusser argues that "if we take seriously what Marx tells us about the real dialectic of history, it is not 'men' who make history . . . but the masses in the relations of class struggle." Louis Althusser, *Politics and History* (London: New Left Books, 1977), p. 168.

[36]Marx and Engels, *The Communist Manifesto*, pp. 77–78.

subsistence economy to one "with inherited property," the man took control in the home, and the woman was degraded and reduced to servitude.[37] Wives are, he argues, worse off than ordinary prostitutes, for they sell their bodies once and for all into slavery.

Although Marx and Engels took it for granted that there had always been a division of labor between men and women, they treat the family as strictly part of the superstructure, determined by the relations of production. The bourgeois family is a product of property; therefore, it will vanish with the vanishing of capital, and with it will vanish women's oppression. Women will be brought back into "public industry," and love will be the basis of relations between the sexes.

Marxist feminists are divided in their response to this analysis. Some feel that orthodox Marxist analysis is essentially correct, although it may need some elaboration. Shelton and Agger, for example, argue that household work needs to be incorporated into the analysis, but that one should "conceptualize (the) double oppression of women (once in the household, a second time in the paid labor force) as a function of capitalism" alone.[38] Others disagree, arguing that explanations must take account of *patriarchy* as something separate from and additional to capitalism. Women's oppression is not, they argue, simply equivalent to the oppression of the proletariat by the bourgeoisie because "domestic slaves are not exploited in the same way as wage slaves. They would have to be paid a wage for this to be true."[39] Instead women's position has to be understood in terms of male supremacy *as well*.[40]

Zillah Eisenstein defines *patriarchy* as the "male hierarchical ordering of society" and argues that it is rooted in biology rather than economics or history.[41] Patriarchal culture exerts control through the "sexual division of labor. . . . It designates the fact that roles, purposes, activity, one's labor, are determined separately."[42] As such it predates—and outlives—capitalism, but the two are nonetheless mutually reinforcing. Thus "patriarchy . . . provides the sexual hierarchical ordering of society for political control . . . while capitalism as an economic class system . . . feeds off the patriarchal ordering."[43]

---

[37]Frederick Engels, *The Origin of the Family, Private Property and the State*, trans. Alick West (New York: Penguin Books, 1972), p. 87. This was written by Engels using notes left by Marx before his death.

[38]Shelton and Agger, "Shotgun Wedding," p. 32.

[39]Zillah Eisenstein, "Developing a Theory of Capitalist Patriarchy and Socialist Feminism," in Zillah Eisenstein, ed., *Capitalist Patriarchy and the Case for Socialist Feminism* (New York: Monthly Review Press, 1979), p. 23. See also Lise Vogel, *Marxism and the Oppression of Women: Toward a Unitary Theory* (New Brunswick, N.J.: Rutgers University Press, 1983).

[40]For a similar critical analysis see the work of Dorothy Smith in Chapter 6.

[41]Eisenstein, *Capitalist Patriarchy*, p. 17.

[42]Eisenstein, *Capitalist Patriarchy*, p. 17.

[43]Eisenstein, *Capitalist Patriarchy*, p. 28.

Marxist feminists of this persuasion argue that "The sexual division of labor and society remains intact even with women in the paid economy."[44] Capitalism has intensified the sexual division of labor by separating the home from the place of work. It creates two distinctive kinds of work, wage labor and domestic labor: "The housewife emerged, alongside the proletariat—the two characteristic laborers of developed capitalist society."[45] Hence abolishing capitalism and the bourgeois ruling class is not, in itself, an adequate solution to women's oppression. At the same time, insofar as the traditional family profits the bourgeoisie as a class, socialism is a necessary precondition to realizing women's potential.

Culture, Ideology, and Alienation

Marx emphasized that feelings and opinions about people in power are important—especially whether their position is viewed as right or whether people feel exploited and oppressed. He thus identified one of the main topics of conflict theory.[46] Marx's own discussion of the role of ideas in establishing control follows from his argument that the legal, political, and cultural superstructure ultimately reflects underlying economic relationships. He argued that people in a class society believe many things that are not correct but are rather a form of *ideology* whose main purpose is to legitimize the position of those currently in control.[47] Such ideology stands in the way of other people realizing what their real interests are, so that, Marxists argue, they suffer from *false consciousness*. To Marx, religion was an excellent example of this process, an "opium of the masses" that muted discontent by focusing attention on a supposedly better world to come.

It is this part of Marx's thought that inspired his and his followers' criticisms of "objective" social reporting and analysis as imbued with the authors' prejudices. However, Marx did not—unlike later theorists such as the symbolic interactionists—reject the possibility of quantitative research as such because he was sure that his own viewpoint was scientifically correct.

---

[44]Eisenstein, *Capitalist Patriarchy*, p. 29.

[45]Eli Zaretsky, "Capitalism, The Family and Personal Life," *Socialist Revolution* 14 (1973): 114. Cited by Eisenstein in *Capitalist Patriarchy*.

[46]As his description of the French peasantry shows, Marx did not believe that only ideology affected people's class consciousness. His remarks here anticipate many of the factors discussed by analytic conflict theorists interested in the way change actually occurs. See pp. 122–25 and 146–47.

[47]The term "ideology" is used in a variety of ways. In Marx's writing it derives from a distinction between what is true and what people may believe through false consciousness; thus ideology involves false ideas. Other writers (including Lenin and Althusser as well as non-Marxists) use the term more generally to represent a specific type of belief system, which is not necessarily true or false, but is associated with a particular historical or social situation. See especially Raymond Boudon, *The Analysis of Ideology*, trans. Malcolm Slater (Cambridge: Polity, 1989).

Thus, in order to obtain adequate information on working-class conditions, he drew up a long questionnaire that was distributed through workers' societies and groups in France. Questions ranged from "Is your work done by hand or with the aid of machinery?" to "Do you know any instances in which the government has intervened to protect the workers against the exaction of the employers and their illegal combinations?"[48]

This questionnaire, devised at the very end of Marx's working life, is concerned entirely with the outward conditions of work. However, Marx also believed that class society was evil because, besides fostering exploitation and false consciousness, the whole nature of its economic life created *alienation*. Marx felt that humanity has an essential nature, which he believed to be realized through creative work. (This notion is, we may note, quite different from Durkheim's, who felt that people needed limits and fixed norms. Durkheim was also concerned at the consequences of modern industrial society for human development; but his concept of *anomie*, or normlessness, appeals greatly to functionalists.[49]) For Marx, the division of labor, the institution of private property, and the whole *cash nexus* of commercial relations alienate people not only from what they produce and the act of producing it, but also from both themselves and their fellows. They view each other in terms of the narrow standards of the workplace rather than as full "species-beings."[50] Consequently the abolition of property and its attendant class relationships would also end this alienation.

This part of Marx's thought has been given increasing attention in recent decades, and its influence is apparent far beyond strictly Marxist writings. Criticisms of the soullessness of modern work, or the actions of people opting for a self-supporting and/or communal life, all belong to the same broad strand of thought as Marx's early writing on alienation. It should be emphasized, however, that Marx did not share the romantic view that the country was inherently superior to the town, and the Industrial Revolution a catastrophe. On the contrary—capitalism and the wealth it produced were the necessary preconditions for the communist utopia.

Although Marx regarded culture and ideology as simply a reflection of the underlying economic substructure, contemporary sociologists generally see the superstructure as important in its own right. Many neo-Marxists, especially in Europe, believe that cultural factors play an independent role in maintaining class inequalities—and potentially in creating revolutionary

---

[48]Results were never published. Apparently few workers were able or willing to work through its 101 items. The questionnaire (the Enquête Ouvrière) is reprinted in *Karl Marx: Selected Writings in Sociology and Social Philosophy*, ed. T. B. Bottomore and Maximilien Rubel (Harmondsworth: Penguin Books, 1961), pp. 210–18.

[49]See Chapter 2.

[50]By "man" Marx, in all his work, means the human species in the collective sense. World history is about the self-realization of generic man, of which the individual is a microcosm. See Tucker, *Philosophy and Myth*, pp. 129–30.

change.[51] In a later section of this chapter we also look in detail at the work of Pierre Bourdieu, whose work on *cultural capital* and the reproduction of class inequalities also draws heavily on Marx's ideas.

Capitalism in America.   American Marxists have been particularly concerned to defend the relevance of core Marxist concepts because they live in a country where class-based parties have been less evident than in any other Western industrialized country, and whose self-image is that of a classless society. Erik Olin Wright's work is of special interest. Wright is currently C. Wright Mills Professor of Sociology at the University of Wisconsin, Madison, and over a period of twenty years has used extensive empirical analysis of both American and other societies to argue for the continuing relevance of Marxist theory, especially the Marxist concept of class.

For Wright, as for Marx, class is defined in relation to property: in other words, whether or not one has property, and what type, is central to one's situation in life, and the sorts of classes that exist are crucial to the nature of a society. He reaffirms the importance of exploitation in explaining why class is so important; and he argues that exploitation exists when

> The material well-being of one group of people depends on the deprivations of another group.
> This comes about because the deprived (the "exploited") are barred from access to certain productive resources.
> There is "appropriation of the fruits of labor of the exploited by those who control the relevant productive resources."[52]

In his *Class Structure and Income Determination* Wright set out to demonstrate that such exploitation continued to occur and, specifically, to use Marxist categories to "explain" (that is, predict) income. By defining classes in terms of their members' control over money and physical capital and over others' labor, he arrived at the classic Marxist distinction between the bourgeoisie, who control capital and direct labor, and the proletariat, who do neither. This, he argued, was a more fruitful way to explain income distribution than the use of such common occupational categories as upper white collar, lower white collar, lower blue collar, farmers, or service workers.[53]

---

[51]See especially the work of Gramsci. American left-wingers of the 1960s also saw students as a revolutionary vanguard. See Samuel Bowles and Herbert Gintis, *Schooling in Capitalist America: Educational Reform and the Contradictions of Economic Life* (New York: Basic Books, 1976).

[52]Erik Olin Wright, "The Continuing Relevance of Class Analysis—Comments," *Theory and Society* 25 (1996): 695–715.

[53]Erik Olin Wright, *Class Structure and Income Determination* (New York: Academic Press, 1979). Data were collected by the Institute for Social Research at the University of Michigan. Wright drew most heavily on the *Panel Study of Income Dynamics* (nearly 6,000 households), the 1969 *Survey of Working Conditions* (1,500 adults), and the 1973 *Quality of Employment Survey* (basically a replication of the *Survey of Working Conditions*).

However, when Wright applies these categories to the modern workforce, only about 1 to 2 percent of workers can be classified as bourgeoisie, and almost half are seen as falling into "contradictory" class locations—that is, not quite one thing or another. The latter are

1. Managers and supervisors (30–35 percent of the workforce)
2. Semiautonomous employees
3. Small employers (with "minimal" control over labor)

With so few cases, by his definition, in existence, the survey data did not actually provide Wright with enough examples of the bourgeoisie for analysis: they were simply omitted.[54] In practice, therefore, he looked at five classes—small employers, managers, supervisors, workers, and petty bourgeoisie (self-employed with no employees). On that basis he found that class *did* affect income:

> People occupying different class positions but with the same level of education and occupational status, the same age and seniority on the job, the same general social background, and working the same number of hours per year, will still differ substantially in their expected incomes. And people in different class positions can expect to receive different amounts of additional income per increment in education credentials, even if they do not differ in a variety of other characteristics.[55]

Figure 3-1 summarizes, for Wright, what these findings imply about the workings of American society.[56]

However, class position actually accounts for only 20 percent of the variation in people's incomes—no worse, but also no better, than the standard (though more complicated) census-based occupational codes. Moreover, as just pointed out, Wright simply *assumes* that the bourgeoisie is important. It does not appear in his data at all.

As Wright has developed his analyses, he has systematized the way in which he conceptualizes classes, taking account of where people stand in terms of the "authority structure of production" as well as property ownership, and also the extent to which they command scarce skills. As a result, in his latest work, he proposes a class structure for modern capitalist societies that includes twelve classes.[57] To his critics, this complexity merely demon-

---

[54]The bourgeoisie control labor as well as investments and the physical means of production; the petty bourgeoisie control only the latter.

[55]Wright, *Class Structure*, p. 162.

[56]The drawing was contributed to *Class Structure* by Luca Perrone.

[57]Erik Olin Wright, *Class Counts: Comparative Studies in Class Analysis* (Cambridge: Cambridge University Press and Maison des Sciences de l'Homme, 1997). See especially pp. 37–57 and Table 2.2, which operationalizes the class structure as involving capitalists, small employers, petty bourgeoisie, expert managers, expert supervisors, expert nonmanagers, skilled managers, skilled supervisors, skilled workers, nonskilled managers, nonskilled supervisors, and nonskilled workers.

FIGURE 3-1   Erik Olin Wright's Analysis of American
Class Structure

strates that class is not, any longer, a helpful concept from which to start analyzing society—that his is "an effort, however genuine, to manufacture class
where it no longer exists as a meaningful social entity."[58] Wright, they would
argue, merely shows what we already know—that your position in the labor
market affects your income.[59] He, conversely, believes that class remains a
critically important concept for understanding how capitalist societies are
shaped by differences in the ownership of property and "differential market
capacity, especially labor-market capacity."[60]

Wright's work is built around the testing of hypotheses derived from
Marxist theory. Thus he notes that Marxist theory would lead one to
predict a "change over time in class distributions . . . toward an expansion
of the working class."[61] He also, for many years, argued in support of the

[58]Jan Pakulski and Malcolm Waters, "The Reshaping and Dissolution of Social Class in
Advanced Societies," *Theory and Society* 25 (1996): 667–91.

[59]An analysis that emphasizes the importance of education in maintaining and legitimating capitalist society is offered in Bowles and Gintis, *Schooling in Capitalist America.*

[60]Wright, "Continuing Relevance," p. 700.

[61]Wright, *Class Counts,* p. 529.

proposition that capitalism would tend to "deskill" jobs—that is, reduce them to routine, which makes it easier to supervise and control workers. "Thus, capitalists look for innovations which tend to reduce skill levels and reduce the autonomy of workers on the job."[62] The combination of over-educated workers and deskilled jobs has been seen by some Marxists as a potentially potent route to class consciousness because it would make workers who traditionally have seen themselves as middle-class realize that their interests lie with the organization of the whole working class. In an article written with Singelmann, Wright predicted that "the rest of the century is likely to be characterized by a continuing and perhaps intensi-fying process of proletarianization."[63]

This prediction differs from that put forward by many economists and politicians, who believe that jobs in developed countries will have to become increasingly highly skilled, especially as competition from lower-wage developing countries increases, and that the occupational structure will increasingly reflect these pressures. Now Wright's own, detailed empirical analyses have led him to modify his position. He reports that—in line with the traditional Marxist view—the "working class remains the single largest location within the class structure" in all the capitalist societies he has exam-ined; indeed, "in terms of relationship to the process of production and exploitation, the majority of the labor force is either in the working class or in those contradictory class locations most closely linked to the working class." However, he also reports strong evidence that "at least in the United States, the working class is declining as a proportion of the labor force and, what is more, this decline is occurring at an accelerating rate. . . . Experts and expert managers, on the other hand, have generally been expanding as a proportion of the labor force."[64]

Wright's recent work also extends the Marxist perspective on one of the themes running through this text: the position of women and, more specifi-cally, their income in the labor market. Feminists have often criticized Marxist theory for not recognizing that gender (as well as race) can be an independent source of stratification and inequality, separate from class. Wright accepts this but also argues that a Marxist perspective would suggest that these different factors will tend to reinforce each other. Marxists will generally expect that *"Nonclass oppression translates into class oppression . . . so*

---

[62]Erik Olin Wright, *Class, Crisis and the State* (London: New Left Books, 1979), p. 65.

[63]Erik Olin Wright and Joachim Singelmann, "Proletarianization in the Changing American Class Structure," in Burawoy and Skocpol, eds., *Marxist Inquiries*, p. 202. Wright also argues that people's class origins are crucial in creating class consciousness and awareness of class interests. Erik Olin Wright and Kwang-Yeon Shin, "Temporality and Class Analysis: A Comparative Study of the Effects of Class Trajectory and Class Structure on Class Consciousness in Sweden and the United States," *Sociological Theory* 6, no. 1 (1988): 58–84; Erik Olin Wright, *Classes* (London: Verso, 1985).

[64]Wright, *Class Counts*, pp. 528–30.

that women and racially oppressed groups should be overrepresented in the working class" and also that *"Class oppression translates into nonclass oppression . . .* at any given level of capitalist development, *the more oppressive and exploitative are class relations within capitalism, the more oppressive these other forms of oppression will tend to be as well."*[65]

Wright concludes that empirical evidence supports the argument that gender inequality translates into class inequality because women in the labor force "are universally much more proletarianized"—a far larger proportion have jobs classified as working class, and a far smaller proportion have managerial jobs. However, there are also some surprises. Wright is especially interested in the idea of the glass ceiling—the idea that, even when women make it into professional and managerial jobs, there is still a limitation placed on their chances of getting right to the top. What Wright finds in his data is that there is indeed a "significant gender inequality in authority," and far fewer women are in high-authority jobs than one might expect from their prior education. However, American women who *are* in the top echelon do not seem to be suffering any additional disadvantage because they are women. In other Western countries, however, such as Sweden, Canada, Australia, or the United Kingdom, they do.[66] More generally, Wright concludes, the results conflict with the idea that gender inequalities will be greatest where class inequalities are also at their highest.[67]

Class, Society, and the State

Marx's belief in classless society rested on his argument that property is the essential determinant of class interest. This implies that if everyone has exactly the same relationship to property, there can be no class divisions. If no one owns land or capital and there are no rents and profits or returns to capital to be paid, labor will get all of its "surplus value," and exploitation will end. In other words, abolishing property will end social conflict. Orthodox Communists share this view, and other Marxists and socialists believe that the abolition of private property will remove many of the systematic conflicts they perceive in social life. Non-Marxists, of course, disagree, as do many Marxian analysts who share Marx's belief in the primary importance of economic factors. They question whether the abolition of property necessarily abolishes systematic differences of interest among social groups. Their reason for questioning this is the existence of the state and state power.[68]

[65] Wright, *Class Counts*, pp. 542–43. Italics original.

[66] Wright, *Class Counts*, chap. 12; and see especially p. 348.

[67] Wright, *Class Counts*, p. 544.

[68] The autonomous role of the state is also the main factor cited by theorists such as Skocpol and Giddens in their critiques of Marxist evolutionary and world-system theory. See Chapter 4.

State Power.   Marx described the state as an instrument of class rule, and he saw political domination as a reflection and expression of conflict between classes. He therefore argued that, with the establishment of a class-less society, the state too would be abolished, and instead of a coercive structure there would remain only routine and uncontroversial administrative tasks.[69] It is not at all obvious, however, that this is likely, as we can see from Marx's own description of the state apparatus.

When Marx discussed the role of the state, with its legal authority, bureaucracies, law enforcement agents, and armed forces, he actually advanced two propositions—although he nowhere recognized them as different. The first was that the state made class exploitation possible by providing stability under which one group was able to remain dominant.[70] The other was that the state was actually an instrument of class rule (in the sense of being an arm of the exploiting class), and its purpose was to advance the exploiting class's interests.[71] These views imply very different interpretations of the role of government officials. The first, unlike the second, implies that officials may be seen as a separate group with independent interests and not merely as part of the ruling class. In that case it is a good deal less plausible to suppose that a coercive state apparatus, the distinction between state and society, and the potential for conflict over state control will disappear.

Marx envisaged communist society as one in which scarcity had vanished—as a result of the achievements of bourgeois capitalism, which in this respect he greatly admired. He also talked as though the abolition of property would also cause all important differences between people to disappear. Consequently, there would be a single social will; economic production would proceed on the basis of universal consent; and a separate, coercive state apparatus would no longer be required. His critics argue that a society without scarcity is nowhere apparent and that even if it were obtainable there is no reason to suppose that people would always agree, for example, on where factories should be sited or whether and for how long school should be compulsory. Moreover, if scarcity did remain and production was no longer the responsibility of private individuals, state power would be far more, not less, important. There would be fierce conflicts over who controlled the powers of the state.[72]

---

[69]This stage would be preceded, however, by a period of great state activity, the "dictatorship of the proletariat," in which communism would be implemented.

[70]A good example is Marx's account of "The Civil War in France," in Marx and Engels, *Selected Works*, Vol. I (see especially pp. 516–18).

[71]See, for example, Marx and Engels, *The Communist Manifesto*.

[72]A society without private property could be organized around workers' control of businesses instead of central government planning. However, there would then be conflicts of interest between successful enterprises, who wished to retain their earnings and expand, and unsuccessful ones, who would favor restraint on competition and income redistribution.

An essentially Marxist analysis of the self-interested use of power in socialist societies is offered by Milovan Djilas in *The New Class*.[73] Djilas, who was a friend of Tito's and vice president of Yugoslavia, was expelled from the Yugoslav Communist Party in 1954 and served long prison sentences for his views. In *The New Class* Djilas argues (following Marx) that classes are essentially based on the property they control. Abolishing private property, however, does not result in the abolition of classes. Instead, he contends, in communist countries it created a new class, the political bureaucracy, which controlled all property (because all property was the state's) and used it to appropriate to itself power and privilege at the expense of the rest of the population:

> As in other owning classes, the proof that [the political bureaucracy] is a special class lies in its ownership and its special relations to other classes. In the same way, the class to which a member belongs is indicated by the material and other privileges which ownership brings to him.
>
> As defined by Roman law, property constitutes the use, enjoyment, and disposition of material goods. The Communist political bureaucracy uses, enjoys, and disposes of nationalized property. . . . In practice, the ownership privilege of the new class manifests itself as an exclusive right, as a party monopoly, for the political bureaucracy to distribute the national income, to set wages, direct economic development, and dispose of nationalized and other property. This is the way it appears to the ordinary man who considers the Communist functionary as being very rich and as a man who does not have to work.[74]

A Marxian analysis that develops Djilas's assessment further is that of Iván Szelényi, a Hungarian sociologist who was forced to emigrate when he would not renounce his views. He argues that with the development of state-socialist economies in the post-Stalin era, a new dominating class developed.[75] This was rather broader than the political bureaucracy described by Djilas. It was the intelligentsia as a whole that grasped class power.

In the early years of Communist rule many senior party functionaries came from working-class backgrounds and owed their position entirely to their party membership. By the 1970s, however, people moved constantly between important bureaucratic and intellectual positions. Thus

---

[73]Milovan Djilas, *The New Class: An Analysis of the Communist System* (New York: Frederich A. Praeger, 1957).

[74]Djilas, *The New Class*, pp. 44–45.

[75]Iván Szelényi, "The Intelligentsia in the Class Structure of State-Socialist Societies," in Burawoy and Skocpol, *Marxist Inquiries*, pp. 287–326. See also George Konrad and Iván Szelényi, *The Intellectuals on the Road to Class Power* (New York: Harcourt Brace Jovanovich, 1979), which the authors wrote in secret, burying the manuscript in the garden of a peasant cottage to forestall police raids.

The present director of one of the comedy theaters in Budapest is a former high-ranking officer of the political police. His former boss in the Hungarian equivalent of the KGB is today the manager of a big salami factory. Today one may be an officer in the political police, but tomorrow one might be the only person licensed to produce political jokes, or one might supervise salami production or sociological research, as a manager or an academic. [I]t is practically impossible to distinguish between the technobureaucracy and the intelligentsia.[76]

Marx, Szelényi argues,

defined his classes on the basis of ownership relations because in a capitalist market economy it was a private ownership of the means of production which legitimated expropriation.[77]

In socialist countries, by contrast, it is not property ownership and the market that define income and the distribution of "the surplus"—defined by Marxists as the difference between what labor produces and what is needed to keep it alive. Instead the state expropriates and allocates the surplus. "Contemporary state socialism might be characterized by the antagonism between redistributors and direct producers."[78] The early redistributors used Marxist ideals to legitimate their seizure of power as creators of a scientifically planned economy; but in mature Communist states allegiance to Marxism alone became insufficient to secure elite status.

Szelényi and his coauthor George Konrad also looked at Hungarian social structure immediately before and after the end of the Communist regime. They argued that the "transformation of the cadre elite"—whereby it became increasingly recruited from and assimilated with "professionalized intellectuals"—continued apace during the 1980s.[79] Such people depended far less, for their position, on rank and patronage within the Communist apparatus: they had educational qualifications and professional skills. Konrad and Szelényi argue that there was such a rapprochement, in terms of recruitment, lifestyle, and attitudes, between officeholders and educated professionals as to provide "an important indication that the formation of a new elite, or even a new class, is well under way."[80]

In his more recent work (often in collaboration with Szonja Szelényi), Iván Szelényi has increasingly called upon elite theory alongside Marxist concepts of class in order to analyze the changing societies of post-Communist

---

[76]Szelényi, "The Intelligentsia in the Class Structure of State-Socialist Societies," pp. 297–98.

[77]Szelényi, "The Intelligentsia in the Class Structure of State-Socialist Societies," p. 300.

[78]Szelényi, "The Intelligentsia in the Class Structure of State-Socialist Societies," p. 301.

[79]George Konrad and Iván Szelényi, "Intellectuals and Domination in Post-Communist Societies," in Pierre Bourdieu and James S. Coleman, eds., *Social Theory for a Changing Society* (Boulder: Westview Press/Russell Sage Foundation, 1991), p. 343.

[80]Konrad and Szelényi, "Intellectuals and Domination," p. 346.

Eastern Europe.[81] At issue is whether the old elite has managed to maintain its position. Those observers who offer an "elite reproduction" theory argue that the old "nomenklatura" elite has indeed managed "to survive at the top of the class structure and is now becoming the new propertied bourgeoise."[82] An alternative view ("elite circulation") is that the transition to postcommunism has changed the sort of people being recruited for what Szelényi calls "command positions."

Most observers of Eastern Europe support some version of the elite reproduction theory; in other words, they believe that the people at the top have remained the same, using their political power to protect their position and obtain equivalent positions in the new order. (An example would be running privatized industries and often obtaining a major shareholding in them too.) The Szelényis conclude, on the basis of a major empirical study, that this is basically true, but not equally so across countries. Most members of the old nomenklatura have retained elite positions; but the nontechno-cratic "bureaucratic faction" of the old socialist elites have been shifted out of the top jobs, and there has also been a substantial inflow of new people, typically from the upper or middle class, not from working-class back-grounds. Rather than revolution, what has occurred, they conclude, is a pri-vatization process that can be more accurately described as a reshuffling of property rights and control positions.

Szelényi (and, by implication, Djilas) contrast socialist countries with Western ones, where they see classes with different relationships to private property as still the major groupings. By contrast, conflict theorists in the Weberian tradition would tend to see their analyses as strengthening the case for discussing power and conflict in terms of several different cate-gories—class being one, political power another. Thus, Djilas's major point can be applied generally to argue that government employees should be viewed as a distinctive group with their own interests and power base[83] and that there are conflicts of interest between those who do and those who do not benefit from increased government spending and activity.[84]

---

[81]See especially Iván Szelényi and Szonja Szelényi, "Circulation or Reproduction of Elites During the Postcommunist Transformation of Eastern Europe," *Theory and Society* 24 (1995): 615–38. See also, in the same issue, Eric Hanley, Natasha Yershova, and Richard Anderson, "Russia—Old Wine in a New Bottle? The Circulation and Reproduction of Russian Elites, 1983–1993," *Theory and Society* 24 (1995): 639–68.

[82]Szelényi and Szelényi, "Circulation and Reproduction," p. 616.

[83]See Alain Touraine, *The Self-Production of Society* (Chicago: University of Chicago Press, 1977), for a Marxian analysis that ascribes an independent role to state organizations.

[84]One can use this approach to explain why, for example, businessmen and doctors gen-erally vote Republican or Conservative, whereas equally "middle-class" teachers and social workers tend to vote Democrat or Labor.

Marxist Analysis: An Assessment

Marx's most important contributions to social analysis in general derive from two sources: his emphasis on the way that people in the same economic position tend to group together for common action and his explanation of why and how societies differ in terms of the characteristics of the groups that are generated by their economic life. As Kolakowski has noted, "No reasonable person would deny that the doctrine of historical materialism has been a valuable addition to our intellectual equipment. . . . [I]f it has become a commonplace, this is largely thanks to Marx's originality."[85]

However, this insistence on the primacy of economics means that Marxist analysts tend to use a catch-22 approach. They assume in advance that economic and business interests lie behind things, proceed to find them, and then offer their explanation as proof of the original proposition. But the fact that on any particular occasion one can generally find businessmen and others seeking to advance their economic interests means neither that this is the "real" explanation of what is going on nor that those involved are necessarily acting in the interests of their class as a whole.

The American South offers a good example of both the strengths and the weaknesses of Marxist analysis. Because of its focus on property relationships, Marxism identifies the pre–Civil War slave-owning South as a distinctive social order based on the ownership of human beings. A great part of the written history of the South and the Civil War has tended to interpret the South as essentially agrarian and therefore threatened by industrialization—or as itself merely a variant of capitalism, based on the plantations. As Eugene Genovese, the leading Marxist historian of the South, argues, neither approach explains the antagonism between North and South or the Civil War. An agrarian hinterland can grow prosperous as a market for manufactured goods and a supplier of food, and competition between farmer and industrialist is hardly a common cause of war. Or if the South was basically capitalist, why could the two sides not reach an accommodation?[86]

However, once we see slavery as the *essence* of Southern society and not just one of its many characteristics, however morally repugnant, it is apparent that the South was fighting to preserve a distinctive world. Much about the politics of the South also becomes comprehensible when we see it as a defense of this slavery-based social structure against not only the blacks who suffered under it but also other potential social groups whose interests it did not serve. Thomas Sowell, for example, points out that forced labor is

---

[85]Kolakowski, *Main Currents of Marxism*, Vol. III, p. 524. He also argues that, as an explanatory system, Marxism is dead: p. 528.

[86]Eugene D. Genovese, *The Political Economy of Slavery: Studies in the Economy and Society of the Slave South* (New York: Pantheon Books, 1965), and *The World the Slaveholders Made: Two Essays in Interpretation* (New York: Pantheon Books, 1969).

always extremely inefficient economically.[87] A Southern slave's labor was potentially worth much more to him than to his owner because he would work far harder and more productively for himself than when forced and driven for someone else. Even without adding in the price he would pay just to be free. "Selling a slave to the highest bidder would mean selling him to himself"[88]—a practice that was common among slave-owning profit-maximizing Romans. However, although this might profit individual slave owners and the slaves themselves, it would certainly have undermined a society whose defining core was plantation slavery and whose ethic was fundamentally anticapitalist. Thus severe legal restrictions developed on the freeing of slaves.

However, Marxist theory does not explain adequately why the white population of the South supported this order so wholeheartedly, even through the terrible rigors of the Civil War.[89] Most whites were not slaveowners, and the poorly functioning Southern economy did not serve their economic interests any more than it did those of nascent industrialists facing a meager home market. Their support, we would argue, can be explained fully by the fact that the racist character of Southern society gave every white an automatic claim to superior *status*, so that "the notion that all men were created equal contradicted the facts of daily experience for most Southerners."[90]

Class interests are an even less adequate explanation of the system of racial segregation that succeeded slavery, under which the old classes of slaves and slaveowners no longer existed. The system of segregation was clearly against the interests of industrialists, for it denied skills to a large section of their potential workforce. Under segregation white and black "proletarians" conspicuously failed to group together to further shared class interests. The system did, however, offer benefits to whites in general—and benefits that were real, not a matter of "false consciousness." Their race alone gave them substantial advantages in power and opportunities—better education, for example, and less chance of being treated unjustly by the courts and police. Moreover, when change did come, it could also hardly be explained in terms of class conflict. Rather, it was the outcome of a civil rights movement, in which blacks of all classes and the power of the federal government were the essential agents of change.

[87]Thomas Sowell, *Race and Economics* (New York: David McKay Company, 1975).

[88]Sowell, *Race and Economics*, p. 16.

[89]Nor, we would add, do we believe that economic interests alone explain the behavior of the North. Moral indignation was one, though not the only, important factor at work.

[90]Barrington Moore, Jr., *Social Origins of Dictatorship and Democracy. Lord and Peasant in the Making of the Modern World* (Boston: Beacon Press, 1966), p. 121. We should emphasize that Moore's account of the South is not identical to our own. For an explanation of the Civil War from a rational choice perspective, see pp. 352–53.

CRITICAL THEORY: THE FRANKFURT SCHOOL

Although all the theorists discussed in this section critique contemporary society, the term *critical theory* is also associated specifically with the theorists of the Frankfurt School. The work of the older Frankfurt theorists only became well known among English-speaking sociologists in the 1960s, but many of their most important writings date from an earlier period. The most important contemporary theorist whose work directly continues their approach is Jürgen Habermas. His ideas are discussed in detail in Chapter 4.

The analyses of the Frankfurt theorists owe a great deal to Marx, and, like him, they emphasize the importance of conflicts of interest based on property relationships. However, they are by no means orthodox Marxists. They owe a major debt to Hegel, and they draw more on Marx's early and more Hegelian work, such as his writings on alienation, than on his later, more economic analyses.[91] In addition, they are interested in uniting psychoanalysis and Marxism, an effort toward which orthodox Marxism (or Marxism-Leninism) is highly unsympathetic. These different influences are apparent in their view of social science and their critique of mass culture and its place in the "administered society."

The Frankfurt School is so called because of its association with a single institution, the Institute of Social Research at the University of Frankfurt in Germany. The institute was founded in 1923 with funds from one of its members, Felix Weil, and his wealthy father; its most important members were Max Horkheimer (1895–1973), Theodor Adorno (1903–1969), Herbert Marcuse (1898–1979), and Erich Fromm (1900–1980). All of them came from comfortable, middle-class Jewish homes, and all had fled Germany for America by the mid-1930s because their political views made the continuation of the institute impossible. Marcuse remained in the United States and worked for the U.S. State Department until the Korean War, when he returned to academic life. He taught at Columbia, Harvard, Brandeis, and the University of California, San Diego. Fromm, who broke with the institute soon after his arrival in America, practiced psychoanalysis in New York and became a founder and trustee of the William Alanson White Institute of Psychiatry, Psychoanalysis, and Psychology. In 1949 he moved to Mexico because of his wife's health. There he started the department of psychoanalysis at the National Autonomous University of Mexico and founded and directed the Mexican Psychoanalytic Institute, while still commuting regularly to the United States and academic appointments in New York and Michigan.

Adorno and Horkheimer were persuaded by the city and the University of Frankfurt to return to Germany, where the Institute of Social

---

[91]Jay, for example, suggests that "on one level . . . the Frankfurt School was returning to the concerns of the Left Hegelians of the 1840s." See Martin Jay, *The Dialectical Imagination* (Boston: Little, Brown, 1973), p. 42.

Research was reestablished in 1949.[92] During the postwar period they became estranged from Marcuse. Horkheimer's attitudes toward liberal capitalism changed; he came to regard it as a form of society to be protected against the encroachment of "totalitarian administration."[93] Marcuse regarded this position as a betrayal of the group's beliefs.[94]

Although the foremost members of the Frankfurt School were not themselves actively involved in politics, their work strongly influenced German student radicals. Furthermore, as we mentioned above, Marcuse was a writer of great importance to the American New Left of the 1960s. Consequently, the Frankfurt theorists remain highly controversial; in fact, they were accused by the minister president of one West German state of being directly responsible for the 1960s wave of urban terrorism in Germany. Nevertheless, Adorno's classes were broken up by students who considered him inadequately revolutionary.

Critical Theory and the Nature of Social Science

At the core of the Frankfurt School's approach to social analysis are two propositions. The first is that people's ideas are a product of the society in which they live. Because our thought is socially formed, they argue, it is impossible for us to reach objective knowledge and conclusions, free of the influence of our particular era and its conceptual patterns. The second proposition is that intellectuals should not try to be objective and to separate fact from value judgment in their work. What they should adopt instead is a critical attitude to the society they are examining, an attitude that makes people aware of what they should do and has as its aim social change. Equally, intellectuals should maintain a critical attitude toward their own work; they should examine and make explicit its relationship to the current state of society and socially created knowledge.

It does not follow, however, that critical theorists consider one critical attitude to be as good as another. Unlike Marx, they admit that because they too are products of a particular society, their own work is subject to its influences and is not uniquely objective. Nevertheless, they also believe that there are such things as truth and knowledge and that their normative approach brings them closer to these than does mainstream, or "positivist," social

[92]Adorno was the most keen to leave, as he was probably the most unassimilated European of the group. A fellow refugee, Paul Lazarsfeld, described him on his arrival in America as "exactly as you would imagine a very absent-minded German professor, and he behaves so foreign that I feel like a member of the Mayflower Society." Donald Flemming and Bernard Bailyn, ed. *The Intellectual Migration: Europe and America, 1930–1960* (Cambridge, Mass.: Belknap Press at Harvard University, 1969), p. 301.

[93]Max Horkheimer, *Critical Theory*, trans. Matthew J. O'Connell et al. Preface to American edition (New York: Herder and Herder, 1972). These essays were written in the 1930s.

[94]Phil Slater, *The Origin and Significance of the Frankfurt School: A Marxist Perspective* (London: Routledge and Kegan Paul, 1977).

science, with its attempts to separate value judgments from analysis.[95] While many of their views are close to those of postmodernists, as discussed in Chapter 9, this last position makes them far more willing to adopt a judgmental position: they are not thoroughgoing relativists.

The ideal standard by which critical theory makes its judgments is closer to the concept of *reason* as it is used by Hegel and other German philosophers than it is to Marx. Horkheimer, for example, argues that "the free development of individuals depends on the rational constitution of society" and that in a rational society there will cease to be a conflict between human potentialities and the organization of society around work.[96] However, what a rational society would be like remains almost totally unclear, and the Frankfurt analysts share none of Marx's confidence that it will one day be realized.

Defenders of traditional social science have always argued in response that, whether or not writers can avoid incorporating their own values into their work, their theories stand or fall by the accuracy of their factual predictions. These—like a bridge built according to twentieth-century science—can be judged objectively. They also question whether critical theory has any reason to claim that it is less context-bound than other approaches.

Culture, Personality, and the Administered Society.   The Frankfurt analysts consider themselves materialists because of their emphasis on the importance of economic organization. During the 1930s, for example, they argued consistently that fascism was rooted in capitalism. For the most part, however, their studies are concerned with aspects of personality, culture, and thought, and not with social institutions. Horkheimer, Adorno, and their colleagues always affirmed that thought and personality are rooted in the economic system, but unlike more orthodox Marxists they also argued that culture and ideology can play an independent role in society and that pure economic determinism is simplistic.

Much of the most important work in critical theory was carried out at a time when psychoanalysis was first becoming widely known and influential. The Frankfurt analysts were very interested in analyzing personality and behavior in terms of the interaction between the "socioeconomic substructure" and basic psychic drives. Their analyses are highly normative, emphasizing the way the economic system distorts or cripples the personality.

---

[95]See especially Max Horkheimer, *Critical Theory*, and Jürgen Habermas, *Theory and Practice*, trans. John Viertel (Boston: Beacon Press, 1972). Members of the Frankfurt School apply the term "positivist" to a wide range of work, most of which does not belong to the philosophical schools of positivism or logical positivism but does share an emphasis on the empirical testing of hypotheses and scientific objectivity. See also Stephen Turner and Regis Factor, *Max Weber and the Dispute over Reason and Value: A Study of Philosophy, Ethics and Politics* (Henley-on-Thames: Routledge and Kegan Paul, 1984); and Anthony Giddens, "Review Essay: Habermas's Social and Political Theory," *American Journal of Sociology* 83, no. 1 (1977): 198–212.

[96]Horkheimer, *Critical Theory*, p. 216.

Erich Fromm showed the greatest interest in psychoanalysis. During the 1930s, when he was a central member of the group, Fromm was interested in the way a particular "libidinal" structure, formed and passed on in the family, could act as a social cement. At this period he argued that, for example, the "capitalist spirit" of rationality, possessiveness, and puritanism was linked to anal repression and orderliness.[97] Later his analyses centered around the idea of "alienation," which he uses rather differently from Marx to describe an individual's psychological experiences of the world.

Fromm argues that alienation is the "central issue . . . [in discussing] the effects of capitalism on personality."[98] Under capitalism, workers and managers alike are alienated because they are denied such basic needs as creativity and identity. Their work is entirely impersonal; their consumption is also alienated, for they acquire possessions whether or not they use or appreciate them. They are motivated by self-interest, not love, in their relationships with others, and they see themselves as "doctors" or "clerks," not people.[99] Moreover,

> The increasing emphasis on ego versus self, on having versus being, finds a glowing expression in the development of our language. It has become customary for people to say, "I have insomnia," instead of saying, "I cannot sleep"; or "I have a problem," instead of, "I feel sad, confused" or whatever it may be; or "I have a happy marriage" . . . instead of . . . "My wife and I love each other." . . . Modern man *has* everything: a car, a house, a job, "kids," a marriage, problems, troubles, satisfactions. . . . He *is* nothing. . . .
> . . . There are no psychological shortcuts to the solution of [this] identity crisis except the fundamental transformation of alienated man into living man.[100]

The Frankfurt analysts indict modern society similarly in their massive study *The Authoritarian Personality*. This study, the most famous of the series on prejudice and anti-Semitism that Adorno, Horkheimer, and their colleagues conducted in America, clearly presented Adorno's views on the connections between personality and social structure.[101] *The Authoritarian Personality* concluded that the most prejudiced and antidemocratic individuals had distinctive personalities and came, on the whole, from homes where relationships between parent and child were characterized by dominance and submission and where family members were intolerant of a lack of conformity. In other words, the factors that precipitate prejudice were

---

[97]Erich Fromm, *The Crisis of Psychoanalysis* (New York: Fawcett World Library, 1975).

[98]Erich Fromm, *The Sane Society* (New York: Rinehart and Winston, 1956), p. 69.

[99]Fromm, *The Sane Society*, pp. 120–91.

[100]Erich Fromm, *The Revolution of Hope: Toward a Humanized Technology* (New York: Harper and Row, 1968), pp. 83–84.

[101]Theodor Adorno et al., *The Authoritarian Personality* (New York: Harper, 1950). The study is rather atypical of critical theory in its use of detailed analysis of questionnaire items and the scaling of people's responses. Most critical theory involves assertions and arguments at a general level, for which little detailed evidence is advanced.

clearly seen as psychological. At the same time, however, Adorno argued that the whole sample showed marked similarities in important degrees. The most prejudiced individuals simply demonstrated more clearly the overall and potentially fascistic cultural pattern produced by the social structure. The prejudiced person "must largely be considered the outcome of our civilization (including) such tendencies in our culture as division of labor, the increased importance of monopolies and institutions, and the dominance of the idea of exchange and of success and competition."[102]

The Critique of Mass Culture.   Critical theory's discussion of culture displays the same deep pessimism as does its analysis of personality. Horkheimer argues that culture and ideology are not a simple reflection of the economic substructure, but a semiautonomous realm. He and his colleagues see popular culture as a means of manipulating the inhabitants of a totally administered society.

Thus Adorno attacked jazz and popular music for its standardization, for distracting people and making them passive, and therefore for strengthening the current social order. Jazz, he argued, increases alienation.[103] He similarly despised astrology and the "attraction to the occult," which he called "a symptom of the retrogression of consciousness."[104] People turn to astrology, he argues, in an attempt to lure meaning out of a "frozen" world where humanity's "domination over nature, by turning into domination over man, surpasses all the horrors that man ever had to fear from nature."[105] Its practitioners exploit their clients, and by providing psychological reassurance they help sustain the current social structure.

In his examination of the *Los Angeles Times* astrology column,[106] Adorno notes that the column's implication that work and pleasure are to be kept strictly apart befits a society in which people's functions as producers are rigidly divided from their consumption. He argues that

> The columnist is very well aware of the drudgery of most subordinate functions in a hierarchical and bureaucratic setup. . . . [People] are encouraged to fulfill little and insignificant set tasks in a machinery. Thus, the admonition to work and not to allow oneself to be distracted by any instinctual interference has frequently the form that one should attend to one's *"chores."*

---

[102]Adorno, *The Authoritarian Personality*, p. 389.

[103]Theodor Adorno, "Über Jazz," *Zeitschrift für Sozialforschung* V, 2 (1936). Adorno's major interest was music, and readers of Thomas Mann's great novel *Dr. Faustus* will be interested to know that Adorno was Mann's major source of information on music. See also Theodor Adorno, *Introduction to the Sociology of Music*, trans. E. B. Ashton (New York: Seabury Press, 1976), for some of Adorno's most interesting analyses.

[104]Theodor Adorno, "Theses Against Occultism," *Telos* 19 (1974): 7.

[105]Adorno, "Theses Against Occultism."

[106]Theodor Adorno, "The Stars Down to Earth, The Los Angeles Times Astrology Column," *Telos* 19 (1974): 13–90.

Dismal early A.M., forgotten by plunging into routine chores. (November 21, 1952, Leo)
    Keeping plugging at chores . . . (December 19, 1952, Sagittarius)
    Stick to attending chores . . . (December 27, 1952, Sagittarius)[107]

In *One-Dimensional Man* Herbert Marcuse paints a bleak picture of modern industrial societies in both the West and the Communist world.[108] Marcuse is more of a technological determinist than his former colleagues; he states that technical progress has made possible a "whole system of domination and coordination" that defeats all protests. Social control in the interests of the status quo, including conditioning by the mass media, is so powerful that even thought provides no source of criticism; it too is subordinated.[109] Culture has been flattened in what Marcuse views as a totalitarian social order that has succeeded the previous liberal one and that has become one-dimensional because it has eliminated alternative ideas.

Marcuse's distaste for modern culture has struck a responsive chord, for many of us have at some time been nauseated by yet more TV advertising or by the thought of life lived in "little boxes all the same." However, Marcuse has also aroused numerous critics. It is frequently pointed out, for example, that Marcuse's own work refutes his claim that all criticism has been suppressed and that his writings generally advance little empirical evidence in support of his claims. Critics also disagree with his assertion that all industrial societies are essentially and similarly totalitarian, and they question his and other critical theorists' conviction that they, unlike the mass of people, know what people's real needs are.

C. WRIGHT MILLS

Among American sociologists, C. Wright Mills (1916–1962) is the best-known modern theorist whose work combines a conflict perspective with a strong critique of the social order. Mills was born and raised in Texas; he never left the state until he was in his twenties, when he won a research fellowship to the University of Wisconsin. Most of his academic career was spent at Columbia, where he was a professor until he died of a heart condition while still in his mid-forties.

---

[107]Adorno, "The Stars Down to Earth," p. 47. The "fragmentation" of modern culture and the "atomization" of experience are still seen by many radical social scientists as both central features of capitalist society and crucial to its continuation. See, for example, David Held, "Crisis Tendencies, Legitimation and the State," in John B. Thompson and David Held, ed., *Habermas: Critical Debates* (London: Macmillan, 1982), especially pp. 189–90.

[108]Herbert Marcuse, *One-Dimensional Man* (Boston: Beacon Press, 1963).

[109]Marcuse, *One-Dimensional Man*, p. 70. Marcuse was also interested in psychoanalysis and argued that an integrated personality is impossible in modern civilization. See his *Eros and Civilization* (New York: Vintage Books, 1955).

Mills was subjected to a barrage of criticism, especially in his later years, when his writing became increasingly accusatory and polemical. He also had many admirers and was never quite the lone wolf he considered himself. Mills was increasingly agonized and pessimistic about the immediate future. He believed that immorality was built into the American system, and he never voted because he considered political parties to be manipulative and irrational organizations. He also bitterly attacked his fellow intellectuals for abdicating their social responsibilities and for putting themselves at the service of those in power while they hid behind a mask of "value-free" analysis.

Mills thought that it was possible to create a "good society" on the basis of knowledge and that people of knowledge must take responsibility for its absence.[110] He believed in a libertarian socialism, and he supported the Cuban revolution (and attacked the U.S. reaction to it) because he hoped that it would combine revolutionary socialism and freedom.[111] In his sociology, his major themes were the relationship between bureaucracy and alienation and the centralization of power in a "power elite." Both these subjects were aspects of his attack on modern American society.

The Sociological Imagination

Mills argues that micro and macro levels of analysis can be linked by the *sociological imagination*. As he describes it,

> The sociological imagination enables its possessor to understand the large historical scene in terms of its meaning for the inner life and the external career of a variety of individuals. It enables him to take into account how individuals, in the welter of their daily experience, often become falsely conscious of their social positions. . . . By such means the personal uneasiness of individuals is focused upon explicit troubles and the indifference of publics is transformed into involvement with public issues.[112]

Mills contends that individuals can only understand their own experiences fully if they can locate themselves within their period of history. Then they become aware of the life chances shared by all individuals in the same circumstances. Thus the sociological imagination enables us to "grasp history and biography and the relations between the two within society."

Mills makes an important distinction between *personal troubles* and *public issues*. Personal troubles are troubles that occur "within the individual as a biographical entity and within the scope of his immediate milieu" and relations with other people. Public issues are matters that have to do with the "institutions of an historical society as a whole," with the overlapping of various milieus that interpenetrate to "form the larger structures of social

---

[110]C. Wright Mills, *The Sociological Imagination* (New York: Oxford University Press, 1959).

[111]C. Wright Mills, *Listen Yankee: The Revolution in Cuba* (New York: McGraw-Hill, 1960).

[112]Mills, *The Sociological Imagination*, p. 5.

and historical life." To explain this distinction Mills presents the example of unemployment. If only one person in a city of 100,000 is unemployed, then it is a personal trouble. But if 5 million people are unemployed in a nation of 50 million, that is a public issue.

Dobash and Dobash used Mills's approach in their study entitled *Violence Against Wives*. They analyzed the laws and ordinances that, throughout history, have legitimized the physical abuse of women, and they combined this study with analysis of nearly a thousand police and court cases of assaults against wives and with hundreds of hours of in-depth interviews with battered women. For each individual, what was involved was a private trouble. The scale of the problem and the law's lack of concern made it a public issue.[113]

Alienation and Bureaucracy

Mills argues that the material hardships of the workers of the past have been replaced today by a psychological malaise rooted in workers' alienation from what they make.[114] He sees white-collar workers as apathetic, frightened, and molded by mass culture. In modern society, he argues, "those who hold power have often come to exercise it in hidden ways: they have moved and are moving from authority to manipulation. . . . The rational systems hide their power so that no one sees their sources of authority or understands their calculation. For the bureaucracy . . . the world is an object to be manipulated."[115]

In a world of big business and big government, the ever-increasing group of white-collar people lives not by making things but by helping to turn what someone else has made into profits for yet another person. Fewer and fewer people own their own productive property and control their own working lives. Stable communities and traditional values, which "fixed" people into society, have disappeared, and their disappearance throws the whole system of prestige or status into flux. Like Veblen, Mills believes that status and self-esteem are closely linked, and the loss of traditional values, he argues, undermines people's self-esteem and embroils them in a status "panic."[116] In fact, Mills's concerns here are curiously like those of Durkheim and the functionalists, who see modern society as threatened by normlessness, or anomie. His critics argue that he ignores the freedom that the breakup of old and restrictive communities can offer.

Unlike Marx, Mills does not believe that work is necessarily the crucial expression of oneself, but he does condemn modern bureaucratic capitalism

---

[113]R. Emerson Dobash and Russell Dobash, *Violence Against Wives: A Case Against the Patriarchy* (New York: The Free Press, 1979).

[114]C. Wright Mills, *White Collar: The American Middle Classes* (New York: Oxford University Press, 1951), pp. xvi–xvii.

[115]Mills, *White Collar*, pp. 110–11.

[116]Mills, *White Collar*, pp. 237–58.

for alienating people from both the process and product of work. This is particularly clear, Mills argues, with white-collar workers like salespeople whose personalities become commodities to be sold and for whom friendliness and courtesy are part of the "impersonal means of livelihood."[117] Thus, he claims, "in all work involving the personality market . . . one's personality and personal traits become part of the means of production . . . (which) has carried self and social alienation to explicit extremes."[118]

Mills's emphasis on alienation derives from his concern with the relationship between character and social structure. Salesmanship, he argues, estranges people from themselves and others because they view all relationships as manipulative.[119] Alienation from work makes people turn frenziedly to leisure, but the entertainment industry produces synthetic excitement, which offers no real release and establishes no deep common values.[120] Other aspects of social structure strengthen psychological tendencies that make modern societies liable to fascist or revolutionary totalitarian success.[121] People's fragmented working environments give them little understanding of how society works, and they believe that the interventionist government is responsible for insecurity and misfortune. An increasingly centralized structure with no remaining traditional beliefs and with permanently anxious people is, Mills argues, highly vulnerable.

The Power Elite

Mills argues consistently that the growth of large structures has been accompanied by a centralization of power and that the men who head government, corporations, the armed forces, and the unions are closely linked. He carries this part of his analysis the furthest in his discussion of the "power elite."[122]

Mills argues that America is ruled by a power elite made up of people who hold the dominant positions in political, military, and economic institutions. "Within the American society," he writes, "major national power now resides in the economic, the political and the military domains. . . . Within each of the big three, the typical institutional unit has become enlarged, has become administrative, and, in the power of its decision, has become central-

---

[117]Mills, *White Collar*, p. xvii.

[118]Mills, *White Collar*, p. 225.

[119]Mills, *White Collar*, p. 188.

[120]Mills, *White Collar*, p. xvii.

[121]Hans Gerth and C. Wright Mills, *Character and Social Structure* (New York: Harcourt Brace, 1953), pp. 460–72.

[122]Mills, *White Collar*, pp. 83 and 349; C. Wright Mills, *The New Men of Power* (New York: Harcourt Brace, 1945); C. Wright Mills, *The Power Elite* (New York: Oxford University Press, 1958); C. Wright Mills, "The Power Elite: Military, Economic and Political," in Arthur Kornhauser, ed., *Problems of Power in American Society* (Detroit: Wayne University Press, 1958).

ized. . . . [The] means of power at the disposal of centralized decision-making units have increased enormously."[123]

Mills argues, moreover, that the three domains are interlocked, so that "the leading men in each of the three domains of power—the warlords, the corporate chieftains, the political directorate—tend to come together to form the power elite of America. . . . The military capitalism of private corporations exists in a weakened and formal democratic system containing an already quite politicized military order."[124] Mills believed that power can be based on factors other than property. However, the unity of the elite's institutional interests brings them together and maintains a war economy.

Mills's analysis coincided with and reinforced an attitude toward American society that was apparent in Eisenhower's denunciation of the "military-industrial complex." Many nonradical sociologists agree that economic life is increasingly intertwined with the activities of the government.[125] However, they argue that it is not simply military expenditures that are important, but rather the increased involvement of government in *all* spheres of economic life. Those of us who live in Washington notice how, month by month, more and more industrial, trade, and labor associations set up headquarters in the city's burgeoning office blocks, close to the federal government and its power.

Moreover, critics frequently disagree with Mills's perception of a single power elite pursuing its united interest and excluding others from influence. They argue that powerful interests may—and frequently do—conflict with each other. Business, for example, undoubtedly has power. It gets some of the measures it wants, and some firms and industries acquire a protected, semimonopolistic position from government regulators. For others, however, plans are delayed or demolished by decisions about environmental quality; prices are set at levels they oppose; or costs are raised by taxes, government paperwork, pollution requirements, and the like.

In general Mills shares with Marxist sociology and the elite theorists a tendency to see a society as divided rather sharply and horizontally between the powerful and the powerless. He also shares Marxist and neo-Marxist theorists' concerns about alienation, the effects of social structure on the personality, and the manipulation of people by the mass media. At the same time, however, Mills clearly belongs to a distinctively American populist tradition, which does not regard property as such as the main source of evil in society. To Mills, small-scale property ownership and the class of independent entrepreneurs are the major safeguards of freedom and security,

[123]Mills, "The Power Elite," pp. 156–58.

[124]Mills, "The Power Elite," p. 164.

[125]See, for example, William Kornhauser, "'Power Elite' or 'Veto Groups'?" in Reinhard Bendix and Seymour Martin Lipset, ed., *Class, Status and Power* (New York: Free Press, 1966); and William V. D'Antonio and Howard J. Ehrlich, ed., *Power and Democracy in America* (Notre Dame, Indiana: University of Notre Dame Press, 1961).

and he regrets the waning of the old American society of independent farmers and businessmen.[126]

PIERRE BOURDIEU

Pierre Bourdieu (b. 1930) is one of the best-known sociologists currently writing within a critical framework, as well as being the best known of all contemporary French sociologists. Seen from one perspective, he is the quintessential eminent French intellectual. Like Durkheim he is a graduate of the École Normale Supérieure, and he is Director of Studies at the École Pratique des Hautes Études (in Paris). He is founder and director of the Centre for European Sociology, holder of the country's senior chair in sociology at the Collège de France, and very much a figure of the Paris intellectual establishment—something entirely compatible with being also a "man of the left" whose work is imbued with Marxist concepts.

From another perspective, however, Bourdieu appears as far more of a critical outsider. France is dominated by a political and business elite drawn overwhelmingly from Paris—an elite that Bourdieu has subjected to detailed analysis but that is not his own original milieu. Instead he comes from a small town in the rural southeast, where he grew up as the son of a minor civil servant close to the surviving world of the southern peasantry. As a student, in an academic culture that was not merely Marxist but heavily Communist and Stalinist, he rejected both of the latter. He subjects his own academic world to a detailed scrutiny and analysis that, he notes, have "separated me from some of my best friends" and led to "dramatic clashes with colleagues."[127] Finally, at a time when Anglo-Saxon and French social science are generally marked by mutual incomprehension and disdain, he has become increasingly well known and widely read by mainstream English-speaking social scientists.

Fields of Conflict.   Bourdieu argues strongly against the Marxist view that society can be analyzed *simply* in terms of classes and class-determined interests and ideologies.[128] Much of his work concerns the independent role of educational and cultural factors; and, like many of the theorists discussed in this text, he emphasizes the importance, in modern societies, of formal educational institutions—the means of his own transformation from the rural Pyranees.

Instead of analyzing societies in terms of classes, Bourdieu uses the concept of a *field*: a social arena in which, just as in a game, people maneuver,

---

[126]Mills, *White Collar*, pp. 7–12.

[127]Pierre Bourdieu and Loic J. D. Wacquant, *An Invitation to Reflexive Sociology* (Cambridge: Polity, 1992), p. 63.

[128]Some commentators see Bourdieu as essentially presenting a "Marxism of the superstructure": see, for example, Randall Collins and Michael Makowsky, *The Discovery of Society* (New York: McGraw-Hill, 1993). While Bourdieu is certainly heavily influenced by Marxist ideas, this seems to us incorrect.

develop strategies, and struggle over desirable resources. Instead of the foot-ball field, we find Bourdieu talking of the academic field, the religious field, the economic field, and the field of power. He states that

> a field may be defined as a network, or a configuration, of objective relations between positions. These positions are objectively defined, in their existence and in the determinations they impose upon their occupants . . . by their . . . sit-uation in the structure of the distribution of power (or capital) whose posses-sion commands access to the specific profits that are at stake in the field.[129]

A field, in other words, is *a system of social positions, structured internally in terms of power relations*: "every field (is) the locus of power relationships."[130] However, whereas Marxists would trace all power relations back to the means of production—the economic field—Bourdieu argues that *different fields can be quite autonomous*, and that more complex societies will have larger numbers of quite different fields. For example, politics in modern soci-eties has become professionalized and autonomous, with its own rules; and the way politics operates, and the power it offers, cannot be seen as simply a function of economic processes. Here Bourdieu is obviously heavily influ-enced by Weber's analysis. However, he adds the argument that power in different fields depends crucially on quite different forms of *capital*.

Marx's great book, *Capital*, was entirely economic in focus. Bourdieu, however, argues that there are three fundamental types of capital—eco-nomic, social, and cultural.[131] The first of these involves command over eco-nomic resources, and the second command over relationships—networks of influence and support people can tap into by virtue of their social position, whether through family or, for example, being a graduate of Harvard. It is the third, however, to which Bourdieu has devoted by far the most attention and that is associated with his most original contributions to sociological theory.

Bourdieu argues that parents provide children with *cultural capital*. He has analyzed in great detail the way in which tastes, and perceptions of what is beautiful or valuable, differ between different classes—and how the elite constantly distances itself from popular taste.[132] However, his most enduring interest has been in how cultural capital is translated into advantages in edu-cational terms.[133] Those from privileged homes have the attitudes and knowl-

---

[129]Bourdieu and Wacquant, *An Invitation to Reflexive Sociology*, p. 97.

[130]Pierre Bourdieu, *In Other Words: Essays Towards a Reflexive Sociology* (Cambridge: Polity, 1990), p. 141.

[131]Bourdieu, *In Other Words*, p. 119. Bourdieu also identifies *symbolic capital*, which inter-sects with these, and can subsume any of them.

[132]See especially Pierre Bourdieu, *Distinction: A Social Critique of the Judgement of Taste* (London: Routledge, 1984).

[133]See especially Pierre Bourdieu and Jean-Claude Passeron, *The Inheritors: French Students and Their Relation to Culture*, trans. R. Nice (Chicago: University of Chicago Press, 1979); pub-lished in France as *Les Héritiers*, 1964.

edge, especially cultural knowledge, that make the education system a comfortable, familiar sort of place in which they can succeed easily. The "formal equality" of competitive examinations encourages people to believe that they succeed—or fail—by their own individual merit. Hence upper-middle-class students have no trouble in reconciling left-wing views with their own privileged position. In fact, though, their position is the result of students' social origins taking effect through "more secret channels."[134] The education system can "ensure the perpetuation of privilege by the mere operation of its own internal logic."[135]

Reproduction and Habitus

Bourdieu's theory is one of class *reproduction*—of how one generation of an (economic) class ensures that it reproduces itself and passes on its privileges to the next generation. Renaud Sainsaulieu, for example, describes reproduction theory as illuminating the "latent ideological functioning of the educational apparatus which, despite its overtly democratic recruitment and the formalization of its rules, carries out in fact a social selection based on the cultural criteria of the dominant class."[136]

Bourdieu argues that what is necessary for educational success is a whole set of cultured behavior. It is this that carries you confidently through higher education, job interviews, boardrooms, and the like. The children of middle- and upper-class families have learned this behavior; their working-class peers have not. Consequently, the former are able to succeed within the educational system, and their families can reproduce their class position from generation to generation in a legitimate and apparently fair way.

The legitimation of this cultural capital is crucial to its effectiveness as a source of power and success and is discussed by Bourdieu in terms of *symbolic violence*, defined as the *"violence which is exercised upon a social agent with his or her complicity."*[137] What this means is that people come to experience systems of meaning (culture) as legitimate; there is a process of misunderstanding or misrecognition of what is really going on. The reproduction of a group's position and the struggle for position in a field are experienced by all players—not only the losers—as being about something quite different: the inculcation of objectively valuable ideas and activities.[138] For example, in one of his more recent books, Bourdieu analyzes in detail the way in which

---

[134]Bourdieu and Passeron, *The Inheritors*, p. 68.

[135]Bourdieu and Passeron, *The Inheritors*, p. 27.

[136]Renaud Sainsaulieu, "On Reproduction," *Revue Francaise de Sociologie*, 13, no. 3 (1972): 339–412; reprinted in Charles C. Lemert, ed., *French Sociology: Rupture and Renewal Since 1968*, trans. P. Lemert (New York: Columbia University Press, 1981), p. 153.

[137]Bourdieu and Wacquant, *An Invitation to Reflective Sociology*, p. 167; italics original.

[138]See especially Pierre Bourdieu, *Reproduction in Education, Society and Culture* (London: Sage, 1990).

students are recruited to the Grandes Écoles, which educate the French elite, and socialized into a "state nobility."[139] Those who succeed in passing the highly competitive examinations are drawn to a very high, and indeed an increasing, degree from professional and upper-class families (see Table 3-1) and from a very few select high schools (lycées).

In a chapter of *La Noblesse d'État* titled "Misrecognition and Symbolic Violence" Bourdieu analyzes in detail the way students in higher education are categorized and labeled as "plodders" or as having flair, and how closely associated with their social origins these verdicts turn out to be. Yet the whole system claims, and *is believed by those involved*, to be one of meritocratic selection and service to the state. Professors and students share the conviction that the "brutal frankness" of the way their work is judged is the only appropriate way for members of an intellectual elite to communicate,[140] and they experience the judgments of merit as objective descriptors.

At the same time as elucidating the statistical link between academic success and social origin, Bourdieu emphasizes that there is nothing mechanical about it. It is the result of "innumerable acts of evaluation—and self-evaluation" whereby students—and professors—bring into play "scholarly taxonomies—those instruments for constructing reality." It is not a question of some outside, deterministic force; on the contrary. "All successful socialization succeeds in making people accomplices in their own fates."[141] A key

---

[139]Pierre Bourdieu, *La Noblesse d'État: Grandes Écoles et Esprit de Corps* (Paris: Les Editions de Minuit, 1989).

[140]Bourdieu, *La Noblesse d'État*, p. 59.

[141]Bourdieu, *La Noblesse d'État*, p. 69; translation ours.

TABLE 3-1   Social Origins of Entrants to a Major Grande École: 1952 and 1982[a]

Father's Occupation	% of Entrants 1952–58	% of Entrants 1978–82
Farmer	2.1	2.2
Manual worker (unskilled)	1.4	0.7
Skilled manual/artisans	10.4	0.5
Senior civil servant (such as diplomat or prefect) [b]	9.0	19.1
Professional	15.3	14.7
Midrank civil servant	24.6	11.0
Businessman	6.6	8.1
White collar/private sector	3.5	1.0

[a]The institution is ENA—the École Nationale d'Administration, the major training ground of the top administrators and senior industrialists in large and state-owned companies in France and of many politicians.

[b]The "prefects" are central government appointees who run the regions and local departments of France.

Source: Adapted from Table 28, Bourdieu: *La Noblesse d'État*. (Figures do not sum to 100%; not all categories are included.)

part of this process is the transformation of people's cultural habits or economic position into symbolic capital that has legitimacy and is seen as somehow real. Bourdieu argues that "symbolic capital is nothing more than economic or cultural capital which is acknowledged and recognized" and then tends to "reinforce the power relations which constitute the structure of social space."[142]

In elaborating his analysis of cultural capital Bourdieu has developed the key concept of *habitus*. Habitus can be defined as "a system of durably acquired schemes of perception, thought, and action, engendered by objective conditions, but tending to persist even after an alteration of those conditions."[143] Bourdieu sees the habitus as the key to reproduction because it is what actually generates the regular, repeated practices that make up social life.[144] It is the "product of social conditionings"[145] and so links actual behavior to the class structure.[146]

In *The Inheritors* Bourdieu and his coauthor argue that a major reason for the rapid growth in higher education is that

> those fractions of the dominant class and middle class who are richest in economic capital (i.e., industrial and commercial employees, craftsmen and tradesmen) have had to make greatly increased use of the educational system in order to ensure their social reproduction. When class fractions who previously made little use of the school system enter the race for academic qualifications, the effect is to force the groups whose reproduction was mainly or exclusively achieved through education to step up their investments so as to maintain the relative scarcity of their qualifications and, consequently, their position in the class structure. . . . [This] generates a general and continuous growth in the demand for education and an inflation of academic qualifications.[147]

In other words, changes in the economic substructure have repercussions for education *because* it is the mechanism for reproducing class advantage. Moreover, education is such a potent and effective mechanism precisely because it does not simply involve learning technical skills or acquiring knowledge. There has to be the accompanying general culture.

---

[142]Bourdieu, *In Other Words*, p. 135.

[143]The definition is Richard Nice's, given on p. 156 of the English edition of *The Inheritors* with reference to Bourdieu's updating epilogue. For Bourdieu's full explanation of the term, see P. Bourdieu, *Outline of a Theory of Practice*, trans. R. Nice (Cambridge: Cambridge University Press, 1977). There are overlaps here with the individual actors' orientations defined by Parsons's pattern variables, as well as Mead's discussion of meaning, but there are also crucial differences in conception. A *habitus* generates coherent actions and behaviors that are specific to a particular group or class and are rooted in the latter's particular economic conditions. It is not universal (unlike Parsons's pattern variables) nor specific for an individual.

[144]Compare the work of Anthony Giddens, who also relates social structure to repeated interpersonal activities. See Chapter 4.

[145]Bourdieu, *In Other Words*, p. 116.

[146]Bourdieu, *Outline of a Theory of Practice*, p. 86.

[147]Bourdieu and Passeron, *The Inheritors*, pp. 77–78.

According to reproduction theory, whenever there is a big increase in the numbers holding a qualification, the major losers are those who do not have the "social capital to extract the full yield" from it.[148]

As well as analyzing the role of education in society as a whole, Bourdieu has also devoted a great deal of attention to internal analysis of the universities. There are two reasons for this: first, his general insistence on the importance of "reflexive sociology" (discussed in the following section), and second, his more specific interest in the ways conflicts take place in the academic field and in the broader "field of power" (champ de pouvoir). Bourdieu's first work was as a social anthropologist, conducting fieldwork in Algeria and in his own home region. He continues to collect and analyze much of his own data, and the university provides a rich source of anthropological data.

Reflexive Sociology and the Idea of "Practice."   Although Bourdieu provides analyses of society at a macro level and draws heavily on empirical and quantitative data, he is extremely critical of sociology that presents itself as supposedly detached and entirely descriptive, based on a scientific model. However, he is also deeply opposed to those who see all theories as simply the product of an individual viewpoint—what he calls the "false radicalism of the questioning of science that is now proliferating . . . those who reduce scientific discourse to rhetorical strategies about a world itself reduced to the status of a text."[149] Instead he rejects what he sees as a false dichotomy between objectivism and subjectivism, and he insists on the importance of a *reflexive sociology* in which sociologists must, at all times, conduct their research with *conscious attention to the effects of their own position, and in particular their own set of "internalized structures."*

Most people, most of the time, Bourdieu argues, take their social world and its way of looking at things entirely for granted.[150] Sociologists are not free from this—for them, too, perceptions and actions are shaped by a *habitus*—and they must be aware of this. Reflexive sociology requires them instead to examine, all the time, "the most essential bias . . . the individual determinations inherent in the intellectual position itself, in the scholarly gaze."[151]

Bourdieu insists that human action and practice must be understood in this way, as a dialectical process involving both the dispositions produced by the habitus and the objective conditions that individuals encounter in the fields where they operate. In this part of his work Bourdieu's debts to Marxist thought are apparent: his concept of practice has direct parallels

[148]Bourdieu and Passeron, *The Inheritors*, p. 90.

[149]Bourdieu and Wacquant, *An Invitation to Reflexive Sociology*, p. 246.

[150]Bourdieu discusses this using the concept of *doxa*—meaning that there is no disjunction between concepts and experience of social reality; the objective structures and the internalized structures coincide. See especially Pierre Bourdieu, *The Logic of Practice* (Cambridge: Polity, 1990).

[151]Bourdieu and Wacquant, *An Invitation to Reflexive Sociology*, p. 69.

with the concept of praxis.[152] However, he also discusses explicitly the work of ethnomethodologists (see Chapter 6), whose ideas about the problematic nature of everyday experience have obvious parallels with Bourdieu's position. Bourdieu sees the work of Garfinkel and other ethnomethodologists as interesting, but he stresses an essential difference between himself and them. They deal with universal principles, he argues; but his theory insists that the particular ways in which things are taken for granted are a function of the particular field of action. Underlying each case are institutions and structured power relations, of which ethnomethodology loses sight.

Summary.   Bourdieu's emphasis on the role of cultural capital may seem exaggerated to readers outside France. However, the French education system is highly centralized and competitive. Almost all members of the elite went not to an ordinary university but to one of the Grande Écoles just discussed—small, selective, autonomous institutions specializing in, for example, engineering or preparation for a government career. For a period in the late 1980s both the French prime minister and the leader of the parliamentary opposition were graduates of the same class of the same selective institution. This is not something that would surprise anyone in France. The cultural processes that Bourdieu emphasizes thus are likely to be more important and more visible in France than in, for example, the United States, with its more open education system. They may nonetheless exist in the United States as well.

Even in France, however, empirical evidence suggests that Bourdieu's argument may be overstated. His own data show that even in the arts faculties, class reproduction is only partial: many students are, in fact, from relatively less privileged homes. In addition, analysis of French survey data by Robinson and Garnier[153] suggests that education has not, in fact, become more important over time in "reproducing" ownership of businesses. Parents who are (large or small) business owners do not "convert" their capital into educational capital as a way of securing their children's position. Conversely, education *can* strongly assist sons of nonsupervisory workers to move up to supervisory positions. The authors also note how different women's life paths are from men's and conclude that if women perpetuate their class position, it is not generally through education.[154] Overall, it would

---

[152]See p. 79. See also the work of Habermas, Chapter 4.

[153]Robert V. Robinson and Maurice A. Garnier, "Class Reproduction Among Men and Women in France: Reproduction Theory on Its Own Ground," *American Journal of Sociology* 91, no. 2 (1985): 250–80.

[154]This may be a misleading conclusion. The survey looked at women's current occupations and related them to their family of origin. However, in France, as elsewhere, women's jobs are often of lower status than either their education or their husband's job would suggest. Conversely, women still acquire status through their husbands, and education may be crucial as a way of meeting a potential husband or becoming a "suitable" wife for a high-status male.

seem, Bourdieu overstates his case for class reproduction, while being quite correct about the independent influence that educational institutions can wield.

Conclusion

Of all contemporary sociological theories, those combining a conflict perspective with social critique are the most clearly associated with arguments current outside academic life, especially among the politically involved. The political importance of these theorists is consequently greater than that of any other group we describe. This is especially evident outside the United States, but it is also true within it, as we can see from the following excerpt from the Port Huron Statement of Students for a Democratic Society, a central document of the student New Left of the 1960s. We find echoes of Marx's economic analysis, Mills's condemnation of the power elite, critical theory's view that society is administered and manipulated, and the concern of all these theories with people's alienation in this statement:

> We regard *men* as infinitely precious and possessed of unfulfilled capacities for reason, freedom, and love. . . . We oppose the depersonalization that reduces human beings to the status of things. . . . We oppose, too, the doctrine of human incompetence because it rests essentially on the modern fact that men have been "competently" manipulated into incompetence. . . .
>
> The American political system . . . frustrates democracy by confusing the individual citizen . . . and consolidating the irresponsible power of military and business interests.
>
> We should replace power rooted in possession, privilege or circumstance by power and uniqueness rooted in love, reflectiveness, reason and creativity. As a *social system* we seek the establishment of a democracy of individual participation. . . . The economic sphere would have [among its] principles:
>
> that work should involve incentives worthier than money or survival . . .
>
> that the economic experience is so personally decisive that the individual must share in its full determination.
>
> Major social institutions should be generally organized with the well-being and dignity of men as the essential measure of success.[155]

As we shall see in the next section, analytic conflict theory shares many of the general orientations of the critical conflict perspectives. The belief in an ideal society and the combination of analysis and moral outrage that the Port Huron Statement embodies are, however, as foreign to it as they are central to the work of the critical theorists we have just discussed.

---

[155]Students for a Democratic Society, *The Port Huron Statement* (Chicago: SDS, 1969). The Port Huron Statement, as will be obvious to the reader from its wording, predates the growth of the feminist movement.

PART TWO

Conflict Theory and Analytic Sociology:
The Legacy of Max Weber

Ralf Dahrendorf, Lewis Coser, and Randall Collins, the theorists discussed in this section, can be grouped as analytic conflict theorists because they share the belief that a conflict perspective is central to the development of an objective, or scientific, sociology. However, they differ from critical theorists in three important respects. First, whereas critical theorists see social science as intrinsically a part of political action and deny that fact and value can or should be separated, analytic theorists consider such a separation to be essential. They argue that it may be difficult or impossible for analysts, particularly those concerned with human society, to frame their hypotheses independently of their own opinions and concerns. Nonetheless, those hypotheses have implications that can be observed and tested objectively with empirical measures. It follows that ideas are not automatically distortions of reality just because they are also the products of particular social circumstances or tend to favor the interests of a particular social group.

Second, analytic conflict theorists do not analyze all societies as stratified along a single dimension, with a ruling group opposed to the masses. Analytic theorists would agree that some societies are of this type. Yet they believe that many others have far more complex power and status distributions and interlocking patterns of stratification that do not line up neatly. This is true, they believe, because society has many different sources of power and position, and one particular set of institutions, such as that based on property, is not always paramount.

Third, the analytic theorists do not contrast the present with a rational or conflict-free ideal for the simple reason that they do not believe in one. On the contrary, they emphasize that conflict and its roots are permanent and that conflicts of interest are inevitable.

In all these respects, modern analytic theorists share Max Weber's approach, just as Marx was the primary influence on the critical approach. Weber believed in the vital importance of objective social science. As we saw earlier, he developed a typology of "class, status, and party" as important influences on people's lives, as opposed to Marx's emphasis on property classes alone. Furthermore, Weber considered the conflicts these generate as permanent features of human society, and he saw modern society tending not toward a communist utopia but toward a bureaucratic society inimical to human freedom. This is not to say, however, that either he or the analytic conflict theorists he influenced are indifferent to political action. In general, conflict theory appeals to sociologists who hold strong political views, and a number of modern analytic theorists have been very involved in politics and social policy, often in direct opposition to the ideas of critical and Marxist theory.

RALF DAHRENDORF

Ralf Dahrendorf (b. 1929) has for many years been widely known and respected in both Europe and North America. As a teenager in Nazi Germany he was sent to a concentration camp for his membership in a high school group opposing the state, and he has continued to be deeply involved in political affairs. He has been a Free Democratic member of the Baden-Württemberg Landtag (Regional Parliament) and the West German Bundestag (Parliament). As a member of the Commission of the European Communities he has been responsible for external relations and for education, science, and research.

Dahrendorf has worked as an academic in Germany, Great Britain, and the United States. From 1974 to 1984 he was Director of the London School of Economics, one of the most prestigious British institutions of higher education. In 1984 he returned to Germany for a while as professor of sociology at the University of Constance. He then became Warden of St. Anthony's College, Oxford University, and now sits in the British House of Lords (the upper house of Parliament) as a life peer, Lord Dahrendorf.[156]

Dahrendorf's work on conflict reveals two major concerns. The first is with what he himself describes as "theories of society"[157]—that is, with setting out the general principles of social explanation. Here Dahrendorf stresses the primacy of power and the consequent inevitability of conflict. Like Marx, his second concern is with the determinants of active conflict—the ways social institutions systematically generate groups with conflicting interests and the circumstances in which such groups will become organized and active.

Power, Conflict, and Social Explanation

There is, Dahrendorf argues, an inherent tendency to conflict in society. Those groups with power will pursue their interests, and those without power will pursue theirs. The interests of the two are necessarily different. Sooner or later, he argues—and in some systems the powerful may be very thoroughly entrenched—the balance between power and opposition shifts, and society changes. Thus conflict is "the great creative force of human history."[158]

---

[156]Although, at the time of writing, many members of the House of Lords sit there by birth (because they have inherited peerages), others—including most of the most active members—hold "life peerages" that cannot be passed on to their children. Ex–prime ministers (including Mrs. Thatcher) generally become life peers and sit in the House of Lords; but most life peers are eminent individuals from nonpolitical walks of life.

[157]Dahrendorf, *Essays*, pp. vi–viii.

[158]Ralf Dahrendorf, *Conflict and Contract: Industrial Relations and the Political Community in Times of Crisis*, the Second Leverhulme Memorial Lecture (Liverpool: Liverpool University Press, 1975), p. 17.

Power.   According to Dahrendorf's theory of society, the distribution of power is the crucial determinant of social structure. His definition of power is Weber's: "the probability that one actor within a social relationship will be in a position to carry out his own will despite resistance, regardless of the basis on which this probability rests."[159] In this view the essence of power is the control of sanctions, which enables those who possess power to give orders and obtain what they want from the powerless. However, people dislike submission. Therefore, Dahrendorf argues, there is inevitably a conflict of interest and an impetus for the powerless to conflict with the powerful, the former in pursuit of power, the latter in defense of it. Power is a "lasting source of friction."[160]

This essentially coercive view of power, which is common to most conflict theorists, is very different from that of functionalism.[161] As we have seen, Parsons believes that power is embodied in political institutions that solve the "functional imperative" of goal attainment.[162] The ability power bestows to get what one wants at others' expense he regards as a secondary, derived phenomenon. Dahrendorf's view is the opposite. Power is necessary if large organizations are to achieve their goals; and at times, such as in a defensive war, the powerful may clearly carry out the common aims of a group. However, what Parsons considers the secondary aspect of power, Dahrendorf considers primary: the powerful are not granted power by the community to carry out some common will, but rather grasp and use that power for their own ends.

Dahrendorf does not see the struggle for power as the sum of social life, however. Weber's (and Dahrendorf's) definition of power includes actors within a social relationship—that is, in situations where other people's actions matter. But people are also at times free to do what they like without other people mattering at all. In his lectures on the current political situation in the West, Dahrendorf has discussed the factors that endow societies with more or less liberty in this sense—with what has been called "negative freedom."[163] In America, for example, you are at liberty to move from

---

[159]Ralf Dahrendorf, *Class and Class Conflict in Industrial Society* (Stanford, Calif.: Stanford University Press, 1959), p. 166; quotation from Max Weber, *The Theory of Social and Economic Organization*, trans. A. M. Henderson and Talcott Parsons (New York: The Free Press, 1964).

[160]Dahrendorf, *Essays*, p. 138.

[161]This view also differs from that of rational choice theory, which is that power is rooted in the exchange of scarce and valuable resources.

[162]See Chapter 2.

[163]Ralf Dahrendorf, *The New Liberty* (London: Routledge and Kegan Paul, 1975). Power and liberty are not, of course, entirely distinct concepts. Some of the most interesting discussions of the two concepts are Brian Barry, ed., *Power and Political Theory: Some European Perspectives* (New York: Wiley, 1976); Stephen Lukes, *Power: A Radical View* (London: Macmillan, 1974); Isaiah Berlin, *Four Essays on Liberty* (London: Oxford University Press, 1969); Friedrich von Hayek, *The Constitution of Liberty* (Chicago: Henry Regnery Company, 1972); John Rawls, *A Theory of Justice* (Oxford: Oxford University Press, 1972).

one city to another without anyone's permission. In China you are not, and whether you get the requisite permission and papers largely depends on your own power and influence.

Norms.   Like other conflict theorists, Dahrendorf argues that societal norms do not define or emerge from social consensus. Conflict theory, he argues, perceives, unlike functionalism, that norms "are established and maintained . . . by power, and their substance may well be explained in terms of interests of the powerful."[164] This may be seen from the fact that norms are backed by sanctions. Vivid examples of what Dahrendorf means can be found in China, where dissidents still risk prison or labor camp, or in the pre–civil rights South, where so-called uppity blacks or nonconforming whites could lose their livelihoods or even their lives. In turn, sanctions involve the control and use of power, particularly the power of law and punishment.[165] "In the last analysis, established norms are nothing but ruling norms," he suggests.[166]

Social Stratification.   Dahrendorf clearly distinguishes between two facts: first, that positions and jobs are different and demand different skills; and second, that different jobs are treated as superior or inferior to one another. There are both "*social differentiation* of positions . . . and *social stratification* based on reputation and wealth and expressed in a rank order of social status."[167] Social stratification is what makes college presidents more generally respected than bus drivers and lies behind claims that teachers "ought" to be paid more than maintenance workers.

Stratification, Dahrendorf argues, is caused by norms, which categorize some things as desirable and other as not. In every group, norms defining how people should behave entail discrimination against those who do not comply. During the Vietnam War, for example, those who supported the war were ostracized on some campuses, those who opposed it on others. In some adolescent groups drug use and criminal behavior may be the norm, while in others drug use is viewed as a sign of personal weakness. Moreover, every society has *general* norms that define certain characteristics as good (such as being an aristocrat or having more education than average) and that therefore entail discrimination against those who do not or cannot conform. These norms, Dahrendorf argues, are the basis of social stratification, and they are themselves derived from and upheld by power. Once again, therefore, power is the central concept.

---

[164]Dahrendorf, *Essays*, p. 140.
[165]Dahrendorf, *Essays*, p. 141.
[166]Dahrendorf, *Essays*, p. 174.
[167]Dahrendorf, *Essays*, p. 154.

This is a very different explanation from that of functionalists, who argue that social stratification derives from society's need to attract talented people into important positions. The two may not be as totally irreconcilable as Dahrendorf implies, however. Dahrendorf does not explain how a group becomes powerful in the first place, but this will surely often depend, at least in part, on its offering skills and a type of social order that people value. Not all successful ruling groups are military invaders! It is precisely the existence of a relationship between power and general social values that functionalism addresses. Similarly, economics' statement that income differentials are a result of the market value of skills[168] has given rise to theories of stratification linking success with provision of scarce services.[169] However, a group that gains power in this way will almost certainly strive to maintain and take advantage of its position, convince everyone of its legitimacy and importance, and prevent competition from groups with different potential power bases—and Dahrendorf's approach is far better suited than functionalism's to analyzing this process.

The Determinants of Conflict: A Theory of Conflict Groups

In his best-known work, *Class and Class Conflict in Industrial Society*, Dahrendorf addresses the question of when inequalities and conflicting interests will actually produce conflicts. His central argument is that social conflicts will take place, systematically, among groups that differ in the authority they enjoy over others. By *authority*, Dahrendorf (again following Weber) means the sort of power that is attached to a social role or position, that is legitimate in the sense of being defined and delimited by social norms, and that is backed by sanctions up to (and no further than) these limits. A university, for example, has the authority to charge you for your courses, board, and lodging, but not to take all your money. A mugger has the power to do just that—but no authority at all to do so.

Dahrendorf's position is that the stable and recurrent patterns of institutional authority systematically give rise to social conflict between those who have some degree of authority and those who have none. In a departure from conventional economic usage, Dahrendorf labels these groups *classes*. He writes that "the term 'class' signifies conflict groups that are generated by the differential distribution of authority in imperatively coordinated associations"[170]—that is, *organizations in which orders are given and taken.*

---

[168]A good discussion of differing theories of pay inequalities can be found in Henry Phelps Brown, *The Inequality of Pay* (Oxford: Oxford University Press, 1977). See also the review by H. A. Turner, *Times Higher Education Supplement*, January 6, 1978. Janet Chafetz synthesizes alternative theories in her analysis of gender-linked pay inequalities. See this chapter's section on stratification by gender, p. 142.

[169]We shall meet this approach when we discuss rational choice theory.

[170]Dahrendorf, *Class and Class Conflict*, p. 204.

Dahrendorf's theory thus implies that authority is dichotomous: you have it or you do not, and your interests are formed accordingly. Critics have suggested that whether you have more or less authority may be equally important and thus that conflict may form around other groupings. But Dahrendorf affirms, with Marx, that conflict involves only two sides. On the other hand, all classes do not engage in active conflicts all the time. Dahrendorf therefore attempts to explain when people will actually mobilize.[171]

The Mobilization of Classes.   The *structural* requirements for people to form active interest groups are "technical," "political," and "social."[172] *Technically*, Dahrendorf argues, a group requires a founder and a charter or ideology to become active. *Politically*, the more liberal the state, the more likely is the mobilization for active conflict; the more totalitarian the state, the less likely. Finally, three *social* factors are important. Group formation is more likely first, if potential members are fairly well concentrated geographically; second, if they can communicate easily (as modern communications technology makes it easier for them to do); and third, if people who stand in the same relation to authority are recruited in similar ways and come, for example, from the same types of families or educational organizations.

The most important *psychological* requirements are, of course, that individuals identify with the interests associated with their position and that these interests seem important and real to them. Dahrendorf disagrees with Marx's argument that people's class positions (in either the property or the authority sense) determine the whole of their social life and behavior, but he does believe class interests will be more real to people who also share a culture. He also suggests that people are less likely to identify with their class's interests and to mobilize if they belong to many associations.[173] Finally, the greater people's personal chances of leaving their class—in other words, the greater the degree of "intragenerational mobility"[174]—the less likely they are to identify actively with it.

Dahrendorf's structural arguments are fairly convincing, although he pays surprisingly little attention to force. He tends to emphasize that if conflict is not to become explosive, there must be some degree of mobility and freedom to express opposition. But as tyrannies throughout history have shown, a sufficient degree of force can suppress conflict very effectively.

Dahrendorf's discussion of the psychological requirements for class action is less satisfactory. Especially in preindustrial societies, the poor have often shared a culture, led lives confined to the immediate community, had few opportunities for advancement, and yet accepted the existing order of

[171]Dahrendorf, *Class and Class Conflict*, pp. 184–93.
[172]Dahrendorf, *Class and Class Conflict*, pp. 178–93.
[173]Dahrendorf, *Class and Class Conflict*, p. 191.
[174]Dahrendorf, *Class and Class Conflict*, p. 220.

things almost without question. Thus Dahrendorf fails to explain satisfactorily how attitudes of opposition originate.

Chafetz and Dworkin had similarly mixed success in explaining the rise of women's movements across the world, using Dahrendorf's perspective.[175] The appearance and size of "ameliorative" movements, concerned simply with legal and educational reforms, can be related clearly to the breakdown of geographical barriers within a country and to ease of communication—Dahrendorf's structural requirements. However, especially in the United States, the second wave of women's movements was far more ideological and challenged gender roles directly. Dahrendorf's theories are much less successful in explaining why industrialized countries have been so different in the strength of their second-wave feminist movements.

Recent work by Kelley and Evans looks more directly at the way in which people's perceptions of class are actually shaped, and in doing so the work provides a fuller explanation of the psychological requirements and processes that affect class mobilization. They point out that (contrary to Marx's expectations) people's class positions have not determined the nature of politics and of political parties; "despite the numerical dominance of the working class" there has been no dominance by left-wing parties. A major reason for this is, in their view, "reference group processes . . . (which) make most people think they are middle class."[176] People conceive of their own position by comparing it with those around them, who tend to be similar to themselves. Consequently "most people see themselves as average and unexceptional."[177] Kelley and Evans summarize a mass of evidence showing how, across social groups and across countries, people tend to place themselves near the middle of the class hierarchy, with plenty of people above and below them. Moreover, because their intimate contacts are with family, friends, and so forth, their dominant experience is of consensus rather than class conflict. Such experience is hardly conducive to class mobilization.

The Violence and Intensity of Conflict.   Dahrendorf also discusses at considerable length what affects the intensity and violence of class conflict when it occurs. He defines *violence* as "a matter of the weapons that are chosen" and *intensity* as the "energy expenditure and degree of involvement of conflicting parties."[178]

Dahrendorf argues that one preeminent factor affects the degree of violence. This is how far conflict is institutionalized, with mutually accepted "rules of the game": "those who have agreed to carry on their disagreements

---

[175]Janet Saltzman Chafetz and Anthony Gary Dworkin, *Female Revolt: Women's Movements in World and Historical Perspective* (Totowa, N.J.: Rowman and Allanheld, 1986).

[176]Jonathan Kelley and M. D. R. Evans, "Class and Class Conflict in Six Western Nations," *American Sociological Review* 60 (April 1995): 157–178.

[177]Kelly and Evans, "Class and Class Conflict," p. 158.

[178]Dahrendorf, *Class and Class Conflict*, pp. 211–12.

by means of discussion do not usually engage in physical violence."[179] For example, the days of extreme violence in strike breaking and picketing in America predate the general acceptance of unions.

Dahrendorf also identifies three important factors influencing the intensity of a conflict. Of these, the first (which he also considers to be the most important)[180] is the degree to which those who are in positions of subjection in one association are in the same position in their other associations. The second and parallel factor is the degree to which authority in an organization is held by people who are also "on top" in other respects—in Dahrendorf's terms whether positions are "pluralist" or "superimposed." Thus if the managers of firms are also the owners and if they also use their wealth and position to control politics, one can expect particularly intense industrial conflicts.

Dahrendorf's third argument is that the greater the mobility between positions, the less intense the conflict will be. This is true not only when individuals themselves can move, but also when their children are mobile. This is partly because mobility makes it less likely that a class will have a common culture and partly because people are less inclined to attack a class their children may one day join. On the other hand, if there is little or no mobility, the struggle becomes more intense.

Conflict in Industry.   During the last hundred years there have been increasing numbers of "joint stock" companies, in which ownership by shareholders is divorced from management control. As we have seen, modern Marxist sociologists generally argue that the change is not very important because the firms still represent and are run in the interests of the owners. Other writers, such as Burnham,[181] believe that it signifies a far-reaching change in social structure and the roots of power.

Dahrendorf argues that his approach demonstrates both what has really changed and what has not. He suggests that because nineteenth-century managers and owners were generally the same people, Marx mistakenly ascribed to property differences a conflict that actually centered on authority, although it was intensified by the superimposition of industrial authority, wealth, and political influence.[182] Today, he continues, industrial conflict will be less intense both because ownership and control are separate and because of industry's "institutional isolation"[183] (which means that one's position in industry has less to do with the rest of one's life than before). At the same time, the split in authority and the conflicts of interest it generates

---

[179]Dahrendorf, *Class and Class Conflict*, p. 228.

[180]Dahrendorf, *Class and Class Conflict*, p. 214, p. 317.

[181]James Burnham, *The Managerial Revolution* (London: Putnam, 1942).

[182]Dahrendorf, *Class and Class Conflict*, p. 136.

[183]Dahrendorf, *Class and Class Conflict*, p. 267.

remain. Arguments that the divide between workers and management has blurred are quite mistaken.

A study with direct relevance to Dahrendorf's argument is *The Affluent Worker in the Class Structure*.[184] This intensive survey of affluent British industrial workers was largely aimed at determining whether there had been a breakdown of the old social division between the working and the middle classes. The results cast doubt on the degree to which industry is, as Dahrendorf suggests, "institutionally isolated." The workers' family-centered social life, for example, remained quite separate from that of white-collar families. However, although union organization was stronger in the plants studied than in many much less wealthy areas, these workers were only rarely committed to the union movement as a national working-class force; instead they were extremely involved in union affairs at the level of the workplace.[185] Only 8 percent attended union branch meetings often enough to vote regularly in branch elections, but 83 percent voted regularly for their shop stewards. In other words, they were closely involved in union organization at the level where they were given orders directly and where they grouped together, to face and face down the managers who gave them, but not in questions of union and economic policy or class politics at the national level.

Conflict and the State.   Dahrendorf argues that in the state, as in industry, the crucial lines of conflict are between those who give and those who receive orders. The state is the most powerful association in society, and the "ruling class" is, in a sense, the elite group that holds the positions at the top of the state hierarchy. But the ruling class is not composed solely of this group. The bureaucracy, too, belongs to a chain of command, and this command of authority makes it part of the ruling class even though it does not define the concerns and objectives of a bureaucratic state. Dahrendorf's argument helps explain the enormous stability of such bureaucratic states as Byzantium and the Egypt of the Pharaohs. The larger the authority-bearing class, the larger the group that will marshal against any threat to it from an organized conflict group of subordinates.[186]

Dahrendorf's argument also implies that the state and bureaucracy are together a separate institution, not simply a reflection of other social groupings, and that other powerful social groups will necessarily oppose the state's authority and try to influence it and restrict its control over them. Thus, in Washington, from the 1970s onward a building boom transformed

---

[184]John H. Goldthorpe, David Lockwood, Frank Bechhofer, and Jennifer Platt, *The Affluent Worker in the Class Structure* (Cambridge: Cambridge University Press, 1969).

[185]Goldthorpe et al., *The Affluent Worker,* pp. 168–69.

[186]It also enabled one of the authors to predict correctly during the 1970s power struggles in China that the bureaucrats, who favored stability and industrialization, would defeat the radicals, who favored continuous revolution, Red Guard iconoclasm, and extreme egalitarianism.

the downtown area. The new offices house thousands of registered lobbyists, as well as law firms that are expanding in response to more and more regulatory legislation. In Dahrendorf's own recent analyses of British politics[187] he argues that "clearly there is today a conflict between government and industry"[188] in which the trade unions are the most visible protagonists but that also involves the giant companies.

A number of modern commentators echo Dahrendorf when they write that growing government activity will have consequences for the range and intensity of political conflict. For example, Christopher DeMuth, a faculty member at Harvard's Kennedy School of Government who formerly worked for Conrail, discussed in the *Wall Street Journal* the behavior of the huge Greyhound bus company. He described how Greyhound lobbied vigorously against the federal subsidies given to passenger trains, with which the buses must compete, while it attempted with equal vigor to stop the Interstate Commerce Commission from allowing new bus companies to start competing with Greyhound and tried to prevent any general deregulation of bus transport. DeMuth argues, "There is no reason to expect Greyhound or any other company to compete in the economic marketplace while abstaining from the political marketplace. . . . [When the government involvement] becomes . . . sufficiently large, it alters fundamentally the nature of competition in the private part [of the economy]—increasing the relative importance of political as opposed to economic competition."[189]

Summary

Dahrendorf provides an illuminating account of the close and permanent relationship between power, or authority, and conflict. He also presents a concrete theory of conflict group formation, which provides a good starting point for explaining people's objectives and identifying potential confrontations. He describes a number of the important factors that either create mobilized conflict groups and intense conflicts or, correspondingly, tend to reduce social conflict. However, his theory of conflict group mobilization fails to explain what makes people aware of themselves as a group with common interests and common grievances. This crucial shift from what Marx characterizes as a class "in itself" to a class "for itself" occupies most conflict theorists,[190] and it is also addressed by the rational choice perspective.[191] No one

---

[187]Dahrendorf, *The New Liberty* and *Conflict and Contract*.

[188]Dahrendorf, *Conflict and Contract*, p. 14.

[189]Christopher C. DeMuth, "Tubthumping in the Political Marketplace," *The Wall Street Journal* (1977). See also Chapter 7.

[190]See p. 85 and p. 130 (Coser's analysis). See also Durkheim on the role of religion and ritual in creating group identification.

[191]See pp. 336–37.

theorist provides a fully satisfactory answer, probably because both micro and macro psychological and sociological variables are involved.

LEWIS COSER

Like many other conflict theorists, Lewis Coser (b. 1913) combines a distinguished academic career with a strong interest and involvement in social policy and politics. He was born in Berlin into a Jewish family of bankers, against whom he reacted strongly. Because of his involvement with the socialist student movement, he left Germany when Hitler came to power. There followed some miserable years in Paris, where, without a work permit, Coser survived at just above starvation level. However, enrollment at the Sorbonne[192] was free, and Coser studied comparative literature. He proposed a dissertation topic comparing nineteenth-century French, English, and German novels in terms of their countries' different social structures. "This is sociology, not comparative literature," a horrified professor exclaimed. So, Coser explains, "I switched to sociology and have been stuck with it ever since."[193]

On the outbreak of war, Coser was interned as an enemy alien.[194] Aided by a local socialist mayor, he managed to get a visa as a political refugee, and reached New York via Spain and Portugal.[195] After the war he taught at the University of Chicago for a while, before earning a Ph.D. at Columbia. He spent nearly twenty years at Brandeis University, and from 1968 to 1988 he was Distinguished Professor of Sociology at the State University of New York (SUNY) at Stony Brook. Since retirement in 1988 he has been Professor Emeritus of Sociology at SUNY at Stony Brook and Adjunct Professor of Sociology at Boston College.

Coser remains a socialist, though no longer a Marxist. His writings have always reflected his concern with politics and the links between ideas and the nature of society. With Irving Howe he founded *Dissent* "during the darkest years of the McCarthy nightmare, to dissent from the intolerance and cowardice of so many intellectual spokespersons that marked this dismal episode."[196] Coser has also contributed frequently to other serious nonspe-

---

[192]University of Paris.

[193]Lewis A. Coser, "Notes on a Double Career," in Matilda White Riley, ed., *Sociological Lives*, Vol. 2: *Social Change and the Life Course*, American Sociological Association Presidential Series (Newbury Park, Calif.: Sage, 1988).

[194]Fortunately the camp was in the Vichy zone, which was run by a collaborationist French regime after the defeat of France by Germany, rather than in the part of France occupied directly by the Germans.

[195]On arrival he visited the International Relief Committee. The young woman handling his case, Rose Laub, herself a refugee, was to become his wife and fellow sociologist.

[196]Coser, "Notes on a Double Career," p. 69.

cialist journals, such as *Partisan Review* and *Commentary*, and is coauthor of a history of the American Communist Party dedicated to Milovan Djilas.[197]

Some of Coser's more recent work is about "greedy institutions" that demand total involvement from their members. Coser says that in the face of recent "indiscriminate" condemnations of the "differentiated, segmented and 'alienated' character of modern life,"[198] he felt bound to point out the threat to human freedom inherent in total involvement. "I wish it to be clearly understood," he writes, "that I consider it essential that an open society be preserved above all."[199]

Of the modern theorists discussed in this chapter, Coser is the closest to Simmel. He is the most concerned with the "web of conflict," or the cross-cutting allegiances that can both bind a society together and generate struggles and confrontations. Indeed, Coser's major book on conflict theory, *The Functions of Social Conflict*,[200] is an exposition and development of Simmel's own rather fragmented insights. Coser emphasizes that conflict, although important, is only one side of social life and no more "fundamental" than consensus.[202]

Coser's contributions to conflict theory are also distinctive in two other respects. First, he discusses social conflict as a result of factors other than opposing group interests. Second, he is concerned with the *consequences* of conflict. As we have seen, Dahrendorf's major concern is with the origins of conflict, which, he argues, then creates social change. Coser has less to say about the institutional roots of conflict, but he distinguishes among its different possible consequences, which include greater social stability as well as change. His discussion of the conditions under which conflict is likely to be divisive or cohesive adds considerably to Dahrendorf's analysis of conflict's characteristics.

The Origins and Functions of Social Conflict

In his discussion of the origins of conflict, Coser pays far more attention than do most conflict theorists to the role played by people's emotions.[202] He agrees with Simmel that there are aggressive or hostile impulses in people, and he

---

[197]Irving Howe and Lewis Coser with the assistance of Julius Jacobson, *The American Communist Party: A Critical History 1919–1957* (Boston: Beacon Press, 1957). See earlier in this chapter for a description of Djilas's critical analysis of Communist societies.

[198]Lewis Coser, *Greedy Institutions: Patterns of Undivided Commitments* (New York: The Free Press, 1974), p. 17.

[199]Coser, *Greedy Institutions*, p. 18.

[200]Coser, *The Functions of Social Conflict* (New York: The Free Press, 1956).

[201]Lewis Coser, *Continuities in the Study of Social Conflict* (New York: The Free Press, 1967), p. 139.

[202]The arguments of *The Functions of Social Conflict* are presented in the form of sixteen separate propositions. Coser's discussion of the origins of conflict can be found under propositions 3, 4, 5, and 8.

emphasizes that in close and intimate relationships both love and hatred are present. Close proximity, he points out, brings ample opportunities for resentment to develop; hence, conflict and disagreement are integral parts of people's relationships, not necessarily signs of instability and breakup.

At the same time, Coser argues, the nature of hostility and conflict varies for sociological reasons. A good example of what Coser means is the differences among countries in how much children fight with their parents. This is the sort of close relationship in which some resentments are inevitable; but these are affected by whether the children have financial independence; whether the steps by which children assume well-defined adult roles are clearly laid down by the society; and whether other family members provide practical and emotional support outside the nuclear family. Coser's work addresses the way such structural factors interact with people's underlying emotions.

Coser argues that conflict often leads to change.[203] For example, it can stimulate innovation[204] or, especially in war, increase centralization.[205] For the most part, however, Coser concentrates on conflict's role in maintaining group cohesion. This is, of course, the subject that most concerns functionalists. However, Coser is a functionalist only in the sense of sharing this interest. He does not imply that it is necessarily desirable for a group to survive and remain cohesive or that conflict occurs *because* it may be functional for the group. He sees cohesion as only one of conflict's possible results.

In this context Coser distinguishes between conflicts that are external and conflicts that are internal to a group. Both types, he argues, can define a group, establish its identity, and maintain its stability and increase its cohesion.

External Conflict.   In his most unqualified statement about the relationship between conflict and cohesion, Coser argues that external conflict is essential in establishing a group's identity. In this he is following not only Simmel but also Marx, who felt that only conflict makes a class self-aware. Coser states, with Simmel, that "conflict sets boundaries between groups within a social system by strengthening group consciousness and awareness of separateness, thus establishing the identity of groups within the system."[206] However, he also distinguished expressly between hostile sentiments and actual conflict,[207] and we would suggest that it is hostile sentiments, rather

---

[203]See especially Coser, *The Functions of Social Conflict*, propositions 9, 13, 15, and 16.

[204]Coser suggests that conflict between employers and unions over wages was one of the forces encouraging innovation because it gave employers a strong incentive to develop the labor-saving technology that increased the economy's productivity. Lewis Coser, "Social Conflict and the Theory of Social Change," *British Journal of Sociology* VIII, no. 3 (1953); reprinted in Coser, *Continuities in the Study of Social Conflict*, pp. 17–35.

[205]Coser, *The Functions of Social Conflict*, pp. 89–95.

[206]Coser, *The Functions of Social Conflict*, p. 34.

[207]Coser, *The Functions of Social Conflict*, p. 37.

than actual conflict, that are essential to group formation. A religious group or utopian agricultural settlement of the type common in American history may coexist with other parts of society without overt conflict.

Coser also argues that external conflict can often strengthen a group. It makes group members conscious of their identity by introducing a strong negative reference group to which they contrast themselves; it also increases their participation.[208] Nonetheless, the process is not inevitable. If internal cohesion before the outbreak of conflict is very low, the conflict may simply hasten disintegration. Coser contrasts the disruptive effects of the Second World War on French society with its unifying effect in Britain.[209] A less dramatic but similar example is America during the Vietnam War as compared to the Second World War. However, because Coser offers no way of telling in advance which development is likely, his arguments here are not very useful in explaining actual conflicts.

Internal Conflict.   Coser follows Durkheim, Mead, and even Marx in arguing that a group's opposition to and conflict with "deviants" makes apparent to group members what they ought to do.[210] In this sense internal conflict is central to defining a group's identity, which is embodied in norms that define correct behavior.

Coser also argues that internal conflict can increase a group's survival, cohesion, and stability. He again follows Simmel when he argues that internal conflict is a crucial safety valve under "conditions of stress . . . preventing group dissolution through the withdrawal of hostile participants."[211] If opposition to one's associates were not possible, people would, in Simmel's words, "feel pushed to take desperate steps . . . opposition gives us inner satisfaction, distraction, relief."[212] Indeed this is one of the few occasions when Coser falls into the trap of implying that because something is functional it will automatically happen, and that because safety valves are important all societies will provide them.[213]

Coser's argument here seems to confuse a group's survival or stability with its cohesion. He implies that whatever promotes survival also promotes cohesion. However, if it uses brute force and terror to support imbalances of

[208]Coser, *The Functions of Social Conflict*, p. 90.

[209]Coser, *The Functions of Social Conflict*, p. 93.

[210]Lewis Coser, "Some Functions of Deviant Behavior and Normative Flexibility," *American Journal of Sociology* LXVIII, no. 2 (1962); reprinted in *Continuities in the Study of Social Conflict*, pp. 111-33.

[211]Coser, *The Functions of Social Conflict*, p. 39. Coser also argues that violent conflicts, such as ghetto riots, serve the function of calling attention to neglected conditions. However, social stability would surely be better served if the discontented accepted their position. See *Continuities in the Study of Social Conflict*, pp. 93–110.

[212]Georg Simmel, *Conflict*, trans. Kurt H. Wolff (Glencoe, Ill.: The Free Press, 1955). Quoted in Coser, *The Functions of Social Conflict*, p. 39.

[213]Coser, *The Functions of Social Conflict*, p. 48.

power, a society can survive and even remain stable in the face of a great deal of internal hostility: witness Haiti, Cuba, Stalin's Russia, or Saddam Hussein's Iraq. Although conflict *may* help maintain a society by providing a safety valve, this pattern is hardly a necessary or universal one. On the other hand, Coser is probably correct in emphasizing the close links between internal conflict and group *cohesion*. In rigid social structures with no channels for expressing hostility, when conflict occurs it is disruptive and violent.

Finally, Coser argues that internal conflict can be important because "stability within a loosely structured society . . . can be viewed as partly a product of the continuous incidence of various conflicts crisscrossing it."[214] When people belong to many different groups, each of which pursues its own interests and is consequently involved in its own conflicts, they are less likely to devote all their energies to a single conflict that could break the society apart. Thus, Coser suggests, "one reason for the relative absence of 'class struggle' in this country is the fact that the American worker, far from restricting his allegiance to class-conflict groupings and associations, is a member of a number of associations and groupings . . . [and] the lines of conflict between all these groups do not converge."[215]

In this context Coser admires Max Gluckman's work on the importance of crosscutting conflicts in African tribes. Gluckman notes that "all over the world there are societies which have no governmental institutions. . . . Yet these societies have well-established and well-known codes of morals and law. . . . We know that some of them have existed over long periods with some kind of internal law and order, and have successfully defended themselves against attacks by others."[216]

These "feuding" societies rely on private vengeance instead of government. The process does not tear them apart, Gluckman argues, because they "are so organized into a series of groups and relationships that people who are friends on one basis are enemies on another. [For example,] a man needs help in herding his cattle: therefore he must be friends with neighbors with whom he may well quarrel over other matters. . . . And through his wife he strikes up alliances with relatives-in-law which are inimical to a whole-hearted one-sided attachment to his own brothers and fellow-members of his clan. . . . A man's blood-kin are not always his neighbors; the ties of kinship and locality conflict. . . . These allegiances . . . create conflicts which inhibit the spread of dispute and fighting."[217]

[214]Coser, *The Functions of Social Conflict*, p. 77.

[215]Coser, *The Functions of Social Conflict*, p. 77.

[216]Max Gluckman, *Custom and Conflict in Africa* (Oxford: Basil Blackwell, 1933), pp. 2–3.

[217]Gluckman, *Custom and Conflict in Africa*, pp. 4, 17–18. A situation of this type may not be stable. Marc Bloch suggests that the inability of people in medieval Europe to obtain reliable protection through kinship relations was important in creating the feudal system, under which the lords provide such protection. Differences in military technology and the inability of ordinary people to combat mounted swordsmen probably help explain the different outcomes in Europe and Africa. See Marc Bloch, *Feudal Society*, trans. L. A. Manyon (Chicago: University of Chicago Press, 1962).

Divisive Social Conflict

In discussing conflict's role in defining a group and maintaining its cohesion, Coser makes the proviso that internal conflict has this role only if it is not about basic values and principles. This, in turn, depends on the rigidity of a society and, once again, the degree to which its members are interdependent.

Coser argues, first, that an internal conflict is more likely to involve basic principles (and so be socially divisive) in a rigid society that allows little "expression of antagonistic claims."[218] We have already noted Coser's belief that some conflict is functional because it serves as a safety valve, without which social hostility would eventually erupt violently. Here he suggests that when conflict emerges after having been suppressed for a long time, it will also split the group around basic issues and values.

Second, Coser returns to the theme of crosscutting allegiances and argues that "interdependence checks basic cleavages."[219] Interdependence therefore makes divisive internal conflict much less likely and reduces the likelihood that external conflict will find a noncohesive group. As we have already discussed, the basic reason is that interdependence means that people with common interests in one respect are opposed in another, so that an overriding and polarizing issue is less likely. However, there is also a related psychological process involved. Conflicts are much more intense, Coser argues, when they involve exclusive groups; this further increases the likelihood that divisive conflicts will occur in societies that have nonoverlapping groups.

Such conflicts are intense because it is in close relationships that love and hate coexist. "The coexistence of union and opposition in such relationships makes for the peculiar sharpness of the conflict," Coser argues.[220] The fewer the groups people belong to, the more likely they are to become intensely involved in the ones they have. An intense involvement affects the nature of conflicts both within the group itself and between it and others. Although Coser, a sociologist, makes this point formally, the leaders of sects and the founders of revolutionary parties have always been aware that the more a person's relationships all lie within the group, the more his or her loyalties and energies will be at its disposal.[221]

The most dramatic and horrifying illustration of this principle in recent times occurred at Jonestown in Guyana in 1978. Jim Jones, leader of a community called the People's Temple, moved the community wholesale from California to a jungle site where members' isolation was total. There,

[218]Coser, *The Functions of Social Conflict*, p. 45.

[219]Coser, *The Functions of Social Conflict*, p. 76.

[220]Coser, *The Functions of Social Conflict*, p. 71.

[221]Coser also related violence to these factors. Violent conflict is most likely, he argues, when groups are *both* unorganized *and* involve people with few other relationships—for example, poor urban blacks. *Continuities in the Study of Social Conflict*, pp. 93–110. See also Coser, *Greedy Institutions*.

one November day, 911 adults and children lined up to drink a lethal punch laced with cyanide. Its effects were clear to all but the very first drinkers; yet almost none resisted or attempted to escape from an agonizing death.

Coser and his wife, discussing the Jonestown horror, argue that, like other communes, the People's Temple was "an experiment in the total absorption of personality. Communes have an innate tendency to become . . . *greedy institutions.*"[222] Jones's means were classic ones. Members were isolated from any contact with the outside world. Before leaving the United States they signed away all their possessions, leaving themselves no independence and nowhere else to go. A combination of promiscuity and enforced abstinence forced couples apart; people were submitted to public confessions, humiliations, and "catharsis." Jonestown "succeeded not merely in totally absorbing members within its boundaries but in reducing them to human pulp as well."[223]

The final tragedy was precipitated by U.S. investigators, who posed a threat to Jones but had no quarrel with his followers. It was the nature of the group that made his conflicts theirs and left them incapable of resistance or escape. More recently, similar pressures precipitated the tragedy at Waco, Texas, where seventy-seven followers of cult leader David Koresh died when federal agencies[224] decided to storm their headquarters after a fifty-one-day siege.

Coser's arguments about interdependence follow reasoning similar to James Madison's in *The Federalist Papers.* One of Madison's reasons for urging voters to adopt the American Constitution was that the resulting union of states would be one of considerable size and diversity. This would reduce the likelihood of one faction trampling over its fellow citizens and of oppression of a minority by the majority. He argued,

> The smaller the society, the fewer probably will be the distinct parties and interests composing it; the fewer the distinct parties and interests, the more frequently will a majority be found of the same party; and the smaller the number of individuals composing a majority . . . the more easily will they concert and execute their plans of oppression. Extend the sphere, and you take in a greater variety of parties and interests; you make it less probable that a majority of the whole will have a common motive to invade the rights of other citizens.[225]

Finally, Coser notes that, in addition to social rigidity and people's interdependence, ideas also affect the divisiveness of conflicts. Conflicts will

---

[222]Rose Laub Coser and Lewis Coser, "Jonestown as a Perverse Utopia: A 'Greedy Institution' in the Jungle," *Dissent* (Spring 1979): 159.

[223]Coser and Coser, "Jonestown as a Perverse Utopia," p. 163.

[224]The FBI and Bureau of Alcohol, Tobacco and Firearms.

[225]*The Federalist,* with an introduction by Edward Mead Earle (New York: The Modern Library, n.d.), pp. 60–61.

be more intense when those involved feel that they are fighting on behalf of the group and not just for themselves —when, in consequence, they feel that what they are doing is morally legitimate. They also then feel strengthened by power derived from the collectivity with which they have identified and which they embody.[226] This is why Coser argues that intellectuals increase the bitterness and the radicalism of conflicts between labor and management; in Mannheim's words, they transform "conflicts of interest into conflicts of ideas"[227] and provide just this moral impetus.

Summary

The major importance of Coser's conflict theory lies in its demonstration that conflict can often be neither socially divisive nor a source of change. This is especially clear in his comparison of societies with or without many independent and overlapping groups and of the differing natures and consequences of conflict within them. However, Coser's account is not fully satisfactory. Complex and interdependent societies that are not particularly rigid may experience conflicts that are highly divisive, and rigid, hierarchical societies may survive for centuries without explosive conflict. The recent history of political strife in Central America, Chile, and Argentina illustrate our first point; the thousand-year history of the Byzantine Empire our second. In addition, Coser's emphasis on the functions of conflict, although a useful corrective, is one-sided. At the beginning of his work he described social conflict as a struggle in which opponents attempt "to neutralize, injure, or eliminate their rivals."[228] Thereafter, one looks in vain for him to pay much attention to such behavior or to recognize the stability of many situations based on force and oppression.

RANDALL COLLINS

Randall Collins (b. 1941), the last of the conflict theorists we shall discuss, is also the youngest, and his work exemplifies the growing interest among American sociologists in a conflict perspective. We noted earlier the renewed interest in Marxism and the discovery of the Frankfurt School by younger, left-wing sociologists, who see their sociology as inextricably entwined with their desire for social change. Many of their contemporaries, whose aim in their sociology is scientific explanation and not political action, also now

---

[226]Coser, *The Functions of Social Conflict*, p. 118.
[227]Coser, *The Functions of Social Conflict*, p. 116.
[228]Coser, *The Functions of Social Conflict*, p. 8.

believe that a conflict perspective is the most fruitful way to approach sociological analysis.[229]

Collins's work is the most far-reaching theoretical synthesis based on this approach to date. Unlike Marx's or Dahrendorf's, Collins's work is not a conflict theory in the sense of describing when social conflict will actually occur. Indeed, in many of the situations he describes there is no overt conflict at all. Rather, he sets out to show that one can explain a wide range of social phenomena on the basis of a general assumption of conflicting interests and an analysis of the resources and actions available to people in particular social situations.

Collins took a B.A. at Harvard, an M.A. at Stanford, and a Ph.D. at the University of California, Berkeley. While still a student working as a research assistant at the Institute for International Studies at Berkeley, he began publishing.[230] He taught at the University of California, San Diego, at the University of Virginia in Charlottesville, and at the University of California, Riverside, and is currently at the University of Pennsylvania.

Collins's work incorporates all the major elements of conflict theory: an emphasis on people's interests, a view of society as made up of competing groups whose relative resources give their members more or less power over each other, and an interest in ideas as a weapon of social conflict and domination.[231] As he acknowledges, Collins's major debts are to Marx, "the great originator of modern conflict theory,"[232] and above all to Weber,[233] whose analytic framework, comparative historical approach, and nonutopian outlook he adopts.

In addition, of all the conflict theorists we have discussed, Collins draws most on Durkheim, who is commonly seen as the father of functionalism. Collins has little good to say about functionalism, but he believes that Durkheim explains a great deal about the ways in which emotional bonds and loyalties are created among people. The most original aspect of Collins's work is the way he incorporates a theory of how social integration is achieved into a conflict approach. Unlike most conflict theorists, Collins also draws on the work of such theorists as Mead, Schutz, and Goffman, who are generally associated with such microsociological perspectives as symbolic interactionism and phenomenology. This is the result of his

---

[229]See, for example, Jonathan Kelley and Herbert S. Klein, "Revolution and the Rebirth of Inequality: A Theory of Stratification in Post-Revolutionary Society," *American Journal of Sociology* 83, no. 1 (1977): 78–99.

[230]For example, J. Ben-David and R. Collins, "Social Factors in the Origins of a New Science: The Case of Psychology," *American Sociological Review* 31 (1966): 451–65.

[231]Collins's most recent work is on how ideas develop and are disseminated. Randall Collins, *The Sociology of Philosophies: A Global Theory of Intellectual Change* (Cambridge 1998).

[232]Randall Collins, *Conflict Sociology: Toward an Explanatory Science* (New York: Academic Press, 1975), p. 428.

[233]Collins, *Conflict Sociology*, pp. 58–59.

concern with exactly how individual loyalties and emotional bonds develop.

The Nature of Conflict Sociology

Collins's basic assumptions are that there are certain "goods," namely wealth, power, and prestige, that people will pursue in all societies,[234] and that everyone dislikes being ordered around and will always do his or her best to avoid it.[235] That is, he assumes that people have certain basic interests wherever they live and that they will act accordingly.

From this it follows that there will always be social conflict. This is true even though not everybody is equally greedy, simply because power, in particular, is inherently unequal: if I have a great deal of power, other people must necessarily have less, and they must obey me. "Since power and prestige are inherently scarce commodities and wealth is often contingent upon them, the ambition of even a small proportion of persons for more than equal shares of these goods sets up an implicit counterstruggle on the part of others to avoid subjection and disesteem," Collins concludes.[236] Such social conflict can take many forms, but at the very heart of it, he believes, lies direct coercion. Force is something people can always turn to, and some people always fare better at it than others. "Above all else, there is conflict because violent coercion is always a potential resource, and it is a zero-sum sort."[237]

As part of his analysis of the determinants of social structure and change, Collins provides a typology of the resources people bring to this struggle. First are material and technical resources, which include not only property, tools, and such skills as literacy but also—very importantly— weapons. Second, he stresses the role that strength and physical attractiveness play in personal relationships. Third, he mentions the sheer numbers and types of people with whom individuals have contact and with whom, therefore, they have the possibility of negotiating for material goods and status.[238] Fourth, Collins emphasizes the resources people possess in their "store of cultural devices for invoking emotional solidarity."[239] By this he means their ability to create and maintain a shared view of how things are and should be, which also sustains the favored position of those promoting that view.

---

[234]Collins, "Functional and Conflict Theories of Educational Stratification," *American Sociological Review* 36 (1971): 1009; and *Conflict Sociology*, chap. 2.

[235]Collins, *Conflict Sociology*, p. 59.

[236]Collins, "Functional and Conflict Theories," p. 1009.

[237]Collins, *Conflict Sociology*, p. 59.

[238]See rational choice theory's discussion of monopoly in Chapter 7 for a related analysis.

[239]Collins, *Conflict Sociology*, p. 60.

We can see what Collins is talking about if we compare the position of a rural Indian untouchable with that of, say, a nineteenth-century Hindu maharajah. The untouchable has almost no skills he could market in a city, for he is barred by the caste system from all but certain "unclean" jobs, such as curing hides or cleaning latrines. For him to work with caste Hindus would pollute them. His social contacts are extremely limited, so he knows little about whether he has any alternatives; he is dirty and undernourished; and his religion, dominated by the priestly caste of the Brahmins, teaches him that his lot is the inevitable result of his conduct in previous lives and must be accepted as such. By contrast, the maharajah has enormous resources and breadth of opportunities and social contacts. Being better fed, he is almost certainly bigger and more attractive physically. Moreover, although he has little or no control over the conduct of the Hindu religion and the influence of its priests, his cosmopolitan contacts may well have weakened the priests' influence over him. Obviously the maharajah is in a position of enormous power compared to the untouchable, and he is in a position to achieve a much wider range of objectives. If you compare two very dissimilar people in America, such as a mother on welfare and a company president, you will find that there are again big differences—but also that they are less extreme. This is because the two societies distribute their resources differently.

Collins follows Weber in suggesting that there are three main areas of life in which people obtain more or fewer resources and are more or less dominant or subjected. Together these create the patterns of social stratification. They are first, people's occupations, where they can be grouped into different *classes*; second, the communities where people live, with their different *status groups*, including age, gender, ethnic, and educational groupings; and third, the political arena, where different *parties* seek political power.[240] In every case what is crucial for social behavior is the degree to which people are in a position to control others and so obtain wealth, status, and overt deference. Collins does not regard one aspect of stratification as primary; people's overall position is simply the sum of their resources and positions in a number of different areas. In other words, Collins prefers Weber's pluralist model to Marx's unicausal one, arguing that "different orders of stratification do not line up neatly."[241]

The major part of Collins's work sets out propositions about the concrete ways in which the distribution and use of resources result in different sorts of social behavior and institutions. He also discusses in detail what creates a shared culture and a "legitimate" social order.

---

[240]Collins, *Conflict Sociology*, pp. 79–87.
[241]Collins, *Conflict Sociology*, p. 50.

Social Institutions and the Balance of Resources

Some of Collins's most interesting arguments about the relationships among conflicting interests, the distribution of resources, and the nature of social institutions concern modern education, organizational theory, the state, and the causes of gender stratification. In each case we shall find that his method is drawn from Weber: for the most part, he discusses general principles in terms of concrete historical settings and the balance of power within them.

Stratification by Education.   Collins has always been interested in how educational qualifications have been used as a resource in the struggle for power, wealth, and prestige, and he has used a conflict perspective to carry out empirical research on the role of education in people's careers. He treats education as one important basis of status-group differences, a sort of pseudo-ethnicity that socializes people into a particular form of culture.[242] The educational elite, which shares a given culture, will use it as a criterion for employment in elite positions, he argues. As educated people themselves, it is in their interests for educational institutions to serve a gatekeeping function, with only those who have passed through successfully allowed to proceed to the next level of the social hierarchy. Similarly, the elite will try to instill respect for its culture in the society as a whole.[243]

Modern industrial societies have longer periods of formal education and require far higher educational credentials for jobs than preindustrial ones. The usual explanation given is that more jobs require more skills than in the past, but Collins argues that this is, at best, only part of the truth. The evidence shows that education "is not associated with employee productivity on the industrial level, and job skills are learned mainly through opportunities to practice them"[244] and not at school at all. Differences among industrial countries are marked but not obviously related to technological progress. For example, in the postwar period American education has, on average, gone on far longer than that of the Japanese or West Germans. Moreover, Collins points out, engineers are the one professional group with real technical skills that industry needs. If the technological explanation of modern education were correct, one would expect the engineering schools to have the highest prestige on campus, and engineering training to dominate education. Nothing of the sort has occurred. Indeed, America, at the under-

---

[242]Compare the work of Pierre Bourdieu, especially his *Homo Academicus*, trans. Peter Collier (Cambridge: Polity, 1988); Collins, *Conflict Sociology*, pp. 86–87.

[243]See Collins, "Functional and Conflict Theorist of Educational Stratification," and Randall Collins, *The Credential Society: An Historical Sociology of Education and Stratification* (New York: Academic Press, 1979).

[244]Collins, *The Credential Society*, p. 48.

graduate level, has "the most massively nonvocational system of education in the modern world."[245]

The best way to understand the enormous growth of the "credential system" is to see education as a way of setting up entry requirements for jobs (and so limiting competition) and creating exclusive occupational cultures that are defined as prerequisites for doing a job. Thus, if you do not speak the same language (or jargon) as established workers, having learned it during "professional" training, then this provides evidence against your competence. This process can quickly create the sort of "credential inflation" that we have experienced in recent years. The highly educated set up job requirements that favor them; people recognize the importance of education as a route to success and acquire ever more of it; employers raise entry requirements yet further to screen out the flood of applicants—and so on.

Organizational Theory.   Collins's general approach to organizations is to view them as arenas for struggle in which superiors try to control their subordinates. He argues that, in consequence, one can best understand the structure of an organization by looking at the sanctions available to those in charge.

The three main types of sanction that can be used are coercion; material rewards given in return for appropriate activities and behavior; and normative control, which invokes people's loyalty to ideals. Each has distinct consequences. People dislike and resist coercion, and subordinates in the organizations that rely on coercion resort to "dull compliance and passive resistance."[246] Forced labor camps are extremely unproductive, and slaves consistently appear stupid and irresponsible to their masters. Material rewards, Collins suggests, are less alienating, but they produce organizations where there are continual fights over pay and piece rates, where informal groups control the work pace and prevent people from working "too hard," and where people tend to do things only if and insofar as they are paid.[247]

Normative control is the most desirable for superiors because if subordinates share superiors' goals they will be far more motivated to cooperate, obey, and work hard.[248] However, it too has costs attached. One of the most effective ways to create normative control is to spread authority because the more people give orders in an organization's name, the more they identify with it. Superiors can, for example, "co-opt members into responsible positions; a related method is to offer them a chance to be promoted."[249] Both

[245]Collins, *The Credential Society*, p. 162. Industrial countries vary markedly in the relative status of engineers, with the French, for example, having created an engineering elite educated outside the universities in the "grandes écoles."

[246]Collins, *Conflict Sociology*, p. 299.

[247]Collins, *Conflict Sociology*, p. 300.

[248]Collins, *Conflict Sociology*, pp. 300–301.

[249]Collins, *Conflict Sociology*, p. 301.

these approaches, however, tend to reduce the superior's own centralized power.

An alternative tactic is to recruit members who have a feeling of solidarity or friendship. Nepotism, the recruitment of family members, is a traditional way of creating organizational loyalty,[250] and recruiting people with similar backgrounds also makes friendships and thus loyalty to the organization more likely.[251] Collins also argues that the more an organization emphasizes rituals, is isolated from the world, and feels itself to be in danger from outside,[252] the more it will reinforce identification and loyalty. In discussing the extreme case of Jonestown, the community whose members died after taking cyanide en masse, we noted the importance of ritual in conjunction with total isolation.[253]

However, Collins points out, people who like each other tend to form strong informal groups, which may disagree and conflict with their leaders. Organizations that rely on normative control can expect continual conflicts about policy and factional fights about who is best able to implement the group's goals. "Astute organizational politicians, then, always attempt to mix normative incentives with material rewards and perhaps subtle coercive threats, since the latter can be administered much more routinely and kept under more stable control."[254] To transform the revolutionary Bolshevik party into the bureaucratic Communist Party, Stalin changed from the normative control of shared ideals, with its intense ideological disputes, to control by the material rewards available to party members and the underlying fear of the secret police.

The State. In using a conflict perspective to analyze the state, Collins again emphasizes that coercion is at the core of social life and social conflict. The state, he suggests, is a special sort of organization because it is "the way in which violence is organized"[255] and "*is*, above all, the army and the police."[256] To analyze political systems, Collins suggests, one must ask how violence is organized and which interest groups control and influence the state's policy.

Collins argues that the resources enabling people to win control of the state include systems of belief, property, networks of communication, and military technology.[257] Indeed, of all the theorists discussed in this chapter

---

[250]Collins, *Conflict Sociology*, p. 303.
[251]Collins, *Conflict Sociology*, p. 305.
[252]Collins, *Conflict Sociology*, p. 304.
[253]See the prior section on Coser.
[254]Collins, *Conflict Sociology*, p. 315.
[255]Collins, *Conflict Sociology*, p. 351.
[256]Collins, *Conflict Sociology*, p. 352.
[257]Collins, *Conflict Sociology*, p. 353.

Collins is the most sensitive to the effects of military technology and military organization of political and social life. A society in which a large proportion of households fight with their own cheap weapons will be far more demo-cratic, he argues, than one in which a small group with expensive individual equipment, like the medieval knights, monopolizes warfare. Similarly, whether an army is supplied and paid from central stores, like the Roman army, or requisitions locally and takes conquered lands as its reward, is crucial in determining whether there is a centralized state or a loose-knit feudal order.

Unlike Collins's analysis of military force, his discussion of economic resources as a basis for political power is sketchy. Collins sees coercion and military power as primary, and in discussing economic underpinnings of political systems, he uses a rather Marxian typology, adapted from Lenski, in which techniques of production are the major causal factor.[258] Collins's dis-cussion tends to neglect the effect of different forms of property and eco-nomic organization on political structure. He also ignores the different laws and systems of law in which these forms are rooted, although law is as essential a function of the state as is the use of force. Curiously enough, Weber, the greatest influence on Collins's work, gave considerable emphasis to economic organization and its legal basis. For example, he pointed to the historical and political consequences of the ability of European townsmen to own their own labor and property and to govern their towns, and he showed the consequences of the way the Chinese were legally tied to the village-based sibs or clans while their towns had no rights to self-government.

Stratification by Gender.   In all societies one of the most important status groups for determining people's life chances has been their gender. In almost every case women are markedly inferior to men in their access to wealth, power, autonomy, and other valued resources; in no known case are they actually superior.[259]

Collins outlines a theory to explain both this general situation and the *variations* in the general status of women.[260] He argues that the generally lower status of women results ultimately from human beings' strong drive for sexual gratification and from the fact that males are for the most part larger and stronger. However, between societies there are great variations. For example, in strict Islamic societies, women are kept veiled, in purdah; whereas in hunting and gathering and technologically simple tribal soci-eties, women may enjoy relative equality. These variations, Collins argues,

---

[258]See Chapter 4, p. 162.

[259]Rae Lesser Blumberg notes that the very few societies in which sexes appear to be equal are small and noncomplex. Rae Lesser Blumberg, *Stratification: Socioeconomic and Sexual Inequality* (Dubuque, Iowa: W. C. Brown, 1978).

[260]Collins, *Conflict Sociology*, chap. 5.

are a result of two major factors: women's market position and the way coercion operates in a society. Women are relatively well off in subsistence economies and affluent market economies, but worse off in "surplus-producing" economies of an intermediate sort. They are better off in nation-states where the state has a monopoly on coercion, and worse off where individuals are able to use force with no legal recourse for their victims or where coercion is delegated to the household level.

A number of feminist theorists have disagreed with Collins's argument that male strength is at the root of women's lower status while sharing his basic approach to explaining variations in women's circumstances.[261] Both Janet Saltzman Chafetz and Rae Lesser Blumberg argue that it is women's biological role as childbearers that is crucial. Its impact can be minimized but not eliminated.[262] All societies have found it to be more efficient for those who bear and nurse children to do the caretaking too. In no society do women "as a category . . . specialize solely in productive/public sector roles."[263]

Chafetz's theory about sex stratification is very much an example of the analytical conflict approach. She defines the degree of inequality between the sexes in terms of access to scarce and valued resources, and she argues that a relatively small number of variables accounts for most of the observed variance. Among them are the average percentage of the female life cycle devoted to childbearing, the distance between work and home, the ideological/religious support for sex inequality, and the degree of threat (and of more or less formal warfare). Thus, Chafetz argues, for example, that "the higher the average fertility rates in a society and the greater the distance between worksite and homesite, the less involved women will tend to be in productive activities."[264]

Factors like these affect not only the number of women involved in productive activities, but also the ways in which they are involved. And this is crucial, because "the greater the involvement of females in the most important (highly valued) productive roles in their societies, the less the degree of sex stratification will tend to be, and vice versa."[265]

---

[261]See, for example, Janet Saltzman Chafetz, "Some Thoughts of an Unrepentant 'Positivist' Who Considers Herself a Feminist Nonetheless," paper presented to the 1990 Annual Meeting of the American Sociological Association, Washington D.C. Hill Collins (see Chapter 5) also emphasizes the importance in stratification of race, class, and gender—that is, of multiple variables.

[262]Janet Saltzman Chafetz, *Sex and Advantage: A Comparative, Macro-Structural Theory of Sex Stratification* (Totowa, N.J.: Rowman and Allanheld, 1984) and "Gender Equality: Toward a Theory of Change" in Ruth A. Wallace, ed., *Feminism and Sociological Theory* (Newbury Park: Sage, 1989); Rae Lesser Blumberg, *Stratification: Socioeconomic and Sexual Inequality* and "A General Theory of Gender Stratification," in Randall Collins, ed., *Sociological Theory 1984* (San Francisco: Jossey-Bass, 1984), pp. 23–101.

[263]Chafetz, *Sex and Advantage*, p. 21.

[264]Chafetz, *Sex and Advantage*, p. 68.

[265]Chafetz, *Sex and Advantage*, p. 52.

Chafetz does not see property as central in the way that Marxist theorists do. However, she does believe that women's participation in production is absolutely central to their status.[266] She analyzes their continuing low pay and low participation in high-status occupations but also believes that "the gender division of labor" is *potentially* amenable to manipulation and change.[267]

Pay inequalities are a perennial topic of debate in the social sciences as well as in national politics.[268] For example, in recent years, as female participation and pay have increased, many commentators nonetheless identify a "glass ceiling" that stops women from reaching the top echelons of pay. Chafetz notes that most explanations of pay inequality fall into one of two categories. Human capital theory argues that people's pay is a reflection of their skills along with employers' "tastes" or requirements. If women have the skills employers want, then, according to this theory, they will be hired. It would be unprofitable for them not to be. Dual labor market theorists reject this explanation as a conservative apologia for the market system. They argue instead that the labor market falls into two parts. The primary sector, dominated by men, has security and good wages. Women and minority groups are forced into the secondary sector, marked by insecurity, short-term employment, and low returns.

However, Chafetz points out, the two theories are not really incompatible.[269] Many factors, including childbearing, home tasks, and ideological attitudes toward girls' education, may affect dramatically women's ability to offer what employers require. Equally, gender stereotypes will affect employers' tastes and hiring practices, at least for as long as a shortage of labor does not force them to change. It is also true that workers in high-status occupations have every incentive to protect their position by making it as hard as possible for them to be replaced by alternative workers (such as women). Structuring jobs so that it is difficult for them to be done by people who cannot work at all and any hours, or who take a break during early child-rearing years, is an obvious strategy. It protects one's interests as an occupational group and keeps one's income level high.

Rae Lesser Blumberg also offers an analysis of gender stratification that, while it differs from Collins's in key propositions, shares his analytic concerns and incorporates elements both of a rational-choice perspective and of Marx's theory of surplus value. Like Chafetz, Blumberg argues that "the most important of the many factors . . . influencing women's overall equality is economic,"[270] and she also emphasizes the importance of looking

[266]Chafetz discusses this in terms of the "nature of work organization."

[267]She also criticizes many contemporary gender theories for "conceptually exaggerating male-female difference . . . and ignoring the enormous variability within each gender." Chafetz, "Some Thoughts," p. 9.

[268]The low pay of women graduates in the United Satates is one of the themes to which we return throughout this text. See especially Chapters 1 and 9.

[269]Chafetz, *Sex and Advantage*, pp. 74–76.

[270]Rae Lesser Blumberg, "Toward a Feminist Theory of Development," in Wallace, ed., *Feminism and Sociological Theory*, p. 163.

at the internal organization of households. What is key is *control of economic resources*: "mere work in economic activities or even ownership of economic resources does not translate into economic power if the person derives no control of economic resources thereby."[271]

Such control is affected by a number of different factors, inside and outside the household, including ideological beliefs, and Blumberg emphasizes the effect of macro-level variables on individual and household behavior. For example, she points out, "Khomeini's decrees drastically restricting the occupational options, dress, and legal situation of Iranian women have apparently diminished their position *within the household* as well as the larger society."[272] Conversely, the greater a woman's economic power, the more she will decide when to have children (and how many); and the greater her control over "marriage, divorce, sexuality, household authority, and various types of household decisions."[273]

However, Blumberg also believes that unless gender issues are confronted explicitly, existing inequalities will tend to reproduce themselves, even among people who consciously reject them. The kibbutz, she argues, is a clear example of this. In spite of a commitment to communal child-rearing that was intended to foster equality, there has been a return toward traditional gender roles. In Blumberg's view the key point was that children's quarters were placed in the inner core (for safety as well as social reasons); the field crops at the farthest perimeter. However, women still came in from the fields during the day to breast-feed or because they were "pressured by Freudian-tinged beliefs"; and so their productivity decreased, to the field team managers' irritation. No one intended a return to traditional sex stereotyping of roles; indeed, at the "micro level, men and women enjoy full, guaranteed economic equality." However, because no one explicitly took action to prevent it, over time, women drifted away from the fields into traditional jobs in or near to the children's houses. Micro-level factors were inadequate to secure equality because macro-level factors worked against it.[274]

Culture, Ideology, and Legitimation

Collins is continually at pains to remind his readers that his subject is ultimately individual people. Writers in the tradition of social phenomenology, such as Mead and Goffman, have, he believes, a great deal to tell us about social interaction because they focus on individual experiences and recognize that these are not something given, fixed, and immutable.[275] Instead, our

[271]Blumberg, "Toward a Feminist Theory of Development." See Chapter 7, pp. 294–95 and 366, for a further discussion of internal household organization.

[272]Blumberg, "Toward a Feminist Theory of Development"; italics ours.

[273]Blumberg, "Toward a Feminist Theory of Development," p. 165. See Chapter 7, pp. 335–36, for Blood and Wolfe's similar analysis from an overtly exchange perspective.

[274]Blumberg, "Toward a Feminist Theory of Development," pp. 186–89.

[275]See Chapters 5 and 6 for a full discussion of this approach.

experiences are in large part a result of our own perceptions and values, so that "men live in self-constructed subjective worlds."[276] These worlds determine whether we see a photograph, for example, as harmless, as a way of stealing our souls, or as a transgression of God's commandment against graven images. They also affect whether we experience our societies as *satisfactory* or *oppressive*.

Collins argues that the sorts of perceptions we have are themselves subject to regular and identifiable influences. We can identify the sorts of individual experiences that make people view a social order as real and as *legitimate*. Legitimacy, in turn, affects the nature of conflict.

The experiences Collins identifies are first, and most important,[277] the giving and taking of orders; and second, the sorts of communications people have with others.[278] He argues that because of the nature of human psychology, those who *give orders* will tend to identify with the ideal of the organization in which they hold power and in whose name they justify their orders. Also, because of their experiences, they will be self-assured and generally formal in manner. By contrast, the more people *receive orders*, the more alienated from organizational ideals they are likely to be and the more fatalistic, subservient, concerned with extrinsic rewards, and distrustful of others they will be. Those in the middle of the authority hierarchy, who give *and* receive commands, tend to combine subservience with organizational identification, but they are little concerned with an organization's long-term objectives.

Collins's basic premise is that people wish to maximize the degree to which they give rather than receive orders. Hence, he argues, a midlevel official or bureaucrat "attempts to transform order-taking situations into orders that he passes on to others."[279] This explains the proverbial inflexibility of midlevel bureaucrats compared to their superiors, who see rules as a means to more distant ends. On the other hand, Collins's general emphasis on the relationship between one's outlook and whether one gives or receives orders implies a world in which everyone works in large organizations. In fact, if you think about people's occupations, you will find that many people—such as farmers, insurance salesmen, and many housewives—are not much involved with "orders" on a day-to-day basis at all.

The types of communication that people have with others are extremely important, Collins argues, because they may reinforce or (and this is crucial for social control) offset the effects of people's experiences of command. They, above all, are what determine the degree to which people accept as real the ideas and norms around which their society is organized. They determine whether people see the social order as legitimate. Collins

---

[276]Collins, *Conflict Sociology*, p. 60.
[277]Collins, *Conflict Sociology*, p. 73.
[278]Collins, *Conflict Sociology*, pp. 75–76.
[279]Collins, *Conflict Sociology*, p. 74.

points out that human beings, like all animals, have automatic emotional reactions to certain gestures, sounds, and signals, and he suggests that social ties are fundamentally based on shared reactions, which differ from those of animals because they involve symbols (such as flags or salutes) rather than genetically programmed sounds and gestures.[280] The strength of these reactions depends on two aspects of people's communications with each other: the amount of time people spend together, or their "mutual surveillance," and the diversity of their contacts. These, Collins argues, correspond to what Durkheim called "social density" in his analyses of how society creates loyalty and identification among its members.[281]

Social Density.   Collins argues that the greater the degree of *mutual surveillance*—the more people are in the physical presence of others—the more they accept the culture of the group and expect precise conformity in others.[282] Conversely, the less they are around others, the more their attitudes are explicitly individualistic and self-centered.[283] This is in large part because being physically together makes it more likely that "automatic, mutually reinforcing nonverbal sequences" will develop. These increase "emotional arousal," and "the stronger the emotional arousal, the more real and unquestioned the meanings of the symbols people think about during that experience."[284]

The *diversity* or *cosmopolitanism* of people's contacts similarly affects the way they think. Collins argues that the more different sorts of communication people are involved in, the more likely they are to start thinking in abstract terms and in terms of long-range consequences. On the other hand, the less varied people's contacts, the more likely they are to think only about particular people and particular things and to see the world outside their own familiar circle as alien and threatening. Thus limited contact will tend to create shared, local views of reality and a feeling of identification with familiar local people vis-à-vis the outside world.[285]

Ritual.   Collins believes that mutual surveillance and limited communications counteract the effects of being on the receiving end of orders. They create emotional ties that bind a group together and make the way it is organized unquestionably real. Thus they strengthen the position of the dominant members of a group. In addition, Collins argues, *rituals* or "stereotyped sequences of gestures and sounds,"[286] can make people's emotional

---

[280]Collins, *Conflict Sociology*, pp. 152–53.
[281]Collins, *Conflict Sociology*, p. 76.
[282]Collins, *Conflict Sociology*, p. 75.
[283]Collins, *Conflict Sociology*, p. 75.
[284]Collins, *Conflict Sociology*, p. 153.
[285]Collins, *Conflict Sociology*, pp. 75–76.
[286]Collins, *Conflict Sociology*, p. 153.

arousal more intense and so commit them more strongly to certain views of reality. Emotional arousal is also affected, he suggests, by the sheer number of people involved.[287] If we look at the ceremonies to which groups and societies attach great importance, we can see that they generally combine highly stereotyped rituals with large gatherings of people. Durkheim pointed this out in his discussion of aboriginal religious ceremonies and their role in integrating society;[288] Hitler's Nuremberg rallies, graduation ceremonies, and the use of particular songs and symbols at civil rights or antiwar demonstrations are also good examples.

The empirical evidence gives Collins's arguments considerable but far from total support. Politics, about which Collins says surprisingly little, provide useful confirmation, because party activists often occupy a position in the party that is quite different from their day-to-day occupations in breadth of communication and power—and as Collins's theory would indicate, this affects their outlook substantially. Parents who are manual workers and who are active in politics and unionism tend to have upwardly mobile children who become managers and professionals.[289]

On the other hand, evidence on working-class union militancy and the development of revolutionary ideologies suggests that Collins's analysis is too simple. His account of how "ritual communities" are created would lead one to expect that military, revolutionary doctrines and a commitment to working-class solidarity are most likely to develop among isolated, homogeneous groups of workers with their own tight-knit communities. For a number of years sociologists have argued that this is indeed the case, citing the study by Kerr and Siegel that argued that isolated masses of workers are more militant and strike-prone.[290] More recently, however, this view has been challenged by a new research group interested in strikes and political violence and, in particular, by the work of Shorter and Tilly. Their study of France between 1830 and 1968 shows that militancy was a characteristic of the metropolis, not the isolated enclave—and of the relatively cosmopolitan skilled worker at that.[291] It is similarly true, we might add, that tight-knit, fanatical, revolutionary political parties of the right and left have been born in heterogeneous cities, not in small, cohesive communities.

---

[287]Collins, *Conflict Sociology*, p. 153.

[288]Émile Durkheim, *The Elementary Forms of the Religious Life* (New York: Collier Books, 1961).

[289]Brian Jackson and Dennis Marsden, *Education and the Working Class* (London: Routledge and Kegan Paul, 1963).

[290]Clark Kerr and Abraham Siegel, "The Interindustry Propensity to Strike," in Arthur Kornhauser, Robert Dubin, and Arthur M. Ross, ed., *Industrial Conflict* (New York: McGraw-Hill, 1954). Dahrendorf's arguments about mobilization are also along these lines.

[291]Edward Shorter and Charles Tilly, *Strikes in France 1830–1968* (London: Cambridge University Press, 1974). See also David Snyder and Charles Tilly, "Hardship and Collective Violence in France 1830–1960," *American Sociological Review* 37 (1972): 320–32.

This suggests a serious imbalance in Collins's treatment of ideas. In his emphasis on the way ideas can be used to support the ruling order, he neglects the origins of ideas and beliefs that oppose it. Indeed, his arguments sometimes leave one wondering why all ruling groups have not been able to assure themselves of permanent legitimacy by manipulating ritual! Tribal societies seem almost never to generate ideas of "revolution" (changing the entire order) as opposed to "rebellion" against individual leaders,[292] but in Europe and America such ideas have been a part of social life for many centuries, and they are held with quite as much passion and conviction of their reality as the beliefs of a tribal "ritual community." A full account of the origins of beliefs and worldviews needs to explain this process, too, and indeed, conflict sociology in general needs to take more account of the origin and force of ideas as tools of opposition as well as domination.

Military Force and Geopolitics

We noted earlier that Collins is highly sensitive to the importance of military technology and organization.[293] His work on geopolitics[294] pays particular attention to such factors—and is notable for its prediction of the Soviet empire's decline and internal fragmentation.

Among sociologists the best-known work on geopolitics is Wallerstein's "world-system theory," discussed in Chapter 4. Wallerstein predicts the development of a unified world empire as a result of economic changes and changes in military technology. Collins disagrees. There has been no basic change, he argues, in the principles that determine the rise and fall of states and empires: first, size and resources; second, geographical position; and third, military overextension.

Collins argues, first, that "other things being equal, larger and wealthier states will win wars against smaller and poorer states, and hence will expand while the latter contract."[295] This may not happen all at once: aggressive, militarized states such as Hitler's Germany, imperial Japan, or Sadam Hussein's Iraq can have the advantage of surprise. In the longer term, however, sheer weight of numbers and wealth can and will tell. Added to this, however, must be the key factor of geography—what Collins calls "positional advantage." In particular, "states with militarily capable neighbors in fewer directions . . . have an advantage over states with powerful neighbors in more directions."[296] Collins calls those favored states, which are

[292]Max Gluckman, *Custom and Conflict in Africa*, p. 28.

[293]See p. 142.

[294] Randall Collins, *Weberian Sociological Theory* (Cambridge: Cambridge University Press, 1986). See especially chap. 7 (originally published in the *Journal of Political and Military Sociology* 9 (1981): 163–77); and chap. 8.

[295]Collins, *Weberian Sociological Theory*, p. 187.

[296]Collins, *Weberian Sociological Theory*, pp. 187–88.

in a peripheral and so relatively unthreatened position, "marchland" states. The term was used by the English of the Middle Ages, whose "marcher lords," their estates backing onto the wild territories of Wales and Scotland, were notoriously difficult for the king to control; and also by Tolkein in describing the wilder border regions of "Middle Earth." In contrast to such states, interior states that are caught between a number of relatively secure marchland neighbors tend to fragment, Collins argues, often in the course of showdown wars that mark a major geopolitical shift.[297]

Both these factors remain, Collins argues, as germane as in the past. There is also a third principle at work. "Even 'world empires' with no equivalent rivals have undergone weakening and long-term decay," he points out. "A major reason is that military overextensions beyond the resources of a territorial heartland result in disintegration of state power."[298]

In predicting the imminent decline of the Russian empire, Collins drew on all three principles. At the time of its expansion, he notes, it had an advantage of population size and wealth over relevant neighbors and potential foes.[299] This changed; in particular, it was caught in arms rivalry with both a stabilized, huge China and an enormously much wealthier United States. Moreover, its very success had abolished its marchland benefits: "the result of its having eliminated virtually all weak buffer states (is) that it now faces powerful enemies in all directions,"[300] including China, Japan, and Western Europe (and so, by proxy, the United States). Its overextension was shown by the extremely high percentage of GNP going to the military budget even in peacetime. The result, Collins predicted, was that the Russian empire was set for decline and was in a position where quite small incidents had the potential to act as a "tipping phenomenon," setting off a process of internal fragmentation and the breakaway of satellite states. In 1994, less than ten years after Collins published his predictions, the independent states of Eastern Europe, the Baltic, Ukraine, Beloruss, and Central Asia were witnesses to their accuracy.

Summary

Collins provides an excellent exposition of the basic assumptions of analytic conflict theory. His work is also important because it provides a large number of concrete propositions that relate institutional structure to the resources available to different groups. Further, it incorporates the insights

---

[297]Collins, *Weberian Sociological Theory*, p. 168.

[298]Collins, *Weberian Sociological Theory*, p. 190.

[299]China was very poor, mired in internal strife, and not immediately concerned with Russian conquests in the south and west.

[300]Collins, *Weberian Sociological Theory*, p. 195.

of microsociological perspectives, especially in its account of how social experiences affect people's outlooks and hence the nature of social behavior, conflict, and change.

Not surprisingly, Collins's major weaknesses are the weaknesses of conflict theory as a whole. The most important are, we would suggest, an overemphasis on the "zero-sum" aspects of social interaction; too mechanistic a view of ideas as an offshoot of the existing social structure; and an inadequate account of the nature of the state. It is to these general weaknesses of conflict theory, as well as its major strengths, that we now turn briefly in conclusion.

CONCLUSION

Conflict theory's major strength lies in the way it relates social and organizational structure to group interests and the balance of resources. This analytical framework is often very productive. Moreover, whereas functionalism never really identifies a mechanism of change, conflict theory does when it points to shifts in resource distribution and power. Conflict theory insists fruitfully that values and ideas must be related to their social environment and not treated as autonomous. Finally, it avoids explaining things simply in terms of their results. By tracing social behavior back to individuals' interests and the purposive way they pursue them, it shows how changes may actually occur.

However, conflict theory also has important weaknesses. Its insistence that power is people's main objective and the primary feature of social relationships is too limited. One can hardly account for the behavior of the Pilgrim Fathers in terms of self-interest or the search for power, as conflict theory commonly uses those terms. Moreover, the way in which they define and discuss power leads many conflict theorists to imply that the whole of social life is essentially "zero-sum": that is, that one person's gain is by definition made up from others' equal loss.[301] In fact, this is not necessarily the case.

Suppose that we take a hypothetical self-interested ruler who wishes to get as much money out of his subjects as possible. He can either seize whatever he can find by brute force, or he can set up a well-defined tax system in which people know in advance exactly how much they will owe—and that nothing more will be demanded. In the latter case it is still ultimately the ruler's ability to coerce that ensures that his subjects pay up. However, they will also find it far more worthwhile to work hard, save, invest, and create

---

[301]Some of Dahrendorf's recent work, notably *Conflict and Contract*, observes that situations may be "positive-sum" but does not address fully what this implies for his theories of power and the state.

economic growth than they will if anything they produce is liable to arbitrary confiscation. For that reason the ruler may ultimately do better for himself by choosing the less arbitrary course. Certainly his subjects will fare much better if he does.[302]

Of course, no ruler ever has a completely free hand to choose one alternative or the other. However, societies can and do vary systematically in how far they provide the sort of environment that gives people security, encourages economic growth, or creates some degree of the "positive sum" in their affairs. Contemporary conflict theory tends to ignore such important differences in how state power is exercised and in how far it provides people with a secure and predictable framework for their actions.[303] Consequently, it also tends to produce an inadequate theory of the state and to treat laws—the product of the state—oversimplistically, as though they were merely a reflection of group interest rather than systems with their own dynamic and influence.[304]

The same oversimplification is apparent in conflict theory's treatment of values and ideas. It is important to analyze the degree to which ideas are rooted in a social order and the way ideologies reflect people's interests; but it is also important to be aware—as functionalism is—that ideas have a degree of autonomy. Conflict theorists tend to treat ideas as though they were simply a reflection of the interests of the powerful, but narrow self-interest often does not fully explain events. Self-interest would have suggested the total extermination of the Native Americans. That this did not happen was largely the result of notions of justice and morality that, however compromised, were universal in their application.

Similarly, conflict theory tends to emphasize how ideas maintain stability, when in fact the ideas in a given society often criticize and undermine the current order.[305] For example, Christianity produced figures like St. Francis and Luther whose teachings created massive social upheavals; and the Kremlin suppressed Russian dissidents brutally for decades because it feared their ideas so much.

Finally, although conflict theory specifies a mechanism of change, it does not provide an entirely satisfactory account of it. This is because conflict theory is far better at explaining how a group maintains power than it

---

[302]These arguments over the nature of society and the rule of law derive essentially from Thomas Hobbes (*Leviathan*) and John Locke (*The Second Treatise of Civil Government* and *A Letter Concerning Toleration*).

[303]It is important to note that none of this requires altruistic behavior "for the good of the people" or implies that systems of law and government exist that are equally good for everyone.

[304]By contrast, Weber pays a great deal of attention to differing legal systems. For an elaboration of this argument, see Douglass C. North, *Structure and Change in Economic History*, chap. 3 (New York: W. W. Norton, 1981). North argues (p. 21) that "one cannot develop a useful analysis of the state divorced from property rights" and treats the state as essentially wealth-maximizing (on its *own* behalf).

[305]This is not universally true, as Schumpeter and Habermas show.

is at showing how it acquired it in the first place. Collins, for example, argues that educational qualifications are an important source of privilege without saying very much about why they are now a more significant resource than they were in the past. Yet groups do not acquire resources and power at random, and we had occasion to suggest earlier in the chapter that the origins of a group's power can often be explained by the services they provided. Educational qualifications may be used to protect and strengthen positions more than in the past *because* education is also necessary to provide the technical skills on which modern wealth depends. At a number of points we have noted the way in which sociologists using an essentially conflict perspective also incorporate arguments of this type drawn from exchange or rational choice theory. These are discussed further in Chapter 7.

CHAPTER FOUR

Evolution and Modernity: Macrosociological Perspectives

INTRODUCTION

An interest in social evolution is as old as sociology itself. Robert Nisbet has argued that the concerns of the early sociologists can best be understood as an attempt to comprehend the almost total transformation of society taking place around them.[1] The "two revolutions"—the dramatic upheaval of the French Revolution and the gradual but even more far-reaching Industrial Revolution—signaled the disappearance of both the old aristocratic political order and the agrarian society in which the vast bulk of the population tilled the soil, as their parents and grandparents had before them. Intellectuals living in such an era could hardly fail to think in terms of the development and evolution of society from one form to an entirely new one.

An interest in social evolution remained characteristic of sociological theory throughout the twentieth century; but it is particularly strong again today. Anthony Giddens, one of the theorists whose work is dealt with in this chapter, writes that

> We live, as everyone knows, at a time of endings. There is, first of all, the end not just of a century but of a millennium: something which has no content, and which is wholly arbitrary—a date on a calendar—has such a power of reification that it holds us in thrall. . . . (But this) is certainly not the whole story. We are in a period of evident transition—and the "we" here refers not only to the West but to the world as a whole.[2]

This chapter brings together the most important evolutionary theories offered in sociology. It includes the conflict perspective of Marx and the functionalism of Parsons: but it also discusses the work of Habermas, Giddens, and Beck, who draw on the ideas of Marx, Weber, and Durkheim to offer an analysis of where society is tending in the "global village" of the late twentieth century. These writers are not postmodernists, who, as we shall see in Chapter 9, believe that the whole nature of social science (and, indeed, intellectual thought) is undergoing a fundamental change. Instead the theorists described here draw on a number of important established perspectives, largely macro, but also including phenomenology and Goffman's form of symbolic interactionism, to analyze the nature of modernity. The turn of the millennium is indeed an appropriate moment to evaluate these ideas.

[1]Robert A. Nisbet, *The Sociological Tradition* (New York: Basic Books, 1966). See also Geoffrey Hawthorn, *Enlightenment and Despair: A History of Sociology* (Cambridge: Cambridge University Press, 1976).

[2]Anthony Giddens, "Living in a Post-Traditional Society," in Ulrich Beck, Anthony Giddens, and Scott Lash, *Reflexive Modernization: Politics, Tradition and Aesthetics in the Modern Social Order* (Cambridge: Polity, 1994), p. 56.

INTELLECTUAL ROOTS

Evolutionary thinking in sociology was central to its very beginnings. August Comte (1798–1857), the creator of sociology, believed that humanity progressed through three states of thought and corresponding types of society: theological, metaphysical, and the dawning positivist model.[3] Ways of thought were crucial in defining the nature of a society because they also affect views of what is a legitimate authority; and this theme of legitimacy recurs frequently in the work of contemporary theorists such as Habermas.

Herbert Spencer (1820–1903) subsequently adopted the concepts of Darwin's evolutionary theory, arguing that societies, too, progress from simpler to more complex forms.[4] He believed that there is an inexorable tendency toward differentiation both in the case of organisms into species and in the case of societies into more differentiated (specialized) structures. This differentiation was equivalent to what economists identified as the division of labor and was, Spencer argued, facilitated by increases in the size of societies. Talcott Parsons incorporated this process of differentiation into his evolutionary model.

Émile Durkheim (1858–1917), whose work has influenced many contemporary theoretical perspectives, also argued for a clear evolutionary tendency in social organization.[5] He wrote that growing population density undermined "mechanical" solidarity, whereby societies are held together because individual differences are minimized and people have common beliefs and similar occupations. Over time it is replaced by the "organic" solidarity of more advanced societies, which are held together by the interdependence that results from a highly complex division of labor.[6] For example, a preindustrial village whether in central Africa or coastal Scandinavia would be largely self-sufficient, with all families involved in the same tasks of food production and collection; whereas today, in an urban environment, each of our individual lives depends on the thousands of different people involved in specialized tasks of producing and distributing electricity; maintaining roads and public lighting; policing the streets; preparing foods for supermarket sales; and so on.

Karl Marx (1818–1883).   Of all the early evolutionary theorists, the one whose ideas had the most importance for future events was Karl Marx. In Chapter 3, we described in detail Marx's theory of class formation, ideology,

---

[3]Auguste Comte, *The Positive Philosophy*, trans. Harriet Martineau (New York: Calvin Blanchard, 1958).

[4]Herbert Spencer, *The Principles of Sociology* (New York: Appleton, 1896).

[5]See Chapter 2 for a fuller description of Durkheim's ideas.

[6]Émile Durkheim, *The Division of Labor in Society* (Glencoe, Ill.: The Free Press, 1964).

alienation, and the state. Marx also developed a theory of history in which society was seen as evolving inevitably, through conflict, toward the communist utopia. It was this utopian vision that inspired the revolutionary communist parties that, during the twentieth century, seized power in many countries, among them Russia, China, Cuba, and Vietnam. Because of its historical importance and continuing influence on Marxist sociologists, Marx's evolutionary theory is discussed in detail in this chapter.

Joseph Schumpeter (1883–1950). The Austrian Joseph Schumpeter developed Marx's ideas about *changes* in the distribution of power but also, and most particularly, expanded on Max Weber's concern with legitimacy and with how a group's success is rooted in its social position. Schumpeter associated social change or evolution with changes in the power of different "classes"—a term he used loosely to describe more or less organized and distinctive social groups. Classes achieve power because they command skills that are either new and innovative or that (because of changing circumstances) are far more important than they were in the past.[7] Their position can then be used to obtain further wealth and privilege, dispose of older groups, and protect themselves from competition.

Ultimately, however, because they fail to continue providing valued services and because new innovatory groups rise up, powerful classes are replaced by others. The new classes attack the old successfully and deny the legitimacy of their position. Thus late–twentieth-century America contains many people whose occupations simply did not exist a short time ago. The success of, for example, the industries of Silicon Valley has created major shifts in the economic—and political—power of various states.

Two of Schumpeter's own most interesting examples are the rise of imperialist warrior groups and the decline of the capitalist bourgeoisie. He argues that the medieval feudal aristocracy developed from warrior groups. They attained power in a society where war was continual, where people consequently sought armed protection, and where fighting skill had to be acquired and maintained over a lifetime.[8] As this situation changed with the rise of the modern state, modern arms, and the conscript army, the aristocracy's position declined.

At present, Schumpeter argues, the capitalist class, which ascended because of its economic achievements, is in decline in its turn. Technological innovation has become institutionalized, and independent entrepreneurs are less important. Meanwhile, a new class of intellectuals with its own group attitudes and group interests has arisen, undermining the legitimacy of the

---

[7]Joseph Schumpeter, *Imperialism and Social Classes* (Cleveland: Meridian Books, 1955).

[8]Schumpeter, *Imperialism and Social Classes.* The history of ancient Egypt is similar, Schumpeter suggests. The repulsion of the invading Hyksos created a new warrior class that then, under the "New" Empire, wrested power from the independent landlords of the "Old" and "Middle" periods.

old order and creating for itself a new power base in the increasingly important government bureaucracies.[9] The influence of Schumpeter's ideas, and especially those about capitalism's loss of legitimacy, is apparent in the work of Jürgen Habermas.

PART ONE

Karl Marx and the Classless Society

The whole of Marx's theory is essentially one of change and evolution; it looks back over the whole of history and forward to the future and claims to explain and understand both. A given economic system has within it, Marx argued, the seeds of change: its own logic and the way it works necessarily produce its successor.

Marxists describe this process in terms of a given order's "contradictions," which develop over time until the whole system becomes unworkable and there is a violent, revolutionary shift to another order altogether, the "negation" of the previous one. This view of development and change as a pattern of inner conflict is known as *dialectical*.[10] Like many other elements in his theory, including alienation, Marx's idea of the dialectic is a reworking of a Hegelian concept. However, Hegel was interested in the development of self-awareness and "Spirit." Marx's concern was the evolution of human society through economic stages.

Marx identified four major types of class society, each with its "primary classes"—Asiatic, ancient, feudal, and bourgeois. The Asiatic mode is based on state-controlled irrigation and a system of royal despotism and ownership of all land; but Marx treats only the last three in detail as part

---

[9]Joseph Schumpeter, *Capitalism, Socialism and Democracy* (London: Unwin University Books, 1943), pp. 131–55. Schumpeter's central argument is that current social trends and conflicts will lead in the end to some form of socialism.

[10]It is often expressed in terms of a "thesis" and its opposite, or "antithesis," producing a new "synthesis"; thus

See Shlomo Avineri, *The Social and Political Thought of Karl Marx* (Cambridge: Cambridge University Press, 1968), p. 171. We have described the dialectic in a way we consider faithful to Marx's own use. However, we should note that it is also used in a more complicated and philosophical sense by a number of writers influenced by the Marxist philosopher George Lukács to discuss the relationships between human consciousness and historical reality.

of Western history. In each case change involves the appearance of new classes. The barbarian military chieftains who overran the Roman empire replaced ancient society with a society of feudal overlords and serfs; in turn they were replaced by the capitalist bourgeoisie, the adversaries of the proletariat. The next stage, however, would be different, Marx prophesied, for the contradictions inherent in capitalism would usher in an ideal communist society, in which property and classes were abolished and alienation replaced by self-realization. In dialectical terms, communist society would "emerge phoenixlike from the ashes of capitalist society."[11]

THE END OF CAPITALISM

Marx argued that over time many smaller capitalists, along with the other distinctive groups of previous eras—small shopkeepers, peasants, crafts workers—would be swallowed up into the proletariat, their skills obsolete or their capital too small for them to compete. Only two ever more strongly differentiated classes would remain. At the same time capitalists would produce more and more on the backs of the exploited workforce without the market expanding correspondingly. Competition would then force the capitalists to cut prices and wages, and the rate of profit would decline toward zero. The outcome would be misery for the masses—but also revolt and the end of capitalism.

Thus, Marx argues, "along with the constantly diminishing number of the magnates of capital, who usurp and monopolize . . . grows the mass of misery, oppression, slavery, degradation, exploitation; but with this too grows the revolt of the working class, a class always increasing in numbers, and disciplined, united, organized. . . . The knell of capitalist private property sounds. The expropriators are expropriated."[12]

Marx's forecasts clearly have not been borne out. There has been neither increasing misery in the West nor a steady decline in the rate of profit. Moreover, although production is more concentrated, ownership is not, and shareholders are more and more often trade unions or pension funds. Marxist analysts, however, have been at pains to show that the survival of capitalism is temporary.[13]

Lenin's theory of imperialism is the most influential such argument. In his great work *Capital*, Marx remarks that capitalist countries use their

---

[11]Avineri, *The Social and Political Thought of Karl Marx*, p. 182.

[12]Karl Marx, *Capital*, Vol. I, trans. Samuel Moore and Edward Aveling, ed. F. Engels (London: Lawrence and Wishart, 1961), chap. 32 (Historical Tendency of Capitalist Accumulation), pp. 762–63.

[13]Serge Mallet, in *La Nouvelle Classe Ouvrière*, 4th ed. (Paris: Editions du Seuil, 1969), suggests that class consciousness will increase in automated enterprises because workers will develop a calculated awareness of their joint interests.

colonies as providers of raw materials, captive markets for their products, and treasure-grounds to loot.[14] From these remarks Lenin developed a Marxist theory of imperialism. He argued that advanced capitalism's need for ever-expanding markets and profitable investment opportunities would dictate a foreign policy of imperialism and of destructive wars among individual rivals for colonial possessions.[15] Imperialism would temporarily stave off the time when profits vanished and capitalism disappeared.

Clearly governments often act in pursuit of the economic interests of home investors and consumers. Western governments' prompt response to Iraq's occupation of Kuwait, as compared to their vacillations in former Yugoslavia, provide a recent instance. However, critics argue that the specific Marxist theory of imperialism is inadequate and frequently wrong. They point to the frequently imperialist policies of noncapitalist countries (for example, China's seizure of Tibet or the Soviet Union's occupation of the Baltic states); and they also note that imperialism was characteristic of the early days of capitalism, before falling profits should have threatened. Modern capitalist states, by contrast, have withdrawn from their former colonies.

Closely related to Marxist ideas about imperialism is *dependency theory*, which views the world as divided into *core* and *periphery*.[16] Like Marx and Lenin, dependency theorists analyze events as part of a particular historic process: the global expansion of capitalism. The core is industrially advanced and develops as a result of its own internal dynamics. In the dependent countries of the periphery, by contrast, what happens depends on the demands and requirements of the core.

World Systems Theory

These ideas have been developed furthest by Immanuel Wallerstein in his work on the "modern world-system." He argued that what exists under capitalism is, for the first time, a truly global system held together by economic, not political or military, ties.[17] The growth of the modern capitalist world economy was made possible by the geographical expansion of the core countries of Western Europe. The exploration and conquests of the sixteenth century were followed by economic domination.

According to Wallerstein, different parts of the world-system specialize or have different functions. Thus the periphery supplies raw mate-

---

[14]Marx, *Capital*, Vol. I, Chapter 33 (The Modern Theory of Colonization).

[15]Vladimir I. Lenin, *Imperialism: The Highest State of Capitalism* (New York: International Publishers, 1939).

[16]See especially André Gunder Frank, *Dependent Accumulation and Underdevelopment* (London: Macmillan, 1978).

[17]In the past there were world *empires*, such as that of Rome, but they were held together militarily, not economically.

rials for the enterprises of the core.[18] This difference is mirrored in the way labor is controlled in different areas. "Free labor is the form of labor control used for skilled work in core countries whereas coerced labor is used for less skilled work in peripheral areas. The combination thereof is the essence of capitalism."[19]

Wallerstein also argues that core areas developed strong states, and peripheral areas weak ones. In the early development of capitalism, states provided important social stability through their growing bureaucracies and monopoly of force. However, the capitalist world-system is one of *economic* integration, and it is through economic mechanisms that the core controls the periphery.

Globalization is a term used frequently, and often imprecisely, to describe the late–twentieth-century world. It is not obvious, for example, that there is an unstoppable convergent or globalizing trend in the way countries run their political affairs, education systems, or family lives. However, the growth of free trade, fast and cheap international transport, the development of the East Asian economies, and the size and importance of multinational corporations make the economies of most countries more intertwined than ever before. In world-system terms, however, critics query whether underdeveloped countries were or are exploited in the sense of being impoverished by capitalist production. They point out that nineteenth-century America was a major recipient of foreign investments, as are today's fastest-growing countries,[20] and that some of the richest countries in the core—such as Australia—are predominantly exporters of raw materials. More generally, Wallerstein's work has been criticized by Randall Collins for exaggerating the importance of changes in military technology;[21] by feminists for treating women as "appendages of men in households";[22] and for

---

[18]Wallerstein also talks of the "semiperiphery," halfway between exploiter and exploited.

[19]Immanuel Wallerstein, *The Modern World-System I: Capitalist Agriculture and the Origins of the European World-Economy in the Sixteenth Century* (New York: Academic Press, 1974), p. 127. See also his *The Modern World-System II: Mercantilism and the Consolidation of the European World-Economy 1600–1750* (New York: Academic Press, 1980), and *The Modern World-System III: The Second Era of Great Expansion of the Capitalist Economy, 1730–1840* (New York: Academic Press, 1988).

[20]For a more detailed presentation of the arguments, see Irving M. Zeitlin, *Capitalism and Imperialism: An Introduction to Neo-Marxian Concepts* (Chicago: Markham, 1972); Irving Louis Horowitz, *Three Worlds of Development*, 2nd ed. (New York: Oxford University Press, 1972); P. T. Bauer, *Dissent on Development* (London: Weidenfeld and Nicolson, 1971) and *Equality, the Third World and Economic Delusion* (London: Weidenfeld and Nicolson, 1981); and Robert W. Tucker, *The Inequality of Nations* (New York: Basic Books, 1977). Of course, it does not follow that because Marx's specific predictions were inaccurate, he was also wrong about the inevitable disappearance of capitalism. Many analysts, including Joseph Schumpeter, have agreed that it will disappear—but not because of the falling rate of profit.

[21]See Chapter 3, pp. 149–50.

[22]Kathryn B. Ward, "Reconceptualizing World System Theory to Include Women" in Paula England, ed., *Theory on Gender: Feminism on Theory* (New York: Aldine de Gruyter, 1993): p. 53.

economic determinism, or underemphasizing the importance of political organization and other noneconomic factors.

Among these critics, Theda Skocpol and Anthony Giddens are notable because they draw on Marxist theory themselves to analyze historical developments worldwide. In her own work on social revolutions, Skocpol argues that the ability of *states* to cope with both internal problems and the international system is of central importance. Because Wallerstein sees differences between states as simply reflections of economic conditions, he cannot explain satisfactorily either the origins of capitalism or the very different histories of different nations that supposedly share a core position.[23]

Giddens, whose own ideas on evolution are discussed later in this chapter, praises Wallerstein for emphasizing that in capitalism we have a truly global phenomenon, integrated economically. However, he also urges recognition of "specifically political and military factors."[24] We can talk of a world capitalist economy, he argues, provided we remember that it is only one aspect of the world-system and that the "globally encompassing nation-state system" is equally important. Unlike traditional states, the modern nation-state is a "power-container" that has swept other forms of state organization before it. This is partly because industry was from the beginning harnessed to provide new weaponry and partly because of the vast expansion of such states' administrative power.[25] They, as much as capitalism, define the nature of our modern world.

Other theorists influenced by Marx draw attention to technological factors in social evolution. For example, Gerhard Lenski's work looks at the change from hunting and gathering societies, which are seen as the most politically (and financially) equal in the world to date, but because of poverty, not wealth; there is not enough wealth to support a large group not directly involved in producing essential goods. The horticultural and agrarian societies that followed are more unequal, because the greater wealth and concentration of population permit a military aristocracy or priests, ruling through religion and ritual, to extract more; industrial societies are less unequal because power must be dispersed to run complex organizations.[26] Marx himself sometimes argues that the actual techniques of production determine social structures. However, his evolutionary theory focuses more on issues of ownership and class—the 'relations of produc-

---

[23]Theda Skocpol, "Wallerstein's World Capitalist System: A Theoretical and Historical Critique," *American Journal of Sociology* 82, no. 5 (1977): 1075–90, and *States and Social Revolutions* (Cambridge: Cambridge University Press, 1979).

[24]Anthony Giddens, *The Nation-State and Violence: Vol. II of a Contemporary Critique of Historical Materialism* (Cambridge: Polity, 1985), p. 168. Giddens also criticizes Wallerstein for functionalism, as when "the existence of semiperipheral regions is explained by reference to the 'needs' of the world system": *The Nation-State and Violence*, p. 167.

[25]Giddens, *The Nation-State and Violence*, pp. 170–72, 255–311.

[26]Gerhard E. Lenski, *Power and Privilege: A Theory of Social Stratification* (New York: McGraw-Hill, 1966).

tion'—rather than the technology. In general the evolutionary theorists who follow are influenced by him but offer a more multifaceted view of what drives evolution and of the nature of modern societies. This is certainly true of Talcott Parsons, to whose evolutionary theory we now turn.

PART TWO

Talcott Parsons's Evolutionary Model

Parsons's ideas on social change were not fully developed until the early 1960s, when he wrote *Societies: Evolutionary and Comparative Perspectives*. The publication of this work marked a renewed interest in the evolutionary development of human society. Although Parsons's work was pitched at a very general level, it also integrated the Western social patterns that typified the midcentury into an evolutionary framework; and it did so just at the time when social patterns were about to change again following the upheavals of the 1960s.[27]

Basically, Parsons's ideas on evolution were an outgrowth of his pattern variable typology and his four-function paradigm, and they further extended Durkheim's ideas. Like Durkheim, Parsons saw the primitive or prehistorical stage, when kinship relations and a religious orientation in the world were prominent, as the first stage of societal evolution. In addition, he posited an intermediate stage characterized by a written language and therefore the availability of documents and history. The modern, or third, stage is characterized by formal relationships and procedures and—most important—the institutionalization of law and full adult literacy.[28]

Echoing Durkheim and using Spencer's concept of differentiation, Parsons argued that continually increasing differentiation (that is, the division of a unit or system into two or more units or systems "which differ in both structural and functional significance for the wider system"[29]) is the key to evolution of social systems. In other words, in the change from primitive societies to modern societies, the change from a situation in which roles are

[27]A group of cultural anthropologists has also revived the biological analogies of Spencer. Among the most important are Marshal Sahlins, Elman Service, and David Kaplan, who argue that one can classify the degree of society's evolution in terms of its overall potential for appropriating nature's energy—something to which, in their view, culture is crucial. See Marshall D. Sahlins and Elman R. Service, ed., *Evolution and Culture* (Ann Arbor, Mich.: University of Michigan Press, 1960). For an alternative theory of economic evolution and its implications for social development, see John Hicks, *A Theory of Economic History* (Oxford: Oxford University Press, 1969).

[28]Parsons, *Societies: Evolutionary and Comparative Perspectives* (Englewood Cliffs, N.J.: Prentice-Hall, 1966), pp. 26 and 27. See also Talcott Parsons's *The System of Modern Societies* (Englewood Cliffs, N.J.: Prentice-Hall, 1971).

[29]Parsons, *Societies; Evolutionary and Comparative Perspectives*, p. 22.

fused to a situation in which roles have been allocated to different role incumbents is what creates and signifies the shift to a different evolutionary level. This shift is crucial, above all, because it permits greater control of the environment. Parsons pointed out, for example, that economic production is more efficient in specialized factories than in self-sufficient households.[30]

Evolutionary Universals

In elaborating on and extending this basic model of evolution, Parsons identified a number of evolutionary "universals," which he defined as "any organizational development sufficiently important to further evolution that, rather than emerging only once, it is likely to be 'hit upon' by various systems operating under different conditions."[31]

First of all, he argued, language, kinship organization, religion, and rudimentary technology are prerequisites if communities are to break out of the primitive stage at all and become what we think of as full societies. Then follow, in order, the six major evolutionary universals: social stratification, cultural legitimation, bureaucratic organization, money economy and markets, generalized universalistic norms, and democratic associations. This evolutionary sequence starts from and is made possible by greater differentiation, and as societies develop and acquire these structures they become still further differentiated (as well as changing in other ways).

Parsons's evolutionary model incorporates both structures and processes.[32] The *structures* (patterned and stable relationships) are social stratification, cultural legitimation, bureaucratic organization, money and markets, generalized universalistic norms, and democratic associations. The *processes* (evolutionary changes taking place in the system) are differentiation, adaptive upgrading, inclusion, and value generalization.

Parsons proposed social stratification as the first structure likely to evolve from an increase in *differentiation*.[33] Thus he added the notions of ranking and of occupations carrying higher and lower prestige to role differentiation as such. Earlier in his career Parsons presented a theory of stratification in which he said that certain jobs have high prestige and are the best paid because of the amount of talent and skill they require; the money, time, and energy spent in training people for them; and the need to attract the most capable individuals to them.[34] Thus Parsons believed that modern schools

---

[30]Parsons, *Societies: Evolutionary and Comparative Perspectives*, p. 22.

[31]Parsons, "Evolutionary Universals in Society," *American Sociological Review* 29 (1964): 339–57.

[32]See the introduction to Chapter 2.

[33]See Talcott Parsons, ed., *Sociological Theory and Modern Society* (New York: The Free Press, 1967).

[34]Talcott Parsons, "An Analytic Approach to the Theory of Stratification," *American Journal of Sociology* 45 (1940): 843.

serve a crucial function for society, not only in teaching values but also in acting as stratifying agents that identify children's skills and so determine their future occupations. Parsons's basic argument here is that a stratification system is both desirable and necessary in a complex industrial society; it fills occupations effectively and keeps the entire social system functioning smoothly. Consequently, social stratification is an evolutionary "universal" because without it a highly differentiated society cannot be maintained.

This functionalist analysis of social stratification is one of the most debated parts of Parsons's theory. Conflict theorists, in particular, disagree with Parsons's analysis.[35] Some regard a stratification system as the antithesis of the classless society they believe in and consider possible. They think that functionalism, by emphasizing the necessity of stratification, takes an essentially conservative stance. Others agree with functionalists that stratification is inevitable; but they disagree with the functionalist explanation of how and why it occurs. They see stratification as an aspect of the unequal distribution of power in society, with those who have more power, for whatever reason, using it to secure greater prestige and wealth. Finally, a number of sociologists see the functionalist view as one-sided rather than completely wrong. It tends to imply a perfect meritocracy and to ignore the fact that the talent of people born into lower status groups, such as the poor, women, or minority groups, often goes undiscovered.[36]

As we have mentioned, Parsons saw differentiation as the key to the evolution of social systems. Without differentiation of role allocation and, he would argue, the accompanying social stratification, specialization and technological development would be impossible. The second evolutionary process, *adaptive upgrading*, involves the idea of control or dominance of the environment,[37] and this, too, is advanced by the development of each of the "universals." Although Spencer's influence is apparent here, Parsons also relies on Weber's notion of rationalization to conceptualize the main trend of social change. In Weber's view modern society has rationalized and made calculable and predictable what in primitive society had seemed to be governed by chance. Robert Bellah, in *The Good Society*, also uses Weber's concept of rationalization, defining it as "a process of systematically organizing all social relations so as to make them the most efficient possible means to maximizing wealth and/or power. Its characteristic institutions were the self-regulating market and the bureaucratic state."[38]

---

[35]See Chapter 3.

[36]See Mark Abrahamson, *Functionalism* (Englewood Cliffs, N.J.: Prentice-Hall, 1978), pp. 57–74, for a full treatment of the functional theory of stratification. He discusses the arguments of Davis and Moore, Tumin, and others.

[37]Here there is a similarity between Parsons and the conflict theorist Habermas on evolutionary change. See Part Three of this chapter.

[38]Robert Bellah, Richard Madsen, William M. Sullivan, Ann Swidler, and Steven M. Tipton, *The Good Society* (New York: Knopf, 1991), p. 233.

Parsons argued that the second process of evolutionary change, adaptive upgrading, enhances societies' adaptive capacities—their ability to attain a wide variety of goals despite environmental difficulties.[39] For example, Parsons states that bureaucratic organization, which involves further differentiation, gives societies an adaptive advantage because the specialization it entails means better utilization of talent and a more flexible response to environmental exigencies. A society also has an adaptive advantage when it has cultural legitimation—when the cultural definition of "we-ness" is expanded well beyond the kinship group to the larger society; as when the notion of "nation" not only emerges but is accepted by its citizens.[40]

In addition to differentiation and adaptive upgrading, Parsons adds two more processes to his model of evolutionary change. One is a sort of desegregation process that he calls *inclusion*.[41] For adaptive upgrading to take place in the United States, for example, people can no longer be excluded from certain jobs because of race, gender, age, sexual orientation, physical handicap, religion, or national origin. Society must recognize that groups that have been excluded are capable of contributing to the functioning of the system. In other words, the more skills that are developed without regard to ascriptive characteristics, the more specialized members there will be, resulting in a more productive society.

To inclusion Parsons adds *value generalization*. The new type of social system emerging in this evolutionary process must have a value pattern that is "couched at a higher level of generality in order to legitimize the wider variety of goals and functions of its subunits."[42] In other words, higher levels of differentiation, adaptive upgrading, and inclusion cannot coexist with a parochial value system that is shared by only some members of the social system. Robert Bellah's idea of the civil religion in America is an example of value generalization. Whatever its label, this religion is neither Protestant, Catholic, nor Jewish; it can encompass an extremely wide variety of believers and nonbelievers because it is basically a religion of patriotism.[43] A civil religion that espouses the values of life, liberty, and the pursuit of happiness legitimizes a much wider variety of goals and functions than does any one of the three major religions in America. It also provides a more general value pattern that is necessary for a society with a wide variety of members.

The direction of the evolutionary processes is from differentiation to adaptive upgrading to inclusion to value generalization. Figure 4-1 shows an example of how each of these processes has occurred in American society. A

---

[39]The term "adaptive capacity" is borrowed from Spencer (*The Principles of Sociology*).

[40]Echoing functionalism's stress on shared values, Bellah et al., in *The Good Society*, argue that a shared understanding of the common good leads to a vital democracy.

[41]Parsons, *Societies: Evolutionary and Comparative Perspectives*, p. 22.

[42]Parsons, *Societies: Evolutionary and Comparative Perspectives*, p. 23.

[43]Robert N. Bellah, "Civil Religion in America," *Daedalus* 96 (1967): 1–21.

Processes:	differentiation	→	adaptive upgrading	→	inclusion	→	value generalization

| Examples: | from medicine man to nurses, pharmacists, surgeons, and so forth | from epidemics to control of disease | from WASP M.D.s to minority, female, M.D.s | from Protestantism to civil religion |

FIGURE 4-1   Parsons's Evolutionary Model Applied to Processes in the United States

change from medicine man to nurse, pharmacist, or surgeon is an illustration of differentiation in medicine; a progression from epidemics to control of disease illustrates adaptive upgrading in the health field; a change in medical school enrollments (and in higher education in general) from discriminating in favor of white Anglo-Saxon male Protestants to opening professions to racial and ethnic minorities and females illustrates inclusion; and finally, in the religious area, a shift from a predominantly Protestant value system to American civil religion is an example of value generalization.

Miriam Johnson uses Parsons's four evolutionary processes to explain the rise of the feminist movement in the United States.[44] She cites Parsons's argument that modernization brings about a clearer *differentiation* between personality and society that is related to the increasing autonomy of individuals.[45] She then argues that "the perception of gender inequality itself depended in part on a process of differentiation by which people's identities and sense of self-worth became separable from the roles they played and the activities they pursued." The process of differentiation, according to Johnson, "made possible the understandings that have characterized Western feminism."[46]

Johnson further argues that the *inclusion* of educated women into the occupational world outside the home on an equal basis with men has led to *adaptive upgrading* because it released more trained capacity into the system. However, she is quick to add that inclusion has not been a smooth process; women's wages are still far below those of men; and, regardless of whether they work outside the home, women continue to take major responsibility for child care. Finally, she makes the point that much of feminist writing could be described as an effort to redefine dominant (male) societal values; in Parsonian terms, it has been an effort to achieve *value generalization*.

The limited success of the women's movement illustrates a weakness in Parsons's model of social change: strain, tension, and resistance to the

---

[44]Miriam Johnson, "Feminism and the Theories of Talcott Parsons," in Ruth A. Wallace, ed., *Feminism and Sociological Theory* (Newbury Park, Calif.: Sage, 1989), pp. 101–118.

[45]Parsons, *Societies: Evolutionary and Comparative Perspectives*, p. 24.

[46]Johnson, "Feminism and the Theories of Talcott Parsons," p. 108.

inclusion process should be inserted. This, then, raises the question about resistance to differentiation, adaptive upgrading, and value generalization as well. In fact, we would argue that Parsons's evolutionary theory would be strengthened if strain, tension, and resistance to change were inserted into each of the four change processes.[47]

Parsons rejects the older evolutionary view that all societies follow an inevitable and uniform course of development, but he does assume that human history reveals an evolutionary trend toward an increase in adaptive capacity.[48] He is not claiming that societies all progress gradually and evenly through these evolutionary processes. Rather, he identifies a number of crucial characteristics, which he sees as central to the way societies develop and which cannot be grafted onto any existing society in an arbitrary fashion.[49] Parsons would argue that if we want to understand the differences between modern society and the Aztecs, we should find out which of these central institutions they possess and then see how they differ. We should consider each society's degree of adaptive upgrading, inclusion, and the rest. Similarly, Parsons would be dubious about efforts to introduce democracy or a modern legal system into a tribal, kin-based society.[50]

Parsons is cautiously optimistic about possibilities for social change. In his theory, evolution and progress emerge as synonymous, and democracy is a logical and stable social development. Though he does not conceal his admiration for American democracy, Parsons synthesizes his American pragmatism with the pathos of European theory. For example, Parsons and Jürgen Habermas, whom we discuss in the next section, consider many of the same features to be central to social evolution, though the overtones are quite different.

Parsons's theory of social change, which emphasizes gradual, smooth adjustments if the institutions of liberal democracy are to be retained, is not a departure from his functionalist perspective; it is an elaboration of it. Parsons does not think an evolving social order is dysfunctional; it leads to change within, but not to change of, the system. Parsons never attempted to

---

[47]In addition, neofunctionalist Frank Lechner, in "Modernity and Its Discontents," in Jeffrey C. Alexander, ed., *Neofunctionalism* (Beverly Hills, Calif.: Sage, 1985), pp. 157–76, argues that we should turn Parsons on his head and use his social change theory as a basis for conceptualizing four functional sources of disorder. For instance, Lechner argues that inclusion can create resistance. It means breaking up what were once closely knit groups, bound together by collective sentiment. Such a process will cause pain, tension, and opposition. Women and other groups occupying a marginal position in society will be quick to recognize that this interpretation helps to explain the unevenness of their inclusion.

[48]See Benton Johnson, *Functionalism in Modern Sociology: Understanding Talcott Parsons* (Morristown, N.J.: General Learning Press, 1975), p. 41.

[49]Parsons, "Evolutionary Universals in Society," pp. 339–57.

[50]For a study that tested Parsons's evolutionary theory, see G. L. Buck and A. I. Jacobson, "Social Evolution and Structural-Functional Analysis: An Empirical View," *American Sociological Review* 33 (1968): 343–55.

explain either sudden or total societal change. A communist coup would be difficult to explain in the Parsonian framework.[51]

Throughout his work Parsons was indebted to Émile Durkheim. Societal progression, as Durkheim saw it, was from the undifferentiated structures of primitive societies (characterized by mechanical solidarity) to structural differentiation in modern societies (characterized by organic solidarity). In summarizing Parsons's thinking on change, we can see that his vital interest in the problem of order is much like Durkheim's preoccupation with integration.[52]

PART THREE

Jürgen Habermas: Rationalization and Communicative Action

Jürgen Habermas is probably the best-known contemporary German social theorist. He was born in 1929 in Gummersbach, near Dusseldorf, where his father was a pastor and head of the local Bureau of Industry and Trade. He studied philosophy at Göttingen and in 1956 became Assistant to Adorno in Frankfurt. In 1961, at an unusually young age for a German academic, he became the professor of philosophy and sociology at Heidelberg, and in 1964 he was awarded the chair at Frankfurt and made codirector of the Philosophical Seminar. He left Frankfurt in 1971 to direct Munich's Max Planck Institute for the Study of Life in Technical and Scientific Society. He has since returned to Frankfurt.

Habermas is strongly interested in politics and in the relevance of sociology and social thought to political affairs. He became generally known in the 1960s, when German student radicalism was at its height. He emphasized repeatedly his solidarity with the movement as a whole, but he also denounced the views of some of its extremist leaders as "left-fascism," defended the importance of democratic institutions and the rule of law, and attacked the use of violence. In this he resembled some (though not all) of the older members of the Frankfurt School (discussed in Chapter 3), with whom he is often associated.

It is true that, like the older Frankfurt theorists, Habermas is heavily influenced by Marx; and he also shares with them a belief in "reason" as a standard by which to judge—critically—our society and a concern with the links between culture, social structure, and personality. However,

---

[51]See Chapter 3. See also Kenneth Bock's critique in his article, "Evolution, Function, and Change," *American Sociological Review* 33 (1968): 343–55.

[52]See Robert N. Bellah, "Durkheim and History," *American Sociological Review* 24 (1959): 447–61, for a description of Durkheim as evolutionist and functionalist.

Habermas's work must be seen not simply as an elaboration of Marx but as an ongoing argument with Max Weber. He returns again and again to Weber's metaphor of bureaucratized society as an "iron cage,"[53] and one sympathetic commentator has described the *Theory of Communicative Action* as being "conceived as a second attempt to incorporate Max Weber into the spirit of Western Marxism."[54] Like Weber (and like the older Frankfurt School analysts),[55] Habermas must also be understood in terms of a German tradition in which there is no strict separation of sociology from philosophy. In this tradition the concept of "reason" is far wider-ranging and imbued with values than our English use of the word implies.

Habermas has also always paid great attention to the role of individuals' perceptions in maintaining or realizing social change. This emphasis is increasingly marked over time, notably in his massive *Theory of Communicative Action,*[56] in which the influence of phenomenology is apparent. This section summarizes his comprehensive theory of social systems and evolution and especially his ideas on the rationalization of the lifeworld.

EVOLUTION AND CRISIS

The major achievement of Habermas's earlier work (especially *Legitimation Crisis* and *Communication and the Evolution of Society*) was to recast Marx's theory of evolution.[57] Although his recent work modifies and expands the earlier model—for example, by changing some of the labels used—the basic categories have remained.

Habermas identifies a number of social formations, shown in Figure 4-2. "Primitive" societies are comparable to Marx's tribal ones; "traditional" societies would include both ancient and feudal ones; "liberal capitalist" describes the nineteenth-century capitalism Marx knew; and our own

[53]See p. 72.

[54]Michael Pusey, *Jürgen Habermas* (Chichester, West Sussex: Ellis Horwood, 1988), p. 105. We are indebted to Pusey's excellent review for pointing up the central role of Weber's diagnosis in Habermas's work. For commentaries on Habermas's work, see also Richard J. Bernstein, ed., *Habermas and Modernity* (Cambridge: Polity, 1985), and Thomas McCarthy, *The Critical Theory of Jürgen Habermas* (London: Hutchinson, 1978).

[55]See the section of Chapter 3 that discusses the Frankfurt School. The older Frankfurt analysts, however, did not engage so directly with Weber.

[56]Jürgen Habermas, *The Theory of Communicative Action,* Vol. I: *Reason and the Rationalization of Society,* trans. Thomas McCarthy (London: Heinemann, 1985), and Vol. II: *Lifeworld and System: A Critique of Functionalist Reason,* trans. Thomas McCarthy (Cambridge: Polity, 1988).

[57]Jürgen Habermas, *Legitimation Crisis,* trans. Thomas McCarthy (Boston: Beacon Press, 1975), and Jürgen Habermas, *Communication and the Evolution of Society,* trans. Thomas McCarthy (London: Heinemann, 1979). See also Jürgen Habermas, *Knowledge and Human Interests,* trans. Jeremy J. Shapiro (London: Heinemann, 1972).

Western societies are examples of "organized capitalism." Habermas classi-fies "state-socialist" societies as "postcapitalist" class societies "in view of their political-elitist disposition of the means of production."[58]

Habermas's mode of analysis is similar to Marx's in that he sees social evolution as a result of crises or contradictions inherent in a given system. These create "steering problems," which eventually make the system unten-able. However, like other critical theorists, Habermas emphasizes the role played by people's ideas and consciousness. Underlying structural changes and contradictions manifest themselves in the breakdown of shared values or "normative structures," and the old social system disintegrates because such changes threaten people's feeling of social identity (and therefore social integration).[59]

In discussing such breakdowns, Habermas focuses on the political organization of societies and on their legitimacy, meaning *a political order's worthiness to be recognized.*[60] In emphasizing legitimation, Habermas is like both Weber, who analyzed the comparable notion of authority,[61] and Parsons, who saw ideas or norms as central to system maintenance.[62] He argues that "problems of legitimacy are not a speciality of modern times. . . . In traditional societies, legitimation conflicts typically take the form of

[58]Habermas, *Legitimation Crisis,* p. 17.

[59]Habermas, *Legitimation Crisis,* p. 3. Following Durkheim, Habermas describes this situ-ation as anomic.

[60]Jürgen Habermas, "Legitimation Problems in the Modern State," in *Communication and the Evolution of Society,* p. 178 (italics original).

[61]See p. 73.

[62]In Parsons's AGIL terms, we can see legitimation as involving systems of ideas that both support the political system's mobilization of resources for goal attainment (G) and also promote "latent pattern maintenance-tension management" (L)—the process of keeping a common value system intact. See above pp. 38–39.

FIGURE 4-2 Social Formations
(Adapted from Jürgen Habermas, *Legitimation Crisis* (Boston Beacon Press, 1975), p. 17.)

Social Formations

Primitive

Traditional Civilizations

Class Societies {
Modern Civilizations
   Capitalist
     Liberal Capitalist
     Organized Capitalist
   Postcapitalist

Postmodern

prophetic and messianic movements that turn against the official version of religious doctrine."[63] It is here that the contradiction between the privileges of the dominant ruling class and the normative system of ideas that is supposed to legitimize them becomes apparent. Examples are the Hebrew prophets or the heretical movements of the Middle Ages. This does not, however, make legitimation crises in the state something separate from class conflicts. On the contrary, it is *through* the development of the state that societies moved away from production by and for families to a situation in which a dominating class appropriated wealth.

Habermas's focus on ideas as the mechanism of change makes his treatment very different from that of Marx, who treats the development of modern industry as a *deus ex machina* that catapulted humanity from feudal into capitalist society. Instead, it displays interesting parallels both with Schumpeter's approach, where the way capitalism destroys its own legitimacy was discussed as the central force behind its inevitable demise, and with that of some leading nonradical economic historians, who also focus on the role of the state and of "ideology" in determining how wealth is distributed.[64]

According to Habermas, the distinctive characteristic of liberal capitalism is the "depoliticization of the class relationship."[65] Before, control of the state by a small group was of central importance. Liberal capitalism features self-regulated market commerce, and the state simply maintains the general conditions of capitalistic production, especially civil law. Like Weber or Marcuse, Habermas notes the cumulative process of "rationalization" under capitalism and the corresponding disintegration of both traditional habits and the justification of practices by an appeal to tradition. Moreover, like Talcott Parsons (to whom he acknowledges an intellectual debt),[66] he notes the general expansion of the secular domain and a shift from "tribal particularism to universalistic and at the same time individualistic orientations."[67]

However, in analyzing the probable development of modern society, Habermas believes that the trend from myth, through religion, to philosophy and ideology is of prime importance.[68] It means that "normative validity claims" (that is, arguments that something ought to be so) must be justified more and more explicitly. Instead of relying on appeals to tradition and authority, capitalism has based its claim to legitimacy on the notion that market exchange between equals is just. However, in a society where legiti-

---

[63]Habermas, "Legitimation Problems in the Modern State," p. 181.

[64]Unlike Habermas, they are also extremely interested in the effects of these on how much is *produced*. See E. L. Jones, *The European Miracle: Environments, Economies and Geo-politics in the History of Europe and Asia* (Cambridge: Cambridge University Press, 1981), and Douglass C. North, *Structure and Change in Economic History* (New York: W.W. Norton, 1981).

[65]Habermas, *Legitimation Crisis*, p. 21.

[66]See p. 45.

[67]Habermas, *Legitimation Crisis*, p. 12.

[68]Habermas, *Legitimation Crisis*, p. 11.

macy rests on the workings of the market, economic fluctuations are direct threats to social integration. Such fluctuations may create very high unemployment or inflation, which wipes out people's savings, or may result in the virtual disappearance of a city's or state's traditional industries. In the process such fluctuations make it clear to everyone involved that market ideology is incorrect. The market is not, in fact, a meeting place of equals; rather it is a form of institutionalized power where some are better placed than others.[69]

In his discussion of contemporary "organized capitalism," Habermas is concerned above all with whether it has resolved this "fundamental contradiction." His answer is that it has not. There are serious crisis tendencies in modern Western societies, the most important of which undermine its legitimacy.

Habermas believes that the transition from liberal to organized capitalism involves two changes. The first is the rise of huge, oligopolistic firms and the disappearance of *competitive* capitalism. The second is the reemergence of the state, which increasingly replaces and intervenes in the market (thus signaling the end of *liberal* capitalism). The state's reemergence is largely a response to economic fluctuations and "steering problems." The state attempts to regulate the economic cycle and maintain growth and full employment; spends on education and research; provides the infrastructure of roads and utilities; and reduces the "social and material costs resulting from private production" through unemployment benefits, welfare, and the like.[70] The profit motive and the "continued private appropriation . . . of surplus value" remain crucial, however.[71]

The "recoupling" of the state and the economic system creates, Habermas argues, an increased need for legitimation, and in a rationalistic age the legitimation must be formal and explicit. Since the old bourgeois ideology of fair exchange has broken down, the alternative is a system of *formal* democracy.[72] *Genuine* participation in decision making would, he argues, make people aware of the contradictions in a society where production is the state's concern, but surplus value is individually appropriated. Such participation is not on offer.

This system is fragile, however. Habermas, following Marx, believes that the economic system itself is threatened by a falling rate of profit. Moreover, there is likely to be insufficient loyalty to the political system and a consequent legitimation crisis. In its early days, capitalism had the remnants of tradition to maintain it. Now its own rationality has undermined traditions, and previously unquestioned norms and loyalties are publicly discussed and thereby weakened.

[69]Habermas, *Legitimation Crisis*, p. 11.
[70]Habermas, *Legitimation Crisis*, pp. 33–35.
[71]Habermas, *Legitimation Crisis*, p. 36.
[72]Habermas, *Legitimation Crisis*, p. 36.

Related changes within the family further destroy the residues of tradition and the casts of mind that upheld the capitalist order.[73] While prebourgeois, authoritarian patterns of upbringing survived, people accepted rule by an elite rather than demanding participation;[74] but these patterns are vanishing, helped on their way by a self-conscious analysis of the ways we socialize children. Such an analysis further reduces the effectiveness of traditional child rearing because the latter's force depended on people not questioning it. Finally, the ideology of achievement is also disappearing. The welfare state makes hard work less important, and in a modern economy it is increasingly difficult to reward people for individual effort and hold them personally accountable.

RATIONALIZATION OF THE LIFEWORLD

Habermas elaborates his evolutionary theory by looking at it in terms of communication and the lifeworld—that is, in terms of how evolutionary change is actually experienced by individuals. Here, too, a direct line between Habermas and Weber is apparent. Weber argued that in social science we need subjective understanding of how other people see the world and of their "webs of meaning."[75] Habermas similarly argues for "intersubjective" projection into others' lifeworlds—that is, for understanding what it would be like to be inside someone else's skin, experiencing the world as he or she does.

To an even greater extent, however, Habermas draws on the phenomenological tradition.[76] Edmund Husserl (1859–1938), the German philosopher who was the first to use the term "phenomenology," also employed the concept of *Lebenswelt*, or *lifeworld*.[77] Husserl was referring here to the most fundamental levels of consciousness, levels of which we are not aware. These levels of consciousness structure all our perceptions and determine how we actually experience reality. Adults in modern society, for example, take it for granted that time proceeds in one direction only and that once you have had your twentieth birthday, you can never be nineteen again. A three-

---

[73]Habermas, *Legitimation Crisis*, pp. 48–49. These are discussed by Habermas in terms of the "social-cultural system" and "motivational crisis."

[74]Habermas, *Legitimation Crisis*, p. 76.

[75]For a discussion of Weber's concept of *verstehen* see Chapter 5.

[76]This reached America primarily through the writing of Alfred Schutz. See Chapter 6.

[77]See also the writings of Thomas Luckmann, who in *Lifeworld and Social Realities* (London: Heinemann, 1983) states that "the lifeworld forms the setting in which situational horizons shift, expand, or contract. It forms a context that, itself boundless, draws boundaries. . . . Lifeworld analysis [is] an attempt to describe reconstructively, from the internal perspective of members, what Durkheim calls the *conscience collective*" (pp. 132–33). Luckmann's work is discussed in Chapter 6. For Durkheim's definition of "conscience collective," see p. 21.

year-old experiences reality differently and may declare that she wants to be two again after she has been twelve.

Seen this way, the process of modernization becomes coterminous with the rationalization of the lifeworld. Tribal societies are environments in which the taken-for-granted lifeworld is highly encompassing. People mix only with others who share the same lifeworld, so they are always able to communicate with each other and have no reason to become self-conscious about the structure of shared experience. One cannot conceive of meeting a phenomenologist amongst our hunting and gathering forebears or in a Viking settlement. Today the lifeworld is increasing rationalized: instead of "knowing" that certain animals are unclean or that chiefs have a right to rule, we demand that things be justified in terms of general principles— what Talcott Parsons calls "value generalization."

Habermas is concerned with the lifeworld as an aspect of his theory of *communicative action*. It is through the action of communicating, he argues, that society actually operates and evolves; this process is encompassed and structured by the actors' lifeworlds.[78] One of his own examples is that of an older worker at a German building site telling the newest recruit to go and get a midmorning beer. The actual remark would probably be brief, almost offhand, but it has built into it all sorts of assumptions. It takes for granted that a midmorning beer break is a normal and acceptable custom and that there is a natural hierarchy based on age or length of service at the building site. A young English carpenter working in Germany might be extremely surprised at the order because beer is not readily available at 11 A.M. in the United Kingdom. He would nonetheless probably share enough of the underlying lifeworld knowledge to understand, act accordingly, and, in so doing, become more integrated into German life.[79]

This is why Habermas argues that communicative action

> is not only a process of reaching understanding; . . . actors are at the same time taking part in interactions through which they develop, confirm, and renew their memberships in social groups and their own identities. Communicative actions are not only processes of interpretation in which cultural knowledge is "tested against the world"; they are at the same time processes of social integration and of socialization.[80]

---

[78]Habermas's concerns here are, as he recognizes, close to those of many modern philosophers, including, notably, John Searle. See J. R. Searle, *Speech Acts* (Cambridge: Cambridge University Press, 1969).

[79]Anthony Giddens offers a similar analysis in his structuration theory. See the Giddens section of this chapter.

[80]Habermas, *Theory of Communicative Action*, Vol. II, p. 139.

Lifeworld and System

In his earlier work on evolution (discussed previously) Habermas empha-sized the move from tribal to class societies, the emergence of state organi-zations, and the way in which the economy becomes self-regulated, with the state ensuring general conditions rather than being directly involved. He later reformulated this somewhat using the concept of lifeworld and the neo-Parsonian "system" framework of Niklas Luhmann.[81]

Habermas argues that as social evolution progresses, there develops a system of institutions—markets steered by money and state organizations steered by power. It is then possible for more people to be involved with each other *without sharing meanings or the same lifeworld.* The social system becomes increasingly complex and differentiated; the lifeworld becomes increasingly rationalized; *and the two are uncoupled to a large degree.*[82] In tribal society, by contrast, system integration and social integration remain tightly interwoven because structures of "linguistically mediated, normatively guided interac-tion immediately constitute the supporting social structures."[83]

Within our contemporary state and market structures, one obeys not people (Weber's "traditional" authority) or even officeholders but general principles and abstract laws. "Social relations are regulated only through money and power. Norm-conformative attitudes and identity-forming social memberships are made peripheral."[84] Lifeworlds get more provincial as the social system gets more complex. This means that "the burden of social inte-gration [shifts] more and more from religiously anchored consensus to processes of consensus formation in language."[85] Only by explicit "rational" discussion do we agree on how things should be carried out—whether it is the way a course is graded or a major foreign policy decision.

Habermas's account is meant to make explicit what to Weber "was still self-evident," namely "the intrinsic (that is, not merely contingent) relation-ship between modernity and what he called 'Occidental rationalism.' "[86] However, what actually most interested Weber was the conditions for the emergence of modern industrial society. What this century has shown—

---

[81]See Chapter 2.

[82]See Chapter 2 for a discussion of Luhmann's work. We can relate Habermas's and Luhmann's work to Parsons's AGIL paradigm by noting that the social system corresponds to Parsons's A (the economy) and G (political institutions). The educational, family, and religious institutions that make up Parsons's L are also the level of the lifeworld and, as such, become progressively detached from A and G. Compare modern work patterns with those of previous societies, where the family home was also the workplace, and the aristocratic home was a center of political power.

[83]Habermas, *Theory of Communicative Action,* Vol. II, p. 156.

[84]Habermas, *Theory of Communicative Action,* Vol. II, p. 154.

[85]Habermas, *Theory of Communicative Action,* Vol. II, p. 180.

[86]Jürgen Habermas, *The Philosophical Discourse of Modernity: Twelve Lectures,* trans. Frederick Lawrence (Cambridge: Polity, 1987), p. 1.

most notably in the case of Japan and its East Asian neighbors—is that the countries in which modernity first develops may differ greatly from those that modernize successfully thereafter.

Habermas's analysis, by contrast, seems to imply that all modern societies will be similar in the lifeworlds that evolve. Habermas's analysis also treats as basically self-evident the claim that a society must have one consistent legitimating set of norms accepted by its inhabitants—a very Parsonian view. However, as van den Berg has pointed out, Habermas does not actually provide any proof of this. It is thus possible to argue that "different value orientations can and do exist within the same system without any disastrous effects on its stability"[87]—that contradictions do not necessarily produce systemic change.

Habermas also uses this communicative perspective on social evolution to elaborate on the development of crises. They are to be found, he argues, at the "seam," where lifeworld and system meet. Continuing rationalization can become pathological if it goes so far as to endanger the whole process of social integration and socialization by which society reproduces itself. For example, the competitive individualism of the marketplace may destroy family structures. The bureaucratic welfare state can be equally destructive. "The deformations of a lifeworld that is regulated, fragmented, monitored, and looked after are surely more subtle than the palpable forms of material exploitation and impoverishment; but internalized social conflicts that have shifted from the corporeal to the psychic are not therefore less destructive."[88]

Reason and Rationalization

Habermas's analysis of rationalization is often very similar to Weber's. Yet he is not a Weberian: this is a dialogue and argument, not an exegesis. In his approach to reason and to the pessimism of Weber's "iron cage," Habermas stands directly in a line that goes through the Frankfurt School to Marx.

The Frankfurt theorists believed in the possibility of a "rational," not merely a "rationalized," society, and in the validity of critical theory compared to the products of other ideologically tainted theories. Marx, too, identified ideologies and argued that they were self-interested rather than true, while believing in the special status of his own theories. To skeptics[89] this has always seemed inconsistent, for if other people's beliefs reflect self-interest and socialization, this must be equally true of critical theorists. Moreover, the latter cannot *prove* that their values are the right ones. We can all discuss

---

[87]See especially Axel van den Berg, "Critical Theory: Is There Still Hope?" *American Journal of Sociology* 86, no. 3 (1980): 449–78, especially p. 465.

[88]Habermas, *Philosophical Discourse*, p. 362.

[89]See the discussion of Marcuse on pp. 100–105.

values and look at their empirical consequences, but they are not subject to proof. We accept them or we don't.

Habermas, however, in critical theory tradition, argues that you *can* provide grounding for the ultimate norms that govern our lives and thereby replace the void left by modernity's "disenchantment" of the world. His earlier work in this area centers on the concept of an "ideal-speech situation."[90] This is a situation in which everyone would have an equal chance to argue and question, without those who are more powerful, confident, or prestigious having an unequal say. True positions would prevail under these circumstances because they are more rational.

The theory of communicative action further develops the argument. Communicative action, Habermas argues, is a distinctive type of social interaction because it is oriented to mutual understanding and not to success or "purposive" achievement of ends.[91] Thus

> the goal of coming to an understanding is to bring about an agreement that terminates in the intersubjective mutuality of reciprocal understanding, shared knowledge, mutual trust, and accord with one another. Agreement is based on recognition of the corresponding validity claims of comprehensibility, truth, truthfulness, and rightness.[92]

The claim that Habermas makes here is common to his earlier and later work. It is that people can, in principle, agree on correct ways of proceeding and arguing. If we do accept and follow such procedural norms, we will then reach substantive agreement because the position of reason will win. More specifically, critical theory and its judgments will appear as objectively correct because they are based on less distorted communication than other approaches; in Giddens's paraphrase, they will be defensible as "meaningful, true, justified and sincere."[93]

Is this really the case? The writer Salman Rushdie lives under permanent police protection because his writing was seen by many Moslems as blasphemous, and some Islamic religious leaders have therefore pronounced it a holy act to kill him. Most Western intellectuals believe that writers should have the freedom to write about whatever they wish, and they therefore condemn the Moslem position. It is not obvious why rational communicative action would shift people's positions on this issue or on others, such as abortion, divorce, defense expenditure, or the government's role in the

---

[90] Habermas, *Legitimation Crisis* and *Knowledge and Human Interests.*

[91] There are echoes here of Aristotle's distinction between "techne," or the purposive action involved in making things, and "praxis," the distinctive human interaction exhibited in intersubjective communication. Compare Marx's use of "praxis," p. 79.

[92] Habermas, "What is Universal Pragmatics?" in *Communication and the Evolution of Society*, p. 3.

[93] Anthony Giddens, "Jürgen Habermas" in Quentin Skinner, ed., *The Return of Grand Theory in the Human Sciences* (New York: Cambridge University Press, 1985), p. 129.

economy. Habermas's critics, and indeed most social scientists, believe that value differences are ultimately irreconcilable.[94]

It is because of his belief in "reason" that Habermas does not consider the progressive rationalization of the world to be entirely negative. Because it demands that meaning and action be justified explicitly, it *also* creates the potential for rational discourse and noncoercive argumentation. Whereas purposive rationality in the arena of the system indeed creates an "iron cage," communicative rationality, Habermas argues, does not.[95]

This may be true; but Habermas has not actually provided us with examples of communicative rationality at work in groups. Nor does he grapple with the potential for conflict in such situations, however "reasonable" the participants. How can we assume that people are equally able to conduct the required discourse? Or that people's desire to be fair and just will really overcome not simply individual ends but family ties, sexual jealousy, the national and religious hatreds that tore apart Bosnia, and indeed the whole gamut of emotions from love to grief to hatred? Habermas's rejection of Weber's pessimistic conclusions seems as much a product of faith as argument.

This is not to imply that Habermas's concern with reason is a matter of academic philosophizing. One reason why European sociologists are so concerned with people's ideas and concepts, and their relationship to social systems, is that it is hard to explain the terrible history of the continent, especially in this century, in purely economic (or functionalist) terms. Habermas tells us that his own crucial formative experience was that of listening, as a German adolescent, to radio broadcasts of the Nuremberg trials of Nazi leaders and war criminals. Around him his elders disputed the justice of the trials by referring to general principles of procedure and questions of who had jurisdiction. They used concepts that were the product of rational modernity, he tells us, to close off the "collectively realized inhumanity" of Nazi Germany.

For a German of Habermas's generation, questions about social evolution must include questions about recent German history. Equally, academic discussion of the subject is not in present-day Germany something for amicable coffee-shop discussion (or, indeed, anything that looks much like ideal communicative action). In 1987 the intellectual and newspaper community was riven by a historians' dispute over whether fascism should be seen as a reaction to Bolshevism and Auschwitz and other death camps as rooted in the Russian Gulag. Predictably, Habermas was heavily involved in the attack on any such views.

---

[94]See, for example, van den Berg, "Critical Theory: Is There Still Hope?"
[95]See Pusey, *Jürgen Habermas*, p. 109.

PART FOUR

Anthony Giddens: Structuration Theory and High Modernity

One of the most widely read analysts of modernity is Anthony Giddens, a prolific British theorist who was professor of sociology at the University of Cambridge and is now director of the London School of Economics and an adviser to the British Prime Minister, Tony Blair. He has commented extensively on the writings of the classical theorists, such as Durkheim, Weber and most notably Marx; but also emphasizes the importance of integrating macro and micro perspectives. Giddens argues that most theorists have tended to be imperialists, claiming all the ground for their own favored concepts—whether these be structure and its constraining qualities (in the case of structuralism and functionalism) or action and meaning (as with symbolic interactionism and phenomenology).

> One of my principal ambitions . . . is to put an end to each of these empire-building endeavors. The basic domain of study of the social sciences . . . is neither the experience of the individual actor, nor the existence of any form of societal totality, but social practices ordered across space and time.[96]

To this end he has drawn particularly strongly on such writers as Erving Goffman and Alfred Schutz, whose micro-level ideas about social reproduction are discussed in Chapter 6. They inform Giddens's macro-level theories of structuration, evolution, and the nature of modernity.

The fullest exposition of Giddens's ideas appears in his *Constitution of Society*,[97] in which he sets forth his *theory of structuration*. He stresses the importance of recognizing that social theory must reconceptualize its subject matter "as a duality—the duality of structure."[98] It is as misleading to concentrate only on the activities of a "free agent" as it is to look only at structural constraints that set limits to free activity.[99] Both are necessary.

Giddens's key point is that human actors re-create through their actions the very social practices (and institutions) *that in turn constrain those actions*. They may also modify and change them. Thus human social life is formed and reformed in the course of the most normal routine activities.

---

[96]Anthony Giddens, *The Constitution of Society: Outline of the Theory of Structuration* (Cambridge: Polity Press, 1984).

[97]Giddens, *Constitution of Society*, passim.

[98]Giddens, *Constitution of Society*, p. xxi. Giddens defines structure as "rules and resources recursively implicated in the reproduction of social systems." *Central Problems in Social Theory: Action Structure and Contradiction in Social Analysis* (London: Macmillan, 1979), p. 64.

[99]Giddens, *Constitution of Society*, p. 139. Giddens's view of the individual as a "knowledgable actor" resembles that of George Herbert Mead. See Chapter 5.

Giddens expresses this by describing human action as essentially *transformational* and argues that "the structural properties of social systems exist only in so far as forms of social conduct are reproduced chronically across time and space."[100] This emphasis on social practices' continuation from day to day or year to year—"time"—and in different places—"space"—runs through all Giddens's writings.

So, too, does Giddens's insistence that this is not a mechanistic repetitive process in which we simply reproduce exactly what came before. Because social practices are modified as well as reproduced, we must reject "the presumption that it is possible to formulate theorems of structural causation which will explain the determination of social action in general."[101] The creative aspects of human action—the individual side of the duality— makes this impossible.[102] It follows that Giddens's ideas on evolution are also less deterministic than those of Marx.

SOCIAL STRUCTURE

Giddens's concern with the dynamics of institutional survival is similarly evident in his definition of social structure: "Structure refers, in social analysis, to the structuring properties . . . which make it possible for discernibly similar social practices to exist across varying spans of *time* and *space* and which lend them 'systemic' form."[103] Structure consists of the "rules and resources recursively implicated in the reproduction of social systems"[104]—that is, the rules that are articulated in social interaction and tell people how to "do" social life, and the resources on which people can call to achieve their objectives.[105]

One distinctive aspect of Giddens's discussion is the emphasis he places on the physical dimensions of human action and social structure. He is aware that we are biological creatures and that our bodies are very important to us and central to the whole process of "transformational" or social human action: "all social interaction is expressed at some point in and

[100]Giddens, *Constitution of Society*, pp. xxi and xxiii.

[101]Giddens, *Constitution of Society*, p. 227.

[102]It follows that all social research must include important parts that are particular to that situation and not to be deduced from general laws; it has a "necessarily cultural, ethnographic, or 'anthropological' aspect to it." Giddens, *Constitution of Society*, p. 237.

[103]Giddens, *Constitution of Society*, p. 17 (italics ours). Similarly, "social systems . . . are organized as regularized social practices, sustained in encounters dispersed across time-space": their existence encompasses different days, weeks, years, and decades, as well as different places. *Constitution of Society*, p. 83.

[104]Giddens, *Central Problems in Social Theory*, p. 64.

[105]"Resources" refer to a wide range of phenomena, similar to those itemized by Collins. See Chapter 3 of this text. Giddens also emphasizes the importance of unevenly distributed resources.

through the contextualities of bodily presence."[106] However, Giddens does not seem to believe that important regularities derive directly from the biological as such—he is no sociobiologist in the making. Rather, his formulation of the "problem of order" as how "it comes about that social systems 'bind' time and space, incorporating and integrating presence and absence",[107] directs him to the physical context of interaction.

The same perspective informs Giddens's rather distinctive classification of social types.[108] Giddens focuses not simply on economic forms of ownership but also on a way in which societies today are quite different from any before. In the past, although some societies were (partially) literate and developed books and even a rudimentary postal system, *communication was essentially and overwhelmingly face-to-face*. Politicians' "whistle-stop tours" by railroad were a way of meeting potential voters. Conversely, emigrants to the New World knew that farewells were, literally, forever.

In the developed societies of our world, none of this is true. Presidential candidates communicate by television commercials, not by hour-long speeches to large crowds (and Romeo and Juliet could use mobile telephones today). Change has been very rapid: for the first edition of this book we shared typed manuscripts and depended on the mail service, but now we collaborate by e-mail and send whole documents electronically to our publishers. In Giddens's terms, the "contemporary world system is, for the first time in human history, one in which absence in space no longer hinders system coordination."[109]

Giddens sees the past as dominated first by tribal and then by class-divided societies.[110] In tribal, and particularly *oral* (preliterate) societies, the dominant structural principle involves tradition and kinship, depending on large amounts of direct interaction between people. In class-divided societies, tradition and kinship remain very important, but there is some disentangling of the two from the institutional spheres of politics (with its standing armies, government officials, and formal legal codes) and economics (with markets, currency, and formal property rights).[111]

Giddens's habitual concern with the "binding together" of social life over time and over space leads him here to focus on the role of writing and of the city. Thus he argues, "Life is not experienced as 'structures' but as the

---

[106]Giddens, *Central Problems in Social Theory*, p. 297. His high opinion of Goffman's work is in considerable measure linked to Goffman's analyses of body management—for example, as seen in the discussion of front and back regions mentioned in Chapter 5.

[107]Giddens, *Central Problems in Social Theory*, p. 181.

[108]See especially Anthony Giddens, *A Contemporary Critique of Historical Materialism*. Vol. I: *Power, Property and the State* (London: Macmillan, 1981); see also Giddens, *Constitution of Society*, chap. 4.

[109]Giddens, *Constitution of Society*, p. 185.

[110]Here his analysis is in many respects similar to that of Habermas.

[111]Giddens emphasizes the differentiation of city from countryside in such societies.

durée of day-to-day existence. . . . In tribal and class-divided societies, the routinization of daily life is governed above all by tradition. . . . [T]he significance of tradition in purely oral cultures is different from those in which some form of writing exists. . . . [It expands] the level of time-space distanciation."[112]

Viewed from this same perspective,

> the city cannot be regarded as purely incidental to social theory but belongs at its very core. . . . [T]he city is . . . a *storage container* that permits time-space distanciation well beyond that characteristic of tribal societies. . . . The city is the generator of the authoritative resources out of which state power is created and sustained. . . . [Cities] are the basis of whatever administrative-political integration is achieved in that society as a whole. . . . In class-divided societies cities are crucibles of power.[113]

It follows, then, that modern capitalism was not just another, more "developed"[114] form of class-divided society, but rather the "first genuinely global type of societal organization in history."[115] In it, state and economic institutions are fully "disembedded" from the family and from orally transmitted traditions. The administrative concerns and reach of the state expand enormously, while the economic system has a built-in continuing tendency to produce technological innovation and greater wealth in a self-sustaining fashion.[116]

High Modernity

It is in the nature of the modern capitalism, as Giddens describes it, that change will continue. "Modern institutions differ from all preceding forms of social order in respect of their dynamism," he argues.[117] As the resulting changes accumulate, in the late twentieth century and "late modern" world what Giddens terms "the question of modernity" becomes a fundamental sociological issue once again.[118] The "globalizing tendencies of modernity," for example, reach a point at which major changes in society result.

---

[112]Giddens, *A Contemporary Critique of Historical Materialism*, Vol. I, p. 150.

[113]Giddens, *A Contemporary Critique of Historical Materialism*, pp. 140, 144, and 145.

[114]Giddens objects to accounts that portray history in strongly evolutionary form, pointing out that the "dissolution of states is no less common an occurrence than their initial formation" (*Constitution of Society*, p. 248). However, his own account does not differ much in its essentials from those of less self-conscious writers.

[115]Giddens, *Constitution of Society*, p. 183.

[116]Anthony Giddens, *The Class Structure of the Advanced Societies* (London: Hutchinson, 1973), p. 252.

[117]Anthony Giddens, *Modernity and Self-Identity: Self and Society in the Late Modern Age* (Cambridge: Polity, 1991), p. 1.

[118]Giddens, *Modernity and Self-Identity*, p. 1.

One of the most important aspects of modernity is that tradition is replaced with *expertise*. The effects of this are increasingly global: no one can avoid the attendant "disembedding" mechanisms entirely. As Giddens explains it, tradition is bound up with memory and ritual: it is formulaic and accepted as true, and as a guide to action, because of the "combined moral and emotional content"[119] that goes with it. "Tradition . . . is an *organizing medium of collective memory*,"[120] and it is attended by "guardians" whose authority derives from their relation to this collective memory.

In its earlier phases, Giddens argues, modernity has destroyed tradition but then rebuilt it. In fact, "the persistence and recreation of tradition were central to the legitimation of power. . . . (T)radition placed in stasis some core aspects of social life—not least the family and sexual identity—which were left largely untouched."[121] Now, however, this has changed. Traditions are destroyed and not rebuilt—in part because of the spread of modern institutions worldwide, and thus the sheer scale of the modernization process, and in part because of internal changes that undercut traditions' legitimacy.

What replaces tradition are experts, expertise, expert systems. These are what Giddens calls "disembedding": they relate to principles outside the concrete local environment, and they demand trust in abstract arguments and universal principles. However, looking to disembedded expertise as a source of legitimate authority and to provide guidance on what one should do (or eat, or say to one's partner) sets up tensions of its own, which are central to the current period of high modernity.

"The accumulation of expert knowledge involves intrinsic processes of specialization," Giddens points out. Whereas "guardians" were special in all aspects of their lives, people who are "experts" in one sphere are themselves simply laypersons looking for guidance in most of the things that affect them. Moreover, the whole nature of expert knowledge is unsettling. It is marked by a *"mixture of skepticism and universalism. . . .* [e]xperts disagree" as an integral part of developing and refining their expertise; "traditions of thought are understood by sympathizer and critic alike to be relatively arbitrary."[122] All knowledge is open to correction and continuing refinement; so society is left with the feeling of resting on shifting sand. Moreover, the nature of globalization means that now everyone in the world experiences this disembedding for at least some aspects of their lives.[123]

Many of the processes that Giddens identifies resemble those discussed by, for example, Parsons or Habermas: the undermining of traditional sources of legitimacy, the growth of specialized knowledge, and the impor-

---

[119]Giddens, *Living in a Post-Traditional Society*, p. 63.
[120]Giddens, *Living in a Post-Traditional Society*, p. 64.
[121]Giddens, *Living in a Post-Traditional Society*, p. 56.
[122]Giddens, *Living in a Post-Traditional Society*, p. 86 (italics original).
[123]Giddens, *Modernity and Self-Identity*, p. 22.

tance of universalism. Giddens's argument, however, is that the accumulation of these processes over time has brought us to a new phase in social evolution; that global "high modernity" is characterized by changes in the nature of personal identity and experience of the world. In understanding these changes, he emphasizes the importance of risk and of self-identity as "a reflexively organized endeavor."[124]

RISK AND REFLEXIVITY: GIDDENS AND BECK

Giddens's ideas on risk have been heavily influenced by the work of Ulrich Beck, professor of sociology at the University of Munich, Germany, whose book on Risk Society brought him considerable fame in Germany. Both Beck and Giddens argue that the concept of risk is fundamental to understanding modern society—not because life is inherently more risky than in the past, but because "the concept of risk becomes fundamental to the way both lay actors and technical specialists organize the social world."[125]

Beck attacks those who see twentieth-century societies as somehow the pinnacle of modernity when in fact they are already dissolving and *"another modernity is coming into being."*[126] Beck sees risk as the defining characteristic of the form of society that is now developing and replacing its precursor, industrial or class society. According to him,

> The driving force in the class society can be summarized in the phrase: *I am hungry!* The movement set in motion by the risk society, on the other hand, is expressed in the statement *I am afraid!* The *commonality of anxiety* takes the place of the *commonality of need.*[127]

In industrial society people were prepared to accept the side effects of modernization because of the rewards it offered in a struggle against scarcity. Now people are no longer hungry, and meanwhile they face risks and hazards that are "a *wholesale product* of industrialization and are systematically intensified as it becomes global."[128] The risks to which Beck refers are above all those of pollution, "nuclear and chemical productive forces,"[129] and their attendant ecological damage. He believes that these introduce risks into

[124]Giddens, *Modernity and Self-Identity*, p. 5.

[125]Giddens, *Modernity and Self-Identity*, p. 3. For a similar analysis see the work of Niklas Luhmann, discussed in Chapter 2.

[126]Ulrich Beck, *Risk Society: Towards a New Modernity* trans. Mark Ritter (Thousand Oaks, Calif.: Sage, 1992), pp. 10, 11. Italics original.

[127]For a somewhat contrasting analysis of how late–twentieth-century people build up beliefs in their personal control over their lives, see Albert Bandura, ed., *Self-Efficacy in Changing Societies* (New York: Cambridge University Press, 1995).

[128]Beck, *Risk Society: Towards a New Modernity*, p. 21.

[129]Beck, *Risk Society: Towards a New Modernity*, p. 22.

our world that are quite different in scale and potential effects from those of other eras, and that growing awareness of this on the part of the public withdraws legitimacy from the whole process of modernization.

Beck's identification of ecological issues as defining and creating the new form of society seems, to a non-German reader, to reflect the far greater importance of Green issues (and of public anxiety about pollution and food additives) in German politics than in most other countries. Giddens's concept is a rather more general one, although he also emphasizes that the whole nature and conception of risk among human beings is changing profoundly. In our societies, "the concept of risk becomes fundamental to the way both lay actors and technical specialists organize the social world. Under conditions of modernity, the future is continually drawn into the present by means of the reflexive organization of knowledge environments."[130] People in the past lived at constant risk of disease, crop failure, and warfare; but they were not able, as we are, to try to quantify the risks, set out alternative scenarios, and insure and plan their lives accordingly. The whole way they conceived of their options and future lives was different.

Giddens also agrees with Beck that under "high modernity" we face the possibility of *global* dangers, such as nuclear warfare or ecological catastrophe, in a way that previous generations did not.

> On the global level . . . modernity has become experimental. We are all, willynilly, caught up in a grand experiment, which is at the one time our doing—as human agents—yet to an imponderable degree outside of our control. . . . It is not an experiment in the laboratory sense . . . more like a dangerous adventure.[131]

This new modernity, where we feel out of control, differs from the conception of, for example, Weber, who saw modern societies as increasingly controlled through "rational" bureaucracies. The result is that we all, worldwide, come to share a framework of experience and perceived risk. It also means that the way we experience the world, as individuals, undergoes profound changes toward what Giddens calls "self-identity" as a "reflexively organized endeavor."[132] Alongside the perception that anything in the world can be changed—though often not in the way that anyone intended—there comes a view of oneself and one's identity as something that involves choices, decisions, and creation. The loss of tradition means that people have to decide on their lifestyle, their relationships with people, and the sort of person they are going to be.

This even applies to our bodies, Giddens argues. "The reflexivity of the self . . . affects the body as well as psychic processes. The body is less and

---

[130]Giddens, *Modernity and Self-Identity*, p. 3.
[131]Giddens, *Reflexive Modernization*, p. 59.
[132]Giddens, *Modernity and Self-Identity*, p. 5.

less an extrinsic 'given' . . . but become itself reflexively mobilized."[133] This is a theme to which we will return in Chapter 8 in discussing the way that sociologists have rediscovered the body.[134] Of course, as the micro perspectives to which we now turn would emphasize, there has always been, in human activity, a central element of self-interaction, of thinking about what one is doing and how it affects oneself and others. What Giddens argues, however, is that the reflexivity of modernity is something different. It means knowing—or at least assuming—that almost all aspects of social activity, and of the material world, are susceptible to "chronic revision in the light of new information or knowledge."[135] This is not something that our ancestors felt; and it is only recently that this attitude has reached every corner of our social lives and physical being.

CONCLUSION

The renewed interest in evolutionary theories reflects, in large measure, a sense that technological and social change is now extremely rapid and that mid–twentieth-century industrial society is no longer a guide to what life will be like in the new millennium. At the same time the evident globalization of the economy makes it plausible to argue for global developments of a more general kind. However, the younger theorists discussed here do not have the same confidence as Marx that they can predict the future; nor do they even share Parsons's view that evolutionary change to date has in some ways been inevitable in its direction and nature.

In this they reflect the general intellectual climate. Developments such as chaos theory emphasize the major effects that tiny changes can have on the physical world; while in psychology and through perspectives such as phenomenology, the emphasis is on the nondetermined and creative aspects of human action and perception. As a result sociologists have come to emphasize the limitations of grand theories and especially when they aim to predict the future. Seymour Martin Lipset, for example, argues that

> we have to face a general limitation of social science, its inherent inability to predict the particular. . . . Social science is at its best in advancing what Robert Merton has called "middle-range" theories and in explaining developments limited in time and space—particularly in the past—where at least there is some possibility of analyzing real data.[136]

---

[133]Giddens, *Modernity and Self-Identity*, p. 7.

[134]Giddens himself is especially interested in anorexia as an indication of this new "reflexivity of self." See Chapter 8, Part 1 for a variety of perspectives on anorexia.

[135]Giddens, *Modernity and Self-Identity*, p. 20.

[136]Seymour Martin Lipset and Gyorgy Bence, "Anticipation of the Failure of Communism," *Theory and Society* 23.3 (1994): pp. 169–71.

Evolutionary theories thus have tended to concentrate on identifying salient and defining aspects of modernity rather than predicting the future. In doing so, however, they provide an interesting but somewhat unbalanced picture. For example, the emphasis placed by Habermas on the legitimacy crisis in modern societies might lead a reader to expect higher levels of overt dissatisfaction with modern systems of government than in the past. In fact, the last decade of the century has proven singularly *unrevolutionary* compared to the periods that produced the American and French revolutions or those of Russia, China, Cuba, and Vietnam.

Similarly, the emphasis on risk in Giddens's and Beck's work seems to reflect the priorities and concerns of a subset of Western populations rather than a major issue for most politicians and voters. Are our societies really more prone to anxiety over uncontrollable external forces than was the case in previous periods (such as the seventeenth century, characterized by witchcraft scares, or the nineteenth, with its widespread belief in spiritualists' ability to make contact with the dead)? The reflexive nature of modern self-identity, and the belief that one can make oneself anew as one chooses, emphasized by Giddens, certainly reflect major social changes; but even they seem less distinctive from the perspective of the United States, a "new" nation to which most people[137] came voluntarily in pursuit of a new life and identity, than from a European standpoint.

Nonetheless, in spite of these criticisms, the evolutionary theorists discussed here provide a stimulating overview of how our societies are developing, and they identify major and far-reaching differences between our "reality" and that of our ancestors. The microsociological perspectives to which we now turn deepen our understanding of the links between these macro-level changes and the way we actually experience life in our changing society.

---

[137]The major exception is, of course, those brought as slaves.

CHAPTER FIVE

Symbolic Interactionism

INTRODUCTION

The term *symbolic interactionism* originated with Herbert Blumer, who describes it as "a somewhat barbaric neologism that I coined in an offhand way in an article written in *Man and Society*. The term somehow caught on and is now in general use."[1]

Man and Society was designed to survey the field of the social sciences and to serve as an "introduction to the spirit, the methods, and the subject matter of each of the social sciences."[2] Herbert Blumer, invited to write the chapter on social psychology, coined the term *symbolic interactionism* in an attempt to clarify how social psychologists differed in their views of human nature. Blumer explained that social psychology was largely interested in the social development of the individual and that its central task was to study how the individual develops socially as a result of participating in group life.

To study the social development of the individual, Blumer proposed, it is necessary to consider the "nature of the equipment with which the human infant begins life."[3] First he discussed two views of original nature with which he disagreed: instinct psychology, which emphasizes the importance of unreasoned natural impulses, and the stimulus-response approach, which sees behavior as acquired but essentially involuntary responses to external stimuli.[4] Blumer contrasted these with the position he held, explaining that his approach pictures the newborn infant as unorganized and dependent on adults for direction and survival. According to his view,

> the development of the infant into childhood and adulthood is fundamentally a matter of forming organized or concerted activity in place of its previous random activity, and of channelizing its impulses and giving them goals or objectives. This view, then, . . . recognizes original nature to be important, but not determinative of its subsequent development. It emphasizes the active nature of the child, the plasticity of this nature, and the importance of the unformed impulse. It is substantially the view taken by the group of social psychologists who may be conveniently labeled "symbolic interactionists."[5]

Thus the term was born. However, for all his later remarks, Blumer's use of the word *symbolic* reflects an important theoretical viewpoint, not the offhand labeling of a perspective. In *Man and Society* Blumer identifies the

---

[1]Blumer, Herbert, *Symbolic Interactionism: Perspective and Method*, 1969, p. 1. Other excerpts from pp. 75, 70, 71, 62, 37, 40, 34, 87. Prentice Hall, Upper Saddle River, New Jersey. Used by permission.

[2]Emerson P. Schmidt, ed., *Man and Society* (Englewood Cliffs, N.J.: Prentice-Hall, Inc., 1937), p. v.

[3]Schmidt, *Man and Society*, pp. 146–47.

[4]See Chapter 7, where we discuss the stimulus-response approach in relation to the work of George C. Homans.

[5]Schmidt, *Man and Society*, pp. 151–52.

cornerstone of symbolic interactionism: a common set of symbols and understanding possessed by people in a group.[6] Symbolic interactionists assume that the key elements in children's milieus are the symbols and understandings that guide the individuals around them. This common set of symbols and understandings that make a child's social environment symbolic are given great prominence by this perspective.

Symbolic interactionism, then, is essentially a social-psychological perspective; it focuses primarily on the individual "with a self" and on the interaction between a person's internal thoughts and emotions and his or her social behavior. Most of the analysis is of small-scale interpersonal relationships. Individuals are viewed as active constructors of their own conduct who interpret, evaluate, define, and map out their own action, rather than as passive beings who are impinged upon by outside forces.[7] Symbolic interactionism also stresses the processes by which the individual makes decisions and forms opinions.

According to symbolic interactionists, the form interaction takes emerges from the particular situation concerned. This contrasts with what Blumer calls the "straitjacket" approach of functionalists, whose stress on norms implies that most interaction is fixed in advance. Although symbolic interactionists admit the influence of social rules, these are not their primary concern, and neither are the average behavior and the general shape of institutions, which other theorists concentrate on.[8] Rather, they are primarily concerned with fully explaining individuals' particular decisions and actions and with demonstrating the impossibility of explaining these by predetermined rules and external forces.

INTELLECTUAL ROOTS: MAX WEBER AND GEORG SIMMEL

The forerunners of and direct contributors to the symbolic interactionist perspective include George Simmel, Robert Park, William Isaac Thomas, Charles Horton Cooley, John Dewey, and George Herbert Mead.[9] Max Weber should also be cited, for in his definition of sociology he emphasized the importance of *verstehen* (interpretive understanding or subjective meaning):

[6]Schmidt, *Man and Society*, p. 159.

[7]Anthony Giddens, whose work on structuration theory is discussed in Chapter 4, borrows from symbolic interactionism the role of human agency, the view that social life is an active accomplishment of purposive, knowledgeable actors. See Anthony Giddens, *Central Problems in Social Theory* (Berkeley: University of California Press, 1979), p. 50.

[8]See, for example, "Conflict Theory" (Chapter 3).

[9]In addition, Blumer mentions E. W. Burgess, Florian Znaniecki, Ellsworth Faris, James Mickel Williams, and William James. See Blumer, *Symbolic Interactionism*, p. 78.

Sociology is a science which attempts the *interpretive* understanding of social action in order thereby to arrive at a causal explanation of its course and effects. In "action" is included all human behavior when and insofar as the *acting individual* attaches a *subjective meaning* to it. Action in this sense may be either overt or purely inward or subjective; it may consist of positive intervention in a situation, or of deliberately refraining from such intervention or passively acquiescing in the situation. Action is social insofar as, by virtue of the *subjective meaning* attached to it by the *acting individual* (or individuals), it takes account of the behavior of others and is thereby oriented in its course.[10]

Weber's action theory, with an emphasis on the individual's interpretation of a situation and on the importance of subjective meaning, influenced the emergence of symbolic interactionism. Earlier in the text we highlighted Weber's contribution to conflict theory.[11] His significance to the symbolic interactionist perspective is an illustration of the breadth of his theoretical contributions and, in particular, his ability to bridge macro and micro perspectives.

Georg Simmel, Robert Park's intellectual mentor, was also of central importance to the development of this perspective. We can understand Simmel's influence on the early symbolic interactionists by examining his defense of many of the tenets of this approach to sociological analysis:

To confine ourselves to the large social formations resembles the older science of anatomy with its limitation to the major, definitely circumscribed organs such as heart, liver, lungs, and stomach, and with its neglect of the innumerable, popularly unnamed or unknown tissues. Yet without these, the more obvious organs could never constitute a living organism.

Similarly, Simmel says, society is pieced together by "countless minor syntheses." He describes some of these human linkages:

That people look at one another and are jealous of one another; that they exchange letters or dine together; . . . that gratitude for altruistic acts makes for inseparable union; that one asks another man after a certain street, and that people dress and adorn themselves for one another—the whole gamut of relations that play from one person to another and that may be momentary or permanent, conscious or unconscious, ephemeral or of grave consequence, . . . all these incessantly tie men together. Here are the interactions among the atoms of society. They account for all the toughness and elasticity, all the color and consistency of social life, that is so striking and yet so mysterious.[12]

---

[10]Max Weber, *The Theory of Social and Economic Organization*, trans. and ed. A. M. Henderson and Talcott Parsons (New York: Oxford University Press, 1964), p. 88. Emphasis ours. Copyright 1947, 1975 by Talcott Parsons. Reprinted by permission of The Free Press, a division of Macmillan, Inc.

[11]See Chapter 3.

[12]Kurt H. Wolff, ed. and trans., *The Sociology of Georg Simmel* (New York: The Free Press, 1950), pp. 1–10. Copyright 1950, 1978 by The Free Press, a division of Macmillan, Inc. Reprinted by permission of the publisher.

Simmel's words are encouraging for sociologists interested in analyzing individual behavior, as contrasted with those whose interests lie in analyzing social systems. This is so not only because the details of individual behavior are themselves of interest, but because some crucial decisions are made on the individual level, among the "atoms of society," which can cause reverberations throughout an entire nation. These decisions help us, as Simmel puts it, "to piece together the real life of society as we encounter it in our experience." One dramatic example is a decision made by Frank Wills, a security guard at the Watergate complex, who noticed some tape on the lock of a door on the evening of June 17, 1972. On his first round of inspection, he simply removed the tape. On the second round, when he saw the same door taped again, he reinterpreted the situation and decided to phone the police. Some sociologists are interested in analyzing behavior like this, which triggered a series of events leading to the resignation of the late President Nixon and to changes in party structure, such as campaign financing limitations. For many of them, the inspiration for such analysis is supplied by Georg Simmel, and Simmel's formal sociology, the "geometry of social space," has become a blueprint.[13]

Two of Simmel's key concepts are the *dyad* and the *triad*. In stressing the significance of numbers for social life, Simmel argues that in a dyadic relationship, each of the two participants is confronted by one other. Hence neither can deny responsibility by shifting it to the group. Because a dyad depends on only two participants, a withdrawal of one will destroy the whole.[14] The transformation of a dyad into a triad, however, causes a major qualitative change. In a triadic relationship an individual participant is confronted with the possibility of being outvoted by the majority. Thus the triad can impose its will upon one member through the formation of a coalition by the other two. Three types of strategy are open to the third participant: playing the role of mediator between the other two and helping to keep the group intact; turning a disagreement between the other two to his or her own advantage; or intentionally creating conflicts between the others for his or her advantage. Simmel's microsociological examples of triadic relationships include the competition of two men for one woman. Other examples of a triad would be the addition of a third roommate in a college dorm, an aged parent moving in with a married son or daughter, or an adult returning to live in the parents' home.

The link from Georg Simmel in Germany to a group of social psychologists at the University of Chicago was forged when Robert Park spent one semester in Simmel's classroom. "It was from Simmel," Park wrote, "that I

---

[13]See Lewis A. Coser, *Masters of Sociological Thought* (New York: Harcourt Brace Jovanovich, 1977), p. 215.

[14]Wolff, *The Sociology of Georg Simmel*, p. 124.

finally gained a fundamental point of view for the study of the newspaper and society."[15]

Simmel's conception of society as a system of interaction, his interest in the geometry of social space, and his stress on social process were adopted by Park and passed on to his students and colleagues at the University of Chicago, which became the birthplace of symbolic interactionism.

A significant theoretical contribution to symbolic interactionism is William Isaac Thomas's notion of the "definition of the situation." Thomas believed that individuals have the power to ignore a stimulus that they responded to at an earlier time and that "preliminary to any self-determined act of behavior there is always a stage of examination and deliberation which we may call the definition of the situation."[16] Even more important is Thomas's belief that people's definitions of the situation have behavioral consequences. Thomas's theorem was stated this way: "If men [sic] define situations as real, they are real in their consequences."[17] Thomas argued that unless researchers pay attention to subjective meanings or definitions of the situation, they cannot understand human activity. In her study of gender differences in law firms, for instance, Jennifer Pierce quotes a male litigator's definition of the situation regarding the adversarial role:

> You have to be aggressive and sneaky in this business. It's part of the job. People who don't like it should stop whimpering and get the hell out. . . . Women just don't have the balls to be tough litigators. It's just one of those things that men do better. . . . Women are good at writing briefs.[18]

In our own everyday lives we know that women and men, younger and older people, upper- and lower-class workers, will often present different definitions of the same situation. Witness the various ways people interpret and evaluate news items, episodes in a movie, segments of sports events, even common cultural objects like a flag, a dishwasher, or a computer. Young children, for instance, often create an imaginary playmate. The playmate, who is real for the child, may have consequences for other family members as well. They may interact with the playmate, even to the point of setting an extra place at the dinner table.

Together with Thomas, Park encouraged students to study various aspects of the social processes in their own city. Rather than examining social structure with a camera producing "still" pictures of social life, Park's stu-

---

[15]Paul J. Baker, "The Life Histories of W. I. Thomas and Robert E. Park, with an Introduction by Paul J. Baker," *American Journal of Sociology* 79 (1973): 256.

[16]William I. Thomas, *The Unadjusted Girl* (Boston: Little, Brown, 1923), p. 41.

[17]William I. Thomas (with Dorothy Swaine Thomas), *The Child in America* (New York: Alfred A. Knopf, 1928).

[18]See Jennifer L. Pierce, *Gender Trials: Emotional Lives in Contemporary Law Firms* (Berkeley: University of California Press, 1995), pp. 136–37.

dents used the "moving camera" of the naturalistic approach to catch life as it was happening. The Chicago School produced Thomas and Znaniecki's classic piece of research on the adjustment of first-generation Polish immigrants, *The Polish Peasant in Europe and America*; Frederick M. Thrasher's research on juvenile delinquency, *The Gang*; Louis Wirth's investigation of the densely populated district where most of Chicago's first-generation Jewish immigrants lived, *The Ghetto*; and Harvey W. Zorbaugh's analysis of the juxtaposition of affluent and slum sections of Chicago, *The Gold Coast and the Slum*.[19]

Charles Horton Cooley, who taught all his life at his alma mater, the University of Michigan at Ann Arbor, was also a forerunner of symbolic interactionism. One of his important contributions is his conception of the "looking-glass self"—that is, the self you understand as a result of the information reflected back at you in the judgments of others with whom you interact. Cooley's three elements of the looking-glass self are "the imagination of our appearance to the other person; the imagination of his judgment of that appearance; and some sort of self-feeling, such as pride or mortification."[20]

As Cooley points out, the looking glass does not suggest the imagination of the other's judgment of our appearance, but he sees this as an essential element. In fact, Cooley states, "the imaginations which people have of one another are the solid facts of society, and to observe and interpret these must be the chief aim of sociology."[21] In other words, both the larger social structure and such constructs as industrial organizations and political parties ultimately rest on these "solid facts."

However, symbolic interactionism was systematized not by these forerunners but by two major theorists, George Herbert Mead and Herbert Blumer. Although Blumer is viewed as the intellectual leader of symbolic interactionism among social theorists, he owes a great deal to his teacher, George Herbert Mead. Most of the elements of symbolic interactionism are

---

[19]See Faris's description of the "golden era" of Chicago sociology. R. E. L. Faris, *Chicago Sociology 1920–1932* (Chicago: University of Chicago Press, 1970). Mary Jo Deegan, "Symbolic Interaction and the Study of Women: An Introduction," in Mary Jo Deegan and Michael Hill, eds., *Women and Symbolic Interaction* (Boston: Allen and Unwin, 1987), pp. 3–15, has suggested that Jane Addams, who described the world of Chicago during the founding years of the Chicago School of Symbolic Interaction, should be listed as a major figure of this school. See Jane Addams, *Twenty Years at Hull-House* (New York: Macmillan, 1910). See also Mary Jo Deegan, *Jane Addams and the Men of the Chicago School: 1890–1918* (New Brunswick, N.J.: Transaction Press, 1986), for an analysis of Addams's relation to the work of Mead and Thomas. See also Patricia Madoo Lengermann and Jill Niebrugge-Brantley, *The Women Founders: Sociology and Social Theory, 1830–1930* (New York: McGraw-Hill, 1998) for an eye-opening account of fifteen hitherto unknown women sociologists who contributed to classical sociological theory, including Jane Addams.

[20]Charles Horton Cooley, *Human Nature and the Social Order* (New York: Charles Scribner's Sons, 1902), p. 184.

[21]Cooley, *Human Nature and the Social Order*, p. 121.

Meadian in origin, and Blumer acknowledged Mead as the most important influence on his thinking.

PART ONE

George Herbert Mead: The Self

It has been said of George Herbert Mead (1863–1931) that "he may now well be reckoned as one among a handful of American thinkers who have helped to shape the character of modern social science."[22] Mead's father was a Puritan clergyman who taught homiletics at Oberlin, where Mead received a B.A. in 1883. His mother was president of Mount Holyoke College after her husband's death. After one year of additional study in philosophy and Greek, Mead received a second B.A. at Harvard in 1888.[23] While at Harvard Mead studied under Josiah Royce and was converted to pragmatic philosophy. In Europe he did graduate studies under Wilhelm Wundt at Leipzig, where he also met G. Stanley Hall; he later studied at Berlin but never completed his doctorate. On returning home Mead taught for two years at the University of Michigan, Ann Arbor, where he met and became friends with John Dewey and Charles Horton Cooley. When Dewey moved to the University of Chicago, Mead decided to follow him, and he taught in the philosophy department there until his death in 1931.

Mead published over eighty articles in his lifetime. More than half of his writing concerned reform issues, such as immigrants, settlement houses, women's suffrage, labor, education, and democracy. On many of these issues he was deeply influenced by his friend and colleague, Jane Addams. Deegan reveals that Mead spoke at a suffrage meeting in 1912, and a few years later "he marched down Michigan Avenue in the company of John Dewey, Jane Addams, and other distinguished Chicago citizens, for the same cause."[24]

But Mead's most famous book was published posthumously, taken from the lecture notes of his students who gathered them for publication. This book, *Mind, Self and Society*, will be one of our chief sources for the basic components of Mead's theory. The four elements we have chosen to highlight are the self, self-interaction, the development of the self, and symbolic meaning.

---

[22]Coser, *Masters of Sociological Thought*, p. 347.

[23]We wish to thank Professor Harold L. Orbach for supplying us with a copy of a page from the 1908–09 Annual Register from the University of Chicago, listing Mead's educational background (p. 26).

[24]See Deegan, *Jane Addams and the Men of the Chicago School*, pp. 106 and 116.

THE SELF

Mead's view of the self is central to symbolic interactionism. He sees the self as an acting organism, not as a passive receptacle that simply receives and responds to stimuli. Blumer explains:

> For Mead, the self is far more than an "internalization of components of social structure and culture." It is more centrally a *social process*, a process of self-interaction in which the human actor indicates to himself matters that confront him in the situation in which he acts, and organizes his action through his interpretation of such matters. The actor engages in this social interaction with himself, according to Mead, by taking the roles of others, addressing himself through these roles, and responding to these approaches. This conception of self-interaction in which the actor is pointing out things to himself lies at the basis of Mead's scheme of social psychology.[25]

The self, then, is active and creative; there are no such ingredients as social, cultural, or psychological variables that determine the actions of the self. Blumer often depicted social scientists' different views of the self in his own classroom teaching by means of a drawing like Figure 5-1, as he enthusiastically transmitted Mead's ideas to his students. Here one can see what the symbolic interactionists are rejecting in the functionalists' view of the individual. Functionalists like Parsons tend to look at human beings as passive agents impinged upon by social and psychological forces. According to Blumer, "the process of self-indication by means of which human action is formed cannot be accounted for by factors which precede the act."[26] In

---

[25]Herbert Blumer, "Comments on 'Parsons as a Symbolic Interactionist,'" *Sociological Inquiry* 45 (1975): 68.

[26]Blumer, *Symbolic Interactionism*, p. 82.

FIGURE 5-1   Blumer's View of the Individual

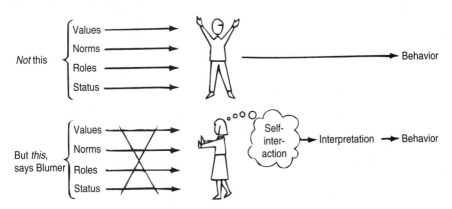

Blumer's estimation, social exchange theorists like George Homans share this passive view of human beings. Blumer writes,

> The self, or indeed human being, is not brought into the picture merely by introducing psychological elements, such as motives and interests, alongside of societal elements. Such additions merely compound the error of the omission. This is the flaw in George Homans's presidential address on "Bringing Men Back In."[27]

In contrast to this passive view of the individual, Mead stresses people's ability, through the mechanism of self-interaction, to form and guide their own conduct. Mead's position is that individuals act on their own environment, and in so doing they create the objects that people it. He distinguishes between "things," or stimuli that exist prior to and independent of the individual, and "objects," which exist only in relation to acts. "Things" are converted to "objects" through the acts of individuals.[28] A tomato, for instance, serves as an object of nutrition when it is eaten and as an object of an expression of anger when it is thrown. The individual, by acting on it, designates the tomato as food in one instance and as a weapon in another. The tomato is not intrinsically either of these; it is simply a "thing" before the individual acts on it. Thus, Mead's "person" is more active and more creative than is social exchange and functional theorists' "person" or "ego."

Symbolic interactionism avoids a deterministic stance by refusing to treat the self as something that is undifferentiated. Specifically, Mead outlines two "phases" of the self. One phase is the "I," which Mead sees as the unorganized response of the organism to the attitudes of others, the spontaneous disposition or impulse to act. The other is the "me," a set of organized attitudes of others that the individual himself assumes in turn; that is, those perspectives on oneself that the individual has learned from others.[29] Mead says, "The attitudes of the others constitute the organized 'me,' and then one reacts toward that as an 'I.'"[30] The "me" guides the behavior of the socialized person, and this aspect of the self brings the influence of others into the individual's consciousness. On the other hand, the incalculable spontaneity of the "I" allows for a certain degree of innovation and creativity as well as a degree of freedom from control by others.[31] As Mead puts it:

---

[27]Blumer, *Symbolic Interactionism*, p. 64. We discuss Homans's address in Chapter 7.

[28]See George J. McCall and J. L. Simmons, *Identities and Interaction* (New York: The Free Press, 1966), pp. 50–51.

[29]See the discussion in McCall and Simmons, *Identities and Interaction*, p. 55.

[30]George Herbert Mead, *Mind, Self & Society from the Standpoint of a Social Behaviorist* (Chicago: University of Chicago Press, 1934), p. 175.

[31]By contrast, functionalism allows only for the "me"; the "I" is Mead's addition to the view of the self. See Chapter 2. In our estimation, the "I" disappears in the work of Kuhn's "Iowa School" of symbolic interactionism, which is one reason we omitted it in this text.

The "I," then, in this relation of the "I" and the "me," is something that is, so to speak, responding to a social situation which is within the experience of the individual. It is the answer which the individual makes to the attitude which others take toward him when he assumes an attitude toward them. Now, the attitudes he is taking toward them will contain a novel element. The "I" gives the sense of freedom, of initiative.[32]

The self, then, consists of the acting "I" when the self is the subject and of the acted-upon "me" when the self is the object. Mead concludes,

The self is essentially a social process going on with these two distinguishable phases. If it did not have these two phases there could not be conscious responsibility, and there would be nothing novel in experience.[33]

SELF-INTERACTION

Because he makes room for what is "novel in experience," Mead offers social scientists a perspective that enables them to analyze behavior that is "unstructured" and not affected by previously established conventions. For instance, symbolic interactionists would be interested in analyzing Roentgen's accidental discovery of X-rays. According to Thomas Kuhn,

The physicist Roentgen interrupted a normal investigation of cathode rays because he had noticed that a barium platinocyanide screen at some distance from his shielded apparatus glowed when the discharge was in process. Further investigations—they required seven hectic weeks during which Roentgen rarely left the laboratory—indicated that the cause of the glow came in straight lines from the cathode ray tube, that the radiation cast shadows, could not be deflected by magnet, and much else besides. Before announcing his discovery, Roentgen had convinced himself that his effect was not due to cathode rays but to an agent with at least some similarity to light.[34]

Kuhn adds that this discovery was greeted with surprise and shock, principally because X-rays violated deeply entrenched expectations.[35]

As Kuhn explains it, a discovery like Roentgen's necessitates "paradigm change" and changes in expectations and laboratory procedures. He defines *paradigms* as "universally recognized scientific achievements that for a time provide model problems and solutions to a community of practi-

---

[32]Mead, *Mind, Self and Society*, p. 177.

[33]Mead, *Mind, Self and Society*, p. 178.

[34]Thomas S. Kuhn, *The Structure of Scientific Revolutions* (Chicago: University of Chicago Press, 1970), p. 57. Copyright © 1962, 1970 by The University of Chicago Press. Reprinted by permission.

[35]Kuhn, *The Structure of Scientific Revolutions*, p. 59.

tioners," and he stresses that changes meet considerable resistance at all times.[36]

Why is it so rare for an investigator like Roentgen to make such an accidental discovery—to perceive that something has happened that his paradigm has not prepared him to perceive and cannot explain? According to Kuhn, such a discovery goes against the idea of normal science, which does not aim at novelties of fact or theory. Rather than abandon the theories and ideas they use to perceive and understand the world, people will try to explain away anomalous findings, to show that they do not really disprove the current paradigm. So Kuhn suggests that a discovery that commences with an awareness of anomaly must continue with a more or less extended exploration of the area of the anomaly, which then results in an adjustment of paradigm theory.[37]

In analyzing why Roentgen continued investigating and discovered X-rays instead of explaining them away, Mead would emphasize Roentgen's self-interaction. What did Roentgen say to himself during those fateful days before he was finally convinced that he had made a discovery? First of all, he had to persuade himself that in spite of the existing paradigm he had indeed seen the glow, that it was not a figment of his imagination, a mirage caused by his own fatigue, or an inconsequential oddity. During those seven weeks in the laboratory, Roentgen must have been asking himself, over and over again, how the phenomenon happened, where it came from, what produced the glow, under what conditions, and why it occurred. Through this kind of self-interaction, combined with repeated experimentation, Roentgen finally convinced himself of his discovery; and the nature of this dialogue determined whether he did so.

The internal conversations one has with oneself are an essential part of the Meadian perspective because they are the means by which human beings take things into account and organize themselves for action. Self-interaction is also the basis for role-taking, which is at the heart of Mead's conception of the human act. Mead explains that communication is a process whereby each person "takes the role of the other"; that is, each person "assumes the attitude of the other individual as well as calling it out in the other," which would be impossible without self-interaction. Mead's description of role-taking underlines the importance of individuals "putting themselves in the other's shoes." As he puts it,

> He himself is in the role of the other person whom he is so exciting and influencing. It is through taking this role of the other that he is able to come back on himself and so direct his own process of communication. This taking the role of the other, an expression I have so often used, is not simply of passing impor-

[36]Kuhn, *The Structure of Scientific Revolutions*, p. viii.
[37]Kuhn, *The Structure of Scientific Revolutions*, pp. 52–53.

tance. . . . The immediate effect of such role-taking lies in the control which the individual is able to exercise over his own response.[38]

One of the attractions of the Meadian conception of self-interaction is that it makes sense in terms of one's daily experiences. If you think back to the last time you walked somewhere by yourself (on the way to class for example), there are probably things you can remember talking to yourself about—reminding yourself to do or to refrain from doing something, making a phone call, stopping at the grocery store, going to the library. Again, people need not think back very far to find a time when they talked to themselves about how to approach a certain situation or whether to confront someone and how to do it. In such a situation you are, in a sense, rehearsing for future action and organizing yourself by an internal conversation, which prepares you to take the role of others. For instance, people who have been through the anxiety of preparing themselves for an encounter with a friend who has recently lost a loved one will recognize that the more they talked to themselves about what to say and how to approach their friend, the more able they were to take the role of the other, and the more effective the interaction was. If we assess the resulting action and ask ourselves whether the internal conversation affected the interaction, we can see that Mead's conception of the human act probably does make sense.

Blumer summarizes Mead's idea of the human act like this:

> The human act is formed through self-interaction, in the course of which the actor may note and assess any feature of the situation, or any feature of his involvement in the act. . . . The subjection of the act to the process of self-interaction imparts a career to the act—the act may be stopped, restrained, abandoned, resurrected, postponed, intensified, concealed, transformed, or redirected.[39]

THE DEVELOPMENT OF THE SELF

Mead outlines the three stages by which the self develops in his writings on the play, the game, and the generalized other. The first stage of self-development, the "preplay" stage at about age two, is marked by meaningless, imitative acts. In Meadian vocabulary, the word *meaning* appears regularly and has a unique connotation. Mead explains, "Meaning as such, i.e., the object of thought, arises in experience through the individual stimulating himself to take the attitude of the other in his reaction toward the object."[40]

[38]Mead, *Mind, self and Society*, p. 254.
[39]Blumer, "Comments on 'Parsons as a Symbolic Interactionist,' " p. 60.
[40]Mead, *Mind, Self and Society*, p. 89.

In other words, when individuals share symbolic interpretations, the act is meaningful to them. The are "speaking the same language" or "looking through the same eyeglasses." Meaning is, then, the wedding of different attitudes and the use of significant symbols that have the same import for all concerned.

The reason Mead labels acts in the preplay state "meaningless" is that the child at that age lacks the ability to take the attitude of the other. As Mead outlines it, this ability gradually evolves as the child develops a self. The second stage, the "play" stage, which appears later in childhood, is the stage when the child can put himself in the position of another person but cannot relate the roles of the other players. The connection between play, on the one hand, and the development of the "me" and the ability to take the role of the other, on the other hand, is particularly apparent when small children scold their toys for being bad or warn them that they are getting dirty or doing something dangerous. Similarly, children at this stage act out others' parts in simple role-taking, such as playing teacher, and games, such as hide-and-seek or tic-tac-toe, that involve only one or two roles and participants. At the play stage, the player has only one alternative role in mind at a time. Nevertheless, this is the time, according to Mead, when the child begins to form a self by taking the roles of other people.

At the game stage, several players act together. This happens in complex, organized games in which the team member must anticipate all the attitudes and roles of all the other players. The person playing first base in a baseball game, for instance, must have a generalized knowledge of what the other team members will do in a given situation. At the game stage, the relevant other is an organization of the attitudes of all involved in the game, so that what the person on first base does is controlled by everyone else on the team. In a wider context, this generalized other includes the organized attitudes of the whole community. Mead explains, "The mature self arises when a generalized other is internalized so that the community exercises control over the conduct of its individuals. . . . The structure, then, on which the self is built is this response which is common to all, for one has to be a member of a community to be a self."[41]

Critics of Mead have reevaluated the concept of "generalized other" and argue that it is somewhat like Parsons's definition of socialization because it means that individuals internalize the norms and values generated by the dominant institutions. Feminists point out that the generalized other incorporates the existing distribution of power in society within the individual.[42] In short, it is the people in power—males, upper classes, educational elites—who define the generalized other.

[41]Mead, *Mind, Self and Society*, p. 163.

[42]Kathy E. Ferguson, *Self, Society, and Womankind* (Westport, Conn.: Greenwood Press, 1980), p. 56.

In a study of sex differences in children's games, Janet Lever found that boys played outdoors more, played more in larger groups, played in more age-heterogeneous groups, and played more often in competitive games than girls.[43] Lever suggests that boys' games teach them to take the role of the generalized other, thus preparing them for successful performance in a wide variety of work settings. By contrast, girls learn the role of the particular other in their play groups, preparing them for their roles as wives and mothers in the private sphere of the home. Thus the way children's play is organized serves to protect the traditional gender-role division in our society.

Lever reports that boys, who were more involved in playing competitive games, learned that emotional discipline and self-control were necessary for team goals. Girls, who were more involved in play that involved turn-taking rather than competition, also showed affection to their best friends more often. Lever states,

> Most girls interviewed said they had a single "best" friend with whom they played nearly every day. They learn to know that person and her moods so well that through nonverbal cues alone, a girl understands whether her playmate is hurt, sad, happy, bored, and so on. There is usually an open show of affection between these little girls.[44]

SYMBOLIC MEANING

The meaning of *symbol* is derived from Mead's definition of "gesture," which is not only the first element of an act but also a sign for a whole act. For instance, when a smoker reaches for a pack of cigarettes, that gesture can be enough to prompt a nonsmoker to leave the room, to open windows, to request that smoking be prohibited, or to engage in other kinds of behavior to avoid what the nonsmoker knows will follow. In this situation the gesture, the first component of the act, can be enough for the nonsmoker, who does not have to wait to see the rest of the act. Thus reaching for the pack of cigarettes is not only a gesture; it becomes a significant symbol, because the gesture calls out in the nonsmoker the meaning of the entire act and signals the beginning of his or her adjustments to it. As Mead puts it, "Gestures thus internalized are significant symbols because they have the same meaning for all individual members of a given society or social group, i.e., they respectively arouse the same attitudes in the individuals making them that they arouse in the individuals responding to them."[45]

[43]Janet Lever, "Sex Differences in the Games Children Play," *Social Problems* 24 (April 1976): 478–87.

[44]Lever, "Sex Differences," p. 484.

[45]Mead, *Mind, Self and Society*, p. 47.

Mead defines a symbol as "the stimulus whose response is given in advance." Consider the situation in which a person threatens you and you knock him down. Mead says that in doing this you are taking the attitude of the community and responding to it in a conversation of gestures. Mead explains how an insulting word is a symbol:

> There is a word, and a blow. The blow is the historical antecedent of the word, but if the word means an insult, the response is one now involved in the word, something given in the very stimulus itself. That is all that is meant by a symbol. Now, if that response can be given in terms of an attitude utilized for the further control of action, then the relation of that stimulus and attitude is what we mean by a significant symbol.[46]

A key element is the meaning of the word (in this case, an insult). It becomes "the stimulus whose response is given in advance" because in the community in question, the connotations of that word and the intentions implied by its use evoke a blow as the appropriate response from the person so addressed. Another crucial element is the self-interaction that is occurring in this process, the conversation of gestures that is going on in the mind of the individual. Mead explains:

> We often act with reference to objects in what we call an intelligent fashion, although we can act without the meaning of the object being present in our experience. One can start to dress for dinner, as they tell of the absent-minded college professor, and find himself in his pajamas in bed. A certain process of undressing was started and carried out mechanically; he did not recognize the meaning of what he was doing. He intended to go to dinner and found he had gone to bed. The meaning involved in his action was not present. The steps in this case were all intelligent steps which controlled his conduct with references to later action, but he did not think about what he was doing. The later action was not a stimulus to his response, but just carried itself out when it was once started.[47]

Why was this *not* a case of symbolic interaction? Obviously, some crucial elements are missing. The individual did not recognize the meaning of what he was doing. The act does not include, in Mead's words, "the adjustive response of one organism to the gesture of another."[48] Because the professor was not interpreting his gestures (he was not going to bed because it was late or because he was sick), there was no meaning in the gestures of the act.

In addition, the professor did not think about what he was doing; he was not talking to himself about what he was doing. Significant symbols, according to Mead, are gestures (such as the smoker reaching for the pack of cigarettes) that possess meaning. A significant symbol is that part of the act

[46]Mead, *Mind, Self and Society*, p. 181.
[47]Mead, *Mind, Self and Society*, p. 72.
[48]Mead, *Mind, Self and Society*, p. 78.

that calls out the response of the other. This assumes interpretation of the symbol, as in the case of the insult.

The relationship between significant symbols and the self becomes clearer when Mead considers the case of Helen Keller, who recognized that it was "not until she could get into communication with other persons through symbols which could arouse in herself the responses they arouse in other people that she could get what we term a mental content, or a self."[49] Let us recall the scene in Helen Keller's life in which her teacher and friend, Annie Sullivan, is pumping water, and Helen, feeling the running water, realizes that water has a name, the very name Annie is finger-spelling in the palm of her hand. She finally understands what the gesture for "water" means. The water episode is a dramatic example of the beginning of the process of symbolic meaning through communication. For Keller, this moment marked the beginning of her acquisition of a set of common symbols.[50]

The Keller case is an illustration of all the components of George Herbert Mead's theory, for once Helen Keller was capable of symbolic interaction, she not only possessed a "me" as well as an "I," but she could also "take the role of the other" and could internalize the "generalized other." This means that she could possess a social self.

PART TWO

Herbert Blumer: Interpretation and Methodology

Herbert Blumer (1900–1987) was on the sociology faculty at the University of Chicago from 1927 to 1952, having finished his doctoral dissertation in 1928 under the direction of Ellsworth Faris, whom Blumer describes as a profound and faithful disciple of George Herbert Mead. Blumer studied under Mead as a regular student and auditor in several of his graduate courses.[51] Mead manifested his confidence in Blumer's interpretation of his thought shortly after the beginning of Mead's last quarter of instruction at the University of Chicago, when he had to withdraw because of illness. On that occasion Mead asked Blumer to take over his major course, "Advanced Social Psychology."[52]

---

[49]Mead, *Mind, Self and Society*, p. 149.

[50]See Helen Keller, *The Story of My Life* (New York: Doubleday, 1902).

[51]Blumer has stated that he was "tremendously influenced at the University of Chicago by George H. Mead." He also "worked closely with Professor Robert E. Park," whom he regards as "the best sociological research scholar produced in the United States." (Personal communication, 1976.)

[52]See Herbert Blumer, "Going Astray with a Logical Scheme," *Symbolic Interaction* 6 (1983): 127–37.

Blumer carried on Mead's tradition for twenty-five years at the University of Chicago and for another twenty-five years at the University of California at Berkeley, where he taught until his retirement. During his Chicago era Blumer was involved in such diverse activities as playing professional football, serving as a mediator in labor disputes, and interviewing underworld figures from the Al Capone gang. Blumer's stature in the profession and the profound respect he commands are indicated by his editorship of the *American Journal of Sociology* from 1941 to 1952, his presidency of the American Sociological Association in 1956, the festschrift in his honor,[53] and several memorial sessions at professional meetings after his death on April 15, 1987.

Blumer's chief contributions to the symbolic interactionist perspective are his work on interpretation, the three basic premises of symbolic interactionism, structure and process, and methodology. We will discuss each of these contributions in turn.

INTERPRETATION

Blumer's discussion of interpretation is an elaboration of Mead's argument against Watsonian behaviorism or any mechanical stimulus-response approach.[54] Like Mead, Blumer argues for the necessity of including subjective experience, or covert behavior, as well as observable behavior in scientific explanations of human interaction. This argument logically follows from the importance symbolic interactionism places on understanding things from the point of view of the actor.

In Blumer's estimation interaction involves something more than simple stimulus-response. Blumer explains that symbolic interactionism inserts a middle term into the stimulus-response couplet so that it becomes stimulus-interpretation-response. "Thus," he says, "A acts; B perceives this action and seeks to ascertain its meaning, that is, seeks to ascertain A's intention; B responds according to what meaning or interpretation he has attached to A's act; in turn, A responds according to the meaning which he sees in B's response."[55] Thus the stimulus alone cannot account for B's action or A's response to it.

As Figure 5-1 showed, symbolic interactionism views the process of self-indication as essential to interpretation. Blumer rejects behaviorism

---

[53]See Tamotsu Shibutani, ed., *Human Nature and Collective Behavior: Papers in Honor of Herbert Blumer* (Englewood Cliffs, N.J.: Prentice-Hall, 1970). This festschrift includes papers by many of Blumer's former students, as well as a complete bibliography of Blumer's work up to 1970.

[54]See Mead, *Mind, Self and Society*, pp. 4–5. Also see Chapter 7, where we discuss Skinner's behaviorism in relation to exchange theory.

[55]In Schmidt, *Man and Society*, p. 171.

because it leaves out interpretation and thus reduces the individual to responding to environmental stimuli.

Blumer explains that in the process of self-indication, individuals point out certain stimuli to themselves and then interpret the appearance of the stimuli to themselves. For instance, people may note that certain social demands are being made on them, that they are hungry, that they want to purchase something, that they are eating with people they despise. In all these examples, Blumer pictures people as acting, not being acted upon. He concludes,

> By virtue of indicating such things to himself, he places himself over against them and is able to act back against them, accepting them, rejecting them, or transforming them in accordance with how he defines or interprets them.[56]

Comic strip artists frequently employ self-indication in their depiction of their characters. Sometimes they differentiate the conversation between two individuals from the conversation an individual is having with himself by drawing a different link or boundary between the character and the words; for instance,

is often used to illustrate self-indications, as opposed to

Gestures are a key element in the interpretation process. Earlier we discussed Mead's definition of gestures, which are significant symbols because they have the same meaning for all concerned, such as the smoker reaching for a pack of cigarettes. To interpret and understand the meaning of the interaction, each of the parties must take the role of the other; in other words, each must "get into the other's shoes." Instead of merely reacting to each other's action in an automatic way, human beings interpret or define each other's actions, and they perform this interpretation on the basis of symbols. Thus the stimulus-interpretation-response process could be translated as a process of meaningful interaction.

When people from different societies wish to understand and communicate with each other, the process of interpretation can be a doubtful and difficult one. Indeed, governments employ full-time experts to help them interpret the meaning of other societies' gestures and symbols.

[56]Blumer, *Symbolic Interactionism*, p. 81.

A study by two symbolic interactionists that illustrates the process of interpretation is *Awareness of Dying* by Glaser and Strauss. They have documented some rather painful and moving examples of a situation in which the ability to pick up on even very subtle cues is crucial—interaction between nurse and dying patients at the time when mutual pretense about the patient's true condition changes to open awareness. The following describes an actual conversation between a dying patient, in great pain and obvious bodily deterioration, and her nurse, Mary.

> There was a long silence. Then the patient asked, "After I get home from the nursing home will you visit me?" I asked if she wanted me to. "Yes, Mary, you know we could go on long drives together . . . " She had a far-away look in her eyes as if daydreaming about all the things we could do together. This continued for some time. Then I asked, "Do you think you will be able to drive your car again?" She looked at me, "Mary, I know I am daydreaming; I know I am going to die." Then she cried, and said, "This is terrible, I never thought I would be this way."[57]

The nurse in this scene recognized a gesture that was a significant symbol; she correctly interpreted the patient's daydreaming gesture, the "far-away look in her eyes." One could speculate that the nurse's second question precipitated the breaking of the pretense. From that moment on, the patient was no longer hanging onto a semblance of her former physically healthy self; she was admitting that she was a dying person. This is a good illustration of the relationship between the interpretation of symbolic gestures and the change in the patient's self-image.

By contrast, nonsymbolic interaction occurs when an individual responds directly to the action of another without interpreting that action. An example of nonsymbolic interaction would be a dog fight, in which the "gestures" of one dog have no "meaning" for the other angry participants but are simply attacks to be beaten off in the cause of survival. If the dog were interpreting the meaning of the action, then it would be devising all sorts of different responses. Similarly, human beings in a moment of anger or in self-defense engage in nonsymbolic interaction.

Now that we have looked at Blumer's elaboration of the interpretative process in symbolic interaction, let us examine his synthesis of the perspective—what he calls the three basic premises of symbolic interactionism.

THE THREE BASIC PREMISES

Blumer's three premises address the importance of meaning in human action, the source of meaning, and the role of meaning in interpretation.

---

[57]Barney G. Glaser and Anselm L. Strauss, *Awareness of Dying* (Chicago: Aldine, 1965), p. 75.

1. Human beings act toward things on the basis of the meanings that the things have for them.

As Blumer explains it, consciousness is a key element in understanding meaningful action:

> Anything of which a human being is conscious is something which he is indicating to himself—the ticking of a clock, a knock at the door, the appearance of a friend, the remark made by a companion, a recognition that he has a cold. . . . To indicate something is to extricate it from its setting, to hold it apart, to give it a meaning. . . . In any of his countless acts—whether minor, like dressing himself, or major, like organizing himself for a professional career—the individual is designating different objects to himself, giving them meaning, judging their suitability to his action, and making decisions on the basis of the judgment. This is what is meant by interpretation or acting on the basis of symbols.[58]

An illustration of Blumer's first premise was provided by one of our students, who was traveling by plane and talking to himself. When observed by another passenger, the student explained that he was boning up on aspects of the termite control business, attempting to memorize the essentials and putting himself in the shoes of potential customers, so that he would be successful in selling people on termite control. His greatest anxiety, he explained, was the health of his older brother, who had two small children and was the new owner and manager of a termite control business. This older brother lay gravely ill in the intensive care unit of a hospital. The younger brother had been enlisted to fill in and aid the floundering business; he had just taken a semester's leave from college and was frantically trying to learn the ropes of a business that heretofore had been almost totally unfamiliar to him.

The student in the above illustration, aware that he had a formidable task ahead of him, was so conscious of every aspect of the termite business, which now had considerable meaning for him, that he was not even conscious that his internal conversation was being overheard until he was so informed by his fellow passenger. Everything he had been indicating to himself was related to his success in keeping the business going; thus he was guiding his future behavior. He was enabling himself to act toward things (aspects of termite control) on the basis of the meanings that the things had for him, because in this process he was giving meaning to, or making himself conscious of, the essential aspects of the business.

Another example, this time from Glaser and Strauss, will also illustrate Blumer's first premise. In the study of the situation of dying, the researchers observed various strategies nurses used to avoid the later stages of the dying

---

[58]Blumer, *Symbolic Interactionism*, p. 80.

scene: avoiding the night shift on wards where many patients die, taking vacation time, or getting sick themselves at the crucial moment. They explain the avoidance strategies thus: "Nurses find the death scene upsetting; the threat to the sentimental order of the ward increases with the number of deaths and the number of nurses who must witness them."[59] Through interviews with these nurses, the researchers discovered the meaning that the death scene had for them. Because they defined it as upsetting, some of the nurses act toward the death scene by avoiding it if at all possible.

2. The meaning of things arises out of the social interaction one has with one's fellows.

Meaning is a social product; it is created, not inherent in things; it is not a given. Blumer elaborates, "The meaning of a thing for a person grows out of the ways in which other persons act toward the person with regard to the thing. Their actions operate to define the thing for the person."[60]

An example of this would be the meaning of a baseball bat to an American teenager as compared to its meaning to a member of a pygmy tribe in Africa, who has never seen a baseball game.[61] Another example is the meaning of the molimo, an instrument for song, to a member of the pygmy tribe as compared to its meaning for an American. Through interaction with others of their culture, individuals learn the different uses of the implements, one for the purpose of sport and the other for religious festivals. The baseball bat would be no more puzzling to the pygmy youth than the molimo would be to the American, who has never witnessed the sacred ritual of which it is an integral part. Both are important cultural implements, and the meaning of both arises out of interaction with others in the society.

In his study of a boys' grammar school in an industrial town in England, Colin Lacey found two striking examples of meaning in interaction processes.[62] On the one hand, he observed the first-year boys in the process of becoming committed to the school, so much so that they would engage in rivalry among themselves. For instance,

> First-year boys adhere rigidly to school uniforms; caps and blazers are proudly displayed, and they attend school functions and clubs in disproportionate numbers. Their behavior in the classroom is characterized by eagerness, cooperation with the teacher, and competition among themselves. "Please sir, Willy Brown is copying my sums" is a remark that could only come from a first-year boy.[63]

[59]Glaser and Strauss, *Time for Dying* (Chicago: Aldine, 1968), p. 202.

[60]Blumer, *Symbolic Interactionism*, p. 4.

[61]See the excellent anthropological study of the BaMbuti by Colin Turnbull, *The Forest People* (New York: Doubleday, 1962).

[62]Colin Lacey, *Hightown Grammar: The School as a Social System* (Manchester: Manchester University Press, 1970). A "grammar school" is an academic high school.

[63]Lacey, *Hightown Grammar*, p. 5.

On the other hand, Lacey found that the teachers stereotyped working-class children as a "bad lot" or "lazy." Their consequent estimation of them as "harder to teach and more difficult to control within the classroom situation" resulted in a situation wherein working-class children would "escalate downward" or drop out.[64]

In both examples the meaning of things for the students, whether school loyalty or a negative label, arose out of the social interaction among students and school staff. In the case of the working-class children, the interaction with teachers, how they interpreted each other's words and actions, and the way they behaved on the basis of these interpretations were crucial because they tended to result in students' failure or their dropping out of the system.

3. **The meanings of things are handled in and modified through an interpretative process used by the person in dealing with things he encounters.**

How does this work? Blumer says that a person communicates and handles meanings through a process of talking to himself. Someone who gives an account of personal worries and anxieties is interpreting what is disturbing to him or her; and Blumer says that it is in the process of making indications to oneself that someone arrives at such an account.

Blumer uses the example of a situation in which a checker at a grocery store is confronted by a (student) customer who tries to bargain for a lower price.[65] In examining and explaining what takes place, symbolic interactionists would focus on the indications the clerk is making to herself, or what she is saying to herself as she decides how to interact with this customer.

Suppose, for instance, that the clerk rejected the idea of asking the manager for help in dealing with the customer. To explain why she did so, one would have to understand the world of the clerk. This particular clerk may have had an argument with the manager recently and may therefore avoid asking for help. The clerk's decision may also depend whether she could afford the time to bargain with the customer, and this, too, must enter the explanation. Indeed, the answer depends on a number of things—the size and physical strength of both parties, for example, and the financial resources of the clerk, who may decide that the simplest thing to do is to let the customer have the item for the lower price and make up the rest out of her own pocket.

The interpretative process, Blumer would point out, would also include the indications the clerk is making to herself about the other people

[64]Lacey, *Hightown Grammar*, p. 181.

[65]This is the same example used by Garfinkel in his student experiments. See Chapter 6. Blumer used this example in a personal interview, 1975.

who are touched by this situation; thus to understand what goes on, we must know the history of the particular clerk concerned. Has this ever happened to her before? If so, what solutions did she come up with then? Were these solutions successful? Together, the basic premises of symbolic interactionism stress the ways human interaction emerges from an individual's ability to confer meaning to a situation.

STRUCTURE AND PROCESS

Blumer often refers to structure as a "straitjacket." Like Mead, he views people as ever active, ever striving, ever adjustable beings, and he sees a drastic difference between Mead's conception of society and the "widespread sociological conception of it as a structure." On the other hand, Blumer explains that Mead's view does not reject the existence of structure in society. In fact, Blumer points to the importance of such structures as "social roles, status positions, rank orders, bureaucratic organizations, relations between institutions, differential authority relations, and the like." Though admitting that such structures are important, Blumer argues that they do not determine behavior:

> It is ridiculous, for instance, to assert, as a number of eminent sociologists have done, that social interaction is an interaction between social roles. Social interaction is obviously an interaction between *people* and not between roles; the needs of the participants are to interpret and handle what confronts them—such as a topic of conversation or a problem—and not give expression to their roles. It is only in highly ritualistic relations that the direction and content of conduct can be explained by roles. Usually, the direction and content are fashioned out of what people in interaction have to deal with. That roles affect in varying degree phases of the direction and content of action is true but is a matter of determination in given cases. This is a far cry from asserting action to be a product of roles. The observation I have made in this brief discussion of social roles applies with equal validity to all other structural matters.[66]

For further clarification, consider the difference between "interactive roles" and "social roles," as discussed by McCall and Simmons. When symbolic interactionists speak of role, they do not mean a social role that is specified by the culture; rather they mean something more flexible and capable of improvisation. What they call an "interactive role" is "a plausible line of action characteristic and expressive of the particular personality that happens to occupy the given position and represents that person's mode of

---

[66]Blumer, *Symbolic Interactionism*, p. 75. Barbara Lal argues that Blumer's essays (1969) were not only a statement of the theory and methodology of symbolic interactionism but also "a polemic attacking the inadequacies of social system and other holistic theories." See Barbara Lal, "Symbolic Interaction Theories," *American Behavioral Scientist* 38.3 (January 1995): 421–44.

coming to grips with the general expectations held toward someone in his position."[67]

Erving Goffman, an important contributor to the symbolic interactionist perspective,[68] illustrates the meaning of interactive role in his work on role distance, which he defines as "denying not the role but the virtual self that is implied in the role for all accepting performers"; that is, "actions which effectively convey some disdainful detachment of the performer from a role he is performing."[69]

Using a merry-go-round as the situation, Goffman shows that riders on the merry-go-round at age three or four throw themselves into the role in a serious way and play the role with verve and an admitted engagement of all their faculties. But this changes at age five, when the riders exhibit a detachment from the role. Goffman describes the resulting role distance:

> To be a merry-go-round horse rider is now apparently not enough, and this fact must be demonstrated out of dutiful regard for one's own character. Parents are not likely to be allowed to ride along, and the strap for preventing falls is often disdained. One rider may keep time to the music by clapping his feet or a hand against the horse, an early sign of utter control. Another may make a wary stab at standing on the saddle or changing horses without touching the platform. Still another may hold onto the post with one hand and lean back as far as possible while looking up to the sky in a challenge to dizziness.[70]

To Goffman, the five-year-old rider is apologizing for the entire role and withdrawing from it by actively manipulating the situation. As children grow older, they increase the distance between themselves and the role; at ages seven and eight they dissociate themselves self-consciously by riding no-hands, and at ages eleven and twelve they "define the whole undertaking as a lark, a situation for mockery."[71]

The important point here is that the clues to role distance are the immediate audience as well as the age of the rider. Because the strategies of the merry-go-round riders were directly influenced by the immediate audience, one could say that the riders were taking them into account. One could, for instance, expect a considerable amount of role distance to be exhibited by teenagers if their peers were in the audience. At the same time, the concept

[67]McCall and Simmons, *Identities and Interactions*, p. 67.

[68]In Part Three we discuss Goffman's contributions in more detail. See other important contributors to this perspective in the following: Jerome G. Manis and Bernard N. Meltzer, ed., *Symbolic Interaction: A Reader in Social Psychology* (Boston: Allyn and Bacon, 1972); Nicholas C. Mullins, *Theories and Theory Groups in Contemporary American Sociology* (New York: Harper and Row, 1973); and the festschrift by Shibutani mentioned previously, *Human Nature and Collective Behavior*.

[69]Erving Goffman, *Encounters: Two Studies in the Sociology of Interaction* (Indianapolis: Bobbs-Merrill, 1961), pp. 108–10.

[70]Goffman, *Encounters*, p. 107.

[71]Goffman, *Encounters*, pp. 108–109.

of "interactive role" allows for many improvisations in the execution of role distance because it takes into account one's particular personality.

Blumer does not deny the existence of structure; what he decries is the overemphasis on the importance of structural matters in determining people's conduct. In their view of human nature, symbolic interactionists believe the human being possesses a self, which is an object to itself. This means that the individual can act toward himself or herself as he or she confronts the world. Action is pieced together as the individual takes the setting of the act into account in making decisions. As acting human beings, people do not simply respond to others in a structured manner. Blumer says that human action is preceded by the individual briefly sketching out plans and intentions. Human action, for the most part, is constructed by people making indications to themselves of what confronts them.

"For the most part" is an important qualifier, however. We have seen that neither Blumer nor Mead totally denies structured action or defined situations. After all, human behavior would be far too complicated and would have too many potentially disastrous opportunities for mutual misunderstanding if every activity had to be defined from scratch! What the symbolic interactionist perspective points out is that there are many unstructured or undefined situations in which human beings must devise their own conduct. Further, even situations in which much is defined in advance include action that is not.

Problematic situations or situations that demand new interpretations are the foci of analysis for symbolic interactionism, whereas some other perspectives tend to deny, sidestep, or acknowledge them without elaboration or substantive analysis. Blumer cites specific examples of such situations. For instance, he points to playful situations where sentiments play a major role—highly personal and informal situations, such as infectious humor or dancing crowds; and adversary relations, such as quarrels and conflicts.

This last category of problematic situations, adversary relations, is the one Blumer uses most often, and he suggests that only symbolic interactionism has the tools for analyzing it. Blumer often brings in the example of a football game, which emphasizes ingenuity at winning or gaining the advantage.[72] Although most football plays can be predefined and precharted, when the ball is intercepted the situation becomes undefined, and self-indication and interpretation are necessary.

Other adversary relations involving undefined situations are crises, dilemmas, droughts, fires, earthquakes, wars, riots, lynchings, and panics. How, asks Blumer, could the social scientist analyze such situations without examining self-indication and interpretation?

---

[72]One suspects that this example stems from Blumer's own experience as a professional football player.

It is precisely because Blumer sees cultural structure and social structure as constraints or "straitjackets" that he chooses to focus on process in his analysis. He is especially adamant regarding the inability of structural analysis to explain anything about problematic situations. For instance, he acknowledges that Parsons's use of the pattern variables does assume some degree of self-interaction, but Blumer sees this as a very restricting form of self-interaction because the "either-or" choice has been decided beforehand.

We will recall that each pattern variable represents a dilemma that must be solved by the actor before action can take place. As an illustration for one of the pattern variables, we presented the case of the employer who is expected to choose achievement over ascription when making a decision about a potential employee.[73] Parsons's position is that there is an appropriate choice to be made by the actor; the decision is not arbitrary but related to the norms and values of the employer's society. Blumer, on the other hand, likes to point out that many situations are unprecedented, and appropriate behavior cannot be spelled out beforehand. He has also recently remarked, with respect to the pattern variables,

> If human beings had to stop and choose between each of the alternatives in each of the five variables before they could interpret and act in each and every one of their situations, they would become paralyzed and human group life would come to a halt.[74]

The more unstructured the situation, Blumer argues, the more likely it is that symbolic interactionist analysis is indispensable to its understanding.

Given his position on structure, how does Blumer move from an analysis of the individual with a self to the group? Translating Mead's term *social act* into *joint action*, Blumer describes it as

> the larger collective form of action that is constituted by the fitting together of the lines of behavior of the separate participants. Illustrations of joint action are a trading transaction, a family dinner, a marriage ceremony, a shopping expedition, a game, a convivial party, a debate, a court trial, or a war. . . . Each participant necessarily occupies a different position, acts from that position, and engages in a separate and distinct act. It is a fitting together of these acts and not their commonality that constitutes joint action.[75]

Blumer then states that each joint action has a career, or history, which is "orderly, fixed and repetitive" because of its common definition by the participants:

---

[73]See Chapter 2.
[74]Blumer, "Comments on 'Parsons as a Symbolic Interactionist,'" p. 59.
[75]Blumer, *Symbolic Interactionism*, p. 70.

Such common definitions serve, above everything else, to account for the regularity, stability, and repetitiveness of joint action in vast areas of group life; they are the sources of the established and regulated social behavior that are envisioned in the concept of culture.[76]

At this point it seems that Blumer may be admitting that there is a great deal of structured social action. However, he quickly points to many possibilities of uncertainty in the career of joint actions. First, joint actions, like picketing by striking workers, have to be initiated; then, once started, they may be interrupted, abandoned, or transformed; the participants may not make a common definition of the joint action; and, finally, new situations may arise in the joint act. As we would expect, Blumer's emphasis is on the "uncertainty, contingency, and transformation" that are "part and parcel of the process of joint action."[77]

Blumer contrasts himself with those sociologists (functionalists or conflict theorists) who stress the importance of social structure in explaining behavior. His discussion of joint action does include some references to rather structured role interaction; and if we examine his examples of joint action, we can find some in which (although far from being highly ritualistic) much can be explained by roles. For instance, a trading transaction could be the grocery clerk who is confronted by the bartering customer. Blumer would have to admit that her role as a grocery clerk could explain at least some of her behavior. Nevertheless, the importance of roles in determining behavior is never central to his mode of analysis; rather, he sees

> the joint act as primarily an "organizing" action instead of an "organization" of action; it is an "organization" only in retrospect. A joint act represents the effort of the participants to work out their lines of action in the light of what they observe each other to be doing or about to do. Thus, the coordination of lines of action (which is the mark of social organization) is something to be achieved in and through the interaction instead of being merely an expression of systemic factors underlying such interaction.[78]

The statement graphically illustrates how Blumer uses a quite different kind of lens from the one a structural theorist such as Parsons would use when looking at the social world. In contrast to that of a camera that produces a still picture taken from a distance, Blumer's lens is similar to a camcorder, which he uses because he wants a close-up view where he can see and hear what is going on in the interaction process between individuals.

In September 1964 the Free Speech Movement erupted on the Berkeley campus. This was a student protest against a university administration ruling that barred campus political activities aimed at the larger community,

---

[76]Blumer, *Symbolic Interactionism*, p. 71.

[77]Blumer, *Symbolic Interactionism*, p. 72.

[78]Blumer, "Comments on 'Parsons as a Symbolic Interactionist,'" p. 59–60.

such as tables set up on campus to recruit students to help on voter registration efforts in the southern states. As Orlans and Wallace describe it, "Some 750 students occupying administrative offices were arrested; graduate teaching assistants went on strike; students boycotted classes; faculty committees and the Academic Senate drafted bitter proposals and counterproposals."[79] During the rallies of the Free Speech Movement at Berkeley, Blumer could be seen mingling with the crowds, observing from an upper-level window, and later talking at length with students involved. As a symbolic interactionist his approach to explaining students' involvement was to find out how individuals perceived and interpreted events and how they had decided to become involved. An illuminating contrast can be found in the work of sociologists such as Etzioni, who are more concerned with social structure. They approach such an event not by looking at individual decisions and actions that went into making up the Free Speech Movement, but by looking for general social phenomena that explain why the sixties were a period of campus turmoil. Etzioni, for example, emphasizes the fact that young people numbered more and were a higher proportion of the population than before or since. In contrast, Blumer's "camcorder lens" gives us a close-up of the action so that we can see and hear what the individuals involved are doing and saying while organizing it.

METHODOLOGY

One of Herbert Blumer's chief contributions to symbolic interactionism has been his elaboration on the methodology of this perspective. In 1983 Blumer received the American Sociological Association Award for a Career of Distinguished Scholarship. The citation stated that Blumer's discussion of methodological issues deeply affected "the adoption and diffusion of field methods, ethnography, and qualitative sociology."[80] As early as 1937 Blumer discussed the techniques researchers used in analyzing the "inner career of action":

> One would expect that starting from such a view, actual study and research would use methods and techniques that aim to penetrate into the area of inner experience. Such is the case. We find that much use is made, in social psychology, of such devices as the life history, the interview, the autobiography, the case method, diaries, and letters. These devices are employed for three purposes. First, to gain a picture of the inner and private experience of the individual that seems to constitute the background for the emergence and existence of a given form of conduct. Thus the account given by a delinquent of his life history is held to reveal the texture of personal happenings, which

[79]Kathryn P. Meadow Orlans and Ruth A. Wallace, ed., *Gender and the Academic Experience: Berkeley Women Sociologists* (Lincoln: University of Nebraska Press, 1994), p. 4.

[80]American Sociological Association, *Footnotes* 2, no. 8 (October 1983): 1.

presumably has given rise to, and which sustains, his delinquency. Second, to show the nature of the individual's subjective slant on life—the world as he views it, the values and meanings which different objects have for him, his "definitions" with which he seems to meet situations, his stock of attitudes, and the way in which he views himself. Third, to throw light on the life and operation of the imaginative process: fantasying, evading, planning, deciding, and the different ways in which, in his imagination, he meets difficulties, frustrations, and problematic situations.[81]

Inductive Approach

In a statement made thirty-eight years later, Blumer reveals the consistency of his position when he explains that symbolic interactionism is committed to an inductive approach to the understanding of human behavior, in which understanding or explanations are induced from data with which the investigator has become thoroughly familiar. Again he compares his position to functionalism. He explains that the scientific approach of symbolic interactionism starts with a problem regarding the empirical world, and it seeks to clarify the problem by examining that empirical world. He concludes,

> The isolation of relations, the development of propositions, the formulation of typologies, and the construction of theories are viewed as emerging out of what is found through constant observation of that world instead of being formed in an *a priori* fashion through deductive reasoning from a set of theoretical premises.[82]

Blumer shows that unlike functionalism, symbolic interactionism is not a deductive theory that begins with a set of hypotheses. Because its methodological approach precludes much of what is considered to be proper research activity, symbolic interactionists run into difficulty when it comes to funding and/or publishing their research.[83]

Blumer discusses this problem in his major explication of symbolic interactionism:

> See how far one gets in submitting proposals for exploratory studies to fund-granting agencies with their professional boards of consultants, or as doctoral dissertations in our advanced graduate departments of sociology and psychology! Witness the barrage of questions that arise: Where is your research design? What is your model? What is your guiding hypothesis? How are you operationalizing the hypothesis? What are your independent

---

[81]In Schmidt, *Man and Society*, pp. 193–94. Barbara Lal ("Symbolic Interaction Theories," p. 425) also includes "newspapers, sermons, and other material that reveals the subjective life of the actor from his or her own point of view."

[82]Blumer, "Comment on 'Parsons as a Symbolic Interactionist,'" p. 62.

[83]Some new journals have emerged to help solve this problem, like *Symbolic Interaction* and *Journal of Contemporary Ethnography*.

and dependent variables? What standard instruments are you going to use to get the data for your variables? What is your sample? What is your control group? And so on. Such questions presume in advance that the student has the firsthand knowledge that the exploratory study seeks to secure. Since he doesn't have it the protocolized research procedure becomes the substitute for getting it![84]

By contrast, the method advocated by symbolic interactionism is to look at the processes by which individuals define the world from the inside and at the same time identify their world of objects. How this works in practice can be illustrated by those aspects of a lawyer's role that demand the use of a symbolic interactionist perspective. For instance, a criminal lawyer defending a client is likely to utilize many of Mead's insights. When Clarence Darrow defended Thomas Massie on charges of fatally shooting the man who had beaten and raped Massie's wife, central to Darrow's defense was the jury's ability to take the role of Massie. Darrow is speaking to the jury:

> We contend that for months Massie's mind had been affected by all that was borne upon him: grief, sorrow, trouble, day after day, week after week, and month after month. What do you think would have happened to any one of you under the same condition? We measure other people by ourselves. We place ourselves in their place and say, "How would we have acted?" We have no further way of telling, except perhaps from the conditions of the life in which we live.
> ... No man can judge another unless he places himself in the position of the other before he pronounces the verdict.
> If you can put yourself in his place, if you can think of his raped wife, of his months of suffering and mental anguish; if you can confront the unjust, cruel fate that unrolled before him, then you can judge—but you cannot judge any man otherwise.
> If you put yourself in Tommy Massie's place, what would you have done? I don't know about you, or you, or you, or you—but at least ten out of twelve men would have done just what poor Tommy Massie did. The thing for which you are asked to send him to prison for the rest of his life.[85]

Darrow thus eloquently communicates his client's definition of the situation to the members of the jury, and he cleverly attempts to get the jury to take the role of the other when he pleads with them to "put yourself in his place." Without identifying it as such, Darrow adopts the methodology of symbolic interactionism.[86]

---

[84]Blumer, *Symbolic Interactionism*, p. 37.

[85]See Arthur Weinberg, ed., *Attorney for the Damned* (New York: Simon and Schuster, 1970), pp. 104–17.

[86]Another profession illustrating the lay use of this perspective is acting.

Modes of Inquiry

For social scientists who attempt to gather data from this perspective, Blumer has clarified its methodology. He sketches the two modes of inquiry by means of which the researcher will be able to get "close to the empirical social world and dig deeply into it." Blumer refers to these modes as the "direct naturalistic examination of the empirical social world," and he terms one "exploration" and the other "inspection."

Exploration.   The exploratory phase has a twofold purpose: first, to provide the researcher with a "close and comprehensive acquaintance with a sphere of social life which is unfamiliar and hence unknown to him"; and second, to develop, focus, and sharpen the researcher's investigation so that the research problem—what is noticed and what is ignored, what are recognized as data, and the way the data are interpreted and analyzed—will be grounded in the empirical world.

Blumer defines exploration as a flexible procedure

> in which the scholar shifts from one to another line of inquiry, adopts new points of observation as his study progresses, moves in new directions previously unthought of, and changes his recognition of what are relevant data as he acquires more information and better understanding. In these respects, exploratory study stands in contrast to the prescribed and circumscribed procedure demanded by current scientific protocol. The flexibility of exploratory procedure does not mean that there is no direction to the inquiry; it means that the focus is originally broad but becomes progressively sharpened as the inquiry proceeds.[87]

The various techniques utilized in this phase are directly observing, interviewing people, listening to conversations and to radio and television, reading local newspapers and journals, securing life-history accounts, reading letters and diaries, and consulting public records. For example, in her study of skid-row alcoholics, Jacqueline Wiseman combined direct observation, both participant and nonparticipant, with the examination of records and unstructured depth interviews to attain a close and full familiarity with the world she was examining.[88] Her developmental stages are a good illustration of the flexibility of this approach because she was able to shift the lines of inquiry during the exploratory phase. When words like, "I never worry when a friend of mine is missing [from skid row]; I know he's out making the loop and will be back," kept recurring in the interviews, she discovered the importance of "making the loop." Although it had not

---

[87]Blumer, *Symbolic Interactionism*, p. 40.

[88]For an excellent explanation of symbolic interactionist research methods, as well as a frank discussion of decisions made in the field, see Wiseman's "Methodology Appendix" in her *Stations of the Lost* (Englewood Cliffs, N.J.: Prentice-Hall, 1970).

occurred to her before she began interviewing, she soon found that "making the loop"—going to one or more institutions or stations in the skid-row environment to "make it better"—was a means of survival for homeless men on skid row. The analysis of these "stations" in the loop became the main focus of her study.

Blumer also urges the researcher to find experts or "participants in the sphere of life who are acute observers and who are well informed" in the exploratory phase. Arranging discussion groups of a small number of these experts is another technique that Blumer feels is "more valuable many times over than any representative sample."[89] Blumer consistently used the "panel of experts" in his own research efforts. For instance, in his study of a drug rehabilitation program in Oakland, California, Blumer and his associates sought to "form a core of youthful drug users, enjoying prestige and respect among their peers."[90] Over a period of time Blumer claims that his staff "established excellent rapport with these central figures, gaining their confidence and respect and working in close relation with them." In the following excerpt, Blumer explains how these central figures influenced him in his decision to change the focus of the study:

> We were able to have continuing group meetings with them (the central figures), as well as close personal association—and we sought through both of these channels to form a nucleus group committed to abstinence. Our line of attack was to have full and frank discussions of their drug use and to seek and make them aware of the hazards to their careers that were set by drug use.[91]

However, the tables were turned on the research staff when they discovered that the central figures "were so well anchored in drug use and well fortified in their beliefs against all the 'dangers' of drug use" that a program of abstinence was impossible. The research staff, thus faced with such opposition, decided to shift from the proposed abstinence program to a study of the world of youthful drug use, which would enable the researchers to "see how it was woven into the life style of drug-using youths." The staff's reasoning was that if they were to hope to do anything effective regarding juvenile drug use, they would first have to "understand realistically the world of such drug use."[92]

Although this incident illustrates one of the advantages of the exploratory phase—namely, a flexibility that allows the researcher to shift the focus of the study—it also reveals a possible drawback of the use of a

[89]Blumer, *Symbolic Interactionism*, p. 41.

[90]Blumer, "The World of Youthful Drug Use" (Manuscript, University of California, Berkeley, School of Criminology, 1967), p. i.

[91]Blumer, "The World of Youthful Drug Use", pp. i–ii.

[92]Blumer, "The World of Youthful Drug Use", p. 11.

panel of experts. The experts can give the researcher an overconfidence that he or she has an edge on the truth about the phenomenon under study.

Inspection.   If, as Blumer predicts, the exploratory phase succeeds in providing a comprehensive and accurate picture of the area of study, then the researcher is ready to move to the next procedure, inspection:[93]

> By "inspection" I mean an intensive focused examination of the empirical content of whatever analytical elements are used for purposes of analysis, and this same kind of examination of the empirical nature of the relations between such elements.[94]

To elaborate, Blumer introduces the term *sensitizing concepts.* In his view, the progression from the exploratory phase to the inspection stage is a movement from description to analysis, when sensitizing concepts are crucial. Blumer contrasts a sensitizing concept with a *definitive concept,* a clear definition of attributes that identifies the individual instance of a class of objects. A sensitizing concept, on the other hand, lacks such a specification of attributes, and it "does not enable the user to move directly to the instance and its relevant content." It does give the user "a general sense of reference and guidance in approaching empirical instances." In summing up this discussion, Blumer says, "Whereas definitive concepts provide prescriptions of what to see, sensitizing concepts merely suggest directions along which to look."[95]

In developing their theory of the awareness of dying, Glaser and Strauss employed sensitizing concepts, which, they reported, enabled medical and nursing personnel to grasp the theory in terms of their own experience. As they explain it,

> For example, our categories of "death expectations," "nothing more to do," "lingering," and "social loss" designate general properties of dying patients that unquestionably are vividly sensitizing or meaningful to hospital personnel; at the same time, they are abstract enough to designate properties of concrete entities, not entities themselves. Further, these concepts provide a necessary bridge between the theoretical thinking of sociologists and the practical thinking of people concerned with the substantive area, so that both may understand and apply the theory. The sociologist finds that he has "a feeling for" the everyday realities of the situation, while the person in the situation finds he can master and manage the theory.[96]

---

[93]See William F. Whyte's *Street Corner Society* (Chicago: University of Chicago Press, 1943) for examples of inspection.

[94]Blumer, *Symbolic Interactionism,* p. 43.

[95]Blumer, *Symbolic Interactionism,* pp. 148–49.

[96]Barney G. Glaser and Anselm L. Strauss, *The Discovery of Grounded Theory: Strategies for Qualitative Research* (Chicago: Aldine, 1967), pp. 240–41.

Another illustration of the inspection stage is provided by Howard Becker's "Becoming a Marihuana User," which has become a classic example of symbolic interactionist research. From the data he obtained in personal interviews with fifty individuals, Becker arrived at a career model of marihuana users. This model, which was composed of sequences of changes in attitudes and experiences, guided Becker's analysis. He describes the career model thus:

> In summary, an individual will be able to use marihuana for pleasure only when he goes through a process of learning to conceive of it as an object which can be used in this way. No one becomes a user without (1) learning to smoke the drug in a way which will produce real effects; (2) learning to recognize the effects and connect them with drug use (learning, in other words, to get high); and (3) learning to enjoy the sensations he perceives. In the course of this process he develops a disposition or motivation to use marihuana which was not and could not have been present when he began use, for it involves and depends on conceptions of the drug which could only grow out of the kind of actual experience detailed above.[97]

Qualitative Analysis. Becker's study illuminates the analytic procedure involved in the inspection stage, but it would be a mistake to assume that the two stages, exploration and inspection, are mutually exclusive. Qualitative researchers, who believe that the two phases overlap, use the term *naturalistic inquiry* to embrace both phases. Wiseman, for instance, describes the interconnections of the stages as a "web" in her article "The Research Web":

> This constant interplay of data gathering and analysis is at the heart of qualitative research. It is therefore difficult indeed to discuss coding, processing, analysis, and writing without also discussing planning and data gathering, for in no other approach is the interrelatedness of all portions of the research act quite so obvious. For me, with the possible exception of the early planning stages, all aspects of the research act are going on almost simultaneously. Early fragments of analysis and of conceptual insights make their appearance both in the organization or coding of material and in the most current decisions I make about what field material to gather in the future.[98]

As Wiseman explains, when the researcher makes a decision about which data will be the primary foci of the study and which will serve as background, this decision paves the way for the next consideration. That consideration, the general design or model, becomes the organizing scheme of the analysis. Even at this point, exploration and inspection are going on

[97]Howard S. Becker, "Becoming a Marihuana User," *American Journal of Sociology* 59 (1953): 41–58.

[98]Jacqueline P. Wiseman, "The Research Web," *Journal of Contemporary Ethnography* Vol. 3, pp. 317, 321, copyright © 1973 by Sage Publications, Inc. Reprinted by permission of Sage Publications, Inc.

simultaneously, for the model comes out of the data already gathered and it also aids in the collecting and categorization of data yet to come.

Wiseman describes several models of behavior used by qualitative researchers:

1. The time order or career model, in which everything has a natural history with a beginning, a middle, and an end, like Becker's career model
2. The cyclical model, which suggests a "constant renewal and replay of the phenomenon, often resulting in acceleration," like Wiseman's "loops"
3. The social types model, "a description of the various types of people that populate a setting and interact within it," like Blumer's different types of drug users
4. The social actions and interactions model, used in comparing behavioral variations, such as the awareness contexts used by Glaser and Strauss
5. The social settings or scenes model, which focuses on behavior settings and includes descriptions of the special culture and activities that take place in these social "subscenes"[99]

Blumer rates naturalistic inquiry as superior to other modes of inquiry because it directly examines the empirical world and its natural, ongoing activity rather than abstracted and quantified data. Nonetheless, Blumer recognizes that his call for direct examination of the empirical social world is not likely to make sense to most social scientists, who are committed to quantitative analysis. He says,

> They would hold that they are examining the empirical world directly when they do such things as collect and analyze various kinds of census data, make social surveys, secure declarations from people through questionnaires, use polls, undertake discriminating clinical examination, employ scales and refined measuring instruments, bring social action into controlled laboratory situations, undertake careful computer simulation of social life, and use crucial empirical data to test hypotheses.[100]

Obviously this is not what Blumer sees as direct examination of the empirical social world. What Blumer wants is a "close and reasonably full familiarity with the area of life under study."[101] This involves none of the mentioned techniques but rather a free exploration in the area: "getting close to the people involved in it, seeing it in a variety of situations they meet, noting their problems and observing how they handle them, being party to their conversations, and watching their life as it flows along." Blumer's position puts him at variance with the social scientists he mentions, who advocate collecting "hard" rather than what they term "soft" data.

---

[99]Wiseman, "The Research Web," p. 321.

[100]Blumer, *Symbolic Interactionism*, p. 34.

[101]Blumer, *Symbolic Interactionism*, p. 87.

In one of his most graphic arguments against the quantitative approach, Blumer attacks the IQ test. He asks how a given intelligence test can yield a satisfactory picture of intelligence, which is present in such varied forms as

> the ingenious exploitation of a market situation by a business entrepreneur, effective methods of survival by a disadvantaged slum dweller, the clever meeting of the problems of his world by a peasant or a primitive tribesman, . . . and the construction of a telling verse by a poet.[102]

Blumer's objection to the IQ test is that such formal, out-of-context instruments cannot measure satisfactorily the kind of contextually rooted behavior he describes. He questions the value of the quantitative approach:

> The basic criticism usually made of the experimental approach, and of the objective, quantitative approach in the form of questionnaires, schedules, and tests, is that they fail to catch the "meanings" which mediate and determine the way in which the individuals respond to objects and situations. The items on a questionnaire, on a schedule, and on a test may be clear and precise; and, the individual may answer in the categorical and definite way that is needed for the quantitative treatment of the responses. But the point is made that the responses to these items do not tell what is the meaning of these items to the individual; hence, the investigator is not in a position to state what are the individuals' attitudes or to know what would be his likely behavior if he were actually to act toward the objects to which the items refer.[103]

For example, a female-headed family of six with an annual income of $7,500 may correctly be classified as in the "under $10,000 a year" category of families. For many researchers, interested in (for example) the statistical relationship between the percentage of poor homes in an area and the average achievement of schoolchildren, these data are enough. Researchers like Blumer, however, are interested in different questions. They want to know what that $7,500 income means to the mother in terms of how she behaves toward her children or makes decisions about looking for work, or how creative she is in stretching her budget in order to put food on the table three times a day. Symbolic interactionists do not deny the usefulness of a quantitative national census; but for the research questions they want to ask, census questions and response are inadequate. Their approach and emphasis on meaning are simply not conducive to quantitative methods.

However, to us it seems unnecessary to select one approach at the expense of another. Qualitative research can contribute to quantitative research. It can generate fruitful hypotheses and uncover heretofore unknown areas of needed research, and it can provide necessary typologies.

---

[102]Blumer, *Symbolic Interactionism*, p. 30.
[103]In Schmidt, *Man and Society*, p. 194.

We want to argue that these two research approaches should cooperate rather than compete with each other.

Microsociology

In speaking of the limitations of the symbolic interactionists' microsociological approach, Skidmore says, "Research with this perspective tends to be the elaboration of ever-different situations and activities, with a consequent lack of emphasis on relating these works into a coherent view of whole societies."[104]

However, in a response to Jonathan Turner's article, "Parsons as a Symbolic Interactionist," Blumer denies the charge that the methodology of the symbolic interactionists "emphasizes microinteractive processes." Blumer argues that the symbolic interactionist approach is capable of studying large organization, and he refers the reader to his article, "Sociological Theory in Industrial Relations."[105]

A perusal of Blumer's article is a little disconcerting, for it fails to set forth a clear and complete methodology. Blumer states,

> The observations necessary to sharpen and fill in this vague perspective must meet the two requirements of intimate familiarity and broad imaginative grasp. . . . It is unfortunate that observation in the field of industrial relations has to be made in the form of large intricate patterns—but it has to be, in order to be realistic. In a way, the necessities of observation in industrial relations are quite similar to those required in modern warfare. The individual soldier in his single observation post, regardless of how competent he may be as an observer, can understand little of what is taking place over the broad area of a campaign. A sociological investigator making observations in a single factory suffers, I believe, from a corresponding limitation. Effective observation requires the observer to sense the movement in the field, to take many varied roles, to size up a variety of different situations and in doing so to perform the difficult task of fitting such things into somewhat of an integrated pattern. This type of observation, whether we like it or not, requires a high degree of imaginative judgment in order to be accurate.[106]

As he concludes the article, Blumer says that we need a scheme of treatment that is suited to the analysis of collective and mass interaction—but that sociologists have not begun this task. Thus what Blumer calls an article that will clarify symbolic interactionism's capability of studying the interaction among macro organizations is not that at all. Though he sets forth some blurred outlines, readers are left not much further along in their under-

---

[104]William Skidmore, *Theoretical Thinking in Sociology* (New York: Cambridge University Press, 1975), p. 236.

[105]Blumer, "Comment on 'Parsons as a Symbolic Interactionist,'" 61. See also Blumer's article, "Sociological Theory in Industrial Relations," *American Sociological Review* 12 (1947): 271–78.

[106]Blumer, "Sociological Theory in Industrial Relations," p. 277.

standing of how symbolic interactionists go about the study of groups at the macro level.[107] Microsociology is, after all, home base for symbolic interactionists. We turn now to Blumer's student, Erving Goffman, who specialized in face-to-face interaction.

PART THREE

Erving Goffman: Dramaturgy and the Interaction Order

BACKGROUND

In this section we take a systematic look at Goffman's theoretical contributions. His work has influenced several theorists outside the symbolic interactionist perspective. Peter Blau, for instance, applied Goffman's concepts of impression management and role distance to his social exchange theory. Goffman's work has also inspired ethnomethodologists,[108] and Randall Collins incorporated many of Goffman's ideas into his book *Conflict Sociology*.[109] In fact, Collins paid the highest tribute to Goffman when he argued that Robert Merton was "the best-known figure in professional American sociology during the middle of the twentieth century," C. Wright Mills had "the greatest political impact," and Talcott Parsons was the "major comprehensive theorist," but Erving Goffman was the sociologist who "contributed most to intellectual progress."[110]

Born in Mannville, Alberta, in 1922, Goffman earned his B.A. at the University of Toronto in 1945 and his M.A. and Ph.D. at the University of Chicago in 1949 and 1953. Shortly after completing his dissertation, Goffman joined his former teacher Herbert Blumer at the University of California, Berkeley, where he taught until 1969.[111] He then accepted a position as

---

[107]For a well-documented argument to the contrary, see David Maines, "Myth, Text, and Interactionist Complicity in the Neglect of Blumer's Macrosociology," *Symbolic Interaction* XI (1988): 43–57. Maines argues that the analysis of societywide organizations was a major concern of Blumer's.

[108]See Paul Attewell's "Ethnomethodology Since Garfinkel," *Theory and Society* I (1974): 179–210.

[109]See Collins's references to Goffman in Chapter 3.

[110]Randall Collins, *Sociology Since Midcentury* (New York: Academic Press, 1981), p. 297.

[111]While at Berkeley, Goffman became interested in the work of Harold Garfinkel, and he encouraged his students to read Garfinkel's published and unpublished work. Some of Goffman's students traveled from Berkeley to Los Angeles in the late 1960s to attend Garfinkel's seminars.

Benjamin Franklin Professor of Anthropology and Sociology at the University of Pennsylvania, where he taught until his untimely death in 1982.[112]

Like Blumer, Goffman was most influenced by Mead, and this is evident in his focus on the self, particularly in his first book, *The Presentation of Self in Everyday Life*, which informed much of his later work. In true Meadian fashion Goffman treats human beings as active and knowledgeable. In *Stigma* he illumines for us the creativity of deviants or stigmatized persons who manage to preserve a sense of self when the cards are stacked against them. His keen observations in a mental institution in *Asylums* led him to create the concept *total institution*, "a place of residence and work where a large number of like-situated individuals, cut off from the wider society for an appreciable period of time, together lead an enclosed, formally administered round of life."[113] He found that inmates invented many ingenious strategies to preserve their own selfhood rather than surrender to an acceptance of the role and the self that the institution prescribed—and this takes place in a very structured institution. He gives many examples in his discussion of "secondary adjustments," which he defines as "any habitual arrangement by which a member of an organization employs unauthorized means, or obtains unauthorized ends, or both, thus getting around the organization's assumptions as to what he should do and get and hence what he should be."[114]

Some of the secondary adjustments were "make-do's" (converting a bathroom sink and radiator to a private laundry system) and "free places" (a patch of woods behind the hospital used as a cover for drinking or the shade of a large tree near the center of the hospital grounds used as a cover for poker games). These secondary adjustments illustrate ways in which human beings meet situations and devise their own conduct. Furthermore, Goffman says,

> The practice of reserving something of oneself from the clutch of an institution is very visible in mental hospitals and prisons but can be found in more benign and less totalistic institutions, too. I want to argue that this recalcitrance is not an incidental mechanism of defense but rather an essential constituent of the self. . . . Our sense of being a person can come from being drawn into a wider social unit; our sense of selfhood can rise through the little ways we resist the pull. Our status is backed by the solid buildings of the world, while our sense of personal identity often resides in the cracks.[115]

Goffman's research revealed an underlife in a mental hospital where inmates resisted every effort to strip away the old self. His work, which is

---

[112]His key publications include *The Presentation of Self in Everyday Life, Asylums, Encounters, Behavior in Public Place, Stigma, Interaction Ritual, Relations in Public, Strategic Interaction,* and *Gender Advertisements.* (See the selected bibliography.)

[113]Erving Goffman, *Asylums: Essays on the Social Situation of Mental Patients and Other Inmates* (New York: Doubleday, 1961), p. xii.

[114]Goffman, *Asylums,* p. 189.

[115]Goffman, *Asylums,* pp. 319–20.

informed to a large extent by Mead's "I," is replete with analyses of situations in which individuals are "resisting the pull" and "residing in the cracks."

In his work Goffman combined several methods used by symbolic interactionists: participant observation supplemented by data from case histories, autobiographies, letters, newspaper articles, and journal advertisements. He describes his approach in *Asylums* as a "symbolic-interaction framework for considering the fate of the self."[116] Mead's concept of the self is, in fact, a central theme in much of Goffman's work.[117]

Durkheim's writings, in particular his analysis of ritual in *The Elementary Forms of the Religious Life*, fascinated Goffman. Not only did he publish a book on the topic (*Interaction Ritual*), but the theme of ritual appears in several of his works. For example, he cites Durkheim in *Asylums* when he discusses the ceremonial practices in a total institution like shows, sports events, and dances. As Goffman puts it, "These ceremonial practices are well suited to a Durkheimian analysis: a society dangerously split into inmates and staff can through these ceremonies hold itself together."[118]

While it may be true that Goffman self-consciously adopted a Durkheimian perspective in some of his early works,[119] this was neither permanent nor all-inclusive. The aerial view of large social structures was not for Goffman; his focus was on the "countless minor syntheses" of Simmel that we described at the beginning of this chapter, the human linkages that Simmel labeled the "atoms of society." Goffman's great interest in the forms of interaction and his ingenuity in fleshing out sociological concepts in his descriptions of face-to-face interaction were indeed reminiscent of Georg Simmel.

However, some of Goffman's later work, in particular *Frame Analysis*, represented a shift toward a variant of structuralism. We turn now to a discussion of two of Goffman's chief contributions to the symbolic interactionist perspective: his dramaturgical ideas and what he calls the "interaction order."

DRAMATURGY AND EVERYDAY LIFE

Webster defines dramaturgy as "the art of dramatic composition and theatrical representation."[120] In his early and often-cited work *The Presentation of Self in Everyday Life*, Goffman takes the familiar sociological concept, role,

---

[116]Goffman, *Asylums*, p. 47.

[117]Goffman did not approve of classifying scholars by their membership in schools of thought. He called this practice "a case of guilt by pigeonholing." See Erving Goffman, "Reply," *Contemporary Sociology* X (January 1981): 61.

[118]Goffman, *Asylums*, p. 109.

[119]Whitney Pope and Barclay D. Johnson, "Inside Organic Solidarity," *American Sociological Review* 48 (October 1983): 691.

[120]*Webster's New Collegiate Dictionary* (Springfield, Mass.: Merriam, 1961), p. 250.

and puts it back on stage by placing the analysis of human behavior in a theatrical setting. He takes the dramatic situation of actors and actresses on stage and applies this theatrical representation to the everyday lives of ordinary women and men who are acting out their roles in the real world.

Goffman looks at the ways individuals in their everyday lives present themselves and their activities to others; in particular, he focuses on *impression management*, the ways in which the individual guides and controls the impressions others form of him or her. Two additional dramaturgical concepts are the *front* and *back regions*. The front is "that part of the individuals' performance which regularly functions in a general and fixed fashion to define the situation for those who observe the performance."[121] Front includes setting (furniture and other items supplying the scenery and stage props) and "personal front"—items of "expressive equipment," like insignia of office or rank, clothing, sex, age, racial characteristics, size, posture, speech patterns, facial expressions, and body gestures.[122]

Goffman makes the point that the standards that women are obliged to maintain regarding a disarray of personal front (clothing and appearance) are stricter than for men. "After all," Goffman says, "for a woman to appear in public with her costume disarrayed can be taken as a sign of accessibility and looseness of morals."[123]

Ask yourself, for instance, when you last carried a briefcase. You may have needed it to carry your books, but you may also have used it to impress a job interviewer, the dean of your college, or even your sociology professor. You may also recall how, in that situation, you carefully articulated each sentence and how you used other aspects of your personal front, like your clothing, posture, facial expressions, and body gestures, to present yourself in the best light. The front region, then, includes anything observed by the audience while the actor is on front stage that makes for a successful performance. The front region is the place where the actor is seriously playing out the script of impression management. In the front region the actor avoids anything that is inappropriate according to the script. Such behavior brings to mind Parsons's pattern variables, where the actor also carefully makes the appropriate choices. Goffman's actors are not improvising when they are on front stage.

What happens in the front region, then, is an attempt to manipulate the audience. An article in a London newspaper concerning a scripted system of

---

[121]Erving Goffman, *The Presentation of Self in Everyday Life* (Garden City, N.Y.: Doubleday, 1959), p. 22.

[122]Goffman, *The Presentation of Self in Everyday Life*, p. 24.

[123]Erving Goffman, "The Arrangement Between the Sexes," *Theory and Society* 4 (Fall 1977): 329. Giddens applauds Goffman's analysis of spatial divisions, a major feature of class differentiation. The front/back region contrast demonstrates how the setting is controlled, and Giddens argues that the capability to control settings is one of the major prerogatives of power. See Anthony Giddens, *Central Problems in Social Theory* (Berkeley: University of California Press, 1983), pp. 206–209.

selling cars describes this manipulation as it occurs in the automobile industry. The article explains that salespersons are taught a script that they must follow "like an actor has to learn his part in a play." One of the best scripts cited is entitled "Playing Harris": (Speaking to customer) "I've got Mr. Harris on the phone wanting to know if the car has been sold. Shall I say yes?"[124]

The front stage performance above would work best if the telephone rang at the strategic moment (prop) and if the script were delivered in a convincing tone of voice (personal front). The front would then have a better chance of defining the situation for the potential customer, who then quickly would answer, "Yes."

The back region, by contrast, is the place closed to and hidden from the audience where the techniques of impression management are practiced. Many forms of assistance to the actors are given in the backstage region, for example, adjustment of costumes and prompting. It is also a place where the performer can relax. As Goffman puts it, "He can drop his front, forego speaking his lines, and step out of character."[125] Backstage is where the actors do not need to engage in impression management; they can be themselves.

In a study of social interaction at the Laundromat, Kenen used Goffman's concept of the front region to analyze some of the activity she was observing. She found customers engaged in "behind the scenes work" in a front stage setting as they attempted to conceal some of the items they were washing. As she put it, "Padded bras, torn underwear, stained garments, and even designer bedsheets can reveal too much about one's habits and tastes to a stranger, and may contradict the intended presentation of self."[126] While Laundromats and automobile salesrooms may seem to be a far cry from the theater, keep in mind that Goffman's dramaturgy is concerned with the lives of ordinary women and men as they act out their daily roles on the stage of life.

By drawing our attention to the backstage region, Goffman helps us to understand all of the hidden work involved in accomplishing successful presentation of self in public. He shows us how, in the drama of everyday life, individuals manage to look good when they present themselves to others at home, school, work, neighborhood, and in other microinteractive settings.

Randall Collins uses Goffman's dramaturgical concepts to analyze organizational politics, which at lower levels involve "presenting a united front to the supervisor, appearing to comply with the supervisor's demands while giving the workers a breathing space in which to control their own work pace." These encounters with authority are front stage. The workers on

---

[124]*The Daily Telegraph* (London), April 5, 1984, p. 7.

[125]Goffman, *Presentation of Self in Everyday Life*, p. 112.

[126]See Regina Kenen, "Soapsuds, Space and Sociability: A Participant Observation of the Laundromat," *Urban Life* 11, no. 2 (July 1982): 178.

their own are backstage, engaging in conversation about such things as "how the boss was fooled, how a member of the team almost blew its cover; jokes are made and anecdotes are exchanged, creating an entire conversational culture of a particular backstage world."[127]

Here Collins, a sociologist, is consciously applying Goffman's ideas to an organizational structure. How does a nonsociologist use them? In a newspaper article on the on- and off-the-record statements of politicians, a journalist writes, "What we call the record often tends to be the precise opposite of a record. It is, rather, the artifice, the cooked-up part, the image that the politician, with our connivance, hopes to convey and generally does. The off-the-record part is where the reality and the authenticity are to be found and where they are generally supposed to remain forever obscure."[128] This journalist is alerting the reader to two important dramaturgical points: first, that on-the-record is, for the politician, front stage, where, as she puts it, "little tricks and big deceptions are being practiced." Second, the real record is in the backstage region, where the politicians speak candidly about what they really think. She is alerting us, the audience, to the attempt on the part of politicians to define the situation for us by their front-stage performances.

What happens when front and back stage activities are not well coordinated is that the actor does not perform well, and the performance is less successful in varying degrees. In some cases the goof may be relatively minor, as when a prompter fails to act quickly enough to supply a forgotten line or when a portion of the costume or other props come crashing down on the stage. Such minor hitches can be covered up and the performance completed. But what happens when backstage *becomes* front stage, when the audience suddenly sees all the hitherto hidden backstage activity? Goffman's analysis of fatefulness is illuminating on this point. In *Interaction Ritual* he argues that in situations where coordination and concealment are vital, "a whole range of minor unanticipated hitches lose their usual quality of correctability and become fateful." He presents the following story as illustration:

> Three robbers who completely botched what was supposed to be a simple little bank robbery in Rodeo were sentenced in Federal Court here yesterday. . . .
>
> All three were nabbed by some 40 police officers Jan. 7 as they struggled to make off with $7710 stuffed into a laundry sack they had just taken out of the United California Bank, the only bank in Rodeo. . . .
>
> Pugh walked in with a sawed-off shotgun and lined up the 13 employees and two customers, while Fleming, carrying a pistol, went to the vault and started filling the laundry bag with currency and, alas, coins.
>
> "The coins can't be traced," he said cleverly. He kept piling in coins until the bag weighed about 200 pounds. Then he dragged the bag across the floor to the door—and the frayed rope snapped.

[127]Randall Collins, *Conflict Sociology: Toward an Explanatory Science*, p. 118.

[128]Meg Greenfield, "Must Reality Be off the Record?" *Washington Post*, April 11, 1984, p. A21. Thanks to William Sandmeyer for drawing our attention to this article.

Both men then lugged the bag through the door, but it caught and ripped a hole, letting coins trail behind them as they dragged the bag to the getaway car, with Duren at the wheel.

Duren, though, had parked too close to the high curb, so the three could not open the door to get the loot inside. Finally, they did, by moving the car, and raced away—around the corner. There the car stopped when the three saw the clutter of sheriff, Highway Patrol, and police cars.[129]

Here a strategic prop (laundry sack) breaks down, and backstage assistance fails to come through on time. As Goffman explains, this is fateful for the individuals involved because the criminal enterprise has a much narrower reserve for correctability. A high price must be paid for bad breaks or goofs—situations in which backstage assistance is inadequate. Here the tables are turned, as the actors have the situation defined for them by the audience.

Goffman's dramaturgical ideas help us examine those countless instances when we have used all the equipment of our front and back regions to create the best possible impressions of ourselves. His basic question to us is, "Aren't we all con artists, after all?" There is no doubt that we use impression management in our own everyday lives, for example, when we succeed in "acing" a job interview, when we regale a group of strangers at a social gathering, when we convince the person we love to be our spouse, or when we do our best to be the "Rock of Gibraltar" for other family members at the funeral of a close relative. In each of these examples we want to be the one who defines the situation for the other individuals present, and Goffman's ideas show how this is possible.

In a more recent book Goffman presents 500 magazine advertisements and analyzes the often unspoken social assumptions about gender conveyed by these pictures. Assuming that the ads represent advertiser's views of how women and men can be profitably pictured, Goffman's analysis could be described as focusing on the front stage.

One of the themes emerging from Goffman's analysis, for instance, was "function ranking," the male performing the executive role both within and outside occupational specialization. Goffman asks the reader to examine how males are

> pictured when in the domains of the traditional authority and competency of females—the kitchen, the nursery, and the living room when it is being cleaned. One answer, borrowed from life and possibly underrepresented, is to picture the male engaged in no contributing role at all, in this way avoiding either subordination or contamination with a "female" task. Another answer, I think, is to present the man as ludicrous and childlike, unrealistically so, as if perhaps in making him candidly unreal the competency image of real males

[129]*San Francisco Chronicle*, March 10, 1966, in Erving Goffman, *Interaction Ritual* (Garden City, N.Y.: Doubleday, 1967), pp. 165–66.

could be preserved. A subtler technique is to allow the male to pursue the alien activity under the direct scrutiny of she who can do the deed properly, as though the doing were itself by way of being a lark or a dare, a smile on the face of the doer or the watcher attesting to the essentially unserious essayed character of the undertaking.[130]

In contrast to sociobiologists who emphasize the influence of heredity, Goffman stressed the sociocultural factors that create and maintain structures of human interaction, like gender inequality. In his article entitled "The Arrangement between the Sexes," he argues that women's breastfeeding is a biological constraint that is extended culturally. Thus, he says, "A whole range of domestic duties come (for whatever reason) to be defined as inappropriate for a male to perform," and correspondingly "a whole range of occupations away from the household come to be defined as inappropriate for the female." [131]

Goffman pictures the household as a socialization depot and presents the example of a middle-class pair of cross-sexed siblings:

> The home training of the two sexes will differ, beginning to orient the girl to taking a domestic, supportive role, and the boy to a more widely based competitive one. . . . (For instance,) . . . the larger portion at mealtime is given to the male "because he's a boy" or the softer of two beds is allocated to the female "because she's a girl," or a male is accorded harsher negative sanctions than a female because his is the coarser nature and it will take more to get through to him.[132]

In contrast to Marx, Goffman argues that

> The deepest sense of what one is—one's gender identity—is something that is given its initial character from ingredients that do not bear on ethnicity or socioeconomic stratification. . . . Brothers will have a way of defining themselves in terms of their differences from persons like their sisters, and sisters will have a way of defining themselves in terms of persons like their brothers, in both cases turning perception away from how it is the sibs of one family are socially situated in a fundamentally different way from the sibs of another family. Gender, not religion, is the opiate of the masses. . . . A man may spend his day suffering under those who have power over him, suffer this situation at almost any level of society, and yet on returning home each night regain a sphere in which he dominates. And wherever he goes beyond the household, women can be there to prop up his show of competence.[133]

Barrie Thorne's study of elementary schoolchildren draws on Goffman's work in the article just cited. She refers to the term "genderism,"

---

[130]Erving Goffman, *Gender Advertisements* (New York: Harper and Row, 1979), pp. 36–37.

[131]Goffman, "The Arrangement Between the Sexes," p. 313.

[132]Goffman, "The Arrangement Between the Sexes," p. 314.

[133]Goffman, "The Arrangement Between the Sexes," p. 315.

defined by Goffman as "a sex-linked individual behavioral practice,"[134] and her study uncovered moments in social life that evoke stereotypic beliefs about masculinity and femininity. Her observations on the playground revealed many instances where boundaries were created and maintained between girls and boys. Thorne labels this emerging pattern of spatial separation "borderwork." The various types of borderwork included contests, chasing, pollution rituals, and invasions. For instance, contests like math and spelling games in the classroom invited gender antagonisms when the teacher labeled the teams as "Beastly Boys" and "Gossipy Girls." On the playground she observed a gender asymmetry in "cootie tag" where girls were treated as an ultimate source of contamination, while boys were exempt. Thorne writes,

> Recoiling from physical proximity with another person and their belongings because they are perceived as contaminating is a powerful statement of social distance and claimed superiority. Pollution beliefs and practices draw on the emotion-laden feeling of repugnance that accompanies unwanted touch or smell. Kids often act out pollution beliefs in a spirit of playful teasing, but the whimsical frame of "play" slides in and out of the serious, and some games of cooties clearly cause emotional pain.[135]

Likewise, invasions took on an asymmetric form because boys tended to invade girls' groups much more often than the reverse. Tomboys, however, were an exception. For example, fifth graders Tracy and Sheila skillfully played group sports less divided by gender, like handball, dodgeball, and kickball. However, in the spring they were serious players in the city's predominantly male youth baseball league, and that spilled over to their participation at school, where Tracy and Sheila "joined predominantly male games of baseball out on the grassy diamond, and they carried their mitts around school as a kind of badge of involvement."[136]

Thorne presents instances in which some creative teachers attempted to correct the damage caused by the various types of borderwork by encouraging a collaborative rather than competitive climate between boys and girls in the classroom. For instance, they organized permanent seating by hearing, sight, and height rather than by gender, and some instructed the children to form their lines by other characteristics, like the color of shoes.[137] Like Goffman, Thorne is also drawing on Georg Simmel's work on the importance of social space. In the next section we turn to Goffman's analysis of the interaction order, his final legacy to sociology.

[134]Goffman, "The Arrangement Between the Sexes," p. 321.

[135]Barrie Thorne, *Gender Play: Girls and Boys in School* (New Brunswick, NJ: Rutgers University Press, 1993), p. 75. See also Myra and David Sadker, *Failing at Fairness: How America's Schools Cheat Girls* (New York: Scribners, 1994).

[136]Thorne, *Gender Play*, p. 125.

[137]Thorne, *Gender Play*, pp. 160–61.

THE INTERACTION ORDER

When Erving Goffman developed cancer in the summer of 1982, he was preparing the address he was scheduled to deliver as president of the American Sociological Association at the annual meeting in September. Although he was not able to present the address orally, he completed the paper before his death on November 19, 1982. The title of this final work, "The Interaction Order," which was published in the *American Sociological Review*, is the label Goffman gives to his focus over his entire career, the domain of face-to-face social interaction, "where two or more individuals are physically in one another's presence."[138] As John Lofland explains, "He showed us with a detail and poignancy no one had before how our sense of ourselves, of what is real, and how we feel is bound up in—is inextricably knotted to—the ever-moving microdynamics of the immediate interaction order in endlessly complicated ways of which we are not aware." Goffman was fascinated with discrepancies between appearances and realities and with "deception and manipulation."[139]

Goffman's presidential address, which sums up his life's work, is his attempt to make the case that the interaction order should be treated as a substantive domain in its own right. It outlines some of the basic units and recurrent structures and processes of the interaction order, from the smallest to the largest: (1) *persons*, whether single, couples, files, processions, or queues; (2) *contacts*, either through physical co-presence, telephone conversation, or letter exchange; (3) *encounters*, or arrangements in which persons come together into a small physical circle as participants in a consciously shared, interdependent undertaking (for example, card games, meals, love-making, and service transactions); (4) *platform performances*, where activity is set before an audience (for instance, a talk, a context, a formal meeting, a play, a musical offering); (5) *celebrative social occasions*, or gatherings of individuals in honor of some jointly appreciated circumstance where participants arrive and leave in a coordinated way. This last unit is the largest interactional one Goffman mentions, one that can be engineered to extend over a number of days.

Although the persons, contacts, encounters, performances, and celebrations outlined are essentially microscopic units, Goffman argues that the interaction order has direct bearing on the macroscopic order. We presented an instance of such a repercussion earlier in this chapter in the Watergate example, where the phone call to the police made by Frank Wills led to the resignation of President Nixon. Goffman states that a good deal of organiza-

---

[138]Erving Goffman, "The Interaction Order," *American Sociological Review* 48 (February 1983): 8.

[139]John Lofland, "Erving Goffman's Sociological Legacies," *Urban Life* 13 (April 1984): 7, 22.

tional work is done face-to-face, and he suggests, for example, that complex organizations are so dependent on particular personnel, especially those in governing roles, that they are extremely vulnerable when key personnel are abducted or injured. At such a time an organization may make every effort to conceal the absence of the administrator in order to keep the system operating. The question "Who is in charge?" raised at the time of serious illnesses of heads of state, like that of Boris Yeltsin in Russia or Ronald Reagan in the United States, are cases in point. Another example is the disorder experienced (or created) by elementary school students when a substitute teacher takes over during the illness of the regular teacher. Reverberations reach beyond the classroom to other parts of the school, including supervision of playground and lunchroom activities and the policing of bus lines and hallway traffic.

Another element of the interaction order that has a direct effect on a person's life chances is what Goffman labels "processing encounters." These include interviews conducted by school counselors, personnel department staff in business organizations, psychologists, and courtroom officials. These processing encounters can affect the relevant social institution as well as the person involved. How an individual performs on a job interview, for instance, affects her or his occupational future. For example, Shirley Hartley, who earned a doctorate at the University of California, Berkeley, in 1969, describes her experience in the early 1960s when she was being interviewed by a faculty member at Stanford University soon after applying to their Ph.D. program in sociology. She explains, "The faculty member made it clear that 'Stanford doesn't accept middle-aged women (I was thirty-three) who just happen to live in the area. We expect our Ph.D.s to teach at Harvard and Columbia.' "[140]

On the other hand, the type of people who are processed successfully can change the face of the institution itself, as is evidenced in the increasing diversity among both graduate students and faculty. For instance, while Shirley Hartley was a graduate student at Berkeley, there were no women full-time faculty members in the sociology department; by 1991 seven of twenty-nine faculty members (24 percent) were women.[141]

Goffman also points to the importance of first impressions for friendship relationships and marital bonds. In fact, he suggests that such close bonds often "can be traced back to an occasion in which something more was made of an incidental contact than need have been made."[142] One need only read the February 14 (Valentine's Day) issue of a newspaper for some "love at first sight" stories to illustrate Goffman's point here.

---

[140]Shirley F. Hartley, "Multiple Roles, Multiple Selves," pp. 113–24 in Orlans and Wallace, *Gender and the Academic Experience.*

[141]See Orlans and Wallace, *Gender and the Academic Experience*, p. 249.

[142]Goffman, "The Interaction Order," p. 8.

In his final article Goffman also attempted to synthesize symbolic interactionism. His examples of the small-scale linkages recommended to our attention by Simmel are found in the interaction order, which consists of persons, contacts, encounters, platform performances, and celebrations. Goffman also claims that forms of face-to-face life, because they are constantly repeated, are more open to systematic analysis than many macroscopic entities. This article represents his final argument for the significance of the microinteractional level for sociology.

However, Goffman's analysis, for the most part, leaves out an important ingredient of the symbolic interactionist perspective: self-interaction. He pays lip service to it when he states that these face-to-face forms are "anchored in subjective feelings and thus allow an appreciable role for empathy."[143] Here he is reiterating the value of taking the role of the other, which is at the core of symbolic interactionism. Goffman's own work, nonetheless, reveals much more about face-to-face interaction than about subjective feelings. He obviously believes in the central premise of symbolic interactionism, that actors interpret, map out, evaluate, and then act; that is, that human beings are active, not passive. However, while Goffman has enriched sociology with a number of important concepts based on his keen observations, his chief interest is not in what actors are saying to themselves as they map out their actions, but in how they succeed in manipulating the definition of the situation. Though his data include sources for subjective meaning, for example, letters and autobiographies, these data are not central to his analysis. He has chosen a narrower focus than that of Blumer, but the depth of his analysis compensates for this.

Goffman's legacy to sociology emerged at the conclusion of his presidential address in the form of advocating a new direction for research on the interaction order. He who spent a substantial part of his career studying the "underdog," focusing on people in subordinate positions and on disenfranchised or discredited groups, recommends something different. Goffman suggests that sociologists pursue "unsponsored analyses of the social arrangements enjoyed by those with institutional authority—police, generals, government leaders, parents, males, whites, nationals, media operators, and all those well-placed persons who are in a position to give official imprint to versions of reality."[144]

Here we see Goffman address the realm of power in the social order and the management of social reality. In order to understand the recurrent patterns of interaction between subordinate and superordinate individuals, Goffman directs the attention of sociologists to the world of the latter. In his recommendation for an all-out effort to examine people in positions of power in our society, he is forcing microsociological researchers to deal with

---

[143]Goffman, "The Interaction Order," p. 9.
[144]Goffman, "The Interaction Order," p. 17.

a key concept of conflict theorists—power relationships. In the last analysis this could be an important effort toward bridging the micro and macro levels of sociological analysis.

PART FOUR

Arlie Russell Hochschild and Patricia Hill Collins: Expanding the Horizons of Symbolic Interactionism

When it turned the spotlight on gender and women's concerns, the contemporary women's movement encouraged sociologists to uncover new research topics and new concepts, thus enlarging the horizons of sociological theory. In Chapter 3 we introduced feminist theorists influenced by Marx and Engels: Zillah Eisenstein, Janet Chafetz, and Rae Lesser Blumberg. In the next chapter we look at that portion of Dorothy E. Smith's work that emerged from phenomenology. Here we examine the work of two feminists who have expanded the horizons of symbolic interactionism. Arlie Russell Hochschild's work on the sociology of emotions has introduced a new micro-level perspective. Patricia Hill Collins analyzes the intersection of race, class, and gender as they affect African-American women, using concepts such as self-definition that make her work quite distinct from older conflict theorists' discussion of power and oppression.[145]

BACKGROUND

Many social theorists tend to overlook, ignore, or dismiss people's emotions as irrelevant.[146] "What," they ask, "do individual feelings have to do with explaining the social world?" However, because symbolic interactionists focus on subjective meaning, we should expect that they will also take the emotions more seriously than any other theorists and supply us with many other ingredients for a social theory of emotion. As we briefly review the material presented thus far in this chapter, we can detect a number of references to emotions, some explicit and some implicit.

Weber's discussion of the importance of subjective meaning in his definition of sociology allows for the relationship between individual emotions and social interaction without making it explicit. We would argue that the subjective meaning that an active individual ascribes to a situation includes

---

[145]See also M. J. Deegan and M. Hill, ed., *Women and Symbolic Interactionism* (Boston: Allen and Unwin, 1987).

[146]As we pointed out in Chapter 3, Lewis Coser is an exception in this regard among conflict theorists.

an emotional element. The feelings people have toward those with whom they come in contact is a factor that can and does enter into the individual's definition of the situation, and this, in turn, influences people's decisions about whether to interact, to withdraw, or, as Weber puts it, to "passively acquiesce" in the situation.[147]

Taking another look at Simmel's description of human linkages, we discover that he explicitly includes two emotions—jealousy and gratitude—as examples of the "countless minor syntheses" that incessantly tie people together.[148] Likewise Cooley, defining the looking-glass self, explicitly mentions "self-feeling, such as pride or mortification," which results from how we imagine the other to be judging our appearance.[149]

Blumer's discussion of the process of self-indication whereby individuals point out certain stimuli to themselves and then interpret the appearance of the stimuli to themselves includes implicit mention of the emotions.[150] For instance, his example of a person who notes that he or she is eating with someone they despise includes an emotional element. As we explained earlier,[151] someone who gives an account of personal worries and anxieties is interpreting what is disturbing to him or her.[152] Examples of emotional self-interactions range from a young child who tells himself "I'm scared!" when he experiences a thunderstorm for the first time, to the adult who says to herself "I can hardly wait to see him!" as her train pulls into the station. Worries, anxieties, jealousy, pride, love, contempt—a whole array of emotions—are often included in the conversations people have with themselves. Thus what people are feeling and their self-indications about those feelings help them to devise or map out their conduct. In short, human beings often choose one behavior over another because it "feels good."

Two other major theorists who include emotional elements are Erving Goffman and Randall Collins. Goffman's impression management is essentially a strategy for avoiding embarrassment or shame and is inspired by pride, a desire to look good. When Goffman asks, "Aren't we all con artists, after all?" this points to one of the reasons why we want to control others' impressions of us—to avoid being embarrassed.

Randall Collins discusses how rituals can intensify emotional arousal and commit participants more strongly to certain views, and how, as a consequence, these rituals tend to strengthen and legitimize a given social

---

[147]See p. 192 in this text.

[148]See p. 192.

[149]See p. 195.

[150]See Part Two of this chapter.

[151]See Part Two of this chapter, p. 207.

[152]In a personal interview (1975) blumer suggested, as a teaching device that might help students to understand the importance of the symbolic interactionist perspective, one might ask students about their own immediate worries, anxieties, and fears, and how those feelings, in turn, affect their behavior.

order.[153] More recently, Collins, influenced by Goffman as well as by Durkheim's work on rituals, has inserted emotional energy as an essential ingredient in his model of "the interaction ritual chain." He argues that the most basic ingredient in interactions is "a minimal tone of positive sentiment toward the other." Thus the individual who is accepted into a conversation, for instance, acquires not only an increment of positive emotional energy from that experience but also additional emotional resources (confidence, warmth, enthusiasm) with which to negotiate successfully in the next interaction. Such chains, Collins argues, "extend throughout every person's lifetime."[154]

ARLIE RUSSELL HOCHSCHILD: EMOTIONAL LABOR

Among sociologists who have done serious theoretical work on emotions, Arlie Russell Hochschild is a dominant figure. In fact she is considered the founder of a new subfield in sociology: the sociology of emotions. Born in 1940, she received degrees from Swarthmore (B.A.) and the University of California at Berkeley (M.A. and Ph.D.). After two years at the University of California at Santa Cruz, she began teaching at the Berkeley campus, where she is now professor of sociology. Her book *The Managed Heart: Commercialization of Human Feeling* is the pioneering theoretical work. As Hochschild explains in a recent autobiographical piece, "The idea of taking the world of emotions and feelings seriously went along with taking women's experiences and public perceptions of that experience seriously."[155]

Although neither Mead nor Blumer developed a theory of emotions, this new social theory is, in part, an expansion of the symbolic interactionist perspective. Hochschild draws from a number of theorists, including Dewey, Goffman, and Freud. She makes the point that Goffman and Freud each provide a limited view of the emotions, as Goffman specialized in studying embarrassment and shame, while Freud specialized in analyzing anxiety.[156] By contrast, Hochschild's theory encompasses a whole range of emotions, from grief, depression, frustration, anger, fear, contempt, guilt, anguish, envy, jealousy, embarrassment, shame, and anxiety to love, compassion, nostalgia, joy, gratitude, pride, and ambivalence.

---

[153]See Chapter 3.

[154]Randall Collins, *Sociology Since Midcentury: Essays in Theory Cumulation* (New York: Academic Press, 1981), pp. 276–81.

[155]Arlie Russell Hochschild, "Inside the Clockwork of Male Careers," in Kathryn P. Meadow Orlans and Ruth A. Wallace, ed., *Gender and the Academic Experience: Berkeley Women Sociologists* (Lincoln: University of Nebraska Press, 1994), p. 137.

[156]Arlie Russell Hochschild, *The Managed Heart: Commercialization of Human Feeling* (Berkeley: University of California Press, 1983), p. 216. See also her more recent books, *The Second Shift: Working Parents and the Revolution at Home* (New York: Viking Penguin, 1989) and *The Time Bind: When Work Becomes Home and Home Becomes Work* (N.Y.: Henry Holt, 1997).

Hochschild focuses specifically on *emotional labor*, which she defines thus:

> I use the term *emotional labor* to mean the management of feeling to create a publicly observable facial and bodily display; emotional labor is sold for a wage and therefore has *exchange value*. I use the synonymous terms *emotion work* or *emotional management* to refer to these same acts done in a private context where they have *use value*.[157]

Jobs calling for emotional labor share three characteristics: (1) the worker must have face-to-face or voice-to-voice contact with the public; (2) the worker is required to produce an emotional state in another person, such as gratitude or fear; and (3) the employer is allowed to exercise a degree of control over the emotional activities of employees.

Hochschild researched the emotional labor required by two occupations: flight attendants (mostly women) and bill collectors (mostly men). She found that the flight attendants were asked to "feel sympathy, trust, and good will," whereas the bill collectors were asked to "feel distrust and sometimes positive bad will."[158]

The following is an illustration from an interview with a flight attendant:

> Even though I'm a very honest person, I have learned not to allow my face to mirror my alarm or fright. I feel very protective of my passengers. Above all, I don't want them to be frightened. If we were going down, if we were going to make a ditching in water, the chances of our surviving are slim, even though we (the flight attendants) know exactly what to do. *But I think I would probably*—and I think I can say this for most of my fellow flight attendants—*be able to keep them from being too worried about it.* I mean my voice might quiver a little during the announcements, but somehow I feel we could get them to believe . . . the best.[159]

Hochschild learned that the struggle to maintain a difference between feeling and feigning led to a strain for the people in occupations calling for emotional labor, a strain that she labeled "emotive dissonance." She states, "We try to reduce this strain by changing what we feel or by changing what we feign."[160] The emotive dissonance involved in the management of feelings that Hochschild discovered in her research resulted in a recasting of the theory of cognitive dissonance, extending its margins to include emotive dissonance as well.[161]

[157]Hochschild, *The Managed Heart*, p. 7.

[158]Hochschild, *The Managed Heart*, p. 137.

[159]Hochschild, *The Managed Heart*, p. 107.

[160]Hochschild, *The Managed Heart*, p. 90. See Chapter 7 for a discussion of Leon Festinger's theory of cognitive dissonance, a situation in which either some of the facts that someone faces are in conflict with others, or someone's experiences are not in line with what "ought" to be happening.

[161]See Robert K. Merton, *On Theoretical Sociology* (New York: Free Press, 1967), in chap. 5, "The Bearing of Empirical Research on Sociological Theory," where he discusses the recasting of theory as a consequence of new data exerting pressure for the elaboration of a conceptual scheme (pp. 162–65).

Hochschild's next two books, *The Second Shift: Working Parents and the Revolution at Home*, and *The Time Bind: When Work Becomes Home and Home Becomes Work*, are extensions of her effort to highlight the importance of the emotions for a better understanding of social interaction in everyday life. In *The Second Shift* she analyzes how two-paycheck parents manage their emotions when they experience the stresses involved in sharing the child-rearing and housekeeping duties involved in their second shift at home. Hochschild found that most women were grateful if their husbands shared at least some of the less valued work of the second shift.

In *The Time Bind* she focused on parents who tended to lengthen their time at work. Her discovery that relatively few workers were taking advantage of family-friendly policies like flexible time, part-time work, and parental leave led her to pursue this research effort. By interviewing and observing parents both at home and at their workplace, and by following some of them as they went about juggling their time for an entire day, Hochschild was able to uncover real surprises and unexpected explanations for the trend toward spending more time at work and less at home.

What she found, for instance, was that the supportive networks at work replaced the mother's neighborhood networks that they no longer had time for. Whereas mothers of an earlier era tended to talk to other mothers who were their neighborhood friends in order to blow off steam and to strategize about their dilemmas at home, the working mothers in Hochschild's study often used what she calls "feel good" sessions at work (coffee breaks, lunchtime, and other periodic rituals like birthday and pre-holiday parties) to help them solve their dilemmas on the home front.

The third shift she describes as the parents' need to notice, understand, and cope with the emotional consequences of the compressed second shift. Cutting back on family time created more emotion work at home because parents had to make up for the lost time with their children. An added complication was that many of the parents' immediate bosses were not committed to the family-friendly policies, and this made it especially difficult for the mothers who tended to carry the major burden of the third shift. Hochschild elaborates on the emotional work of the third shift:

> Parents are then obliged to hear their children's protests, to experience their resentment, resistance, passive acquiescence, to try to assuage their frustrations, to respond to their stubborn demands or whining requests, and in general to control the damage done by a reversal of worlds. This unacknowledged third shift only adds to the feeling that life at home is hard work.[162]

Here Hochschild is applying Goffman's dramaturgical concepts, as Randall Collins recently argued. What is being played out in the lives of these families is the tension between the official front-stage ideals as to how

---

[162]Arlie Russell Hochschild, *The Time Bind*, p. 218.

parents are expected to deal with their children, and the backstage reality of "how people make out amid the pressures of institutions."[163] In Collins's view, Hochschild is pointing to the cutting edge of social change, "a way of making sense of what has happened to the entire complex of work-and-home as we pass a historical watershed."[164]

Sociologists who favor quantitative research, however, tend to downplay the importance of Hochschild's work because her findings are not based on a national survey of working parents. One such critic quoted the latest national surveys that reveal job satisfaction is not declining throughout the United States. However, he conceded there is value in her approach because her study revealed that good day care and other policies to support working families are still inadequate. He said, "By showing how these problems persist even among the most progressive segments of corporate America, Hochschild has contributed to our understanding of the challenges that remain in resolving the conflicts between work and family demands."[165]

In addition to studies on the "emotional geography" of the workplace, Hochschild argues for an extension of research efforts beyond one's place of employment. She writes, "I believe we can apply the sociology of emotions perspective to a variety of issues of the day—both to try to press the theoretical frontiers of sociology, and to clarify the human story beneath social policy."[166]

OTHER CONTRIBUTIONS TO SOCIOLOGY OF EMOTIONS

Another feminist who has made an important contribution to the sociology of the emotions is Nancy Chodorow. In her book *The Reproduction of Mothering*, Chodorow, drawing on and expanding Freud's psychoanalytic theory, argues that male children see themselves as unlike the mothers with whom they have had their first emotional relationship, and they learn to repress and deny female qualities in order to accomplish their individuated male identity. Thus males grow up with an underdeveloped relational capacity, and they tend to see the feminine as inferior. Female children, on the other hand, strongly and continuously identify with the mother, accept their emotions, and develop a high relational capacity.[167]

---

[163]Randall Collins, "The Sociological Eye and Its Blinders," *Contemporary Sociology* 27 (January 1998): 5.

[164]Collins, "The Sociological Eye and Its Blinders," p. 6.

[165]William T. Bielby, "Firm Commitments," *Contemporary Sociology* 27.1 (January 1998): 34.

[166]Arlie Russell Hochschild, "A Sociology of Emotions Approach to the Workplace," *Sociology of Emotions Newsletter* 6 (February 1994): 3. An illustration that the process of pressing theoretical frontiers has already begun can be found in the April 1993 issue of *Rationality and Society*, devoted entirely to the special topic of "Emotions and Rational Choice."

[167]See Nancy Chodorow, *The Reproduction of Mothering* (Berkeley: University of California Press, 1978), and her *Feminism and Psychoanalysis* (New Haven: Yale University Press, 1989).

In her participant-observation study of boys and girls in a grammar school environment, Raphaela Best found many examples of how children learn the meaning of gender through interaction. She observed the girls bustling around the classroom, busy with helping and housekeeping chores, while the boys were typically the passive recipients of this help. On occasion the boys would defy the teacher (a woman), insisting on repeatedly going to the bathroom or claiming to have turned work in when they hadn't. Both in the classroom and outside the girls would openly express emotions, crying, hugging, and comforting each other, whereas the boys kept a tight lid on emotions and expressed affection only in rough play. Younger boys often created various "clubs," from which boys perceived as sissies, crybabies, mama's boys, and teacher's helpers were excluded.[168]

One would expect that the sociology of the emotions would be an appropriate topic for symbolic interactionists who take self-interaction and subjective interpretation seriously, or for critical conflict theorists, who are interested in the relationship between personality and social structure and who often draw heavily on Freudian theory. Yet theorists in these traditions tend to pay little attention to the emotions. It is primarily women sociologists who, in the past two decades, have expanded our awareness of how important emotions are to an understanding of social interaction.

Meisenhelder's analysis of Habermas and feminism can shed some light on this question. He argues that because Habermas, like other critical theorists, holds that a core characteristic of the human being is the potential to reason, it does not occur to him to investigate human experiences of emotionality—such as the caring, affect, and solidarity within the private sphere of the family. Meisenhelder states,

> Habermas admits moral aesthetic values into the totality of human reason but not feelings. In the end he never frees himself from the presumptive dualities of patriarchal thought. . . . His conception of reason remains formal and fails to adequately represent the experience of really existing men *and* women.[169]

Lillian Rubin, in her study of working-class families, quotes from one of her interviews which reveals the male denial of feelings and a husband's view of his wife's emotionality:

> She's like a kid sometimes, so emotional. I'm always having to reason with her, to explain things to her. If it weren't for me, nothing would happen very rational around here.[170]

---

[168]Raphaela Best, *We've All Got Scars: What Boys and Girls Learn in Elementary School* (Bloomington: University of Indiana Press, 1983).

[169]See Thomas Meisenhelder, "Habermas and Feminism: The Future of Critical Theory," in Ruth A. Wallace, *Feminism and Sociological Theory* (Newbury Park, Calif.: Sage, 1989), p. 125.

[170]Lillian Breslow Rubin, *Worlds of Pain: Life in the Working Class Family* (New York: Basic Books, 1976), p. 117.

Rubin then presents her analysis:

> This equation of emotional with nonrational, this inability to apprehend the logic of emotions lies at the root of much of the discontent between the sexes, and helps to make marriage the most difficult of all relationships.
>
> Her lifetime training prepares her to handle the affective, expressive side in human affairs; his, to handle the nonaffective, instrumental side. Tears, he has been taught, are for sissies; feelings, for women. A real man is the strong, silent type of the folklore—a guy who needs nothing from anyone, who ignores feelings and pain, who can take it on the chin without a whimper. For a lifetime, much of his energy has gone into molding himself in that image—into denying his feelings, refusing to admit they exist. Without warning or preparation, he finds himself facing a wife who pleads, "Tell me your feelings." He responds with bewilderment. "What is there to tell?"[171]

The work of Hochschild and others[172] on the emotions has enormous implications for what Goffman described as the "interaction order," for when "two or more individuals are physically in another's presence" the feelings they have toward each other will have consequences for the behavior that ensues.

PATRICIA HILL COLLINS: BLACK FEMINIST THOUGHT

Patricia Hill Collins earned her B.A. at Brandeis (1969), her M.A. at Harvard (1970), and her Ph.D. in sociology at Brandeis (1984). She is presently associate professor of African-American studies at the University of Cincinnati. Her book, *Black Feminist Thought: Knowledge, Consciousness, and the Politics of Empowerment*, represents, as she explains it, "one stage in my ongoing struggle to regain my voice."[173] The American Sociological Association presented the Jessie Bernard Award to Patricia Hill Collins and Dorothy E. Smith in 1993 in recognition of their scholarly work that "has enlarged the horizons of sociology to encompass fully the role of women in society."[174]

Collins presses for a reconceptualization of social theory in which analysis starts from the distinctive visions of outsider groups, and in which conventional concepts of race, class, and gender are informed and changed

---

[171]Rubin, *Worlds of Pain*, p. 117.

[172]See also Norman Denzin, *On Understanding Emotion* (San Francisco: Jossey-Bass, 1984); Theodore Kemper, *A Social Interactional Theory of the Emotions* (New York: John Wiley, 1978); Theodore Kemper, ed., *Research Agendas in the Sociology of Emotions* (Albany: State University of New York Press, 1990); Irwin Deutscher, Fred P. Pestello, H. Francis, and G. Pestello, *Sentiments and Acts* (New York: Aldine de Gruyter, 1993).

[173]Patricia Hill Collins, *Black Feminist Thought: Knowledge, Consciousness, and the Politics of Empowerment* (Boston: Unwin Hyman, 1990), p. xi. Copyright © 1990. From *Black Feminist Thought* by Patricia Hill Collins. Reproduced by permission of Routledge, Inc.

[174]See Chapter 6, p. 284 for the wording of the award citation.

by including the concrete experiences and definitions of subordinate groups. While she was growing up Collins was surrounded by children like herself—daughters and sons of laborers, domestic workers, secretaries, and factory workers—whose families affirmed her. She presents an example of this affirmation on the occasion of her performance in a play when she was five years old: "Their words and hugs made me feel that I was important and that what I thought, and felt, and accomplished mattered."

Later, as she became "one of the few" or the "only" African-American working-class woman in her schools, communities, and work settings, the daily assaults she experienced left her with the feeling that she was growing smaller in a world where she was not only different, but considered less important. As a result, she became quieter and was virtually silenced.

Collins's book is an attempt to capture the interconnections of race, social class, and gender, based on the experiences of African-American women from the literature both about them and by them. She argues that white male interests pervade the thematic content of traditional scholarship, and "As a result Black women's experiences with work, family, motherhood, political activism, and sexual politics have been routinely distorted in or excluded from traditional academic discourse." Therefore, she states, "To support my analysis, I cite few statistics and instead rely on the voices of Black women from all walks of life."[175]

A related objective, Collins states, is "to develop an epistemological framework that can be used both to assess existing Black feminist thought and to clarify some of the underlying assumptions that impede the development of Black feminist thought." The definition of epistemology includes the study of the nature and grounds of knowledge, especially with reference to its limits and validity. Included among the four dimensions of Collins's Afrocentric feminist epistemology are: (1) concrete experience as a criterion of meaning; (2) the use of dialogue in assessing knowledge claims; (3) the ethic of caring; and (4) the ethic of personal accountability.

Like Goffman, Collins draws on a variety of sources, including autobiographies and novels to illustrate her concepts. For example, she uses traditional black church services to illustrate the interactive nature of all four dimensions. She cites the widespread use of the call-and-response discourse mode in these services as an illustration of the importance of dialogue, and describes it thus:

> Composed of spontaneous verbal and nonverbal interaction between speaker and listener in which all of the speaker's statements, or "calls," are punctuated by expressions, or "responses," from the listener, this Black discourse mode pervades African-American culture. The fundamental requirement of this interactive network is active participation of all individuals. For ideas to be tested and validated, everyone in the group must participate. To refuse to join

[175]Collins, *Black Feminist Thought*, pp. 201 and 202.

in, especially if one really disagrees with what has been said, is seen as "cheating."[176]

She argues that these church services represent "more than dialogues between the rationality used in examining biblical texts and stories and the emotion inherent in the use of reason for this purpose." The rationale for such dialogues, she explains, "involves the task of examining concrete experiences for the presence of an ethic of caring." Collins concludes that emotion, ethics, and reason are used as interconnected and essential components in assessing knowledge claims in these services.[177] This illustration sheds some light on the limitations of Habermas's "ideal speech situation" discussed previously.[178] In the African-American dialogue mode, the listener's responses are not limited to the realm of the rational; instead the whole gamut of emotions, from love to grief to hatred, are included as well.

Patricia Hill Collins makes it clear that she is not grounding her analysis in any single theoretical tradition. However, one can readily detect Blumer's classic three premises as she records African-American women acting on the basis of meanings, discovering meaning in interactions with others, and engaging in the interpretative process in their daily encounters.

A key concept in Patricia Hill Collins's work that is central to the symbolic interactionist perspective is African-American women's self-definition. The elements of this self-definition include self-reliance, self-esteem, and independence. Collins links the emergence of this self-definition to their rejection of the controlling images of African-American women that originated during the era of slavery: mammies, matriarchs, welfare mothers, and sexually denigrated women.

She argues that the controlling images of black womanhood "are designed to make racism, sexism, and poverty appear to be natural, normal, and an inevitable part of everyday life. . . . Such images . . . not only keep Black women oppressed but are key in maintaining interlocking systems of race, class, and gender oppression."[179]

Collins discusses three factors that led to the rejection of these controlling images: black women's relationships with one another, the black women's blues tradition, and the emerging influence of black women writers who offer alternative definitions. Collins presents an example of the rejection of the mammy role from Bonnie Thornton Dill's research on child-rearing patterns among black domestics. The participants in Dill's study

[176]Collins, *Black Feminist Thought*, p. 213.
[177]Collins, *Black Feminist Thought*, p. 219.
[178]See Chapter 4.
[179]Collins, *Black Feminist Thought*, p. 68.

encouraged their children to avoid domestic work and "discouraged them from believing that they should be deferent to whites."[180]

Like Simmel, Collins's work includes elements of both symbolic interactionism and conflict theory. For instance, the concepts of domination and subordination are central to Collins's analysis of the oppression of African-American women. She states, "I approached Afrocentric feminist thought as situated in a context of domination and not as a system of ideas divorced from political and economic reality. . . . I examined the situated, subjugated standpoint of African-American women in order to understand Black feminist thought as a partial perspective on domination."[181]

Collins rejects approaches to domination that see its dimensions as separate and additive: as when, for example, gender relations are viewed as a basis for domination to which age, sexual orientation, race, ethnicity, social class, and religion are added. Instead she views relations of domination as a system of interlocking race, class, and gender oppression. Her focus is on the interconnections of these systems.

Collins states, "African-American women have overtly rejected theories of power based on domination in order to embrace an alternative vision of power based on a humanist vision of self-actualization, self-definition, and self-determination."[182] She points to the recent resurgence of black feminist thought within such social institutions as schools, churches, and the media, and the outpouring of black feminist thought in history and literature that "directly challenges the Eurocentric masculinist thought pervading these institutions."[183]

Collins's work points to the distinctive angle of vision provided by those who have been prevented from becoming full insiders in mainstream academic discourse, "outsiders within," like black women intellectuals, who call into question either/or dichotomous thinking.[184] However, she admits that there has never been a uniformity of experience among African-American women, and she challenges black feminist scholars to "rearticulate these new and emerging patterns of institutional oppression that differentially affect middle-class and working-class Black women."[185]

Other people of color, Jews, Catholics, the poor, white women, and gays and lesbians can also provide distinctive angles of vision. Collins argues, "Placing African-American women and other excluded groups in the center of analysis opens up possibilities for a both/and conceptual stance,

---

[180]Collins, *Black Feminist Thought*, p. 73.

[181]Collins, *Black Feminist Thought*, p. 236.

[182]Collins, *Black Feminist Thought*, p. 224.

[183]Collins, *Black Feminist Thought*, p. 229. This definition of power is similar to some of the elements of critical conflict theory exemplified in the Port Huron Statement quoted in Chapter 3.

[184]Collins, *Black Feminist Thought*, p. 12.

[185]Collins, *Black Feminist Thought*, p. 66.

one in which all groups possess varying amounts of penalty and privilege in one historically created system."[186]

Patricia Hill Collins disagrees with neofunctionalist Niklas Luhmann's view that social theory should concern itself with the reduction of the extreme complexity of the world.[187] She points to new directions in the physical sciences that demonstrate an increasing commitment to the concept of complexity that might prove extremely useful for the social sciences. By contrast with Luhmann, Collins argues that in order to explain apparent disorder and chaos, social scientists should develop new conceptual and methodological tools to understand complexities rather than attempt to reduce them. For example, in a recent statement she cites the new area of race, class, and gender studies and its emerging paradigm of intersectionality. Collins explains,

> Examining how racial meaning is constructed in gendered terms and how gender shapes class formations allows a complex web of understandings and social relationships to emerge. Moreover, this emerging paradigm of intersectionality moves beyond race, class, and gender to encompass additional categories such as nation, sexuality, ethnicity, age, and religion.[188]

CONCLUSION

In this chapter we discussed the basic premises and assumptions of the symbolic interactionist perspective introduced by George Herbert Mead and his forerunners, elaborated by Herbert Blumer and Erving Goffman, and expanded recently by Arlie Russell Hochschild and Patricia Hill Collins. The perspective's views of the self, especially Mead's stress on the "I," and discussions of self-interaction, taking the role of the other, interpretation, gestures, and symbolic meaning lead to an emphasis on studying processes of interaction between individuals and a methodology that is primarily inductive, qualitative, and geared toward microsociological analysis. Given the interests of symbolic interactionists and the types of questions arising from these interests, we can see that the perspective is basically a social-psychological one, focusing on Simmel's interactions among the "atoms of society." The result could be described as a moving picture rather than a still photograph of human behavior, and a close-up rather than an aerial picture.

---

[186]Collins, *Black Feminist Thought*, p. 225. In Chapter 2 we raised the problem of generalization with respect to Parsons's AGIL model, which emerged from research on small groups made up of white upper-class male Harvard undergraduates.

[187]See Luhmann, Chapter 2.

[188]Patricia Hill Collins, "On Book Exhibits and New Complexities: Reflections on Sociology as a Science," *Contemporary Sociology* 27.1 (January 1998): 11.

Although still not considered to be in the mainstream of sociology, symbolic interactionism has been less marginal over the past two decades, and many of its core concepts have been accepted.[189] In addition, some inter-actionists have developed concepts that connect to the macro and structural demands of sociology. It has recently been argued that only the rare microso-ciologist "disdains interest in questions of larger institutions."[190] Symbolic interactionism has experienced a resurgence since the founding of the Society for the Study of Symbolic Interactionism and the publication of the journal *Symbolic Interaction*. In addition, leading sociological journals now typically include symbolic interactionists on their editorial boards and, as a result, these journals are publishing more research articles informed by this tradition. A perspective that places a primary value on subjective meaning and on process as opposed to structure, combined with a methodology that takes great pains to capture the world of the other as seen by that other, asks important sociological questions that cannot be answered by mainstream sociology. Symbolic interactionism can be seen as an alternative perspective providing theoretical tools missing in other perspectives. It therefore deserves recognition as an approach that makes important and distinctive contributions to sociology.

---

[189]Gary Alan Fine, "The Sad Demise, Mysterious Disappearance, and Glorious Triumph of Symbolic Interactionism," *Annual Review of Sociology* 19 (1993): 61.

[190]Fine, "The Sad Demise, Mysterious Disappearance, and Glorious Triumph of Symbolic Interactionism," pp. 65, 69.

CHAPTER SIX

Phenomenology

INTRODUCTION

Compared to the other sociological perspectives we discuss in this book, phenomenology is one of the more recent. The term "phenomenological sociology," like conflict theory, encompasses several types of sociological analysis. However, we will limit ourselves to a discussion of the three most prominent: Harold Garfinkel's ethnomethodology, Peter Berger's social reality construction, and Dorothy E. Smith's feminist standpoint theory.

The word *phenomenonon* derives from the Greek meaning "appearance." *The Encyclopedia of Sociology* defines phenomenology as "a method in philosophy that begins with the individual and his [sic] own conscious experience and tries to avoid prior assumptions, prejudices, and philosophical dogmas. Phenomenology thus examines phenomena as they are apprehended in their 'immediacy' by the social actor."[1] Suppose someone walked over to you now as you are reading this book and asked you how the object that you are reading appears to you. You would most likely label it an absurd question because everyone knows what a book looks like. We arrive at the notion of a book through socialization, the process whereby we learn how to perceive and how to interpret the world, or as phenomenologists put it, "how to *be* in the world." If the person who asked you the absurd question had just arrived from outer space, you would probably take the question seriously and proceed to explain clearly the meaning of the term "book." Why would you respond in this way? You would do so because you would know that the visitor's social world differed from yours and you would want to help such a person learn how to be in your world.

Phenomenology asks us not to take the notions we have learned for granted, but to question them instead, to question our way of looking at and our way of being in the world. In short, this perspective asks us to assume the role of the stranger, like a visitor from a foreign country, or our extraterrestrial visitor just mentioned. Phenomenological sociologists study how people define their social situations once they have suspended or "bracketed" their learned cultural notions. The basic proposition states that everyday reality is a socially constructed system of ideas that has accumulated over time and is taken for granted by group members. This perspective takes a critical stance with regard to the social order, and, in contrast to functionalism, it challenges our culturally learned ideas.

For example, phenomenologists would view the realities of women's nature, needs, role, and place in society as systems of ideas constructed in past interactions and sustained by present ongoing interaction.[2] Phenomenologists

---

[1]*The Encyclopedia of Sociology* (Guilford, Conn.: Duskin, 1974), p. 210.

[2]See Patricia M. Lengermann, Katherine M. Marconi, and Ruth A. Wallace, "Sociological Theory in Teaching Sex Roles: Marxism, Functionalism and Phenomenology," *Women's Studies International Quarterly* 1, no. 4 (1978): 375–85.

would ask, "Is it 'natural' that women, in addition to bearing children, also take sole responsibility for nurturing and rearing them?" "Do they have an innate 'need' to be rooted in the private sphere of the home while men's 'needs' are in the public sphere of wage work?" Contemporary feminists not only challenge these taken-for-granted ideas but also interject alternative definitions of female identity and propose other "realities" for women.[3] People who question the way their world is ordered or who are members of a subordinate group, like racial, ethnic, and religious minorities, the poor, women, and gays and lesbians, will acquire many insights into their situation if they put on the lens of this perspective.

INTELLECTUAL ROOTS: EDMUND HUSSERL AND ALFRED SCHUTZ

The roots of phenomenological sociology are primarily in European phenomenological philosophy, especially in the work of the German philosopher Edmund Husserl (1859–1938), who was the first to use the term *phenomenology*. Husserl defined phenomenology as interest in those things that can be directly apprehended by one's senses. This is the essential point about phenomenology: It denies that we can ever know more about things than what we experience directly through our senses. All our knowledge comes directly from these sensory phenomena. Anything else is speculation, and Husserl argued that we should not even try to speculate.

Phenomenological sociologists consequently see the task of sociology as describing precisely how we see the world, although they emphasize that our perceptions are molded intrinsically by our concepts. They also examine the ways we come to have similar perceptions to those of others—how we put together the phenomena we experience in such a way that we all construct a similar or shared everyday world. The most important influence on their approach, however, is less Husserl's work directly than Alfred Schutz's developments of his arguments. Schutz (1899–1959) was a social philosopher who left Germany in 1939 to escape the Nazis, took a daytime position in a New York bank to support himself, and began to teach evening courses in social philosophy at the New School for Social Research in 1943.[4] He became professor of sociology and philosophy in 1952 and taught at the New School until his death in 1959. Schutz introduced phenomenology to American sociology.

---

[3]See Dorothy Smith, *The Everyday World as Problematic: A Feminist Sociology* (Boston: Northeastern University Press, 1987). Smith's approach, a sociology based on women's experience, combines the materialist method developed by Marx and Engels with Garfinkel's ethnomethodology. We discuss Smith's contribution to phenomenological sociology in Part Three of this chapter.

[4]See Nicholas C. Mullins, *Theories and Theory Groups in Contemporary American Sociology* (New York: Harper and Row, 1973), p. 186.

What precipitated the emergence of phenomenology? As we have seen, Edmund Husserl wrote in the shadow of Nazism in Germany, and Alfred Schutz came to the United States in order to escape the Nazi regime. Subsequently, the contemporary sociological theorists, Harold Garfinkel, Peter Berger, and Dorothy E. Smith, began to write their major works during a period of social unrest in the 1960s, in the wake of the American civil rights movement, the antiwar movement, and the contemporary women's movement. It is not surprising that a great deal of questioning about our way of looking at the world would coincide with these events. The "bracketing" or suspending of taken-for-granted assumptions by oppressed groups makes sense in such situations, and the time was ripe for the emergence of a new perspective with the conceptual tools to analyze these situations.

In his attempt to adapt Husserl's philosophy to sociology, Schutz incorporated Weber's concept of *verstehen* (subjective understanding).[5] For Schutz, the meaning that the individual imparts to situations in everyday life is of prime importance; he puts the spotlight on the individual's own definition of the situation.

For Schutz, the definition of the situation includes the assumption that individuals draw on a common *stock of knowledge*, that is, social recipes of conceptions of appropriate behavior that enable them to think of the world as made up of "types" of things like books, cars, houses, clothing, and so on. Schutz's idea of the stock of knowledge is similar to Mead's *generalized other*. Schutz thus views individuals as constructing a world by using the typifications (or ideal types) passed on to them by their social group.

Schutz illustrates the typification process in his discussion of the assumptions involved in mailing a letter.[6] He explains that in mailing a letter one takes for granted that there will be types of persons involved in processing the letter, like postal carriers, sorters, and deliverers. People who mail letters, by means of a process of self-typification, see themselves cooperating with postal workers, even though they do not know them personally. By using such "recipes" individuals are able to see the work of their everyday world as orderly, especially when the process is successful, as, for example, when the letter reaches the desired destination.

Anthony Giddens, whose theories borrow from a number of the perspectives, both macro and micro, was also influenced by Schutz.[7] In his analysis of everyday action, Giddens draws attention to the "vast bulk of the 'stocks of knowledge,' in Schutz's phrase, or what I prefer to call the *mutual*

---

[5]See pages 191–92 for a discussion of *verstehen*.

[6]Alfred Schutz, *Collected Papers: The Problem of Social Reality* (The Hague: Martinus Nijhoff, 1962), p. 17. Schutz also corresponded with Talcott Parsons on their different points of view on a number of topics, including subjectivity. These letters provide an insight into the divergence between functionalism and phenomenology. See Richard Grathoff, ed., *The Theory of Social Action* (Bloomington: Indiana University Press, 1978).

[7]See Chapter 4, where we discuss Giddens's contributions to evolutionary theory.

knowledge incorporated in encounters."[8] This knowledge is essentially outside what Giddens calls "discursive consciousness," by which he means that people are not normally self-conscious about it or conscious of knowing it. Indeed, the knowledge about which they are self-conscious and about which they can hold forth is only a small part of that with which they operate. An enormous amount of other mutual knowledge is used automatically.

Giddens himself gives an excellent example of what he means in the following transcript from a courtroom:

Public defender (PD):	Your honor, we request immediate sentencing and waive the probation report.
Judge:	What's his record?
PD:	He has a prior drunk and a GTA (grand theft, auto). Nothing serious. This is just a shoplifting case. He did enter the Kmart with intent to steal. But really all we have here is petty theft.
Judge:	What do the people have?
District Attorney (DA):	Nothing either way.
Judge:	Any objection to immediate sentencing?
PD:	Eighty-three days.
Judge:	I make this a misdemeanor by PC article 17 and sentence you to ninety days in County Jail with credit for time served.[9]

Each speaker here, as Giddens points out, assumes that the other participants know a vast amount about what a legal system is and how this particular one operates, as well as about "drunkenness" and "Kmarts." (You, as an almost twenty-first-century reader, also can understand the passage without too much difficulty. Imagine the reaction of a ninth-century Viking to this passage.) What Giddens also underlines is that "by invoking the institution to render what they do intelligible and coherent to one another—they thereby contribute to reproducing it."[10] Such exchanges are a necessary precondition of a legal system's continued existence.

For the same reasons, Giddens lays great emphasis on the idea of routinization. Following Schutz again, he points out how we use formulae, or "typified schemes," in the course of our social life in order to get through routine, recurrent situations. People know general rules for doing particular types of social activity, and into these the particulars of a certain situation can be slotted. Moreover, "those types of rules which are of most significance for social theory are locked into the reproduction of institutionalized

---

[8]Anthony Giddens, *The Constitution of Society* (Cambridge, England: Polity, 1984), p. 4.

[9]Giddens, *Constitution of Society*, p. 330.

[10]Giddens, *Constitution of Society*, p. 331.

practices."[11] That is why studying everyday life is an integral part of any analysis of how institutional practices—macro topics—are maintained or reproduced.

Giddens also stresses the way in which routinization is crucial to the individual for reasons that go beyond those of rational convenience. He argues that routine, *"psychologically linked to the minimizing of unconscious sources of anxiety,* is the predominant form of day-to-day social activity. . . . In the enactment of routines agents sustain a sense of ontological security."[12] In other words, they maintain a sense that their world is real. Routine is important for ensuring the continuity of our own personalities, not just the continuity of institutions. We therefore have a "generalized motivational commitment"[13] to sustaining the routine and tactfulness of ordinary social intercourse.

Giddens demonstrates the importance to us of routine, and the trust it engenders, by describing the effects of its absence. In particular,[14] he draws on Bruno Bettelheim's famous account of his experiences as a prisoner in Dachau and Buchenwald, two Nazi concentration camps. The camps were a place where the ordinary routines of life were systematically and deliberately destroyed. Violence against an individual was an ever-present threat and might descend without warning. All toilet activities were carried out in public, under the control of the guards, as a deliberate way of denying people control and privacy. Prisoners—torn from their families and familiar environments frequently without warning—were in many cases tortured and set to senseless tasks, without any ability to plan for the future. In these circumstances, Bettelheim records, "I . . . saw fast changes taking place and not only in behavior but personality also." Those who managed to maintain some small control in their daily lives were able to survive—albeit with regression to childlike attitudes and with marked and volatile mood swings; but with time, prisoners' personalities were "reconstructed" so that they actually came to identify with their oppressors, the camp guards.

Giddens sees the camps as an extreme example of critical situations in which normal routine is radically disturbed. Study of critical situations and their effects leads us to a deeper understanding of the role of routine. We can see that socialization is not something that occurs once and for all during childhood. Instead, it is by creating and re-creating the familiar, through social relations, that our (acquired) personalities are sustained and anxiety

---

[11]Giddens, *Constitution of Society,* p. 22.

[12]Giddens, *Constitution of Society,* p. 282. Italics ours.

[13]Giddens, *Constitution of Society,* p. 64.

[14]Anthony Giddens, *Central Problems in Social Theory* (Berkeley: University of California Press, 1979), pp. 125–26.

contained. "Continuity of social reproduction involves the continual 'regrooving' of established attitudes and cognitive outlooks."[15]

Schutz, whose work inspired Giddens, also believes that the meaning one imparts to the interaction situation may be shared by the person with whom one is interacting; he calls this the "reciprocity of perspectives." For example, because the musicians in an orchestra share their meanings of the situation with the conductor, the musicians could exchange positions with the conductor and experience the situation in the way the conductor does. In Schutz's scheme, then, shared meanings may be both assumed and experienced in the interaction situation.

Schutz says that in these situations people are acting on the basis of taken-for-granted assumptions about reality. They suspend doubts that things might be otherwise, and interaction proceeds on the assumption of the reciprocity of perspectives. Here we can detect some similarity to Mead's concept of "taking the role of the other," which Schutz also incorporated into his framework.[16] Thus Schutz's thinking was heavily influenced by Husserl, but he was also responsible for introducing some of Weber's and Mead's ideas into phenomenological sociology.

In this chapter we introduce three types of phenomenological sociology. The first is Harold Garfinkel's ethnomethodology, the second is Peter Berger's social construction of reality theory, and the third is Dorothy Smith's feminist standpoint theory.

PART ONE

Harold Garfinkel: The Founder of Ethnomethodology

Harold Garfinkel is recognized as the founder of ethnomethodology and its leading figure since the publication in 1967 of his book *Studies in Ethnomethodology*. Since then we have seen a proliferation in the number of sociologists who consider themselves ethnomethodologists.[17] Although it cannot be considered a mainstream perspective, ethnomethodology has been influential enough to be the subject of attack in a presidential address

---

[15]Giddens, *Central Problems in Social Theory*, pp. 126–27.

[16]See Chapter 5.

[17]We are aware that there are other interpretations of this perspective by ethnomethodologists, but we have decided to sidestep a discussion of the various directions and controversies among ethnomethodologists and to restrict our attention to an explication of Harold Garfinkel's ethnomethodology. See Harold Garfinkel, *Studies in Ethnomethodology* (Englewood Cliffs, N.J.: Prentice-Hall, 1967).

of the American Sociological Association—another reason we should attempt to understand the perspective better.[18]

BACKGROUND

Born in 1917, Garfinkel completed his Ph.D. at Harvard in 1952. Aside from two years of teaching at Ohio State and a brief interim on a research project at the University of Chicago (the jury deliberation project mentioned later), Garfinkel has spent his entire career at the University of California at Los Angeles, where he currently holds the title of professor emeritus. Because of Garfinkel's leadership, UCLA became a training center for ethnomethodologists. Both the University of California at Santa Barbara and the University of California at San Diego were seen as its branches because of the presence of such ethnomethodologists as Aaron Cicourel, an important student of Garfinkel who was at UCSB from 1966 to 1971 and has been at UCSD since 1971. Garfinkel spent 1975–1976 at the Center for Advanced Studies in the Behavioral Sciences near Stanford University, where he put together a manual of ethnomethodological studies that have been published since 1967, when his *Studies in Ethnomethodology* appeared.[19]

Garfinkel names four persons whose "writings have provided me with inexhaustible directives into the world of everyday activities."[20] They are Talcott Parsons, under whom he studied at Harvard; Alfred Schutz, whom he visited and studied under at the New School for Social Research; and the phenomenological philosophers Aron Gurwitsch and Edmund Husserl.[21] *Studies in Ethnomethodology* is replete with references to Schutz, and Garfinkel says that his own work is heavily indebted to him.

Garfinkel wanted to construct a perspective that would fill in one aspect of Parsons's theory of action, the motivated actor. He wanted to "remedy the sketchy treatment of the actor's knowledge and understanding within the voluntaristic theory."[22] Garfinkel himself attests to Parsons's influence, stating that ethnomethodology had its origins in Parsons's four-volume *Structure of Social Action* and that ethnomethodology's "earliest initiatives were taken from these texts."[23] Parsons's influence relates to a point that is fundamental

[18]Lewis Coser, "Presidential Address: Two Methods in Search of a Substance," *American Sociological Review* 40, no. 6 (December 1975).

[19]Personal interview, September 1975. This book, *Ethnomethodological Studies of Work in the Discovering Sciences*, was published in 1987 (London: Routledge and Kegan Paul).

[20]Garfinkel, *Studies in Ethnomethodology*, pp. ix and 31–37.

[21]Mullins, *Theories and Theory Groups*, p. 185.

[22]Garfinkel, *Studies in Ethnomethodology*, pp. ix and 31–37.

[23]Harold Garfinkel, "Evidence for Locally Produced, Naturally Accountable Phenomena of Order, Logic, Reason, Meaning, Method, etc. in and as of the Essential Quiddity of Immortal Ordinary Society (I of IV): An Announcement of Studies," *Sociological Theory* 6 (1988): 103–109.

to both functionalism and ethnomethodology: an underlying trust as the basis of human behavior. As we will see in the following section, Garfinkel wants to break the taboo on questioning the social order and uncover the taken-for-granted assumptions or myths that operate in the interaction situation.[24]

ETHNOMETHODOLOGY DEFINED

The beginnings of ethnomethodology can be traced to Harold Garfinkel's analysis of tapes of jury deliberations, which he conducted in 1945. It was when he was writing up the materials on these deliberations that he "dreamed up the notion underlying the term 'ethnomethodology.'"[25] What interested Garfinkel about the data was "how the jurors knew what they were doing in doing the work of jurors"; in other words, he was interested in "such things as jurors' use of some kind of knowledge of the way in which the organized affairs of the society operated—knowledge that they drew on easily, that they required of each other"[26] in doing the work of jurors. This is the concern underlying the practice of ethnomethodology.

The term itself was coined when, working with the Yale cross-cultural files, Garfinkel came to a section entitled "ethnobotany, ethnophysiology, ethnophysics." It occurred to him that on the jury deliberation project he was "faced with jurors who were doing methodology," and he decided that the label that seemed adequate to convey the notion was *ethnomethodology* because "ethno" refers to the "availability to a member of commonsense knowledge of his society as commonsense knowledge of the 'whatever.' "[27] In the case of the jurors, it was their use of available commonsense (as opposed to scientific) knowledge of what was expected of jurors, as a result of which they were able to be jurors, that interested Garfinkel.

If we translate the "ethno" part of the term as "members" (of a group) or "folk" or "people," then ethnomethodology can be defined as members' (or people's) methods of making sense of their social world. Ethnomethodology's interest is in how people make sense of everyday activities. Obviously a lot of everyday activity is normally taken for granted, so the question of making sense of it is not even raised. Indeed, if people take reality for granted, why should they attempt to make sense of it? Garfinkel's approach, by contrast, is to treat as problematic what is taken for granted in order to understand the commonsense everyday world.

---

[24]See Randall Collins, *Conflict Sociology*, pp. 106–107 for a discussion of Parsons and Garfinkel.

[25]See Roy Turner, ed., *Ethnomethodology: Selected Readings* (Baltimore: Penguin Books, 1974), p. 16.

[26]Turner, *Ethnomethodology: Selected Readings*, p. 16.

[27]Turner, *Ethnomethodology: Selected Readings*, p. 16.

Suppose you were sitting in a classroom in the middle of a semester, waiting for class to begin as usual. The professor entered the room and, without speaking, proceeded to perform some seemingly nonsensical action, such as placing sheets of newspaper on the floor, drawing obscure symbols on the blackboard, raising and lowering the window shades repeatedly and unnecessarily, and the like.[28] How would you and other students describe the professor's actions? No doubt many students would attempt to make sense of this highly unusual situation. In other words, students would look for ways to describe this behavior as an unusual example of behavior that is recognized as normal and familiar to Americans, in the way that placing pieces of paper on desks is quickly interpreted as meaning that a test is on the way.

In fact, this was the result in a number of experiments conducted by one of the authors of this book. Some students suggested that the professor was "doing free form" or "attempting to evoke reactions"; one student said the professor was "performing mysterious rituals."

What the professor was doing was making the taken-for-granted situation of coming into class obviously problematic; she was shattering the social world of students. What the students were doing was assembling the appearance of social order in that situation; they were attempting to put it all back together. It is to this process that ethnomethodology directs its attention. It puts the taken-for-granted everyday world on center stage and asks, "How do people present to others an orderly social scene?" or "How do people render scenes or situations intelligible or reasonable?"

From the classroom experiment we can see that the students interpreted the rather bizarre behavior of the professor in ways that gave meaning to the situation for them. They devised interpretations that illustrated some underlying order, interpretations that made it clear to themselves and others that what they experienced was comprehensible and in line with the underlying rules and conventions they shared with each other about a professor's behavior. Ethnomethodology examines the methods by which people do this. By making sense of events in terms of a preconceived order for society, people create a world that is indeed ordered.

Ethnomethodology is not simply a new methodology that can solve problems raised by traditional theoretical perspectives. It is a theoretical perspective that focuses on a completely different set of problems from those of most sociological inquiry. In setting out to understand these problems, ethnomethodologists use some methods that are similar to those used by other perspectives and some that are different.

Garfinkel disagrees with Durkheim's view that social facts, the subject matter of sociology for Durkheim, have objective reality, are *sui generis*, and are "out there somewhere." Instead, Garfinkel says, ethnomethodology sees

---

[28]We are indebted to Robert Moran for this idea.

the objective reality of social facts as an "ongoing accomplishment of the concerned activities of everyday life."[29] By this he means that in everyday situations individuals invoke or recognize social facts, such as taken-for-granted norms or values, that interpret the meaning of the situation for them. When they make sense of the situation by recognizing implicit social norms, individuals are constructing social reality. In other words, they are ordering their experiences so that they are in line with what we consider the everyday social world to be like. Garfinkel proclaims that ethnomethodological studies "analyze everyday activities as members' methods for making those same activities visibly-rational-and-reportable-for-all-practical-purposes, that is, 'accountable' as organizations of commonplace everyday activities."[30]

What Garfinkel is saying, essentially, is that ethnomethodology denies the functionalists' suggestion that social facts have a reality of their own that impinges on the individual. Suppose we take as an example the role expectations of a professor. Functionalists believe these include preparing and giving lectures, reading and grading exams and papers, engaging in research, and publishing books and articles. These expectations impinge on the professor.

By contrast, ethnomethodologists do not treat order as "out there somewhere," created by society independently of the individuals experiencing and living within it. Neither does ethnomethodology study how role expectations are created in the interaction process, as does symbolic interactionism. Instead, ethnomethodology studies the process by which people invoke certain taken-for-granted rules about behavior with which they interpret an interaction situation and make it meaningful. To ethnomethodology, in fact, the interpretive process itself is a phenomenon for investigation. In the professor's case, ethnomethodology would be concerned with which rules professors invoke as they go about doing the work of professors. Thus, for functionalists, norms and values are explicit and "out there" acting on the individual; for symbolic interactionists, norms and values emerge from the interaction process; but for ethnomethodologists, the origin of norms and values is not of primary interest. Instead, their interest is in the process by which human beings interact and prove to each other that they are following norms and values.

Schutz's essay on the "stranger" may help to clarify the area of social life that is of interest for ethnomethodology. Schutz discusses

> the typical situation in which a stranger finds himself in his attempt to interpret the cultural pattern of a social group which he approaches and to orient himself within it. For our present purposes the term "stranger" shall mean an

---

[29]Garfinkel, *Studies in Ethnomethodology*, p. vii. See also Warren Handel, *Ethnomethodology: How People Make Sense* (Englewood Cliffs, N.J.: Prentice-Hall, 1982).

[30]Garfinkel, *Studies in Ethnomethodology*, p. vii.

adult individual of our times and civilization who tries to be permanently accepted or at least tolerated by the group which he approaches. The outstanding example for the social situation under scrutiny is that of the immigrant, and the following analyses are, as a matter of convenience, worked out with this instance in view. But by no means is their validity restricted to this special case. The applicant for membership in a closed club, the prospective bridegroom who wants to be admitted to the girl's family, the farmer's son who enters college, the city-dweller who settles in a rural environment, the "selectee" who joins the army, the family of the war worker who moves into a boom town—all are strangers according to the definition just given, although in these cases the typical "crisis" that the immigrant undergoes may assume milder forms or even be entirely absent.[31]

Later Schutz says that the stranger becomes "essentially the man who has to place in question nearly everything that seems to be unquestionable to the members of the approached group." Thus the situation of the stranger is one that is ripe for ethnomethodological analysis; it is the perfect problematic situation.[32]

Schutz's work on the existence of seen but unnoticed background experiences or the taken-for-granted world is, as we have noted, the cornerstone of ethnomethodology. He wondered how these background expectancies, or implicit rules, could be brought to light. His suggestion was that somehow one must take the role of a stranger, a foreigner, someone who is unfamiliar with the taken-for-granted aspects of everyday life, so that those aspects become problematic. Similarly, Garfinkel's aim is to understand commonsense everyday situations by treating them as problematic. Following Schutz, he argues that a "special motive" is necessary if the "world known in common and taken for granted" is to be brought in question.[33] Only when sociologists can estrange themselves from the "attitudes of everyday life," as Schutz puts it, can they discover the expectancies that give commonplace scenes their familiar, life-as-usual character. As we will see later, the "special motive" is exemplified in Garfinkel's experiments, in which he attempts to make trouble or violate the scene, as the professor did in the example at the beginning of this section.

It should be clear by now that ethnomethodology does not aim to explain human behavior or to show, for example, why places and generations vary in their suicide and divorce rates or why religion exists. The emphasis in this perspective is on description, and the subject matter—people's methods of making sense of their social world—poses different questions from those asked by traditional sociology.

[31]See Alfred Schutz, "The Stranger: An Essay in Social Psychology," in Open University, *School and Society: A Sociological Reader* (London: Routledge and Kegan Paul in association with Open University Press, 1971), p. 32. See also Simmel's essay on the stranger in Kurt Wolff, trans. and ed., *The Sociology of Georg Simmel* (Glencoe, Ill.: The Free Press, 1950), p. 402.

[32]Schutz, "The Stranger," p. 34.

[33]Garfinkel, *Studies in Ethnomethodology*, p. 37.

Ethnomethodologists are interested in the interpretations people use to make sense of social settings. Hugh Mehan provides us with a graphic illustration of the incorrect assessments made about students by teachers who interpret test results without examining the children's own perceptions and understanding of the testing materials:

> The California Reading Test consists of a number of words, sentences, and paragraphs along the left side of the page contained in an arrow which points to a series of three pictures arrayed along the right side of the page. The child is told to "mark the picture that goes best with the words in the arrow."
> One question has the word "fly" in the arrow pointing to pictures of an elephant, a bird, and a dog. The correct answer to this (obviously) is "the bird." The answer sheets of many of the first grade children showed that they had chosen the elephant alone or along with the bird as a response to that question. When Mehan asked them why they chose that answer, they replied, "That's Dumbo." Dumbo, of course, is Walt Disney's flying elephant, well known as an animal that flies, to children who watch television and read children's books.[34]

Mehan concludes that when children apply the word *fly* to an elephant, this may be "evidence to the tester that this child cannot abstract the similar features of objects and has 'impoverished' conceptual abilities. But this conclusion denies the actual complexity and richness of the child's day-to-day lived life." According to the way the tester views and interprets the test, the child has shown an inability to use some of the background skills of conceptual thought. But the children, who do not yet necessarily know the right way to answer the test, may have made sense of it—differently, yes, but on the basis of conceptual skills nonetheless. Incorrect answers, therefore, can result from a discrepancy between adult and student views of the world. Rather than take the question and the responses on the test sheet at their face value, as the teachers did, Mehan probed for the way the student interpreted the question and the answer. The child's response told Mehan what meaning that particular student got out of the situation; in a real sense, the student was accounting for a previous action by showing how she or he had made sense of the task. This notion of accounting is one to which Garfinkel has devoted considerable attention.

ACCOUNTING

Accounting is people's ability to announce to themselves and others the meaning they are getting out of a situation. Accounting involves both language and meaning; people are constantly giving linguistic or verbal accounts as they

---

[34]Hugh Mehan, "Ethnomethodology and Education," in D. O'Shea, ed., *Sociology of the School and Schooling* (Washington, D.C.: National Institute of Education, 1974), p. 20. See also Hugh Mehan, "Structuring School Structure," *Harvard Educational Review* 48 (1978): 50–51.

explain their actions. Garfinkel urges ethnomethodologists to call attention to reflexive practices: "by his accounting practices the member makes familiar, commonplace activities of everyday life recognizable as familiar commonplace activities; . . . on each occasion that an account of human activities is used . . . they [should] be recognized for 'another first time.' "[35]

For instance, when a child is asked to tell about his or her own creative production and then proceeds to interpret the figures, shapes, and colors in the drawing to another person, the child is giving an account. If an art teacher is truly interested in the student's own interpretation of a drawing, that teacher will not bluntly ask "What is it?" and embarrass the student, but instead will carefully phrase the request as something like "Tell me about it" so as to invite an interpretation from the student's own world of meaning. From the account will emerge the student's meaning.[36]

Much of the accounting that people make to each other about their behavior is done in an abbreviated form because commonplace conversation assumes a common understanding of many things that are left out of the conversation. Terms that require mutual understanding and that are not explicated verbally Garfinkel calls *indexical expressions*. One of the assignments Garfinkel gives to his students is to "report common conversations by writing on the left side of sheet what the parties actually said and on the right side what they and their partners (in the conversation) understand that they were talking about."[37] The result is that much more is written on the right side than the left side. What is "left out" on the left side is related, as Garfinkel states, to "the previous course of the conversation, or the particular relationship of actual or potential interaction that exists between user and auditor."[38] Garfinkel refers to this practice of filling in the meanings to talk as the *et cetera* principle; it is a shorthand way of talking.

Accounts and meanings in any situation largely depend on the nature of the situation. Garfinkel points out that the meanings two people attach to any interaction are linked to its location and time, the persons present, the purpose or intention of the actors, and their knowledge of each other's intentions—all of which are aspects of indexicality. Garfinkel is saying that social interaction is explicable only in context, and contextual relevance is at the heart of ethnomethodology's concerns.

Garfinkel mentions a related issue, the "sanctioned properties of common discourse."[39] This refers to people's expectation that there will be no

[35]Garfinkel, *Studies in Ethnomethodology*, p. 9. See also John Heritage's excellent chapter titled "Accounts and Accounting" in his *Garfinkel and Ethnomethodology* (Cambridge, England: Polity, 1984).

[36]See Marvin B. Scott and Stanford M. Lyman's much-cited article, "Accounts," *American Sociological Review* 33 (February 1968): 46–62.

[37]Garfinkel, *Studies in Ethnomethodology*, p. 38.

[38]Garfinkel, *Studies in Ethnomethodology*, p. 40.

[39]Garfinkel, *Studies in Ethnomethodology*, p. 41.

interference with the conduct of everyday affairs in the form of questions about what is really said. In other words it is expected and required that people will understand plain, everyday talk so that common conversational affairs can be conducted without interference. To illustrate the sanctioned character of these properties, Garfinkel presents the following experiment: "Students were instructed to engage an acquaintance or a friend in an ordinary conversation and, without indicating that what the experimenter was asking was in any way unusual, to insist that the person clarify the sense of his [sic] commonplace remarks."[40]

Below is one student's account of this experiment:

> The subject was telling the experimenter, a member of the subject's car pool, about having had a flat tire while going to work the previous day.
> (S) I had a flat tire.
> (E) What do you mean, you had a flat tire?
> She appeared momentarily stunned. Then she answered in a hostile way. "What do you mean, 'What do you mean?' A flat tire is a flat tire. That is what I meant. Nothing special. What a crazy question."[41]

This account is a good illustration of sanctioned character because the subject actually became hostile. Also, she attempted to make sense of the situation by treating it as a "crazy question." Obviously, on many occasions the question "What do you mean?" is perfectly acceptable and, in fact, is expected for purposes of clarification. But there are other occasions, like the one just described, when the question becomes a "violation of the scene" for the subject. The student actually made trouble by questioning indexical expressions based on mutual understanding, and the question introduced a sense of distrust into the situation. The subject attempted to make order of a disorderly scene. Her announcement that it was a "crazy question" was her way of assembling an orderly scene.

It is important to study how people build accounts of social action while doing that action, because making sense of a situation is involved in giving linguistic accounts of social interaction. (As Garfinkel puts it, "To do interaction is to tell interaction.") It is not surprising, therefore, that many ethnomethodologists are engaged in conversational analysis, for these endeavors are at the heart of ethnomethodology's concerns.

For instance, Fishman analyzed conversational activities of couples in their homes from the perspective of the socially structured power relationships between men and women. She found several general patterns. For instance, both men and women regarded topics introduced by women as tentative, and many of these were quickly dropped. By contrast, topics intro-

[40]Garfinkel, *Studies in Ethnomethodology*, p. 42.
[41]Garfinkel, *Studies in Ethnomethodology*, p. 42.

duced by men were treated as topics to be pursued, and they were seldom rejected.[42]

Roy Turner has made the point that exchanges of utterances can be regarded as doing things with words. As examples he cites the "I do" of a wedding ceremony, the "I apologize" after stepping on someone's toe, and the "I'll bet you five dollars that Chris Evert will win." Turner argues that these utterances are clearly activities.[43] Because accounts are in the form of talk, descriptive sentences of actual conversations and respondents' own interpretation of conversations, word-for-word, are important data for ethnomethodologists. This is illustrated by the methods used by sociologists who are doing ethnomethodology, to which we now turn.

DOING ETHNOMETHODOLOGY

The various methods that have been used by ethnomethodologists to gather data for analysis include open-ended, or depth interviews; participant observation; videotaping; the documentary method of interpretation; and ethnomethodological experiments, often called "breaching experiments." The meaning that the individual imparts to everyday life situations is of prime importance to ethnomethodologists. Therefore, we can expect to see them conducting open-ended depth interviews with people because this is an excellent way of gathering data that convey subjective meaning. Two projects employing this methodology were Garfinkel's jury deliberation study and Mehan's school testing study. Garfinkel had taped sessions of the actual jury deliberations, but the personal interviews with the jurors revealed the sources of the knowledge that they drew on in order to do the work of jurors. Thus Garfinkel's interviews with jurors revealed the following about how the jurors knew what they were doing in doing the work of jurors:

> Jurors learned the official line from various places: from the juror's handbook; from the instructions they received from the court; from the procedure of the *voir dire* when jurors were invited by the court to disqualify themselves if they could find for themselves reasons why they could not act in this fashion. They learned it from court personnel; they learned it from what jurors told each other, from TV, and from the movies. Several jurors got a quick tutoring by their high school children who had taken courses in civics.[44]

[42]Pamela M. Fishman, "Interaction: The Work Women Do," *Social Problems* 25 (1978): 397–406.

[43]Roy Turner in Jack D. Douglas, ed., *Understanding Everyday Life* (Chicago: Aldine, 1970), p. 170.

[44]Garfinkel, *Studies in Ethnomethodology*, p. 110.

In like manner, Mehan used personal interviews with students who had been tested to get at their own interpretations of the test questions as well as their own meaning of their responses to the test questions. Another example is the case study of a transsexual reported by Garfinkel in "Passing and the Managed Achievement of Sex Status in an Intersexed Person."[45] Most of the data presented there were gleaned from thirty-five hours of tape-recorded conversations with Agnes, a nineteen-year-old girl raised as a boy, who was constantly experiencing the risks and uncertainties involved in learning to act and feel like a woman. Agnes learned from her fiancé's direct admonitions to her and from his critiques of other women that she should not insist on having things her way and that she should not offer her opinions or claim equality with men. From her roommates and other women friends Agnes learned "the value of passive acceptance as a desirable female trait."[46]

Depth interviewing combined with participant observation can highlight the problematic areas of an individual's everyday life, areas that might otherwise have never been brought to light. For instance, in his study *Passing On*, David Sudnow says that his ethnomethodological perspective enabled him to spot the ambiguity of the bereaved status and thus to highlight the "essentially troublesome character of the normative elements in grief."[47] Sudnow notes,

> Bereaved persons apparently have considerable difficulty in their management of the properties of their own situation. They frequently don't know at what point they should undertake activities typically engaged in prior to death, and a large part of their difficulty derives from the sheer fact of their known status as a bereaved, which leaves them open to being treated sorrowfully no matter how they might conduct themselves. It is felt that only with time do they lose their status as bereaved in the eyes of others and cease to encounter treatments as a grievous person, and that time can often come long after they have ceased regarding themselves in that fashion.[48]

Functionalists like Parsons, for instance, maintain that grief is functional for the release and reduction of tension, and they assume that the roles of the bereaved and those around the bereaved are societally clear-cut. Ethnomethodologists like Sudnow may be revealing to us the limits of the culturally created role. There are wide gaps in the cultural prescription, and individuals experience the gaps sharply. For example, Sudnow's research shows that the bereaved person may be anxiously asking, "How am I supposed to act here?"

---

[45]Garfinkel, *Studies in Ethnomethodology*, pp. 116–85.

[46]Garfinkel, *Studies in Ethnomethodology*, p. 147.

[47]David Sudnow, *Passing On: The Social Organization of Dying* (Englewood Cliffs, N.J.: Prentice-Hall, 1967), p. 140.

[48]Sudnow, *Passing On*, p. 137.

Another method used by ethnomethodologists is called the *documentary method of interpretation*. Garfinkel credits Mannheim with the label and quotes his definition as the search for "an identical homologous pattern underlying a vast variety of totally different realizations of meaning." Garfinkel says,

> The method consists of treating an actual appearance as "the document of," as "pointing to," as "standing on behalf of" a presupposed underlying pattern. Not only is the underlying pattern derived from its individual documentary evidences, but the individual documentary evidences, in their turn, are interpreted on the basis of "what is known" about the underlying pattern.[49]

To Garfinkel, the documentary method is something people are constantly using as they continually interpret and reinterpret each other's behavior and look for the patterns that emerge from that behavior. One use of the documentary method by an ethnomethodologist is found in a study of the convict code by D. Lawrence Wieder.[50] As a participant observer at a halfway house, Wieder—after several months and many conversations with residents—detected a code that was operative. The code included prohibitions against snitching, copping out, taking advantage of other residents, messing with other residents, and trusting staff, as well as positive injunctions to share what you had and to help and show loyalty to other residents. "Telling the code" did not simply describe, analyze, and explain a situation in that environment. It was also the way residents actually guided conduct. For instance, when a resident terminated a conversation by saying, "You know I won't snitch," he was not only negatively sanctioning the prior conduct of the person with whom he was interacting and thereby terminating the conversation; he was also pointing out potential consequences if his associate persisted. Thus "telling the code" was extremely persuasive.

Wieder describes an instance of the use of the documentary method and the discovery of an underlying pattern that emerged from the behavior he observed:

> An example of the use of this method is provided by the interpretation of a remark I overheard during my first week at halfway house. I passed a resident who was wandering through the halls after the committee meetings on Wednesday night. He said to the staff and all others within hearing, "Where can I find that meeting where I can get an overnight pass?" On the basis of what I had already learned, I understood him to be saying, "I'm not going to that meeting because I'm interested in participating in the program of halfway house. I'm going to that meeting just because I would like to collect the reward of an overnight pass and for no other reason. I'm not a kiss-ass. Everyone who is in hearing distance should understand that I'm not kissing up to staff. My

---

[49]Garfinkel, *Studies in Ethnomethodology*, p. 78.
[50]See Turner, *Ethnomethodology: Selected Readings*, pp. 144–72.

behavior really is in conformity with the code, though without hearing this (reference to an overnight pass), you might think otherwise."[51]

Wieder continues,

> I thereby collected another "piece" of talk which, when put together with utterances I had heard up to that point (which permitted me to see the "sense" of this remark) and used with utterances I had yet to collect, was employed by me to formulate the general maxim, "Show your loyalty to the residents."[52]

Wieder explains that to be able to see an utterance like that as an expression of an underlying moral order, he had to know some of the particulars of that underlying pattern to begin with, so his participant observation and interviews with residents were crucial.

An example of the use of the documentary method by nonsociologists is presented by Jeffrey Alexander. "Reporters," he says, "employ the documentary method in their own perceptions of events, and the products of their investigations document the events for their readers."[53]

A final way of doing ethnomethodology is to engage in a *breaching experiment*, in which researchers disrupt ordinary activity, or, as Garfinkel puts it, "violate the scene." When they do this, the researchers are interested in what the subjects do and what they look to in order to give the situation an appearance of order or to make sense of the situation.[54] The professor's experiment with her class that we mentioned at the beginning of this section is an example of such an experiment.

However, although some ethnomethodologists find ways to make trouble themselves so that they can study how people attempt to bring order out of chaos—and many of Garfinkel's own student assignments are this type of endeavor—we would like to enter a note of caution. We suggest that a rather acute sensitivity is required for researchers who decide to violate the scene and thus create ethnomethodological data. For example, when one of the authors gave Garfinkel's "boarder" assignment to her students, there were some disturbing results. To summarize briefly, in this assignment the students were to spend "from fifteen minutes to an hour in their homes imagining that they were boarders and acting out this assumption. They were instructed to conduct themselves in a circumspect and polite fashion.

---

[51]Turner, *Ethnomethodology: Selected Readings*, p. 160.

[52]Turner, *Ethnomethodology: Selected Readings*, p. 160.

[53]Jeffrey C. Alexander, "The Mass News Media in Systemic, Historical and Comparative Perspective," in Elihu Katz and T. Szecsko, eds., *Mass Media and Social Change* (London: Sage, 1981), pp. 17–51.

[54]We have found, incidentally, that students tend to get a better grasp of what ethnomethodology is all about by completing some of the experiments or assignments mentioned by Garfinkel. (See especially the experiments on pp. 38, 42, 47, 79, and 85 in *Studies in Ethnomethodology*.)

They were to avoid getting personal, to use formal address, to speak only when spoken to."[55]

A distressing result we found with our own students is related to the question of sensitivity and trust. One of the students who attempted to complete the boarder assignment was a recently divorced woman with two young children. The children were so threatened by the shattering of their world at home when the mother began to act out the boarder role that the mother ended the experiment immediately. However, it took her at least a month to reassure the children that their world was not shattered; she went to great lengths to prove herself with them after that incident, until they finally came to the point where they felt they could trust her again. In retrospect she felt that it was too soon after their father's departure from the home. When the mother became a boarder, she was, in a sense, leaving the children also.

Garfinkel's concept of trust explains how people comply with a certain order of events and is, as we have seen, close to Parsons's idea of shared normative expectations. How do people perceive and interpret their daily lives, and how do objects and events and facts come to be seen as normal, as making sense? Garfinkel's answer is "trust." That is, rules are ambiguous, and they are perceived and interpreted differently; but the actor trusts the environment in the face of this uncertainty.[56]

The notion of trust is an important element in the incident with the divorced mother and her children. Their reaction to her taking on the role of boarder should underscore the complexities involved in the decision to violate the scene. Our position is that certain ethical questions should be addressed in advance, well before the ethnomethodologists go out into the field to make trouble. In fact, according to the Code of Ethics of the American Sociological Association, such conduct is no longer acceptable, and not only is the informed consent of the subject required, but also they must be informed by the researcher about the assurance of confidentiality and about their right to refuse to answer questions posed by the researcher.[57]

The ways ethnomethodologists conduct research underscore the differences between what they do, how they go about doing it, and the way other sociologists do their work. The differences between ethnomethodology and symbolic interactionism are particularly interesting because both are inductive social-psychological perspectives limited primarily to the microsociological level, and both use qualitative data.

---

[55]Garfinkel, *Studies in Ethnomethodology*, p. 47.

[56]Aaron V. Cicourel, *Method and Measurement in Sociology* (New York: The Free Press, 1964), p. 206.

[57]See *Code of Ethics: American Sociological Association* (June, 1997).

METHODOLOGICAL COMPARISON

Like symbolic interactionism, ethnomethodology is a social-psychological approach concerned with individuals rather than roles and social structures. However, its questions differ from those of symbolic interactionism. Cicourel points out that notions like Cooley's "looking-glass self" and Thomas's "definition of the situation" presuppose that meanings can be accepted as self-evident. What ethnomethodology is interested in, according to Cicourel, is the properties of meanings, or the structure of the rules of the game. The ethnomethodological question is "How do the rules of conduct (or the rules of the game) inform the actors about the nature of their environment?" Or, as Cicourel puts it, "How does the actor go about making sense of his environment in socially acceptable ways?"[58]

Though the methods used by symbolic interactionism and ethnomethodology are essentially the same, they are used in a different way because ethnomethodology asks different questions. Ethnomethodologists, for instance, are constantly seeking situations where they can analyze subjects who are making sense of a situation—situations in which meaning is problematic. What are obvious places for such phenomena? Many data would be available to any researcher who could follow immigrants around during their first few weeks in a new country. The same could be said for the first few weeks in a college student's campus life, or the days and months after a family has been informed that their son or daughter has AIDS. Places where new or unexpected situations occur frequently (like the wards frequented by David Sudnow, where announcements of deaths were made) are also rich in ethnomethodological data.

Let us recall the example of the baseball player and Mead's "generalized other," which we discussed in Chapter 5. Mead's analysis dealt with the ability of the player to have the mind-set of all the other players on the team. Thus the player on first base would automatically know the meaning of the situation regardless of whether a fly, a strike, or a walk occurred at home plate.

Ethnomethodologists view the meaning of such a situation as problematic. Someone working from an ethnomethodological perspective would be more interested in the ways players make sense of the situation, as evidenced by their reactions when the umpire or another player acts unexpectedly, than in what was going on in the minds of the players. For instance, with regard to the unusual behavior of a basketball player who makes a basket in the opponent's court, the ethnomethodologist asks, "What methods would the player use in constructing and maintaining a sense of order?"

Sudnow explicitly points to this problematic stance as an important difference between symbolic interactionism and ethnomethodology. He con-

---

[58]Cicourel, *Method and Measurement in Sociology*, p. 198.

trasts his own study of death and dying with that of Glaser and Strauss (*Awareness of Dying*), which we discussed in Chapter 4, and states,

> Their analysis is not treated as a problematic phenomenon. Their central interest, of considerable social-psychological importance, is the management of information in interaction. . . . I have found it necessary, being less concerned with interaction between staff and patient and more concerned with the organization of ward activities, to regard the very phenomenon of dying as troublesome, an understanding of its sense requiring location of those practices which its use warrants.[59]

Sudnow adds that he feels that, from an organizational perspective, awareness of dying is irrelevant for a considerable number of people. If one is interested, as ethnomethodologists are, in studies of naturally organized activities of an everyday nature, then the degree of the patient's awareness of dying is, for ethnomethodologists, not important. What is important to Sudnow is how people in the ward make sense of a dying situation—that is, the ways all the people involved present to the world an orderly social scene on the ward.

The differences in approach are again apparent if we recall the experiment in which students were instructed to bargain with a sales clerk for merchandise that had a standardized price.[60] This is another of the experiments Garfinkel uses, although when we discussed it in Chapter 4, we did not identify it with him. What was Garfinkel's focus in this experiment? Quoting Parsons, Garfinkel argues that because of the internalization of the standardized expectancy of the institutionalized one-price rule, that is, because of background expectancies, student-customers would be fearful and shamed, and sales clerks would be anxious and angry. (An important piece of contextual information is the location of this experiment. It took place in the United States rather than in Mexico, for instance, where the standardized expectation is bargaining.) Though many of Garfinkel's students were fearful, many of those who completed six bargaining episodes learned that they could bargain successfully and planned to do so in the future, thus illustrating that the internalization of the one-price rule was, in fact, problematic. In this respect they were constructing a new social reality for themselves and for the merchants.

As we stated in Chapter 4, the symbolic interactionist perspective would concentrate instead on the self-interaction of the sales clerk and on what the sales clerk was saying to herself as she confronted this surprising situation. The sales clerk's definition of the situation and its meaning for her would be the focus for symbolic interactionism; all Garfinkel says about the clerk is, "A few showed anxiety; occasionally one got angry."[61] Ethnomethodologists

---

[59]David Sudnow, *Passing On*, pp. 62–63, fn. 2.
[60]Garfinkel, *Studies in Ethnomethodology*, pp. 68–70.
[61]Garfinkel, *Studies in Ethnomethodology*, p. 69.

would want to know what methods or accounting practices the sales clerk looks to in order to give this situation a semblance of order. Does she ask the student-customer questions; impute motives; consult an oracle, a god, or an astrology calendar; ask for a repeat of the request; label the student-customer crazy; or simply ignore the incident? The taken-for-granted, or the contextual, features of the situation would certainly be a central part of the ethnomethodological interpretation of the action. Because Garfinkel emphasizes the fact that meanings are situationally dependent—that is, that interaction is characterized by indexicality—such contextual features as the location and time of the interaction between the sales clerk and customer, the persons present during the incident, and the sales clerk's knowledge of the intentions of the customer would have to be fleshed out to get to the meaning of the situation.

Basically, both perspectives deal with qualitative data, but neither would argue that quantitative data has no value. Some, like Cicourel, are known for their sophisticated use of quantitative data. In his article "The School as a Mechanism of Social Differentiation," Cicourel employs such "hard" data as SCAT scores and grade-point averages in his analysis of school counselors' rating and student achievement types, and he shows that the students' progress is contingent upon the interpretations, judgments, and action of school personnel.[62] However, Cicourel attacks the overconfident stance of the survey researcher when he says, "The nature of the inferred role of the other is a problem seldom addressed by sociologists. (For example, how does the subject decide the meaning of questionnaire items?)"[63]

Questions like this are important for those who deal only with hard data. You may recall that we discuss the problem of misinterpretation of test items in the study of schoolchildren by Mehan.

Like Blumer,[64] Cicourel raises serious questions about measurement systems used in sociology. He says that even the written word is "subject to the differential perception and interpretation of actors variously distributed in the social structures."[65] Moreover, quantitative analysis leaves out what Cicourel calls the "inner horizon" of subjective social action as outlined by Weber; instead it concentrates on the "outer horizon," or distributions like occupational prestige scales or social class rankings. The "inner horizon," which both symbolic interactionism and ethnomethodology highlight, includes "idiomatic expressions, course of action motives, institutional and innovational language"—all of which are unclarified in the "outer horizon"

[62]Aaron V. Cicourel and John I. Kitsuse, "The School as a Mechanism of Social Differentiation," in Jerome Karabel and A. H. Halsey, ed., *Power and Ideology in Education* (New York: Oxford University Press, 1977), pp. 282–92; and Aaron V. Cicourel and John I. Kitsuse, *The Educational Decision-Makers* (New York: Bobbs-Merrill, 1963).

[63]Cicourel, *Method and Measurement in Sociology*, p. 212.

[64]See Chapter 5.

[65]Cicourel, *Method and Measurement in Sociology*, p. 221.

of distributions.[66] Cicourel says that without the inner horizon, social research is a "closed enterprise rather than an open search for knowledge relative to a given era."[67]

A good example of the value of the inner horizon is given by Sudnow in *Passing On* when he discusses the counting of deaths. He mentions the value the hospital administrators place on a general demographic inventory of deaths, but he notes that the ward personnel do not add up the daily death counts in any systematic way. However, rather special varieties of death are not only counted but remembered in some detail; these include suicides, death from barium enema exams, deaths of very young children, mothers who die in childbirth, and patients who die during the course of a doctor's routine morning round. What Sudnow brings to our attention are *noteworthy deaths*, "those which take place in settings where death is uncommon, those which result from accidents or diagnostic and treatment errors, and those which result in the very young patient."[68] In other words, these are the deaths that don't make sense and that are correspondingly ripe for ethnomethodological analysis, because they offer the possibility of learning how people manage the discrepancies between what is expected or appropriate and their own unsettling experiences.

As will be apparent from its stress on participation and the inner horizon, ethnomethodology also resembles symbolic interactionism in that it must deal with researchers' possible biases as they interpret the subjective data they have collected. To his credit, Sudnow admits that his descriptions are made by a middle-class observer; he concludes that ethnography is "continually plagued by the import of such descriptive biases."[69] The problem of bias, of course, must be dealt with by all researchers, no matter what perspective they espouse. However, the bias is probably more problematic for ethnomethodologists because they tend to become practitioners in a deeper sense than the other perspectives, so the danger may be more acute.

Finally, both ethnomethodologists and symbolic interactionists use participant observation, case studies, depth interviews, and biographies as methodological techniques. However, in discussing participant observations, Garfinkel stresses the role of the researcher as practitioner and emphasizes the participant over the observer's role. He says that researchers must be part of the world they are studying and must know it well.[70] Another way of putting it is to say that ethnomethodology is

---

[66]Cicourel, *Method and Measurement in Sociology*, p. 223.

[67]Cicourel, *Method and Measurement in Sociology*, p. 224.

[68]Sudnow, *Passing On*, pp. 40–41.

[69]Sudnow, *Passing On*, p. 176.

[70]Personal interview, September 1975.

involved in "studies of activities, not theories about activities."[71] As Psathas describes it, it is like learning how to swim. Though a person can learn a lot from reading books about swimming, the only way to become a swimmer is to do it, to get in the water and swim. We sense that what ethnomethodologists are really saying is that to know what ethnomethodology is you must do ethnomethodology.

PART TWO

Peter Berger: The Social Construction of Reality

BACKGROUND

Another branch of phenomenological sociology is represented by the work of Peter Berger. Born in 1929 in Vienna, Austria, Berger earned his B.A. at Wagner College in 1949 and his M.A. and Ph.D. in 1950 and 1954 at the New School for Social Research, where he studied under Alfred Schutz. Subsequently he taught at the Hartford Seminary Foundation, the New School for Social Research, Rutgers, and Boston College. Currently he is university professor at Boston University.

The theoretical underpinnings for Berger's work appear in *The Social Construction of Reality* (1966), which he coauthored with Thomas Luckmann. Much of Berger's writing has focused on the sociology of religion, and here his most important work is *The Sacred Canopy* (1969). Berger's interest in religion is not accidental; he studied for a time at Lutheran Theological Seminary in Philadelphia and at Yale Divinity School. A past president of the Society for the Scientific Study of Religion, Berger has published numerous articles and a half-dozen books on religious topics.[72] He has also developed an interest in the area of social change, as is evidenced in his books *The Homeless Mind* (1973) and *Pyramids of Sacrifice* (1975). A later work, coauthored with his wife, Brigitte Berger, is *The War over the Family* (1983). We will look first at the key concepts of Berger's theory and then at some applications of his phenomenological position.

---

[71]See George Psathas, "Misinterpreting Ethnomethodology." Paper presented at American Sociological Association annual meeting, New York, 1976, p. 5.

[72]For example, *The Noise of Solemn Assemblies, The Sacred Canopy, Rumor of Angels,* and *The Heretical Imperative.*

KEY CONCEPTS

In *The Social Construction of Reality*, Berger and Luckmann take a sociology of knowledge approach. They focus on the "processes by which *any* body of 'knowledge' comes to be socially accepted *as* 'reality.' "[73] By reality construction they mean the process whereby people continuously create, through their actions and interactions, a shared reality that is experienced as objectively factual and subjectively meaningful. They assume that everyday reality is a socially constructed system in which people bestow a certain order on everyday phenomena, a reality that has both subjective and objective elements. By subjective they mean that the reality is personally meaningful to the individual. By objective they refer to the social order, or the institutional world, which they view as a human product.[74]

An excerpt from Berger's book *The Sacred Canopy* may help clarify their position:

> Worlds are socially constructed and socially maintained. Their continuing reality, both objective (as common, taken-for-granted facticity) and subjective (as facticity imposing itself on individual consciousness), depends upon specific social processes, namely those processes that ongoingly reconstruct and maintain the particular worlds in question. Conversely, the interruption of these social processes threatens the (objective and subjective) reality of the worlds in question. Thus each world requires a social "base" for its continuing existence as a world that is real to actual human beings.[75]

According to Berger and Luckmann, alienation is defined as a loss of meaning: there has been a disintegration of the socially constructed knowledge system. Developing nations, for instance, where modernization is eroding traditional worlds, and new nations arising from the collapse of the Soviet Union are experiencing this kind of alienation.[76] Only by reconstructing a knowledge system so that it brings with it a rediscovery of meaning can these nations' alienation be alleviated.

The heart of this theory deals with the question of how everyday reality is socially constructed. As Berger and Luckmann put it, "How is it possible that subjective meanings *become* objective facticities?"[77]

---

[73]Peter L. Berger and Thomas Luckmann, *The Social Construction of Reality* (New York: Doubleday, 1966), p. 3.

[74]The subjective element is borrowed from Weber's *verstehende*, and the objective from Durkheim's social facts. See pp. 191–92 and 21–22.

[75]Berger, *The Sacred Canopy* (New York: Doubleday, 1969), p. 45.

[76]See Peter Berger, Brigitte Berger, and Hansfried Kellner, *The Homeless Mind* (New York: Random House, 1973). This concept of alienation is very different from the Marxist concept discussed in Chapter 3 and is closer to Durkheim's notion of anomie.

[77]Berger and Luckmann, *The Social Construction of Reality*, p. 18.

Berger and Luckmann's phenomenological analysis is focused on the subjective experience of the reality of everyday life, the here and now. This reality also includes past and future. As they explain it, "My attention to this world (of everyday life) is mainly determined by what I am doing, have done, or plan to do in it." But their focus is not on a self-contained world, for the reality of everyday life is described as an "intersubjective world, a world that I share with others."[78] Berger and Luckmann are, like Goffman, convinced that face-to-face interaction is where the real action is. In fact, they state that face-to-face interaction is the prototype of social interaction and that all other cases of social interaction derive from it.[79] In contrast to Goffman, whose actors appear to be reading scripts that were written by others, Berger and Luckmann's actors improvise and create their own scripts.

The fact that Berger and Luckmann include objective reality as well as subjective reality in their framework makes it more than a purely microsociological approach. Instead their theory can be viewed as an attempt to bridge the micro- and macrosociological levels of analysis, an attempt made by only a few social theorists.[80] The key concepts of Berger and Luckmann's theory, which they describe as "moments" of a dialectical process, are *externalization*, *objectivation*, and *internalization*.

Externalization

Berger and Luckmann label the first moment in the continuing dialectical process of the social construction of reality *externalization*, wherein individuals, by their own human activity, create their social worlds. They view the social order as an ongoing human production. The social order is the "result of past human activity" and "exists only and insofar as human activity continues to produce it."[81] Thus externalization has two dimensions. On the one hand, it means that human beings can create a new social reality, like forming a new friendship or starting a new business. On the other hand, it means that human beings can re-create social institutions by their ongoing externalization of them, like maintaining and renewing old friendships or paying income taxes.

In order to understand externalization better, let us look at the creation of a new friendship. Two people who find their interaction mutually rewarding become friends. This friendship is a new social reality; their

---

[78]Berger and Luckmann, *The Social Construction of Reality*, pp. 22 and 23.

[79]Berger and Luckmann, *The Social Construction of Reality*, p. 28.

[80]See, for instance, Randall Collins, p. 136, Peter Blau, p. 328, C. Wright Mills, pp. 106–107, Anthony Giddens, pp. 180–81, and Pierre Bourdieu, pp. 115–16. We discuss Dorothy E. Smith's contribution to the effort to bridge the micro and macro levels in the next section of this chapter.

[81]Berger and Luckmann, *The Social Construction of Reality*, p. 52.

newly forged "we-ness" is a social reality that did not previously exist. The friends themselves actively and willingly produced this new social entity. Friendship is an ongoing human production in the sense that every time the friends interact, they re-create their friendship. Thus friendship is an institution that is both external to and produced by human beings. Other examples of externalization are creating and maintaining a marriage, a new business, or a new occupation.

In a study of Catholic parishes headed by laywomen, Wallace found that the women pastors practiced collaborative leadership, which involves a guiding rather than commanding mode; and they drew on the talents of parishioners, recruiting them as coworkers. The women pastors accomplished this by a combination of strategies: visiting homes, learning the first names of each member of the family, mentioning parishioners' concerns when they preached, and making themselves accessible. This type of leadership directly contrasted with previous priest pastors, who tended to practice hierarchical leadership, typically performing like a "one-man band" rather than a conductor leading an orchestra. On their part, the parishioners were willing accomplices in the creation of this new social reality, partly because they wanted to avoid the alternative, a closing of their parish due to the priest shortage. One of the parishioners explained, "It's hard to say no to (her) because people respect her and you want to help her. And she just has a way of asking you that puts you at ease. It's not a demanding sort of way at all. She always *asks*, never says '*Do* this.' "[82]

The moment of externalization, then, is the moment of production in the dialectical process. It is in the externalization phase of reality construction that Berger and Luckmann see individuals as creative beings, capable of acting on their own environment. This concept is akin to the "I" phase of the social self, an idea borrowed from George Herbert Mead.[83] In short, externalization means that individuals create society.

Objectivation

Objectivation is the process whereby individuals apprehend everyday life as an ordered, prearranged reality that imposes itself upon but is seemingly independent of human beings. For the individual, as Berger and Luckmann put it, "the reality of everyday life appears already objectified, that is, constituted by an order of objects that have been designated as objects before my appearance on the scene."[84]

---

[82]Ruth A. Wallace, "The Social Creation of a New Leadership Role: Catholic Women Pastors," *Sociology of Religion* 54, no. 1 (Spring 1993), 37.

[83]See Chapter 5.

[84]Berger and Luckmann, *The Social Construction of Reality*, p. 22.

Language is the means by which objects are so designated. Berger and Luckmann explain, "The common objectivations of everyday life are maintained primarily by linguistic signification. Everyday life is, above all, life with and by means of the language I share with my fellowmen [sic]. An understanding of language is thus essential for any understanding of the reality of everyday life."[85]

The role of language in maintaining common objectivations suggests that changes in language will be resisted. Consider the continuing confrontations over the use of inclusive language that are currently taking place in some quarters.

To return to the example of friendship again, objectivation means that the friendship between two people that resulted from their interactions confronts the two friends as a social reality. When the friends refer to this reality as "we," they are using language to designate the friendship as an objective social reality. Other people, hearing that the two are friends, understand what the relationship means.

In his fieldwork at a nursing home, Gubrium used the concept of objectivation to analyze the status of senility among the patients. He argued that knowledge about senility and incipient senility emerged in the process of the everyday work done by health care personnel to categorize behavior as senile or nonsenile. When senility is realized in this way people seem to accept the natural objective status of senility.[86] Once designated as such, the status of senility acts back on those who have been so labeled. For instance, Gubrium found that patients tend to believe senility is contagious. He quotes two patients: (1) "You spend too much time around 'em, you get to be nuts before your time." (2) "That crazy stuff is catchy, you know. They'll set you as goofy as they are."[87] To illustrate the social construction of reality in the case of senility, Gubrium makes the point that it is taken for granted that confused, disoriented, or agitated behavior is considered senile when the individual engaging in such behavior is aged. However, the manifestation of the same symptoms in a younger individual is believed to be obviously something else.[88] Thus senility is an objective reality that has consequences for the people so labeled. In short, objectivation means that society is an objective reality that has consequences for the individual because it acts back on its creator. And this brings us to our next concept.

---

[85]Berger and Luckmann, *The Social Construction of Reality*, p. 37.

[86]Jaber F. Gubrium, "Notes on the Social Organization of Senility," *Urban Life* 7, no. 1 (April 1978): 27.

[87]Gubrium, "Notes on the Social Organization of Senility," p. 38.

[88]Gubrium, "Notes on the Social Organization of Senility," p. 26.

Internalization

The third moment of the dialectical process is *internalization,* a kind of socialization by which the legitimation of the institutional order is assured. For Berger, successful socialization means that there is a high degree of symmetry between both objective and subjective reality and objective and subjective identity. Whereas "objectivation implies the production of a real social world, external to the individuals inhabiting it; internalization implies that this same social world will have the status of reality within the consciousness of these individuals."[89] Internalization for Berger is what socialization is for Parsons in that individuals internalize (make their own) the objectivated social reality, with the result that "everyone pretty much is what he is supposed to be." There is no problem of identity, for "everybody knows who everybody is and who he is himself."[90]

A study of the reentry of Vietnam veterans illustrates some of the problems caused by a lack of symmetry between objective and subjective identity. As the researchers put it, "There is a change of identity as one moves from the war world. The civilian turned soldier has an acute sense of the war as having made him different through and through, not merely identifiably different." And though the veteran wants to be reincorporated into the taken-for-granted social reality of home, he finds that his war world cannot be mutually shared in his home world. He must "get his head out of Nam," as one veteran put it.[91] In short, he is *not* what he is supposed to be, and the identity problem is acute.

As we have mentioned, Berger's definition of socialization is similar to Parsons's, that is, the internalization of social norms and values. Berger, however, distinguishes between primary and secondary socialization. Primary socialization refers to what individuals undergo in childhood when they encounter the significant others with whom they identify emotionally. "The child takes on the significant others' roles and attitudes, that is, internalizes them and makes them his own."[92] Secondary socialization is "any subsequent process that inducts an already socialized individual into new sectors of the objective world of his society."[93] Basically secondary socialization is a later phase in the acquisition of knowledge, and it concerns more specific roles. It takes place under the auspices of specialized agencies, like modern educational institutions.

[89]Peter Berger, *The Sacred Canopy,* p. 83.

[90]Berger and Luckmann, *The Social Construction of Reality,* p. 164.

[91]Robert R. Faulkner and Douglas B. McGaw, "Uneasy Homecoming: Stages in the Reentry Transition of Vietnam Veterans," *Urban Life* 6, no. 3 (October 1977): 308 and 315.

[92]Berger and Luckmann, *The Social Construction of Reality,* pp. 131–32.

[93]Berger and Luckmann, *The Social Construction of Reality,* p. 130.

The social construction of reality theory argues that whenever individuals engage in internalization, they are conforming to the expectations of existing social institutions, and they are also re-creating that social institution. The creation of a new institution occurs in the moment of externalization; once externalized, it is objectified; and once objectified, it acts back on the individual as an internalized entity. As Berger and Luckmann sum it up: "Society is a human product" (externalization); "society is an objective reality" (objectivation); and "man is a social product" (internalization).[94]

Returning once again to our example of friendship, let us consider its institutionalization. When two individuals create a friendship in the moment of externalization, it becomes an object (objectivation), which then acts back on them as something they have internalized. Thus forming a friendship can have various consequences for the friends in question, such as the use of a friend's time, energy, and other resources. Consider for a moment the whole gamut of behaviors expected of a friend: visiting a friend in the hospital or caring for a friend when she or he is sick, giving advice to a friend, lending money, giving gifts, writing letters, and even spending whole days with that friend. In short, an institution that I helped create is acting back on me whenever a friend demands my time (objectivation); and when I choose to meet those demands (internalization), I am re-creating (externalizing) that institution again. As an individual I can act and react; I can create new institutions and re-create (and thus maintain) old ones; but in either case reality is grounded in the ongoing process of interaction and negotiation.

As we mentioned above, Berger and Luckmann see the central question for sociological theory as "How is it possible that subjective meanings become objective facticities?"[95] Their primary interest is in the factors that make a given world more or less real and fully internalized.

An issue related to internalization is what Berger and Luckmann call *reification*, "the apprehension of the products of human activity *as if* they were something else than human products—such as facts of nature, results of cosmic laws, or manifestations of divine will. Reification implies that man is capable of forgetting his own authorship of the human world, and further that the dialectic between man, the producer, and his products is lost to consciousness. The reified world is, by definition, a dehumanized world."[96]

In *The Sacred Canopy* Berger pictures the individual who reifies his social world as one who is living an alienated and meaningless life. As Berger puts it, "The actor becomes *only* that which is acted upon."[97] The dialectic is lost, and the individual is no longer free but is a prisoner of his or her destiny. Berger discusses the role of religion in this reification process:

[94]Berger and Luckmann, *The Social Construction of Reality*, p. 61.
[95]Berger and Luckmann, *The Social Construction of Reality*, p. 18.
[96]Berger and Luckmann, *The Social Construction of Reality*, p. 89.
[97]Berger, *The Sacred Canopy*, p. 86.

> One of the essential qualities of the sacred, as encountered in 'religious experience,' is otherness, its manifestation as something *totaliter aliter* [totally other] as compared to ordinary, profane human life. . . . The fundamental 'recipe' of religious legitimation is the transformation of human products into supra- or non-human facticities. The humanly made world is explained in terms that deny its human production.[98]

Thus, to the degree that religious beliefs convince individuals that they are *not* masters of their own fates, or that priestly roles are reserved for males, or that patriotism or anticommunism are sacred beliefs, or that blind obedience is a moral duty—to that degree religion, according to Berger, aids and abets the reification process.

Finally, the theory of the social construction of reality argues that roles as well as institutions can be reified. For instance, when an individual says, "I must act in this way because of my position. I have no choice," that individual is demonstrating a reified lockstep mentality. Such a mentality minimizes the choices available to people, and it exemplifies the situation wherein individuals have, indeed, forgotten their authorship of the human world. For example, daughters or sons who feel they must follow in their parents' footsteps regarding the choice of an occupation or of a school or college exemplify the reification process.

This does not mean that responsible behavior and firm commitments imply reification. Berger's theory takes account of individuals who reaffirm their responsibilities and choices while being mindful of other alternatives available to them. A friend who willingly gives scarce time or money in the name of friendship and a parent who says, "I must do this because of my responsibility to my child," are consciously re-creating social reality rather than reifying their positions.

We now turn to Dorothy Smith, a theorist who was strongly influenced by phenomenology, but who also used concepts from critical conflict theory in her effort to bridge the micro and macro levels of analysis.

PART THREE

Dorothy E. Smith: Feminist Standpoint Theory

BACKGROUND

Born in Great Britain in 1926, Dorothy E. Smith worked as a secretary before enrolling at the London School of Economics, where she earned her bachelor's degree in 1955. Shortly thereafter she moved to the United States,

---

[98]Berger, *The Sacred Canopy*, pp. 87 and 89.

where she earned her doctorate in sociology at the University of California, Berkeley, in 1963, returning there as lecturer between 1964 and 1966. Other academic appointments include the University of Essex in Great Britain, the University of British Columbia in Canada, and the University of Toronto, where since 1977 she has held the rank of professor in the Department of Sociology in Education at the Ontario Institute for Studies in Education.

Dorothy Smith's writings are widely read and increasingly cited.[99] She has been thrice honored by the American Sociological Association: (1) the Spring 1992 edition of *Sociological Theory* featured a symposium on her work; (2) in 1992 the ASA theory section organized a special session devoted to her books that demonstrated the depth and breadth of her theoretical work, *The Everyday World as Problematic: A Feminist Sociology, The Conceptual Practices of Power: A Feminist Sociology of Knowledge,* and *Texts, Facts, and Femininity: Exploring the Relations of Ruling;* (3) and in 1993 the American Sociological Association presented the Jessie Bernard Award to Dorothy Smith and Patricia Hill Collins[100] in recognition of their "scholarly work that has enlarged the horizons of sociology to encompass fully the role of women in society." The award further reads,

> Together these award recipients are part of a transformation of sociology. Together they have extended the boundaries of sociology to include the standpoint, experiences, and concerns of women; together they have extended the boundaries of gender scholarship to include the intersection of race, class, and gender. Together they represent a sociology which seeks to empower women through a dialectic of theory and practice.[101]

As we mentioned in Chapter 5, Patricia Hill Collins drew on Smith's work when she extended standpoint theory to include race and class as well as gender, and proceeded to analyze the more complex forms of oppression experienced by African-American women. Here we look at the key elements of Dorothy Smith's theoretical work, followed by a discussion of the methodological implications.

STANDPOINT THEORY DEFINED

Dorothy Smith's standpoint theory explores the everyday/everynight worlds of individuals situated in subordinate positions. Although hers is a feminist standpoint theory, focusing on the perspectives of women, a stand-

---

[99]Leading feminist theorists like Joan Acker have acknowledged their debt to Smith's work. See Acker's "Making Gender Visible," pp. 65–81 in Ruth A. Wallace, *Feminism and Sociological Theory* (Newbury Park, Calif.: Sage, 1989).

[100]See Chapter 5, Part Four, where we discuss the theoretical contributions of Patricia Hill Collins.

[101]See "ASA Award Winners Reflect Broad Spectrum of Sociology," *Footnotes* 21, no. 7 (October 1993): 13.

point theory could take the perspectives of other subordinated individuals, like the black women analyzed by Patricia Hill Collins. Other standpoint theories could focus on poor white women and men, nonwhite women and men, homosexual women and men, and individuals belonging to minority ethnic and religious groups outside contemporary Western society.

Smith's feminist standpoint theory includes both social-structural and social-psychological elements. Like C. Wright Mills, Anthony Giddens, Pierre Bourdieu, and Randall Collins, her work bridges the macrostructural and microinteractional levels of analysis. She describes her perspective as "a conjunction of the materialist method developed by Marx and Engels and Garfinkel's ethnomethodology."[102] Smith is interested in the structures of male domination as experienced by women in their everyday experiences and in how women think and feel about those experiences.

Like Garfinkel, Smith wants to break the taboo regarding the questioning of the social order, and to uncover the taken-for-granted assumptions or myths operating in the interaction situation. Her work is similar to the phenomenologists we mentioned at the beginning of this chapter, who would view the realities of women's nature, needs, role, and place in society as systems of ideas constructed in past interactions and sustained by present ongoing interaction. Following Garfinkel, her approach is to treat as problematic what is taken for granted in women's everyday/everynight world.[103] Smith's aim is to develop a sociology founded on an investigation of the problematic of the everyday world; in particular she wants to develop a sociology not *about* women but *for* women, one that will give them a voice.

Inspired by Marx and Engels, who propose in *The German Ideology* to ground social science in the activities of actual individuals and their material conditions, Smith explains the origins of her feminist standpoint theory:

> I began thinking through how to develop sociological inquiry from the site of the experiencing and embodied subject as a sociology from the standpoint of women. In the women's movement, we began to discover that we lived in a world put together in ways in which we had had very little say. . . . We discovered that we had been in various ways silenced, deprived of the authority to speak, and that our experience therefore did not have a voice, lacked indeed a language, for we had taken from the cultural and intellectual world created largely by men the terms, themes, conceptions of the subject and subjectivity, of feeling, emotion, goals, relations, and an object world assembled in textually mediated discourses and from the standpoint of men occupying the apparatuses of ruling. We came to understand this organization of power as

---

[102]Dorothy E. Smith, "Sociological Theory: Methods of Writing Patriarchy," in Wallace, *Feminism and Sociological Theory*, p. 60. See also *The Everyday World As Problematic: A Feminist Sociology of Knowledge* (Boston: Northeastern University Press, 1987), pp. 8–9, where, in addition to Garfinkel and Marx and Engels, she acknowledges the influences of George Herbert Mead and Maurice Merleau-Ponty.

[103]See the beginning of this chapter, where we discuss Garfinkel's approach.

"patriarchy," a term that identified both the personal and the public relations of male power.[104]

As a result of their powerlessness in the patriarchial order, Smith argues that women experience a *line of fault* between what they know and experience in their everyday/everynight lives and what is official knowledge, as expressed in the symbols, images, vocabularies, and concepts of the patriarchal culture. Consequently women tend to live with a bifurcated consciousness. Smith's debt to phenomenology is exemplified as she strives to decode the taken-for-granted assumptions in social institutions. Smith's subjective experiences as the wife of a graduate student are an illustration. She states,

> I was hooked on sociology; he was not. He loved the life, the good talk, and was passionately interested in people, but had little interest in sociology as inquiry or in its scholarly side. We had it the wrong way round in terms of the husband-wife relations of those times. We were constantly involved in pretending it was otherwise; I worked on learning to displace, subdue, or conceal my interests, trying, though never very successfully, to acquire the styles of subordination proper for an American woman toward her husband. Never being successful, I was guilty and anxious; Bill impugned, angry, and embarrassed.[105]

A key concept in Smith's standpoint theory is the *relations of ruling*, or the ruling apparatuses, which include not only the state but also institutions of administration, government, management, and the professions that organize, lead, and regulate contemporary societies. Women and others who are not members of the dominant white male minority participate only marginally, if at all, in the relations of ruling. Another autobiographical reflection illustrates Dorothy Smith's marginality as a faculty member during her two years of teaching at the University of California, Berkeley:

> For one term Shirley Starr was there as a visiting professor. Shirley was one of the older generation of women scholars whose statistical brilliance had enabled them to establish themselves in research positions. On the margins. She gave me some advice. She saw me one day running off my course outlines in the departmental office. "Don't do your own mimeographing," she said. "People will think you're a secretary." Since I'd been a secretary, that didn't exactly freak me out, but I got the point. The department was a caste system; faculty were male. Forty-four men. And me . . . and Shirley for one semester.[106]

---

[104]Smith, *Texts, Facts, and Femininity: Exploring the Relations of Ruling* (New York: Routledge, 1990), pp. 1–2.

[105]Dorothy E. Smith, "A Berkeley Education," in Kathryn P. Meadow Orlans and Ruth A. Wallace, ed., *Gender and the Academic Experience* (Lincoln: University of Nebraska Press, 1994), p. 46.

[106]Smith, "A Berkeley Education," pp. 47–48.

Smith argues that the ruling apparatus is an organization of class implicating the dominant classes, which excludes not only the working class but also women and "the many voices of women and men of color, of native peoples, and of homosexual women and men. From different standpoints different aspects of the ruling apparatus and of class come into view."[107] Smith argues that the standpoint of women is a place for the social scientist to start, opening up for exploration "the conceptual practices of the extralocal, objectified relations of ruling of what actual people do."[108]

While this aspect of Smith's work is an extension of the critical conflict tradition, her call for a woman-centered sociology could also be labeled by ethnomethodologists as a violation of the scene for mainstream sociologists because her questions challenge taken-for-granted assumptions. She agrees with Schutz's critique of the scientific attitude that "brackets" or suspends "the subjectivity of the thinker as a man among fellow men, including his bodily existence, as a psychophysical human being within the world."[109] Smith therefore argues that exploring the "objectivity" that supports the ruling apparatus is a way for women and other subordinate groups not only to make sense of their social world but also possibly to change it. The following descriptions of her approach reveal her debt to Garfinkel:

> It proposes an insider's sociology, that is, a systematically developed consciousness of society from within. . . . Beginning from where the subject is actually located returns us to a social world arising in and known in and through the ongoing actual activities of actual people.[110]
>
> An insider's strategy takes concepts, ideas, ideology, and schemata as dimensions and organizers of the ongoing social process that we can grasp only as insiders, only by considering our own practices.[111] . . . An alternative sociology, from the standpoint of women, makes the everyday world its problematic.[112]

As we discussed earlier in this chapter, phenomenology questions the taken-for-granted assumptions, challenges culturally learned ideas, and treats as problematic what is taken for granted in order to understand the everyday world. An illustration of this stance is found in Smith's discussion of femininity. She argues that a feminist exploration of femininity "means a shift away from viewing it as a normative order, reproduced through socialization, to which somehow women are subordinated. Rather femininity is

[107]Smith, *The Everyday World as Problematic*, p. 107.

[108]Dorothy E. Smith, *The Conceptual Practices of Power: A Feminist Sociology of Knowledge* (Boston: Northeastern University Press, 1990), p. 28.

[109]Alfred Schutz, "On Multiple Realities." In *Collected Papers*, Vol. 1 (The Hague: Martinus Nijhoff, 1962), p. 249, quoted in Smith, *The Everyday World as Problematic*, p. 70.

[110]Smith in Wallace, *Feminism and Sociological Theory*, p. 38.

[111]Smith, *The Conceptual Practices of Power*, p. 202.

[112]Smith, *The Conceptual Practices of Power*, p. 27.

addressed as a complex of actual relations vested in texts."[113] By texts Smith is referring to official accounts that transmit and re-create the institutional order.[114] Like Berger and Luckmann, Smith views gender relations as socially constructed.

In her analysis of a cosmetic display in a shopping mall, Smith employs the documentary method to show how the cosmetic displays document the underlying pattern, or the underlying social order. She explains how the use of pastel colors (cream-colored containers with pale pink tops surrounded by pink and white flowers) and the expressions of softness through the use of lace and other delicate fabrics code femininity:

> "Softness" in the discourse of femininity expresses a tenet of its doctrines—the feminine woman is yielding, pliant, and compliant. The structuring of the coded image within the discourse enables its local appearances to function expressively. She who wears the delicate, the floating, the diaphanous fabrics, the pastel colors, presents herself as a text to be read using the doctrines of femininity as interpretive schemata.[115]

The emphasis on insider's sociology, the importance of seriously looking at the actual location of the subject, suggests that there might be a number of methodological implications to Smith's standpoint theory. Indeed, Smith admits that she is primarily concerned with the methods of writing sociology.[116]

METHODOLOGICAL IMPLICATIONS

In addition to the example of her use of the documentary method in analyzing the cosmetic display mentioned above, Dorothy Smith also employs the inner horizon. Earlier in this chapter we discussed Cicourel's critique of quantitative researchers, based on their focus on what he calls the outer horizon of scales and rankings, and the consequent omission of the inner horizon of subjective social action.

---

[113]Dorothy E. Smith, *Texts, Facts, and Femininity: Exploring the Relations of Ruling* (New York: Routledge, 1990), p. 163.

[114]Smith contrasts the difference between an account that arises directly from the local historical experience of an individual with an official account (text). She gives the example of an account of what a witness to a confrontation between police and street people saw that was published in the form of a letter in an underground newspaper, and a rebuttal of that story from the mayor's office, the product of an official inquiry. The latter was produced in an institutional process, an objectified account (text) that was not located in the perspective and experience of any particular individual. See Smith in Wallace, *Feminism and Sociological Theory*, pp. 39–40.

[115]Smith, *Texts, Facts, and Femininity*, pp. 176–77. There is some similarity here to Goffman's analysis of unspoken social assumptions about gender conveyed in magazine advertisements in his book *Gender Advertisements*. See Chapter 5.

[116]Smith, *The Everyday World as Problematic*, p. 106.

In her analysis of the work of a commission of inquiry into unexplained deaths on an infant ward in 1983, Dorothy Smith notes the discounting of women as speakers in public discourse.[117] Both doctors and nurses were called in as witnesses, but the former were treated as authorities and as equals of the judges and lawyers on the commission. By contrast, the nurses were interrupted and badgered: "one was asked if she were willing to submit to hypnosis, another if she would take a lie detector test, and yet another if she were willing to take 'truth serum.'" As a consequence the inner horizon of the nurses was discounted and omitted in the inquiry. Smith explains,

> They were never treated in any way as professional authorities whose observations of the situation on the ward, of the children's conditions, or of the actual routines of the work organization of care would be of equal relevance to the inquiry as the observations of physicians. Their knowledge was never made use of. It was not recognized as knowledge.[118]

One would assume that most or all of the doctors in the above inquiry were male, though there is no mention of it in the account. At that time the association of low status with females and high status with males was so taken for granted that it was not necessary to comment on the gender of the individuals involved.

Smith proposes that researchers organize their inquiry by asking their subjects two questions: "How does it happen to us as it does?" and "How is the world in which we act and suffer put together?"[119] An example from a recent collection of writings by scholars who worked or studied with Smith illustrates the institutional ethnography approach that she advocates.[120] Didi Khyatt, who studied the social relations of schooling experienced by lesbian high school students in Toronto, found that the work and activities of other students, teachers, guidance counselors, and administrators made lesbian and gay sexuality invisible. While these practices were not always deliberate, they were effective in creating and maintaining both the appearance that lesbian and gay sexuality did not exist, and a silence surrounding the subject inside and outside the classroom that generated a feeling of isolation in the lesbian students. One of the students, who had previously been well liked and nominated for the student council, experienced an immediate backing off on the part of the students after her coming out. She said,

> When I sit down (in the auditorium) no one will sit around me, that's the worst. They'll leave a space . . . and that's hurting me inside, because I think it's my

[117]Smith, *The Conceptual Practices of Power*, p. 102.

[118]Smith, *The Conceptual Practices of Power*, p. 102.

[119]Smith, *The Everyday World as Problematic*, p. 154.

[120]See Didi Khyatt, "Compulsory Heterosexuality: Schools and Lesbian Students," pp. 149–63 in Marie Campbell and Ann Manicom, ed., *Knowledge, Experience, and Ruling Relations* (Toronto: University of Toronto Press, 1995).

choice to come out or not, but I did come out and I'm glad of it. That's what you get when you come out.[121]

Khyatt analyzes it thus: "Their most profound sense of isolation came from being marginalized, from never being able to speak freely about their sexuality, and from almost always feeling that an essential part of their being was either dismissed, despised, or deleted from the everyday life of being a high school student."[122]

Dorothy Smith's contributions, however, go far beyond the use and clarification of phenomenological research methods. In fact, much of Dorothy Smith's work can be depicted as an enlarging and repatterning of sociological inquiry. She has stated that she does not see her work as a "totalizing theory" but rather as "a *method of inquiry*, always ongoing, opening things up, discovering . . . an inquiry relevant to the politics and practices of progressive struggle, whether of women or of other oppressed groups."[123] In this sense she is extending beyond the methodology of phenomenology and drawing heavily on the critical conflict approach.

The standpoint of women that Smith proposes does not forget the body; "it never leaves the actual location of the subject." She argues that women's experience of oppression is "grounded in male control, use, domination of our bodies." She explains,

> The knowing subject is always located in a particular spatial and temporal site, a particular configuration of the everyday/everynight world. Inquiry is directed toward exploring and explicating what she does not know—the social relations and organization pervading her world but invisible in it.[124]

It is here that Smith reveals the transformational direction of her inquiry. She makes it clear that her major concern is with "what we confront in transforming oppressive relations." She wants a sociology that is capable of "exploring and mapping actual organization and relations that are invisible but *active* in the everyday/everynight sites where people take up resistance and struggle, capable of producing a knowledge that extends and expands their and our grasp of how things are put together and hence their and our ability to organize and act effectively."[125]

Although Smith states that she uses this method of inquiry primarily from the standpoint of women in contemporary capitalism, she presents some examples of researchers who have deployed this method on other

[121]Khyatt, "Compulsory Heterosexuality," p. 152.

[122]Khyatt, "Compulsory Heterosexuality," p. 160.

[123]Dorothy E. Smith, "Sociology from Women's Experience: A Reaffirmation," *Sociological Theory* 10, no. 1 (Spring 1992): 88.

[124]Smith, "Sociology from Women's Experience: A Reaffirmation," pp. 89 and 91.

[125]Smith, "Sociology from Women's Experience," p. 96.

topics related to the relations of ruling: a "study of late nineteenth-century Bengali theater in the formation of ruling-class consciousness"; an "investigation of how teachers' work is shaped by the economic status of the homes of the children they teach"; and "the investigation of the experience of gay students in high school, which explores through that experience the distinctive social organization of their oppression."[126]

CONCLUSION

As we have seen, phenomenology is far from being conventional or traditional sociology. It is distrusted by many mainstream sociologists, particularly those who favor quantitative research. It is not surprising that phenomenologists found it difficult to get their work published in the 1970s, a dilemma they sometimes shared with symbolic interactionists. The emergence of journals like *Journal of Contemporary Ethnography* (formerly called *Urban Life and Culture*) was extremely important because it created a channel for the publication of ethnographic studies. Now, however, even a mainstream journal like *American Sociological Review* has phenomenologists serving as editors and associate editors.

In addition, an increasing number of publications devoted exclusively to theory publish the work of phenomenologists, for example, *Sociological Theory, Current Perspectives in Sociological Theory, Theory and Society*, and *Theory, Culture and Society*. For sociologists interested in applying the ideas of feminists like Dorothy Smith and Patricia Hill Collins, a number of new journals, many interdisciplinary, have emerged since the explosion of research on gender beginning in the 1960s, including *Gender and Society, Signs, Feminist Studies, Sex Roles, Resources for Feminist Research*, and *Women's Studies International Forum*.[127]

Other characteristics shared by symbolic interactionism and phenomenology include the view of the individual as an active, knowledgeable (and even sometimes emotional) subject and a disdain for any research methodology in which the individual is passive. To use C. Wright Mills's terms, both perspectives have a negative view of "grand theory" and "abstracted empiricism." Phenomenology and symbolic interactionism have different and complementary contributions to make at the level of microsociological analysis.

One of the things ethnomethodology shares with functionalism is that it has been the subject of an attack by a president of the American Sociological

---

[126]Smith, "Sociology from Women's Experience," p. 97.

[127]For an overview of the journals launched by feminists in the late 1960s and early 1970s, see Jessie Bernard, "The Dissemination of Feminist Thought: 1960 to 1988," pp. 23–33, in Wallace, *Feminism and Sociological Theory*.

Association in a presidential address. Recall that George C. Homans used his presidential address as an occasion to attack Parsons, Smelser, and the functionalists. In like manner, Lewis Coser chose in his presidential address to attack path analysis and ethnomethodology. His chief criticism was that the ethnomethodological perspective ignores "institutional factors in general, and the centrality of power in social interaction in particular."[128]

Why does Garfinkel, for instance, make trouble or violate the scene? He aims not to change the social system but simply to see what people do to bring back a semblance of order when their social world is disrupted. Garfinkel doesn't make trouble to illustrate that the social system is exploitative or to point up imbalances in power and resources, as does Dorothy Smith. Rather, in functionalist terms, Garfinkel is introducing strain into a situation and is interested in how people bring this particular situation back to equilibrium.

Berger's theory of the social construction of reality is like functionalism in defining socialization as the internalization of society's values and norms. Berger's position, however, differs from Parsons's in that the former views the individual as capable of taking a critical stance toward the social order. Berger reminds us that the social order is a human product, but unlike Dorothy Smith, he fails to address the question of whether some people are in a better position than others to create social reality. Berger's theory lacks the tools necessary for the analysis of power relationships, a shortcoming shared with ethnomethodology and symbolic interactionism. It was for this reason that Dorothy Smith combined Marx and Engels with phenomenology in order to analyze the standpoint of women and other groups who are in a subordinate position in the relations of ruling.

Phenomenology's concerns would not appeal to macrosociologists, whose main interest is in distinguishing among the origins of different social institutions and studying social change. Neither would it appeal to social scientists like George Homans, who give priority to establishing general explanatory propositions.

What is the future of phenomenology? One of the indicators that its early demise is unlikely is the current increase in publications and the continued interest in sessions devoted specifically to this perspective at annual sociological meetings, both regional and national.

---

[128]Coser, "Presidential Address: Two Methods in Search of Substance," p. 696. See Chapters 2 and 3.

CHAPTER SEVEN

Theories of Rational Choice

INTRODUCTION

Theories of rational choice assume that people are rational and base their actions on what they perceive to be the most effective means to their goals. In a world of scarce resources this means constantly weighing alternative means to alternative ends and choosing between them; hence the term rational *choice*.

Theories of this type are most closely associated with economics. Indeed, the approach can be expressed through the commonplace phrase that "there is a price for everything and everything has its price." This is not to imply, however, that conventional economic affairs—production, employment, and the sale of goods—are the only truly important facts in explaining social behavior. Rather, what rational choice theorists suggest is that the way to understand much of how people behave toward each other is by seeing them as rational decision makers in a world of scarcity.[1]

We can give a good example of how this perspective works by examining the rise in the divorce rate in recent years. Commentators have suggested a number of possible influences: affluence, changing moral values, and legal changes that make the process of divorce easier. Social scientists using a rational choice perspective start, instead, with the fact that all divorces involve individuals making choices about whether to stay married. They then ask what it is that makes many more people than in the past choose divorce.

Imagine two women in their late thirties, the first a farmer's wife in the nineteenth-century American Midwest and the second a contemporary woman in Los Angeles or Paris. The first is almost bound to stay with her husband, even if he is frequently drunk and violent. In her area there are almost no jobs open to single women, let alone divorced women with children (and no welfare benefits either). The whole family, adults and children, must work to gain a livelihood on the farm.

The modern woman, by contrast, probably has at least secretarial skills, and she can go out and look for a salaried job. She could, for example, get a job as a medical secretary and take a small apartment in a modern high-rise building. Because of the development of modern contraceptives, she need not resign herself to celibacy. Changes in the divorce law mean that, if there is property, she is clearly entitled to a share of it; current debates are about how much each side should receive, not about the principle that both should receive a share. And if there is no property to divide, she can still probably support both herself and her children on her salary alone. If a woman finds

---

[1] And of uncertainty. The fact that I cannot predict the future does not mean that I have to act at random and cannot adopt perfectly rational strategies based on what I do know. See the following discussion of the *Principles of Rationality*.

that her relationship with her husband is unsatisfactory, the choice of divorce is therefore a much more attractive one.

You can probably think of several people you know who have made that choice, and of others who do not see any reason to marry at all. For others, the decision to have children outside marriage is itself a rational one today where it would not have been a century ago, because of changes in government programs and spending. As Elijah Anderson points out, in the urban ghettos "in cold economic terms, a baby can be an asset which is without a doubt an important fact behind exploitative sex and out-of-wedlock babies. Public assistance is one of the few reliable sources of money."[2] Rational choice theorists approach divorce, the decision whether to marry, and a wide range of other social behavior in terms of people's choices and the considerations that enter into them.

In contemporary sociology, rational choice approaches first became widely known in the context of "exchange theory." Exchange theorists conceptualize social interaction as an exchange of tangible or intangible goods and services, ranging from food and shelter to social approval or sympathy. People choose whether to participate in an exchange after they have examined the costs and the rewards of alternative courses of action and have chosen the most attractive. In Simmel's words, "all contacts among men rest on the schema of giving and returning the equivalence."[3]

The best-known works on exchange theory were written in the 1960s, after which, for a number of years, interest in a rational choice perspective declined among sociologists. In other disciplines the opposite was true. Political scientists are increasingly concerned with "public choice," or the application of the rational choice perspective to the public goods with which political science is concerned. Thus topics such as voting behavior and union membership have been analyzed in terms of the exchange of votes or membership for specific rewards,[4] while the "game theory" aspects of rational choice dominate current work on international relations and military strategy.[5] In social psychology Thibault and Kelley's analysis of groups is based on the premise that whether people choose to have anything to do with each other depends on whether they get more out of the relationship

---

[2]Elijah Anderson, *Streetwise: Race, Class and Change in an Urban Community* (Chicago: University of Chicago Press, 1990), p. 136.

[3]Georg Simmel, *The Sociology of Georg Simmel* (Glencoe, Ill.: The Free Press, 1950).

[4]Key texts include Anthony Downs, *An Economic Theory of Democracy* (New York: Harper and Row, 1957), and Mancur Olson, *The Logic of Collective Action: Public Goods and the Theory of Groups* (Cambridge: Harvard University Press, 1965).

[5]Game theory, formulated in terms of rational expectations and strategies for winning, is the variant of rational choice analysis that is most important here; see pp. 322–27. Stewart Wood and Iain McLean provide an overview in "Recent Work in Game Theory and Coalition Theory," *Political Studies* 43 (1995): 703–17. See especially Michael Nicholson, *Rationality and the Analysis of International Conflict* (Cambridge: Cambridge University Press, 1992), and Peter Ordeshook, *A Political Theory Primer* (London: Routledge, 1992).

than they would from alternatives.[6] Much recent work in biology and, especially, sociobiology, similarly starts from a rational choice perspective.[7]

Perhaps because the approach seems so productive in other disciplines, there is now a renewed interest in rational choice among sociologists. Work directly concerned with social exchange and rational choice is growing in volume, for example, in the journal *Rationality and Society*. While most is concerned with individual and small group behavior, a number of works on institutional, macro-level issues also start explicitly from a rational choice perspective. In particular, James Coleman's massive work *The Foundations of Social Theory* makes the case for explaining social systems by working upward from a theory of rational individual behavior.[8]

Within the sociological tradition, small group analysis is most strongly associated with the theories of George Homans, and institutional analysis with the exchange theory of Peter Blau. This chapter discusses the work of both theorists in some detail, relating it to that of other theorists working from a similar perspective, including Richard Emerson, Raymond Boudon, and Michael Hechter. It also considers the related approach of network theory, which, like much of exchange theory, concentrates on the "emergent properties" of interactions between individuals. The final section discusses the work of James Coleman and sets it in the context of the growing interest of rational choice theorists in explaining institutional development.

INTELLECTUAL ROOTS

Exchange theory's stress on people's rationality bears a strong resemblance to the outlook of many nineteenth-century thinkers. In the nineteenth century both economists and many philosophers emphasized individual activity and choice. The utilitarians, for example, described people as self-interested in the sense of desiring pleasure, being averse only to pain, and actively pursuing their desires. They also argued that behavior was more or less moral according to the amount of utility it bestowed on numbers of individuals. Economics built upon the work of Adam Smith and retained his emphasis on understanding economic activity as the result of individuals' myriad choices and decisions.[9]

---

[6]Harold H. Kelley and John W. Thibault, *Interpersonal Relations: A Theory of Interdependence* (New York: John Wiley, 1978). See also John W. Thibault and Harold H. Kelley, *The Social Psychology of Groups* (New York: John Wiley, 1959).

[7]See Chapter 8.

[8]See Part Three of this chapter.

[9]Welfare economics, the normative part of mainstream economics, assumes, with the utilitarians, that courses of action should be judged according to the total amount of utility they bestow on individuals.

Early sociologists, by contrast, showed little interest in an exchange perspective. The sole major exception was Georg Simmel, who, as we have seen,[10] was interested in identifying universal characteristics of human behavior. He was particularly concerned with why and how people move from isolation to different forms of contact with each other.[11] Like modern social exchange theorists, he argued that their motive was to satisfy needs and pursue individual goals. Simmel also suggested that although people may not receive equal returns, their interactions are always characterized by some form of reciprocity and should therefore be viewed as kinds of exchange. Blau, in particular, uses Simmel's work.

However, Simmel's concept of interaction as exchange was not elaborated or much used by the succeeding generation of sociologists. The major intellectual influences on those sociologists who have adopted a rational choice perspective are found instead in other areas of social science: anthropology, economics, psychology, and, more recently, public choice theory in political science and the theory of games.

Anthropology and the Importance of the Gift

Many of the great twentieth-century anthropologists have been concerned with the central role exchange plays in social life. One of the most important was Bronislaw Malinowski (1884–1942), whose emphasis on long periods of fieldwork and intimate acquaintance with a particular culture played a crucial role in the development of modern anthropology. He spent many years among the Trobriand Islanders of the Melanesian Islands, where he concluded that mutual exchange is the basis of social cohesion.

> Trobriand society is founded on the principle of legal status . . . [involving] well-balanced chains of reciprocal services. The whole division into totemic clans, clans of a local nature and into village communities, is characterized by . . . a game of give and take. . . . [Moreover] reciprocity, the give-and-take principle, reigns supreme also . . . within the nearest groups of kinsmen. . . . [The] most unselfish relation, that between a man and his sister, [is] founded on mutuality and the repayment of services.[12]

The Gift. In examining exchange we can draw a distinction between, on the one hand, institutions that have no independent purpose outside of exchanging or gift giving and, on the other, "instrumental" exchange, which

[10]Chapter 3, "Intellectual Roots."

[11]D. Levine, E. Carter, and E. Miller, "Simmel's Influence on American Sociology II," *American Journal of Sociology* 81 (1976): 112–32.

[12]Bronislaw Malinowski, *Crime and Custom in Savage Society* (London: Routledge and Kegan Paul, 1926), pp. 46–48.

characterizes interactions that take place primarily so that people may obtain things they want. Anthropology has paid special attention to the former.

Among the best-known examples of institutionalized reciprocal gift giving is the Kula, a Trobriand ceremony that fascinated Malinowski. At regular intervals the men from an island community would row out toward another island, meet its inhabitants, and exchange bracelets for necklaces of shells. These bracelets and necklaces were highly prized, but they had no obvious use. Instead they were kept until the next exchange and then passed on again, so that the same ceremonial jewelry traveled year after year around the Kula Ring.

Anthropologists and exchange theorists argue that a crucial aspect of such exchanges is the way they bind society together through mutual obligations and so increase social cohesion. It is not difficult to find other examples. Homer's Greek kings exchanged gifts continually,[13] and so do modern Americans—Christmas is unlikely to be uncommercialized in a hurry. Indeed, the role of gifts in establishing friendly relations is demonstrated every time we offer a visitor coffee. The reciprocal friendly gesture of accepting makes endless cups of tepid liquid an occupational hazard for social workers or the clergy.

Anthropologists have argued that there are also less obvious exchanges of a similar kind: the exchanges of marriage partners. Tribal societies generally have complex and precise rules about marriage—for example, that a girl should always (or never) marry a father's sister's son and a boy, conversely, a mother's brother's daughter. Claude Lévi-Strauss, the famous French anthropologist, attempted to make sense of these rules by analyzing kinship groups and marriages as a system of alliances. From this viewpoint, wives are the most valuable gifts of all and hence the most effective exchange with which to cement an alliance and ensure social cohesion.[14]

Anthropologists are also aware of the relationship between power and the exchange of gifts. In his book *The Gift* Marcel Mauss (1872–1950) emphasized the "obligatory and interested" nature of gifts and other forms of exchange.[15] Gifts, he argued, are intrinsically bound up with the way power and precedence are determined in a society, for *receivers of gifts are at a disadvantage* vis-à-vis the donor unless they can discharge their obligations by making an equal return. Marshall Sahlins noted the contrast between the generalized reciprocity that occurs within a family, where people do not keep precise count of favors done, and the way in which, within any village or tribe, people keep careful count. Over time there is quite exact balancing

[13]M. I. Finley, *The World of Odysseus*, rev. ed. (Harmondsworth, Middlesex: Penguin Books, 1972).

[14]Claude Lévi-Strauss, *The Elementary Structures of Kinship*, rev. ed. (London: Eyre and Spotiswoode, 1969); Robin Fox, *Kinship and Marriage* (Harmondsworth, Middlesex: Penguin Books, 1967).

[15]Marcel Mauss, *The Gift* (Glencoe, Ill.: The Free Press, 1954), p. 1.

of what is given and received.[16] This concern with the role of exchanges in creating power relationships has been adopted by exchange theorists, especially Peter Blau.

A characteristic of some sociological variants of rational choice theory—and particularly exchange theory—is their concern with the existence of recurrent generalized norms governing social exchange.[17] Most often cited is the existence of a binding *norm of reciprocity*, and for this, too, the debt is to anthropology. Mauss, for example, argues that one must make return or incur hostility or loss of status from people other than those directly involved.[18] Reciprocity is a rule enforced by society. Malinowski is somewhat less precise, but he too implies the existence of a socially enforced obligation to reciprocate.

Economics, Profit, and Price

The central corpus of economic theory developed by such great economists as Adam Smith, David Ricardo, and Carl Menger rests on certain premises about individual psychology and its implications for people's behavior in the marketplace. Rational choice theorists similarly start with individual psychology[19] and apply the same premises to behavior that does not involve the exchange of material goods for money, the production of goods for sale, or the workings of the economy. Like economists, they emphasize how important it is that we live in a world of scarcity, where we cannot have all the goods, or status, or emotional support we might like. Rational choice theorists adopt four of the basic propositions of economics:

1. Individuals are rational profit maximizers, making decisions on the basis of their tastes and preferences.
2. The more of something an individual has, the less interested he or she will be in yet more of it.
3. The prices at which goods and services will be sold in a free market are determined directly by the tastes of prospective buyers and sellers. The greater the demand for a good, the more "valuable" it will be and the higher will be its price. The greater the supply, the less valuable it will be and the lower will be its price.
4. Goods will generally be more expensive if they are supplied by a monopolist than if they are supplied by a number of firms in competition with each other.

[16]Marshall Sahlins, *Stone Age Economics* (Hawthorne, New York: Aldine de Gruyter, 1966/1972).

[17]This is especially striking because, on the whole, rational choice theorists do not like normative explanations.

[18]See Alvin Gouldner, "The Norm of Reciprocity: A Preliminary Statement," *American Sociological Review* 25 (1960): 161–78.

[19]This is most explicit in the case of George Homans's theories of elementary social behavior.

The first two propositions are assumptions about people's basic psychological makeup. For all their apparent simplicity, they can be used to make some concrete predictions about behavior. They are, moreover, far from universally accepted. For example, for many years people have debated whether there exists a "cycle of poverty" in which people are trapped, largely by their own values and actions, for generation after generation. Some proponents of this view have argued that one reason for the continuing poverty of the underdeveloped nations is that peasants in these countries are too conservative and wedded to tradition to adopt new farming techniques.

This argument implies a sort of irrationality in human behavior; after all, what is at stake is not some esoteric objective but a universal human desire for material comfort and security. It is also an argument that economists and rational choice theorists find inadequate. They assume that peasants are as interested in increasing their profits (or "utility") as anyone else, and they are mistrustful of "culture" or the "weight of tradition" as an explanation of behavior. Thus, throughout the world, peasants tend to farm several scattered plots of land, even though, on average, consolidating these plots and strips could raise output by at least 10 percent. For people who are often close to starvation, this seems quite irrational, until you realize that scattered plots make any *particular* family less at risk from local disasters such as mildew, flooding, or wandering animals. The village community has no way of insuring people against the risks of consolidation, so peasants, quite rationally, stick with an "individual-level, safety-first" strategy.[20]

Economists tend to concentrate on situations in which they can compare the financial benefits of alternative courses of action. They can predict with considerable success that shifts in payoffs will produce shifts in people's choices; for example, if the prestige of teaching drops, as it has in the United States and the United Kingdom, and its relative pay also falls or even just fails to improve, there will be a drop in the average quality of people entering the profession.[21] Compared to economists, sociologists often are interested in situations where there is no convenient measure of price or profit.[22] Even here, however, rational choice theorists believe that one can fre-

---

[20]Samuel L. Popkin, *The Rational Peasant: The Political Economy of Rural Society in Vietnam* (Berkeley: University of California Press, 1979). See especially pp. 49–51. Strictly speaking, the problem with consolidation is that it produces *greater variance* in yields from year to year.

[21]This is true irrespective of the fact that some exceptional people will continue to see it as a vocation. It is important to emphasize that economics does not claim to be able to predict what a given individual will do; it predicts general movements "at the margin." For a discussion of the links between wages and teacher quality, see E. Hanushek and S. Rivkin, "Understanding the 20th Century Growth in U.S. School Spending," Working Paper 5547, Cambridge, Mass.: National Bureau of Economic Research Inc., 1996.

[22]Richard Emerson made some attempts to provide a theory of value in social exchange; see p. 310. For a discussion of whether utility maximization is a testable proposition or a tautology, see pp. 310–11.

quently compare the relative payoffs of different actions clearly. Therefore one can explain or predict people's actions accurately even without being able to put an exact value on each possibility.

The second of the propositions listed, which is also a statement about human psychology, is the law of "diminishing marginal utility." This law declares that as the amount of a good consumed increases, its marginal utility (that is, the extra utility that one gains by consuming another unit of it) tends to decrease and so, therefore, does the amount people will pay for it. For example, if it is a hot day and you are very thirsty, you will be prepared to pay a lot for a first cold drink. A second drink, however, will be worth considerably less, and you may well forgo it if you can get it only by paying a lot.

If you think back to high school dating, you can see this same process at work. At first you probably valued any proof that you were not unattractive, and so you dated people in whom you were only mildly interested or who made great demands on you. But every relationship that made you more self-confident correspondingly made a date as such less valuable. You could hold out for more or be prepared to give less, and you could end a relationship that in the past might have been important enough to you to continue. Homans in particular draws on this proposition in his analyses of interpersonal and small group behavior.

The third and fourth of the propositions that rational choice theorists share with economists concern the price at which people will exchange things. Again, sociologists extend these propositions beyond the marketplace and argue that other forms of social interaction or exchange also involve prices that are determined by supply, demand, and the degree to which would-be buyers can get what they want only from a single, monopolistic supplier. For example, theorists analyzing the "marriage market" in these terms would point out that it is successful and wealthy men who, on the average, have the prettiest wives. They explain this by the fact that success (or power) and female beauty are both valued and scarce qualities, each of which can therefore command a high price. When people refer to a younger, pretty second (or third) wife as a "trophy wife" they are acknowledging exactly this phenomenon.

An individual who monopolizes valued qualities and powers is in an even better position. A pre–twentieth-century monarch, for example, could obtain as casual mistresses women who would hold out for marriage with any other men. Recent work in the rational choice tradition has focused increasingly on the importance of complete or partial monopolies as a way of analyzing power and dependence.

While anthropology contributes a view of society as a network of exchanges regulated by the norm of reciprocity, it is from economics that rational choice theorists draw most of their basic propositions. Consequently, their approach also shares economics' limitations. Its users are generally not concerned with explaining the origins of people's beliefs, values, and tastes but take them as given and address themselves to the behavior that follows. Their focus on rational and purposive actions also limits what they have to say about the role of the emotions in explaining human behavior. Fortunately, this is not as restrictive as it sounds because there are a good number of basic and universal human desires that people seek to realize in a more or less consciously purposive way. Assuming no more than that people value money, power, social esteem, and, of course, survival, rational choice theorists can build up quite detailed theories about friendship, status differences, and social discontent—just as similar assumptions about what makes up "self-interest" underlie conflict theorists' detailed analyses of inequality, conflict, and change.

Behaviorist Psychology and the Theory of Games

Especially in analyses of individual behavior and its consequences, there are two final but important influences on the rational choice approach. Behaviorist psychology was important for the development of earlier versions of exchange theory, while, in more recent years, concepts and models drawn from the theory of games have increasingly been adopted.[23]

In formulating his version of exchange theory, George Homans turned to the behavioral school of experimental psychology founded by his friend B. F. Skinner. He wanted direct evidence of the validity of propositions that economists tend to treat as assumptions. Behavioral psychology takes the position that in studying behavior, one can avoid hypotheses about unobservable phenomena. Experimental psychologists of this school try to avoid making statements about the "black box" of a human (or animal) mind that cannot be directly tested or falsified. Instead they attempt to construct a satisfactory theory of behavior that deals only with the overt responses that result from observable stimuli—not with the thoughts or feelings that lead people or animals to react to stimuli in a particular way. Mead and the symbolic interactionists argue against this theory vehemently, stressing instead the importance of internal and unobservable perceptions and meanings.

In fact, exchange theory, in common with rational choice theories as a whole, does make statements about unobservable phenomena, especially about people's values. For exchange theory, the importance of behavioral psychology's propositions is that they are consistent with economics; thus Richard Emerson, to whose work we refer later in this chapter,[24] uses the

---

[23]The theory of games has itself reached a wider audience because its approach is used by many of the most influential writers on public choice. The way in which rational choice theories cross disciplinary boundaries is encapsulated in the award of a Nobel Prize for Economics to James Buchanan, whose work on public choice has had an enormous effect on political science.

[24]See the section on *Power, Equity, and Games.*

vocabulary of operant conditioning in much of his exchange theory. The congruence of economics and psychology strengthens exchange theory's argument that these principles apply to all areas of social life. Homans writes, "We believe that the propositions of behavioral psychology are the general explanatory propositions of all the social sciences. Accordingly, they are the general propositions of economics."[25]

Psychology is also an important influence in the area in which sociological variants of rational choice theory are most distinct: their concern with the "morality of social exchange."[26] Either "economic man" does not recognize the existence of a raw deal—or a fair price—or he takes what comes to him in silence. This hardly describes the people we know (and are), full of ideas and disagreements about what is our due or what we ought to pay or get. The more the issue in question affects our daily lives, the more vehement our concern with what is right or fair. The debate about the division of property after a divorce (and the justification for palimony) offers a fruitful hunting ground for those in search of conflicting notions of justice.

Although experimental psychologists are not concerned with justice per se, they are interested in what happens when expectations are not fulfilled—for example, when a looked-for reward fails to materialize. Their evidence on the way people and animals react is the basis of much of Homans's discussion of "distributive justice."[27]

The theory of games, by comparison, is much concerned with particular sets of choices and alternatives and with identifying recurrent dilemmas and strategies. In discussing conflict theory, we noted that it tends to see social life as a zero-sum game in which one person's gain is necessarily another's loss. However, games theory as a whole is concerned with a far wider range of situations than this. Its best-known example is the "prisoner's dilemma," discussed in detail in this chapter,[28] but the theory's value and interest to sociologists lie not in the range of different possible games devised but in the number of social situations that can be seen as examples of one or another type. Sociologists interested in phenomena as diverse as the expansion of higher education, the lobbying success of the Sierra Club,

---

[25]George C. Homans, *Social Behavior: Its Elementary Forms*, rev. ed. (New York: Harcourt Brace Jovanovich, 1974), p. 67. Copyright 1974 by Harcourt Brace Jovanovich, Inc. Reprinted by permission of the publishers. See also George C. Homans, "Fundamental Social Processes," in Neil J. Smelser, ed., *Sociology* (New York: John Wiley, 1967), pp. 27–78.

[26]Anthony Heath, *Rational Choice and Social Exchange* (Cambridge: Cambridge University Press, 1976). In discussing the distinction between the rational and the moral elements in social exchange, as well as for his numerous other perceptive remarks, we are indebted to Anthony Heath's analyses of exchange theory.

[27]In recent years sociobiologists have speculated about the extent to which there may be a biological basis for the norm of reciprocity, given its universal nature (see pp. 299 and 391). However, although sociobiology and rational choice theory are both influenced by game theory and use similar types of model, few rational choice theorists put forward biological factors as major explanatory variables.

[28]See the section on *Power, Equity, and Games*.

and the prospects of peace between the superpowers have discovered that finding the underlying "game structure" helps them to analyze both past events and likely developments.

Most of the perspectives discussed in this text concentrate on either the micro *or* the macro level. Although this division applies to most individual theorists working in the rational choice tradition, it is not true of the perspective as a whole. While some of the best-known work covered here—especially that associated with exchange theory—is focused on small group behavior, other theorists are expressly concerned with structural and institutional analysis.

Part One of this chapter covers theory and research work that are concerned predominantly with individual actions and behavior. It looks first at the basic propositions associated with exchange theory, especially the work of George Homans, and then at the way in which a number of other theorists, including Richard Emerson, have extended the analysis of individual behavior. Part Two looks at rational choice perspectives on social structure as exemplified by the exchange theory of Peter Blau, and describes the related analyses offered by network theorists. Part Three discusses the work of James Coleman, which incorporates and builds on an influential body of theory about the way in which social interaction and exchange can create trust and generate social order. Finally, the conclusion summarizes the strengths and weaknesses of the rational choice approach.

PART ONE

Rational Choice, Social Exchange, and Individual Behavior

GEORGE HOMANS: ELEMENTARY SOCIAL BEHAVIOR

Modern social exchange theory is associated primarily with two sociologists: George Caspar Homans and Peter M. Blau. George Homans (1910–1989) was a Boston Brahmin, born—most unusually for a sociologist—into one of the city's great Yankee families.[29] In his autobiography Homans notes,

> To use words that now provoke scorn, the Brahmins were gentlemen and ladies. Other people were not. . . . We were not able to muster up "pride in our port, defiance in our eye"—whom were we going to defy?—and seldom talked about class. Nevertheless we were class conscious. By profession all sociologists are class conscious but usually about other persons' classes, not their own.[30]

[29]Homans's mother was a niece of Henry Adams.
[30]George Caspar Homans, *Coming to My Senses: The Autobiography of a Sociologist* (New Brunswick, N.J.: Transaction Books, 1984).

At Harvard Homans studied English, not sociology. Nonetheless, he maintained,

> If I learned no theoretical, I learned much practical sociology. One of the routes by which a person gets interested in this subject is by living in an environment in which people are highly conscious of social relations. This rule holds good more often of microsociologists like me, who are concerned with the face-to-face interactions of persons, than of macrosociologists, concerned with the characteristics of whole societies. For us microsociologists the laws of sociology are the laws of snobbery, and an undergraduate of my background found Harvard to a high degree "socially conscious"—in the bad sense of the phrase.[31]

The "final clubs" were at the core of prewar Harvard, and membership depended on a mixture of qualities—personal as well as those related to class, religion, and ethnic background. (Homans himself, intellectual and rather sardonic, was by no means the "right" sort of person.) The structure of small groups and the way in which social approval is engendered—the core, in fact, of Homans's later theory—are indeed typified in the operation of "final clubs," fraternities and sororities.

Homans spent his whole academic career at Harvard, interrupted only by four and a half years in the wartime navy. He came to sociology "because I had nothing better to do" when a postgraduation newspaper job disappeared with the Depression. Unemployed and in Cambridge, he accepted an invitation to attend a seminar on Pareto, whose sociology was then almost unknown in America. Homans ended up collaborating with Charles Curtis on *An Introduction to Pareto* and soon thereafter was elected to the Harvard Society of Fellows as a sociologist. Homans, who never earned—or studied for—a doctorate, was a president of the American Sociological Association, and in 1988, while professor emeritus at Harvard, he was awarded the association's Distinguished Scholarship Award. In an obituary notice in the Harvard Gazette, his colleagues noted that

> Homans was a dedicated teacher who generously gave time to his students. In the way he related to students and colleagues, it was difficult to detect any difference based on their age, sex, rank, or social status. He had little patience in the late 1960s with the "wafflings of the foolish, hypocritical, and self-righteous 'liberals,' " but he believed in civility without regard to status and numbered among his friends, students and colleagues of all political persuasions.[32]

The influence of Pareto remains clear in Homans's later work, notably in his concern with the basic laws of psychology that underpin human behavior, his receptiveness to concepts generally associated with economics,

[31]Homans, *Coming to My Senses*, p. 9.
[32]Minute placed upon the records at a meeting of the Harvard Faculty of Arts and Sciences, February 11, 1992; reprinted in the Harvard Gazette, March 6, 1992.

and his desire to establish full deductive theories or explanations. However, Homans's work was also always stimulated by his wide range of friends working in other disciplines and involved both anthropology and English history, in which he taught a course for many years.

The results of Homans's interest in small group research were synthesized first in *The Human Group*.[33] He then turned to the basic principles of human activity, which he came to see as underlying small group behavior. These he set out in his most important book on what has come to be known as exchange theory, *Social Behavior: Its Elementary Forms*.[34]

By "elementary social behavior" Homans means behavior that appears and reappears whether or not people plan on its doing so. Homans believed elementary social behavior can be explained by basic propositions about individual psychology and motivation. He argued consistently that satisfactory explanations of social phenomena must ultimately be psychological explanations; that psychological principles are the basic building blocks of explanation in all the social sciences; and, indeed, that there are no such things as purely sociological explanations—something, he points out, that is also true of history without apparently causing historians much discomfort.[35]

Presidents of the American Sociological Association frequently have used the presidential address to make controversial statements about the state of sociology. In 1964 Homans employed his to argue that because functionalism had rejected psychological propositions, it had been unable to generate explanations. "Let us get men back in, and let us put some blood in them," he argued.[36] His theory is a worked-out statement of this position.

The general statements that Homans presents are accepted, more or less intact, by other social exchange theorists and sociologists in the rational choice tradition. However, Homans's work sets them out most clearly as an interlocking deductive system. As most recently stated, they are:

1. *The success proposition.* For all actions taken by persons, the more often a particular action of a person is rewarded, the more likely the person is to perform that action.
2. *The stimulus proposition.* If in the past the occurrence of a particular stimulus, or set of stimuli, has been the occasion on which a person's action has been rewarded, then the more similar the present stimuli are to the past ones, the more likely the person is to perform the action, or some similar action now.
3. *The value proposition.* The more valuable to a person is the result of his action, the more likely he is to perform the action.

---

[33]George C. Homans, *The Human Group* (New York: Harcourt Brace Jovanovich, 1950).

[34]George C. Homans, *Social Behavior: Its Elementary Forms* (New York: Harcourt Brace and World, 1961). Reprinted by permission of the publishers. References in this chapter are mostly to the 1974 revised edition, which incorporates substantial changes in Homans's theories.

[35]George C. Homans, "A Life of Synthesis," in Irving L. Horowitz, ed., *Sociological Self-Images: A Collective Portrait* (Beverly Hills, Calif.: Sage, 1969).

[36]George C. Homans, "Bringing Men Back In," *American Sociological Review* 29, no. 5 (December 1964), 809–18.

The rationality proposition (combining 1 through 3). In choosing between alternative actions a person will choose that one for which, as perceived by him at the time, the value, V, of the result, multiplied by the probability, p, of getting the result, is the greater.

4. *The deprivation-satiation proposition.* The more often in the recent past a person has received a particular reward, the less valuable any further unit of that reward becomes for him.

5. *The aggression-approval proposition.*
   a. When a person's action does not receive the reward he expected, or receives punishment he did not expect, he will be angry; he becomes more likely to perform aggressive behavior, and results of such behavior become more valuable to him (the frustration-aggression hypothesis).
   b. When a person's action receives the reward he expected, especially a greater reward than he expected, or does not receive punishment he expected, he will be pleased; he becomes more likely to perform approving behavior, and the results of such behavior become more valuable to him.[37]

We have noted that Homans is known as a major exchange theorist, but in these propositions the term "exchange" nowhere appears. This is because Homans is talking not about a particular sort of exchanging behavior but about universal principles, applying to all forms of social activity, and incorporating human emotions as well.[38] In doing so he envisages "social behavior as an exchange of activity . . . between at least two persons."[39] He sees his main task as explaining "the repeated exchanges of rewards between men which we shall refer to as interpersonal relationships."[40] However, Homans actually disliked the way "my theory . . . got stuck with the name of 'exchange theory.' . . . This was too bad . . . because it suggested that the theory was a special kind of theory, whereas it is a general behavioral psychology."[41]

An emphasis on general principles of human action lies at the core of all theories of rational choice. This section examines in some detail Homans's application of his five propositions, as well as related work on individual behavior and its wider social consequences.

The Principles of Rationality

The first three principles of human behavior that Homans advances are essentially a statement of human rationality. To argue that people repeat rewarding actions, respond to stimuli associated with such rewards, and act

---

[37]Homans, *Social Behavior*, rev. ed., pp. 16–50.

[38]Sociologists are increasingly aware of the importance of emotion in explaining human behavior, although such work mostly falls outside the rational choice paradigm. See especially the conclusion to this chapter, and Chapter 5 Part 4.

[39]Homans, *Social Behavior*, 1st ed., p. 13.

[40]Homans, *Social Behavior*, rev. ed., p. 51.

[41]Homans, *Coming to My Senses*, p. 338.

on the basis of the values they attach to things is, in fact, to state that they are rational—though *not* to say that they are always right about what the most rewarding or rational choice would be.

This sounds tame and obvious enough, but it is not necessarily either. Criminology draws on this principle when examining the deterrent effects of arrest rates and sentencing. A principle of rational behavior implies that, other things being equal, the more often crimes succeed, the more people will commit them. The evidence is largely consistent with this argument, and the obverse is also true.[42]

Parts of the Washington, D.C. area have in recent years experienced a murder epidemic involving, for the most part, young men buying and selling drugs (especially crack). In an interview with the *Washington Post*, the city's then Assistant Chief of Police made the point that, given the dealers' values and opportunities, what we were seeing was purely rational behavior:

> Something has changed to produce the kids that I see. Let me give you an example. Not long ago, I went with the homicide squad to arrest a kid who was 18 years old. This kid had a hardworking mother who is doing her best . . . a working family that is trying to give him the benefit of a good value system. And yet this kid . . . is defining himself in terms of material things—not in terms of his mother's values . . . He's got to have it all, right now. He's got to have a 4 × 4 truck, he's got to have a big car, he's got to have the most expensive jewelry, he's got to have designer clothes. . . . He's got to get what he wants, right now.
>
> I went back to my alma mater, Eastern High School, a couple of years ago, and talked to some students about drugs and money. One kid said to me, "Chief Fulwood, you're full of bullshit. Why should I go and make $3.50 or $4.25 an hour at a regular job? I can make that in one minute on the street . . . How much do you make, Chief?" I told him . . . He smiled. "I can make more than that." *Those kids can make as much money as they're willing to take risks.*[43]

The rational choice approach proves similarly useful in looking at another of our cities' enduring problems: the poor education so many children obtain in inner-city schools and the overt war between teacher and pupils that characterizes many inner-city classrooms. If people are basically rational, those pupils who are most involved in warfare and disruption and least interested in studying and cooperating with the teacher presumably find studying less valuable than its alternatives. Leaving aside for the

[42]See, for example, Isaac Erlich, "Participation in Illegal Activities. A Theoretical and Empirical Investigation," *Journal of Political Economy* 81 (May–June 1973): 521–65; and "The Deterrent Effect of Capital Punishment: A Question of Life and Death," *American Economic Review* LXV, no. 3 (June 1975): 397–417; Gennaro F. Vito and Ronald M. Holmes, *Criminology: Theory, Research and Policy* (Belmont, Calif.: Wadsworth, 1994); D. A. Smith and P. A. Gartin, "Specifying Specific Deterrence: The Influence of Arrest on Future Criminal Activity," *American Sociological Review* 54 (Feb. 1989): 94–106.

[43]Extracted from the transcript of an interview with Isaac Fulwood, Jr., assistant chief of police for field operations, Washington, D.C. *Washington Post* (Outlook section), January 1, 1989. Italics ours.

moment the reasons for their choice, this implies that if you increase the rewards of studying and thereby alter the relative value of pupils' alternatives, you will also increase the number who choose cooperation over war.

George Richmond taught in just such a New York elementary school, where both his arguments and pleas for cooperation and his threats and punishments failed. Looking for some way out of the impasse, he came to see the traditional schoolroom as a feudal society, where students were "tied to the land—to room 308," having no private property and requiring his permission to exercise their most basic liberties. His response was to devise what he called the "microeconomy game" and to use it in the classroom, as he describes here:

> The next morning I arrived in 308 with a plan, and with some materials. I immediately began a discussion that eventually altered everything. . . .
> "From now on, I'm going to buy compositions with this." I held up a bundle of paper money that I had mimeographed the day before. "These are soul dollars. They come in ones, fives, twenties, hundreds, and five hundreds. You'll also get a dollar for each point that you score on a spelling or a math test."
> "Hey, Mr. Richmond," Sandoval called. "You expect us to get rich off that phony stuff? Man, if I take that phony-baloney down to the candy store all it gonna buy me is a kick in the ass."
> "Patience, Sandoval, patience. You want to know what you get for this money, right?"
> "Yeah," they chorused.
> "At the end of each month, I'm going to bring books, brownies, cookies, soda, and other things to school and auction them off to the highest bidder. That means that the people with the most of this phony-baloney get what they want."
> "You mean this money buys things, real things?"
> "Yes. . . . Your parents work, right?"
> A couple of kids shook their heads.
> "Well, some of them do. They trade their work for dollars. Then they trade their dollars for food that somebody else's work produced. Well, you work too, but in school. And I'm going to pay you for your work because it's valuable to me. Then I'm going to bring stuff—candy, soda, and other things—and you'll trade your work for food just the way your parents do."[44]

Students could also be paid for classroom jobs, and those who wanted them found them. The results were spectacular. "Those who took jobs performed enthusiastically. Students doubled their academic output."[45]

In spite of its apparent usefulness in explanation, the idea of rationality, especially the idea that people choose courses of action on the basis of their potential value, has come under more attack than any other part of exchange theory. This is partly because Homans originally advanced the value propo-

[44]George Richmond, *The Micro-Society School: A Real World in Miniature* (New York: Harper and Row, 1973), specified excerpts from pp. 15, 24–26, 31, 33–35. Copyright 1973 by George Richmond. Reprinted by permission of John Hawkins and Associates, Inc. The microeconomy game, described fully in Richmond's book, was rather more complicated and closer to Monopoly than this excerpt implies.

[45]Richmond, *The Micro-Society School*, p. 31.

sition as an empirically verifiable proposition.[46] Many of his critics argued that it was a tautology and so true by definition; or, in practice, untestable; or, in some cases, both at once! More recently, the late Richard Emerson attempted to develop a theory of value in social exchange. He noted that economics focuses almost entirely on transactions where money is involved and where there is therefore an agreed unit of value; and he argued that sociology needed something more. Because it is concerned with the "interpersonal comparison of benefits from exchange," it also needs a "concept of subjective value or utility possessing a nonarbitrary origin and unit of measure."[47] In other words, we need a way of measuring the value of things to people that goes beyond deducing things after the event, using the benefit of hindsight—beyond, for example, saying that "we know she prefers a business career to helping people *because* she took business courses and chose a business internship."

If we had such an independent measure of how much people value things, we could, of course, test the value proposition directly. However, Emerson did not succeed in establishing one; and we would question whether this is ever a viable proposition. In the final section of this chapter we return to the question of whether the assumptions of a rational choice perspective are open to serious challenge, as well as to the issue of its sociological scope. Here we note simply that sociologists in the rational choice or exchange theory tradition can plausibly assume that certain values and objectives are very common, if not universal. They can and do, like conflict theorists, assume that people value survival, approval, and power; and they can then predict behavior accordingly. Assumptions are, after all, not arbitrary. They stand or fall by whether theories incorporating them produce the goods, and here the value proposition does rather well.[48]

What *is* true is that the value proposition on its own is often an inadequate explanation of—or guide to—behavior. On many occasions people are in a situation of uncertainty or risk, where they cannot be sure of the outcomes of their actions or, therefore, which is the most valuable alternative. It

[46]Homans, *Social Behavior*, 1st ed., p. 43.

[47]Richard M. Emerson, "Toward a Theory of Value in Social Exchange," in Karen S. Cook, ed., *Social Exchange Theory* (Newbury Park, Calif.: Sage, 1987), p. 12.

[48]Those interested in following up the debate are referred to R. Maris, "The Logical Adequacy of Homans's Social Theory," *American Sociological Review* 35 (1970): 1069–81; Morton Deutsch, "Homans in the Skinner Box," in H. Turk and R. L. Simpson, ed., *Institutions and Social Exchange: The Sociologies of Talcott Parsons and George C. Homans* (Indianapolis: Bobbs-Merrill, 1971); Stephen Turner, "The Logical Adequacy of 'The Logical Adequacy of Homans' Social Theory,'" *American Sociological Review* 36 (1971): 706; K. Cook and M. Levi, ed., *The Limits of Rationality* (Chicago: University of Chicago Press, 1990); *Sociological Theory* 9.2 (1991); Michael Inbar, "The Violation of Normative Rules and the Issue of Rationality in Individual Judgments" in Jon Clark, ed., *James S. Coleman* (London: Falmer, 1966); Anthony Heath, *Rational Choice and Social Exchange*; and Homans, *Social Behavior*, rev. ed., pp. 33–37. Neither Homans nor a number of his critics seem to distinguish clearly between an untestable proposition and a strictly tautologous one. However, in either case, the proof of the pudding lies in the hypotheses it can generate.

is a great strength of Homans that he addresses this point. His rationality proposition, which is based on the first three propositions we quoted, states that people will multiply the value of an action's possible reward by the probability of it actually materializing and then choose on the basis of these results.[49]

As stated, the principle sounds extremely complicated, and, of course, no one is suggesting that we stand around with calculators all the time. However, much of people's behavior does seem to be explained by their making approximate comparisons of this kind; indeed, as we saw in Chapter 4,[50] some of the most important theorists who write about modernity see the pervasive assessment of probabilities and risks as one of the defining characteristics of modern societies. For example, when you make decisions about what to major in or what career to choose, your estimates of the probable rewards are among the things you take into account. During the 1970s and 1980s, there were enormous rises in house prices in both the United States and much of Europe, partly as a result of people estimating that inflation was likely to remain high or get worse—in other words, that the probable reward of putting money into housing was higher than the probable reward of investing in stocks or depositing the money in a (regulated) savings account. Given past inflation rates, this was not unreasonable; but when it turned out to be wrong, many people took a serious loss in the housing market. Again, the rationality principle can perfectly well accommodate people's use of "rules of thumb"—shortcuts to decision making that work most of the time and that we use rather than incur the very real costs of working out, on the basis of inadequate evidence, exactly what the best option is likely to be.

The Deprivation-Satiation Proposition

The deprivation-satiation proposition is a straightforward counterpart of the economists' principle of declining marginal utility, which we have described. Blau, in particular, presents it in economists' language. It states that if you have recently received something you value, you will be decreasingly interested in more of the same, at least in the short term. Economists

---

[49]In economics the rationality proposition is discussed in terms of "maximizing expected utility." Actually, both Peter M. Blau (*Exchange and Power in Social Life* [New York: John Wiley, 1964], p. 18) and Homans (*Social Behavior*, rev. ed., p. 33) suggest, rather curiously, that people's preferences are not necessarily transitive or consistent; in other words, the fact that they prefer A to B and B to C does not necessarily imply that they prefer A to C. Neither makes much of this, but if true, it would make much of people's behavior indeterminate or unpredictable and undermine their whole approach. In fact, there is some evidence, described by Heath, that people's preferences *are* transitive and thus that one of the basic assumptions of utility theory is justified.

[50]See especially the section on *Risk and Reflexivity: Giddens and Beck.*

accept this proposition because and insofar as it produces correct predictions, and exchange theory's position is basically the same.[51]

Declining marginal utility plays a central role in the economic theory of price. Correspondingly, the deprivation-satiation proposition is central to exchange theory's discussion of how exchange rates are set and exchange relationships entered into and left. Obviously, rational individuals will do something only if its value to them is greater than what they give up to get it, in either direct costs or forgone opportunities (in other words, if they make a net profit). However, because the first unit of something is worth more to people than the second, and the second is worth more than the third, they may quickly reach a situation where it is no longer worthwhile to go on paying. At that point the exchange relationship is likely to come to an end.

Aggression and Approval

Homans expressed his fifth basic proposition in behavioral psychology's terms. It states that if people's expectations are disappointed, they become angry and often aggressive, whereas if their expectations are fulfilled or exceeded, they are pleased. The proposition is important for sociology because many of people's expectations are rooted in customs and social norms that define what ought to happen and what is right and just. This fifth proposition moves well beyond the concerns of economics to questions of norms and the morality of social exchange.

Homans proposes an actual rule of distributive justice, *which applies in all societies*. It states that what matters to people is that "reward should be proportional to investment and contribution."[52] Peter Blau, whose application of exchange theory to macrosociology is discussed next, similarly argues that "people compare themselves in terms of their investments as well as in terms of their rewards, and expect differences in the rewards to correspond to differences in the investments."[53] This is an ambitious claim that goes beyond the more general proposition that there is some sort of norm of reciprocity.

In support of his argument that there is a rule of distributive justice, Homans describes a research study that showed that supermarket workers did not like to "bundle" (pack a shopper's goods into bags) for cashiers whose status was lower than theirs. They felt, for example, that a part-time worker attending college ought not to bundle for one still in high school.

---

[51]In his earlier work Homans included some discussion of laboratory pigeons in this context. George C. Homans, "Social Behavior as Exchange," *American Journal of Sociology* LXII (1958): 597–606.

[52]Homans, *Social Behavior*, rev. ed., p. 250.

[53]Peter M. Blau, *Exchange and Power in Social Life* (New York: John Wiley, 1964), p. 156. Copyright 1964 by John Wiley and Sons. Reprinted by permission of John Wiley and Sons, Inc.

Supermarkets where status and job relationships were generally congruent were also noticeably more efficient and profitable.[54]

Homans's own work included an extensive study of office workers in the Customers' Accounting Division of the "Eastern Utilities Company." There were three main groups of workers, all women. One group consisted of the address file workers, who kept customers' addresses up-to-date; another of the cash posters, who recorded how much customers had paid on their bills; and the third of the ledger clerks, who did everything else necessary to keep the accounts up-to-date. The address file workers were the youngest and also had the most boring and worst-paid jobs. The clerks and cash posters were paid the same as each other; but the clerks tended to be older and to have more seniority. They also had more varied and responsible work; but because the managers felt that cash posting had to be kept up-to-date, some of the clerks were set to work helping the posters in the afternoon.

Homans found that the address file workers, although they grumbled about the dreariness of their jobs, did not compare their situation unfavorably with the others. It was the ledger clerks who did that. They complained constantly about being paid the same as the cash posters and about being "taken off their own jobs and put down to work on posting." Homans interprets these results in terms of distributive justice:

> The investments of the ledger clerks were greater than those of the cash posters: they had put in more time in the company; they had learned to do a more responsible job, one that the cash posters could not do. Distributive justice accordingly demanded that their rewards should be greater than the posters' and some of them were: their work was more varied and interesting. But not all were: they got the same pay as the cash posters, and they were allowed even less autonomy—whereas the bosses left the posters alone, they took the ledger clerks off their "own" job and put them "down" on posting. Apparently distributive justice demands not just that higher investment should receive higher reward in one respect but that it should do so in all.[55]

In a direct study of distributive justice at work, Adams and Jacobson paid people to do an identical proofreading job. On the basis of a "test," they told some of the readers that they were qualified for a full rate and others that they were not qualified but would be paid the full rate anyway.[56] The result was that the "unqualified" group found more errors and marked more nonerrors, such as lighter type. Apparently they felt guilty at being overpaid and thus morally obligated to redress the balance by working hard.

---

[54]Homans, *Social Behavior*, rev. ed., pp. 202–208.

[55]Homans, *Social Behavior*, 1st ed., p. 240.

[56]J. Stacy Adams and Patricia R. Jacobson, "Effects of Wage Inequities on Work Quality," *Journal of Abnormal and Social Psychology* 69 (1964): 19–25.

Homans originally suggested that people recognized some very precise rules governing the relationship between rewards, costs, and investments.[57] More recently he argued simply that people believe the relative amount they put into something—including costs, contributions, and investments—should be in line with the relative amount they get out. "The condition of distributive justice is satisfied when the ratio of the measures of the persons is equal to the ratio of the measures of their respective rewards. That is, if the two persons are equal, they should, in justice, receive equal rewards; if one is better than the other, he should receive the larger reward."[58] If we look back to the Eastern Utilities Company or Adams and Jacobson's proofreaders, we find their attitudes compatible with this rule.

However, such a rule is also little more than a general statement that costs and investments also matter in social exchange. It does not provide any guidance to what people in different societies will define as relevant contributions. Moreover, there is no guarantee that, even within a society, people will put the same value on things. In February 1998 Lorna Wendt made the cover of *Fortune* magazine when a Connecticut judge ruled on her divorce settlement claim for half of the net worth of her CEO husband. The question of what a corporate wife contributes and deserves is one on which Americans disagree strongly. As *Fortune* noted, "Increasingly, women have been asserting that it isn't just the spouse who brings home a paycheck who provides economic value," and Lorna Wendt's lawyers argued that her role in her husband's success deserved recognition. She feels that she complemented him in an equal partnership; but many, if not most, high earners consider that "the contribution of the at-home spouse is important but not equal," and that someone like Lorna Wendt certainly does not deserve 50 percent of Gary Wendt's net worth.[59] Moreover, there are major differences here between the views of men and women. A poll for *Fortune*, reported in the same issue, found that 51 percent of American women but only 28 percent of American men felt that the duties of a corporate wife were extremely important to his success. So while they might all subscribe to Homans's rule of distributive justice, the very different ways in which they interpret it—and the changes over time in what is seen as fair in divorce cases—means that the rule can in itself do little to predict how people will react or behave.

Approval and Social Conformity   Homans does offer some theories about how norms and opinions develop. In these, social approval plays a key role, comparable to that of money in economics and market exchanges.

---

[57]Homans, *Social Behavior*, 1st ed., pp. 234–45, and Heath, *Rational Choice and Social Exchange*.

[58]Homans, *Social Behavior*, rev. ed., p. 249.

[59]Betsy Morris, "It's Her Job Too," *Fortune*, February 2, 1998.

Social approval is not as ideal a unit of exchange, of course; it cannot easily be measured or counted, banked, lent, and passed from hand to hand. Nonetheless, it is the one thing that can be offered in almost any exchange situation, on the assumption that everyone finds it a desirable commodity, and it can also be used by one side or other to balance an exchange. We can see how this works in Homans's favorite example, in which one person requests and receives advice from another. The individuals concerned, "Person" and "Other," work in the same office.

> Person is new to the work and unskilled at it. . . . Other seems to be experienced in the job and he has time to spare. . . . Therefore, Person seeks out Other and asks him for advice about a problem he has run into in his work. Other does give him help and in return Person gives Other approval in the form of heartfelt thanks.[60]

Homans uses the assumption that people value approval to explain how conformity is created and maintained in informal groups. Group members can supply each other with social approval, he argues. They will therefore have good reason to behave in a way their friends approve and to conform with their wishes in order to obtain approval and esteem.

In support of his case Homans cites a study of married students living in Westgate, a housing project at M.I.T.[61] The buildings in Westgate were built in clusters facing grass courts, although a few corner buildings faced in the other direction with doors on the street. When the investigators examined attitudes toward the tenants' organization, they found that a majority of the couples in each court shared the same attitude but, at the same time, that attitude differed from court to court. The way housing assignments were made could not explain this. It was a group norm.

The investigators then looked at friendship patterns within Westgate. They found that the more cohesive a court—that is, the more couples selected their friends from among their neighbors—the smaller the number deviating from the group norm. Within each court, moreover, deviates consistently received fewer friendship choices than did conformers. Finally, deviates were especially likely to live in the corner houses that faced away from the court center.

Homans suggests that couples whose houses faced onto the court were likely to see each other often and therefore to establish friendships. This, in turn, set up the process (the feedback loop) by which conformity could be established and maintained. People wanted to continue being friends and therefore had a motive for conforming; moreover, conforming would bring them yet more approval and strengthen the friendship. Couples in the

---

[60]Homans, *Social Behavior*, rev. ed., p. 54.

[61]Leon Festinger, Stanley Schachter, and Kurt Back, *Social Pressures in Informal Groups* (New York: Harper, 1950).

corner houses, by contrast, saw less of the others. They were less likely to have friends there, and consequently the group had less hold on them. If people have little to lose, they also have little reason to change their opinions; and, of course, if they do not, the group will hardly be more welcoming than before. Other forces, Homans notes, must also have affected friendships and opinions. Nonetheless, because of its effect on the frequency of their interaction with others, a couple's geographical position "'caused' its social acceptance and its social acceptance in turn 'caused' its conformity to the court norm . . . if, moreover, social acceptance 'caused' conformity, conformity also 'caused' social acceptance."[62]

What Homans advances is a convincing account of the dynamics of friendship and conformity in small groups. One can see the same process at work in the groups of young inner-city unmarried mothers observed by Elijah Anderson.[63] They form "baby clubs," through which they can obtain value and status in a way that inverts the normal bases for social approval. Mature women disapprove of the way the girls spend huge sums on clothes for their babies:

> Oh they can't wait until check day . . . so they can go the store. I listen at 'em, talking about what they gon buy *this* time. . . . And that's exactly what they will do, expensive stores, too. The more expensive the better. . . .
> . . . there was a sale at the church . . . some baby clothes for sale. They were some cute clothes, but they weren't new. The young girls would just pass them by. . . . No hand-me-downs. . . . And the babies sometimes are burning up in the clothes, but they dress them up anyway.[64]

But as Anderson explains, this "irresponsibility" evolves logically. The "baby clubs" formed by young unmarried mothers give social support; but their members also compete through their babies. If the baby looks good, the mother gets compliments and feels pride. The result is "an ideology counter to that of more conventional society,"[65] which provides approval for the way the mother is leading her life.

However, such a process does not adequately explain "social integration" in the wider sense because conformity to the norms of a large society requires more than people's desire for companionship and approval from their immediate associates. In this respect Homans's version of exchange theory is a theory of small groups, not social institutions. Later in this chapter we evaluate how far other rational choice theorists have succeeded in explaining the emergence of social, rather than small-group, norms.

[62]Homans, *Social Behavior*, rev. ed., p. 152.

[63]Anderson, *Streetwise*.

[64]Anderson, *Streetwise*, p. 125.

[65]Anderson, *Streetwise*, p. 126.

POWER, EQUITY, AND GAMES

Power

In discussing friendship and conformity, Homans identifies social approval as the good people offer when they have nothing else desirable to exchange. This same situation of imbalance—when one party or other has relatively little to offer—is at the root of exchange theory's analysis of power.

Homans defines power as the ability to provide valuable rewards. His analysis explains someone's potential power in exactly the same way that economists explain something's price:

> Power depends on an ability to provide rewards that are valuable because they are scarce. . . . Yet the objective scarcity of the reward is not what counts. The ability to whistle well may be scarce, but probably no one has ever acquired power through the ability to whistle well. Only if a large number of persons found it valuable to listen to concert whistling would the ability to whistle be a basis for power—a means, for instance, of getting people to pay money. What determines the scarcity value of a reward is the relation between the supply of it and the demand for it.[66]

Thus power is seen as reflected in the price people can get for their services. This price may be paid in the form of some concrete exchange, such as money, or in a more generalized form, such as obedience to orders. However, having resources that are generally valuable does not necessarily give someone power over any given individual. For that there has to be some imbalance.

Homans's conception of power can be applied to coercive power, which depends on the ability to punish, and to noncoercive power, in which both sides obtain some degree of extra reward. Mugging victims generally believe their choice to be between losing life (and thus money too) or just losing money; they perceive muggers as unlikely to be caught and therefore willing to take the additional small risk of a murder charge. The victims' potential reward is therefore greater than the muggers'; and they will usually pay up. However, Homans argues, noncoercive power is not only more common, it is also more effective. Carrots are more reliable than sticks.[67]

---

[66]George C. Homans, *Fundamental Social Processes*, p. 571. Put more succinctly:

The end is easily foretold.
When every blessed thing you hold
Is made of silver or of gold
You long for simple pewter
When you have nothing else to wear
But cloth of gold and satins rare
For cloth of gold you cease to care
Up goes the price of shoddy.
(Gilbert and Sullivan, *The Gondoliers*)

[67]Homans, *Fundamental Processes*, p. 571.

Threats of punishment often stir rebellion, and they may not elicit the behavior you want unless all other routes are blocked.

An example of the process Homans describes is given by George Richmond in his account of the microeconomy game from which we have already quoted. As part of the Monopoly-like game, players were allowed to borrow money, either to pay off debts they had not done enough work to cover immediately or because they had an eye on profitable investments. The change in the rewards available to pupils, and therefore in the resources and skills they valued, shifted the distribution of power.

> Ramon became 308's banker. . . . Frankly, I would never have predicted that Ramon, of all people, would get the job. When I first began teaching in P.S. 484, he caused me so little trouble that I barely knew him. Ramon was quiet, well-mannered, but uncoordinated; he played only a nominal role in the daily skirmishes that claimed our energies. In the order of selection for a punchball team, Ramon was often the last to be chosen. Sometimes team captains refused to let him play.
>
> In one respect, Ramon's passivity was an effective strategy for survival. As every hack in the schoolhouse knows, if you keep to yourself and take few gambles, teachers and other students don't bother you. No one was threatened by Ramon. He made no challenges, so few calls were made for him to defend himself in the brutal infighting that went on in 308. At least, this description fitted Ramon until we started playing Micro-Economy.
>
> After I introduced money to the classroom, all that multiplying, adding, and subtracting began to make sense, and Ramon's life began to change. He was unanimously chosen to be banker, not for his popularity, only possibly for his anonymity or his prosperity, but chiefly because he could add, subtract, and multiply better than anyone else. He became rich by getting a hundred on his math tests, and after I began paying for points on spelling tests, he scored perfectly there too. . . . Instinctively entrepreneurial, Ramon turned a part of his cash holdings into property; the rest he loaned to his classmates. Both investments earned him enviable returns.
>
> As Ramon got richer and richer, he began to pay a price for his success. The cloak of anonymity came off; he became important and powerful; his advice, previously ignored, was now sought by other children. . . . His natural business head and his common sense were important ingredients in a new social order. The fiefdom was breaking down in favor of commercial baronies, and whether he liked it or not, Ramon was 5-308's first commercial baron. . . .
>
> Intellect was now competing with muscle for dominance. It came as no great shock to anyone when Ramon hired Raoul, the strongest kid in the class, to protect his interests, to collect his debts, to run his errands. No one but me saw the significance of that seemingly inconsequential reversal of the student hierarchy. Muscle had surrendered to commerce. . . . There were other signs of change. The first indication of Ramon's emergence had been a line of children waiting to see him with their financial problems. The second sign, however, shook me just a little. Ramon was now among the first to be chosen for punchball.[68]

---

[68]Richmond, *The Micro-Society School*, pp. 33–35.

In Richmond's classroom a shift in what the children valued made Ramon the source of scarce rewards for which, within the context of the game, the others had relatively little to offer in return. As a way of balancing things, his classmates altered other parts of their behavior in ways that Ramon would like. Ramon, that is, acquired the power to affect their behavior in a noncoercive way.

The exchange analysis of power differs from both conflict theory's (the ability to coerce on the basis of one's command of resources) and from functionalism's (the means by which society organizes and implements decisions). Instead it emphasizes the relationship between power and individuals' provision of valued services. It has been developed fully in the work of Richard Emerson, who emphasizes the link between power and whether one partner in an exchange is *dependent on the other* for services and values those services more than the other person values anything he can offer.[69]

In a much-cited article that appeared in 1962,[70] Richard Emerson listed the conditions determining the extent to which the supplier of a good or service (such as weekly wages or companionship) exerts power over those receiving the supplies. The supplier's power is greater the more it is true that (1) the individual who wants a service has nothing the supplier needs that he or she can offer in return; (2) the recipient has no alternative to turn to; (3) the recipient cannot use direct coercion to extract the services he or she needs; and (4) the recipient cannot resign himself or herself to doing without the services or find a substitute. The second and fourth conditions echo the conditions economists use to describe monopoly. However, in economic exchange the result is simply that the buyer pays more, whereas in social exchange the supplier can make general demands and secure submission and compliance.[71]

The exchange perspective explains why group leadership on a desert island will shift to the individual with survival skills, even if, beforehand, he was an unemployed mechanic and his companions lawyers, bankers, or corporate executives.[72] However, it does not address the institutional bases of power in society—the circumstances that make particular goods and services valuable in our and other societies, or the means by which some groups consistently acquire or monopolize valued resources and leave others with nothing to bargain for. Conflict theorists, by contrast, tend to ignore the independent importance of the fourth condition—that the recipi-

---

[69]See pp. 320–22 and 334–37.

[70]Richard M. Emerson, "Power-Dependence Relations," *American Sociological Review* 27 (1962): 31–41. See also Karen S. Cook and Richard M. Emerson, "Power, Equity and Commitment in Exchange Networks," *American Sociological Review* 43 (1978): 721–39. See the general discussion of network analysis in Part Two of this chapter.

[71]Homans's work generally emphasizes power's noncoercive aspects—the fact that someone may pay a high price but nevertheless obtain something he or she wants.

[72]We are indebted to Ociola Newby for this example.

ents of services are not prepared to do without them—and focus almost entirely on one type of power, which rational choice theorists might call monopolies; in other words, the ways groups establish and maintain a position of control over scarce and valued resources. This type of institutional analysis tends to be lost in exchange theory's focus on anchoring power relationships in myriad individual actions.

At the same time, the exchange approach pays far more attention to the coercive and monopolistic aspects of power and its resulting inequalities than do most functionalists. The functionalist theory of social stratification, for example, argues that higher rewards for some occupations than for others are "functional" in that they induce people with rare talents and skills to fill those occupations. The exchange perspective similarly identifies a link between power and exchange of goods or services and relates the value of a service to the price its supplier can command. However, functionalism pays little attention to the fact that people and groups may, in effect, distort the market, whereas exchange theory's discussion of coercive power does recognize the importance of distortions.

Power and Equity: The "Social" Mix

What most distinguishes sociologists' versions of rational choice theory from the approach of economists is their insistence on a moral or normative dimension to social exchange. This is especially evident in the theoretical work on social exchange of Richard Emerson, Karen Cook, and their collaborators.[73]

As has been described, Emerson emphasizes the concepts of power and dependence and the alternatives available to people. The dependence of individual or group A on individual or group B is analyzed as a function of how much A values the resources to be obtained from an exchange with B, and how many alternative sources exist for that same resource. The power (P) of B over A, Emerson states, is the mirror image of the dependence (D) of A on B:

$$P_{ba} = D_{ab}$$

The greater your power in an exchange relationship, the greater your potential for profit: "The existence of alternatives is the key factor in defining dependence."[74] So far, this accords with economists' theory that monopolies will raise the price of goods. However, social exchange theorists argue, the existence of notions of equity and justice also feed directly into power relations, *constraining the use that people make of their power.*

[73]For an overview of this work, see especially Karen S. Cook, Jodi O'Brien, and Peter Kollock, "Exchange Theory: A Blueprint for Structure and Progress," in George Ritzer, ed., *Frontiers of Social Theory: The New Synthesis* (New York: Columbia University Press, 1990), pp. 158–81; and Karen Cook, ed., *Social Exchange Theory* (Newbury Park, Calif.: Sage, 1987).

[74]Karen S. Cook, "Emerson's Contributions to Social Exchange Theory," in Cook, *Social Exchange Theory*, p. 215.

Cook and Emerson illustrated this directly through laboratory studies of exchange relationships.[75] People were recruited to take part in a study of trading relationships and were paid according to the profits they made during "trading" sessions. Trading was conducted via computers, through which they could receive and send messages to trading partners. However, some participants were in a far more favorable situation to make profits than others—their potential rewards from a deal were greater and their alternatives more numerous.

At first, participants had no idea what situation their partners were in and, therefore, had no reason to do anything but maximize their own profits—that is, take advantage of their potential power and the others' dependence. They duly did so. However, when the situation was changed, so that participants knew not only what their own earnings would be from a deal but also how their partners would fare, their behavior changed. Constrained by concerns for equity, *those in potentially powerful positions ceased to make full use of their power.*

Studies of exchange situations also show how the experience of frequent exchange creates a positive feeling toward other members of the exchange network. For example, Edward Lawler and his colleagues have investigated the way in which exchange may create what they call "relational cohesion": the perception that the exchange involves a real group or unit. They argue that "instrumentally based exchange relations actually foster emotionally based, expressive ties between actors. . . . [A] theory of relational cohesion suggests that exchanges build the foundation for perceptions of similarity . . . between actors and for the interpersonal relations within which their economic behavior is embedded."[76] Thus "if a network repeatedly brings the same two people together and the two accomplish a joint task they are likely to experience an "emotional buzz. . . . [This makes] the dyadic relation . . . more salient and more real . . . [and] leads to commitment behavior."[77]

Insofar as people experience positive feelings associated with the exchange, they will want to understand the source of these and replicate them. This is why they tend to objectify the exchange relationship and see it as something outside themselves, a target for "attachment and commitment."[78] This in turn makes them "more likely to stay in their exchange relation, give each other token gifts, and contribute to a new joint venture."[79]

Empirical studies such as those of Emerson, Cook, Lawler, and others have extended Homans's formulations and underlined the distinctive characteristics of social exchange. Moreover, while there are no really funda-

---

[75]See especially Karen S. Cook and Richard M. Emerson, "Power, Equity and Commitment in Exchange Networks," *American Sociological Review* 43 (1987): 721–39.

[76]Edward J. Lawler and Jeongkoo Yoon, "Commitment in Exchange Relations: Test of a Theory of Relational Cohesion," *American Sociological Review* 61 (February 1996): 89–108.

[77]Lawler and Yoon, "Commitment in Exchange Relations," p. 103.

[78]Lawler and Yoon, "Commitment in Exchange Relations," p. 95.

[79]Lawler and Yoon, "Commitment in Exchange Relations," p. 106.

mental differences in Homans's and Emerson's conceptions of power, Emerson's focus on what he calls the "exchange domain"—the continuing series of actual and possible transactions with different partners—highlights the crucial fact that social relationships may exist over long periods. Thus, in the study described above, participants' concern for equity was related to the fact that they developed longer-term relationships with—and commitments to—trading partners.

In Parts Two and Three of this chapter we discuss at greater length the way in which rational choice theorists, by studying relationships over time, have contributed to our understanding of such social characteristics as interpersonal trust and group norms. First, however, we look at how the theory of games has affected the way in which rational choice theorists conceptualize individual or "elementary social" behavior.

Games Theory and the Prisoner's Dilemma

Games, with rules, strategies, and, usually, winners are a quintessential human activity. Games theorists analyze human behavior by arguing that many situations can be seen as manifestations of one or other quite simple "game."

The *prisoner's dilemma* is the best known of all such "games." This is partly because in the original "one-off," or one-occasion, formulation there is a wonderfully inevitable awfulness to its outcome. However, it is also because the parallels with many social situations can be grasped easily.

In the classic version of the game, two prisoners have committed a crime together. They are both under arrest and unable to communicate with each other. In order to force a confession, the authorities offer each prisoner, *separately*, the following deal:

> If you confess and your companion does not, he will get nine years in prison, and you will be let off scot-free.
> If you both confess, you will get five years each.
> If neither of you confesses, you will get two years each.

Figure 7-1 summarizes the choices facing each prisoner. Each quadrant shows the consequences of given actions for each prisoner separately and the combined number of years in prison that will follow. The box in the upper left corner shows the consequences if both confess. It is clearly the second-worst choice for each individual—and the worst of all in terms of the *total* number of years' imprisonment that it implies. Yet this is, quite inevitably, the choice that their dilemma will lead the prisoners to make. Why?—because each prisoner will, in isolation, reason this way:

> If I don't confess, and the other guy doesn't either, we will get only two years each.
> But it is also quite possible that I'll keep quiet and then find the other guy has confessed. I'll then end up with nine years in prison. So not confessing is really risky.

PRISONER B

	Confesses	Doesn't confess
Confesses	5 years / 5 years / Total −10	9 years / Goes free / Total −9
Doesn't confess	Goes free / 9 years / Total −9	2 years / 2 years / Total −4

FIGURE 7-1 The Prisoner's Dilemma

On the other hand, if I do confess, I may strike lucky—he may stay silent, and I'll get off completely. At worst, I'll get five years, which is better than nine. I'll confess.

The paradox that makes the prisoner's dilemma so intriguing is that both participants end up defecting even though they both know that they would be better off cooperating. Raymond Boudon, one of the foremost contemporary French sociologists, believes that the unintended consequences of social action, especially what he calls "perverse effects," can often be understood as variants of a prisoner's dilemma or other game.

Raymond Boudon and "Perverse Effects." Boudon defines perverse effects as "individual and collective effects that result from the juxtaposition of individual behaviors and yet were not included in the actors' explicit objectives."[80] Some such effects may be beneficial,[81] but the "mechanisms that

---

[80]Raymond Boudon, *The Unintended Consequences of Social Action* (London: Macmillan, 1982), p. 5.

[81]The most influential work on unintended beneficial effects is that of Adam Smith, who pointed out that "it is not from the benevolence of the butcher, the brewer, or the baker that we expect our dinner, but from their regard to their own interest." Adam Smith, *An Inquiry into the Nature and Causes of the Wealth of Nations*, Edwin Cannan edition (London: Methuen, 1904), Vol. I, bk. 1, chap. 2, p. 18.

are most significant socially are those that end up producing *undesirable* effects, those that are in everyday parlance called perverse."[82]

Boudon's major interest is in one of the recurrent themes of this text: the role of formal education in modern industrial societies. In France, as in the United States and Great Britain, the expansion of higher education has been seen as a way of increasing opportunities for children from poorer and lower-class homes. In France, as in other countries, these hopes have largely been disappointed, while at the same time people experience the kind of certification spiral analyzed by conflict theorists such as Randall Collins.[83] Boudon argues that the structure of individual options and choices makes such outcomes quite inevitable.[84]

As an example, Boudon takes the French government's decision to create institutes of technology offering two-year degrees in technical subjects.[85] Since 1945 higher education in France has been marked by big increases in numbers of students and in the average length of time for which people study. Most students, moreover, take rather general degrees—arts and social sciences rather than science and technology. Boudon rejects the idea that people are studying longer because of some large increase in the body of knowledge they need to acquire. Rather, it is that

> economic and social remuneration tends to vary positively, on average, with a person's amount of education. Each student, therefore, seeks to obtain the largest possible amount of education for himself. If everyone pursues the same strategy, this results in a rise in the demand for education; the supply of educated persons increases beyond the demand for particular skills in the labor market. This in turn leads to underemployment, with its attendant devaluation of qualifications, and this gives a further twist to the spiral by again increasing the demand for education.[86]

France's technical institutes (IUTs) were a conscious attempt to break this cycle by offering students the chance to acquire technical skills in intensive two-year courses, using newer teaching methods and with closer ties to industry, commerce, and the job market. Students would spend fewer years obtaining a degree; it would cost them less; and in the eyes of the government, the IUTs would provide an education closer to the "the aspirations of contemporary youth and the demands of the modern world." French students complain regularly about the amount of time they have to spend

---

[82]Boudon, *Unintended Consequences*, p. 5.

[83]See Chapter 3.

[84]Boudon, *Unintended Consequences*, p. 101. Boudon takes issue here with fellow French sociologist Pierre Bourdieu, who emphasizes class-related cultural factors and whose work is discussed in Chapter 3.

[85]Raymond Boudon, "Educational Institutions and Perverse Effects: Short-Cycle Higher Education," in Boudon, *Unintended Consequences*, pp. 77–104.

[86]Boudon, "Educational Institutions and Perverse Effects," p. 83.

studying and about the costs—both direct and in income forgone. The government correspondingly forecast that within eight years of their establishment, the institutes would be educating 21 percent of all students in higher education. In fact, it was a bare 7 percent. What went wrong?

Looking at the incomes of French university graduates at first makes this even more puzzling. The *average* salary of graduates from "long" university and "short" institute courses is the same. However, the pattern of salaries is very different. Institute salaries are more clustered together. Some university graduates earn considerably less than institute ones, but some earn considerably more. This gives Boudon his clue to solving the problem, which he does by casting it in the form of a game. Each high school graduate can be seen as choosing, *in isolation*, a strategy that will maximize his or her chances of a high payoff from higher education.

Suppose you are a French student. You don't *want* to spend many years in crowded, expensive lecture halls and classrooms. If you and your peers could get together and quit the universities for the institutes *en masse*, then all employers would have to accept your institute degrees as adequate qualifications. You would be able to compete for any jobs, and your costs would be considerably lower than those of current students.

However, at present, the best jobs in France go not to IUT graduates, but to university ones—even though there are too many of them and some end up worse off than the technically qualified institute students.[87] This means that you, as an individual student, would like *other* people to go to the institutes while *you* attend university and get an increased chance of one of the plum jobs. Conversely, you dare not risk going to one of the institutes while your peers all go to the university. If that happens, they will shoulder you out of the market for the jobs you want and think you have a chance of getting.

With every potential student weighing possible choices or strategies in this way, one quickly ends up, as Figure 7-2 shows, with something close to the classic prisoner's dilemma. People choose the long university courses even though they know that if they all agree to cooperate and choose the short institute courses, they would all be better off. Comparable processes are at work elsewhere. Americans grit their teeth and proceed to endless graduate degrees. The British government finds it impossible to persuade more students to take socially important engineering degrees because in the United Kingdom it is generalists, not technical graduates, who get a crack at the best jobs.

Boudon's model emphasizes the paradoxical effects of multiple individual decisions, rather than looking for cultural factors such as the devalu-

---

[87]In fact, the very best jobs in France go to graduates not of the big universities but of the small and highly selective Grandes Écoles. However, the general argument holds, both for France and for other countries.

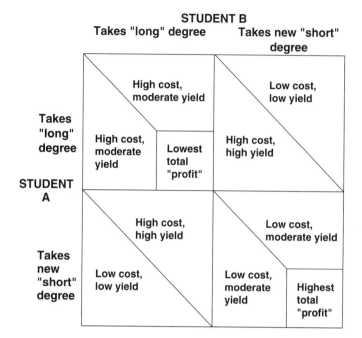

FIGURE 7-2   The Student's Dilemma

ation of technical training.[88] This emphasis is central to the rational choice perspective. Mary Brinton, for example, uses it to examine education in Japan, and in particular the different paths followed by men and women.[89]

In Japan far more young men than women go to university. Moreover, when one looks at the aspirations parents have for their children, it turns out that it is the mothers, far more than the fathers, who "favor" their sons over their daughters. Table 7-1 underlines the huge gender-related gap in Japanese mothers' aspirations compared to other countries.

Brinton tries to go beyond explanations phrased in terms of values and sex discrimination; she looks at how individual decisions can be explained "rationally" in terms of the choices Japanese parents face. Two things, in her view, are crucial: the low levels of state support for the elderly (there is nothing like Social Security or European state pensions available) and the structure of the Japanese labor market. The former means that parents expect to depend on their children in old age and have a strong motive to concentrate their own support on children who will be able to get high returns—good future earnings—from the education their parents underwrite.

---

[88]Boudon, *Unintended Consequences*, p. 101.

[89]Mary C. Brinton, "Intrafamilial Markets for Education in Japan," in Michael Hechter, Karl-Dieter Opp, and Reinhard Wippler, ed. *Social Institutions: Their Emergence, Maintenance and Effects* (Berlin: Walter de Gruyter 1990), pp. 307–29.

TABLE 7-1   Mothers' Aspirations for Sons and Daughters: Number stating that they hoped their son/daughter would go to a university[90]

	Sons (%)	Daughters (%)
Japan	73.0	27.7
USA	68.9	65.8
Sweden	87.3	84.5
West Germany	31.3	30.8
Philippines	48.1	44.1

Moreover, women live longer. Mothers are the ones most likely to end up living with their children for substantial periods of time and are therefore particularly interested in the returns to their educational investments. At the same time, the structure of the Japanese economy means that the children who can offer help will almost always be sons; that is why their mothers favor them. Big Japanese companies invest heavily in training their staff but expect permanent commitment and lifelong employment in return; and this works against women, who may want to interrupt their careers for child-rearing.

Brinton's approach is very much in the rational choice tradition, with its insistence that external incentives—in which financial considerations figure large—are far more important than values as an explanation. Multiple individuals making rational decisions of this type can clearly have major social effects, as Table 7-1 illustrates. However, skeptics have queried the use of a rational choice perspective to analyze *groups*, or institutions that operate and cooperate over time. The following sections review work that attempts just such an analysis.

PART TWO

Rational Choice and the Analysis of Social Structure

The work described in the previous section focuses on the origins and nature of individual choices and does so almost entirely within a small group setting. However, among the major sociological perspectives, rational choice theory is notable for encompassing both macro- and microsociologists. In the following section we look at the work of Peter Blau on social integration and power, and then more generally at the ways in which sociologists have brought rational choice perspectives to bear on institutional structure and the development of collective values.

[90]Adapted from Brinton, "Intrafamilial Markets," p. 308. Source of figures: Office of the Prime Minister, Japan, 1982.

PETER BLAU: EXCHANGE AND SOCIAL INTEGRATION

Peter Blau and George Homans are the two sociologists most responsible for establishing exchange theory and alerting sociologists to the potential of a rational choice approach. However, of the two, Peter Blau has been closer to the mainstream of American sociology. Born in Vienna in 1918, he received his sociology degrees from Elmhurst College and Columbia University. After teaching at Wayne State, Cornell, and then, for many years, at the University of Chicago, he became professor of sociology at Columbia in 1970 and is now at the University of North Carolina, Chapel Hill. In 1964 Blau became president of the American Sociological Association. He has been largely concerned with analyzing bureaucracies, from federal regulatory agencies to the modern university, and with the general characteristics of social structure and established social institutions rather than with small or informal groups. His writings are particularly notable for their combination of original empirical research with general or theoretical propositions.

Blau's interest in social structure is common to both his theories of social exchange and his later work, in which he is no longer directly concerned with exchange per se. Thus, in a discussion of structural analysis, he emphasizes his concern with occupational variation (the division of labor) as compared to particular individuals' occupations and with "the distribution of incomes in a society which reflects income inequality" rather than with "the income of individuals."[91] Whereas Homans believes that such properties are ultimately explained by psychological factors, Blau argues that distinctively social factors are involved as well. Nonetheless, he also believes that the study of the "simpler processes that pervade the daily intercourse among individuals"[92] is crucial to understanding complex social structures. Social exchange is such a process.

Exchange and Power in Social Life is the only book that Blau presented as a direct contribution to exchange theory. Its analysis of the origins and principles governing exchange behavior is close to Homans's. However, Homans is essentially concerned with setting out a deductive theory of behavior in general. By contrast, Blau sees exchange as one particular aspect of most social behavior. He deals with all "voluntary actions of individuals that are motivated by the returns they are expected to bring"[93] but does not see these as comprising all social activity. Correspondingly, his analyses suggest how an exchange perspective can provide explanation rather than offering strict deduction and exposition.

---

[91]Peter M. Blau, ed., *Approaches to the Study of Social Structure* (New York: The Free Press, 1975), p. 14.

[92]Blau, *Exchange and Power*, p. 2.

[93]Blau, *Exchange and Power*, p. 91.

Blau extends Homans's analyses of interpersonal relationships with a more explicit discussion of price mechanisms in social exchange and an analysis of people's general objectives in friendship and love. His major contributions to exchange theory, however, concern the relationship between exchange and the integration of society at large, and the exchange basis of power in large institutions as well as small groups. In describing Blau's exchange theory, we shall also refer to his own empirical studies of bureaucracy, which are among the best analyses of exchange processes in institutional settings.[94]

The Distinctive Nature of Social Exchange

Like the anthropologists we have discussed, Blau believes that social exchange is extremely important in social integration. He also argues that one of the two general functions of social—as compared to economic—exchange is the creation of bonds of friendship. The other function is to establish subordination or domination. Blau argues that exchanges increase social integration by creating trust, encouraging differentiation, enforcing conformity with group norms, and developing collective values.

Blau clarifies some of the distinctive social factors that affect "price" in noneconomic exchanges. For example, he points out that some social associations are intrinsically valuable. "It is not what lovers do together but their doing it together that is the distinctive source of their special satisfaction," he argues.[95] This aspect of exchange means that what we ask in return for a given service is likely to vary depending on who is involved; we will require a smaller return from a friend than from a stranger. Because there is no unit of account (like money), it is harder for social exchange theory to compare the value of alternative actions than it is for economics. The importance of the intrinsic elements of social exchange reduces exchange theory's precision even further.

Blau also emphasizes the importance in social exchange of "impression management," or how people present themselves to others. People want to be seen in two ways—as associates who promise rewarding extrinsic benefits and can therefore command favorable returns and as companions whose presence is intrinsically rewarding. Impressions are therefore crucially important to the "prices" at which social exchange is conducted.[96] Blau draws here on the work of Erving Goffman, an important contributor to symbolic interactionism, who emphasizes the creative aspects of human behavior. Goffman's work on how people control their images includes the

---

[94]See especially Peter M. Blau, *The Dynamics of Bureaucracy: A Study of Interpersonal Relationships in Two Government Agencies* (Chicago: The University of Chicago Press, 1955).

[95]Blau, *Exchange and Power*, p. 15.

[96]Blau, *Exchange and Power*, pp. 34–43.

concept of "role distance"—how people impress others by distancing them-selves from a task and demonstrating how easily they can perform it.[97] Blau believes that role distance is especially relevant to social exchange because people wish to demonstrate how skilled they are and thus how valuable their services must be.[98]

Blau also discusses the determinants of friendship and love. He starts with the assumption that people value status; he defines *status* as the common recognition by others of the amount of esteem and friendship that someone receives.[99] This means, first, that sociable intercourse and friend-ship generally occur among people whose social standing is roughly equal; and second, that relationships between unequals are less strained when the inequality is clear and marked.

The first of these points is easily explained. Quite apart from the fact that people in different social positions are less likely to have interests and lifestyles in common, status requires that inferiors cannot be allowed to get away with ignoring the deference they owe to superiors. A situation in which people are worried that subordinates might be perceived as equals clearly impedes easy socializing.

Blau argues that the second proposition holds because people whose status is not very secure are most threatened by being seen with lower-status people, especially lower-status people who may not even recognize them-selves as such. By contrast, people whose status is firmly established are unaffected by such exposure. In a modern office one often finds that man-agers are much more relaxed with their secretaries than with immediate sub-ordinates, who, they fear, may make claims of friendship and equality. Similarly, modern social scientists infer correctly that overt racial prejudice is strongest among those whites whose own status is least secure.

Blau argues that exchange considerations also apply to the most romantic of love relationships and that equality of status is as important to lovers' relationships as to friends'. Although much of what lovers exchange, such as affection and companionship, is intrinsic to the relation-ship, few people are entirely indifferent to conventional valuations of looks, potential career success, athletic ability, and the like. Successful men tend to have beautiful wives and are able to attract and marry such women well into old age.

Blau discusses the effect on love relationships of an imbalance such that one partner contributes more than she or he receives and finds the rela-tionship less important and valuable than does the other. Like Homans and Emerson, Blau considers an exchange imbalance of this type to be the

---

[97]Erving Goffman, *Encounters* (Indianapolis: Bobbs-Merrill, 1961). See Chapter 5 of this text for full discussion of Goffman's work.

[98]Blau, *Exchange and Power*, pp. 40–41.

[99]Blau, *Exchange and Power*, p. 70. Blau's analysis of status is close to Homans's.

essence of power. He cites Willard Waller's "principle of least interest," whereby the partner who is less involved in a relationship is in an advantageous position.

> Costly possessions are most precious, in love as elsewhere. . . . A woman whose love is in great demand among men is not likely to make firm commitments quickly, because she has so many attractive alternatives to weigh before she does. . . . A woman who readily gives proof of her affection to a man, therefore, provides presumptive evidence of her lack of popularity and thus tends to depreciate the value of her affection to him.[100]

Exchange, Trust, and Reciprocity. Blau argues that social exchange is different from economic exchange because it creates trust between people and integrates individuals into social groups. Because it is so difficult for anyone precisely to measure and value what they are exchanging, exchanges tend to start small and evolve slowly. This tendency is strengthened, according to Blau, by the fact that in social exchange obligations cannot be specified and stipulated in advance, and one has no formal recourse against freeloaders. Reciprocation and expanded exchange are "accompanied by a parallel growth of mutual trust. Hence, processes of social exchange, which may originate in pure self-interest, generate trust in social relations through their recurrent and gradually expanding character."[101]

In the previous section we presented analyses of how commitment and sharing emerge over time within informal groups. Blau expands this to look at trust in larger, institutional settings. For example, in his analyses of a federal enforcement agency and of a state employment agency, Blau found that a work group's social cohesion, as shown by whether they lunched or spent rest periods together, was directly related to whether they cooperated in their work. The more they exchanged advice or services, the more they liked each other. By contrast, workers who competed head-on did not seek each other's company away from their desks.[102] In the employment agency, this was apparent in the case of staff members who tried to maximize the number of unemployed workers they placed by concealing vacancies from their colleagues.

Underlying this process of social exchange, in Blau's view, is the fundamental *social norm* of reciprocity. As we discussed earlier, anthropology stresses the existence of such a norm, and Blau, in turn, argues that the "need to reciprocate for benefits received in order to continue receiving them serves as a 'starting mechanism' of social interactions."[103] Group norms,

---

[100]Blau, *Exchange and Power*, pp. 78–79. For an economist's approach to the same issues, see Gary S. Becker, "A Theory of Marriage Part I," *Journal of Political Economy* 81 (July/August 1973): 813–46.

[101]Blau, *Exchange and Power*, p. 94.

[102]Blau, *Dynamics of Bureaucracy*, pp. 61–62 and 132–36.

[103]Blau, *Exchange and Power*, p. 92.

"including the fundamental and ubiquitous norm of reciprocity," regulate exchange transactions, and a known failure to reciprocate brings with it group sanctions. At the same time, social exchange differs from economic exchange in that the nature of the return cannot be bargained over, and social exchange (unlike economic exchange) entails "unspecified obligations . . . while there is a general expectation of some future return, its exact nature is definitely not stipulated in advance."[104]

Blau provides a convincing account of how trust and social integration can be promoted by social exchange; and, as we will see in later parts of this chapter, other theorists have extended and built upon the explanation he offers. It may even be possible to account for the emergence of a generalized norm of reciprocity in this way[105]—either instead of, or alongside, Homans's psychological account of people's desire for "justice." However, Blau tends to overstate the difference between economic and social exchange and understate the extent to which people keep tabs on whether favors have been reciprocated. You may have little formal recourse against a freeloader on a specific, isolated occasion, but failure to reciprocate will often deprive the culprits of services they may want in the future because of social disapproval and reluctance to trade with them. In situations like this, the balance of chance and sanctions is not so different from the balance in economic exchange.

Social Conformity and the Development of Collective Values

In using an exchange perspective to explain conformity in the wider society, Blau points out that one distinguishing characteristic of large institutions is that exchange is increasingly indirect. Rewards come to you in a roundabout fashion, often from someone who does not even know the individual who received your services. Blau believes that this type of indirect exchange depends on the strength and internalization of social norms, which in turn depend on the fact that people receive approval in exchange for their conformity.

> The condemnation of rate busters in factories, of apple polishers and teacher's pets in schools, of traitors to their country, of stool pigeons and informers in groups of any kind—all these reflect social norms designed to suppress conduct that advances the individual's interest by harming the collective interest. . . .
>
> Social norms substitute indirect exchange for direct transactions between individuals. The members of the group receive social approval in exchange for conformity. . . . By adhering to . . . moral principles, individuals establish a good reputation which stands them in good stead in subsequent social interaction . . . [and] is like a good credit rating.[106]

[104]Blau, *Exchange and Power*, p. 93.
[105]See Chapter 8 for a sociobiological perspective on the norm of reciprocity.
[106]Blau, *Exchange and Power*, pp. 257–59.

Blau's analysis here is similar to that of Homans, who also sees social approval as the main force creating conformity. It is certainly difficult to account for large parts of social behavior without admitting the force that such approval—and disapproval—may possess. For example, in her preface to "The Maimie Papers," a unique collection of letters written between 1910 and 1922 by a prostitute, Maimie Pinzer, Ruth Rosen points out just how well prostitution paid. "Most prostitutes interviewed in this era were unskilled workers who, prior to entering prostitution, had earned a weekly wage of four to six dollars. But authorities generally agreed that a woman living without a family needed a weekly wage of nine dollars. How then was a woman without a family to survive? Both unions and employers refused to train women for the more highly paid skilled jobs. . . . (However) as a prostitute a woman's earnings soared. On the average, prostitutes in American cities during the first fifteen years of the century earned from fifty to four hundred dollars a week."[107] At one stage Maimie abandoned prostitution for the supposed economic security of marriage. However, she explains, when she saw how meager and bare a living she would obtain this way, "I gave up in disgust and . . . began to use what charms I might possess to make it possible to have a few of the luxuries."[108]

The mystery, it might seem, is not why she did so, but why so many people did not. A probable major reason is the reaction of their families and friends. In Maimie's own case, for example, her brothers either avoided all contact or showered her with insults and accusations; while her mother was so angry at her daughter's behavior that she had her arrested and imprisoned. However, this in itself underlines a major problem for the use of approval to explain social conformity. The family is, in essence, a small group, and one that takes a great interest in the behavior of its members. In many cases, especially in large institutions and mobile societies, it seems unlikely that people will know enough about each other's actions for approval and disapproval to have much force.

The Development of Collective Values.   Blau also proposes an "emergent process" by which shared experiences actually produce group norms and values. The mechanism is not direct exchange, but rather people's dislike for the psychological state of *cognitive dissonance.* This term is used by social psychologists to describe a situation in which either some of the facts that someone faces are in conflict with others, or someone's experiences are not in line with what "ought" to be happening. Leon Festinger, who coined the term, suggests that people dislike this dissonance and try to avoid and

---

[107]Ruth Rosen and Sue Davidson, ed., *The Maimie Papers* (New York: The Feminist Press in cooperation with the Schlesinger Library of Radcliffe College, 1977), pp. xxvii–xxviii.

[108]Rosen and Davidson, *The Maimie Papers*, p. 52.

reduce it—for example, by denying or arguing away the facts and opinions behind it.[109]

Blau suggests that when this happens in a group context, individual responses and rationalizations can be strengthened and transformed into common values and norms. People who find themselves in the same situation of cognitive dissonance are likely to discuss it with each other and to seek and get support for their arguments. In the course of such mutual discussion, individual rationalizations are transformed into social consensus and, indeed, social norms. In his empirical analyses of bureaucracy, for example, Blau describes how interviewers in the state employment agency would commonly discuss troublesome cases and decisions *after* the event in order to elicit colleagues' assent and approval and to allay their own doubts.[110] More generally, Blau (like Homans) believes that intensive group discussion and interaction create shared values. The process Blau describes here goes beyond the basic approach of exchange theory. That people discuss situations of dissonance because they want reassurance can be fully accounted for by the idea of rational choice. However, Blau suggests, emerging from this process are new, shared values and norms whose origins lie not in individual utility maximization but in some aspect of group psychology. Blau's account of the process is somewhat sketchy and far from conclusive, but it does seem plausible that rational choice alone cannot explain the development—as opposed to the consequences—of our values.

Exchange and Power

Blau follows the approach of Emerson[111] in seeing power as rooted in exchange relationships and also in looking beyond individual (or dyadic) relationships to larger structural settings. Blau defines power as

> the ability of persons or groups to impose their will on others despite resistance through deterrence either in the form of withholding regularly supplied rewards or in the form of punishment, inasmuch as the former as well as the latter constitute, in effect, a negative sanction.... If [a person] regularly renders needed services [others] cannot readily obtain elsewhere ... their unilateral dependence obligates them to comply with his requests lest he cease to continue to meet their needs.[112]

---

[109]Leon Festinger, *A Theory of Cognitive Dissonance* (Evanston, Ill.: Row, Peterson, 1957). See also pp. 281–83 for a related discussion by Peter Berger.

[110]Blau, *Dynamics of Bureaucracy*, pp. 89–90. Lewis Coser (see Chapter 3) argues that conflict may similarly give rise to new norms because it encourages people to discuss ideas explicitly and refine these ideas—and because it creates new social formations. Coser, *The Functions of Social Conflict*, (Glencoe, Ill.: The Free Press, 1956), p. 125.

[111]See pp. 320–22.

[112]Blau, *Exchange and Power*, pp. 117–18.

Indeed, considerable evidence supports a general link between relative power and the supply of services. Of particular note is Blood and Wolfe's study of the balance of power between husbands and wives.[113] Blood and Wolfe argue that the more crucial the husband's skills to the family's survival and well-being and the more complete his control of its wealth and resources, the more patriarchal the family. They suggest that this is because the husband's or wife's say in decisions is a direct result of what each contributes—not through some conscious calculation of relative power but because the partner who receives more than he or she gives feels both indebted for the past and dependent on future contributions. In a study of decision making in over 700 Detroit families,[114] Blood and Wolfe found evidence of just this pattern at work:

> Although society no longer insists upon a particular balance of power in marriage, the larger community still affects husband-wife relationships. Today, the more successful the husband is in the eyes of the community, the more dominant his part in marital decision-making . . . [although the] husband's earnings are an even more sensitive indicator of his power than his occupation. . . . Bringing home the bacon is a prime example of contributing a resource to marriage. That top-income-bracket husbands should be most influential in marriage reflects the magnitude of their contribution to the family exchequer. By contrast, where the total income of the family (rather than the husband's alone) is taken into consideration, the balance of power is altered in the wife's direction. . . . So, high-income husbands are most powerful if their wives contribute no income.
>
> . . . [Another] index of individual resources is the couple's stage in the family-life cycle. . . . Having a young child creates needs for the wife which lead her to depend more on her husband for help, financial support, and making decisions. . . . Childlessness allows a continuation of the honeymoon state of mutual emotional and financial interdependence with the husband. [By contrast] the mother of a new baby . . . gives up her job and is confined to her home by the heavy demands of child care. Not only is she cut off from contact with her fellow workers but even the opportunity to participate in recreational activities and organizational meetings is impaired by her baby-sitting responsibilities. . . . It is no wonder, therefore, that the wife's dependence increases.[115]

[113]Robert O. Blood, Jr., and Donald M. Wolfe, *Husbands and Wives: The Dynamics of Married Living* (New York: The Free Press, 1960). For similar analyses and findings, see John Scanzoni, *Power Politics in the American Marriage* (Englewood Cliffs, N.J.: Prentice-Hall, 1972); M. Anderson, *Family Structure in Nineteenth Century Lancashire* (Cambridge: Cambridge University Press, 1971); and C. Safilios-Rothschild, "The Study of Family Power Structure, A Review 1960–1969," *Journal of Marriage and the Family* 32 (1970): 539–52. See the conclusion to this chapter for a discussion of divergent findings and their lessons for rational choice theory.

[114]The decisions studied were (1) what job the husband should take; (2) what car to get; (3) whether to buy life insurance; (4) where to go on a vacation; (5) what house or apartment to take; (6) whether the wife should go to work or quit work; (7) what doctor to have when someone was sick; and (8) how much money the family could afford to spend per week on food. See Blood and Wolfe, *Husbands and Wives*, p. 19.

[115]Blood and Wolfe, *Husbands and Wives*, pp. 30–32 and 41–43.

Blood and Wolfe tend to emphasize the relationship between power and obligations. However, there is also evidence that normative factors affect how people behave; and Blau believes that power can rest on either basis. For example, in families where the wife is the major breadwinner there is a tendency for the women to cede some of their financial power to their husbands. A study by David Morley of family television viewing habits in Great Britain showed that, when either men or children were at home, women almost invariably deferred to them in their choice of program. The women felt that they ought to be the peacemakers in the family, giving other members power to choose by default.[116]

Blau would see this as an example of power based on normative factors; but in fact, examples like this—and Blau's willingness to identify two completely different bases for power—comprise a serious problem for the exchange theory of power. If it is only sometimes the case that power is a direct outcome of exchange and dependence relationships, and that one cannot predict when, and how far, normative considerations will alter the balance, then the theory is, in fact, not very helpful as a predictive approach; and it is reduced to ad hoc explanations after the event. We return to this issue in detail in the concluding section.

Power, Legitimacy, and Opposition.   A major theme of this chapter has been the ability of rational choice theories to explain the emergence of norms that hold beyond the confines of a small group. Blau, whose own interest is in large-scale social structures, offers an exchange analysis of just such a process: the development of legitimate institutional power.[117]

Blau argues that the major determinant of legitimacy is found in the exchange aspect of power—namely, whether subordinates feels that power is being exercised not merely fairly but generously. "If the benefits followers derive . . . exceed their expectations of a fair return for the costs they have incurred . . . their collective approval of [the] leadership legitimates it," he states.[118] Legitimacy transforms power into authority because legitimacy makes it right and proper to obey; in other words, the group develops norms that help to enforce members' obedience. By contrast, superiors who perform their tasks well or even make major contributions to the achievement of common goals will command respect and power but not necessarily legitimation and authority.

---

[116]Peggy Stamp, "Research Note: Balance of Financial Power in Marriage: An Exploratory Study of Breadwinning Wives," *The Sociological Review* 33 (1985): 546–57; David Morley, *Family Television: Cultural Power and Domestic Leisure* (London: Comedia, 1986). See also the conclusion to this chapter.

[117]See Chapters 3 and 4, especially the sections on Weber and Habermas, for discussions of legitimacy and authority.

[118]Blau, *Exchange and Power*, p. 202.

The mechanism is the one we described earlier. People find that deference and submission create costs of a substantial order and will question whether they should comply with others' commands. To resolve their state of cognitive dissonance in situations involving deference or obedience, they will discuss and seek support for their opinions from others. From this, social consensus and group norms will emerge. When power is exercised generously, Blau argues, individual rationalizations of obedience will be transformed into a collective norm that mandates obedience to legitimate authority. The development of opposition ideologies follows a parallel course. When subordinates experience collectively the unfair exercise of power, their collective disapproval generates opposition movements based on appropriate values.[119]

Blau's argument is an interesting one, but unfortunately little evidence either supports or contradicts it; it remains suggestive rather than conclusive. Indeed, this is generally true of his attempts to use exchange theory to explain social structure and emergent processes. In the next section we examine some more recent attempts to apply a rational choice perspective to institutional analysis, with particular reference to social norms and social and exchange networks.

NORMS AND NETWORKS

Although Blau himself moved away from exchange theory in his later work, a considerable number of younger sociologists continued to elaborate the links between individual exchanges and macrosociological variables. They saw the exchange perspective as a variant on the more general rational choice approach, offering an alternative to the older macro perspectives with which they were dissatisfied.

Michael Hechter, for example, criticizes "structuralist" explanations, among which he includes variants of conflict theory, and "normative" explanations such as functionalism.[120] Normative theories like functionalism explain the fact that we behave in particular ways, cooperate, and carry out social roles by referring to the internalization of social norms. However, Hechter argues, such a theory fails completely to explain why we obey norms only sometimes and why norms change over time. Why, for example, if little girls are so well socialized in "feminine" ways, did the contemporary women's movement emerge?

A conflict theorist, unlike a functionalist, would emphasize the restraints under which different groups operate. Oppressed classes are qui-

---

[119]Blau, *Exchange and Power*, p. 230.

[120]Michael Hechter, *Principles of Group Solidarity* (Berkeley, Calif.: University of California Press, 1987).

escent, in this view, because they are effectively coerced; equally, we should expect that groups with common interests will act in common to pursue these. But if that is the case, retort the rational choice theorists, why do groups that could act often not do so? Why is it, in Marx's terms, that a "class in itself" only rarely mobilizes as a "class for itself"? And does the implicit claim that when people share the same social position, individual differences wash out, really hold up? If women are so alike in their class position, why do we find that the majority of the most committed activists on *both* sides of the abortion debate are women?

Rational choice theory, in our view, also provides only a partial answer to what holds societies together and explains group behavior. However, by starting from the viewpoint of a rational individual, it recasts the question. In doing so, it makes apparent just how difficult it is to explain both social order and group, or "collective," action.

Collective Action and the Problem of "Free Riders"

Rational choice theory's distinctive approach to macrosociology can best be introduced by looking at the types of questions that it poses. Take, for example, its best-known puzzle: Why do people turn out to vote?[121]

Imagine that it is the morning of an election day. Our rational individuals, if they decide to vote, will have to take time to do so—perhaps get up early, or go out in the evening after supper, or miss a favorite TV program. Why should they?

In his classic analysis of voting behavior, Anthony Downs assumed that everybody is aware of (can calculate) their "party differential." This is a measure of how much better off they will be if one party or candidate wins rather than another—or of how much they care about the result—and will affect their willingness to vote. However, even if someone's party differential is high, he should also, rationally, take into account whether his vote is likely to make a difference. Thus he may much prefer one candidate over another, but what are the chances that his vote, and his alone, will decide the issue? Even in a school board election, the odds are fairly low, "and in an electorate of millions this probability is so small that the value of voting will be infinitesimal, even for someone who has a large party differential. Thus, it seems to follow that rational citizens would not vote if there are costs involved—and it always take time and energy to cast a vote."[122] If you calculate your party differential and then multiply it by the odds that your vote

---

[121]See especially Anthony Downs, *An Economic Theory of Democracy* (New York: Harper and Row, 1957); Brian Barry, *Sociologists, Economists, and Democracy* (London: Collier-Macmillan, 1970); and Howard Margolis, *Selfishness, Altruism, and Rationality* (Cambridge: Cambridge University Press, 1982).

[122]Barry, *Sociologists, Economists, and Democracy*, p. 15.

will be the crucial one, the result is likely to be less than the cost in shoe-leather of walking to the polls.[123]

Of course, the fact is that large numbers of people do vote; in the United States about half the eligible population does so. Some critics have taken this to prove that the rational choice perspective has to be abandoned and that we need to revert to an explanation in terms of norms—people believe they ought to vote, and so they do. However, it is equally the case that a lot of people don't vote, when, according to normative explanations, they should. Moreover, the people who do—or don't—aren't always the same, so it cannot simply be a question of good (or failed) internalization.

Rational choice theory, by contrast, can easily explain why, in an election where you don't much care who wins, a rainstorm may well tip the balance.[124] Equally, it can suggest why people vote more in presidential elections, where their vote really can hardly matter, than in school board or parish council ones, where it might. The theory points out that people's party differential is generally greater in the former than in the latter case; in other words, they care more about the result. However, we are still left with the question of why anyone votes at all.[125]

A common response of people, when asked why they (or anyone else) vote is "Well, what if everyone stopped voting?" The implication is that they are, in fact, being rational, helping to maintain a system that benefits them in the long term. Unfortunately, there is a difference here between what seems rational in a small group and rational in a large one. In the previous section we described how a rational choice perspective can explain cooperative behavior and conformity quite well in small groups, because those who do not cooperate and conform are quickly identified and repaid in kind. In a large group this isn't true. It is quite possible, and apparently rational, to *free ride*: Let everyone else vote and keep the system going while I go to the movies.

Blau got around this problem by simply invoking a general norm of reciprocity. Other theorists, discussed next, examine the importance of *selective benefits and sanctions*. Before turning to these ideas, one should emphasize that while it remains puzzling (and a challenge to rational choice theory) that anyone does vote, or collect for charity, or write to their senator,

> the logic of collective action is overwhelmingly successful in predicting negligible voluntary activity in many realms such as, say, the contemporary envi-

---

[123]See Iain McLean, *Public Choice: An Introduction* (Oxford: Basil Blackwell, 1987), p. 46.

[124]Rational choice theories as a whole share with economics an emphasis on what happens at the margin. Thus the point is not that a rainstorm will make everybody stay at home: but that those to whom voting was only marginally worthwhile on a dry day will find it (marginally) unworthwhile on a wet one.

[125]A further twist is added by those people who, having had a vague feeling that they ought to vote, gave up doing so with a clear conscience once they knew about public choice theory.

ronmental movement. Then what about the Sierra Club and other environmental organizations? The answer is that environmentalists contribute woefully little to their cause given the enormous value to them of success and given the repeated survey results that show high commitment by a large percentage of Americans to that cause. Environmentalists annually spend less on their apparently great cause than 25,000 two-pack-a-day smokers spend on cigarettes. . . . One could go on to note even more embarrassing statistics on how little Americans have spent on such honored causes as civil rights, the contemporary women's movement, gun control (as opposed to anti-control), and so forth.[126]

Rational Choice and Group Solidarity.   In their explanations of collective behavior, rational choice theorists emphasize the differences between public goods and selective benefits. With *public goods*, there is no way of stopping noncontributors from benefiting. Thus, in the voting example given above, if most people vote and in doing so preserve a democratic system, there is no way of stopping the nonvoters from enjoying its (presumed) benefits.

By contrast, *selective benefits* can be kept for group members who pay their dues.[127] Take a common form of organized group, a trade union to which members pay regular dues. If a union negotiates with management and obtains a pay increase or change in working conditions, all workers in a plant or industry benefit, regardless of whether they are union members. Why, then, should anyone ever join a union?

Rational choice theory suggests that much of the answer lies in the selective benefits that only members receive. Thus, if a union member is involved in a dispute with management, the union officials will get involved on his or her behalf. The union may provide legal advice and representation and may also offer other benefits, such as low-cost insurance packages. Selective benefits of this type can be substantial. For example, in Great Britain, the cost of joining the Association of University Teachers is about the same as the reduction in automobile insurance you can receive as an AUT member.

The benefits of legal staff and negotiated insurance packages are not something that individuals can obtain on their own; they are essentially collective goods, produced by groups.[128] Michael Hechter argues that this situation can provide us with a satisfactory rational choice theory of group formation and solidarity.

> The starting point of this theory is the assumption that actors initially form groups, or join existing ones, in order to consume various *excludable jointly produced* goods—goods whose attainment involves the cooperation of at least two (but usually far more) individual producers. The survival of any group there-

---

[126]Brian Barry and Russell Hardin, ed., *Rational Man and Irrational Society? An Introduction and Source Book* (Beverly Hills, Calif.: Sage, 1982), p. 21.

[127]This point was made most forcibly by Mancur Olson in *The Logic of Collective Action: Public Goods and the Theory of Groups* (Cambridge: Harvard University Press, 1965).

[128]Selective incentives don't on their own explain the emergence of public interest groups. See Part Three of this chapter.

fore hinges on the continuous production of such goods. But this is a highly problematic outcome. It requires the establishment of several different kinds of rules—rules about how to make rules, rules that serve to coordinate members' productive activities, and rules that govern each member's access to those goods once they have been attained.[129]

In many cases people will obey the rules of the group because, and only insofar as, they are compensated for doing so. People's rule-abiding behavior at work is very much related to direct compensation in the form of money now and/or the prospect of promotion in the future. If something better offers itself,[130] people quit.

Rational choice theorists also emphasize the need for constraints and sanctions—ways of preventing or at least controlling the "free rider" problem of individuals who take benefits and make no contributions. Hechter, for example, argues that visibility is an important way of solving this: "For a joint good to be maximally excludable, both individual production and distribution must be highly visible."[131] He points out that in tribal hunting and gathering societies, the collection and the distribution of food is always a highly visible, shared social affair. In such situations people can see that everyone is contributing as well as gaining. "Both in their roles as producers and consumers, individuals must be highly visible to one another to reduce the severity of the free-rider . . . problems."[132]

This process helps to explain how cooperative ventures such as baby-sitting circles, trade unions, or wagon trains to the West might develop successfully; but what about "solidaristic" groups—the sort of tight-knit group with shared patterns of living associated with Durkheim's concept of "mechanical solidarity" or Toennies' *gemeinschaft*? Why do people conform with their often pervasive demands?

Hechter defines solidarity as "compliance in the absence of compensation" and agrees that, in varying degrees, it characterizes many groups whose members act in accordance with group norms, many of them demanding and restrictive. However, rather than explaining this in terms of internalization or identification with the group, he argues that "individual compliance and group solidarity can be attained only by the combined effects of dependence and control."[133]

[129]Hechter, *Principles of Group Solidarity*, p. 10.

[130]Allowing for exit costs.

[131]Michael Hechter, "The Emergence of Cooperative Social Institutions" in Michael Hechter, Karl-Dieter Opp, and Reinhard Wippler, ed., *Social Institutions: Their Emergence, Maintenance, and Effects* (Berlin: Walter deGruyter, 1990), pp. 13–34, 18.

[132]Hechter, "The Emergence of Cooperative Social Institutions," p. 21.

[133]Hechter, *Principles of Group Solidarity*, p. 11.

Hechter's notion of dependence is the same as that used by Emerson and Cook in their discussion of power.[134] It is a function of how much someone wants the joint good produced by the group *and of how many alternative sources exist.* The more dependent someone is, the more compliance for the less compensation the group can extract. In effect, the "more dependent people are, the more tax they must pay for access to the same quantity of a given good."[135] The economists' formulation, quoted at the beginning of this chapter, is only slightly different: Goods will generally be more expensive if they are supplied by a monopolist than by a number of firms in competition.

Compare, Hechter suggests, the extent of the group obligations incurred by Orthodox and Reform Jews in return for group membership and support. "When the bulk of Eastern European Jews were confined to the shtetl, they subscribed to a religion with extensive obligations. Once individual Jews were granted full citizenship and became less dependent upon their coreligionists for their life chances, Reform Judaism began to supplant the Orthodox variety."[136] More and more Jews abandoned the strict dietary laws, restrictions on Sabbath activities, and requirements for daily prayer.

At the same time, dependence is not enough to ensure that people meet the obligations the group demands. The reason it is not—especially in larger groups—is the same: the incentive to free ride. The larger the group, the more it must rely on formal controls and sanctions for noncompliance. This is true, Hechter argues, however great the members' dependence and however much the group is one that offers community and support rather than material goods.

In an analysis that recalls Coser's discussion of such "greedy institutions" as sects and revolutionary parties,[137] Hechter examines "intentional" communities, where people who are not kin live together—places such as the communes of the 1960s or monastic and semimonastic communities (such as the Shakers). They are "quintessential obligatory groups whose members seek to provide joint goods—like a sense of community, friendship, love, and the feeling of security—all of which flow from the existence of social harmony."[138] They also survive *to the degree that they use exactly the sort of compliance mechanisms that succeed elsewhere.*

Communities that reject hierarchy, do not make their members highly dependent on the group for food and shelter, and do not enforce specific obligations rarely last long. Conversely, those that are able to monitor members' actions in great detail—for example, through communal living quarters and regular, ritualized meetings; that impose high costs on leaving;

---

[134]See pp. 320–22.
[135]Hechter, *Principles of Group Solidarity*, p. 46.
[136]Hechter, *Principles of Group Solidarity*, p. 57.
[137]See pp. 133–35.
[138]Hechter, *Principles of Group Solidarity*, p. 148.

and that make all rewards collective, notably by insisting on communal property, are also more likely to survive in the long term. Hechter concludes, "The *Gemeinschaft* is more solidary than the *Gesellschaft*, not because it entails more extensive normative internalization or promotes greater commitment, but because its institutional arrangements permit members' behavior to be controlled more economically."[139]

In work that he carried out in the decade after his work on exchange theory, Peter Blau uses a comparable approach and offers a direct reworking of Durkheim's theory of social integration.[140] Durkheim believed that, whereas primitive societies were held together by "mechanical solidarity" (shared beliefs), modern societies are held together by the interdependence that comes with the division of labor—"organic solidarity."[141] Essentially, Durkheim's argument is that division of labor, that is, increasing specialization, comes about through population growth and more frequent social interaction. The greater the division of labor, the more we depend on each other and the less self-sufficient we are. As the unions in a number of Western European countries have discovered, a group of workers in, for example, the water or electricity industry can hold a country or government for ransom. Fifty-five million Britons and two hundred seventy million Americans could not become self-sufficient hunters and gatherers even if they wanted to do so.

However, Blau argues, although division of labor may make for functional interdependence, it does not, in and of itself, create integration. That depends, ultimately, on actual association between different members of a society, and it is perfectly possible to have high levels of interdependence without many of the workers involved actually meeting each other.

What really matters for integration, Blau reiterates, is the degree of social association between people in a society. Thus it is quite true that "*the advancing division of labor increases the probability of social associations among different occupations,*"[142] but not equally and automatically in all circumstances. That will depend on the form it takes. Social integration will be greater the more increases in the division of labor involve "outmobility" from groups—for example, peasants moving into the towns. It will be lower as more "salient parameters" are "consolidated," or, in ordinary English, the more particular jobs are reserved for or preempted by people from particular well-defined groups, with few or no social bonds to other groups. South Africa provided an extremely clear case of such a society in the apartheid era; and is also, and equally clearly, still not a well-integrated

[139]Hechter, *Principles of Group Solidarity*, p. 167. See the section on Coser in Chapter 3 for a complementary analysis of "greedy institutions."

[140]Peter M. Blau, *Inequality and Heterogeneity: A Primitive Theory of Social Structure* (New York: The Free Press, 1977).

[141]See Chapter 2, pp. 21–25.

[142]This is known as "Theorem 28." Blau, *Inequality and Heterogeneity*, p. 201.

society. The legacy of apartheid is a lack of social association among different racial groups.

Altruists and Zealots.   Hechter's arguments may explain some of the taken-for-granted behavior that is actually puzzling and that seems to be at odds with the rational choice view of human behavior. People who belong to groups on which they are very dependent will also find that the group can extract a high behavioral "tax" from them. Much of the puzzling behavior that we identified cannot be explained in this way, however. For example, in Great Britain blood supplies are provided entirely through voluntary contributions; in the United States huge proportions of the population give time to "volunteer" activities; and in neither the United States nor most other Western countries are there any penalties for failing to vote. The people involved are living in fluid urban societies where their neighbors hardly know what they are doing—a situation far removed from Hechter's intentional communities or Coser's greedy institutions.

Public choice theory does, in fact, offer some explanations of why people behave like this and, by analogy, of why public interest groups may emerge in the first place. James Coleman, whose work is discussed in detail in the next section, provides a formulation that is very close to that of the conventional model of rationality and to Homans's exchange theory. Coleman argues that if your actions benefit others, then those others have an incentive to provide rewards—in the form, say, of social approval.

> Thus, one's efforts [may] directly help to satisfy one's interests (even if not enough to outweigh the costs of those efforts) and . . . also bring rewards from others for helping to satisfy their interests. In some cases the combination of these two benefits is far greater than the costs of the activity to the person. This is the rationality of the zealot.[143]

An explanation of this type works quite well for small groups. Often, however, the sort of behavior we are dealing with is effectively invisible. Who knows that we vote, give blood, or give to charity, let alone rewards us for doing so? Rational choice theory thus has to admit that truly altruistic behavior exists and must try to account for it and for the norms that underpin it.

We saw earlier that Blau (and a number of earlier writers) invoke a general norm of reciprocity at this point. Because people feel it is morally unacceptable to free ride, they feel guilty when they do and assuage their guilt when they don't. However, this isn't much of an explanation on its own. Without showing how the norm arose, the theorists seem to be simply importing factors to fill awkward gaps.

---

[143]Coleman, "Free Riders and Zealots," in Cook, ed., *Social Exchange Theory*, p. 63.

Margolis approaches the issue by suggesting that most of us are altruistic in two ways.[144] The first is that we want people to have things; this is "goods altruism." We therefore tell the polls that we approve of government doing things for people; give (a bit) to charity; and may take into account not just what we will gain from our party's winning but also what other people will.[145] We also act on the basis of a second "participation altruism"—that is, we get a good feeling from actually taking part in things for what we feel are nonselfish reasons. Many blood donors express this feeling when asked why they volunteer.[146]

Homans's argument that laws of social behavior must be ultimately psychological would certainly seem to apply to any explanations of human altruism. One possible approach is that taken by sociobiology,[147] which looks at the reproductive advantage that certain behavior—such as moderate degrees of altruism—might bestow on a species. However, some recent sociological work suggests that we can also learn a lot by combining a rational choice perspective with the way microsociology—such as symbolic interactionism or phenomenology—views human identity.

Kristin Luker studied women activists on both sides of the abortion debate: women who gave considerable amounts of their time either to the pro-life movement or to pro-choice activism.[148] She concluded that the activities of both groups were bound up with the way they defined not only their individual identity, but their whole worldview. Participating in a political movement was a way of having both of these validated and made more real by other people.

Pro-life people, Luker found, see the world as inherently divided into a male and female sphere. Abortion on demand, for them, breaks up a whole set of social relationships in which women and children are protected and everyone loses out. A pro-life doctor told Luker that

> I think women's lib is on the wrong track. . . . The women have been the superior people. They're more civilized, they're more unselfish by nature, but now they want to compete with men at being selfish. And so there's nobody to give an example, and what happens is that men become *more* selfish.[149]

---

[144]Margolis, *Selfishness, Altruism, and Rationality.*

[145]As McLean points out, this changes the whole arithmetic of voting decisions. Even if my party differential is minuscule, the combined differential of all supporters is huge. Multiply $50,000,000 rather than $2,500 by even the minuscule chance that my vote will make a difference, and you will get quite a respectable sum of money.

[146]See R. M. Titmuss, *The Gift Relationship* (London: Allen and Unwin, 1970); and Iain McLean and Jo Poulton, "Good Blood, Bad Blood, and the Market: *The Gift Relationship* Revisited," *Journal of Public Policy* 6, 4 (1988): 431–45.

[147]See Chapter 8.

[148]Kristin Luker, *Abortion and the Politics of Motherhood* (Berkeley, California: University of California Press, 1984).

[149]Luker, *Abortion and the Politics of Motherhood*, p. 163.

Pro-life people also feel that there is a lot of antichild feeling in modern society and that this is encapsulated in the cultural norm of small families and the idea that births should be timed to fit in with adults' career plans. Their own position is the opposite. They value traditional roles and believe that if you take on the responsibilities of marriage and parenthood, other parts of your life should be subordinated to these. Most pro-life activists are, themselves, wives and mothers for whom these roles are the most important in their lives.

Taking an active part in the pro-life movement enables these people to defend and reinforce their whole worldview and self-concept. Being among others who share their values and attitudes is a crucial part of the process and provides a strong, if unconscious, motive for their behavior. Exactly the same holds for pro-choice activists, although their worldview is, obviously enough, a very different one.

Thus Luker ties collective and altruistic behavior to the process by which people get their chosen selves confirmed and approved. This provides a fully rational explanation for the time activists give up. However, by drawing on insights from symbolic interactionism and phenomenology, which examine how we develop a self and experience our world as real and substantial,[150] Luker's work provides both a synthesis and an indication of the limitations of rational choice as an all-embracing perspective.

Networks and Emergent Processes

Because exchange and other rational choice theorists are interested in linking the development of institutions and norms to the exchange-based links among individuals, they also tend to be concerned with the underlying structure of contacts in and between social groups. For example, in the previous section we discussed how Hechter links group solidarity to a situation where members are dependent on the group and have few alternative sources for what they want. He is describing a dense network of contacts within a group but few links between it and the outside. Simmel discusses the "web of group affiliations";[151] but in contemporary sociology the term "networks" is more commonly used.

Network analysis is rather like a traffic engineer using nighttime photography to estimate traffic flows. If you take a long-exposure aerial photograph of a city's traffic at night, you get a pretty but seemingly shapeless pattern of thicker and thinner lines of light (from headlights) interspersed with dark. The pattern is not shapeless, however. If you take a series of pho-

---

[150]See Chapters 5 and 6.

[151]Georg Simmel, "The Web of Group Affiliations," trans. Reinhard Bendix, in Kurt H. Wolff, Reinhard Bendix, et al., *Simmel: Translation of Chapters from "Soziologie"* (New York: The Free Press, 1964).

tographs and superimpose them, the differences between thick and thin lines will become increasingly clear, reflecting differences in the volume of traffic.

Network analysts do something like this with social relationships, building up a pattern rather like a drawing based on aerial photographs. They also, and most importantly, try to specify "how this ramification influences the behavior of the people involved in the network."[152] To stretch our own metaphor a little further, drivers react to what they know about traffic patterns (such as by trying to avoid busy roads) and are affected by them (such as being held up especially often at places where traffic flows tend to produce accidents). Social networks are things to which we react and which affect us. Just as particular types of road junctions may be *generally* associated with high or low accident rates, so there may be *general* characteristics of social networks that[153] produce recurrent, patterned events and behavior.[154] Often a key factor is the opportunities that networks do or do not offer for interpersonal exchange; equally, it is often possible to account in rational choice terms for the way people do or do not activate potential links with others in their network.

Clyde Mitchell suggests that network analysis is potentially most helpful in explaining what is going on in large-scale social situations (which, as we have seen, are the ones that seem least suited to conventional exchange theory approaches).[155] In modern, fluid societies, referring to the "occupational structure" or the "economic system" is just not adequate to explain what is going on at the individual level and how different people behave, he argues. People do not live within hermetically sealed occupational or economic groups, and one needs to look beyond, to how and where their lives crosscut them. Individual ties outside their main groups may be of prime importance for them, as the poet Dylan Thomas pointed out: "If you want to be a proper newspaperman," I said, "You got to be well known in the right circles. You got to be *persona grata* in the mortuary, see."[156]

Claude Fischer and his associates used network analysis to examine critically one of the most durable views of modern life: that in the process of moving from agricultural village to urban industrial life we have been cut off from any authentic community and have become a "nation of

[152]J. Clyde Mitchell, "Social Networks," *Annual Review of Anthropology* 3 (1974): 279–99.

[153]Other things being equal.

[154]Sociometry, or the study of patterns of friendship and liking, encouraged the development of statistical techniques for network analysis. Early sociometric studies generally asked people to name others they liked most and then mapped out the results, gradually revealing the structure of friendship in a group.

[155]Mitchell, "Social Networks," p. 280.

[156]Dylan Thomas, *Return Journey to Swansea*, a spoken recording (London: Caedmon, 1972).

[157]Claude S. Fischer, with Robert M. Jackson, C. Ann Steve, Kathleen Gerson, Lynne McCallister Jones, and M. Baldassare, *Networks and Places: Social Relations in the Urban Setting* (New York: The Free Press, 1977). The phrase "a nation of strangers," cited by Fischer, is from Vance Packard, *A Nation of Strangers* (New York: McKay, 1972). See pp. 30–31 for a discussion of the related ideas of Gemeinschaft and Gesellschaft.

strangers."[157] It should follow, Fischer argues, that it is from local social relations that people get intimate friendship and support and that people who have moved recently are more likely to be isolated and suffer psychologically.

In fact, however, data from Detroit did not indicate that men whose friends came from a local neighborhood group were a distinct or especially fortunate minority.[158] Modern communications enabled people to maintain friendships over distances and gain real support from them—in part, no doubt, because friendships that are established and maintained in modern societies are truly chosen by both parties rather than wished upon them by propinquity. The twenty years since Fischer's study have brought us millions of people "surfing the net" and joining like-minded and global discussion groups, cellular telephones used in the fields by Indian peasants, and local telephone networks crashing under the volume of e-mail. Technology is thus further reducing the link between people's emotional networks and geographical distance.[159]

Granovetter's notion of the "strength of weak ties" is concerned with the effects of network density: that is, with the number of links among the various members of someone's acquaintance.[160] He argues that people with dense networks in which friends all know each other will, for that reason, tend to be relatively cut off from information and from contact with the wider population. Loosely knit networks and weak ties are important not only in spreading information and fostering cohesion in a large society but also in furthering individuals' goals.[161] For example, "mere acquaintances" are more likely to give you a lead to a job opening than are your close friends because by definition they move in different circles and have access to different information than you. Weak ties are also one important reason why middle-class communities generally do better at protecting themselves from undesired development than working-class ones. Somebody in a middle-class neighborhood usually knows somebody who can "drop a word" in the right place, or who is great at presenting evidence at a tribunal, or who can get coverage in the local press.[162]

In his research on how people find jobs, Granovetter notes that it is sometimes assumed

[158]Fischer, et al., *Networks and Places*, p. 165.

[159]See Frances Cairncross, *The Death of Distance* (Cambridge: Harvard University Business School Press, 1997).

[160]Mark Granovetter, "The Strength of Weak Ties," *American Journal of Sociology* 78, 6 (1973): 1360–68, and "The Strength of Weak Ties. A Network Theory Revisited," in Collins, ed., *Sociological Theory 1983* (San Francisco: Jossey-Bass, 1983), pp. 201–32.

[161]See pp. 343–44 for Blau's similar argument. Another classic proposition of network theory is that multistranded relationships are more likely to be intense than single-stranded ones. In other words, the more numerous the links that join people, the more likely it is that they will honor obligations and be able to demand help successfully.

[162]Mitchell, "Social Networks," p. 283.

that the advent of "modernization" leads to a widespread use of formal and "universalistic" procedures, liberating individuals from the limitations once imposed by particular social milieus. But empirical sociological studies continually demonstrate the crucial importance of informal interaction in systems that are formally rationalized.[163]

Granovetter (like Fischer) questions the conceptualization of modern societies as comprehensively different from old-style communities, arguing that the "particular" and the personal remain vitally important in explaining what happens to individuals.[164] In his research on professional, technical, and management-level workers who had changed jobs in the previous five years, he found that only 19 percent had found out about their new posts through formal channels such as advertisements; 19 percent had approached the employer directly, and no less than 56 percent obtained information from personal contacts. In line with the general importance of weak ties, most (over 80 percent) of these contacts were relatively distant acquaintances rather than close family and friends or even teachers.[165]

This makes sense when you consider that, if information is being shared within a tight-knit group, then, by definition, everyone will know it. New information—such as a possible job opening for someone with your particular skills—has to come from outside the group, through weak links with outsiders. One of the reasons why ghetto dwellers find it so hard to find work is that they live in a society with relatively few such ties; instead, theirs is a dense and constricted social network.

Raymond Boudon, whose work on the prisoner's dilemma we have discussed,[166] also emphasizes the way in which social phenomena emerge and can only be understood in terms of underlying networks and individual behavior. He takes as an example the way in which new agricultural techniques spread in a rural community: first very slowly, then accelerating until most people have accepted them, and then slowing down dramatically again.[167] A similar pattern is found for many novelties—rollerblading, purchase of video recorders, viewing figures for a new sitcom, sales of a soft drink.

This pattern is interesting to sociologists and hugely interesting to marketing managers; and it stems from the fact that, with something new,

[163]Mark Granovetter, *Getting a Job: A Study of Contacts and Careers*, 2nd ed. (Chicago: Chicago University Press, 1995), p. 4.

[164]Granovetter is using the language of the Parsons pattern variables in discussing whether modern societies are truly "universalistic."

[165]Granovetter, *Getting a Job*. See also Mark Granovetter and Richard Swedberg, ed. *The Sociology of Economic Life* (Boulder, Col.: Westview, 1992).

[166]See pp. 323–26.

[167]Shown graphically, this gives a rather S-shaped graph; or it may be seen as like an ink blot, spreading out steadily but irregularly from the center. Raymond Boudon, *The Logic of Social Action: An Introduction to Sociological Analysis*, trans. David Silverman (London: Routledge and Kegan Paul, 1981).

people hear about it, then consult their friends to see if the latter are using it or know anything, and only then take action. In other words, personal recommendation and contact are crucial, even in a media- and advertising-saturated society. At the beginning only a very few people—the ones who most like change and novelty—will have the information or have tried the product; so further take-up tends to be slow. Then, as more and more people are involved, it becomes increasingly likely that, if you ask someone in your network, you will meet with a useful reply, or that someone one knows will, unprompted, offer relevant information. But some people will have only tenuous links with the main networks of users, while others will have little taste for novelty. They will never adopt the product or practice in question.

Not all network analysts identify themselves as believers in rational choice or embrace exchange theory; but they do share the same concern to link the micro and the macro and to explain how social phenomena emerge from individual behavior. In doing so they, like Homans or Blau, focus on fundamental psychological phenomena—such as the importance of face-to-face contact and recommendations in forming people's opinions—as well as on the structure of networks, the opportunity they provide for sharing information, and the different aspects of exchange, dependence, and power that have been discussed.

PART THREE

James Coleman and the Foundations of Social Theory

James Coleman (1926–1995) was a sociologist for whom theory and practice, or research and policy, were always deeply entwined. In a speech at his memorial service in 1995, Senator Daniel Patrick Moynihan recalled the controversy in which Coleman was embroiled following the publication of his work for the government on equality of educational opportunity, and the stoicism with which he bore the attacks on his work and on him personally. Moynihan also cited the tribute of a senior government official. "There are a very small number of people who end up defining a major part of the intellectual agenda for their times. . . . An even tinier group of thinkers influence both intellectual and policy debate. James Coleman's work formed the bedrock for scholarship and policy in education and sociology for a generation."[168] Nobel Laureate and fellow University of Chicago professor Gary Becker considered him "the most creative sociologist of his generation" and

---

[168]Cited in Senator Daniel Patrick Moynihan's address at the memorial service for James Coleman, Rockefeller Memorial Chapel, Chicago, May 19, 1995, and reprinted in Jon Clark, ed., *James S. Coleman* (Bristol, Pa.: Falmer, 1996).

greeted his massive work on the *Foundations of Social Theory* as "the most important book in social theory in a long time."[169]

James Coleman was born in Bedford, Indiana; went to high school in Louisville, Kentucky; took his bachelor's degree at Purdue; and then went to work at Eastman Kodak as a chemist. But in 1951, discontented with his work, he enrolled for a Ph.D. at Columbia University. He was to say, later, that after Columbia "I was a different person, with different goals, headed in a different direction."[170] Richard Swedberg of Stockholm University in Sweden has argued that American sociologists have not yet come to appreciate the importance of Columbia and the extent to which it constituted "a *school* in the full sociological sense of this word; a 'living being' . . . made up of scholars and their students with an intellectual style or approach in common."[171] Paul Lazarsfeld, Seymour Martin Lipset, and Robert Merton most influenced Coleman; he was to write later that he "worked *with* Lipset, worked *for* Lazarsfeld, and worked *to be like* Merton"[172]; and it was to "Robert K. Merton, my teacher" that he dedicated *Foundations of Social Theory*.[173]

Functionalism and rational choice are not usually seen as compatible, let alone interconnected; but Merton and Coleman are alike in linking the development of social institutions to individual concerns, and in their interest in social norms. Merton's analysis of political machines[174] is carried out from a perspective that is quite similar to that adopted by Coleman in some of the work described here, such as that on politicians' behavior in Congress. What Coleman argued was that the links between micro and macro levels could best be explained systematically starting from a rational choice perspective. This section summarizes his approach and its relation to related work in the fields of public choice and games theory, drawing on *Foundations of Social Theory* but also on a range of his earlier publications. It looks first at coalition building; then at trust and the formation of group norms; and finally at Coleman's ideas on social capital and corporate actors.

[169]Memorial service address by Gary S. Becker, republished in Clark, *James S. Coleman*.

[170]Unpublished autobiographical sketch cited in Richard Swedberg, "Analyzing the Economy: On the Contribution of James S. Coleman" in Clark, *James S. Coleman*, p. 314.

[171]Richard Swedberg, "Analyzing the Economy: On the Contribution of James S. Coleman" in Clark, *James S. Coleman*, p. 313.

[172]James S. Coleman, "Robert K. Merton as teacher" in J. Clark, C. Mogdil, and S. Mogdil, ed., *Robert K. Merton* (London: Falmer, 1990).

[173]James S. Coleman, *Foundations of Social Theory* (Cambridge, Mass: The Belknap Press of Harvard University Press, 1990). For a review symposium on the book, see *Theory and Society* 21.2 (April 1992).

[174]See pp. 52–53.

COALITIONS, TRUST, AND NORMS

Coalition Building

Coleman was always interested in the way individual decisions, once aggregated, produce what are often unanticipated social effects. He argues that "collective decisions," such as the votes of Congress or Parliament, can be better understood if they are seen in terms of individuals maximizing utility. People care very much about some issues, he suggests, and relatively little about others. They therefore try to do as well for themselves as possible by trading or exchanging their partial control over some matters for greater control over others. For example, members of Congress vote with a colleague on a piece of legislation in return for that colleague's support in receiving an assignment to a particular committee.[175]

Coleman tested some of his theories about coalition building by devising a game in which players played the role of legislators whose constituencies were more or less interested in various issues.[176] Over the period of the game, different issues would come to a vote, and, as predicted, players always formed coalitions, trading "useless" for "useful" power according to their degree of constituency interest. Moreover, the *more issues there were to negotiate*—that is, the more possible exchanges—*the easier it was for players to put together winning coalitions* on the particular issues they cared about.

Situations like this differ crucially from the prisoner's dilemma examples given earlier. Coleman's players were not involved in once-and-for-all decisions but rather in relationships that extended over a long period. Coleman found that as the game continued, all players became trustworthy—that is, if they promised to deliver a vote in a given way, they kept their word.[177] Moreover, players who early on had been tempted into reneging on deals found their reputation for unreliability a handicap. They therefore attempted to restore confidence by making exchanges that were less favorable to themselves than they might be—not as in the Cook and Emerson example quoted previously,[178] because they believed in equity, but because it was rationally self-interested of them to do so.

This sort of analysis, based on individuals' preferences and decisions, obviously works best in situations where people are fairly autonomous.

---

[175]See especially James S. Coleman, "Foundations for a Theory of Collective Decisions," *American Journal of Sociology* LXXI (1966): pp. 615–27; James S. Coleman, *The Mathematics of Collective Action* (Chicago: Aldine, 1973). See also Olson, *The Logic of Collective Action*.

[176]James S. Coleman, *Individual Interests and Collective Action: Selected Essays* (Cambridge: Cambridge University Press, 1986). See also James S. Coleman, "Free Riders and Zealots," in Cook, ed., *Social Exchange Theory*.

[177]See Chapter 8 for sociobiology's discussion of altruistic behavior, which overlaps in many ways with that offered by rational choice theorists.

[178]See pp. 320–21.

Thus contemporary American legislators can and do behave similarly to Coleman's players because they must cultivate their own local political bases. In most other Western democracies, legislators are elected as members of a political party that strictly controls the way they vote. However, here, too, we can apply a theory of coalitions based on rational choice principles. Instead of dealing with individual legislators' votes, it applies to the combinations of policies that politicians stitch together.

Such a theory starts from the fact that politicians are in business to win elections. In order to do so, they build coalitions of voters—groups such as farmers, pensioners, and teachers whose interests they promise to advance. If one party persistently loses, then its politicians will try to find issues with which to break up their opponents' winning coalition and attract enough of its voters over to their side.[179]

American coalitions are easy to study because there have always been two, and only two, parties fighting for power at the national level.[180] At the time of independence the conflicts were between the Federalists, representing the interests of the Northern manufacturers, and the agricultural coalition, which became the Democratic party. However, between 1816 and the eve of the Civil War there was effectively one-party rule. The Democrats' coalition, representing both slave-owning and non–slave-owning farmers from the South and West, was so effective that the cities and Northeast could never win.

Rational choice theorists argue that in this situation the obvious thing for the minority to do was to find a coalition-splitting issue. After failing to split the Democratic coalition over immigration and the role of Freemasons, they hit on a winner—slavery.[181] "A number of northern politicians took up the slavery issue for reasons which their opponents saw as pure expediency. . . . Raising the issue of slavery did break up the Jacksonian coalition and it (also destroyed) the Union."[182] While disgust at slavery had to exist for the maneuver to be workable, rational choice theorists would argue that it took "rational," or self-seeking, actors pursuing votes to translate this into the Civil War.

Trust and the Formation of Group Norms

Coleman's analysis of legislative coalitions is especially interesting because of the way it shows cooperative behavior developing, even though the players in the game remain self-interested. As we noted, the important factor here is that they are also involved in a long-term relationship. Thus in

---

[179]The discussion of coalition theory draws heavily on Iain McLean, *Public Choice: An Introduction* (Oxford: Basil Blackwell, 1987), especially chap. 6, "Winning Elections and Winning Power: The Theory of Political Coalitions."

[180]Or, to be more specific, only two with any real chance of winning.

[181]See especially W. H. Riker, *Liberalism Against Populism: A Confrontation Between the Theory of Democracy and the Theory of Social Choice* (San Francisco: W. H. Freeman, 1982).

[182]McLean, *Public Choice*, p. 107.

Coleman's game players kept their words and behaved in a trustworthy fashion; if they did not, they soon learned that it would be in their interests to do so.

The development of "good behavior" of this type is obviously more likely the longer people are going to spend together and the more they depend on each other. In describing Boudon's work on French students' choices, we saw how these could be modeled using a two-person, prisoner's dilemma–type game. That worked well because the students were making a single decision, albeit one with long-term consequences for themselves.

Coleman elaborates on the effects of long-term relationships in his discussions of *trust*.[183] He emphasizes how fundamental an element of human interaction trust is—not least because the placement of trust allows both parties, the trustor and the trustee, to do something "that would not have been possible otherwise."[184] What makes contacts involving trust different from others is that *the potential loss will tend to outweigh the potential gain if the trustee turns out not to be trustworthy after all*, and that there are time lags involved. The recompense that the person doing the trusting can expect will tend to be a long way in the future.

Mail order transactions illustrate how important trust is to the working of a modern society. One of you has to start: either you pay up front and trust the firm to deliver, or the firm sends the goods and trusts you. Of course, there are legal remedies; but neither of you is likely to want to pay huge lawyers' fees over a $10 or $20 transaction. Coleman also quotes an example from a book on merchant banking by Joseph Wechsberg that illustrates the point exactly. The scene is the merchant bankers, Hambros, in London on a Friday afternoon.

> A prominent shipowner was on the line. He needed help, at once. To be exact, he needed two hundred thousand pounds within the next half hour . . .[185] one of his ships had undergone repairs at a big Amsterdam shipyard. A few minutes ago he'd had a call from his captain. The Amsterdam yard would not release the ship unless a cash payment was made of £200,000. Otherwise the ship would be tied up for the weekend and the owner would lose at least twenty thousand pounds.[186]

The Hambros manager to whom he was speaking was completely unfazed by this request. He did not request a meeting with his superiors or dictate a memo to a loan committee. Instead he simply pointed out to the anxious shipowner that it was late—in Amsterdam the bankers might

---

[183]Coleman, *Foundations of Social Theory*.

[184]Coleman, *Foundations of Social Theory*, p. 97.

[185]This was the early 1960s. The comparable sum today would be at least ten times as much.

[186]Joseph Wechsberg, *The Merchant Bankers* (London: Weidenfeld and Nicolson, 1967), p. 22; quoted in Coleman, *Foundations of Social Theory*, p. 92.

already have gone home for the weekend. However, he would try to get hold of Hambros's "corresponding" bank there. The shipowner should stay on the line; none of it would take very long. He then sent a telex to Amsterdam, and within three minutes a second phone rang. It was the Amsterdam bank. On the basis of a single telex from Hambros they had already telephoned the shipyard and confirmed that the cash for the repair bill was at the shipyard's immediate disposal. The Hambros man then spoke to the shipowner waiting on the other line: he could give his captain sailing orders.

In this transaction Hambros *trusted* the shipowner to pay them back a large sum of money, and the Amsterdam bank *trusted* Hambros to do the same. Moreover, this was done entirely on the basis of telephone calls and a single telex (the equivalent of a fax, but without even a signature). As the Hambros manager explained, if he had asked for confirmation, talked to his supervisors, checked records,

> it would have been too late to arrange the credit in Amsterdam. Our client would have lost twenty thousand pounds over a weekend and we might have lost a good client.[187]

He also commented that "Actually the risk isn't as terrible as it seems." All of the parties involved had a strong interest in a long-term relationship, and all had a great deal to lose if their good faith were ever called into question.

Over the last two decades a great deal has been written by researchers in all the social sciences about human behavior and the extent to which it can be modeled as a game. Interest in the area has been stimulated partly by the discovery that people do not, in most cases, behave like the mythical prisoners. We saw in the previous section how exchange theorists are building up evidence of the way in which exchanges create emotional bonds, and showing that people often do not maximize individual profits, but instead seek to share and benefit their partners.[188]

This work emphasizes the importance of contacts that are part of a long-term relationship. Much of how people behave in these situations can also be modeled as "two-person encounters" or games, and we can see that people generally follow quite simple (and sensible, or rational) rules. For example: "If I cooperate with the other person now, there is a fair chance that she will cooperate with me next time, if there is a next time. . . . [This] is clearly likeliest to work when we both value the future relatively highly and are likely to meet again."[189]

---

[187]Wechsberg, *The Merchant Bankers*, p. 23.

[188]See pp. 321–22.

[189]Iain McLean, "Review Article: Some Recent Work in Public Choice," *British Journal of Political Science* 16 (1989): pp. 377–94.

An obvious rational strategy to adopt is "tit for tat." This means that I will cooperate in the first game (encounter), but after that, I will do exactly what you did the time before. Hence, if you cheat on me, I will cheat right back, and if you cooperate, I will too. Simple as it is, "tit for tat" can be an extremely successful strategy for winning games and, by analogy, for creating stable and cooperative social groups.[190]

Rational choice theorists have taken the analysis furthest in discussing the market for "lemons." Suppose that I am a small used-car salesman and that some of my cars are lemons. If you come in off the street, planning to buy a car, I know that this is probably the only sale I will ever make to you. (I am also a bit mistrustful of you myself and not convinced that your credit is all that good.) Obviously, I have no incentive to tell you that the car you like is one of the lemons. If I can unload on you a car that I wish I'd never bought, so much the better.

Unfortunately, of course, the customer is as aware of this situation as I am. The effect of lemons in the marketplace is actually to shift our behavior—and cost us all money. In the case of secondhand cars, for example, the cheapest way to buy a car is from another individual; the second-cheapest, from a small used-car salesman; and by far the most expensive, from a large established dealership. So why do any of us go to the dealer? Answer: because of the "lemon" problem. A big dealer is going to be around for a long time, values its reputation, and hopes some day to sell us new cars as well. Therefore, we reason, we are less likely to get a lemon. Instead of getting just the car we want from an individual on the next block, we pay more for another, and quite possibly worse, one from the dealer.

What these analyses emphasize is the crucial difference between one-time and continuing relationships. The former, which include house sales as well as used-car sales, are in fact notorious for producing cheating or attempted cheating. Moreover, the people who attempt to cheat in these situations often would not dream of doing so at other times. In other words, whether or not people obey norms will depend on the rational choices facing them—what they can get away with and how much they hope to gain.

A major emphasis in all these games is on how one person perceives the other's behavior. The same is true in ordinary social life, and Coleman discusses in detail the importance of "intermediaries" in creating "systems

---

[190]See especially Robert Axelrod, "The Emergence of Cooperation among Egoists," *American Political Science Review* LXXV (1981): 306–18, and *The Evolution of Cooperation* (New York: Basic Books, 1984); and J. Maynard Smith, *Evolution and the Theory of Games* (Cambridge: Cambridge University Press, 1982). Sociobiology is a major source of insights in this area because of its analysis of reciprocal altruism in animals (see Chapter 8). Richard Dawkins provides an excellent introduction to the implications of different strategies among animals, notably in his analysis of the benefits accruing to "suckers" (who always help), "cheats" (who never do), and "grudgers" (who always help the first time, but then bear a grudge against anyone who doesn't reciprocate). Richard Dawkins, *The Selfish Gene* (Oxford: Oxford University Press, 1976), chap. 10.

of trust"—that is, situations in which we can be confident that it is safe to trust someone about whom we know little or nothing. In the example given above, Hambros was an intermediary; the Amsterdam bank trusted the shipowner because it trusted Hambros. As Coleman also points out, in modern life there is a

> skewed distribution of trust. . . . Certain persons, such as those employed in managerial positions in large respected organizations, find that trust of all sorts is readily placed in them. Their path in life is cleared. . . . In contrast, there is a large set of other persons for whom this is not true: young persons, persons who are out of work, women who do not work outside the home, self-employed persons such as writers and artists, and retired persons. All these persons have more difficulty in carrying out even the everyday activities of life which require some trust on the part of others.[191]

A great deal of work on military strategy[192] focuses on the related concept of *credibility*—in this case not whether one is making a credible offer of a reliable used car, but whether one is making a credible threat that one can be trusted to carry out. Credibility has also become a major interest of management theorists and management consultants, who look at how people make their offers, intentions, and actions credible to others when, for example, they are involved in an important negotiation or bid.[193]

Coleman's approach to trust, and to the development of cooperative behavior, is that it offers a way of discussing the development of social norms within what remains a general rational choice framework. Sociological variants of rational choice theory are distinguished by their concern with the morality of social exchange, including the argument that there exist general social principles of distributive justice and equity.[194] These developing theories of trust and cooperation are fully consistent with Homans's arguments that group norms could emerge easily in small groups because conformity would bring friendship and approval.[195] However, while Homans argues that the explanation for such norms is to be found ultimately in aspects of human psychology (such as an innate belief in distributive justice), the game analysis of Coleman and others suggests that group norms emerge naturally in the course of rational interaction among group members.

[191]Coleman, *Foundations of Social Theory*, p. 185.

[192]Including analyses of the Cold War period and the "mutually assured destruction" doctrine that was at the heart of US strategic policy; see Robert Powell, *Nuclear Deterrence Theory: The Search for Credibility* (Cambridge: Cambridge University Press, 1990); and Michael Nicholson, *Rationality and the Analysis of International Conflict* (Cambridge: Cambridge University Press, 1992).

[193]See A.K. Dixit and B. J. Nalebuff, *Thinking Strategically: The Competitive Edge in Business, Politics and Everyday Life* (New York: W.W. Norton, 1991).

[194]See the introduction to this chapter.

[195]See pp. 314–15.

Norms and Rights.   Coleman is especially interested in the development of social norms because of his underlying concern with "the transitions between micro and macro levels."[196] In *Foundations of Social Theory* he offers a more formal analysis than in his earlier discussions of trust, arguing that, underlying norms, we find fundamental conceptions of *rights*. You can have the right to act; and you can have the right to control another's action. Buying something will generally give you the right to consume it—which, in turn, is what gives you the incentive to engage in an act of exchange and obtain the object in question. For someone to sell it to you, or exchange it for something else, they must have the right to dispose of whatever it is that you want.

Some rights are protected by law, and, most of the time, such legal rights are accepted without serious question. (If you buy a new bicycle from an established store, not many people will question your right to ride off on it.) But in cases where there is no legal protection, and sometimes even where there is, people's conceptions of rights can conflict. Coleman suggests that "an actor has a right to carry out an action or to have an action carried out when all who are affected by exercise of that right accept the action without dispute."[197] In other words, rights do not exist in some absolute sense but are bound up with social consensus; they exist by virtue of being recognized by others.

Coleman illustrates how the idea of people's rights can change over time by using the example of smoking. At the moment it is common for smokers and nonsmokers to have different ideas about smokers' rights, and about who, in a given situation, "holds rights over smoking." Twenty years ago, if a smoker lit up in a room, it was rare for anyone to object; there was general agreement that smokers had the right to light up. Today, the reverse is true indoors, and most smokers accept this; they see it as the right of the non-smoker to decide whether someone can smoke in a room shared by a smoker and a nonsmoker. But most smokers would still deny that nonsmokers have the right to decide whether they can smoke outdoors or in their own homes.

Coleman notes that over time there is a tendency (though by no means a universal one) for conceptions of rights to converge so that people agree on whether a particular right exists. A number of factors may be important, including the processes of giving and withholding social approval that Homans describes and that creates consensus, but also the use of power (which may mean that something becomes a legal right before it is generally accepted.) Coleman emphasizes that the "essential quality of a right lies in its social base. Rights come into existence, vanish, and are taken from one actor and given to another by social recognition. Yet rights are dependent on power for their enforcement."[198] The currently recognized rights of nonsmokers are

[196]Coleman, *Foundations of Social Theory*, p. 21.
[197]Coleman, *Foundations of Social Theory*, p. 50.
[198]Coleman, *Foundations of Social Theory*, p. 63.

enforced in libraries, classrooms, and other public places because the authorities in those places have legally recognized rights, and therefore enforceable powers, to lay down requirements for behavior in them.

In Coleman's view *"a norm concerning a specific action exists when the socially defined right to control the action is held not by the actor but by others."*[199] In other words, when we observe that there is now a social norm that forbids smokers to smoke indoors in the presence of objecting nonsmokers, we are saying that there is a consensus that the smoker's actions can be controlled by others. By contrast, there are currently no general social norms that govern your right, as an adult, to decide what TV channel to watch, what time to go to bed, or what to eat for breakfast. In Coleman's view, the "emergence of norms is . . . a prototypical micro-to-macro transition, because the process must arise from individual actions yet a norm itself is a system-level property."[200] It is also, as he argues at length, a process that typically arises in the course of repeated direct or indirect interactions and exchanges. It requires people to notice what others are doing and to be in a position, over time, to reward conforming behavior and to invoke sanctions against deviants and free-riders; in other words, it requires "small group" behavior.

SOCIAL CAPITAL

One of Coleman's most influential concepts is that of "social capital."[201] By social capital Coleman means those aspects of social structures that make it easier for people to achieve things. He gives as an example the central Kahn El Khalili market in old Cairo, where

> the boundaries between merchants are difficult for an outsider to discover. The owner of a shop that specializes in leather will, when queried about where one can find a certain kind of jewelry, turn out to sell that as well—or, what appears to be nearly the same thing, to have a close associate who sells it, to whom he will immediately take the customer. Or he will instantly become a money changer . . . merely by turning to his colleague a few shops down. . . . (O)ne can see the market as . . . a set of individual merchants, each having an extensive body of social capital on which to draw through the relationships of the market.[202]

Another example of high social capital that Coleman gives is the wholesale diamond market in New York, where merchants are able, with

[199]Coleman, *Foundations of Social Theory*, p. 243; italics ours.

[200]Coleman, *Foundations of Social Theory*, p. 244.

[201]See especially James S. Coleman, "Social Capital in the Creation of Human Capital," supplement to *American Journal of Sociology* 94 (1988): S95–S120. Francis Fukayama made this the central concept in his best-seller, *Trust: The Social Virtues and the Creation of Prosperity* (New York: The Free Press, 1995).

[202]Coleman, "Social Capital," S100.

confidence, to hand bags of stones over to others to be examined at leisure. And we can contrast Coleman's positive examples with the lack of social capital among urban drug addicts, as described by Leon Dash, who records family members stealing from the refrigerator to raise money for cash, or, in one woman's case, accepting a small sum of money—quickly spent on crack—to allow her boyfriend's murderers into his apartment.[203]

Coleman argues that social capital facilitates productive activity. "For example, a group within which there is extensive trustworthiness and extensive trust is able to accomplish much more than a comparable group without that."[204] In analyzing the way social capital operates he identifies the degree of trustworthiness (the extent to which obligations will be repaid) but also the extent to which different individuals ("actors within the same structure") have high levels of obligations outstanding. He suggests that we can think of the latter as credit slips on which people can draw. Coleman contrasts a structure like a Mafia "family," where obligations are almost always repaid, but where the credit slips are concentrated in one man's hands, with the more diffuse structures of the type underpinning safe urban environments where people can walk safely alone at night, and neighbors can be trusted to look out for each other's children.[205]

Echoing Granovetter's work on networks, Coleman emphasizes that an "important form of social capital is the potential for information that inheres in social relations."[206] However, where Granovetter emphasizes the benefits of "weak ties," Coleman tends to emphasize their downside. As we have seen, he argues that norms tend to arise when links between people are close and tight, so that one gets closure in social networks. High levels of social capital require the effective enforcement of social norms; but without "closure of the social structure" this is difficult to achieve. Here, and in his later work, Coleman expresses concern that, in modern societies, closure is increasingly rare, and that this has serious implications for the creation of social capital and for the life-chances of children in families with low levels of social capital.

Coleman's argument is that modern societies, characterized by formal organizations, geographical mobility, and a lack of visibility for people's actions, will inevitably have problems in developing and enforcing social norms. Noticing deviants and wrongdoers and bringing sanctions to bear (for example, chastising or reporting teenagers who are vandalizing property, or passing on information about the nontrustworthiness of a local

---

[203]Leon Dash, *Rosa Lee: A Mother and Her Family in Urban America* (New York: Basic Books 1996).

[204]Coleman, "Social Capital," p. 101.

[205]For an interesting analysis of the Sicilian Mafia as the supplier of protection in a society of danger and distrust, see Diego Gambetta, *The Sicilian Mafia: The Business of Private Protection* (Cambridge, Mass: Harvard University Press, 1993).

[206]Coleman, "Social Capital," S104.

trader) are themselves activities that have costs for the person involved. Equally, bringing up children to behave "well" and internalize certain values and norms is itself a demanding task. Coleman argues that

> norms and values . . . grow slowly and only in stable social systems. The imposition of external sanctions is subject to free-rider problems.[207] When there is not stability . . . the potential future retribution that can overcome the free-rider problem is gone and, as a result, external sanctions that make norms effective vanish. The creation of internal sanctions through socialization is in the socializer's interest only when relations are sufficiently stable to make it possible to reap the benefits of the socialization effort.[208]

In other words, if no one is ever going to know whether you did anything to stop vandalism or other undesirable behavior, and you are not going to suffer in any direct, immediate way for turning a blind eye, why should you put yourself out? You might just bring down trouble on yourself for no good reason. (Ask yourself how willing you would be to reprimand a large and belligerent smoker in a no-smoking area where there was no one else around.) Equally, in Coleman's view, it is irrational to expect paid caregivers to put the same effort into socializing children that their parents and families would. By the time the results are evident, they, the caregivers, will be long gone.

Coleman's analysis echoes Durkheim's[209] in its pessimism about the long-term ability of modern societies to maintain cohesion and enforce social norms; and he emphasizes the enormous impact of a shift away from the family as the organizing institution of society. Families, he argues, are, while not perfect, far better than any other institution at making everyone contribute and pull their weight (that is, at overcoming free-rider problems) and at socializing children effectively so that they internalize social norms. "The means by which they do this appear to be largely social-psychological: the use of stigma to brand noncontributors and the conferring of status and power on those who contribute more than their share. These kinds of incentives appear to be effective only within very small social units."[210]

Natural Persons and Corporate Actors.   As well as echoing some of Durkheim's pessimism, Coleman also revisits some of Durkheim's major ideas. Durkheim, as we have discussed, drew a major distinction between the mechanical solidarity of primitive societies and the organic solidarity of

---

[207]In other words, it is in your interests to have other people who are prepared to keep local teenagers in order, and enforce other social norms, without your having to do anything to make yourself unpopular.

[208]James Coleman, "Constructed Social Organization," in P. Bourdieu and J. Coleman, ed., *Social Theory for a Changing Society* (Boulder, Co: Westview Press, 1991), pp. 1–16.

[209]See Durkheim's discussion of anomie in Chapter 2, p. 23.

[210]Coleman, *Foundations of Social Theory*, p. 657.

advanced ones. Coleman reconceptualizes this by drawing a distinction between societies where both the physical and the social environment are *natural*, and those where they are *constructed*. In the former the actors are simply *natural persons*; but in the latter—our own modern societies—new actors make an appearance: *corporate actors* such as businesses, government departments, law courts, and newspapers. They are new structural elements in a social system, and they also create a new structure for actions and inter-actions. In the past interactions involved only people as individuals (natural persons). Now new, important types of interaction occur: persons with persons still, but also persons with corporate actors, and corporate actors with each other.

Constructed environments, Coleman argues, involve the "unbundling of activities that were once tied together in the family."[211] Welfare and child care duties are increasingly taken over by corporate actors. What Coleman calls "purposively constructed affinity groups"—friends—need no longer be geographically close. As Fischer noted, communication can be maintained over wide distances. However, Coleman is less sanguine than Fischer. He argues that the change in social structure has major effects on patterns and intensity of association—the same variables that interest Blau—and in par-ticular has "major consequences for children."[212]

Children and young people, Coleman argues, need attention and inten-sive contact for support and for constraint. Intense parent-child relations can produce remarkable results, as shown by, for example, a number of recent mathematical and chess-playing prodigies, and by the enormous success of certain immigrant groups. A close relationship with a single parent or parents creates social capital for a child; but so can other, more diffuse sets of relationship *if, taken together, they create a strong set of links*. For this, however, one needs closure—a relationship *among* the adults involved with the child so that they can share information and reinforce (or restrain) each other's behavior. In other words, dense networks and strong ties are needed for child rearing.

Closure of this sort "is part of the primordial social structure that has the family as its building block."[213] It *may* occur in our own, modern, "con-structed" societies—for example, if children are in workplace nurseries, or if teachers and parents meet frequently in the course of community activities. But there is nothing inherent in our new structures that will provide it; and many factors—long journeys to work, frequent moves of house and job, turnover among childcare workers—act in the opposite direction. Coleman has no direct measures of closure (association) among the different adults involved with contemporary teenagers. However, he does cite data that

[211]Coleman, *Foundations of Social Theory*, p. 585.

[212]Coleman, *Foundations of Social Theory*, p. 597.

[213]Coleman, *Foundations of Social Theory*, p. 594.

show how the chances of dropping out of high school increase the less intense the parent-child relationship and the more moves a child makes between houses and schools. In doing so he is advancing hypotheses about the links between structural variables and individual behavior and well-being that epitomize his conception of social theory.

CONCLUSION

Rational choice perspectives have attracted a great deal of attention in recent years. Some argue that they must be given pride of place as the basis of sociological theory in the next century; others criticize them as based on a flawed or incomplete view of human nature, unable to explain many of the major concerns of sociology, and essentially tautological in their propensity to first assume in advance that actions must be rational, and then explain them as such. This final section reviews the achievements of rational choice theorists and the strengths and limitations of the approach.

Overall, rational choice theories (including exchange theory) tend to be most successful when used to analyze behavior in small group situations. Homans, for example, focuses entirely on elementary social behavior. Although Emerson and Cook argue that their work on exchange relations can be generalized to larger groups, they in fact deal almost entirely with small groups rather than institutions. Blau's exchange-based analyses of love and friendship and of the interpersonal imbalances at the root of power are generally more satisfactory than his attempts to explain the origin of collective values, legitimacy, or opposition movements. He, indeed, came to believe that the approach is intrinsically suited only to "face-to-face relations . . . and must be complemented by other theoretical principles that focus on complex structures."[214]

As the last part of this chapter described, a growing body of work now applies the rational choice perspective to structural issues, especially the development and perpetuation of group norms and of trust. This work tends to support theorists such as Coleman and Homans in their contention that psychological propositions underlie all sociological explanation. Nonetheless, it seems likely that most sociologists concerned with social institutions will continue, for good reason, to discuss their subject matter in terms of structural variables, such as class structures or legitimacy, rather than individuals' decisions and reactions.

In this respect it is instructive to look back at the conflict sociology of Randall Collins. Like the rational choice theorists, Collins is concerned with linking the micro and the macro levels and analyzing social institutions with

---

[214]Peter M. Blau, "Interaction IV: Social Exchange," in David L. Sillo, ed., *International Encyclopedia of the Social Sciences*, Vol. 7 (New York: The Free Press, 1968), p. 457.

reference to the motives, experiences, and actions of the people involved. Nonetheless, many of his propositions refer to such constructs as "bureaucratization" or "classes." In other words, in analyzing regularities among societies, Collins uses a structural vocabulary.

Nothing in recent rational choice theory suggests that this will change. A rational choice perspective often works well in explaining people's actions when the institutional setting is largely given and the details of individual behavior are of special interest. It is also valuable in explaining people's reactions to institutional changes when we can assume that their values remain much the same. Examples where the institutional setting is given include the informal groups on which Homans concentrates but also Blau's discussion of modern love, Richmond's experience with the microeconomy game, and Coleman's discussion of congressional voting patterns and alliances.

Moreover, even in these contexts, the rational choice approach is often best supplemented with insights and concepts more often associated with other micro perspectives. For example, we saw how Kristin Luker used a modified rational choice perspective to explain why many women give so much time to political activism on both sides of the abortion debate.[215] In doing so she drew on ideas more often associated with other micro perspectives. Similar points are made by two eminent commentators on the perspective, Randall Collins and Neil Smelser. Both see rational choice as offering a great deal to sociological theory. However, both also emphasize that a view of human action and motivation that sees rationality as an all-encompassing explanatory variable is seriously inadequate.

Collins emphasizes that the power of the rational choice perspective to explain and predict depends on it being more than an empty tautology. "Let us take as the analytical core of the rational approach, the principle that behavior is motivated by maximization under constraint; i.e., what happens in social interaction is determined by the ratio between the rewards of alternative actions, and their costs."[216] Much research on human behavior tends to show that people do not in fact "calculate" very much; the ethnomethodologists' analysis of how much we simply take things for granted comes closer to the texture of the micro situation. As Collins points out, "Human beings . . . operate within restricted cognitive limits, avoiding broad-ranging calculations and sticking conservatively within background assumptions,"[217] and this must temper our view of rational choice as a good model for human behavior. However, it does not necessarily invalidate the approach; rather one must see the term "rational choice" as essentially metaphorical rather than a description of people's conscious mental processes. Over time, within constraints, the drift

---

[215]See pp. 345–46.

[216]Randall Collins, "Can Rational Action Theory Unify Future Social Science?" in Clark, ed., *James S. Coleman*, pp. 329–44.

[217]Collins, "Can Rational Action Theory Unify Future Social Science?" p. 332.

of behavior may be in the direction that the theories predict; moreover, in many situations, material considerations will be overriding, providing the sort of contexts within which accurate predictions can be made.

Many situations—but by no means all. Collins also emphasizes a major weakness of rational choice theories, namely their neglect of the emotions. Many of the things that people want and that motivate them cannot be measured on some common scale and are not purely or even primarily material. The clear sense of self that Luker sees as a reward for activism is a case in point.

As we have seen, Emerson tried and failed to develop some common metric that would enable precise comparisons to be made between things that do not have an established monetary value. Collins suggests a rather different approach: namely, that we should see emotions rather than material rewards as the primary force driving human actions.[218] What he labels "emotional energy" can be seen as a continuum, from confidence, enthusiasm, and happiness through to depression and gloom. Material objectives are then seen as *one* of the things that people seek out in order to sustain or raise their emotional energy level, not as something that should necessarily be seen as primary in explaining incentives and behavior.[219]

Smelser also emphasizes rational choice theory's neglect of the emotions and of "affect"; but he does not see the answer as lying with a different, all-embracing metric based on emotional energy. Instead he criticizes the perspective's assumption that one course of action can be clearly seen as desirable, another as undesirable, and the optimal (rational) choice therefore clear. In fact, human life and human emotions are not like that at all, he argues. One of their psychological foundations is *ambivalence*.

"The nature of ambivalence is to hold opposing affective orientations toward the same person, object, or symbol," he argues.[220] We can have feelings of love and hate toward the same person; and the balance between them is unstable. This chapter has described how Homans and others emphasize the way in which close contacts build up group norms and identity; but tight groups are also resented by their members.[221] "This negative side of dependence has not been given anything like equal time" by rational choice theorists, Smelser believes.[222] Overall, he feels that rational choice models work best in those situations where people have relative freedom of choice—for

---

[218]R. Collins, "Emotional Energy as the Common Denominator of Rational Choice," *Rationality and Society* 5 (1993): 203–30.

[219]Collins's approach risks falling into the same trap of tautological reasoning as rational choice theorists have been charged with. Without an independent measure, how can one tell whether people's actions were motivated by a desire to build up energy levels? Does one simply assume this to be the case?

[220]Neil Smelser, "Presidential Address: The Rational and the Ambivalent in the Social Sciences," *American Sociological Review* 63, no. 1 (February 1998): 5.

[221]See pp. 129–30 for Coser's comparable arguments, derived from Simmel.

[222]Smelser, "The Rational and the Ambivalent," p. 6.

example, to leave a group, to select a university, to vote as they please. Elsewhere, far more weight must be given to psychological models based on the emotions and ambivalence generated by dependence and constraint.

The strengths and weaknesses of a rational choice perspective can best be summarized by turning to an area of active empirical research: who does the housework? We saw earlier in this chapter how a rational choice perspective can successfully predict that decision making within a marriage will be linked to the relative earning power of husband and wife and the degree to which the wife is emotionally and financially dependent on her husband. The seminal work in this area was carried out by Blood and Wolfe in the late 1950s; since then there have been major shifts in marriage patterns, female labor force participation, and social attitudes. One might therefore expect that in, for example, households with two full-time earners, housework would be more or less equally shared.

Instead, survey after survey finds that women continue to do the greater share of the housework.[223] The relative earnings of men and women do explain some of the gap between male and female contributions, but this leaves large amounts unexplained. The presence of children explains a little more; but again, a large gap persists. It is simply not possible to argue that women are doing more of the housework simply because they earn less, nor to see this pattern as a simple result of their dependence on men. (While women whose own earnings are very high do less housework than low-earning women, this isn't because their husbands do more; more often it is that the household buys help and eats out more.) In other words, while the rational choice approach explains some of what is going on, for a fuller explanation we have to look elsewhere.

Housework, it seems, is an activity that is closely bound up with people's self-image and their ideas about how men and women, and particularly husbands and wives, *ought* to behave. Thus the gender gap is highest for married couples and lowest for divorcees and widows/widowers who are cohabiting. Having adult sons at home means that their mothers do more housework; adult daughters at home have the opposite effect. If there is a crossover point in a family's history, where the wife moves from being a large-scale contributor to family income to becoming the primary wage earner, she tends to *increase* her contribution to the housework, as a way of compensating the husband for the undermining of what one analyst calls his "gender-normative identity." In other words, while the economic dependency arguments of rational choice theory provide important insights into the dynamics of the modern family, they go only so far, and they must be supplemented by perspectives that take account of human emotions, values, and socially constructed identities.

---

[223]See especially Julie Brines, "The Exchange Value of Housework," *Rationality and Society* 5.3 (July 1993): 302–40; Scott J. South and Glenna Spitze, "Housework in Marital and Nonmarital Households," *American Sociological Review* 59 (June 1994): 327–47; Arlie Russell Hochschild, with Anne Machung, *The Second Shift: Working Parents and the Revolution at Home* (New York: Viking, 1989).

CHAPTER EIGHT

Rediscovering the Body:The Sociology of the Body and Sociobiology

INTRODUCTION

Sociologists have always been much occupied with defining both sociology and society itself. Among the classical theorists, one of the most influential such discussions was that of Durkheim, whose concept of social facts was summarized in Chapter 2.[1] Durkheim's arguments included the claims that "if . . . we begin with the individual, we shall be able to understand nothing of what takes place in the group" and that social facts "should not be confused with biological phenomena."[2] Durkheim's emphasis on the group rather than the individual has never been fully accepted; hence, in addition to the perspectives offered by symbolic interactionism and phenomenology, we now find rational choice theorists arguing that beginning with the individual is actually a very *good* way to understand group behavior and "emergent" social phenomena. Until recently, however, Durkheim's indifference to the biological has found a ready echo in sociological theory as a whole. The major perspectives discussed so far all share an emphasis on symbol and meaning, on values and norms. This is one of the things that has made them sociological.

In recent years, however, this emphasis has come under attack. Sociology (and anthropology) have been criticized for effectively ignoring the physical and the biological altogether; for implying that society is essentially symbolic, and controlled and shaped entirely by ideas and interests, rather than a world of flesh-and-blood animals whose biology also affects their behavior. The critics argue that we should study the biological aspects of people's social behavior—what Parsons labels the level of the "organism"—which they consider to be far more important than has commonly been admitted.

This new interest in the body and in human beings as a biological species has manifested itself in two quite distinct ways, both of which are discussed in this chapter. The first is a *sociology of the body*, which draws heavily on phenomenology and cultural studies. The second involves the direct application of evolutionary theory to sociology through the medium of evolutionary biology or, as it often known, *sociobiology*.

PART ONE

The Sociology of the Body

The new sociology of the body is, in one sense, quite as concerned with meaning and symbol as its classical predecessors. One of its foremost theorists recently offered his own definition of sociology as concerned with "the

---

[1]See pp. 21–22.

[2]Émile Durkheim, *The Rules of Sociological Method*, ed. George E. G. Catlin (New York: The Free Press, 1938/1966), pp. 104, 3.

meaning of social action, that is, the subjective perspective, emotions, and feelings of human agents as social individuals."[3] What they emphasize, however, is that the body and physical experiences are of central importance to individual and social life. Moreover, while the ways in which we regard illnesses or the process of aging may change over time and between cultures, our perceptions and our experiences are a result of constant interaction between the cultural and the biological. The latter cannot be ignored.

One reason for the growing interest of sociologists in the body is the highly visible and growing interest of the public at large in the whole area of physical health and well-being. There is enormous interest in the effect of different foods on our bodies and health, as evidenced by the explosion of food labeling and the flight of the American population toward any food that is low-fat or fat-free. Diet foods, plastic surgery, and health clubs have been some of the fastest-growing industries of the late twentieth century. Magazines devote enormous amounts of space to issues of health, fitness, and cosmetics.

Chris Shilling links this to the general changes that were discussed in Chapter 4 and in particular to what Giddens and others refer to as high modernity. He observes that

> the position of the body within contemporary popular culture reflects the unprecedented individualization of the body. Growing numbers of people are increasingly concerned with the health, shape, and appearance of their own bodies as expressions of individual identity. . . . (O)f all the factors which have contributed to the visibility of the body, two apparently paradoxical developments seem to have been particularly important. *We now have the means to exert an unprecedented degree of control over bodies, yet we are also living in an age which has thrown into radical doubt our knowledge of what bodies are and how we should control them.*[4]

The growing self-consciousness of modern human beings and their inability to take things for granted have been described at length by, for example, Jürgen Habermas in his analysis of the rationalization of society. The new theorists of the body emphasize how this self-consciousness, allied with the belief that everything can be controlled, encourages us to focus on our own physical selves. Bauman argues that our modern obsession with health and beauty is "an attempt to belie the ultimate limits of the body."[5] Yet in the end those limits hold: we cannot all look like supermodels or champion bodybuilders, and in the end we all die.

[3]Bryan S. Turner with Colin Samson, *Medical Power and Social Knowledge*, 2nd ed. (Thousand Oaks, Calif.: Sage, 1995), p. 3.

[4]Chris Shilling, *The Body and Social Theory* (London/Newbury Park: Sage, 1993), pp. 1–3; italics original.

[5]Zygmunt Bauman, "Survival as a Social Construct," *Theory, Culture and Society* 9 (1): 1–36.

Representing the Body

The work of the postmodernist Michel Foucault (1929–1984) has been important in awakening sociologists' interest in the human body. Foucault was not a professional sociologist in the American tradition: the chair at the prestigious Collège de France that he held at the time of his premature death[6] was in history and systems of thought, and his degrees were in philosophy, psychology, and psychopathology. However, his work has enormously influenced sociological theory, as well as the study of literature and culture. He is particularly interested in the prison and the asylum, which to him exemplify the modern world.

Foucault explores changes in the way people have thought and behaved with respect to a variety of activities and behavior, in all of which the human body plays a central role. His books reproduce vivid contemporary descriptions of torture, madness, and prisons. In premodern times, he notes, torture and public floggings and executions were the state's main tools for securing order.[7] Then came a major transition to the use of confinement—for convicted criminals, but also (and often, at first, in the same place) for the insane and the indigent. An "entire population . . . almost overnight found itself shut up, excluded more severely than the lepers"[8] of the Middle Ages. "In a hundred and fifty years, confinement had become the abusive amalgam of heterogeneous elements."[9] In the early nineteenth century, suddenly "everywhere we find the same outrage, the same virtuous censure"[10] of the way the insane and criminals are imprisoned together. Similarly, throughout Europe and the United States, in the space of a few decades, modern codes of law were drawn up. "At the beginning of the nineteenth century . . . the great spectacle of physical punishment disappeared; the tortured body was avoided."[11]

People came to find disgusting the very idea of public floggings and hangings, or of going on a Sunday outing to view the insane. However, it was not, in Foucault's view, that society was now characterized by "more kindness, more respect, more 'humanity'."[12] Rather, the old ways were incompatible with the whole emerging "scientifico-legal complex."[13] Instead of physical punishment, the new prisons assured "both the real capture of

---

[6]From AIDS.

[7]Michel Foucault, *Discipline and Punish: The Birth of the Prison*, trans. Alan Sheriden (London: Allen Lane, 1977); and *Madness and Civilization: A History of Insanity in the Age of Reason*, trans. Richard Howard (New York: Random House, 1965).

[8]Foucault, *Madness and Civilization*, p. 45.

[9]Foucault, *Madness and Civilization*, p. 45.

[10]Foucault, *Madness and Civilization*, p. 227.

[11]Foucault, *Discipline and Punish*, pp. 7 and 14.

[12]Foucault, *Discipline and Punish*, p. 16.

[13]Foucault, *Discipline and Punish*, p. 23.

the body and its perpetual observation";[14] change was rooted in new, far-reaching "mechanisms and strategies of power."[15]

Foucault's three-volume *History of Sexuality* similarly traces links between physical activities—and what could seem more straightforwardly physical than sexual acts?—and changes in both how people think and underlying structures of power. We have a simplistic view, he argues, that people used to be repressed sexually and no longer are. But human history is far more complicated than that. Take, for example, homosexual relations between men and young boys. In classical Greece this was marked by "intensity," "seriousness," "vitality"[16]; but by the Roman era, attitudes had changed. "What seems to have changed is not the taste for boys . . . (rather) a fading of the importance it was granted in philosophical and moral debate." There was a conflict with the power of the Roman father, who was determined to maintain control over his sons, not cede it to adult lovers; hence "love for boys was practised for the most part with young slaves, about whose status there was no reason to worry."[17] It was not that a partiality for boys was criticized or seen as illegitimate, but that the value attached to it altered.

This in turn paved the way for new perspectives on sexual intercourse, with the Stoics arguing that "an equal exchange of enjoyment" is crucial, and impossible with a boy. Today we view sexual intercourse between adults and minors as reprehensible and unnatural. Foucault's point is that one cannot see these activities as purely physical, the outcome of biological drives that may be "warped" in some people. On the contrary: the sexual activities that we engage in, and that we wish to engage in, are mediated by ideas that themselves relate to underlying structures of power. We must recognize how sex is "historically subordinate to sexuality."[18]

However, although Foucault's work was important in directing attention to the body, his analytical methods and conclusions also tend to deny it any fixed reality, implying, rather, that how we view and how we experience our bodies is *entirely* a social construction. Foucault concentrates on textual analysis, and on how people viewed and talked about the body, because he seeks structures of knowledge. As we discuss further in Chapter 9, Foucault's postmodernist perspective implies that an age is defined by the particular way in which we see and comprehend the world, and that this is also what governs how power is exercised.[19] In the process, as Shilling points

---

[14]Foucault, *Discipline and Punish*, p. 304.

[15]Foucault, *Discipline and Punish*, p. 305.

[16]Michel Foucault, *The Care of the Self: Vol. 3 of The History of Sexuality* (London: Allen Lane, 1988), p. 189.

[17]Foucault, *The Care of the Self*, pp. 189–90.

[18]Michel Foucault, *The History of Sexuality, Vol. 1: An Introduction* (London: Allen Lane, 1976), p. 157.

[19]See Chapter 9, pp. 407–408.

out, the body itself "disappears as a material or biological phenomenon . . . reduced to an inert mass which is controlled by discourses centered on the mind."[20]

Bryan S. Turner also emphasizes that our bodies must be understood as socially constructed; but in his work the biological remains far more apparent and important. Turner is currently dean of the faculty of arts at Deakin University, Australia; he previously held chairs at Essex University, England; Flinders University, Australia; and the University of Utrecht in the Netherlands.[21] He sees his work as symptomatic of a more "general movement in social science . . . which has attempted to come to terms with the embodiment of the human actor and hence with the relationship between emotionality and feeling in relation to purposeful activity."[22] We have encountered this movement at various points in this text—for example, in discussing Hochschild's sociology of the emotions, or Goffman's work on "personal front."[23] However, Turner advances a more systematic theory and classification of the body in society, and he also emphasizes how strongly the model of social actors as intrinsically rational and disembodied still holds sway. "We have to assert that in the beginning was the body" and overcome the still-pervasive mind-body division, he argues.[24]

Turner does not believe that there is some universal scientific way of describing how our bodies "are" in society. On the contrary: how we feel our bodies to be, how others perceive them, and how they function and behave are in large part (not wholly) a function of culture. One of the challenges for a sociology of the body is to distinguish between and relate these different layers: for example, to distinguish between and look at both the "organic" fact of handedness (that is, that people favor one hand over another) and the "cultural representations and social meanings of right-handedness."[25]

Turner defines the sociology of the body as being concerned with the "historical and social consequences of the management of the body in human affairs."[26] He argues that bodies in human societies have to be regulated—trained and disciplined in the appropriate techniques of a given society and culture. Human babies learn to walk and gesture in all societies; but how they carry themselves, how they move, and the sorts of gestures

[20]Shilling, *The Body and Social Theory*, p. 80.

[21]Turner's most important publications in this area are *The Body and Society: Explorations in Social Theory* (Oxford: Basil Blackwell, 1984); *Regulating Bodies: Essays in Medical Sociology* (London: Routledge, 1992); *Medical Power and Social Knowledge*; and M. Featherstone, M. Hepworth, and B. S. Turner, ed., *The Body, Social Process and Cultural Theory* (London: Sage, 1991). The development of the approach is particularly associated with the journal *Theory, Culture and Society*.

[22]Turner, *Regulating Bodies*, p. 162.

[23]See Chapter 5, pp. 241–42 and 230.

[24]Turner, *Regulating Bodies*, p. 7.

[25]Turner, *Regulating Bodies*, p. 9.

[26]Turner, *Regulating Bodies*, p. 15.

they make vary enormously. The body is also an important part of what Bourdieu would describe as "cultural capital": a way of differentiating people within as well as between societies.[27] For example, there have been enormous changes in the last one hundred years in the way tanned skins are perceived in Western societies. They were for a long time the mark of relatively low status—the result of open air work, probably in the fields. Then they became a sign of wealth—the ability first to take summer holidays in the sun, later winter ones too, while poorer people toiled in factories or offices. More recently, as more and more people can do this (or frequent a tanning salon), tans have lost much of their cachet while also starting to acquire undesirable associations with skin cancer.

Turner describes how diet used to be seen as a way of promoting mental stability and reason as well as health but is now promoted in terms of longevity and sexuality.[28] He also notes, "The new emphasis in body-beautiful culture on self-preservation and self-maintenance . . . may . . . be closely associated with the aging of the populations of the Western industrial societies." Thus, the "way in which human bodies are represented in terms of aging processes has changed fundamentally. . . . The image these days is of an endless youth stretching before us. But one knows that these representations of the young body can only be achieved by continuous exercise and athleticism, topped up by the periodic face-lift, draining off human fat, operations on the eyelids, and so on. These 'young' bodies are literally constructed but they are constructed *against* aging."[29]

The emphasis on the "body beautiful" has a far greater effect on women than on men. Young women have always been concerned with their physical appearance prior to marriage. However, social changes, and especially the growing belief that the body is almost infinitely malleable, have had a profound effect on the degree to which women's self-image is associated with physical appearance throughout their lives. In discussing the role of women in society, we have noted, for example, Dorothy Smith's analysis of how femininity is associated with clothes and image.[30] To this must be added physical appearance and especially body weight. Moreover, while in the past being "pretty" or "plain" were seen largely as givens, a matter of luck and fate, the modern belief that one's body can be constructed is associated with an equally strong belief that the shape one is relates to one's inherent worth. A writer who describes herself as "frankly fat" observes that

[27] See Chapter 3 for a discussion of Bourdieu's work.

[28] Turner, *The Body and Society* and "The Discourse of Diet," *Theory, Culture and Society* 1.1 (1982): 23–32, reprinted in Featherstone et al., *The Body, Social Process and Cultural Theory.* See also M. Featherstone, "The Body in Consumer Culture," *Theory, Culture and Society* 1.2 (1982): 18–33.

[29] Turner, *Regulating Bodies*, pp. 165, 262.

[30] See Chapter 6, Part 3. See also Goffmann, "The Arrangement Between the Sexes," *Theory and Society* 4 (1977): 301–32.

Fatism is . . . a hidden prejudice and as such it is perhaps the most vicious of all. . . . Fat is hated and despised and fat people are coerced to the outer limits of mainstream society—that is if they dare to try to be part of it.[31]

Visiting a health and beauty spa, she found that only small, one-size robes were available. This was a policy of the place; they did not want to encourage fat people to come, and many of their clients supported this. As one such client explained,

"They only have small robes . . . because a place like that is not meant for fat women. It's really offensive to have to look at women like that—it must have been awful for everyone else there. . . ."This one woman, whose outburst was prompted by the thought of me, . . . encapsulated the attitude of our society in a single voice.[32]

Mental Illness: Real or Constructed?

Debates about the extent to which physical characteristics and behavior are socially constructed or biologically given have consequences that go well beyond the university and the academic press. One of the most important recent examples of how theories influence public perceptions and policy is to be found in the area of mental illness.

A growing body of writing has made policymakers and the general public aware that the diagnosis of mental illness is not a simple affair based on objective physical criteria on which everyone can agree. Different interpretations of what is acceptable behavior, different attitudes on the part of prospective patients and their families, and different (and often contradictory) theories held by psychiatrists and other doctors, along with how the medical staff see their patients, all influence diagnoses and treatment. Table 8-1 illustrates the situation clearly: in the United States men are much more likely to be admitted to psychiatric hospitals than women, whereas in England the opposite is true. Because these are both rich, industrialized

---

[31]Shelley Bovey, *Being Fat Is Not a Sin* (Boston: Pandora Press, 1989), p. 1.

[32]Bovey, *Being Fat Is Not a Sin*, p. 13. See also Susie Orbach, *Fat Is a Feminist Issue*; and Marcia Millman, *Such a Pretty Face: Being Fat in America* (New York: Berkely Books, 1980).

TABLE 8-1 Number of People per 100,000 Admitted to Psychiatric Hospitals: 1986 Adapted from Table 4.4 in Turner 1995 op cit

	Males	Females	Difference (female rate minus male rate)
England	364	468	104 or +29%
USA	790	551	−239 or −30%

countries, with similar life expectancies and living styles, it is hard to see how this can be explained in purely biological terms.

Some commentators have therefore come to see mental illness as more or less entirely socially constructed. Foucault's work sometimes comes close to this position; and Dorothy Smith (see Chapter 6) has also shown how much perceptions of mental illness follow from the observer's own orientation and framing of the behavior.[33] However, this perspective is most fully enunciated in the work of Thomas Szasz,[34] who sees a psychiatric diagnosis as essentially a measure of how far the individual deviates from the social norm, and treatment as something forced on patients in an attempt to bring them back into line. Arguments such as Szasz's have had a growing impact on public opinion, strengthened by publicity about cases in which people had been incarcerated for decades (and often forcibly sterilized) for no apparent reason other than being an inconvenience to their family or community.

Throughout the 1970s and 1980s the number of patients in mental hospitals fell rapidly in many Western countries, including the United States. Over a twenty-year period, from 1965 to 1985, and when the population as a whole was growing rapidly, the number of residents in state mental hospitals was halved and then more than halved again.[35] Asylums were replaced with care in the community, based around institutions such as Community Mental Health Centers, which were intended to address problems at an early stage and provide a safety net.

To many people, however, the events of the last twenty years have shown that too heavy an emphasis on the socially constructed side of illness can be just as destructive as the view that sees illness as a purely biological phenomenon. Rossi, for example, has estimated that there are up to half a million homeless people in the United States and that 20 to 30 percent of these are mentally ill.[36] In the United Kingdom the crusading organization SANE (Schizophrenia A National Emergency) was founded by the journalist Marjorie Wallace after she completed a series of investigative reports on what was happening to the families of patients released into the community. One of her examples was a young lawyer, Edward Curtis Bennett, who, as schizophrenia developed, neglected himself and focused threats and obsessions on his mother. When she sought help, the psychiatrist "refused to discuss anything about Edward . . . unless Edward himself gave express permission." Soon the mother was so terrified that she was living on the run.

[33]Dorothy Smith, "K Is Mentally Ill: The Anatomy of a Factual Account," *Sociology* 12.2 (1978): 23–53.

[34]Thomas Szasz, *The Manufacture of Madness* (New York: Harper and Row, 1970).

[35]From 475,000 in 1965 to 111,000 in 1986: National Institute for Mental Health statistics quoted in Turner, *Medical Power and Social Knowledge*, p. 65.

[36]P. Rossi, *Down and Out in America: The Origins of Homelessness* (Chicago: University of Chicago Press, 1989).

"[I]n periods of lucidity, (Edward) would beg that when he became deluded he should be given treatment even if he appeared to refuse it. . . . This pattern continued over many months, with Edward begging his psychiatrist for detainment . . . while his psychiatrist argued that if he detained him, he was depriving him of his fundamental civil liberties." The story ended only with Edward's death by suicide.[37]

It has become increasingly clear that psychiatric patients are considerably more likely to commit suicide and homicide than is the population as a whole (and death is still a definitive biological event).[38] Although the greatest threat is to the patients themselves and their families, a number of widely publicized random murders by ex-patients has changed the tenor of policy debate and commentary, and strengthened those who favor what its critics call the "biomedical concept" of mental illness. In the United Kingdom the climate has turned against care in the community; and one of the first decisions of the health minister in the new Labour government elected in 1997 was to halt policies favoring closure of long-stay hospitals. "The move . . . to care in the community has failed to deliver. . . . Mentally ill people should be cared for in safety and security," he announced.[39]

Regulating Populations and Bodies

In Chapter 2 we described Parsons's fourth "system level," that of the behavioral organism, and also his argument that all societies face recurring problems or needs, including the need to integrate or regulate the various different systems. Contemporary sociology of the body has turned back to Parsons's ideas, though without the implication that solutions are in any sense automatically functional or good for a society's members.

Taylor's general theory of the relation of the body to society is encapsulated in the same type of square diagram as Parsons used, reproduced in Figure 8-1. He argues that it is important to think of bodies both individually and in terms of populations; these are represented in the right and left columns of the two square diagrams shown. Populations have to be reproduced over *time* if societies are to survive; they also have to be regulated in *space*. At the individual level the two key dimensions are *internal* and *external*. Bodies have to be disciplined to show internal restraint and discipline; and in particular to discipline their desire for sexual gratification. They also have to be trained to present or represent themselves in the appropriate ways for a given culture.

[37]Marjorie Wallace, *Schizophrenia 1992: Catch 22. The Paradox of Enlightenment* (London: SANE, 1993).

[38]See, for example, the results of the Confidential Inquiry for the U.K. Department of Health carried out by Manchester University; reported in circular 97/396 (London: Department of Health, 1997).

[39]Paul Boateng, minister of health: announcement on September 12, 1997.

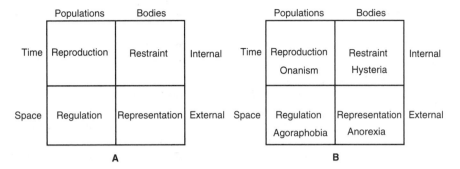

FIGURE 8-1   Regulating Populations and Bodies
(Adapted from Bryan S. Turner, *The Body and Society.*)

The diagram on the left shows the basic theoretical scheme; that on the right adds Turner's examples of ways in which bodies break down under, or break away from, these tasks. These examples illustrate how illnesses and forms of deviance are associated with the different societal tasks involved in managing bodies.

Thus the reproduction of populations (top left) involves the social control of fertility. Masturbation was regarded as deviant by both Christianity and orthodox Judaism[40] and, especially in the eighteenth and nineteenth centuries, was attacked as harmful to health and even likely to lead to madness. Underlying this were societal concerns with maintaining reproductive levels and the consequent "need" to maintain control over young people and tie them into parental responsibility.

Populations also have to be "regulated," Turner argues—controlled in space as well as over time. The family, in which the property-owning head of the household could control its other members, was a powerful mechanism for this purpose; and nineteenth-century urban life was characterized by women—particularly middle-class women—becoming increasingly confined to the home. Agoraphobia—fear of the outside and of leaving home—appears as a recognized medical syndrome in just this society; but it did so, Turner argues, at a time when the cities were in reality becoming safer, and women's freedom potentially greater. "The agoraphobia of married women was . . . metaphorically expressive of the anxieties of husbands regarding their capacity to control the domestic sphere and the economic arrangements of the household in a situation where their wives were potentially more independent . . . there may be a degree of collusion between husband and wife. . . . The woman had the compensation of moral praise in exchange for staying at home, while the husband had his

---

[40]The term "onanism" comes from Onan in the Bible (Genesis xxxviii) who "spilled his seed upon the ground" and was struck dead in punishment.

status and economic power reinforced by the apparent incapacity of his wife."[41]

At an individual level, these same concerns regarding social control and continuity manifest themselves in efforts to make individuals restrain their "sexuality and desire in the interests of public order":[42] in particular, to reproduce only within stable family units and to control sexuality within the family unit. In practice, this has meant the regulating and restraining of women, who were confined within the patriarchal family while a limited amount of sexual deviance by men was tolerated outside it. And here too we find diseases that reflect this social context. Female hysteria—common a century ago, and now almost disappeared—appears in the top right corner of Turner's diagram as a paradigmatic "disease" related to *internal* restraint. It was seen as a major medical problem in the nineteenth century and was an acceptable way for restrained women to adopt a "sick" role.

With the shift away from the powerful patriarchal family, there has been, Turner argues, a relative shift in emphasis from internal restraint to *external representation*—the bottom right box. Alongside this we find a large increase in eating disorders, notably the appearance of anorexia nervosa as a recognized illness and diagnosis.

The growing incidence of anorexia and of bulimia (binge-eating and vomiting) attracts a great deal of attention inside and outside sociology, especially as it is so much more common among women than men. (The current ratio is 10 to 1.[43]) Although the general cult of slimness is one factor, few think it a sufficient explanation. Drawing on the work of Hilda Bruch, Turner argues that "we can see anorexia as a form of adolescent rebellion against parental control where the young woman seeks to assert her individuality against the powerful conventions represented by her mother and her typically absent father. . . . [I]n more general terms anorexia in the twentieth century, like hysteria in the nineteenth century, is expressive of the political limitations on women within a society characterized by inequality between the sexes."[44]

Anthony Giddens, whose work has been discussed in Chapter 4, also sees the "continuing exclusion of women from full participation in the universe of social activity"[45] as an important factor. However, he also emphasizes the importance of choice and reflexivity in modern cultures: the fact that we have so many possible identities open to us, must think about and

---

[41]Turner, *Medical Power and Social Knowledge,* pp. 105–106.

[42]Turner, *Medical Power and Social Knowledge,* p. 101.

[43]Liz Jobey, "Why piglet disappeared," *Times Literary Supplement*, March 20, 1998.

[44]Turner, *Medical Power and Social Knowledge,* p. 107–108. There exist a number of theories about the growth of anorexia and other eating disorders, but nearly all see family dynamics as crucially important.

[45]Anthony Giddens, *Modernity and Self-Identity: Self and Society in the Late Modern Age* (Cambridge: Polity, 1991), p. 106.

make choices about what sort of people we are, and also believe that everything, including any form of "constructed" body, is available to us. Anorexia is a form of protest, Giddens agrees, but "the anorexic individual is not the passive victim of the dietician: on the contrary, anorexia involves body regimes that are highly active and coordinated."[46]

The father of an anorexic who eventually died of the disease describes a period when he was out of work and she was looking after him and her younger sister. "During this period, Catherine became a tower of strength. . . . There was, however, no letting up on her anorexia; she ruled the kitchen and she screamed if I entered it during her meals. . . . Her drive and determination were incredible."[47]

We do not really know why a particular individual becomes anorexic or why Catherine in the end "wanted to die."[48] However, at a macro level, the growth of anorexia in modern society must be related to factors such as Giddens and Turner propose. In general the new sociology of the body attempts to bring together our physical nature with phenomenology's emphasis on how systems of ideas create the everyday world that we inhabit and experience. The sociology of the body shows that our bodies are both a given and a social construct, just as a disease such as anorexia can be both a real and fatal affliction *and* a product of particular societies. The whole approach is especially well exemplified in the following account by Irving Zola, who has written widely about the sociological and phenomenological aspects of disability but is here drawing on his own personal experiences:

> In the pre-vaccine year of 1950, shortly before my sixteenth birthday, I contracted polio. Four years later I was in a serious automobile accident. As a result of both of these incidents, I wear a long leg brace on my right leg and two short ones on my left, use a back support, ambulate with two canes and use a wheelchair for longer trips. . . . When such information appears in someone else's description of my work . . . the phraseology surrounding it is usually something like "*despite* such incidents, he has gone on to accomplish, etc, etc." I want at the very least to bring these personal bodily experiences closer to my center—not to claim that they constitute all of who I am, but that they are a central part of my identity.[49]

For many years, Zola explains, his own attitude to his disability was a similar one: it should be ignored and he should treat it as far as possible as

[46]Giddens, *Modernity and Self-Identity*, p. 107.

[47]Maureen Dunbar, *Catherine: The Story of a Young Girl Who Died of Anorexia Nervosa* (London: Penguin, 1986), p. 127.

[48]Dunbar, *Catherine*, p. 128.

[49]Irving Kenneth Zola, "Bringing Our Bodies and Ourselves Back In: Reflections on a Past, Present, and Future Medical Sociology," *Journal of Health and Social Behavior* 32 (March 1991): 1–16.

something separate from himself to be shrugged off and overcome. Thus, in the 1960s,

> when questioned about the physical difficulties of airline travel for someone like myself, I described them as relatively minor or nonexistent. . . . My ordinary mode of travel was to drive to the airport, park in the most convenient spot, and then limp, often with my baggage strapped to my back, to what often seemed the most distant terminal in the airport.
>
> Twenty years later, though my physical condition . . . was essentially unchanged, my reactions were quite different. By the end of the 1970s and the early 1980s the women's movement . . . and the disability rights and independent living movements . . . were in full swing, and with them came some interesting changes in self-perception. . . . Though I was still quite capable of walking long distances, I no longer felt that it was necessary to do so. And so . . . I would get into either my own wheelchair or the airline's and roll to that distant terminal. Completely unanticipated was the difference in my physical condition at the end of my trip: I now arrived *untired . . . not* sore . . . *not* cramped.
>
> My conclusion was straightforward: I had *always* been tired, sore, and cramped, but with no pre-polio and pre-wheelchair experience for comparison, these experiences had been cognitively inaccessible. . . . Only after the rise of the independent living movement . . . and the resulting change in self-consciousness was I "able" to use a wheelchair. Only then did I realize how much of my travel "experience" inhered not in my disability but rather in the society in which I lived—socially maintained and constructed.[50]

Feminism, Consumerism, and the Body. The growth of feminism is an important reason for sociologists' growing interest in the body. Arthur Frank argues that "feminism now sets much of the theoretical and empirical agenda" in this area. "Bringing bodies back in is, as a theoretical and empirical research program, made thinkable and imperative by the practical political program of women bringing themselves back in."[51] If one ignores or takes for granted the gender of the people under discussion one can also ignore the fact of their being bodily creatures.[52] Once gender becomes a focus of attention, the body inevitably does so too.

In describing Turner's theories we cited examples of how social control of women was associated with phenomena such as agoraphobia and hysteria. In contemporary society many feminists are particularly critical of the promotion of thinness as a virtue, and the implication that one can and should discipline oneself to acquire a different, "better" body. Turner also focuses on the link between these ideas and a society characterized by "inequality between the sexes." He argues that "to control women's bodies

---

[50]Zola, "Bringing Our Bodies and Ourselves Back In," p. 4.

[51]Arthur W. Frank, "For a Sociology of the Body: An Analytical Review," in Featherstone et al., *The Body, Social Process and Cultural Theory*, p. 41.

[52]See, for example, Dorothy Smith's discussion of the "embodied subject" and of medical attitudes, pp. 288–89.

is to control their personalities" and notes the implication that an "obese woman is a woman (who) is out of control because the unrestrained body is indicative of moral laxity."[53]

Feminists tend to see gender as socially constructed; whereas Gervase Le Bon, in the nineteenth century, not only stressed fixed biological differences between men and women, but used skull measurements to "prove" women's mental inferiority. This is now seen as ridiculous; but there is still vigorous argument about whether men and women learn in different ways, and whether this means that certain types of examination are unfair to women.[54] In the early twentieth century, boards of education saw the menstrual cycle as causing a (temporary) reduction in girls' mental efficiency, and as therefore requiring a differentiated school curriculum.[55] Few people would accept that today; yet many regard premenstrual tension as having major effects on behavior, which may be admitted as relevant evidence in evaluating someone's legal responsibility for their actions. As we saw in, for example, Chapter 3, conflict theorists such as Collins, Chafetz, and Blumberg argue that biological characteristics, such as child-bearing and strength, are an important part—though only a part—of any theory of gender stratification. Others see these as arguments advanced by patriarchal societies to justify male domination. Some feminists regard women as intrinsically non-violent compared to men; others, again, consider this a cultural artifact.

Popular writers tend to hedge their bets by discussing male-female differences in an ambiguous way; that is, they leave it open whether differences are biologically determined or the result of culture and upbringing. John Gray, author of the best-seller *Men are from Mars, Women are from Venus*, provides a good example of this, arguing, for example, that women ("Venusians") "are very intuitive. They have developed the ability through centuries of anticipating the needs of others."[56] Does he mean that they are inherently more intuitive than men—that the differences are genetic? Or that girls, but not boys, learn at home and school how to be intuitive and caring about the needs of others, and pass it on, with more to teach (and learn) in each passing generation?[57]

[53]Turner, *Medical Power and Social Knowledge* (London: Sage, 1987), p. 108.

[54]J. Elwood, "Undermining Gender Stereotypes: Examination and Coursework Performance," *Assessment in Education* 2.3 (1995): 282–303. N. G. McCrum, "Gender and Social Inequality at Oxford and Cambridge Universities," *Oxford Review of Education* 22.4 (December 1996).

[55]See, for example, Board of Education, London: Report of the Consultative Committee on Differentiation of the Curriculum for Boys and Girls Respectively in Secondary Schools (London, 1923); quoted in Shilling, *The Body and Social Theory*, p. 46.

[56]John Gray, *Men Are from Mars, Women Are from Venus: A Practical Guide for Improving Communication and Getting What You Want in Your Relationships* (New York: Harper Collins, 1992).

[57]For arguments that this indeed occurs, see discussions of the work of Best, Goffman, and Chodorow, Chapter 5, pp. 233–35 and 244–45.

Gray is careful never to commit himself to one position rather than the other; but an increasingly influential area of scholarship *is* committed to clarifying exactly that issue—what is genetically based and what is not. Faced with Gray's statement, researchers in this field would note that a few centuries is far too short a time to develop a genetic difference between the sexes; but if that difference really exists, but is cultural, then why don't little boys learn intuition too? The field in question is that of evolutionary biology or "sociobiology," and the following section examines its basic premises and their relevance to sociology.

PART TWO

Sociobiology

The sociology of the body studies the ways in which bodies are socially reproduced and regulated, focusing on common tasks but also on the specific practices and meanings of specific societies. Sociobiology, by contrast, is concerned with the biological bases of behavior: with what is common to all societies, and common, moreover, by virtue of our biological nature and evolutionary history. Over the last few decades there has been an explosion of interest and work in the general area of evolutionary biology and evolutionary psychology and in explaining the behavior of all our planet's species in terms of natural selection, or whether certain types of behavior tend to favor the survival of creatures whose genes predispose them in that direction.[58]

In the process the term "sociobiology" has become less generally used; but we retain it here as familiar to sociologists and as the term that zoologist Edward Wilson used in his massive synthesis of work on "the systematic study of the biological basis of all social behavior."[59] His work made the public fully aware of the existence of sociobiology as a controversial approach to *human* behavior and not something confined to ants, bison, or chimpanzees. In this section we discuss the general arguments advanced by sociobiologists to demonstrate the relevance of biological considerations to the study of societies; and then look in some detail at their theories about

---

[58]For an excellent view of the development of evolutionary biology, see W. D. Hamilton, *The Narrow Roads of Gene Land* (New York: W. H. Freeman, 1996). These are the collected papers of one of the creators of modern biology and include work on kin selection, altruism, and violence. For a recent discussion of evolutionary psychology's insights into human behavior, see Steven Pinker, *How the Mind Works* (London: Allen Lane, 1998).

[59]Edward O. Wilson, *Sociobiology: The New Synthesis* (Cambridge, Mass: The Belknap Press of Harvard University Press, 1975), p. 4. In fact, Wilson's work deals almost wholly with animal societies and such features as their "dominance systems" (or pecking orders), rules of territoriality, and parental care.

altruism and trust, and about human reproduction and the very different strategies and interests of men and women.

Sociobiologists argue that the human race is a product of evolution and that vast quantities of information are passed on by our genes. It follows that genes as well as environment play a role in society and that behavior has a biological base. The balance may be different for humans, just as animals and insects differ from one another, but the basic framework of analysis is the same.

> Sociobiology applies natural selection theory to behavior. It asserts that the behavior of an animal, like its anatomy, is the product of a process of biological evolution through natural selection. Any behavioral phenotype is the result of the interaction between genotype and environmental conditions. . . . [F]or man, culture is indeed a whole new evolutionary ball game. . . . However, human culture does not stand apart form biological evolution; it grew out of it and remains inextricably intertwined with it.[60]

Sociobiologists are not simplistic genetic determinists who claim that human behavior is directly controlled by genes. Rather, they believe that biological factors and genetic influences set limits to the range of possible behaviors. These limits and behavioral tendencies, they argue, result from evolution, just as does the behavior of other species, and they must be understood in the context of natural selection.

This approach met with enormous hostility from some sociologists and, indeed, continues to do so, largely because it appears to legitimate aspects of human societies that people wish to reform and to set limits on how far you can change (or perfect) people. Opponents see the human being as *essentially* a creature of cultural norms, in whom biological universals extend no further than such basic activities as eating, excreting, and sleeping. They argue that Wilson, for example, is a product of an alienated culture and his own class prejudices, and he "joins the long parade of biological determinists whose work has served to buttress the institutions of their society by exonerating them from responsibility for social problems."[61] The question of what is biologically or genetically based becomes especially controversial in the context of discussions of gender roles and the origin of differences between men and women; homosexuality (a lifestyle choice? a genetic disposition?); and the extent to which intelligence is inherited or the product of upbringing. Sociobiologists' position is that, as scientists, their job is to understand, and that the importance of people's genes is an empirical question.

The other major criticism of sociobiology is that cultures are so diverse that biology, which deals with the universal, really cannot be much use in

---

[60]Pierre L. van den Berghe, "Sociobiology, Dogma, and Ethics," *The Wilson Quarterly* (Summer 1977): 121.

[61]Letter to the *New York Review of Books*, November 13, 1975, from the Cambridge, Massachusett–based Sociobiology Study Group.

explaining things. As Neuhaus points out, this is a very odd approach to theory construction. "One of the principal functions of theory is to narrow the range of possibilities and suggest where to look," he argues.[62] You can see how mistaken it is to discount biological factors because they are universal "by looking at statements which are logically similar. . . . 'If language is a constant in all cultures, we may safely ignore its effects on human actions.' "[63] Ignoring the effects of language would certainly have deprived us of many of the insights provided by the symbolic interactionist and phenomenological theorists discussed in chapters 5 and 6.

Robin Fox, one of the first social scientists to embrace biological perspectives, describes how as a young student,

> I had the litany chanted at me: "biological universals cannot explain cultural differentials . . . " And of course at one level they cannot. Muslims, I was told, take off their shoes to go into church while Christians take off their hats. Now find a biological explanation for *that*! I was never sure I wanted to find any kind of explanation for it. It seemed to me an arbitrary thing. . . . [Nonetheless] I was plagued by the question: If we do not really know what biological universals there are then how can we study the cultural differentials in the first place? How to study the variables without the constants?[64]

Fox argues that although there is a great deal of difference in the "symbolic disguises" worn by different societies and in the details of their culture and behavior, beneath these differences is a remarkable uniformity of social structure and social institutions. He predicts that if you could bring up children in isolation from any known culture, within a very few generations they would produce a society with a long list of concrete properties: "laws about property, rules about incest . . . a system of social status and methods of indicating it . . . courtship practices . . . associations set aside for men . . . gambling . . . homicide, suicide, homosexuality, schizophrenia, psychosis, and neurosis, and various practitioners to take advantage of, or cure, these, depending on how they are viewed."[65] They would do this, he claims, because it is "in the beast."

In other words, Fox argues, we are not different in kind from other animals because we are "cultural" and they are "biological." Rather we are a special kind of primate; a primate that produces cultures and that has endured as a "cultural animal." As the human being evolved as a biped dependent on brains for survival, the capacity for cultural behavior was at a

---

[62]John William Neuhaus, *Toward a Biocritical Sociology* (New York: Peter Lang, 1996), p. 107. Neuhaus argues at length against the idea that there is anything intrinsically reactionary about a sociobiological perspective; instead it offers the possibility for a new form of critical social science based on a developed theory of human needs.

[63]Neuhaus, *Toward a Biocritical Sociology*, p. 116.

[64]Robin Fox, "The Cultural Animal," *Encounter* XXXV, no. 1 (July 1970): 33.

[65]Fox, "The Cultural Animal," p. 33.

premium. Natural selection favored those who could develop cultural traditions and thus adapt rapidly to changing circumstances—for although cultural traditions may change slowly, they do so very rapidly compared to instinctive behavior and genetic material. The use of brain-dependent cultural activities and the growth of the human brain went hand in hand. Thus "culture does not represent a triumph over nature," Fox argues. Rather, "in behaving culturally we are behaving naturally."[66]

SELFISH GENES AND KIN SELECTION

While increasing numbers of social scientists accept the importance of biological factors in explaining human behavior, it is nonetheless extraordinarily difficult to examine the role of these factors directly and find out just how important they are. No one, after, all is denying that environment and culture both matter. But how are we to separate the inextricably entwined?

One possibility is to look at some of the major theoretical advances that have been taking place in biology and ethnology and ask how far they illuminate human behavior. (If the answer is "very little," this does not, of course, prove that future developments might not do better—but it will at least counsel caution in using biology to help explain social behavior.) Darwin's theory of evolution states that things survive if they are able to compete for resources in a successful—and stable—fashion. We now know that, among living things, the basic unit of survival is the gene because it is genes that replicate themselves. If an organism contains a gene that tends to promote its survival, then that gene will spread gradually.[67] Those descendants of the first organism that inherit the gene will tend to survive and reproduce relatively more successfully, and the gene will be replicated. The cockroach, which has remained unchanged for hundreds of millennia, is produced by a particularly effective and stable set of genes.

This basic theory of natural selection—in which the mechanism for Darwin's theory is provided by Mendelian genetics—is essentially one of what has been called "gene selfishness."[68] This is not to say that genes are *consciously* selfish. Rather the whole theory of natural selection implies that the race goes, by definition, to those who behave in ways that promote the interests (namely the survival) of their genes. This, in turn, means that if a

---

[66]Fox, "The Cultural Animal," p. 40. In a similar vein Groves and Sabater Pi analyze similarities between human and apes in the use of a "fix-point" or home base for sleeping. Colin P. Groves and J. Sabater Pi, "From Ape's Nest to Human Fix-Point," *Man* (n.s.), 20 (1985): 22–47.

[67]Other things being equal.

[68]Richard Dawkins, *The Selfish Gene* (Oxford: Oxford University Press, 1976, and London: Granada, 1978), p. 7. Page references are to the Granada edition.

particular gene tends to promote the survival of an organism, it will be reproduced. If it does not, it will not.[69]

We are all descended from generations and generations of people who looked after their children. People who could think of better things to do than look after crying, demanding infants, and who abandoned them, also tended to have few or no descendants, so their genes died out. It is therefore not surprising to sociobiologists that our societies are full of examples of people looking after, and looking out for, their children. One of the contributions of this approach, in fact, is to show that what we all take for granted is actually worth noticing.

In her autobiography, *Wild Swans*, Jung Chang describes her childhood as daughter of a senior Chinese Communist official. "In China it is assumed that anyone in a powerful position would look after their relatives. There was a well-known saying: 'When a man gets power, even his chickens and dogs rise to heaven.' But my father felt that nepotism and favoritism were the slippery slope to corruption, which was the root of all the evils in the old China."[70] He would not help his family (and ended up offending and alienating many of them); but Jung Chang observes how unusual he was in this. As the revolutionary zeal of the early Communist cadres wore off, family ties reasserted themselves; and those doing business in contemporary China discover that family connections, as well as other personal networks, are critically important.

It is obviously highly plausible to suppose that there is a biological basis for people's tendency to favor their kin; people whose genes predisposed them to do this were also more likely to have descendants. Proving it, however, is another issue. Israeli pioneers who set up the kibbutz system originally raised their children communally; so that although the children knew who their parents were and had special ties with them, they spent little time alone with them. This system has now been abandoned because parents wanted far more involvement in their children's upbringing; but is this biology reasserting itself? or the continuing influence of more general social norms?

Many of these questions are probably impossible to resolve; but we do have one powerful and chilling piece of evidence to indicate that genes are important in explaining the way we help and support our kin. Two American researchers reasoned that if genes and "kin selection" really affected the way we bring up children, then one would expect major differ-

---

[69]Clearly this is not an instantaneous, either-or situation. Rather, over time, organisms with the (more successful) gene A will tend to do better than those with the (less successful) gene B. Over enough time, those with gene B may do badly enough that gene B becomes extinct. The persistence of sickle-cell anemia in parts of Africa shows how complex this process can be. Although sickle-cell anemia is often fatal, the responsible genes also protect against malaria and to this degree promote survival (and themselves survive).

[70]Jung Chang, *Wild Swans: Three Daughters of China* (London: Harper Collins, 1991), p. 180.

ences in the way natural children and stepchildren are treated, and particularly in the risks they run from violence and abuse. They then went out and collected statistics to test their theory and found them fully consistent. Children are far more likely to suffer abuse at the hands of substitute than of biological parents; and stepchildren are *sixty-five times* more likely to die than children living with only their biological parents.[71]

However, while we do, for the most part, build our lives around our families, it is also true both that societies vary in the extent to which family ties dominate economic and social life, and that human beings engage in a great deal of activity that is not obviously in the interests of their relatives or of their own particular genes. The main challenge to the evolutionary view of human behavior has always been the existence of altruistic behavior—that is, behavior that apparently *does not* promote the survival of the creature exhibiting it.[72] Humans are quite often altruistic, but so, apparently, are other animals, and not only where their children are concerned. Worker bees, for example, use their stings as an effective defense of the nest, and they die in doing so. Many small birds use an alarm call to warn of the approach of hawks or other predators—and in doing so draw attention to themselves.

One common explanation that has been offered is that creatures behave in this way "for the good of the species." The individuals concerned may not benefit directly, but the way they act will help other members of the species to survive, reproduce, and replicate altruistic behavior. Robert Ardrey suggested that the world became populated with groups of self-sacrificing individuals because, as a species, they did better than selfish, noncooperating ones.[73] The idea has also appealed to sociologists and social psychologists. J. Phillippe Rushton, for example, in discussing the way in which altruistic behavior develops in society, suggests that the need for mutual defense created "group loyalty and ultimately the altruistic willingness to sacrifice the self for the group."[74]

It is an appealing scenario, but unfortunately it never would have occurred. One reason is that it implies an ability to recognize and identify

[71]M. Daly and M. Wilson, *Sex, Evolution and Behavior* (Belmont, Calif.: Wadsworth, 1983), cited in M. Ridley, *The Red Queen: Sex and the Evolution of Human Nature* (London: Viking, 1993), p. 207. See also M. Daly and M. Wilson, "Children as Homicide Victims," in R. Gelles and J. U. Lancaster, ed., *Child Abuse and Neglect: Biosocial Dimensions* (New York: Aldine de Gruyter, 1987). This is something that traditional fairy stories recognize. See also Laura Betzig, Monique Borgerhoff Mulder, and Paul Turke, ed., *Human Reproductive Behaviour: A Darwinian Perspective* (Cambridge: Cambridge University Press, 1988), p. 12.

[72]It is the consequences of the behavior that are important—"altruistic behavior" is being defined independently of the supposed intentions of the creatures involved. Compare Penelope J. Green, Charles J. Morgan, and David P. Barash, "Sociobiology," in Scott McNall, ed., *Theoretical Perspectives in Sociology* (New York: St. Martin's Press, 1979), pp. 414–30.

[73]Robert Ardrey, *The Social Contract* (London: Collins, 1970). Compare the work of V. C. Wynne-Edwards.

[74]J. Phillippe Rushton, *Altruism, Socialization and Society* (Englewood Cliffs, N.J.: Prentice-Hall, 1980), p. 29.

with one's own species, a characteristic that animals do not display. The second flaw in the group selection theory is also simple. It leaves the field wide open to the mutant gangster who won't play by the rules. He is happy to let others sacrifice themselves for him, but he sees no reason to do the same. He will simply take the pickings and do far better than the altruists at breeding. (Moreover, his offspring will likely be gangsters, too.) This does not mean that *only* gangsters will survive: to continue the analogy, aggressive individuals of this sort fortunately attack each other as much as, or more than, their more timid co-citizens. This may help keep their numbers down and leave space for the rest to go on breeding, too. However, we cannot use the good of the species as a satisfactory explanation for alarm calls, bee stings, and the like, where the behavior is a general characteristic of *all* members of the species.[75] A gene for such self-sacrificing behavior would not last long, let alone give rise to stable and universal traits.[76]

Modern biologists, who mostly look at nonhuman species, use a variety of explanations, arguing that a great deal of cooperative and altruistic behavior can, in fact, be seen as an example of *kin selection* after all. They point out that cooperation is nearly always observed taking place between close relatives: mothers, children, sisters, and so on. As Barash points out:

> The Carnegie Medal for bravery is a peacetime equivalent of the Congressional Medal of Honor, and its bestowers unconsciously recognize the sociobiology of altruism by not giving the medal for bravery in saving the life of a relative. Helping a relative in distress is apparently expected. What is unexpected, and therefore worthy of a medal, is encountering danger to help a nonrelative.[77]

Sociobiology's gloss on this point is to show that altruistic behavior may be highly adaptive even when it does not promote the survival and future reproduction of a given individual, so long as it does benefit *related* individuals.[78]

This is much clearer once we realize that in the long term we are talking about whether particular *genes* survive and are passed on to more or less remote individuals. Suppose, for example, that individual A gives birth to three children (see Figure 8-2), all of whom share with A an altruistic gene α.

---

[75]See the work of J. Maynard Smith for a full discussion of how different categories (such as "hawk" and "dove") can coexist within a species in stable proportions—for example, J. Maynard Smith and G. R. Price, "The Logic of Animal Conflicts," *Nature* 24b (1973): 15–18. See also Dawkins, *The Selfish Gene.*

[76]Rational choice theorists and economists, examining organizations that depend on reciprocity, generally refer to "free riders" or "opportunists." See Chapter 7 pp. 338–44; also Mancur Olson, *The Logic of Collective Action* (Cambridge: Harvard University Press, 1965); and Douglass C. North, *Structure and Change in Economic History* (New York: W. W. Norton, 1981).

[77]Barash, "Sociobiology," p. 135.

[78]In its present form, the theory owes most to the work of W. D. Hamilton; see especially "The Genetical Evolution of Social Behavior" (I and II), *Journal of Theoretical Biology* 7 (1964): 1–16 and 17–52.

They help each other in a number of situations, and eventually poor B^1 perishes, leaving no offspring. However, B^2 and B^3 are luckier; and the results of the cooperative behavior can be seen in the fact that they, between them, raise six children, three of whom possess α. By the fourth generation (D^1, D^2, and so on), there are five copies of α around instead of three; whereas the noncooperating siblings (C^1, C^4, C^6) have only managed three adult offspring among them. In other words, the "sacrifice" of B^1 had a positive payoff in terms of natural selection. It promoted the spread of the relevant gene and was in that sense quite consistent with the "selfishness" of evolution.

What kin selection points out is that something we take for granted—looking after one's children—is really only a special case of something more general. Any genetically based behavior that tends to help one's genes to survive will, by definition, tend itself to survive. If we go back to those kamikaze worker bees, we can see how the same logic applies. Because such behavior promotes the welfare of their genes, they care for and defend each other and the nest, generation after generation. They are sterile themselves; therefore, from the point of view of natural selection, it is the protection and care of the current and future queens (and their mates) that is selected for.[79] Worker bees who look after themselves will not promote the survival of their genes.

Nonetheless, in much of human society, cooperation and altruism go well beyond the bounds of family and relations. It might seem, therefore, that biology cannot be the explanation. However, sociobiological theory does have some interesting suggestions about the development of altruistic behavior, and the extent to which it may, in fact, have a biological and evolutionary foundation. These have strong similarities to rational choice theories described in Chapter 7. There we discussed how collaboration among

[79]The particular social organization developed by ants, bees, and wasps is related to their distinctive system of sexual reproduction, in which, for example, "sister" worker bees share more genes with each other than with their mother. See R. L. Trivers and H. Hare, "Haplodiploidy and the Evolution of the Social Insects," *Science* 191 (1976): 249–63.

FIGURE 8-2 A Model of the Spread of an "Altruistic" Gene

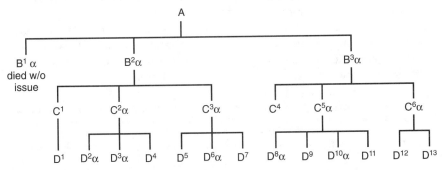

rational self-interested individuals leads to a gradual growth of trust and enduring cooperation. The research discussed in that chapter also indicated how rarely, over the long term, it pays to be seen as untrustworthy.[80]

Trust and Altruism. Most research on the development of trust does not refer to biology; instead it emphasizes the processes by which social interaction consistently leads people to adopt certain strategies. Equally, sociobiology acknowledges the enormous differences among societies in the extent to which there is widespread collaboration outside kin groups, in the degree of trust between fellow citizens, and in their willingness to behave generously or altruistically toward others. However, sociobiologists also point out that one of the common elements in *all* human societies is the existence of widespread sharing, gift giving, and collaborative behavior; and they ask the standard biological question, Is there anything in this for the individual? Would people who had a predisposition toward this sort of behavior actually also be more likely to have descendants, so that over time the race went to those with collaborative and altruistic genes? Might there be a biological, as well as a social, element in the process by which collaboration and trust are built up?

Rational choice theorists point out that while being a free rider or a selfish cheat may make sense if you are never going to see somebody again, in a longer-term relationship it is a bad idea. Sociobiologists make the same point. Using sophisticated models, they demonstrate that, over generations, people who cooperate, but who also play tit for tat and do not help those who have failed to reciprocate, do well; their descendants are not crowded out by individuals who never reciprocate.

They also point out that altruistic behavior is itself a way of telling potential partners that, as a good person, you are also a good risk as a collaborator: you will not cheat and will reciprocate. In other words, "advertised" altruism may serve quite different purposes from altruism concealed. The great medieval Jewish philosopher Maimonides made the same point when he distinguished between the eight degrees in the giving of charity, one higher than the other. "He who gives grudgingly, reluctantly, or with regret" occupies the lowest level; far better is the person "who gives without knowing to whom he gives, and the recipient not knowing from whom he receives."[81]

Some sociobiologists believe that this sort of behavior among humans may have a strong genetic element in it, and that it is not simply something that each generation learns for itself in the day care or playground jungle. Matt Ridley points out that it is very useful to human beings to be able to

---

[80]Patrick Bateson, "The Biological Evolution of Cooperation and Trust," and David Good, "Individuals, Interpersonal Relations and Trust," in Diego Gambetta, ed., *Trust: Making and Breaking Cooperative Relations* (New York: Basil Blackwell, 1988).

[81]Maimonides, *Mishnah Torah*, ed. Philip Birnbaum (New York: Hebrew Publishing Company, 1985), chap. 10, verses 7–14.

spot those with whom it makes sense to collaborate and those with whom we should avoid doing business. He describes an experiment by Robert Frank, who has written widely on the evolution of cooperation, and who

> put a group of strangers in a room together for just half an hour, and asked them to predict privately which of their fellow subjects would cooperate and who would defect in a single prisoner's dilemma game.[82] They proved substantially better than chance at doing so. They could tell, even after just thirty minutes' acquaintance, enough about somebody to predict his cooperativeness.
>
> Frank does not claim that this is too surprising. We spend a good deal of our lives assessing the trustworthiness of others, and we make instant judgments with some confidence. He poses a thought experiment for those unconvinced. "Among those you know (but have never observed with respect to pesticide disposal), can you think of anyone who would drive, say, forty-five minutes to dispose of a highly toxic pesticide properly? If yes, then you accept the premise that people can predict cooperative predispositions."[83]

Ridley points out that individuals have a stronger and stronger incentive to show trustworthiness the better other people are at predicting who will cheat. Moreover, there is now a considerable body of evidence that shows not only that we are good at predicting other people's tendency to cooperate, but also that we are extremely good at spotting cheats and opportunities for cheating. All of this presupposes that we are able to recognize other individuals and to keep score. And "there is no doubt that human beings, with their astonishing ability to recall the features of even the most casual acquaintance and their long lives and long memories, are equipped" to do this far better than any other species.[84]

The "strong" sociobiological view is that the "human brain is not just better than that of other animals, it is different. And it is different in a fascinating way: it is equipped with special faculties to enable it to exploit reciprocity (and) to trade favors."[85] In our view, the theory that there is actually a biological basis for reciprocity remains unproven: general self-interest and an ability to see beyond the short term may be all that is required to generate such recurrent behavior. Equally, a biological element cannot be ruled out on current evidence.

Randolph Nesse, writing about group selection, describes his concern that "some students . . . have left my courses with a naive notion" that this view of inherited behavior and altruism can "justify selfish behavior."[86]

---

[82]For a description of the prisoner's dilemma, see Chapter 7, pp. 322–23.

[83]Matt Ridley, *The Origins of Virtue* (New York: Penguin, 1996), p. 82. The quotation from Frank is from R. H. Frank, T. Gilovich, and D. T. Regan, "The Evolution of One-Shot Cooperation," *Ethology and Sociobiology* 14 (1993): 247–56.

[84]Ridley, *The Origins of Virtue*, p. 83.

[85]Ridley, *The Origins of Virtue*, p. 131.

[86]R. Nesse, Commentary on "Reintroducing Group Selection to the Human and Behavioral Sciences," *Behavioral and Brain Sciences* 17 (1994).

Before leaving the sociobiologists' theories of altruism, it is therefore important to emphasize that they are not denying that the behavior concerned is genuinely altruistic. If their analyses are right, then among our ancestors there were many individuals who behaved altruistically and then, *coincidentally*, found themselves and their children benefiting as a result. They did not behave in this way because it seemed self-interested or necessarily recognize that altruism could also benefit themselves.

Reproductive Strategies: Who Is Cheating Whom?   Another area in which sociobiologists feel that evolutionary theory can help us understand human societies relates to one of the major themes of this text: the differences between men and women. One fundamental and defining difference in that women have a limited number of eggs, each of which, if fertilized, takes a long time to develop, while men can, in principle, father huge numbers of children. Added to this, the mother of a child will rarely be in doubt; its biological father was, until recently, impossible to determine with certainty. These facts, sociobiology argues, set up some fundamental conflicts of interest between the sexes that are likely to have social repercussions irrespective of how different societies allocate actual child care and other responsibilities.

As Matt Ridley points out,

> Cuckoldry is an asymmetrical fate. A woman loses no genetic investment if her husband is unfaithful, but a man risks unwittingly raising a bastard. As if to reassure fathers, research shows that people are strangely more apt to say of a baby, "he (or she) looks just like his father" than to say "he (or she) looks just like his mother"—and that it is the mother's relatives who are most likely to say this.... (M)en are likely to mind even more about their wives' infidelity than vice versa. History, and law, have long reflected just that. In most societies, adultery by a wife was illegal and punished severely, while adultery by a husband was condoned, or lightly treated.... This double standard is a prime example of the sexism of society, and is usually dismissed as no more than that. Yet the law has not been sexist about other crimes: women have never been punished more severely for murder than men, or at least the legal code has never prescribed that they be so.[87]

The point is that adultery by women has different consequences from those of adultery by men. Men's attempts to control the women of their family recognized this. Laws sanctioning the right of husbands to beat their wives have been common and were repealed in the West quite recently; and the tendency to award custody to divorced *mothers* is also a relatively modern development.[88]

---

[87]Ridley, *The Red Queen*, pp. 229–30.
[88]See p. 108 for a discussion of the Dobashs' work in this area.

Because so much of the sociological writing on women emphasizes their role as oppressed, passive victims,[89] one of the striking things about sociobiology's analysis is its emphasis on *women's* reproductive strategies and active behavior. During the 1980s a group of women scientists at the University of California at Davis, led by Sarah Hardy, began to focus on the promiscuous behavior of female chimpanzees—and to note that the female was just as likely to be the initiator as was her male partner. Out of this work has emerged a new way of looking at female reproductive behavior, which can be summarized as "having your cake and eating it."[90] The female finds herself the best available mate, which will be a function of both what she has to offer and what she needs from a "long-term" partner: reliability, wealth, and perhaps complaisance. Then she commits adultery with a higher quality of father, improving her own reproductive success.

Adultery is notoriously difficult to study in humans, but what evidence we have suggests that it is common in all societies—and an obsession in them all as well. Such data as we have on parentage also indicate that a surprisingly high percentage of children's "fathers" are not their fathers at all.[91] This is highly compatible both with the particular theories being advanced and with sociobiology's more general point that sexual behavior and adultery (or unfaithfulness) have more to do with the general organization of society than conventional sociological theory would suggest. Indeed, one of the surprising things about this text is that, with a few notable exceptions (Dorothy Smith, Patricia Hill Collins, Michel Foucault), few authors say much about sexual behavior—something to which most human beings devote large amounts of time, either directly or in thinking, reading, planning, and fantasizing.

More generally, anthropologists have come to focus on reproductive success (measured by numbers of surviving children) in their analyses of social structure.[92] While emphasizing that cultural responses to environmental pressures vary widely, they also identify links between recurrent practices (and supposed "adaptation") and individuals' success (or "enhanced fitness"). They point out the female adultery is more common in societies where men care for their sisters' sons rather than their own. Female adultery is also generally more common the more inheritance is matrilineal (from mother to child rather than father to child).[93]

---

[89]See, for example, Turner's analysis in the previous section on the sociology of the body.

[90]For this description, as for much of this section, we have drawn on Ridley's *The Red Queen*, especially chap. 6 and 7.

[91]In a study of apartment dwellers in the English city of Liverpool, fewer than four in every five people were the children of their ostensible fathers. Ridley, *The Red Queen*, p. 218.

[92]See, for example, Betzig, Borgerhoff Mulder, and Turke, ed., *Human Reproductive Behaviour*; and N. A. Chagnon and W. Irons, ed., *Evolutionary Biology and Human Social Behavior: An Anthropological Perspective* (North Scituate, Mass.: Duxbury, 1979).

[93]In these cases there is less riding on whether a child's paternity is correctly identified.

SOCIOBIOLOGY AND CULTURE

Sociobiological explanations work best in explaining particular cultures and societies when they are combined with other factors and perspectives; and this is becoming increasingly common. For example, in his current work Francis Fukuyama is examining what he has dubbed "The Great Disruption": an enormous change in social norms and behavior that has occurred in the industrialized world since 1965 and that is apparent in the breakdown of the nuclear family, the rise in divorce and illegitimacy, crime rates that continue to be very high compared to earlier periods, and increases in child abuse.[94]

Changes in family patterns are a topic that we have discussed from a number of different theoretical perspectives. They are closely related to one of this text's unifying themes, namely the role of women in contemporary society; and we have, for example, looked at the link between divorce rates and economic opportunities for women when discussing rational choice.[95] Fukayama accepts the importance of such economic factors, but he also argues that biological givens play an important role in explaining these massive changes.

Following the sociobiologists, Fukayama sees men and women as having quite different reproductive strategies; and he argues that the drive in human males to have sex with many partners makes good adaptive sense. "The fact that human males with high status and/or wealth have done this readily in cultures from China to Turkey to present-day corporate America suggests that this drive is very much with us."[96] At the same time, he argues, human beings had to evolve a willingness to invest huge amounts of time and effort into bringing up demanding human children. This is because "the parent-child relationship involves a large, one-way transfer of time, energy, resources and emotional involvement."[97] This was especially necessary for women, because they were generally the ones left, literally, to hold the baby; so it was more important to your survival, as a baby, to have an altruistic mother than an altruistic father. "Evolutionary psychology suggests that male altruism toward offspring, while rooted in biology, is more the product of socially constructed norms than female altruism."[98]

Human societies throughout history managed the bringing up of children through family patterns that gave men legitimate access to sex in marriage and also forced them to provide for the children that resulted. "There

---

[94]Francis Fukayama, *The End of Order* (London: Social Market Foundation and University of Utah Press, Tanner Lectures on Human Values, vol. 18: 1997).

[95]See the Introduction to Chapter 7.

[96]Fukayama, *The End of Order*, pp. 51, 56.

[97]Fukayama, *The End of Order*, p. 109.

[98]Fukayama, *The End of Order*, p. 56.

is evidence that as late as the 1950s in the United States, over 60 percent of all brides were pregnant at the altar and their bridegrooms coerced into marriage."[99] However, two developments blew apart this more or less stable arrangement: contraception and the rise of female employment and relative incomes.

This last point is one that we have discussed before in showing how it changes the nature of the marriage bargain for women because they are not forced to stay in marriage to survive. What Fukayama emphasizes are two *biological* factors that reinforce that trend. The first is that contraception made it possible for women to have sex without worrying about its reproductive consequences; and they were therefore able and willing to take on a far larger range of partners. The second is that this interacted with and reinforced males' natural tendency to take less responsibility for their children and to seek out a wide range of sexual partners. It was easier for them to find sexual partners and easier for them to shrug off the 'norm of male responsibility'. The biological bases of men's behavior were, through human history, quite compatible with the successful rearing of children; but Fukayama worries that they are much less so now, given the dramatically different economic context and the huge changes in sexual behavior following from contraception. "(W)hile these new norms of fatherlessness and male irresponsibility may serve to maximize the interests of mothers and fathers, it is by no means clear that they are in the interests of children."[100]

Biology and Culture

Social scientists who are interested in integrating sociobiology into their own disciplines can be divided roughly into those who are trying to use neo-Darwinian concepts to examine culture—those concerned with "cultural evolution"—and those who are interested in the ways in which "proximate" biological and environmental factors shape and set limits to our social lives. Two presidential addresses—one by the psychologist and statistician Donald Campbell and one by sociologist Alice Rossi—illustrate these two approaches. Both, interestingly, were intended by their authors to convince their fellow professionals of the importance of pursuing evolutionary and biological hypotheses.[101]

Campbell suggests that it may make sense to see human culture as the product of selective evolution, just as it does physical and psychological attributes. The fact that culture is not gene-based in the way that, say, the

---

[99]Fukayama, *The End of Order*, p. 45.

[100]Fukayama, *The End of Order*, p. 111.

[101]Donald T. Campbell, "On the Conflict Between Biological and Social Evolution and Between Psychology and Moral Tradition," *The American Psychologist* (1975): 1103–26; and Alice S. Rossi, "Gender and Parenthood," *American Sociological Review* 49, no. 1 (1984): 1–19.

working of our kidneys is, does not mean that societies select their cultures almost at random. On the contrary, over time, it makes sense to see the "cumulated culture and social system"[102] as the product of adaptive evolution. This is clear enough for, say, tools, but less so for rules of social organization. However, Campbell speculates,

> Since time immemorial, human populations have continually been reorganized under different organizational systems with different beliefs and customs. In this flux, there may well have been a selective retention of organizational principles and ideologies, independent of the fate of individuals, if these organizational forms and belief systems contributed to the social system functionality, as expressed in the conquest and conversion of other people.... [A] complex division-of-labor, urban, apartment-house, stored-food society ... has independently occurred for human beings a half-dozen times.[103]

Such a view of human society as the product of biological and culture evolution is known as "dual inheritance theory"[104] and bears some striking resemblances to functionalism. However, there are some important differences, too. Campbell notes that "the wisdom produced by any evolutionary system is always wisdom about past worlds"[105] and may be quite *harmful* in current circumstances. Moreover, he doubts whether the process is still continuing.

> Adaptive evolution is a negative feedback steering device, and therefore works best when the evolving social organization is a small part of the total environment, so that variations in the social organization do not substantially change the selective system, that is, the overall environment.... [O]ne might well doubt that any adaptive social evolution is going on at the level of nations today ... [because] major nations are so few in number, and so much the dominant part of each other's environment.[106]

More specifically, Campbell and dual inheritance theorists differ from previous sociologists in seeing the interaction between biological and social factors as worth particular and special attention.[107] In discussing altruism earlier we rejected the idea that creatures behave for the good of the species and argued that kin selection and reciprocal altruism also take us only a

---

[102]Campbell, "On the Conflict Between Biological and Social Evolution," p. 1104.

[103]Campbell, "On the Conflict Between Biological and Social Evolution," p. 1106.

[104]For a formal elaboration of the basic postulates, see Peter J. Richerson and Robert Boyd, "A Dual Inheritance Model of the Human Evolutionary Process: Basic Postulates and a Simple Model," *Journal of Social and Biological Structures* 1, no. 2 (1978): 127–54.

[105]Campbell, "On the Conflict Between Biological and Social Evolution," p. 1106.

[106]Campbell, "On the Conflict Between Biological and Social Evolution," p. 1106.

[107]See especially articles by William H. Durham and others in *Human Ecology* 10, no. 3 (Sept. 1982), an issue on "Biology and Culture." Also see Thomas Dietz, "The 'New Environmental Paradigm,' Human Ecology and Environmental Sociology," *Environmental Sociology* (1978): 12–15.

limited way in explaining human behavior. Campbell agrees, emphasizing that *"social evolution has had to counter individual selfish tendencies which biological evolution has continued to select as a result of the genetic competition among the cooperators."*[108]

Campbell argues that religion and morality have to be seen in terms of their evolutionary adaptive value as a way of counteracting necessary selfish human nature and that we can and should look for links between culturally evolved systems and biologically evolved traits. One possibility is that of children's eager conformity, our "suggestibility to majorities and prestige figures," and our obedience to authority. Indeed our "universal tendency for conformity to the opinions of others may be essential to an adaptive social custom cumulation."[109] In other words, we may possess traits that not only help in our socialization but make us want to be socialized.

In a similar spirit Alice Rossi, in her 1983 address to the American Sociological Association, argued that "none of the theories prevalent in family sociology . . . are adequate to an understanding and explanation of human parenting because they do not seek an integration of biological and social constructs."[110] When discussing human reproduction and child rearing, the appropriate response to the fact that socialization may exaggerate biological differences is not, she argues, to pretend they do not exist. Sociologists need no reminder, she goes on,

> that the . . . subpopulation group [of young men] predominates in sexual violence, alcohol and drug abuse, crime, and social deviance. Unattached males roam the interstices between socially cohesive groups, kill and are themselves killed and maimed, but the machine cultures of the West have shown no inventiveness in developing new social institutions capable of providing individual loyalty and social integration to replace the bonds of family. Our only answers have been armies and prisons.[111]

Too often, Rossi argues, sociologists treat behavior differences between the sexes as simply culturally determined. Thus hormones that bring on puberty are treated as though they were simply signals that certain "appropriate" behavior can and should follow. In fact, among young men there are high correlations between testosterone levels and aggression.[112] Although

[108]Campbell, "On the Conflict Between Biological and Social Evolution," p. 1115. Italics original.

[109]Campbell, "On the Conflict Between Biological and Social Evolution," p. 1107. This argument is developed further in Robert Boyd and Peter J. Richerson, "Cultural Transmission and the Evolution of Cooperative Behavior," *Human Ecology* 10, no. 3 (1982): 325–51.

[110]Rossi, "Gender and Parenthood," p. 1. See also Alice Rossi, "A Biosocial Perspective on Parenting," *Daedalus* 106, no. 2 (1977): 1–31.

[111]Rossi, "Gender and Parenthood," p. 5.

[112]Even after allowing for all other factors. Rossi's reference is to J. R. Udry, J. O. G. Billy, N. M. Morris, T. R. Groff, and M. H. Raj, "Serum Androgenic Hormones Motivate Sexual Behavior in Adolescent Boys," *Fertility and Sterility* 43, no. 1 (1985): 90–94.

older men may have greater control, "older men are not all 'mature.' . . . [L]ife pressures can often escalate to the point that our thin veneer of social-ized self-control is lost, with the results we see in our prisons, hospitals, shel-ters for battered wives or homeless men, and treatment centers for child victims of incest. . . . Feelings and thoughts are molecular events in the brain that have chemical consequences"[113] and physical ones.

Biology and Sociology.   Many of the recent theoretical advances of the "new biology" will have limited relevance to sociology. Models deriving optimum ratios of worker bees to drones will hardly be used to explain changes in human family size, nor will middle managers' behavior be best understood in terms of a baboon troop's. What *does* seem likely is that socio-biology's development will encourage social scientists to treat reproduc-tion, scarcity, and environmental uncertainty as factors that are just as important in explaining human behavior as animal behavior—even if we respond differently.

They may also heed Rossi's plea not to see human beings as infinitely plastic. Sociologists tend to take it for granted that society revolves around group membership, even though they are often more interested in social classes than in kinship. They are less happy with the fact that groups require boundaries and the exclusion of people as well as their inclusion. But crea-tures that have lived in groups through millions of years of evolution are very likely to have characteristics that strongly encourage identification with one's own group—and therefore rejection of others. In consequence,

> sociobiology expects *every* racial group to be xenophobic. . . . [I]t expects, if anything, that every group feels itself superior to others.[114] (This is because) when it occurs in natural settings, xenophobia is a functional and adaptive trait in that it maintains the integrity of the social group. It ensures that group members will be socially familiar. . . . Xenophobia has apparently arisen in the course of natural selection and social evolution in those species and popula-tions where discrete social groups are adaptively favored.[115]

What it *may* also leave us with is "a residual and irreducible element of interracial hostility after all other historical, political, economic, social and

---

[113]Alice S. Rossi, "Growing Up and Older in Sociology," in Matilda White Riley, ed., *Sociological Lives*, p. 62. See also Alice S. Rossi, "Sex and Gender in an Aging Society," *Daedalus* 115, no. 1 (1986): 141–69.

[114]Vernon Reynolds, "Sociobiology and Race Relations," in Vernon Reynolds, Vincent Folger, and Ian Vine, ed., *The Sociobiology of Ethnocentrism. Evolutionary Dimensions of Xenophobia, Discrimination, Racism and Nationalism* (London: Croom Helm, 1987), p. 212.

[115]Johan M. G. van der Denneu, "Ethnocentrism and In-Group/Out-Group Differentiation," in Reynolds, Folger, and Vine, *Sociobiology of Ethnocentrism*, p. 22. See also Austin L. Hughes, *Evolution and Human Kinship* (New York: Oxford University Press, 1988). See also Lewis Coser's analysis of conflict and group identity in Chapter 3.

psychological factors have been removed."[116] The implication is the same as Rossi's: not that we should excuse or accept, but that along with their culture we should recognize the biology of human beings and the constraints that this implies.

---

[116]Reynolds, "Sociobiology and Race Relations," p. 211.

CHAPTER NINE

Conclusion: Evaluating Sociological Theory

PART ONE

The Future of Sociological Theory: Modernism and Postmodernism

Introduction

The millennium invites appraisals, in sociology as elsewhere; and sociologists surveying the state of theory offer a variety of views, many positive and optimistic, others far less so.[1] In this volume we have surveyed the most important theoretical perspectives of contemporary sociology. All of these have their roots in the work of great scholars of the nineteenth and early twentieth centuries: sociologists such as Durkheim and Weber, economists and political visionaries such as Marx, philosophers, social reformers, and evolutionary theorists. However, these perspectives are included here not because of their historical interest but because they are living intellectual traditions that continue to develop and contribute to our understanding of societies and how we live within them. Our own view is, as this book's title implies, an optimistic one. Sociological theory is as dynamic a body of ideas today as it has ever been. It continues to borrow from other disciplines *because* it is active and developing; while at the same time it offers a distinctive and unique perspective on human experience. In the final section of this chapter (and of this book) we return to the two themes that have run through each chapter—the role of education and the place of women in modern society—and summarize how each perspective offers different but complementary insights and answers.

We begin this chapter, however, by looking at the way sociology and particularly sociological theory have developed in the latter part of this century, and at what might be meant by the idea that we should be moving into a "postmodern" phase of theorizing. After all, sociological theories and theorists are part of the social scene themselves, and their popularity does not depend on their internal qualities alone. At different times during the last forty years, different approaches have been more or less popular and influential, and the reasons for this are not only concerned with how well they work as explanatory systems.

Historical Trends

In American sociology, particularly, three distinct phases are apparent. In the 1950s functionalism was the most influential perspective, and theorists' con-

---

[1]For contrasting views, see Irving Louis Horowitz, *The Decomposition of Sociology* (Oxford: Oxford University Press, 1994); and Randall Collins, "The Sociological Eye and its Blinders," *Contemporary Sociology* 27.1 (January 1998).

cerns were predominantly macrosociological. In the 1960s and 1970s neo-Marxist and analytic conflict theory were increasingly important, and there often seemed to be more people interested in finding things wrong with functionalism than there were sociologists using its approach. At the same time, especially in the United States, interest in the details of person-to-person encounters increased sharply. Symbolic interactionism and, increasingly, phenomenology influenced even those sociologists whose main interest was in macrosociology.

The result, in the 1980s and 1990s, was a third phase: one of increasing concern with the links between macroanalysis and microanalysis and with ways of integrating the two. Many of the most active contemporary theorists discussed in this book cross this macro-micro divide. At the same time, however, a minority of sociologists and others[2] argued that there had been a decisive shift in the nature of society, from "modernity" to "postmodernity"; that, as a result, the distorted nature of many of the concepts and ideas used by modern theorists (including scientists and social scientists) is increasingly apparent; and that a postmodernist vocabulary and discourse should henceforth be adopted instead.

We cannot pretend to offer a full and original analysis of these changes, but a number of social developments were probably influential. First is the different social experience of different generations of sociologists. One does not have to believe that ideas are straightforwardly determined by people's social positions to agree that the questions sociologists ask, and the perspectives they adopt in trying to answer them, will be shaped by their own lives. So will the degree to which a reader finds the question sensible and interesting or the answer convincing. Many of the sociologists who were active in the 1950s had fathers in the ministry and backgrounds where gradual social reform was advocated as a means of aiding disadvantaged groups and integrating them into society. They were working in a period when there was a general political consensus, and many intellectuals believed in an "end of ideology." Functionalism's emphasis on common norms thus seemed an appropriate way to examine society.

Younger sociologists' interests were formed during the era of the Vietnam War, a period of renewed political and ideological strife. Whatever their own political preferences, they had their attention turned to the origins of conflict and importance of ideology. Meanwhile, the New Left produced a group of young left-wing sociologists with a great interest in the Frankfurt School.[3]

[2]Notably literary critics and theorists in the areas of semiotics and cultural studies.

[3]It is important to remember that the period did not simply produce left-wing critiques. It refueled political and ideological debate across the spectrum, producing not only a new generation of radicals but also a new conservatism concerned about the growth in state power and intervention and the use of the courts to make social policy. This side of the renewed ideological character of intellectual debate is less apparent in sociology than in the intellectual scene as a whole, where, for example, the discovery of Marcuse by some is balanced by the discovery of his contemporary, Hayek, by others.

In addition, during the 1960s old cultural conventions broke down and alternative lifestyles flourished, especially in the United States. There was increasing interest in the way people's relationships with each other are created and affected by their mode of communication. Humanists also attacked science for ignoring the emotional and artistic sides of human experience. Alongside the demonstrations and controversies splitting the United States, many turned away from involvement in any organizations. It seems likely that these currents made younger sociologists more interested in the details of interaction, more aware of how one's world, or one's reality, could be created in an immediate way by oneself and the people around one. By contrast, during the 1950s people were aware of a different sort of social change. The importance in the economy of small businesses and farms was fast shrinking, and increasing numbers of people were being employed by large organizations. This focused the attention of many of the most able sociologists on organizations and the industrial firm—on structural questions rather than microsociological analysis.[4]

A third factor affecting the direction taken by sociological theory was the similar shift in interest taking place in the intellectual world at large. Since 1945 phenomenology has become increasingly well known outside Germany. Its criticisms of mainline social science and its concern with the subjective aspects of reality have influenced many more sociologists than just the self-declared phenomenologists. English and American philosophers have also been increasingly interested in the active, or intentional, aspects of perception and in the way our thoughts and experiences rest on shared assumptions and irreducible concepts.[5] Stephen Toulmin noted a change among philosophers of science (and social science) with similar implications. He argued that during the 1960s they became increasingly concerned with how perceptions and theories were rooted in the "historical temporary world" and in the general conceptual framework of an age.[6]

Curiously enough, the relative decline in sociology's status during the late 1970s and early 1980s probably stimulated the integration of such theories into mainline sociology. With the decline of 1960s-style "counterculture," America and Western Europe alike found students moving to

[4]See, for example, Peter M. Blau and W. R. Scott, *Formal Organization* (San Francisco: Chandler, 1962), or Amitai Etzioni, *A Comparative Analysis of Complex Organization* (New York: The Free Press, 1961).

[5]The work of P. F. Strawson (such as *Individuals: An Essay in Descriptive Metaphysics* [London: Methuen, 1959]) is especially important in this area. Noam Chomsky's work on "depth grammar," in which he has argued for the existence of a grammar shared by all human languages (and rooted in the genes of the individual) also became well known during this period. See Noam Chomsky, *Aspects of the Theory of Syntax* (Cambridge, Mass.: M.I.T. Press, 1965).

[6]Stephen Toulmin, "From Form to Function: Philosophy and History of Science in the 1950s and Now," *Daedalus* 106.3 (Summer 1977): 159.

subjects with more immediate relevance in the job market. The discipline ceased to be highly fashionable and linked with political activism, developing instead into one social science discipline among others. American sociologists, in particular, became more interested in academic developments elsewhere. Especially in the area of theory, they looked more to other disciplines and to other countries—moves that are in any case mutually reinforcing because in Europe the barriers between different social science disciplines are far less defined. A growing interest in such European theorists as Habermas, Bourdieu, and Giddens meant growing influence for theorists who themselves are interested in the micro roots of macrosociology and are well acquainted with phenomenological analysis. Similarly, the growing influence of rational choice theory, reentering sociology via political science and economics, also meant a renewed focus on the micro-macro interface.[7]

What we have described so far implies a coming together of different theoretical perspectives and the espousal of a relatively eclectic approach, in which sociologists draw on whatever seems the most appropriate framework to illuminate the particular question from which they start. A growing number of sociologists have argued for a synthesis of theoretical approaches to the explanation of social phenomena. Peter Berger, Randall Collins, Anthony Giddens, and Dorothy Smith are among those who recognize the strength of a more expansive view of social reality, one that incorporates the macrostructural, microinteractional, and interpretive levels of analysis.

In our view this indeed characterizes the mainstream of sociological theory and of empirical sociological studies. However, as we have noted, a minority argues against this, and indeed against the whole thrust of contemporary sociology and social science and their attempt to make sense of the world. This attack is particularly associated with the term "postmodernism."

The Postmodernist Critique

Charles Lemert, one of the best-known American sociologists to write within a postmodernist perspective, distinguishes a number of different strands of postmodernist writing.[8] One important group is advancing the argument that there has been a major shift in the nature of society, and that the type of society that we have characterized as modern has been succeeded by a very

---

[7]Although sociobiology's influence remains relatively small, it is concerned with the society-wide implications of individual behavior and of gene-based individual characteristics.

[8]Charles Lemert, *Postmodernism Is Not What You Think* (Malden, Mass.: Blackwell, 1997).

different one.[9] This approach is particularly associated with writers who emphasize the profound effect that mass media have had on our experience of the world and on what people experience as real, and who analyze the effect of the mass media on the sorts of people we are, on what are seen as important issues and events, and on the concepts and ideas that define us and our views of others.[10] Another group also examines the concept of modernity from a critical perspective, identifying what they see as its essential components, the ways in which these are changing, often quite dramatically, in the late twentieth century, and the ways in which older and emerging forms of society fail to realize human potential. This latter approach is one we have encountered in earlier chapters, especially in the work of the Frankfurt School (Chapter 3) and of Jürgen Habermas (Chapter 4).

Sociologists and analysts of this type tend to believe that their work should incorporate a critique of contemporary society (hence the term "critical"); but they are nonetheless within the mainstream tradition of sociological analysis. However, there is a third stream of postmodernism, which is the one most clearly associated with the term in both social science and literary studies, as well as the most controversial, and which distances itself markedly from most of the sociological theorists that we have discussed in the preceding chapters.

This third group shares the conviction that there has been a major shift in the nature of contemporary society, so that we inhabit a distinctive postcapitalist—or postmodern—world. However, what distinguishes it, and makes it recognizably different from most sociological theory, and indeed from mainstream scholarship and commentary in general, are two other features: first, its emphasis on discourse (to which we return next), and second, its explicit opposition to the scientific canon of reason and empirical investigation.

Throughout the history of sociology, there has been an active debate about whether the scientific model is appropriate to the study of society. Human behavior is purposive, and if you tell people that something is going to happen because social laws predict it, they may, unlike fruit flies or crystals, set out to

[9]Outside sociology, the adjective "postmodern" is used in a wide range of contexts, becoming almost a synonym for "late twentieth century." For example, as Lemert points out, the skyscraper that Philip Johnson designed for AT&T has become an icon of postmodernist architecture because it is full of surprising and self-conscious nonmodern characteristics, such as the Greek temple style of the pediment. Johnson's building certainly had an enormous influence on the late-twentieth-century move away from pure modernist (twentieth century) architecture, with its extremely severe and simple lines; but it is not obviously different in kind from other architectural developments of the past. The jokey and equally self-conscious style of "Strawberry Hill Gothic" signaled a comparable move away from the clean lines of English Georgian or American colonial architecture toward the heavier styles of the nineteenth century. Postmodernism as a theoretical movement in the social sciences and humanities is making claims to be something much more distinctive and unprecedented.

[10]See especially the work of Jean Baudrillard, but also much of the fast-expanding literature on cultural studies; for example, Norman Denzin, *Symbolic Interactionism and Cultural Studies: The Politics of Interpretation* (Oxford: Blackwell, 1992).

prove you wrong. Nonetheless, the physical sciences offer an impressive model to copy, explaining whole groups of phenomena with a few powerful laws.

The most important component of postmodernism is its rejection of this scientific canon, of the idea that there can be a single coherent rationality or that reality has a unitary nature that can be definitively observed or understood. Instead its exponents stress the "fragmentary, heterogeneous, and plural nature of reality and the inherently unstable and shifting nature of the subject and individual consciousness."[11] As a result, they argue, we "live in a fragmented, diversified, and decentralized discursive framework."[12] This implies an extreme relativism about what is true or not true, and a rejection of the idea that theories or hypotheses can be tested (or disproved) according to rational, universal scientific principles.

Within sociological theory, enthusiasts for postmodernism argue that theory of the traditional type is dead but that a postmodern approach can revitalize theory. Thus Steven Seidman argues,

> To revitalize sociological theory requires that we renounce scientism—that is, the increasingly absurd claim to speak the Truth. . . . Postmodernism gives up the modernist idol of human emancipation in favor of deconstructing false closure, prying open present and future social possibilities, detecting fluidity and porousness. . . . The hope of a great transformation is replaced by the more modest aspiration of a relentless defense of immediate local pleasures and struggles for justice . . . (and) a social analysis that takes seriously the history of cruelty and constraint in Western societies.[13]

There are clear echoes here of the aspirations of, for example, the critical conflict theorists such as Habermas and the Frankfurt school, even though the latter's belief in reason is explicitly rejected. In fact, postmodernists in the social sciences tend to see themselves as automatically of the left, although it is not clear why, if everything is relative, left-wing positions should be any more valid, or have greater claims to truth, than any other.

The second defining characteristic of postmodernism is its concern with "discourse" and with "texts." The idea that words and their meanings are socially produced and constructed is one we have encountered on a number of occasions in the previous chapters—for example, in Marx's discussions of ideology and false consciousness but also, and especially, in the discussions of the micro perspectives associated with phenomenology.[14] However, postmodernism goes beyond this to make language, especially the

---

[11]Andy Green, "Postmodernism and State Education," *Journal of Education Policy* 9.1 (1994): 67–83.

[12]Bryan S. Turner, *Regulating Bodies: Essays in Medical Sociology* (London: Routledge, 1992), p. 142. Turner is here defining postmodern models of science rather than describing his own position.

[13]Steven Seidman, "The End of Sociological Theory: The Postmodern Hope," *Sociological Theory* 9.2 (1991): 132–46.

[14]See, for example, Mehan's discussion of how teachers misinterpreted children's answers to tests because they did not understand the children's own understanding of the vocabulary and materials: p. 264.

language of written texts, its major concern and, in many cases, its sole source of material evidence.

The two most famous names in postmodernism are Jacques Derrida and Michel Foucault, both of them French. This in itself reflects an enduring difference between the French intellectual tradition and what other countries often refer to as the Anglo-Saxon approach of North American, Australasian, and British social scientists. The latter, brought up in an empiricist tradition, tend to concentrate on people's actual behavior in trying to understand society, whereas French intellectuals are far more inclined to look at what people say and how they think.[15] This is itself related to the place of intellectuals in French society, where they write for a general literary public rather than within a particular academic discipline. To the foreign reader the most striking thing about much French social analysis is that it is "all about words,"[16] and this is certainly true of postmodernism.

Derrida himself is a philosopher and essayist rather than a sociologist; but the general popularity of the term *discourse* derives from him.[17] In using this word Derrida and other postmodernists mean to emphasize the primacy of the words we use, the concepts they embody, and the rules that develop within a group about what are appropriate ways of talking about things. They mediate between us and reality; or as Hayden White puts it, "Discourse, in a word, is quintessentially a mediative enterprise."[18]

In contrast to Derrida, Michel Foucault analyses subject matter that is very much that of the sociologist: prisons, asylums, medicine, and changing sexual attitudes and practices. We have referred to Foucault's work earlier in discussing the growing importance of the body as a subject for sociological theory; and he has been by far the most influential postmodernist theorist in sociology. He also encapsulates the perspective's preoccupation with texts.

To Foucault, the prison and the asylum exemplify the modern world. However, while we commonly see the advent of the modern mental hospital and the decline of the death penalty as signs of progress, Foucault sees them as epitomizing a shift in the way power is exercised in a society. They embody discipline, deprive those involved of liberty, and exist to serve the interests of those in power: "the whole differential question of illegalities

---

[15]See Edith Kurzweil, *The Age of Structuralism: Lévi-Strauss to Foucault* (New York: Columbia University Press, 1980).

[16]See also, for example, the work of the anthropologist Claude Lévi-Strauss, which examines the categories that structure people's thoughts and actions: Claude Lévi-Strauss, *The Elementary Structures of Kinship* (London: Eyre and Spottiswoode, 1969); Edmund Leach, *Lévi-Strauss* (London: Collins, 1970).

[17]Derrida is also associated with the term *deconstruction*, which implies the taking of an ironic and critical attitude toward modern culture in order to highlight the way it ignores differences and inequalities.

[18]Hayden White, *Tropics of Discourse* (Baltimore: Johns Hopkins University Press, 1978), p. 4; cited in Lemert, *Postmodernism Is Not What You Think.*

through penalty forms part of those mechanisms of domination."[19] In this they are more extreme than, but nevertheless similar to, the other major institutions of modern life—for example, the factory or the modern school.

In putting forward this view, Foucault concentrates on textual analysis because he seeks structures of knowledge. His sources are books, treatises, legends—*texts*. The particular way in which we see and comprehend the world is to be found in texts, and, in his view, it is such a viewpoint that defines an age and governs the ways in which power is exercised. Doctors, prison governors, lawyers, and politicians are not seen by Foucault as individuals who consciously develop institutions that will secure their positions. Rather, the viewpoint of an age—in our case, the "scientific" view—means that people naturally see things in a certain way. The actions follow.

In *The Order of Things*[20] (the book that made him famous) and in *The Archaeology of Knowledge*,[21] Foucault puts forward the notion of an "episteme" that defines an age. The modern episteme was formed at the end of the eighteenth century and was bound up with the shift of language toward objectivity; but is no more universally valid or permanent than its predecessors.

Having read Foucault once, one cannot look at modern society in quite the same way again. This is not to say, however, that his approach is not open to criticism. The eminent psychologist Jean Piaget, whose work transformed the way we think about the development of children's reasoning, has been one of Foucault's harshest critics, stating that "beneath the cleverness there are only bare affirmations and omissions."[22] There is no real method behind his selection and elaboration of an episteme's characteristics. Rather "he relies on intuition and substitutes speculative improvisation for methodical procedures."[23] One of France's most eminent contemporary sociologists, Raymond Boudon, sees Foucault's underlying thesis as nothing more than a simplistic form of functionalism, in which everything is seen as serving a function—for example, prisons benefit the ruling class of their time—and in which identifying this function is supposed to be an adequate explanation of how the institutions in question came about.[24]

A more general criticism can be applied to the general postmodernist preoccupation with the written and spoken word. Those who write and tell

---

[19]Michel Foucault, *Discipline and Punish: The Birth of the Person*, trans. Alan Sheridan (London: Allen Lane, 1977).

[20]Michel Foucault, *The Order of Things: An Archaeology of the Human Sciences* (London: Tavistock, 1970).

[21]Michel Foucault, *The Archaeology of Knowledge*, trans. A. M. Sheridan Smith (London: Tavistock, 1972).

[22]Jean Piaget, *Structuralism*, trans. and ed. Chaninah Maschler (London: Routledge and Kegan Paul, 1971), p. 130.

[23]Piaget, *Structuralism*, p. 133.

[24]Raymond Boudon, *The Analysis of Ideology*, trans. Malcolm Slater (Cambridge: Polity, 1989). See especially chap. 2.

tales, and whose words survive, are only a fraction of a society. They are unquestionably its products in the sense of being the people they are because of when and where they live. However, especially in the written word, there is much that is individual to the writer and much more that is specific to the outlook of the "writing" classes alone. It is dangerous to believe that one can somehow deduce social institutions directly from ideas, just as it is dangerous to see ideas as simply a superstructure mirroring the economic institutions below.

Postmodernism has been strongly attacked both on theoretical grounds and for having, as yet, provided a great deal of abstract critique of existing theory but rather little that can actually replace it.[25] One general and frequent criticism is that if postmodernists are serious about their claim that there is no unitary reality, and that statements can have only a partial and shifting authority, then this puts in doubt their own position. Their own general statements about society are also by definition partial, fragmentary, and with no greater claim to truth than anyone else's views. (Critics also point out that postmodernists do not seem to carry their own relativist convictions over into the world of science they attack, being no keener than the rest of us to have their medical operations carried out or their houses and bridges built by enthusiasts for alternative paradigms.)

In a previous chapter we noted Neil Smelser's criticism of rational choice theory for tending to ignore the importance of emotion, affect, and ambivalence—in other words, the *nonrational* aspects of human life.[26] Smelser sees postmodernism, however, as something quite different: it is not that it is concerned with the nonrational, but that it is *antirational*.[27] As such it is quite separate from the main tradition of social science and philosophy in which he locates both himself and the vast majority of classical and contemporary theorists we have discussed in these pages: Simmel, Pareto, Goffman, Merton, Coleman, and the like.

Although postmodernism is the subject of frequent comment by sociologists, it is unclear whether it will have a major impact on the practice of sociology.[28] Since the death of Foucault there are no major sociological theorists discussed in this text whom one can categorize as active and unequivocally postmodern. At the same time there *are* important continuities between postmodernism and some of the major concerns and emphases in contemporary sociology and in social science as a whole.

[25]See, for example, Jeffrey C. Alexander, "Sociological Theory and the Claim to Reason: Why the End Is Not in Sight," *Sociological Theory* 9.2 (1991): 146–53; E. Gellner, *Postmodernism, Reason and Religion* (London: Routledge, 1992); Green, "Postmodernism and State Education."

[26]See the conclusion of Chapter 7.

[27]Neil J. Smelser, "Presidential Address: The Rational and the Ambivalent in the Social Sciences," *American Sociological Review* 63, no. 1 (February 1998): 1–15.

[28]The disciplines in which postmodernism is most influential are literary and cultural studies, and, to a lesser extent, history.

We pointed out earlier in this chapter that contemporary theory has involved an increasing integration of micro and macro perspectives, including a growing influence for phenomenology, which itself emphasizes the importance of subjective meaning. Thus Berger analyzes the social construction of reality, and Garfinkel and Smith both focus on the taken-for-granted aspects of people's interactions—aspects that are in fact subject to constant change, construction, and reconstruction. There are continuities here with postmodernism's emphasis on the mediated nature of experience. More generally, some fundamental nonsociological breakthroughs in how we think about ideas and words have affected the way we understand ourselves and the way sociological theorists conceptualize human experience. For example, we have mentioned the work of psychologist Jean Piaget, who has inspired the huge advances made by modern psychology in understanding how we form and modify concepts and hypotheses about the world and act upon them. Similarly, the linguist Noam Chomsky has argued for the existence of a depth grammar shared by all human languages.[29] What this means is that all languages—and therefore the ways in which all human beings understand and communicate about the world—have fundamental features in common. If we can comprehend this underlying structure and its transformational rules, we will have learned something important about the sort of creatures we are. The fact that in all human languages sentences must have subjects and predicates structures our experience.

The common element in this work is the search for the structure of thought and perception. The way we see and conceptualize the world affects the way we act, and understanding social behavior must therefore involve understanding the laws of language and the intellect.[30] There are continuities here with the postmodernist perspective; but few sociological theorists, at least to date, see the postmodern critique as a reason to abandon their belief in testing hypotheses against evidence, or, indeed, for abandoning a belief in reason itself. As Randall Collins has argued eloquently, many sociologists come to their discipline because they are concerned about social issues; but they pursue it in a spirit that is absolutely opposed to those who see every publication as "a move for or against a partisan position." On the contrary: for Collins and most other contemporary sociologists, it is the essence of the "sociological eye" to bring into the open the "unexpected *reality* (others) are afraid to see."[31] In the remainder of this chapter we summarize the different

---

[29]Noam Chomsky, *Cartesian Linguistics, A Chapter in the History of Rationalist Thought* (New York: Harper and Row, 1966), and *Aspects of the Theory of Syntax* (Cambridge, Mass.: M.I.T. Press, 1965). See also the work of Pinker and Danielle Dennett.

[30]Piaget, in his discussion of structuralism, defines it as the search for a whole, self-regulating system of laws. "[T]he elements of a structure are subordinated to laws, and it is in terms of these laws that the structure . . . is defined." Piaget, *Structuralism*, p. 7.

[31]Randall Collins, "The Sociological Eye and Its Blinders," *Contemporary Sociology* 27.1 (January 1998): 6. Italics ours. Collins is referring here to the attacks on Hochschild's findings in *The Time Bind*: see pp. 243–44.

ways in which major theoretical perspectives do just this, with particular reference to the unifying themes of this book: formal education and the role of women in society.

PART TWO

Sociological Theory and Understanding: The Value of Multiple Perspectives

Contemporary sociological theory ranges from the antideterminist inductive and descriptive approach typified by ethnomethodology to the predictive, deductive approach advocated by exchange theory. It encompasses the most detailed microsociological analysis alongside theories of global social evolution. In Chapter 1 (see especially Table 1-1) we summarized the ways in which perspectives differ in what they believe motivates human beings; the extent to which they see behavior as predictable and embrace a scientific, deductive approach to theorizing; and their whole view of sociology, and whether it is about description, prediction, or promoting social change. The chapters of this book have correspondingly discussed theorists as different as Marx and Garfinkel, Coleman and Smith, or Parsons and Goffman.

However, these differences do not mean that the major theoretical perspectives are totally incompatible with each other. Postmodernism presents itself as fundamentally different from other approaches to social science; but where other theoretical perspectives are concerned, the trend among sociologists is to adopt insights that seem appropriate to the problem at hand rather than confining themselves to one predetermined approach. This increasingly eclectic and inclusive approach to theory is especially evident in the trend toward integrating micro and macro levels of analysis.

The insights that different perspectives offer into education and the role of women encapsulate, in our view, the complementary nature of contemporary theories. So, too, does our own experience as empirical sociologists, working on issues that also relate to these themes. Wallace, for example, has looked at the results of changes, at the national level, in a major institution, the Catholic Church; but she has also focused on what these mean, at a micro level, to the individuals concerned. She has drawn on the insights of Peter Berger in studying U.S. parishes headed by laywomen;[32] while in her recent and as yet unpublished research on married men heading Catholic parishes, she draws explicitly on Goffman's work. For example: because living room, dining room, and kitchen are often used for parish

---

[32]See p. 279.

committee meetings, families living in parish rectories are challenged to keep their front-stage work spaces separate from their family backstage region. One of the wives said that the house never really felt like home to her; and her oldest daughter elaborated:

> My mother felt invaded, completely invaded. And there wasn't anything to do about it. She had to have the dishes done when people came for those meetings at 7:00 or people were going to see that she didn't have her dishes done. You know, there was still this "your house is a reflection of you."

Wallace employs Goffman's regional concepts and ideas about impression management in looking at an area that brings together macro and micro phenomena. Wolf's empirical work similarly reflects this trend to integrate different insights and levels of analysis. In explaining the rapid increase worldwide in the number of young people obtaining first degrees, higher degrees, and professional qualifications, she draws on conflict theory's ideas about how groups use education to pass on privilege to their children. She also uses rational choice theory's ideas about how multiple individual decisions produce results that no one predicts, and the ideas of Goffman and others about how individuals perceive the world and the way they present themselves. To understand the size of modern higher education and the very general and nonvocational nature of so many courses, she argues, you have to start with individuals whose decisions are based on the desire to look good to employers as compared to their contemporaries and competitors.[33]

These examples themselves concern the changing role of women and the huge formal education sector: themes that we selected for this text because both are so central to the nature and experience of life in contemporary societies and raise a number of puzzling questions. We have argued that in answering these questions, different perspectives offer important, complementary insights. The remainder of this chapter summarizes the way in which they do so.

Exploring Formal Education: The Role of the School

In Chapter 1, we raised two major questions about education in modern society. The first of these, which can hardly fail to strike any observer, is, What accounts for the enormous size of the modern education system? The second must equally well occur to anyone who has been through formal schooling and thinks back to his or her fellow students: Why do some individuals do well when others fail and drop out? As we can now see, the first question is essentially macrosociological because it poses a question about social structure; consequently, functionalism and conflict theory offer the

---

[33]Alison Wolf, "Growth Stocks and Lemons: Diplomas in the English Market Place 1976–96," *Assessment in Education* 4.1 (1997): 33–49.

most by way of answers. The second question, by contrast, asks why our day-by-day experiences of school add up to academic success in some cases and to dropping out as soon as possible in others. Here the micro approaches of symbolic interactionism and phenomenology along with theories of rational choice prove most enlightening.

One common explanation of our enormous educational establishment refers to the general nature of industrial society. It is meritocratic and impersonal. Technical skills are necessary for many jobs, and, for most people, work and home are miles apart. Such a society, it is argued, demands our sort of school system. Children have to undergo an extensive and prolonged education outside the home so that they will learn to see individual performance, not family ties, as the proper criterion for job placement and success. At the same time they can learn complicated technical skills, and employers can discover, from school certification, who is capable of performing different jobs.

Functionalism analyzes education in just such terms. In Chapter 2 we described Talcott Parsons's classic account of the American school system,[34] in which he discusses how elementary school teaches children the impersonal and achievement-oriented values of an industrial society, accustoms them to a world in which there is none of the unconditional affection and support provided by the family, and thus develops "the commitments and capacities for successful performance of their adult roles."[35] At the same time it performs the equally important function of human resource allocation, identifying children as potentially fitted, or unfitted, for college and for particular jobs—a task that cannot be left to family ascription because special abilities and skills are so important in modern occupations. Other functionalists have extended the analysis, interpreting the continuing growth of the education system as a function of the increasing technical skills required of the labor force.[36] Others discuss the functions of different types of higher education, as when Burton Clark examines the way junior colleges accustom and resign people to limited career ambitions.[37]

Much of this analysis has become part of the way that not just sociologists but almost all those involved with education look at modern schooling, even when they criticize its role. It is, for example, exactly the view put forward by politicians throughout the developed and underdeveloped world when they spend massive sums on education so they can fit their soci-

---

[34]Talcott Parsons, "The School Class as a Social System: Some of Its Functions in American Society," in A. H. Halsey, Jean Floud, and C. Arnold Anderson, ed. *Education, Economy and Society* (New York: The Free Press, 1961). See also Chapter 2.

[35]Parsons, "The School Class as a Social System," p. 434.

[36]This case is argued explicitly by, among other, Burton Clark in *Educating the Expert Society* (San Francisco: Chandler, 1962).

[37]Burton Clark, "The Cooling-Out Function in Higher Education," *American Journal of Sociology* 65 (1960).

eties for the "white-hot technological revolution."[38] Parents similarly try to impress on their children the need to study and acquire a skill if they are to do well in the modern economy.

However, there is also an alternative way of explaining the nature and growth of modern education. According to this explanation, the educational system is essentially a way of securing power and privilege in a technological age. One could argue that instead of directly passing on money or land, successful families today secure the position of their children by giving them education. Either because society considers a long, expensive education to be a superior qualification for holding certain positions or because middle- and upper-class families can provide far greater scholastic help to their children than can other families, a long formal education allows parents to pass on and secure position and status for their children. These same children might fare far less well in a world of self-made entrepreneurs and on-the-job training.

At the same time one could view extended compulsory schooling as indoctrinating children into believing in the current form of society and teaching them the basic skills needed by "factory fodder." In this view schooling is a useful way to maintain the status quo to the benefit of those in charge. Finally, there is the related argument that people who have a lot of education, however acquired, have a stake in increasing the importance of education in the job market. Their efforts to do so encourage the upward spiral of educational requirements and the educational system's continued growth.

The conflict theorists discussed in Chapter 3 analyze education in this way, as a factor in the competitive struggle for resources rather than a contribution to a society's functioning. In general they agree that education has becoming increasingly important in this way, with Konrad and Szelényi, for example, documenting how an education-based class, the intelligentsia, has dominated both Communist and post-Communist Hungary. Norman Birnbaum and Pierre Bourdieu both question the degree to which schooling identifies skills objectively. They argue instead that families with the wherewithal to secure good education for their children use the system to ensure for them a superior social position.[39] Cultural traits mark "top people" so that those without the right habits of speech and manners can be discriminated against by educated insiders. Such "cultural capital" is, such theorists argue, important in securing children an entry into top educational establishments, and is also at least as important a product of education as any technical skills.

Finally, these theorists emphasize the dynamics of conflict, rather than technological change, when they analyze the continuing expansion of edu-

---

[38]The phrase is that of Harold Wilson, former prime minister of the United Kingdom.

[39]Norman Birnbaum, *The Crisis of Industrial Society* (New York: Oxford University Press, 1969); Pierre Bourdieu and Jean-Claude Passeron, *The Inheritors*, trans. R. Nice (Chicago: University of Chicago Press, 1979).

cation. Collins, for example, argues that people with an education, like any other group with particular resources, want to secure for themselves the maximum potential benefits. They attempt to make high educational requirements a prerequisite for job entry and to exclude those without formal certificates. The attempt by large numbers of people to obtain the required certificates and the continuing attempt by educated groups to protect their privileges lead, Collins argues, to an educational spiral, in which the formal educational requirements for job entry are raised continually.[40] Raymond Boudon, from a rational choice perspective, complements Collins's argument by showing how individuals' choices will almost always tend to result in longer courses being taken rather than shorter ones. People calculate that if they take short courses, they risk being pushed aside in the job market by other people who have taken longer ones. Multiply these individual choices, and obviously one is left with a continuing expansion of the average size of higher education and its average length.[41]

Which set of explanations is correct? Probably both and neither. A modern society does demand real and complex skills, and its schools help accustom children to an impersonal environment. At the same time educational qualifications are undoubtedly a resource in people's continual struggle to secure a good life for themselves; and a heavy emphasis on formal education suits those with the qualifications and the ability to help their children get them. What is important for our purposes here is that these two accounts, each embodying very different insights, also derive from two of the major perspectives discussed in this book: functionalism and conflict theory.

In similar fashion, rational choice theory, symbolic interactionism, and phenomenology offer different but complementary answers to our second question: Why does one particular student fail while another succeeds? One possible explanation is that a student's decisions and behavior depend, basically, on the costs and benefits that student perceives. Students who find that hard work and good behavior bring them rewards that they value, including parental approval or respect and status from their peers, will behave in one way. Students who find that they get praise and good grades even when they do little work will respond accordingly. Students whose peer group admires and rewards rebels, who do not see academic rewards as something they can attain, or who believe their school to be so bad that what it offers is not worth acquiring will respond rationally to these very different signals.

Rational choice theorists (Chapter 7) stress the way in which the award of social approval in small groups affects behavior and also, over time, leads to the internalization of norms about what is desirable. Coleman, for

---

[40]Randall Collins, "Functional and Conflict Theories of Educational Stratification," *American Sociological Review* 36 (1971): 1002–19; and *The Credential Society: An Historical Sociology of Education and Stratification* (New York: Academic Press, 1979).

[41]Raymond Boudon, *The Unintended Consequences of Social Action* (London: Macmillan, 1982).

example, argues that for this to work well with small children, you need carers who have a long-term perspective and an interest in how the child will behave years from now; and he argues that unstable child care or family patterns are likely to affect attitudes toward school for this reason. Rational choice theorists also underline the importance of looking at the day-to-day options that face the children themselves. When George Richmond looked in this way at his own ungovernable classroom, he was able to alter affairs dramatically by changing the pattern of rewards.[42] Before, continual war with the teacher at least offered students fun and peer-group status. Once there were tangible benefits to be gained from study, however, the balance swung the other way. Richmond's microeconomy game, by paying students and introducing a competitive game they enjoyed, resulted in a classroom where students worked hard and willingly.

It is also possible, while retaining an emphasis on students' daily experiences, to focus not on rational choice but on the interaction between teachers and students. Teachers may misinterpret such things as students' accents or styles of speech, responding, for example, with a "Don't talk to me like that" when they hear what seems to them cheeky or insubordinate. They may react to behavior that is symbolic to them of a student unlikely to do well in school. Conversely, students may interpret teachers' behavior as evidence that they do or do not take their job seriously, or do or don't care about whether any particular student learns or succeeds. If both sides behave to each other on this basis, both their general relationship and the students' school careers will be influenced accordingly.

Symbolic interactionists address students' success or failure in this way. Their perspective enabled Colin Lacey to explain why some children succeeded and others failed in an English grammar school (academically selective high school). He showed how the interaction between students and teachers created and reinforced both the images each held of the other and the way they behaved. For example, boys whom teachers saw as buffoons or potential dropouts came increasingly to see themselves in this way and to behave accordingly.[43]

Finally, there is yet another way of explaining a particular student's failure or success. One can go beyond looking at how people generally interpret aspects of each other's behavior to look at the minute details of speech and conversation—at how students understand particular questions and

---

[42]George Richmond, *The Micro-Society School: A Real World in Miniature* (New York: Harper and Row, 1973).

[43]Colin Lacey, *Hightown Grammar: The School as a Social System* (Manchester: Manchester University Press, 1970). A good discussion of the scope of educational sociology of this interpretive type can be found in Jerome Karabel and A. H. Halsey, ed., *Power and Ideology in Education* (New York: Oxford University Press, 1977), chap. 1. See also Carl Werthman, "Delinquents in Schools," in *School and Society: A Sociological Reader*, prepared by the Open University School and Society Course Team (London: Routledge with Open University Press, 1971).

problems. Here the emphasis is on the fact that teachers' statements or items on a test do not have a single, shared, and self-evident meaning, even though we all tend to assume that they do. A child's apparent failure on a test may not be a result of ignorance or stupidity. Instead, the child may understand a question in a perfectly coherent but "wrong" way. Similarly, to grasp fully why another child is a "success," we must see how the teacher understands the question and the way the child's answers fit with the teacher's assumptions and preconceptions.

Phenomenology's contribution to understanding scholastic success and failure is to be found in such analysis of the speech patterns, concepts, and assumptions involved in conversations between teacher and child and whether the child's answers or conduct are seen as right or wrong. In his description of how small children's tests were interpreted and graded, for example, Hugh Mehan applied ethnomethodology's concern with underlying assumptions of shared meaning to understanding how teachers assess an answer as correct. He demonstrated how a child's perfectly coherent and accurate reasoning may, because of the way he or she interprets the materials, produce answers different from those the teacher and test compiler consider obviously right. Similarly, Aaron Cicourel and John Kitsuse showed how guidance counselors' interpretations and assumptions result in records being assessed as good or poor and in students being labeled and treated accordingly.[44]

Exploring the Role of Women in Contemporary Society

The second theme that has run through this text is that of gender, in particular the role of women in contemporary society. Here, too, we started with two apparently puzzling questions. The first was why females with one to three years of college in full-time employment in the United States have lower average annual earnings than full-time male workers who are only high school graduates. The second was why men and boys, at home, school, and work, tend consistently to be more aggressive and dominant, and girls and women more caring and supportive. How can the multiple perspectives of sociology build up answers to each of these questions?

One possible explanation for gender-linked income differentials is that they follow from, or contribute to, the complex and interdependent roles undertaken by people in modern industrial societies. As we said in Chapter 2, functionalism does indeed provide such an explanation. Parsons sees sex role differentiation as one important way in which families—and societies—respond to the need of systems to carry out different tasks. In pattern vari-

---

[44]Hugh Mehan, "Ethnomethodology and Education," in D. O'Shea, ed., *Sociology of the School and Schooling* (Washington, D.C.: National Institute of Education, 1974); Aaron Cicourel and John Kitsuse, *The Educational Decision-Makers* (New York: Bobbs-Merrill, 1963).

able terms, there is a need for expressive leadership but also for instrumental leadership. In AGIL terms, there is a need for adaptation—securing enough resources—but also for latent pattern maintenance and the transmission of societal values. Role differentiation, Parsons would argue, is a more effective way of fulfilling system needs than if everyone tried to do everything.

Thus, according to functionalist analysis, primary responsibility for breadwinning and instrumental leadership is allocated to men, and primary responsibility for the family and expressive leadership to women. This gender-based societal response to the need for both kinds of role is, according to this argument, reflected in the labor market. Higher average earnings for men reflect a combination of giving higher pay to people who have the main occupational responsibilities; men doing more overtime (for the same reasons); and women's choice of less well-paid but "caring" occupations that are consistent with their general expressive role.[45]

There is, however, another very different explanation of income inequalities, generally and in this specific, gender-linked case. This explanation is phrased in terms of self-interest and the activities of organized interest groups, and it is presented by the conflict theorists discussed in Chapter 3. Marxist feminists, for example, argue that gender has to be used alongside class in analyzing inequalities and see societies as patriarchies in which power relations favor men at the expense of women. Thus, for Zillah Eisenstein the sexual division of labor is a basic mechanism of control, of preserving men's superior (and better-paid) position. Classifying a job as a "woman's" job is a way to justify paying less and treating the occupation concerned as somehow inferior. Dorothy Smith's work extends this approach to incorporate phenomenological approaches, but she also sees the ruling apparatus as excluding women (among others), and she describes how the university where she worked had "a caste system: faculty were male." Administrative tasks were the job of lower-status, lower-paid females.[46]

Conflict theorists in the analytic tradition are less likely to provide explanations that invoke cohesive patriarchal organization by men to oppress women. Instead, they see gender as one dimension among others in terms of which people organize and act self-interestedly. Collins and Chafetz, for example, both point out that women are almost universally inferior to men in their access to wealth, power, and other valued resources. They note, however, that there are big variations between societies and that one needs to look at factors specific to a situation as well as to universal differences.[47]

---

[45]Miriam Johnson provides a feminist critique, within the general functionalist model, of this analysis. She sees the process of "inclusion" as gradually promoting equal pay and opportunity for women albeit to the accompaniment of tension and strain.

[46]See p. 286.

[47]See Chapter 3, pp. 142–45.

In explaining women's lower average earnings in the contemporary United States, analytic conflict theorists give considerable weight to universal biological differences. All societies, they note, have found it more efficient for those who bear the children also to do the caretaking. It can be arranged otherwise, but this will be more troublesome and less obvious a solution. Thus, women's child-care responsibilities affect their choice of occupation and the time they devote to it in a way that is not true for men. Not only do women more often work part-time, they also choose jobs that—like teaching—fit in relatively well with child care (and other family responsibilities). The fact that women are interested in these jobs for reasons other than the material rewards means, in turn, that employers can offer wages that are lower than they would have to pay otherwise. Women are caught in a double bind, one made worse by such factors as the long distances that, in modern society, often separate home and workplace; the attitudes that encourage them to aim for "women's" jobs; and the fact that established occupational groups have a strong interest in continuing to structure jobs so that they are difficult for women to do. Rae Lesser Blumberg, for example, documents the way in which factors such as child-care responsibilities and distance between home and workplace undermined the original ideals of the kibbutz regarding gender equality.

Rational choice theory provides a perspective on women's earnings that is quite similar to that of analytic conflict theorists such as Janet Chafetz. It looks at the logic of men's and women's choices and shows how they make them freely and rationally *within a set of social constraints and values.* Thus Brinton explains how Japanese mothers come to have much lower aspirations for their daughters' education than for their sons'. Luker found that women in the pro-life movement were often full-time mothers and housewives to whom raising a family and nurturing were the most important things a woman could do.[48]

The individual choices and decisions of women like these will, on a large scale, help to produce and perpetuate average national earnings that are lower for women than for men. Rational choice theory does not posit patriarchy as an explanation, but it does refer to values and decisions that are gender-linked or specific to women—values and decisions that simply do not affect men in the same way.

Exactly these sorts of values inform theorists' answers to the second of our questions about women in contemporary society. At issue here was why men and boys tend to dominate a situation and show aggression, while girls and women tend to assume supporting roles and provide nurture and support. Functionalism's emphasis on shared values, and on the importance of these values being internalized during socialization, provides a macro-level answer. Boys who are aggressive and girls who are nurturing have

[48]See Chapter 7, pp. 326–27 and 345–46.

learned the "appropriate" gender role behavior: the socialization process "worked." Thus in Parsons's view social institutions like the home, school, and church successfully performed the pattern maintenance function.

It is predominantly the micro perspectives that address this question; and their explanations are not conflicting so much as concerned with different levels of analysis. Deferring to men and nurturing can be viewed as quintessentially non–self-interested and therefore not amenable to explanation in rational choice terms. However, rational choice theory does set out to explain such behavior, alongside the altruism of political activists, blood donors, and so on. The women studied by Luker, activists for *and* against abortion, behaved in this way in order to affirm and confirm the values they held and their own self-image. What is interesting about the pro-life group, in particular, is their belief that there are things that it is particularly women's role to provide—that women *should* be the nurturers, the home-makers, the peacemakers.

Similar values are invoked in rational choice theorists' analyses of the dynamics of power within a family. While decision making is to a large extent a function of who earns most, it is also obvious that women defer to men—and to their children—in ways that can only be explained by values. Thus in families where women are the main earners, they are generally careful not to exploit their greater potential power to the full. For example, the way in which men and women divide up housework cannot be explained in terms of their earning power or time commitments outside the home, but only as resting on ideas about what men and women "should" do.

Rational choice theory uses the values that women hold to help explain the pattern and rationality of women's behavior. The theory does not, however, explain how women come to hold these values in the first place. Symbolic interactionists, by comparison, are particularly interested in detailed analysis of the process by which people take on particular identities—such as that of a traditional wife and mother. Nancy Chodorow, notably, argues that female children strongly and consciously identify with their mothers, so they develop, generation by generation, a "high relational capacity." All sorts of signals from society as a whole reinforce them in their belief that this is a suitable thing to do.[49] Thus Raphaela Best points out how girls at school are able to express emotions openly, whereas boys get laughed at as crybabies when they do. Erving Goffman shows how the way men and women are depicted in something as apparently unimportant as advertisements again reinforces people's ideas of what is appropriate male and female behavior, and how gender differences develop between siblings. Barrie Thorne shows how the games children play reinforce and perpetuate traditional gender-based roles

---

[49]Although there is no overt disagreement among microtheorists in their analysis of women's relative lack of aggression, we should note that a number of macrotheorists (male and female) reject Chodorow's theories as inadequate and unable to account for change.

and the separation of the sexes.[50] By contrast, Patricia Hill Collins links the emergence of a self-definition among African-American women that includes self-reliance, self-esteem, and independence to their rejection of the controlling images originating during the era of slavery: mammies, matriarchs, welfare mothers, and socially denigrated women.[51]

Phenomenology, as usual, goes even further into the microstructure of human interaction and the way in which our identities, themselves bound up with our values, are created. In the work of writers such as Pamela Fishman, we can see how women's tentativeness in conversation is reinforced. Similarly, Garfinkel, in his story of Agnes,[52] who undergoes a sex change, describes how she was able to learn, from direct and indirect signals, what the appropriate behavior was for someone who wanted to be a woman. Among the important things Agnes learned were that she should not offer opinions and that passive acceptance is a desirable female trait.[53] Dorothy Smith questions the taken-for-granted assumptions about women's subordinate position and argues that a feminist exploration of femininity involves a shift away from the traditional view. She shows how a cosmetic display in a shopping mall documents the underlying social order through the many expressions of "softness," signaling that the feminine woman should be yielding, pliant, and compliant.[54] Finally, the sociology of the body discusses the possible role of biologically based differences, but also the strong effects of social ideas about femininity on the whole way women construct their bodies and feel about fatness and thinness. The sociology of the body also studies the development of medical conditions such as anorexia, which affect women more than they do men.

In sum, each of the major perspectives of contemporary sociological theory succeeds, in its different way, in helping us understand one of the major determinants of our daily lives and experiences. In doing so, moreover, it complements rather than contradicts the insights provided by others. A similar pattern could be found and traced in many other spheres—for example, voting patterns or the workings of a government bureaucracy or standing army. This is the reason, ultimately, that each perspective is recognized as an important part of modern theory and why so many practicing sociologists are eclectic in their approach, drawing on the insights of different perspectives in accordance with their interests and concerns.

[50]See Chapter 5, pp. 233 and 245.

[51]See chapter 5, p. 249.

[52]Harold Garfinkel, *Studies in Ethnomethodology* (Englewood Cliffs, N.J.: Prentice-Hall, 1967). See also Chapter 6.

[53]A full discussion of male/female differences in behavior carries one into the vexed and uncertain area of biological influences. While these cannot be treated fully within a sociological textbook, sociobiologists such as Alice Rossi warn against the danger for sociology of ignoring physical and biological factors. See Chapter 8.

[54]See Chapter 6, Part 3.

Selected Bibliography

Abrahamson, Mark. *Functionalism*. Englewood Cliffs, N.J.: Prentice-Hall, 1978.

Adorno, Theodor, et al. *The Authoritarian Personality*. New York: Harper and Row, 1950.

Alexander, Jeffrey C. *Neofunctionalism and After*. Malden, Mass.: Blackwell, 1998.

———. *Theoretical Logic in Sociology*. 4 vols. Berkeley: University of California Press, 1982.

———. *Twenty Lectures: Sociological Theory Since World War II*. New York: Columbia University Press, 1987.

———, ed. *Durkheimian Sociology: Cultural Studies*. New York: Cambridge University Press, 1988.

———, ed. *Neofunctionalism*. Beverly Hills, Calif.: Sage, 1985.

Avineri, Shlomo. *The Social and Political Thought of Karl Marx*. Cambridge: Cambridge University Press, 1968.

Beck, Ulrich. *Risk Society: Toward a New Modernity*. Thousand Oaks, Calif.: Sage, 1992.

Beck, Ulrich, Anthony Giddens, and Scott Lash. *Reflexive Modernization: Politics, Tradition and Aesthetics in the Modern Social Order*. Cambridge: Polity, 1994.

Bellah, Robert N. "Civil Religion in America." *Daedalus* 96 (1967): 1–21.

———. "Durkheim and History." *American Sociological Review* 24 (1959): 447–61.

Bellah, Robert N., Richard Madsen, William M. Sullivan, Ann Swidler, and Steven M. Tipton. *The Good Society*. New York: Alfred A. Knopf, 1991.

Bellah, Robert N., Richard Madsen, William M. Sullivan, Ann Swidler, and Steven M. Tipton. *Habits of the Heart: Individualism and Commitment in American Life*. Berkeley: University of California Press, 1985.

Berger, Peter L. *The Sacred Canopy: Elements of a Sociological Theory of Religion*. New York: Doubleday, 1969.

Berger, Peter L., Brigitte Berger, and Hansfried Kellner. *The Homeless Mind*. New York: Random House, 1973.

Berger, Peter L., and Thomas Luckmann. *The Social Construction of Reality*. New York: Doubleday, 1966.

Blau, Peter M. *The Dynamics of Bureaucracy: A Study of Interpersonal Relationships in Two Government Agencies*. Chicago: University of Chicago Press, 1955.

———. *Exchange and Power in Social Life*. New York: John Wiley, 1964.

———. *Inequality and Heterogeneity: A Primitive Theory of Social Structure*. New York: The Free Press, 1977.

———, ed. *Approaches to the Study of Social Structure*. New York: The Free Press, 1975.

Blau, Peter M., and Joseph E. Schwartz. *Cross-Cutting Social Circles: Testing a Macrostructural Theory of Intergroup Relations*. Orlando, Fla.: Academic Press, 1984.

Blau, Peter M., and W. Richard Scott. *Formal Organizations*. San Francisco: Harper and Row, 1962.

Blumer, Herbert. "Comments on 'Parsons as a Symbolic Interactionist.' " *Sociological Inquiry* 45 (1975): 59–62, 68.

———. "Going Astray with a Logical Scheme." *Symbolic Interaction* 6 (1983): 127–37.

———. "Sociological Theory in Industrial Relations." *American Sociological Review* 12 (1947): 271–78.

———. *Symbolic Interactionism: Perspective and Method*. Englewood Cliffs, N.J.: Prentice-Hall, 1969.

———. "The World of Youthful Drug Use" (manuscript). Berkeley, California: University of California, School of Criminology, 1967.

Bock, Kenneth. "Evolution, Function, and Change." *American Sociological Review* 28 (1963): 229–37.

Bott, Elizabeth. *Family and Social Network*. London: Tavistock, 1957 and 1971.

Boudon, Raymond. *The Unintended Consequences of Social Action*. London: Macmillan, 1982.

Bourdieu, Pierre. *Distinction :A Social Critique of the Judgment of Taste*. London: Routledge, 1984.

———. *In Other Words: Essays Toward a Reflexive Sociology*. Stanford, Calif.: Stanford University Press, 1990.

———. *Outline of a Theory of Practice*, trans. R. Nice. Cambridge: Cambridge University Press, 1977.

Bourdieu, Pierre, and James S. Coleman. eds. *Social Theory for a Changing Society*. Boulder, Colo.: Westview 1991.

Bourdieu, Pierre, and Jean-Claude Passeron. *The Inheritors*, trans. R. Nice. Chicago: University of Chicago Press, 1979.

Bourdieu, Pierre, and Loic J. D. Wacquant. *An Invitation to Reflexive Sociology*. Cambridge: Polity, 1992.

Burawoy, Michael. *Manufacturing Consent*. Chicago: University of Chicago Press, 1979.

Burawoy, Michael, and Theda Skocpol, eds. *Marxist Inquiries: Studies of Labor, Class and States*. Chicago: University of Chicago Press, 1982.

Campbell, Donald T. "On the Conflict Between Biological and Social Evolution and Between Psychology and Moral Tradition." *The American Psychologist* (1975): 1103–26.

Campbell, Marie, and Ann Manicom, eds. *Knowledge, Experience and Ruling Relations: Studies in the Social Organization of Knowledge*. Toronto: University of Toronto Press, 1995.

Carey, James, and Norman Denzin. *Symbolic Interactionism and Cultural Studies: The Politics of Interpretation*. Oxford: Blackwell, 1992.

Chafetz, Janet Saltzman. *Feminist Sociology: An Overview of Contemporary Theories*. Itasca, Ill: Peacock, 1988.

———. *Sex and Advantage: A Comparative, Macro-Structural Theory of Sex Stratification*. Totowa, N.J.: Rowman and Allanheld, 1984.

Chafetz, Janet Saltzman, and Anthony Gary Dworkin. *Female Revolt: Women's Movements in World and Historical Perspective*. Totowa, N.J.: Rowman and Allanheld, 1986.

Chodorow, Nancy. *Feminism and Psychoanalysis*. New Haven: Yale University Press, 1989.

———. *The Reproduction of Mothering*. Berkeley: University of California Press, 1978.

Chomsky, Noam. *Aspects of the Theory of Syntax*. Cambridge, Mass.: The M.I.T. Press, 1965.

Cicourel, Aaron V. *Method and Measurement in Sociology*. New York: The Free Press, 1964.

Cicourel, Aaron V., and John I. Kitsuse. *The Educational Decision-Makers*. Indianapolis: Bobbs-Merrill, 1963.

Coleman, James S. "Foundations for a Theory of Collective Decisions." *American Journal of Sociology* LXXI (1966): 615–27.

———. *Foundations of Social Theory*. Cambridge: The Belknap Press of Harvard University Press, 1990.

———. *Individual Interests and Collective Action*. New York: Cambridge University Press, 1986.

———. *The Mathematics of Collective Action*. Chicago: Aldine, 1973.

Collins, Patricia Hill. *Black Feminist Thought: Knowledge, Consciousness, and the Politics of Empowerment*. Cambridge: Unwin Hyman, 1990.

Collins, Randall. *Conflict Sociology: Toward an Explanatory Science*. New York: Academic Press, 1975.

———. *The Credential Society: An Historical Sociology of Education and Stratification*. New York: Academic Press, 1979.

———. "Functional and Conflict Theories of Educational Stratification." *American Sociological Review* 36 (1971): 1002–19.

———. *Sociology Since Midcentury*. New York: Academic Press, 1981.

———. *Weberian Sociological Theory*. New York: Cambridge University Press, 1986.

Comte, Auguste. *The Positive Philosophy*, trans. Harriet Martineau. New York: Calvin Blanchard, 1958.

Cook, Karen, ed. *Social Exchange Theory*. Newbury Park, Calif.: Sage, 1987.

Cooley, Charles Horton. *Human Nature and the Social Order*. New York: Scribner's, 1922.

Coser, Lewis A. *Continuities in the Study of Social Conflict*. New York: The Free Press, 1967.

———. *The Functions of Social Conflict*. Glencoe, Ill.: The Free Press, 1956.

———. *Greedy Institutions: Patterns of Undivided Commitments*. New York: The Free Press, 1974.

———. *Masters of Sociological Thought*. New York: Harcourt Brace Jovanovich, 1977.

———. "Presidential Address: Two Methods in Search of a Substance." *American Sociological Review* 40, no. 6 (December 1975): 691–700.

———, ed. *The Idea of Social Structure: Papers in Honor of Robert K. Merton*. New York: Harcourt Brace Jovanovich, 1975.

Dahrendorf, Ralf. *Class and Class Conflict in Industrial Society*. Stanford, Calif.: Stanford University Press, 1959.

———. *Essays on the Theory of Society*. Stanford, Calif.: Stanford University Press, 1968.

———. *The New Liberty*. London: Routledge and Kegan Paul, 1975.

Davis, Kingsley. "The Myth of Functional Analysis as a Special Method in Sociology and Anthropology." *American Sociological Review* 24 (1959): 757–72.

Dawkins, Richard. *The Extended Phenotype: The Gene as the Unit of Selection*. Oxford and San Francisco: W. H. Freeman, 1982.

———. *The Selfish Gene*. Oxford: Oxford University Press, 1976.

Deegan, Mary Jo. *Jane Addams and the Men of the Chicago School: 1890–1918*. New Brunswick, N.J.: Transaction, 1986.

Deegan, Mary Jo, and Michael Hill, ed. *Women and Symbolic Interaction*. Boston: Allen and Unwin, 1987.

Denzin, Norman. *On Understanding Emotion*. San Francisco: Jossey-Bass, 1984.

Dixit, A. K., and B.J. Nalebuff. *Thinking Strategically: The Competitive Edge in Business, Politics, and Everyday Life*. New York: W.W. Norton, 1991.

Djilas, Milovan. *The New Class: An Analysis of the Communist System*. New York: Holt, Rinehart and Winston, 1957.

Douglas, Jack D., ed. *Understanding Everyday Life*. Chicago: Aldine, 1970.

Durkheim, Émile. *The Division of Labor in Society*. Glencoe, Ill.: The Free Press, 1964.

———. *The Elementary Forms of the Religious Life*. New York: Collier Books, 1961.

———. *Moral Education*. New York: The Free Press, 1973.

———. *The Rules of Sociological Method*. Edited with an introduction by Steven Lukes. Translated by W. D. Halls. New York: The Free Press, 1982.

———. *Suicide*. Glencoe, Ill.: The Free Press, 1951.

Eisenstein, Zillah R. *Capitalist Patriarchy and the Case for Socialist Feminism*. New York: Monthly Review Press, 1979.

Emerson, R. M., "Exchange Theory, Part I: A Psychological Basis for Social Exchange"; and "Exchange Theory, Part II: Exchange Relations and Networks." In J. Berger, M. Zelditch, and B. Anderson, ed., *Sociological Theories in Progress*. Boston: Houghton-Mifflin, 1972.

———. "Power-Dependence Relations." *American Sociological Review* 27 (1962): 31–41.

Engels, Friedrich. *The Origin of the Family, Private Property and the State*. Trans. Alick West. New York: Penguin, 1972.

Etzioni, Amitai. *The Spirit of Community: Rights, Responsibilities, and the Communitarian Agenda*. New York: Crown, 1993.

———. *The New Golden Rule: Community and Morality in a Democratic Society*. New York: Basic Books, 1996.

Faris, R. E. L. *Chicago Sociology 1920–1932*. Chicago: University of Chicago Press, 1970.

Featherstone, M., M. Hepworth, and B. S. Turner, ed. *The Body, Social Process, and Cultural Theory*. London: Sage, 1991.

Ferguson, Kathy E. *Self, Society and Womankind*. Westport, Conn.: Greenwood Press, 1980.

Festinger, Leon. *A Theory of Cognitive Dissonance*. Evanston, Ill.: Row, Peterson, 1957.

Foucault, Michel. *Discipline and Punish: The Birth of the Prison*. Trans. Alan Sheridan. London: Allen Lane, 1977.

———. *The History of Sexuality*. Vols. 1 and 3. London: Allan Lane, 1976–1988.

———. *Madness and Civilization. A History of Insanity in the Age of Reason*. Trans. Richard Howard. New York: Random House, 1965.

———. *The Order of Things: An Archaeology of the Human Sciences*. New York: Vintage Books, 1973.

Fox, Robin. *Kinship and Marriage*. Harmondsworth, Middlesex: Penguin, 1967.

Fromm, Erich. *The Sane Society*. New York: Holt, Rinehart and Winston, 1956.

Fukayama, Francis. *The End of Order*. London: Social Market Foundation and University of Utah Press, 1997.

Garfinkel, Harold. *Studies in Ethnomethodology*. Englewood Cliffs, N.J.: Prentice-Hall, 1967.

Gellner, Ernest. *Postmodernism, Reason and Religion*. London: Routledge, 1992.

Gerth, Hans, and C. Wright Mills. *Character and Social Structure*. New York: Harcourt Brace Jovanovich, 1953.

Giddens, Anthony. *Central Problems in Social Theory*. Berkeley: University of California Press, 1979.

———. *The Constitution of Society*. Cambridge, England: Polity, 1984.

———. *Modernity and Self-Identity: Self and Society in the Late Modern Age*. Cambridge: Polity, 1991.

———. *Profiles and Critiques in Social Theory*. Berkeley: University of California Press, 1982.

———. "Review Essay: Habermas' Social and Political Theory." *American Journal of Sociology* 83, no. 1 (1977): 198–212.

Glaser, Barney G., and Anselm L. Strauss. *The Discovery of Grounded Theory: Strategies for Qualitative Research*. Chicago: Aldine, 1967.

Goffman, Erving. "The Arrangement Between the Sexes." *Theory and Society* 4 (1977): 301–32.

———. *Asylums: Essays on the Social Situation of Mental Patients and Other Inmates*. New York: Doubleday, 1961.

———. *Encounters: Two Studies in the Sociology of Interaction*. Indianapolis: Bobbs-Merrill, 1961.

———. *Gender Advertisements*. New York: Harper Colophon, 1976.

———. "The Interaction Order." *American Sociological Review* 48, no. 1 (February 1983): 1–17.

———. *Interaction Ritual: Essays on Face-to-Face Behavior*. Garden City, New York: Doubleday Anchor, 1967.

———. *The Presentation of Self in Everyday Life*. Garden City, New York: Doubleday Anchor, 1959.

———. *Stigma: Notes on the Management of Spoiled Identity*. Englewood Cliffs, N.J.: Prentice- Hall, 1963.

———. *Strategic Interaction*. Philadelphia: University of Pennsylvania Press, 1969.

Granovetter, Mark. "The Strength of Weak Ties." *American Journal of Sociology* 78 (1973): 1360–80.

Grathoff, Richard, ed. *The Theory of Social Action: The Correspondence of Alfred Schutz and Talcott Parsons*. Bloomington, Ind.: Indiana University Press, 1978.

Habermas, Jürgen. *Communication and the Evolution of Society*. Trans. Thomas McCarthy. London: Heinemann Education Books, 1979.

———. *Legitimation Crisis*. Trans. Thomas McCarthy. Boston: Beacon Press, 1975.

———. *The Philosophical Discourse of Modernity: Twelve Lectures*. Trans. Frederick Lawrence. Cambridge: Polity, 1987.

———. "Talcott Parsons: Problems of Theory Construction." *Sociological Inquiry* 51 (1981): 173–96.

———. *Theory and Practice*. Trans. John Viertel. Boston: Beacon Press, 1973.

———. *The Theory of Communicative Action*. Vol. 1, *Reason and the Rationalization of Society*, 1984; and Vol. 2, *Lifeworld and System: A Critique of Functionalist Reason*, 1988. Cambridge: Polity.

Handel, Warren. *Ethnomethodology: How People Make Sense*. Englewood Cliffs, N.J.: Prentice-Hall, 1982.

Hayek, Friedrich. See Von Hayek.

Heath, Anthony. *Rational Choice and Social Exchange*. Cambridge: Cambridge University Press, 1976.

Hechter, Michael, Karl-Dieter Opp, and Reinhard Wippler, eds. *Social Institutions: Their Emergence, Maintenance, and Effects*. Berlin: Walter de Gruyter, 1990.

Heritage, John. *Garfinkel and Ethnomethodology*. Cambridge: Cambridge University Press, 1976.

Hochschild, Arlie Russell. *The Managed Heart: Commercialization of Human Feelings*. Berkeley: University of California Press, 1983.

———, with Anne Machung. *The Second Shift: Working Parents and the Revolution at Home*. New York: Viking, 1989.

———. *The Time Bind: When Work Becomes Home and Home Becomes Work*. New York: Henry Holt and Company, 1997.

Homans, George C. "Bringing Men Back In." *American Sociological Review* 29, no. 5 (December 1964): 809–18.

———. *The Human Group*. New York: Harcourt Brace Jovanovich, 1950.

———. "A Life of Synthesis." In *Sociological Self-Images: A Collective Portrait*, ed. Irving L. Horowitz. Beverly Hills, Calif.: Sage, 1969.

———. *The Nature of Social Science*. New York: Harcourt Brace Jovanovich, 1967.

————. "Social Behavior as Exchange." *American Journal of Sociology* LXII (1958): 597–606.

————. *Social Behavior: Its Elementary Forms*. Revised edition. New York: Harcourt Brace Jovanovich, 1974.

————. "A Sociologist's Reaction." *The American Sociologist* 12, no. 2 (May 1977): 69.

Horkheimer, Max. *Critical Theory*. Trans. Matthew J. O'Connell et al. New York: Continuum Books, 1972.

Johnson, Benton. *Functionalism in Modern Sociology: Understanding Talcott Parsons*. Morristown, N.J.: General Learning Press, 1975.

Jones, E. L. *The European Miracle: Environments, Economics and Geopolitics in the History of Europe and Asia*. Cambridge: Cambridge University Press, 1981.

Kemper, Theodore. *A Social Interactional Theory of the Emotions*. New York: John Wiley, 1978.

Kolakowski, Leszek. *Main Currents of Marxism*. Oxford: Clarendon Press, 1978.

Konrad, George, and Ivan Szelenyi. *The Intellectuals on the Road to Class Power*. New York: Harcourt Brace Jovanovich, 1979.

Kornhauser, William. "'Power Elite' or 'Veto Groups'?" In *Class, Status and Power*, ed. Reinhard Bendix and Seymour Martin Lipset. New York: The Free Press, 1966.

Kuhn, Thomas. *The Structure of Scientific Revolutions*. Chicago: University of Chicago Press, 1970.

Leach, Edmund, ed. *The Structural Study of Myth and Totemism*. London: Tavistock, 1967.

Lemert, Charles C. *Postmodernism Is Not What You Think*. Malden, Mass.: Blackwell, 1997.

————, ed. *French Sociology: Rupture and Renewal since 1968*. New York: Columbia University Press, 1981.

Lengermann, Patricia Madoo, and Jill Niebrugge-Brantley. *The Women Founders: Sociology and Social Theory, 1830–1930*. New York: McGraw-Hill, 1998.

Lenin, Vladimir I. *Imperialism: The Highest Stage of Capitalism*. New York: International Publishers, 1939.

Lenski, Gerhard E. *Power and Privilege: A Theory of Social Stratification*. New York: McGraw-Hill, 1966.

Levi-Strauss, Claude. *The Elementary Structure of Kinship*, rev. ed. London: Eyre and Spottiswoode, 1969.

————. *Totemism*. Boston: Beacon Press, 1963.

————. "Le Triangle Culinaire." *L'Arc* 26 (1965): 19–29.

Levine, D., E. Carter, and E. Miller. "Simmel's Influence on American Sociology II." *American Journal of Sociology* 81 (1976): 1112–32.

Loubser, Jan J., Rainer C. Baum, Andrew Effrat, and Victor Lidz, eds. *Explorations on General Theory in Social Science: Essays in Honor of Talcott Parsons*. New York: The Free Press, 1976.

Luhmann, Niklas. *The Differentiation of Society*. New York: Columbia University Press, 1982.

————. *Risk: A Sociological Theory*. New York: Aldine De Gruyter, 1993.

————. "Society, Meaning, Religion—Based on Self-Reference." *Sociological Analysis* 46 (1985): 5–20.

————. "Tautology and Paradox in the Self-Descriptions of Modern Society." *Sociological Theory* 6 (1988): 26–37.

Lukes, Steven. *Émile Durkheim: His Life and Work*. New York: Harper and Row, 1972.

Lumsden, Charles J., and Edward O. Wilson. *Genes, Mind and Culture: The Coevolutionary Process*. Cambridge: Harvard University Press, 1981.

Manis, Jerome G., and Bernard N. Meltzer, eds. *Symbolic Interaction: A Reader in Social Psychology*. Boston: Allyn and Bacon, 1972.

Marcuse, Herbert. *Eros and Civilization*. New York: Vintage Books, 1955.

————. *One-Dimensional Man*. Boston: Beacon Press, 1964.

Marx, Karl. *Capital*, Vol. 1, trans. Samuel Moore and Edward Aveling, ed. F. Engels. London: Lawrence and Wishart, 1961.

————. *The Eighteenth Brumaire of Louis Bonaparte*. New York: International Publishers, 1935.

————. *The Poverty of Philosophy*. Moscow: Foreign Languages Publishing House, n.d.

Marx, Karl, and Frederich Engels. *The Communist Manifesto*. Harmondsworth, Middlesex: Penguin, 1967.

Marx, Karl, and Frederich Engels, ed. *Selected Works*, Vol. I. London: Lawrence and Wishart, 1962.

Mauss, Marcel. *The Gift*. Glencoe, Ill.: The Free Press, 1954.

McCall, George J., and J. L. Simmons. *Identities and Interactions*. New York: The Free Press, 1966.

McLean, Iain. *Public Choice: An Introduction*. Oxford: Basil Blackwell, 1987.

Mead, George Herbert. *Mind, Self and Society*. Chicago: University of Chicago Press, 1934.

Merton, Robert K. *Social Theory and Social Structure*. Enlarged edition. New York: The Free Press, 1968.

Michels, Robert. *Political Parties: A Sociological Study of Oligarchical Tendencies of Modern Democracy*. Trans. Eden and Cedar Paul. Glencoe, Ill.: The Free Press, 1958.

Mills, C. Wright. *Listen Yankee: The Revolution in Cuba*. New York: Ballantine, 1960.

———. *The New Men of Power*. New York: Harcourt Brace Jovanovich, 1948.

———. *The Power Elite*. New York: Oxford University Press, 1956.

———. "The Power Elite: Military, Economic and Political." In *Problems of Power in American Society*, ed. Arthur Kornhauser. Detroit: Wayne State University Press, 1957.

———. *The Sociological Imagination*. New York: Oxford University Press, 1959.

———. *White Collar: The American Middle Classes*. New York: Oxford University Press, 1951.

Moore, Barrington, Jr. *Social Origins of Dictatorship and Democracy: Lord and Peasant in the Making of the Modern World*. Boston: Beacon Press, 1966.

Mosca, Gaetano. *The Ruling Class*. New York: McGraw-Hill, 1960.

Mullins, Nicholas C. *Theories and Theory Groups in Contemporary American Sociology*. New York: Harper and Row, 1973.

Munch, Richard. "Talcott Parsons and the Theory of Action, I and II." *American Journal of Sociology* 86 (1981): 709–39 and 87 (1982): 771–826.

Nagel, Ernest. *The Structure of Science*. New York: Harcourt, Brace Jovanovich, 1961.

Nisbet, Robert A. *The Sociological Tradition*. New York: Basic Books, 1966.

North, Douglass. *Structure and Change in Economic History*. New York: W. W. Norton, 1981.

Olson, Mancur. *The Logic of Collective Action: Public Goods and the Theory of Groups*. Cambridge: Harvard University Press, 1965.

Pareto, Vilfredo. *The Treatise on General Sociology*. New York: Dover, 1963.

Park, Robert E., and Ernest W. Burgess. *Introduction to the Science of Sociology*. Chicago: University of Chicago Press, 1921.

Parsons, Talcott. *Action Theory and the Human Condition*. New York: The Free Press, 1978.

———. *Essays in Sociological Theory*. New York: The Free Press, 1954.

———. "Evolutionary Universals in Society." *American Sociological Review* 29 (1964): 339–57.

———. "On Building Social System Theory: A Personal History." *Daedalus* (1970): 826–81.

———. "The School Class as a Social System: Some of Its Functions in American Society." In *Education, Economy and Society*, ed. A. H. Halsey, Jean Floud, and C. Arnold Anderson. New York: The Free Press, 1961.

———. *The Social System*. New York: The Free Press, 1951.

———. *Societies: Evolutionary and Comparative Perspectives*. Englewood Cliffs, N.J.: Prentice-Hall, 1966.

———. *The System of Modern Societies*. Englewood Cliffs, N.J.: Prentice-Hall, 1971.

———, ed. *Sociological Theory and Modern Society*. New York: The Free Press, 1967.

Parsons, Talcott, Robert F. Bales, and Edward A. Shils. *Working Papers in the Theory of Action*. Glencoe, Ill.: The Free Press, 1953.

Parsons, Talcott, and Gerald M. Platt. *The American University*. Cambridge: Harvard University Press, 1973.

Parsons, Talcott, and Edward A. Shils, eds. *Toward a General Theory of Action*. Cambridge: Harvard University Press, 1951.

Piaget, Jean. *The Child's Construction of Reality*. London: Routledge and Kegan Paul, 1958.

———. *Structuralism*. Trans. and ed. Chaninah Maschler. London: Routledge and Kegan Paul, 1971.

Pierce, Jennifer L. *Gender Trials: Emotional Lives in Contemporary Law Firms*. Berkeley: University of California Press, 1995.

Popper, Karl. *The Logic of Scientific Discovery*. London: Hutchinson, 1959.

Reynolds, Vernon. *The Biology of Human Action*. 2nd ed. Reading, England: W. H. Freeman, 1980.

Reynolds, Vernon, and R. E. S. Tanner. *The Biology of Religion*. London and New York: Longman, 1983.

Ridley, Matt. *The Red Queen: Sex and the Evolution of Human Nature*. London: Viking, 1993.

Rossi, Alice. "A Biosocial Perspective on Parenting." *Daedalus* 106, no. 2 (1977): 1–31.

———. "Gender and Parenthood." *American Sociological Review* 49, no. 1 (1984): 1–19.

Sahlins, Marshal D., and Elman R. Service, eds. *Evolution and Culture*. Ann Arbor: University of Michigan Press, 1960.

Schumpeter, Joseph. *Capitalism, Socialism and Democracy*. London: Unwin University Books, 1943.
———. *Imperialism and Social Classes*. Cleveland: Meridian Books, 1955.
———. *Ten Great Economists: from Marx to Keynes*. London: Allen and Unwin, 1952.
Schutz, Alfred. *Collected Papers I: The Problem of Social Reality*. The Hague: Martinus Nijhoff, 1962.
———. "The Stranger: An Essay in Social Psychology." In *School and Society: A Sociological Reader*. Open University. London: Routledge and Kegan Paul, 1971.
Scott, Marvin, and Stanford M. Lyman. "Accounts." *American Sociological Review* 33 (1968): 46–62.
Shibutani, Tamotsu, ed. *Human Nature and Collective Behavior: Papers in Honor of Herbert Blumer*. Englewood Cliffs, N.J.: Prentice-Hall, 1970.
Simmel, Georg. *Conflict*. Trans. Kurt H. Wolff. Glencoe, Ill.: The Free Press, 1955.
———. *The Sociology of Georg Simmel*. Trans. Kurt H. Wolff. Glencoe, Ill.: The Free Press, 1950.
Smelser, Neil J. "Mechanics of Change and Adjustment to Change." In *Industrialization and Society*, ed. Berthhold F. Hoselitz and Wilbert E. Moore. Paris: Unesco-Mouton, 1963.
———. "Presidential Address: The Rational and the Ambivalent in the Social Sciences." *American Sociological Review* 63, no. 1 (February 1998): 1–15.
———. *Social Change in the Industrial Revolution*. Chicago: University of Chicago Press, 1959.
———. *The Sociology of Economic Life*. Englewood Cliffs, N.J.: Prentice-Hall, 1963.
Smelser, Neil J., and R. Stephen Warner. *Sociological Theory: Historical and Formal*. Morristown, N.J.: General Learning Press, 1976.
Smith, Dorothy E. *The Conceptual Practices of Power: A Feminist Sociology of Knowledge*. Boston: Northeastern University Press, 1990.
———. *The Everyday World as Problematic: A Feminist Sociology*. Boston: Northeastern University Press, 1987.
———. *Texts, Facts, and Femininity: Exploring the Relations of Ruling*. New York: Routledge, 1990.
Spencer, Herbert. *The Principles of Sociology*. New York: Appleton, 1896.
Stacey, Judith, and Barrie Thorne. "The Missing Feminist Revolution in Sociology." *Social Problems* 32 (1985): 301–16.
Szelényi, Iván. "The Intelligentsia in the Class Structure of State-Socialist Societies." In *Marxist Inquiries: Studies of Labor, Class and States*, ed. Michael Burawoy and Theda Skocpol. Chicago: University of Chicago Press, 1982.
Szelényi, Iván, with Robert Mancin, Pal Juhasz, Balint Magyar, and Bill Martin. *Socialist Entrepreneurs: Embourgeoisement in Rural Hungary*. Cambridge: Polity, 1988.
Thibaut, John W., and Harold H. Kelley. *The Social Psychology of Groups*. New York: John Wiley, 1959.
Thomas, William I. *The Unadjusted Girl*. Boston: Little, Brown, 1923.
Thomas, William I., with Dorothy Swaine Thomas. *The Child in America*. New York: Alfred A. Knopf, 1928.
Thompson, John B., and David Held, eds. *Habermas: Critical Debates*. London: Macmillan, 1982.
Thorne, Barrie. *Gender Play: Girls and Boys in School*. New Brunswick, N.J.: Rutgers University Press, 1993.
Touraine, Alain. *The Self-Production of Society*. Chicago: University of Chicago Press, 1977.
Trivers, Robert. "The Evolution of Reciprocal Altruism." *Quarterly Review of Biology* 46 (1971): 35–57.
Tucker, Robert C. *Philosophy and Myth in Karl Marx*. Cambridge: Cambridge University Press, 1961.
Turner, Bryan S. *The Body and Society: Explorations in Social Theory*. Oxford: Basil Blackwell, 1984.
———. *Regulating Bodies: Essays in Medical Sociology*. London: Routledge, 1992.
Turner, Roy, ed., *Ethnomethodology: Selected Readings*. Baltimore: Penguin, 1974.
Van den Berg, Axel. "Critical Theory: Is There Still Hope?" *American Journal of Sociology* 86, no. 3 (1980): 449–78.
Veblen, Thorstein. *The Theory of the Leisure Class*. New York: Modern Library, 1934.
Von Hayek, Friedrich. *The Constitution of Liberty*. Chicago: Henry Regnery Company, 1972.
Wallace, Ruth A., ed. *Feminism and Sociological Theory*. Newbury Park, Calif.: Sage, 1989.
Wallerstein, Immanuel. *The Modern World System I: Capitalist Agriculture and the Origins of the European World-Economy in the Sixteenth Century*. New York: Academic Press, 1974.

——. *The Modern World System II: Mercantilism and the Consolidation of the European World-Economy, 1600–1750*. New York: Academic Press, 1980.

——. *The Modern World System III: The Second Era of Great Expansion of the Capitalist Economy, 1730–1840*. New York: Academic Press, 1988.

Weber, Max. *The Protestant Ethic and the Spirit of Capitalism*. Trans. Talcott Parsons. New York: Scribner's, 1958.

——. *The Religion of China: Confucianism and Taoism*. Trans. and ed. Hans H. Gerth. Glencoe, Ill.: The Free Press, 1951.

——. *The Theory of Social and Economic Organization*. Trans. A. M. Henderson and Talcott Parsons. New York: The Free Press, 1964.

Wellman, Barry. "Network Analysis: Some Basic Principles." In Randall Collins, ed., *Sociological Theory 1983*. San Francisco: Jossey-Bass, 1983.

White, Harrison C., Scott A. Boorman, and Ronald L. Breiger. "Social Structure from Multiple Networks: I. Blockmodels of Roles and Positions." *American Journal of Sociology* 81 (1976): 730–80.

Williams, Robin M., Jr. "Change and Stability in Values and Value Systems." In *Stability and Social Change*, ed. Bernard Barber and Alex Inkeles. Boston: Little, Brown, 1971.

Wilson, Edward O. *On Human Nature*. Cambridge: Harvard University Press, 1978.

——. *Sociobiology: The New Synthesis*. Cambridge, Mass.: The Belknap Press of Harvard University Press, 1975.

Winch, Peter. *The Idea of a Social Science and Its Relation to Philosophy*. London: Routledge and Kegan Paul, 1958.

Wright, Erik Olin. *Class, Crisis, and the State*. London: New Left Books, 1979.

——. *Class Structure and Income Determination*. New York: Academic Press, 1979.

Wright, Erik Olin, and Joachim Singelmann. "Proletarianization in the Changing American Class Structure." In *Marxist Inquiries: Studies of Labor, Class and States*, ed. Michael Burawoy and Theda Skocpol. Supplement to Vol. 88 of the *American Journal of Sociology*, 1982.

Zeitlin, Irving M. *Capitalism and Imperialism: An Introduction to Neo-Marxian Concepts*. Chicago: Markham, 1972.

Index

Z